POLITICS IN THE COMMUNIST WORLD

POLITICS

IN THE

COMMUNIST WORLD

LESLIE HOLMES

CLARENDON PRESS · OXFORD

Oxford University Press, Walton Street, Oxford OX2 6DP

Oxford New York Toronto
Delhi Bombay Calcutta Madras Karachi
Petaling Jaya Singapore Hong Kong Tokyo
Nairobi Dar es Salaam Cape Town
Melbourne Auckland

and associated companies in
Beirut Berlin Ibadan Nicosia

Oxford is a trade mark of Oxford University Press

Published in the United States by
Oxford University Press, New York

First published in hardback and paperback 1986
Hardback and paperback reprinted 1987

British Library Cataloguing in Publication Data
Holmes, Leslie
Politics in the communist world.
1. Communist state   2. Communist countries—
Politics and government
I. Title
320.9171'7   JC474
ISBN 0–19–876146–5
ISBN 0–19–876147–3 Pbk

Library of Congress Cataloging in Publication Data
Holmes, Leslie.
Politics in the communist world.
Bibliography: p.
Includes index.
1. Communist countries—Politics and government.
2. Communist state.   I. Title.
JC474.H55   1986   320.9171'7   85–21551
ISBN 0–19–876146–5
ISBN 0–19–876147–3 (pbk.)

Printed in Great Britain
at the University Printing House, Oxford
by David Stanford
Printer to the University

For Beenz (again), G. H., Mary (mind that canary),
Julie, Graham, Hazel, Jenny, and Pauline

PREFACE

COMMUNISM is a powerful force in today's world, and writers who in the past have predicted its imminent demise (for example Burnham, 1950; Guins, 1956) were clearly mistaken. More than a third of the world's population lives in communist systems—considerably more than the number of citizens who live under Western-style democracies—and the number is growing. Moreover, what happens in the communist world, especially in the USSR and China, sometimes has profound effects on ordinary people in the West. For example, poor relations between Moscow and Washington can lead to arms buildups in both the communist world and the West, which means that there is less to spend on health, education, housing, roads, etc. Some knowledge of contemporary communism is thus important and relevant to everyone. Yet there are very few books that treat communism on a comparative basis, and even fewer written by a single author; it was this gap in the literature that led me to write the present volume.

The book is offered as an introductory text on politics—that is, power relationships and conflict—in what I have chosen to call 'the communist world'. The latter term is a contentious one; there has in recent years been a very lively debate on whether or not there is such an entity as 'the communist world' and, if there is, which countries should be included in it (see, e.g. Kautsky 1973, Waller 1979 and 1982, Harding 1981, and White 1983). I do not wish to become deeply involved in this debate at this point. However, the fact that I have referred to 'the communist world' reveals that I do believe that there is a more or less identifiable entity known as a communist system. This does *not* mean that I believe that communist systems are entirely different from other kinds of political, economic, and social system. I would argue that there are both similarities and differences between all kinds of polity, but that there are sufficient distinguishing features to render communist systems discrete. Nor would I be foolish enough to suggest that there is a stereotypical communist system—anyone who has visited, say, the GDR, Yugoslavia, China, and Mozambique will be very aware that there are enormous differences between one communist country and another. But I do maintain that there is a certain 'hard core' of commonalities—namely, a commitment to the building of socialism and eventually communism; an ideology called Marxism–Leninism; and a political system constructed on the principles of 'democratic centralism'—that distinguishes such countries from others which, in many ways, look similar. It might be objected that the term 'communist' is misleading, in that no country has yet claimed to have achieved communism, and in that the countries considered in this book for the most part describe themselves as 'socialist'. Although there is some validity to this argument, it is often important to distinguish Marxist–Leninist systems from others which also claim or have claimed to be socialist (e.g. Libya, Tanzania), but which are different in important ways from the countries considered in this volume. It is for these reasons that I refer to 'the communist world', despite my awareness of the problems this can involve.

The choice of countries to be included in this book was not an easy one. There is a core of sixteen states which are widely accepted as being communist, beyond which scholars begin to disagree amongst themselves. One reason for this is that the political situation in several countries is still very much in flux. Moreover, new countries are joining the ranks of the communist world year by year. Hence there cannot be a definitive list of communist states, and it would be a long and unproductive task to explain why some countries have been included in this study and others excluded; in borderline cases, the final decision often had to be somewhat arbitrary. Suffice it to say that twenty-three countries have been accepted as communist for the purposes of the present volume; these can be listed alphabetically by continent. Thus, included under Europe are Albania, Bulgaria, Czechoslovakia, Germany (East—the GDR), Hungary, Poland, Romania, the USSR (which in fact straddles both Europe and Asia), and Yugoslavia. The Asian communist states are Afghanistan, China (mainland—the PRC), Kampuchea, Laos, Korea (North—the DPRK), Mongolia, Vietnam, and Yemen (South—the PDRY). In Africa, there is Angola, Benin, the Congo, Ethiopia, and Mozambique. Finally, there is one Latin-American communist state, Cuba.

The book is aimed at beginners, and this fact has dictated much of the layout and approach. For instance, I have consciously striven to minimize the use of social science jargon. But it is not always possible to avoid technical language; where such usage _is_ required, I have defined the term the first time it is employed. Moreover, I have learnt from my teaching experience that major concepts of political science—such as the state or ideology or political socialization—are not always as familiar even to third-year undergraduates majoring in politics as they should be. For this reason, several chapters start with a brief overview of general concepts relevant to the particular topic; following this these concepts are related specifically to the communist world.

The book has been organized thematically rather than historically (for useful historical overviews of post-Second World War communism see Westoby 1981 or Seton-Watson 1980) or by country (for individual country studies see Szajkowski 1981a and the series of volumes edited by Bromke _et al_. See Bromke 1965, Bromke and Rakowska-Harmstone 1972, and Bromke and Novak 1978). There is to some extent a logical sequence to the chapters. Thus chapter 1 outlines the classical _theories_ of communism. Chapters 2 to 5 are concerned primarily with the ways in which communists take, consolidate, and maintain power. The people, institutions, and processes of legitimate politics form the core of 6 to 10 while chapters 11 to 13 are concerned more with illegitimate (in this sense meaning not sanctioned by the party-state complex) politics. In the penultimate chapter, we move beyond the domestic political scene to examine relations between communist states, whilst the concluding chapter looks at various approaches to the study and understanding of politics in the communist world.

Any single-volume introduction to the politics of twenty-three countries will necessarily be superficial. This is inevitable, and anyone who feels that they would like to know more about the politics of Romania or Mongolia or Yemen can use the bibliographies in the appendix to guide them to detailed analyses of the individual countries. Conversely, the reader who wants to follow up a particular theme or phenomenon will find a short bibliography (up to a dozen sources) at the end of each chapter. Although a book of this nature has to be relatively general, I have also learnt from my teaching of comparative communism that examples of a given phenomenon dropped at random into a discussion and not elaborated are usually either of little value or else positively confusing. In an endeavour to overcome this problem, the format adopted in most of the following chapters has been to make some introductory comments, give a few reasonably detailed examples, and then provide a genuinely comparative overview of the particular phenomenon; this seems to me to be the optimal method of blending breadth with depth. Examples have not been taken in equal measure from each communist state, and the reader will find much more on some countries than on others. There are a number of reasons for this. First, there is the fact that the two giants of the communist world—the USSR and China—are so much more influential and significant (e.g. in terms of number of people affected) than any of the other countries, so that there are more examples from these two states than from elsewhere. Second, my own knowledge of individual countries varies considerably; broadly speaking, I know more about European communism than about Asian, and more about Asian communism than about African. This is partially a reflection of my own education, but also of the fact that the European communist world as a whole is older than the Asian, which is in turn older than the African. One important ramification of this is that there are, quite simply, more sources available on the more established communist states than the newer ones, and this is another major reason for the imbalance in the treatment of individual countries. Finally, and as mentioned earlier in another context, the very newness of many communist states means that much is still in flux and/or unclear to outside observers; this is another reason for the unequal treatment of countries in this book.

It had originally been my intention merely to present an overview of the literature on a given topic, since I felt that there was a need for this. My position on this has not fundamentally changed, but I began to realize as I continued to write that there comes a point at which, for many topics, one has to opt for one approach rather than another if the chapter is to be more than just an entry in a reference book. Thus I have sought to present the major arguments on any given topic, but have, when appropriate, also made my own views clear. The reader will soon discover that I am by nature a critical animal—critical of many aspects of politics in the communist world (and elsewhere, though this is not my concern here), critical of much Western writing on such politics, etc. I have sought never to be completely negative in my criticism; my principal aim in most cases is to improve our understanding of a given phenomenon or argument through subjecting it to a relatively rigorous examination. This is a practice I learnt above all from my doctoral supervisor, Mary McAuley, and I am deeply grateful to her for it. It should not be assumed, however, that a critical approach represents hostility. I would certainly not wish to be thought of as someone who sees the communist world only in a negative light. The communists have achieved a great deal in many countries, especially in terms of economic development and social legislation, and it should never be forgotten that many of the present communist systems replaced corrupt and dictatorial regimes that had little in common with the values most prized in the liberal democracies.

One technical point that needs to be made concerns transliteration. Many of the proper nouns in this book have to be transcribed from languages not written in Latin script (e.g Korean, Arabic), and there is often disagreement among scholars on the best way of doing this. So many languages are involved that I do not intend to explain why I have opted for one transliteration rather than another. Suffice it to say that I have used the Pinyin system for Mandarin, and what seems to me to be the most commonly used rendering for other languages. I have avoided the use of accents for all languages, since I feel that their inclusion is unnecessary and possibly confusing in an introductory textbook.

The book has been long in the writing, and even longer in my mind. So many people have—often unwittingly—contributed to my thinking on communism over the years that it would be impossible to acknowledge them all. However, I do wish to record my gratitude to my students both at the universities of Wales (Aberystwyth), Kent, and Melbourne and in the Kent branch of the Workers' Educational Association for helping me to clarify my own mind and to see a given problem from yet other angles. I would also like to thank by name people who have read and commented upon all or some of the manuscript of this book—they are, in alphabetical order, Archie Brown, Lloyd Churchward, Bruce Headey, Phil Hodgkinson, Joe Miller, Mary McAuley, David McLellan and David Tucker. I have at least considered all the suggestions made by these friends and colleagues, even if I have not incorporated all of them. The responsibility for any errors, as well as all interpretations, is of course solely mine. My research assistant, Keith Forster, kindly did the donkey-work on the bibliography and the index. For the superb and patient way they transformed my appalling scrawl into neatly typed chapters, I would like to thank Linda Harty and Jan Souter; fortunately, my somewhat belated acquaintance with the dictaphone has made life for my typists a little easier.

There is one other person who deserves very special thanks—my wife, Sue. Not only has she been unbelievably tolerant when I have put other responsibilities to one side in order to work on this book, but she has also been enormously helpful in pointing out confusion and/or blurring in my arguments. Thanks Beenz.

L.T.H.

Melbourne
January 1985

CONTENTS

LIST OF TABLES

LIST OF FIGURES

ABBREVIATIONS

ANZUS	Australia, New Zealand, United States (mutual security pact)
AR	Autonomous Region
AVNOJ	(Anti-Fascist Council of National Liberation of Yugoslavia)
BCP	Bulgarian Communist Party
CCP	Chinese Communist Party
CDM	Committee of Defence Ministers
CDU	Christian Democratic Union
CMEA	Council for Mutual Economic Assistance
Comecon	(same as CMEA)
Cominform	Communist Information Bureau
Comintern	(3rd) Communist International
CPC	Communist Party of Cuba
CPCS	Communist Party of Czechoslovakia
CPK	Communist Party of Kampuchea
CPSU	Communist Party of the Soviet Union
DPRK	Democratic People's Republic of Korea
EEC	European Economic Community
FNLA	(National Front for the Liberation of Angola)
Frelimo	(Front for the Liberation of Mozambique)
FRG	Federal Republic of Germany
GDR	German Democratic Republic
GMD	Guomindang
GPCR	Great Proletarian Cultural Revolution
HSWP	Hungarian Socialist Workers' Party
KAN	(Club of Non-Party Committed)
KGB	(Committee of State Security)
Komsomol	(Communist Youth League)
KOR	(Committee for the Defence of Workers)
KSS	(Committee for Social Self-Defence)
LCY	League of Communists of Yugoslavia
MKS	(Inter-Factory Strike Committee)
MPLA	(Popular Movement for the Liberation of Angola)
NAM	Non-Aligned Movement
NATO	North Atlantic Treaty Organization
NKVD	(People's Commissariat for Internal Affairs)
OEEC	Organisation for European Economic Co-operation
ORI	(Integrated Revolutionary Organization)
PCC	Political Consultative Committee
PDPA	People's Democratic Party of Afghanistan
PDRY	People's Democratic Republic of Yemen
PLA	People's Liberation Army

PRC	People's Republic of China
PSP	Popular Socialist Party
PURS	(United Party of the Socialist Revolution)
PUWP	Polish United Worker's Party
RCU	Revolutionary Communist Union
RSFSR	Russian Soviet Federal Socialist Republic
SED	(Socialist Unity Party of Germany)
UDBa	(State Security Administration)
UK	United Kingdom
UN	United Nations
UNITA	(National Union for the Total Independence of Angola)
US(A)	United States (of America)
USSR	Union of Soviet Socialist Republics
WTO	Warsaw Treaty Organization

1

WHAT IS COMMUNISM?

ACCORDING to a somewhat bitter East European joke, capitalism can be defined as the exploitation of man by man, whereas communism reverses this. To a large extent, the acerbity of this remark can be attributed to the experience of many people living in states that are supposed to be building communism, but where life often seems to be at least as bad and unjust as life under capitalism. In other words, it highlights what some have seen as a great gap between the theory and practice of communism. The bulk of this book is concerned with the practice of communist states, but at various points we shall look at the extent to which such practice coincides with the classical theories of communism; at this point we need to consider the most fundamental tenets of these theories, and indeed the meaning of the word communism.

The origin of the term communism is Latin. The Latin word *communis* is probably a compound of the syllables *com*, meaning 'together', and *munis*, meaning 'serving' or 'obliging'. There is also an Old French word *comuner*, which means 'to share'. Thus the basis of the term is an idea of living together and working for and with each other rather than in competition or in a master-subordinate relationship. It is no mere coincidence that when the hippy movement developed in the late 1960s—with its philosophy of love, equality, and living/working together—the name chosen by these 'flower children' for the place where they lived and worked was 'commune'.

Yet this sort of definition is not very detailed or meaningful as a basis for transforming existing societies, and many writers, particularly in the past century and a half, have attempted to explain what communism is or should be, and, perhaps more importantly at this stage of human development, how this condition is to be reached. It should be noted that this latter point (i.e., that the end goal is only one aspect of communism) is made explicitly by some contemporary communist theoreticians. Thus, a member of the Chinese Politburo wrote recently:

What does Communism refer to? It has two meanings: On the one hand, it refers to a social system to be established in the future; on the other, it means the ideology that elaborates why and how to establish this social system and the practice that aims at realizing this ideology, that is, the communist movement. (Hu Qiaomu, 1982, p. 12.)

This is more or less in line with the following passage from *The German Ideology*, in which Marx wrote:

Communism is for us not a *state of affairs* which is to be established, an *ideal* to which reality [will] have to adjust itself. We call communism the *real* movement which abolishes the present state of things. (Marx and Engels, 1970, pp. 56–7.)

Thus communism can refer to particular kinds of existing political movements, not simply some distant and rather vague goal. In this sense, therefore, it is permissable to talk of communist states even though none of them claims to have obtained the conflictless society of the future.

The body of literature on communism is vast and still rapidly growing, and it is not intended to examine here the sometimes fascinating, sometimes turgid polemics on what Marx or Lenin or Joe Soap *really* meant by 'communism' or 'alienation' or 'the dictatorship of the proletariat'. Rather, the aim is to give the novice a brief introduction to what seem to me to be the aspects of the versions of communist theory and practice which have had the most influence and/or are most frequently cited in the communist states themselves. These versions are Marxism, Marxism–Leninism, Stalinism, and Maoism. However, there is also a brief section on Eurocommunism; although this version of communism does not, in the opinion of most commentators, derive from the communist world, it was seen by many politicians in the communist states themselves as a very important phenomenon and even as a dangerous heresy in the 1970s. Therefore, in view of its significance, and because many readers will wish to have at least a general idea of this conception of communism, the concept is included here.

MARXISM

The most widely-known analysis of communism is the *Manifesto of the Communist Party*, written by Karl Marx and Friedrich Engels, and first published in 1848. Although Engels was involved in the writing of this document, he himself acknowledged in 1888 that the main ideas in it were Marx's; largely for this reason, and perhaps somewhat unfairly, we shall here adopt the practice common in the communist states of calling the body of ideas emanating from both Marx and Engels as Marxism; it should be noted though that this is not acceptable to some writers, such as Gramsci or McLellan.

The term '-ism' usually connotes a consistent, interrelated set of ideas, doctrines, etc. attributed to a person, religion, or political movement. The consistency of such sets of ideas is rarely as high as people believe—for instance, if I am a Methodist and am attacked in the street, do I 'turn the other cheek' or insist on 'an eye for an eye'? Similarly, what we call Marxism is frequently inconsistent and ambiguous; indeed, Marx himself said in 1877 that he was not a Marxist! This very inconsistency and ambiguity is at once intellectually stimulating *and* means that some horrific policies and actions have been pursued in the name of Marxism. This has led many Western Marxists to condemn strongly much of what happens in Eastern Europe, for instance; but East European ideologists can cite Marx in justification of their state's actions, and no one can say definitively whether the Western critics or the Eastern ideologists are more correct in their interpretations of Marx and Engels' writings.

Despite these problems, we can at least bring out those aspects of Marxism which are either relatively uncontentious or are important dimensions of the debate because they concern the actual practice of managing a communist state.

Basically, as was intimated earlier, Marx was less concerned in his writings with what a future communist society would look like than he was with the preconditions for the transition to it. We know that several aspects of the 1871 Paris Commune were attractive to Marx—but not all were, and he specifically stated that the Commune was not an example of the communist society he envisaged. We shall be considering specific aspects of the Paris Commune in a later chapter, when we consider the state; but having made the point that Marx was not very concerned with the end goal itself, let us examine his views on reaching it.

In his introduction to the 1888 English edition of the *Manifesto of the Communist Party*, Engels put down what he considered to be the 'fundamental proposition' of the document,

That proposition is: that in every historical epoch, the prevailing mode of economic production and exchange, and the social organisation necessarily following from it, form the basis upon which is built up, and from which alone can be explained, the political and intellectual history of that epoch; that consequently the whole history of mankind (since the dissolution of primitive tribal society, holding land in common ownership) has been a history of class struggles, contests between exploiting and exploited, ruling and oppressed classes; that the history of these class struggles forms a series of evolutions in which, nowadays, a stage has been reached where the exploited and oppressed class—the proletariat—cannot attain its emancipation from the sway of the exploiting and ruling class—the bourgeoisie—without, at the same time, and once and for all, emancipating society at large from all exploitation, oppression, class distinctions and class struggles. (Marx and Engels, 1967, pp. 20–1.)

What all this means is that for Marx, the history of mankind has been dominated by struggle (or conflict) between, most fundamentally, two groups in society which have antagonistically different relations to the economic basis of society; he calls these groups 'classes'. There are, and have been down the centuries, those that own the main source of wealth—land in a feudal age, factories and machinery in the industrial, capitalist age—and those who work for these owners. The former wish to maximize their profits, and so try to get away with paying the latter as little as possible for working their land or their factories, which leads to hostility and resentment. This relationship and antagonism is for Marx the most basic and important one in society; since it is based on the notion of relationships arising from the means of production, this theory has been called a *materialist* conception of history. According to this, the concrete world around us (i.e., matter), including the economic relationships in it, affects the way we perceive the world and therefore the way in which we structure our political and social system. Our most basic need is to survive—to feed, clothe, and house ourselves; to do this we must work, and this simple fact affects our entire social structure. The Marxist approach is thus radically different from the *idealist* approach—represented, for instance, by Hegel—in which the world around us is merely a reflection of ideas (i.e. mind dominates matter). Despite his basically materialist approach, Marx did not claim that the relationship between the economic base and the socio-political superstructure was a simple one-way process; rather, there is continual interaction between them, with the economic base being the more dominant factor. Marx also realized that scientific discoveries have their effect on society and the relationships within it. Hence discoveries such as the 'spinning jenny' or the steam mill—which helped to make possible the industrial revolution—meant that a new group of individuals arose that not only wanted to build and own factories, but that also needed political power in order to ensure full protection of its economic interests. This kind of development leads to a major clash between the existing owners of the principal means of production (e.g. landowners) and the owners of the new source of wealth (e.g. the factory-owners). Thus there arises a revolutionary situation; the events in France in the period around 1789 constitute a prime example.

This notion of continual interaction—of a moving or dynamic situation—has led some scholars to refer to Marx's approach as *dialectical* materialism. This term was never used by Marx himself to describe his methodology; but in that the method, if not the premiss, was similar to what Hegel referred to as the dialectic, its use is appropriate. According to Engels, the Marxist dialectic represents 'the science of the general laws of motion and development of nature, human society, and thought'. For Marx, society is constantly changing, although all major changes reflect the basic source of conflict in society, the struggle between classes based on their different relationships to the means of production. This application of dialectical materialism specifically to the study of history is known as *historical materialism*.

For Marx, the highest stage of development that man had yet reached was capitalism—the set of economic, social, and political relationships that arose from the development of industry under private ownership. The main classes that existed under capitalism were the owners of the means of production—the *bourgeoisie*—and those that sold their labour to these people—the *proletariat*. Marx did sometimes refer to other classes, and as with so many other concepts, is consistent neither in his use of the term 'class' nor in his analysis of the class structures of actual industrialized societies. Nevertheless, he seems to have believed—certainly in his earlier years—that under capitalism society would increasingly obviously polarize into these two main classes. In Marx's view, one of the most important features distinguishing the ruler/ruled or exploiter/exploited relationship of capitalism from all earlier variants of the theme was that it contained within itself not only the seeds of its own destruction but also the destruction of the antagonistic relationships that had characterized almost all previous societies. Under capitalism, people working on production lines are even more dehumanized and estranged (*alienated*) from the fruits of their own labour, nature, and each other than they are when working in the fields or their own workshops, for instance. More importantly, Marx saw all previous revolutionary changes—e.g. from slavery to feudalism, from feudalism to capitalism—as having been brought about by and in the interests of a *minority*. Under capitalism, the simplification of the social structure into two main classes meant that the *majority* of the population would become proletarians and would eventually bring about the overthrow of capitalism and the bourgeois class; there was, in other words, no new minority likely to arise to replace the bourgeoisie and become simply another élite or ruling class. This kind of argument means that Marx's ideas were quite different from some of the best-known Italian political theorists of recent centuries—Machiavelli, Mosca, and Pareto—who see history repeating itself and believe that not only have there always *been* ruling élites but that there always *will* be.

However, contrary to popular belief, Marx does not appear to have believed that the end of capitalism and hostile class relationships was either imminent or that it would necessarily lead to communism. He did argue that if the wage-labourers (i.e., those who sold their labour to the owners of the means of production) were increasingly antagonized by the bourgeoisie, then a revolutionary situation would develop and the capitalist system be overthrown. Such antagonism could develop because the desire of the bourgeoisie to maximize their own profits, at the same time as competition in the market kept the prices of their products down, meant that they would have to try to pay their workers ever less in real terms. But Marx was not always optimistic that such a polarization of the classes would take place. Already in the mid-nineteenth century he noticed signs which suggested that the proletariat might come to adopt the values of the bourgeoisie to such an extent that they might not be aware of the fundamental differences between them and the owners of the means of production. After all, the bourgeoisie had enormous influence over the educational system, which could be used to instill ideas in proletarians that would make them either sympathetic to capitalism or at least accept it as in some sense the 'natural' order of things. He also began to realize that the bourgeoisie might continue to make what he considered to be relatively minor concessions (e.g. the reduction of the working week, the introduction of sickness benefits, etc.) in order to minimize worker discontent and therefore avoid a socialist revolution. Unless the proletariat were aware of itself as a class and understood its position *vis-à-vis* the bourgeoisie, then it was not going to develop a revolutionary consciousness.

Thus Marx's views on inevitability are neither as crude nor as clear as is sometimes maintained. It must be remembered that although Marx and Engels called their approach 'scientific'—which they contrasted to the views of earlier 'utopian' socialists such as Fourier and Saint-Simon—it was the method that was held to be such; relatively few claims about what would happen in the future were made.

If capitalism were to be overthrown, Marx was again vague on what would ensue. He did give us *some* idea, however, particularly of the immediate aftermath. Thus he envisaged a situation in which the proletariat would have to defend its new position until the former bourgeoisie was finally beaten—spiritually and/or physically. This would necessitate a coercive state machinery for some time after the revolution; Marx called this type of state a 'dictatorship of the proletariat'. Unlike all previous dictatorships, this one would represent the interests of the majority, not an élite minority. Unfortunately, however, the details of how it would be organized and operate were not spelt out by Marx. In the *Manifesto of the Communist Party*, Marx did list some of the policies that would typify this period; since these are of direct relevance to communist parties taking power, it is instructive to reproduce them in full:

1. Abolition of property in land and application of all rents of land to public purposes.
2. A heavy progressive or graduated income tax.
3. Abolition of all right of inheritance.
4. Confiscation of the property of all emigrants and rebels.
5. Centralization of credit in the hands of the State, by means of a national bank with State capital and an exclusive monopoly.
6. Centralization of the means of communication and transport in the hands of the State.
7. Extension of factories and instruments of production owned by the State; the bringing into cultivation of waste lands, and the improvement of the soil generally in accordance with a common plan.
8. Equal liability of all to labour. Establishment of industrial armies, especially for agriculture.
9. Combination of agriculture with manufacturing industries; gradual abolition of the distinction between town and country, by a more equable distribution of the population over the country.
10. Free education for all children in public schools. Abolition of children's factory labour in its present form. Combination of education with industrial production, etc.

Some of these policies have been introduced following revolutions, others have not. But, as has been emphasized, the *nature of the political system* that was to introduce these policies was not elaborated; this is a serious gap in Marx's writings.

Although Marx did not see socialist revolution as inevitable, he did want it for ethical or normative reasons. This is yet another of the sources of contradictions and confusion in Marx's writing—sometimes his analysis of what was happening did not square with what he *wanted* to occur. One thing was reasonably clear in Marx's mind, however: that the sort of social revolution he thought could and certainly should take place would do so only in advanced industrial states. The one time he partially deviated from this idea was when various Russian revolutionaries approached him in the 1870/1880s and asked him for his views on their country. Marx agonized for a long time over this question. In a letter he wrote in 1877, he emphasized that his analyses and prognoses in *Das Kapital* referred only to Western Europe, and were not intended to be a blueprint of the development of all states. As a result, he could make the rather odd statement—seen by Weintraub (1950, p. 501) as an example of Marx betraying Marxism!—that

If Russia continues to pursue the path she has followed since 1861, she will lose the finest chance [i.e. of avoiding capitalist development on the way to communism] ever offered by history to a people, and undergo all the fatal vicissitudes of the capitalist regime. (In Feuer, 1969, p. 477).

Later, in 1881, the revolutionary Vera Zasulich wrote to Marx and asked him if he would confirm that he believed that Russia could reach socialism and communism via the peasant commune. Marx evidently found it difficult to answer this question, producing four drafts of the reply before finally deciding on his position. Eventually, and near the end of his life, he wrote to Zasulich that, first, he wished to reiterate that much of his analysis (especially *Das Kapital*) applied to the capitalist states of Western Europe and not to Russia and, second, that the commune *might* become the basis of Russia's 'social regeneration' if conditions were right. Quite what is meant by 'social regeneration' is left unexplained—certainly it is not obvious that Marx meant by this socialism or communism. This vagueness was later amplified by Engels, who wrote in 1893,

As to the burning questions of the Russian revolutionary movement, the part which the peasantry may be expected to take in it, these are subjects on which I could not conscientiously state an opinion for publication without previously studying over again the whole subject and completing my very imperfect knowledge of the facts of the case. . . . (In Feuer, 1969, p. 480.)

Clearly, then, both Marx and Engels were very circumspect in their comments on Russia. The reason so much space has been devoted to this one point is that, in doing so, it is hoped that the reader will appreciate that it is not *necessarily* true that the revolution in Russia in 1917—the first claiming to be a socialist one—or the Chinese Revolution of 1949 or any other communist accession to power was in some sense 'un-Marxist'. As has been emphasized, although Marx had a reasonably standardized *method* for analysing society, he also said that each particular case must be examined in its own setting and that there were no general *laws* of social development applicable to all countries at all times (this has been called Marx's 'principle of historical specificity'). This, plus the contradictions that sometimes arose between the 'descriptive' and the normative aspects of Marx's approach, make it impossible to say with any certainty how Marx would have reacted to many developments in communist theory and practice of the twentieth century. But one very important point in this connection is that Marx believed that theoreticians should do more than merely explain and/or interpret the world around them. In his *Theses on Feuerbach* Marx wrote: 'The philosophers have only *interpreted* the world, in various ways; the point is to *change* it' (in Feuer 1969, p. 286). This has served as an inspiration to many in the century and a half since Marx wrote it—including the various leaders whose views we are about to examine.

LENINISM

As with Marx, so ambiguities can be found in the writings of Lenin—perhaps the most frequently cited example being the discrepancies between his ideas expressed in *The State and Revolution* and those contained in his writings after the Bolsheviks had seized power. Many of these differences can be explained by the fact that the former document represents one of the very few occasions on which Lenin looked at the long-term aims of a socialist revolution, whereas in most of his writing he is primarily concerned with short-term, specific problems and the way in which the Bolsheviks should deal with them. It is important to note that Lenin was both a practical revolutionary and a theoretician, and at least some of the problems of ambiguity to be found in his works become less so if one realizes that he could be dealing with different types of questions in different tracts. This point also means that Leninism is the first of the major approaches to communism which is based on the practical experiences of directing a revolution and then a country, as well as on theoretical premises.

Most would agree that Lenin's most important contributions to the debates on socialism and how to achieve it were those concerned with the *organization of a revolutionary party*. Marx himself did not write or say very much about the role of such a party; he never founded one himself, and was only a member of one for about sixteen of his sixty-three years (he belonged to the Communist League from 1847 to 1852 and to the First International from 1864 to 1873). However, as McLellan points out, Marx

... did insist that this party should have a completely democratic internal organisation; that it should be the independent creation of the workers themselves; that it was distinguished by a theoretical understanding of working-class goals and that (usually) its organisation was not to be a part of, or dependent on, any other political party. (1980, p. 197.)

On some of these points, Lenin's view differed from Marx's; on others, Lenin spelt out details Marx had not elaborated. The organizational principle of Lenin's party was to be *democratic centralism*, whereby policies were to be discussed at all levels, then finally decided upon by the centre—after which no further discussion was to be tolerated. In order to ensure that the centre did not become too estranged from the rank-and-file, there was to be regular consultation between the various levels, and the lower party members would themselves elect the centre. Lenin had rather less faith in ordinary workers than Marx did, and in the classic statement on party organization, *What is to be Done?* (1902), made it clear that he felt that in a capitalist society most workers could not rise above what he called a trade-unionist or economist mentality without strong leadership. In other words, he argued that the majority of proletarians could only think of improving their own position in terms of trying to secure higher wages or better conditions from their employers, and did not think in terms of a radical political change in society. Only a few workers were able to rise above what he saw as the rather trivial struggle for improved conditions, and these were to become professional revolutionaries—alongside the radical intellectuals in whom Lenin seemed to place most of his faith. This group of professional revolutionaries would form an élite, whose tasks it would be secretly to organize for revolution and to help agitate amongst the working mass. In short, at the beginning of this century, Lenin seemed to be arguing that the Russian working class might eventually become a mass movement for overthrowing the existing regime, but also that it would need a core of clandestine revolutionaries (the party) to *organize* its activities.

Anyone who reads *What is to be Done?* will find that the whole document is related very much to the concrete conditions of autocratic Tsarist Russia in the early twentieth century. Thus one must acknowledge that the sentence so often quoted from this pamphlet to 'prove' that Lenin had no real faith in the workers—'Only an incorrigible utopian would have a *broad* organisation of workers, with elections, reports, universal suffrage, etc.'—actually closes with the words, '. . . . under the autocracy' (Tucker 1975, p. 73). To omit this part of the sentence is to perpetrate a grave distortion of Lenin's ideas in this pamphlet. Lenin later explicitly stated that *What is to be Done?* was related to specific conditions and was not to be taken as a *general* theory of the role of the revolutionary party.

Indeed, if we look for such a statement in Lenin's works, we shall be frustrated. Even the infamous *Resolution on Party Unity* of 1921, in which Lenin forbade factionalism within the party and seemed to be calling for a highly centralized political system, is related specifically to the problems the new Bolshevik state was encountering. This all said, much of the logic of Lenin's view of the party is such that the virtually unassailable position of the party in many communist states can be attributed to his general attitude towards politics. The absence of any proper consideration of the question of the control of the party itself in Lenin's writings means that there is no in-built mechanism in Leninism to overcome abuses within a communist party. Nor is there any mechanism to ensure its eventual disappearance, or its full answerability to either the whole population or even just the proletariat in any given society.

The theory of the party is not the only major contribution Lenin made to communist theory. Another is his theory of *imperialism*, a theory he developed less from the writings of Marx—who only touched upon the subject— than from those of J. A. Hobson, R. Hilferding and N. Parvus. Lenin's theory provided an explanation of the absence of the socialist revolution in the advanced capitalist states, yet suggested that such a revolution was now imminent. Basically, he argued that capitalists had been able to make concessions to the workers in their own countries in recent decades to no small extent because they were colonizing other countries and making such big profits (e.g. because of their ability to obtain very cheap raw materials from these colonies). However, he also argued that this could not go on indefinitely. Once capitalists from the leading industrial nations had divided up the rest of the world, there would be only one way in which they could attempt to continue expanding their markets, their sources of cheap resources, etc., and that was by taking colonies from other capitalists. For Lenin—who was heavily influenced by Parvus on this—evidence that capitalism had reached this stage of inevitable conflict was provided by the outbreak of the First World War in 1914, which for him represented the death knell of capitalism. For this reason, he referred to imperialism as 'the highest stage of capitalism'. However, although he believed that the proletariats of both the advanced and the less developed countries would now begin to realize that they had common interests against the capitalists/imperialists, he also realized that there would need to be some trigger mechanism to set off the international socialist revolution. It was in this context that he developed the *weakest link* argument. According to this, Russia represented the weakest link in the capitalist chain of countries in Europe. Lenin maintained that if revolution were to break out in Russia, thus snapping the chain of capitalist domination, then revolution would be triggered in the leading capitalist states. Russia did have a revolution in February 1917, but this was seen by almost all Russian Marxists, including Lenin, as a bourgeois one, which was therefore not likely to act as a trigger. As it became increasingly clear that this revolution was not leading to a consolidation of bourgeois power, so Lenin began to argue that Russia could move on very rapidly to the next stage of socialist revolution. Although he was aware that the conditions in Russia were not ripe for such a revolution—in terms of the social and economic structure of the country, for instance—he argued that the events in his own country would spark off revolutions in the advanced states, such as Germany, and that the proletariats of those countries would then be able to draw the proletariats of the more backward countries along with them to a new socialist international order. Lenin was not in fact the first of the Russian Marxists to provide this sort of analysis (i.e., of permanent international revolution and of less developed countries missing out or abbreviating stages of development)—Trotsky was; but the credit for turning them into an action plan is more Lenin's than Trotsky's.

In fact, Lenin's theory did not prove to be correct; although there was certainly evidence of some revolutionary consciousness in the proletariats of the leading countries (notably Germany) at the end of the First World War, capitalism proved to be far more resilient than he had anticipated. One reason for this might have been that the attempts by bourgeois ideologists to develop nationalist loyalties among the working classes had been considerably more successful than Lenin had realized. This is a problem to which we shall return later in the book; for now, the most important point to be made is that the international revolution did not materialize and that, for whatever theoretical reason, Lenin had justified an attempt at socialist revolution in a country in which the proletariat was a small minority. Therefore, by most tenets of classical Marxism, Russia was not ready for such a revolution. Put another way, Lenin had set a precedent for attempting a socialist revolution in a country in which the peasantry still constituted the vast majority of the population. Since this is such an important point—in terms of inspiring revolutionaries in so many relatively backward countries in the twentieth century, and permitting a dictatorship in the name of a minority—it is necessary to examine Lenin's views on the political role of the peasantry in a little detail.

On the whole, Lenin—like Marx—had little faith in the socialist potential of the peasants. Nevertheless, he did realize by the early part of this century that the peasantry would almost certainly have to be involved in and attracted to any Russian revolution. Thus he referred in the pamphlet *Two Tactics of Social Democracy in the Democratic Revolution* to the need for a 'revolutionary-democratic dictatorship of the proletariat and peasantry'. The Mensheviks (a group of Russian Marxists who often disagreed with Lenin and his Bolshevik group) argued that this represented a serious distortion of Marxism; Marx had only ever referred to a 'dictatorship of the proletariat'. However, Lenin pointed out that he was referring to an alliance between the peasantry and the urban proletariat in a *bourgeois-democratic revolution*, not a socialist one. It can be argued that this does not overtly contradict anything in Marx, but this is not very convincing; it is clear that the notion of a dictatorship of workers and peasants in a bourgeois democracy would have seemed absurd to Marx, for whom rule by the majority and the sort of political rule typical of capitalist economic systems (i.e., bourgeois government) were mutually exclusive. As for the role of the peasants just before and during a *socialist* revolution—this is not clearly spelt out in Lenin's writings. It is true that Lenin called the new political structure after the October (socialist) Revolution a 'workers and peasants' state', but he did so for reasons of expediency, and he does not appear ever to have changed his basic belief that the peasants—even most of the poorer ones—were innately conservative and oriented towards private property. Thus, although Lenin was forced by historical circumstance into some sort of *modus vivendi* with the peasants, we can say with certainty that he would never have given them the *leading* role in either a bourgeois or a socialist revolution.

Two final points need to be made about Leninism. The first is that it was Lenin who really introduced the relatively sharp distinction that most communists nowadays make between *socialism* and *communism*. Marx had tended to use the two terms interchangeably, usually making a distinction only when he wanted clearly to separate his and Engel's views from those of other socialists with whom they disagreed. But in a passage in *Critique of the Gotha Programme*, Marx referred briefly to the 'first phase' and a 'higher phase' of communism; in *The State and Revolution*, Lenin argued that the first phase should be called 'socialism', and only the higher phase 'communism'. For Lenin, socialist society is primarily one in which there is still a division of labour and inequalities (e.g. in terms of the distribution of wealth, or facilities in town and countryside), but in which the means of production are socially rather than privately owned. Because of such inequalities in socialism, plus the need immediately following the revolution for the suppression of elements hostile to the new economic and political order (the 'dictatorship of the proletariat'), Lenin argued that a state would still be necessary; but it would have a less dominant and certainly ever less oppressive role than in capitalist society, as antagonistic classes slowly disappeared. Thus the state starts to wither away under socialism, but does not disappear completely until true communism is reached. In terms of simple slogans to distinguish the two stages, Lenin continued to use Marx's image of communism ('from each according to his ability, to each according his need'—a slogan Marx took from the French writer Étienne Cabet), but said that under socialism, distribution would be on the principle of 'from each according to his ability, to each according to his work'.

The second point is that Lenin was very much a *voluntarist*. Marxists generally tend to a more voluntarist or a more *determinist* view of the world; expressing this in simple terms, the debate concerns the question of whether Marxists, having understood the 'laws' of their own society's development, should consciously attempt to accelerate processes that are considered inevitable anyway (the voluntarist approach), or else should wait for relationships to mature and for historical change to come about at its own pace (the determinist approach). The question is actually one of degree rather than of qualitative differences, since events in history are largely the result of human actions anyway; so the question is basically one of how much of a boost to development Marxists should give. Lenin adopted a highly voluntaristic interpretation of Marx, whereas the Mensheviks took a more deterministic view. Scholars have subsequently devoted considerable attention to the question of whether Marx himself was really more of a voluntarist or a determinist; although this debate is of great theoretical importance, it is of marginal relevance here. What is important is that Lenin's interpretation has served as a legitimation to many revolutionaries in the twentieth century to seize power in the name of Marxism and the building of communism, even though other Marxists have warned them that conditions are not yet ready for such a take-over and that there might be a backlash.

Having briefly considered some of the main tenets of both Marx's and Lenin's writings, we can make the point that the official ideology in all communist states is called Marxism–Leninism (although some states add other '-isms' or names to this), a term coined by Stalin. More details on this ideology will be given in chapter five; at this point we need merely to note that since Marxism itself is so ambiguous, the combining of these ideas with the mixture of political theory and pragmatism we call Leninism is clearly going to produce a body of ideas prone to widely differing interpretations.

Although Stalin possessed neither a very original nor a penetrating mind, it would be a grave mistake to underestimate his contribution to communist theory and practice. Whilst Marx was concerned with the big problems of understanding social development, and Lenin, above all, with taking his communist Bolsheviks to power and consolidating that power, Stalin actually showed the world one way of developing a country very rapidly without being either a capitalist state or a colony of one. It fell to him, as leader of the USSR, to show in concrete terms what a 'dictatorship of the proletariat' and other important concepts mentioned but not elaborated by Marx would look like; many may have criticized what he did, but it is an unfortunate fact that a highly voluntaristic approach to the building of communism is quite likely to lead to the kind of wilful leadership and human atrocities associated with the name of Stalin. Although Stalinism is not a *necessary* outcome of either Marxism or Leninism, it is a perfectly *feasible* one.

For our purposes, Stalin made two major contributions to communist theory—the concept of *socialism in one country*; and the justification of the strong state and party under socialism. He also made *terror* a major aspect of his 'socialist' system, and developed the *cult of the personality*.

Both Marx and Lenin had conceived of socialism as an international phenomenon; as we saw earlier, Lenin had often argued that the Russian revolution would not be successful unless accompanied by revolutions in the West European states. Although there is evidence to suggest that Lenin was beginning to lose his faith in the imminence of revolution in Western Europe, there was still just enough happening at the time of his death (January 1924) to permit him some optimism; the massive inflationary crisis Germany experienced in 1923 was one such event. But Germany overcame this problem, and following Lenin's death, faith in the impending revolutions began to wane

amongst many Bolsheviks. Trotsky remained convinced that socialism could
be achieved only on an international scale. He argued that the Soviet Union
should continue to push ahead with its own revolutionary change, but also
that it should encourage revolution in other countries, on the grounds that
Russia could only consolidate socialism by linking up with other, more advanced industrial states which had themselves undergone socialist revolutions. Thus one of the key elements of *Trotskyism* is a commitment to
'permanent revolution', which implies internationalism. But for a number of
reasons—the Soviet population's war-weariness, nationalist feelings, and the
fact that successful revolutions abroad were simply not materializing—
Trotsky's idea of 'permanent revolution' found ever less support. Hence,
when Stalin proposed a policy of 'socialism in one country' at the end of
1924, it found immediate and wide support amongst both members of the
communist party and the general population; at this stage, the ramifications
of it, particularly for the peasantry, were very vague. The concept was not
actually Stalin's own—he was merely developing ideas put forward by both
Bukharin and Preobrazhenskii. But it was Stalin who pushed it through as a
policy and hence with whose name the theory is most usually linked.

There is some debate as to whether or not, in advocating 'socialism in one
country', Stalin was in fact renouncing world revolution. Trotsky claimed he
was, but Carew Hunt (1963, p. 217) is probably more accurate when he
argues that both Trotsky and Stalin wanted socialism in Russia and in the
world generally, but that the two men rank-ordered these priorities differently in the 1920s. However, as the years went by, Stalin became less and less
committed to international socialism, and ever more of a traditional Russian
autocrat, to whom Russian dominance in the world was far more important
than the spreading of whatever 'true' socialism might be. In fact, in 1946 he
went so far as to claim that not only socialism but even communism could be
achieved in one country (Carew Hunt 1963, p. 223). One of the most important aspects of 'socialism in one country' was that it provided a new theory of
economic development. Put simply, this stated that an economy could be
modernized without either indigenous capitalists or foreign investment.
Funds for industrial development could be obtained through what is sometimes called 'primitive socialist accumulation' (a term coined by Preobrazhenskii), which basically means that the peasants are exploited by the state in
the name of socialism. This implied a major reorganization of society and the
economy, and led to what Stalin called a 'revolution from above'; whereas
both Marx and Lenin had only ever conceived of revolution from below,
against the existing state, Stalin was now arguing that revolution could
actually be initiated and directed by the existing state powers.

Stalin's theory of 'socialism in one country', and the related concept of
'revolution from above', has held its attractions for the leaders of many
underdeveloped states who have wanted to modernize and to build socialism
and yet be independent of the capitalist world. However, several less attract-

ive features flow almost necessarily from the concept. The first is that, as might be imagined, many Soviet peasants were hostile to the idea that they should bear the major burden for the funding of the transformation of society. As peasant hostility in the USSR grew—in the late 1920s/early 1930s—so Stalin used increasingly harsh measures to overcome it. This snowballed, and by the end of the 1930s, the name of Stalin was synonymous with terror; in one sense, the so-called 'dictatorship of the proletariat' was by now very clearly a dictatorship *over* rather than of the majority.

Second, Stalin used the existence of opposition as part of his attempt to justify not only the continued existence, but indeed the strengthening of the state in what he alleged was a socialist society. Stalin proclaimed in 1936 that socialism had been achieved in the Soviet Union, and the reader could be forgiven for supposing that this would lead to a 'withering away' of the Soviet state. But Stalin argued that there were still shortages of some goods in society, differences between town and countryside, etc., which meant that there would have to be a central government to direct distribution. More importantly, he argued that the class struggle would intensify under socialism (a view Marx would almost certainly have disagreed with) and that there were enemies both within Russia and abroad ('capitalist encirclement'). Both these factors necessitated the continued existence of the state's agencies of coercion (the police) and defence (the army); in fact, the notion of 'capitalist encirclement' led Stalin to conclude that there might be a need for a state even under communism.

For the state to operate in the interests of the working masses, rather than its own officials, there would have to be some form of control or supervisory mechanism. However, instead of entrusting this to the masses, Stalin argued that the communist party would have to perform this task. It is difficult to argue that this goes against the ideas of either Marx or Lenin, since neither of them had provided much detail on the role of the party once socialism had been achieved. The role of the masses was now to carry out, unquestioningly, the directives of the central authorities. Moreover, the masses were to treat the communist leaders as demigods; this elevation of individual leaders to superhuman status is known as the 'cult of the personality', and it was Stalin who introduced this phenomenon to the communist world. He started by creating a cult of the late Lenin, and subsequently developed a cult around himself.

There are a number of other factors that one associates with Stalin, most of them being aspects of the major points we have already considered. In the economy, for instance, there were five-year plans, forced collectivization, excessive concentration on heavy industry at the expense of other sectors—all parts of the 'revolution from above' in the context of 'socialism in one country'. Socially, there were contradictory ideas on equality (on the one hand, Stalin mounted a major campaign against wealthy peasants or 'kulaks'; on the other, he criticized 'bourgeois egalitarianism' and introduced élite, fee-paying schools), harsh labour laws, high levels of social mobility and impressive rises in educational standards. The total package of leadership style and policies has served as a model for a number of communists throughout the world—although many have sought, with varying degrees of success, to achieve the economic development with less repressive political means.

MAOISM

One of those leaders most impressed by Stalinism was the leader of the Chinese communist revolution, Mao Zedong. Although the personal relationship between Stalin and Mao was not always as warm as it might have been, Mao—like many other dissatisfied Chinese intellectuals—was particularly attracted to the concept of 'socialism in one country'. This was largely because Mao was almost as much of a nationalist as a communist, a point that comes out clearly in his 1938 statement that:

Being Marxist, Communists are internationalists, but we can put Marxism into practice only when it is integrated with the specific characteristics of our country and acquires a definite national form . . . For the Chinese Communists who are part of the great Chinese nation, flesh and blood, any talk about Marxism in isolation from China's characteristics is merely Marxism in the abstract, Marxism in a vacuum-
. (Mao, 1965, ii. 209.)

Even in his more abstract theorizing—for instance on dialectics in the essay *On Contradiction*—Mao takes as much from traditional Chinese philosophy (in this particular case, the theory of the yin and the yang) as he does from German (Hegel or Marx). Mao tended to treat the ideas of Marx, Engels, Lenin, and Stalin as methods and political theories but his own ideas as essentially pragmatic and related specifically to the Chinese situation; for this reason he, and the Chinese generally, talk of the ideas of the four 'classical' writers as 'isms', but refuse to refer to Maoism; instead, his writings are always referred to as 'Mao Zedong Thought'. However, this division is unnecessary and unjustified, since the writings of Lenin and Stalin—and to a lesser extent even Marx and Engels—are, like Mao's, a mixture of abstract theorizing and analysis of concrete events. Hence, we shall adopt here the common Western practice of referring to Maoism rather than Mao Zedong Thought.

Although Mao often praised the Stalinist approach to communism, there are in fact a number of significant differences between Mao's ideas and those we have already considered. One of the most important is on the question of the role of the peasantry. In the early 1920s, Mao was a fairly conventional Marxist by most criteria; certainly he looked to the urban, industrial proletariat as the main force in any future revolution. But his own experiences made him turn his attention increasingly towards the peasantry, and already by 1926, he was looking to them for any future revolutionary change. To a large extent, Mao was able to justify his faith in the peasantry because of a fundamentally different conception of class from those we have examined so far. Both the Russian leaders had taken what they considered to be an orthodox Marxist view of class—namely that class is a function of one's relationship to the means of production, an objective criterion. But Mao maintained that class was a more subjective concept—a way of thinking as much as an objective relationship. Taking this as his starting-point, Mao was able to argue that the bulk of the Chinese peasantry were 'blank'—meaning that they had no strong political views and that their minds were therefore relatively easy to mould. In other words, whereas Marx, Lenin, and Stalin believed that our way of perceiving the world is conditioned by our position in the economy, Mao believed that people's minds are much more malleable. It was on the basis of this premiss that Mao argued that the peasantry—and, indeed, other classes—could have proletarian (i.e., pro-communist) ideas instilled in them. Only by appreciating this point can one make any sense of Mao's notion—held at least until the mid-1960s, when he began to question it himself—that it was possible to go right through to communism with a 'four-class bloc' (workers, peasants, petty bourgeoisie, and national bourgeoisie). Thus the concept of a 'dictatorship of the proletariat' was severely modified by Mao, who developed a concept of 'people's democratic dictatorship' in the late-1940s. Although the proletariat (or, in the absence of a proletariat, then a proletarian party), was to play the leading role in this alliance, not only the peasantry but even the bourgeoisie could also be involved if they agreed to accept the new values.

This strong belief in the malleability of people's minds has led writers such as Schram (1969, p. 135) to point out that Mao was even more of a voluntarist than Lenin (and, we might add, Stalin). It also helps to explain the difference between Stalin's and Mao's approaches to change in the post-revolutionary period. Stalin believed that the transformation of the economic base was all important; other changes were secondary to this. In contrast, Mao believed that change in people's consciousness was the top priority. Thus, whereas Stalin sought control and change through physical coercion and terror, Mao tended to rely more on 'thought reform'.

The logic of this approach also led Mao to take a rather different line from Stalin on the question of the role of the ordinary citizen in politics. Although Mao accepted the Leninist concept of 'democratic centralism', he placed greater emphasis than either of the Soviet leaders on the democratic element—here, in the specific sense of involving the masses more in politics. It was in this context that he developed the *mass-line* approach to Chinese politics. This was in line with his views on thought reform, in that he believed that one of the most effective ways to make the population understand and accept a new political system was to encourage them to participate in it. The classic statement on this came in a piece Mao wrote for the Central

Committee in 1943 entitled *Some Questions concerning Methods of Leadership*, in which he argued that:

In all the practical work of our Party, all correct leadership is necessarily 'from the masses, to the masses'. This means: take the ideas of the masses (scattered and unsystematic ideas) and concentrate them (through study turn them into concentrated and systematic ideas), then go to the masses and propagate and explain these ideas until the masses embrace them as their own, hold fast to them and translate them into action, and test the correctness of these in such action. Then once again concentrate ideas from the masses and once again go to the masses so that the ideas are persevered in and carried through. And so on, over and over again in an endless spiral, with the ideas becoming more correct, more vital and richer each time.   (Mao, 1965, iii. 119.)

It should be clear from the above quotation that Mao is not advocating some form of representative democracy, in which the politicians respond to popular demands; rather, the masses are to learn through participation, and the party is to lead—but with an awareness of what the masses are thinking. That this is a long way from Western concepts of democracy is partially borne out by the fact that the post-Mao leadership has criticized Mao's practice of the 'mass-line', on the grounds that mass campaigns, for instance, were merely tools for implementing the leader's will rather than being a symbol of meaningful mass participation.

For third-world revolutionaries, one of the most important practical aspects of Maoism is the analysis of *guerilla warfare*. Marx never dealt with this question, and the Soviets have always been more interested in conventional warfare. Mao began to develop his ideas in the 1930s, initially through his experiences in fighting the Chinese nationalist (Guomindang) forces. He believed that a small army could defeat a much larger one if the tactics and strategy were superior. One of the methods he advocated was that, wherever they happened to be operating, guerillas should always seek to gain the respect and support of local citizens (for instance, by helping them harvest their crops). They should also try to establish bases to which they could retreat in highly inaccessible areas—mountains, jungles, swamps, etc. One other important point in the Maoist approach was that guerillas should always be prepared for protracted wars, and not attempt too rapid a victory: the small army should chip away at the larger one, weakening its morale and resolve. These methods have certainly worked well, not only in China, but also in Yugoslavia, Vietnam, Mozambique, and elsewhere.

Closely linked to the last point is Mao's emphasis on the role of a revolutionary army; as he expressed it in 1938, 'A few small political parties with a short history . . . have no army, and so have not been able to get anywhere . . . Every Communist must grasp the truth, "Political power grows out of the barrel of a gun." '   (Mao, 1965, ii. 224.)

To be sure, Mao also emphasized that the army must be subordinate to the party—'Our principle is that the Party commands the gun, and the gun must never be allowed to command the party' (ibid., p. 224); but in practice the revolutionary army played in many ways at least as important a political role before, during and, to a lesser extent, even after the revolution as the communist party itself.

EUROCOMMUNISM

Nowadays, there is fairly widespread agreement that 'Eurocommunism'—whatever it might mean—is now in decline, perhaps even dead. Nevertheless, there were many in the 1970s who believed that Eurocommunism was an important new political phenomenon with a bright future, and it certainly caused considerable irritation and embarrassment to the USSR. Moreover, the legacy is in some senses still with us, in that communists in the West have in many countries still to heal the rifts in their own ranks that the questioning and the 'new' approach of the 1970s brought about. Finally, the concept is important in that, unlike any of the forms of communism considered so far—with the partial exception of Marxism—Eurocommunism is based on conditions in the most developed countries, not more backward ones; although Marx had envisaged socialism coming about in such countries, many of the descriptions and analyses he produced in the nineteenth century now seem very dated, while it is clear why much in Leninism, Maoism, etc. is irrelevant to the countries of Western Europe or North America. It is thus necessary to consider this 'new' form of communism, if only briefly.

The actual term 'Eurocommunism' seems to have been coined by a Yugoslav journalist in June 1975 (Levi, 1979, p. 9). Unfortunately, we cannot be nearly so precise on its actual meaning, for the simple reason that commentators have interpreted it in different ways. There are those who take a very broad view, referring to any group of communists which is critical of the USSR and calls for a more liberal version of communism as 'Eurocommunist'; this would therefore include, for instance, the Yugoslavs. Then there is the 'middle of the road' approach, represented by writers such as Löwenthal, in which any party that has decided to work very definitely within the existing bourgeois political framework and is critical of the USSR is defined as 'Eurocommunist'. Such a definition would embrace many West European communist parties (the West German being a notable exception), as well as those in Japan, Australia, and elsewhere. Third, there is the 'narrow' definition, in which the term is used almost exclusively to refer to the policies and style of three of the most powerful communist parties in Western Europe in the 1970s—the Italian, French, and Spanish. Finally, there are those, such as the Italian communist Amendola, who believe that there never was such a concept. Given this wide range of views, it is not possible to produce an analysis of the phenomenon that will be acceptable to all. In the description that follows, I have decided to use what seems to me to be the most commonly held view—that Eurocommunism was a widespread phenomenon in the advanced capitalist states in the 1970s, but that the most influential proponents of it were the Italian, French, and Spanish parties (i.e., a mixture of definitions two and three).

In analysing the 'birth' of Eurocommunism, we can isolate both long-term background factors, and more immediate factors from the late-1960s on. Let us now consider these.

One of the salient features of Eurocommunism was a desire on the part of individual communist parties to choose their own way to communism, taking into consideration the specific features of their own society. In the case of virtually all the Eurocommunist parties, with the exception of the French, this involved severe criticism of the USSR and of its insistence on being involved in the affairs of communist parties in other countries. This desire for equality between parties and for the right to choose one's own path was nothing new in the 1960s/1970s; one can cite instances of it at least as early as the 1940s, for instance, and the Italian communist leader Togliatti's concept of *polycentrism* in the mid-1950s was a very clear example. However, little was actually done by communists in Western Europe to back up these calls for greater autonomy, and it was the invasion of Czechoslovakia in August 1968 that finally galvanized many Western communists into action.

Another major event of 1968 which can be seen as one of the watersheds in the development of Eurocommunism was the revolutionary situation in France that peaked in May. For our purposes, it is sufficient to note that the French communists came under heavy attack from other left-wing groups for having helped the French government to placate the workers and thus defuse the revolutionary situation. The reasons for the communists' behaviour are too complex to elaborate here; the salient point is that the communists were now very sensitive to charges that they were a conservative force that did not represent the working class in the way it should. Public support for the party declined sharply, and this led the communist leaders to reassess their position and policies. They had been in a form of coalition with more moderate left-wing parties since 1965, and for a while after 1968 decided that this had been an error; consequently their alliance with other parties was dissolved in 1969. However, the communists very soon realized that they would probably be even more ineffectual on their own than in a left coalition. They therefore decided to join forces with other left-wing parties and to make it absolutely clear to all that they favoured reform—albeit radical reform—rather than violent revolution. In other words, they felt that they could not be accused of the hypocrisy of which they had been accused by the radical students in 1968, since their position was now stated openly. In 1972 they signed a 'Common Programme for Government' with the socialists, thus making their willingness to work within the system clear to all.

While the situation was not quite as dramatic in Italy, the Communists there too had been responding to changes in their own society, as well as to Soviet actions in Eastern Europe. The late-1960s witnessed a polarization of politics in Italy. For instance, student radicalism in 1967 and 1968 was followed by an upsurge of militancy amongst the workers, peaking in the so-called 'hot autumn' of 1969. At the same time, terrorism—from both the extreme left and the extreme right—was becoming a major feature of Italian politics. The communists tried to organize themselves better to lead the left-wing unrest in the early 1970s, but in fact were not very successful; and in the 1972 general election, the left as a whole fared poorly. Italy seemed to be swinging to the right. However, the communists now acquired a new leader, Enrico Berlinguer, who probably correctly argued that it was an over-simplification to suggest that Italy was moving to the right. Rather, a minority of the Italian population was moving in the direction of extremist politics—whether of the left or the right—whilst the majority in the middle believed that the 'conservative' Christian Democrats would be better able to restore order than the somewhat shambolic moderate left. For about a year after the Christian Democrats had secured power in the 1972 election, the communists encouraged the trade unions to show that their members neither over-whelmingly supported the government nor could be put down by that government. Italian society was in even more chaos than usual, and no one group seemed able to bring the situation under control. It was in these circumstances that Berlinguer proposed the so-called 'historic compromise' in the autumn of 1973. Under this, the communists expressed their willingness to work with the moderate right (i.e., the Christian Democrats), as well as the socialists, in order to bring Italy out of chaos.

Although we have so far concentrated on developments in France and Italy, we need now to consider other events of the early 1970s that encouraged the development of Eurocommunism, not only in these two countries but elsewhere too. The first was the rise of *détente*, the marked improvement in East–West relations. Ironically, perhaps, the improving relations between the capitalist and communist worlds was accompanied by a major campaign in the Western media to encourage the regimes of Eastern Europe to show respect for human rights. This led to a concentration on the treatment of dissidents which, of course, tended to make communism look like a very repressive kind of political system. This in turn meant that the Western communists, if they were to increase their popularity, would have to distance themselves even further from the practice of their comrades in the USSR and elsewhere. A second factor was the situation in Chile, where a Marxist regime of sorts—led by Salvador Allende—had come to power through perfectly legitimate means in September 1970, only to be overthrown three years later. The collapse was seen by many as the result of both Allende's failure to reconcile major conflicting interests in Chile and US involvement in his removal. Communists in Europe—especially in Italy—felt that it would not be sufficient just to be elected into power on their own (assuming this were possible anyway), but that some sort of coalition would be necessary in order both to avoid really major clashes of interest, and in order that other regimes would not become unduly concerned and thus attempt to interfere in a given country's domestic politics. Berlinguer was quite explicit that this was one of the reasons behind his proposal for the 'historic compromise' (see Russo, 1979, pp. 78–9 and Lange and Vannicelli, 1981, p. 118).

We have seen how both domestic and international events in the late 1960s/early 1970s led the communists in both France and Italy to reassess themselves and their relations with other parties. But it was events in the two years or so from the autumn of 1973 that really crystallized the phenomenon of Eurocommunism. First, there was the enormous rise in oil prices in November 1973, which had serious repercussions for the Western economies; there was massive inflation and signs that unemployment would reach levels unknown since the 1930s. Shortly after this came the collapse of right-wing dictatorships in Portugal (April 1974), Greece (July 1974), and Spain (following Franco's death in November 1975), and a feeling in some quarters that there would be serious political instability in those countries. These events and developments led the communists, among others, to argue that Western Europe was in a state of crisis—the only solution to which was a move towards socialism. It was in these circumstances that several communist parties in Western Europe (as well as Japan) issued a series of 'joint declarations' between July 1975 and March 1977 (for these, see Lange and Vannicelli 1981, pp. 357–61); these represent some of the clearest and tersest statements we have on the Eurocommunist approach.

As should by now be clear, one of the salient features of Eurocommunism was its pragmatism, its willingness to abandon what many had considered to be sacred tenets of communist theory (e.g. the French communist party's abandonment of its commitment to a 'dictatorship of the proletariat' in February 1976) if such commitments were preventing the communists from appealing to a much wider audience. In fact, the communists seemed now to be adopting an overall stance which is best described as eclectic, in the sense that they seemed to be wanting the best of both socialist *and* bourgeois ideas and ideals. This comes out clearly in the following extract from the 'joint declaration' of the French and Italian communist parties (November 1975), which encapsulates many of the key ideas of Eurocommunism:

Socialism will constitute a higher phase of democracy and freedom: democracy realized in the most complete manner.

In this spirit all the freedoms—which are a product both of the great democratic-bourgeois revolutions and of the great popular struggles of this century, headed by the working class—will have to be guaranteed and developed. This holds true for freedom of thought and expression, for freedom of the press, of assembly, association and demonstration, for free movement of persons inside and outside their country, for the inviolability of private life, for religious freedom and total freedom of expression for currents of thought and every philosophical, cultural and artistic opinion. The French and Italian communists declare themselves for the plurality of political parties, for the

right to existence and activity of opposition parties, for the free formation of majori-
ties and minorities and the possibility of their alternating democratically, for the lay
nature and democratic functioning of the state, for the independence of the judiciary.
In the same way they declare themselves for the freedom of activity and the autonomy
of the trade unions.   (From Lange and Vannicelli, 1981, p. 359.)

Despite all these changes, Eurocommunism never became the major force
its supporters hoped and its opponents feared it might become. There were a
number of reasons for this, and we can mention only a few. One was that
Western governments were better able to deal with the economic crisis than
some had predicted; the welfare state, for instance, cushioned many ordinary
citizens from the worst excesses of a major capitalist crisis which in turn
meant that those citizens did not question their political system as much as
the communists had expected. Another was that many voters felt that 'a leo-
pard cannot change its spots'—i.e., that the communists' declarations of a
commitment to civil liberties, a willingness to work with other political parties, etc. was just a cover-up, and that past experience in other countries suggested that once in power, the communists would show the same lack of
respect for human rights as their colleagues in Eastern Europe had done and
were continuing to do. The Western communists' position was not helped by
the fact that it became evident within months of the signing of the Helsinki
agreement (1975) that many of the East European regimes were totally ignoring the promises to respect civil liberties they had so recently made in signing
that document. Moreover, the Western communists refused to renounce
their commitment to democratic centralism within their own organizations,
and many felt that this revealed that the alleged commitment to a new, much
more open and democratic version of communism was less than total.
Finally, the French communists—unlike their Spanish and Italian comrades—were loath to be too critical of the USSR, which again made voters suspicious. For these and other reasons, the Eurocommunists did not fare nearly
as well in the elections of the mid-to-late 1970s as they had hoped, and by the
early 1980s, Eurocommunism had all but been forgotten.

In one sense, the Eurocommunists were in a dilemma right from the start.
Many of their policies were in fact hardly distinguishable from those of some
of the social democratic and/or socialist parties of Europe—and the latter did
not have to prove that they were committed to legitimate politics. If voters
could get similar policies from parties whose commitment to parliamentary
democracy was not in doubt—and who could thus be removed by the electorate if the latter disliked their style of government—then why should they support the communists, who might stay in power irrespective of the wishes of
the electorate? On the other hand, we have seen how the communists had
already by the early 1970s lost their more radical image amongst those—particularly the young—who did in fact *want* a revolutionary party. In sum, in
attempting to widen their appeal, the communists finished up losing their

identity and appealing to very few. Although the Italian communists have done rather better than the French or Spanish from most points of view, this is largely because there is no major social democratic alternative in that country, a situation which could be changing. Certainly, as a pan-European phenomenon, the future of Eurocommunism is bleak: the Spanish communists are divided and now a minor political force, while the French communists have largely returned to their pro-Moscow stance and have lost much ground to the socialists. Perhaps the hierarchy and élitism that are inherent in most conceptions of communism in power become ever less acceptable and relevant as societies become more complex and as people become better educated and enjoy higher standards of living. It is thus perhaps in Eurocommunism that we see the most glaring contradiction in the Marxist–Leninist argument that communism is both an end goal and a political movement for reaching that end goal.

SUMMARY AND CONCLUSION

So what is communism? On one level, it is a better society in the future, in which there are no classes and hence no fundamental antagonisms. This is because there will be no private property, at least in terms of ownership of the means of production, which most communists see as the basis for class divisions and hence conflict. It is a society in which there is enough for all, and in which people will voluntarily and willingly contribute what they can for the good of society as a whole. People will not be alienated from each other or from their work, which they will enjoy—partially because there will be no rigid division of labour, so that when one becomes bored with one task, one can move on to another. This is brought out nicely in one of the few passages in Marx in which we catch a glimpse of the future society:

... in communist society, where nobody has one exclusive sphere of activity but each can become accomplished in any branch he wishes, society regulates the general production and thus makes it possible for me to do one thing today and another tomorrow, to hunt in the morning, fish in the afternoon, rear cattle in the evening, criticise after dinner, just as I have a mind ...   (Marx and Engels, 1970, p. 53.)

This is not a totally idealistic (this word here being used in its everyday rather than its philosophical sense) picture, since Marx envisaged such a society emerging from a highly industrialized one, in which machines had taken over all the really tedious work. Communism as an end goal is also a world-wide society, in which there are no meaningful national differences and no more wars.

  In many ways then, communism as a distant target is surely a very attractive concept. But it has been emphasized that the end goal was rarely examined or described in detail by any of the theorists whose ideas we have examined; for all of them, communism was also a method for understanding the world around them, and a political movement for reaching the distant, vague—if highly desirable—goal. The bulk of their writings—certainly of the twentieth century communists—has been concerned with the practicalities of seizing and maintaining power. This has led some communists in power to produce some very strange 'popular' definitions of communism—one of the most extraordinary of all being the North Korean slogan 'Rice is Communism' (cited in Shuhachi, 1984, p. 83). Such eccentricities aside, we have also seen that there are profound differences between communist theoreticians on some very basic questions such as class, the nature of revolution, revolutionary tactics, the role of the peasantry, nationalism and internationalism, the functions of the party and the state, etc. And of course we have looked at only a tiny number of the communist theorists that could have been included. In one sense, therefore, the examination of communism in practice in the following pages will help to give the reader a clearer understanding of what communism is; beyond this, unfortunately, there is no brief, universally acceptable and thus satisfactory description of communism.

Basic further reading

R. N. Carew Hunt, 1963
S. Carrillo, 1977
L. Feuer (ed.) 1969.
N. Harding, 1983.
L. Kolakowski, 1978.
M. Liebman, 1975.

D. McLellan, 1975; 1977; 1979; 1980
A. Meyer, 1984.
S. Schram, 1969.
P. F. della Torre et. al., 1979
R. Tucker (ed.), 1975; 1977; 1978.

2

HOW COMMUNISTS COME TO POWER

THERE is no 'standard' path by which communists come to power. Nevertheless, the more examples we study, the more obvious it becomes that certain factors keep recurring, even though the particular mix and balance of such factors is in each case unique. This recurrence of factors has led several Western analysts to attempt to classify the various types of communist takeover, although the very fact that such typologies sometimes differ quite considerably from each other tends to endorse the point about uniqueness. In this chapter, we begin by considering three of the best known typologies, following which we examine the transition to communist power in six countries. At the end of the chapter, the variables which seem most frequently to be contributory factors to a successful takeover by communists will be listed.

TYPOLOGIES

In an article published in 1968, Robert Tucker argued that there have in fact been only three basic types of communist takover. The first was the takeover of Russia by the Bolsheviks, which for Tucker is *sui generis* (i.e., unique). The takeover was enacted by indigenous revolutionaries, but—in the beginning at least—was virtually bloodless, and there was no protracted resistance offered by the previous regime. Tucker's second category—revolution by armed struggle—differs from the first type primarily in that the communists had to wrest power against considerable resistance, either from indigenous contestants for power and/or foreign forces. In this category are included Albania, China, Cuba, Vietnam, and Yugoslavia. The third and final category for Tucker is what he calls 'imposed revolution'; included here are Bulgaria, Czechoslovakia, East Germany, Hungary, North Korea, Mongolia, Poland, and Romania. Tucker argues that in these cases the communists would not have been able to take power on their own, and in fact owe their position to the assistance of an external agent—in all cases, the USSR. This imposition actually came in very differing ways in the countries listed—reluctantly and somewhat surreptitiously in Czechoslovakia, very slowly in Mongolia, and crassly in Poland—but the general pattern was similar.

R. V. Burks (1964), admittedly only considering communist takeovers in Eastern Europe (excluding the USSR), also produced a three-category typology—viz. guerilla conquest (Albania and Yugoslavia), parliamentary infiltration (Czechoslovakia, Hungary, and, in slightly different form, Bulgaria) and finally 'baggage-train' government (East Germany, Poland, and Romania). In the first type, the country was occupied by an invader and the communists built up their resistance movement. This movement used guerilla tactics not only against the invading forces, but also against rival indigenous movements. Although the communists did not themselves oust the invader, they had, by the time the allies defeated the invader, built up a reputation for representing the national interest. Moreover, the anti-communist guerilla movements collaborated with the invading forces in the later stages of the Second World War which meant that, ironically perhaps, the communist guerilla movement was the one supported by the Western allies. At the same time, many of the anti-communist guerilla movements in the later stages seemed more interested in fighting the communists than the invaders, and thus lost considerable support at home. In the second type (parliamentary infiltration), the communists did not create a guerilla movement. Their popularity and strong position was based largely on traditional (pre-Second World War) attitudes towards the communists, both native and Soviet, and the shadow of Soviet presence in the country. The communists here tried to build up popular support by parliamentary means, only forcibly seizing power when the parliamentary road did not appear to be bringing the desired results. By 'baggage-train government', Burks means takeovers by communists in states where they were clearly unpopular and where they secured their victory only with massive Soviet backing.

A more complex typology than either Tucker's or Burks's is Thomas Hammond's (1975b, pp. 638–40). In the most detailed study yet of communist takeovers (for others see Seton Watson, 1960, p. 330; Dallin and Breslauer, 1970, p. 14; Black, 1964, pp. 417–25), Hammond identifies no less than eight different paths by which communists have come to power.

(1) *Outright annexation of territory by a communist state.* In this case, an existing communist regime annexes geographically contiguous territory and incorporates it into a new, larger communist state. Russia did this on a large scale in the early years after 1917, and also during the period of the Nazi–Soviet non-aggression pact (1939–41). China also did this with Tibet.

(2) *Installation of a communist regime outside of Russia by the Soviet Army.* The states included by Hammond under this category are Bulgaria, East Germany, Hungary, North Korea, Mongolia, Poland, Romania, and Tannu Tuva (which some see as being part of Mongolia).

(3) *Counter-revolutions in heretical communist countries by the Soviet Army.* Hammond's third category does not in fact refer to communist takeovers (although he classifies them as such) if by these we understand a situation in which communists take power from some other political force. Rather, he is referring to a reassertion of communist power following some crisis in an existing communist state. In some cases, this reassertion will be accompanied by a change in the communist leadership, although this is not invariably so. The reassertion always involves the Soviet Army. Under this category Hammond includes East Germany in 1953, Hungary in 1956, and Czechoslovakia in 1968.

All the types so far described have been examples of what Hammond calls *exported* revolution. There are, in addition, five types of primarily *indigenous* revolution.

(4) *A revolution in the urban centres, based largely on the proletariat, followed by conquest of the countryside.* The USSR is the only country to have followed this path.

(5) *A revolution in the countryside, based mainly on the peasants, followed by conquest of the urban centres.* Under this heading Hammond includes Albania, China, North Vietnam, and Yugoslavia.

(6) *A completely legal takeover through free elections.* According to Hammond, this has happened only in three small areas (West Bengal, Kerala, and San Marino), and in all three the communists were later voted out of office.

(7) *A semi-legal takeover through considerable popular support, combined with armed threats.* The sole example of this is Czechoslovakia.

(8) *A non-communist leader seizes power and then decides to adopt communism.* Once again, Hammond cites one such case—Cuba.

It emerges from the above typologies that writers disagree not only on how many basic types of communist takeover there are (this is only partially explained by the fact that Hammond was writing later and about more states than Tucker and Burks) but even on what types of takeover some countries have experienced (cf. Burks' classification of Hungary and Bulgaria with Hammond's and Tucker's) and one wonders how many more categories and disagreements there would be were the analyses to be updated. There has certainly emerged at least one new type of takeover which we should note. This is where one communist regime is ousted by an external force—itself a communist state, but hostile to the existing rulers—and a new one installed; in 1979, the pro-Chinese Pol Pot regime in Kampuchea (formerly Cambodia) was forced out of office by the Vietnamese, and a pro-Vietnamese/pro-Soviet government sworn in.

In sum, existing typologies reveal disagreements amongst analysts and, if we were able to update them, would in any case become so complex that there seems little point in attempting the exercise; in arguing this, we are broadly in agreement with Szajkowski's (1982, p. 15) view that typologies of communist takeovers are of very limited value. Instead, it is more useful to look at several examples of communist accessions to power, and to extrapolate from these the variables which most frequently seem to contribute to the success of communist bids for power. In the analyses that follow, takeovers will be considered in terms of long- and short-term factors and the main events.

THE USSR

Russia experienced two revolutionary changes of government in 1917—one in February and one in October. The first testified to the ripened disillusionment amongst the Russian people with the tsarist autocracy, the second to the disillusionment with the government that replaced that autocracy. Russia was ruled by the Romanov dynasty from 1613 to 1917. There had been signs of dissatisfaction in the past—the Pugachev rebellion of 1773, the Decembrist movement of 1825, etc.—but none until the 1905 revolution (see below) had seriously undermined the legitimacy of the Tsar in the eyes of the overwhelming majority of the Russian population. The Russian peasantry at the turn of the century accounted for some 80 per cent of the population; they were mostly religious, and believed in the divine right of kings. This is not to say that they were fully satisfied with their lot, but they did not organize themselves in any political sense to improve their situation.

However, many nineteenth-century Russian intellectuals were of the opinion that there was considerable room for improvement in their country and wrote various tracts calling on the Tsar and his government to improve the peasant situation. Their calls appeared to have been heeded with the passing of the Land Reform Act, better known as the Serf Emancipation Act, in 1861. The expectation was that this act would liberate the serfs from their dependence on the great landlords, and in this it was largely successful. However, there proved over time to be two major drawbacks to the reform. First, the act required compensation to the landlords, which meant that many peasants found themselves enormously in debt. Second, the village commune now in effect became a surrogate landowner, and many peasants felt that there was little if any more freedom than in the pre-1861 period. There was one other aspect of the reform which was eventually to have important consequences for the tsarist regime. Whereas it had been very difficult indeed before for peasants to move away from their villages, they could now—subject to the permission of the village commune—move to the towns. This greater freedom was an important factor in the industrialization of Russia, which took off again in the late nineteenth century (having started in the 1820s but stagnated from the 1840s) and which had profound social and political effects.

As it became clear to many Russian intellectuals that the 1861 act had not in fact emancipated the peasants to any meaningful extent, political movements and groups blossomed. At first, such groups wanted to found a new society based on the peasant commune; they were called *Narodniki* or populists. Some preferred an essentially peaceful pursuance of their aims. Others opted for terrorist tactics and indeed succeeded in assassinating Tsar Alexander II in March 1881. But as time passed, and the works of Marx and Engels were read in Russia, so some intellectuals came to believe that revolutionary change would come from the newly emerging urban proletariat rather than the territorially deconcentrated and politically conservative peasantry. Plekhanov was the first of the major Russian Marxists, but by the turn of the century it was one of his students who had come to dominate the movement. That man was Lenin.

By 1905, there was thus a less than satisfied but still essentially loyal peasant majority; a small but rapidly growing proletariat; a few landowners; a tiny bourgeoisie; and the professional and other (e.g. petty bourgeois) classes. From amongst these groupings—primarily the last—various illegal political groups had been formed. All of these wanted change of some kind, but some preferred reform to revolution, and some had more faith in the peasantry than in the urban working class. But the events of 1905 had a profound effect on the whole of Russia and must be seen as a watershed in the lead-up to the events of 1917. At the beginning of the year, following several Russian defeats in its war with Japan, a peaceful demonstration led by a priest (Father Gapon) called on the Tsar to improve the lot of the masses. Although the demonstrators declared their loyalty to the Tsar, troops fired on the crowd and several demonstrators were killed; the event is known in Russian history as 'Bloody Sunday'. This led to further demonstrations and political agitation throughout Russia for much of the rest of 1905. The government eventually responded in two ways. First, there was the issuance in October of a Manifesto. According to this, Russia was to have an elected national parliament (the Duma) for the first time. As a corollary, political parties were legalized and trade unions officially sanctioned, although in practice both continued to be harassed. A less direct result was that the government seems to have felt that it should ensure that the more enterprising and intelligent peasants—those a government should have as supporters rather than opponents—more definitely identify with the tsarist regime. Partly for this reason, and partly to improve agriculture and so help to avoid the kind of situation (notably food shortages) which had sparked off the 1905 events in the first place, a set of agrarian reforms was announced in 1906. The basic point of these was to encourage enterprising peasants to leave the peasant communes and set themselves up as individual farmers. It was hoped that this would lead to greater satisfaction in the countryside and subsequently in the towns. However, by the outbreak of the First World War, the development of private farms had not proceeded very far. In fact, whilst the economic benefits of the policy had not really materialized, the policy had had the undesirable social effect of stratifying the peasantry.

If we now consider the towns at the outbreak of the war we see that industrial growth had taken off again from 1907, following a period of very slow growth from the turn of the century; Russia was unquestionably on the way to becoming an industrial state. However, there were two dimensions of this development which distinguished it from the industrialization process in Western Europe and the USA and which had important political repercussions. The first is that Russian development was almost entirely funded either by the state itself or by foreign investors. As a result, there was virtually no capitalist or bourgeois class in Russia. Second, Russian industry was far more highly concentrated than foreign industry. A relatively small number of very large enterprises were located in a few industrial centres. The political significance of this is that it is much easier to agitate in a few centres than many, and that if this agitation is successful, its impact can be greater and more immediate. One final point about the industrialization is that living conditions in the towns were often very poor. Peasants would take advantage of their greater relative freedom to leave the communes and try their luck in the towns. There they would find poor housing, and work that was both more monotonous and more consistently onerous (i.e., in that they had to work hard all year round, instead of mainly at sowing and harvest time). This made urban life unattractive to many, and there was widespread disillusionment.

So by 1914 there was considerable dissatisfaction in Russia, and changes in the economic base (i.e., industrialization) were having important political and social consequences. At the same time, the Tsar had undermined his own legitimacy once he had agreed to an elected parliament; he had in effect renounced his divine right as the source of all wisdom and hence policies. Despite this, he did not allow the Dumas any significant powers, so that even right-wingers and liberals, whose political stance was very different from that of the Bolsheviks, were increasingly disappointed with the Tsar.

In 1914, Russia entered the First World War. Her losses over the next three years were enormous. The tsarist regime had already suffered one significant defeat in its 1904–5 war with Japan; now, with a poorly trained and badly equipped army, she was suffering even more serious defeats. Almost half the army was either killed, wounded, or imprisoned. Morale sank to a disastrous low, and there were no less than one and a half million desertions in 1916 alone. At the same time, so many men had been drafted that both agriculture and industry were short of labour. Consequently, the army was not only suffering from low morale but also food shortages and insufficient ammunition. There were also food shortages and generally worsening conditions in the towns. Russia was in a potentially revolutionary situation.

In February 1917, serious bread riots broke out in Petrograd. At first, the troops obeyed the Tsar's orders to shoot demonstrators. But by the end of the month, many soldiers had rebelled and sided with the rioters. The Duma politicians implored the Tsar to act more reasonably. He refused, and these politicians decided that the time had come for them to take power from the monarchy. Nicholas II was pressured into abdicating and Russia had a new provisional government.

When the new regime took over in February 1917, many people both inside and outside Russia believed that the country would now become much more like the liberal parliamentary democracies of Britain or the USA. It was thought by most—including many socialists—that this period would be a long one, and that Russia was going to experience the same sort of bourgeois development and institutions that the advanced countries had. Why was it then that such predictions proved wrong, and that by the end of the year the provisional government had been replaced by Lenin and the Bolsheviks?

There is, of course, no single answer to this. But at the most general level, we can say that the October Revolution was a result of the failure of the provisional government combined with the determination, skills and suitability of the Bolsheviks to take power. Let us consider this statement in more detail.

The Russian population had high hopes of the new government that replaced the Tsar. They expected the new regime to put more food in their bellies, to overcome the age-old problems of the countryside, and to end the war that, particularly since the collapse of the monarchy and the concomitant 'loyalty to the crown', people felt was not their concern anyway. But the government did none of these things, and indeed seemed to be characterized by its inability to govern firmly. In the eight months of its existence, its composition was changed three times; it had two heads (Prince L'vov, then Kerensky); it continued Russia's war effort; it failed to enact an expected land reform; it did not significantly improve the food situation. It also shared power with a rival organization, in the form of the Petrograd Soviet (the term 'soviet' is the Russian word for council); as Trotsky wrote, Russia at this time was characterized not by dual power, as some had argued, but rather by dual powerlessness. However, weak governments can continue for long periods in the absence of rival alternatives, even in a period of great expectancy such as Russia was in during the spring and summer of 1917. It is at this point that we need to see what was so special about the Bolsheviks.

The Bolsheviks had emerged in 1903, when disagreements in the Russian Social Democratic Labour Party (founded 1898) resulted in a split into what became in essence two parties, the Bolsheviks and the Mensheviks. In addition to the Mensheviks and a plethora of tiny parties, there were by 1917 the conservative Octobrists, the liberal Cadets, and by far the biggest party in terms of membership and support, the Social Revolutionaries. The unique feature of the Bolsheviks relative to all these other parties was that they were the only group to have refused consistently to participate in the provisional government—most of the time (other than when it seemed that even these bodies were turning against them) supporting instead the soviets. Thus when the time came, they were the only party who could justifiably reject the provisional government and proclaim an alternative government. But there were several other important factors that contributed to the Bolsheviks' success. One was Lenin's strong leadership qualities, which not only inspired other Bolsheviks, but also added credibility to the notion of an alternative to the vacillatory provisional government. Another is that Lenin, in particular, had a superb understanding of mass psychology; this is perhaps best revealed in his ability to promulgate simple but extremely effective slogans. Thus, when the Bolsheviks summarized their policies as 'Bread, Peace, Land' and 'All Power to the Soviets', they succinctly encapsulated the main aspirations of the vast majority of the population. Communications were such that not everyone was familiar with these slogans, and amongst those peasants who were, there was some scepticism about a party which had always claimed to represent the workers rather than the peasants. Nevertheless, the Bolsheviks' support did increase rapidly, particularly in key cities and amongst soldiers and sailors; this was another very important factor in their success. Then there was the failure of General Kornilov to march the army into Petrograd and take power in August 1917. Kornilov's failure meant that the military and the right wing appeared no more able to give Russia the strong leadership so many were looking for than the provisional government. Bolshevik success amongst the soldiers and sailors owed much to the skills of Trotsky as head of the so-called Military Revolutionary Committee in Petrograd. The Bolsheviks benefited, too, from the absence of a powerful, organized bourgeois class. The final factor is that the Bolsheviks promised the kind of political arrangements that many had hoped the provisional government would introduce. Thus there were contested elections in Russia in the autumn of 1917, *after* the Bolsheviks had taken power; it was to be some time before the Russians and the world would see the new regime become a one-party state.

EASTERN EUROPE—YUGOSLAVIA AND POLAND

The Second World War broke out in September 1939. The USSR had seen this coming, and was anxious not to become involved in it; indeed, had it been able to, it would have been quite content to watch the 'imperialist' powers destroy each other. In order to ensure this non-involvement—as well as to gain control of the Baltic states—the Soviets signed a non-aggression pact with the Nazis just before the outbreak of war, in August 1939. But the Soviet attempt to stay out of the war failed. In June 1941, the Nazis broke the treaty and invaded Belorussia and the Ukraine. The Soviets now decided that it was in their interests to side with the Western Allies, and so became part of the combined effort against the Axis (fascist) powers. In the early 1940s, the Soviets often fared better than the West in their struggle against the Nazis, but at enormous cost in terms of lives lost. These points about losses and the Soviet contribution to the overall defeat of Nazism need to be borne in mind when attempting to understand how Eastern Europe came under communist rule in the mid-to-late 1940s. In fact the emergence of a communist Eastern Europe was a highly complex process, and all we can do here is to produce an impressionistic sketch of what happened.

In the period 1943–5, the Western Allies (mainly the USA and the UK) were involved in a number of discussions and negotiations with the Soviets on how Europe should be administered following the defeat of the Nazis. The most famous of these meetings were those held in Teheran (late 1943), Yalta (February 1945), and Potsdam (July–August 1945). The future of Eastern Europe was just one of many items on the agenda at these meetings, and in some ways the question was essentially glossed over. Stalin insisted that countries surrounding the USSR should not have political systems that could produce anything like the Nazis again, and the West basically accepted this.

On the other hand, the West insisted that the regimes be 'democratic'. There was thus broad agreement that the regimes in Eastern Europe would be 'friendly and democratic', but neither side probed too deeply as to how the other side understood this term. Only later did it become clear that the phrase meant something rather different to the Soviets than it did to the West.

But there is one other meeting which must be mentioned if we are to understand the fate of Eastern Europe after the war, and this is the one that took place in Moscow between Churchill and Stalin in October 1944. It was at this meeting that the notorious 'percentages agreement', based on a proposal first made by the British in June 1944, was concluded. Churchill himself described part of the October meeting as follows:

The moment was apt for business, so I said, 'Let us settle about our affairs in the Balkans. Our armies are in Roumania and Bulgaria. We have interests, missions, and agents there. Don't let us get at cross purposes in small ways. So far as Britain and Russia are concerned, how would it do for you to have ninety per cent predominance in Roumania, for us to have ninety per cent say in Greece, and go fifty-fifty about Yugoslavia?' While this was being translated I wrote out on a half-sheet of paper:

Roumania	
Russia	90%
The others	10%
Greece	
Great Britain	90%
(in accord with usa)	
Russia	10%
Yugoslavia	50–50%
Hungary	50–50%
Bulgaria	
Russia	75%
The others	25%

I pushed this across to Stalin, who had by then heard the translation. There was a slight pause. Then he took his blue pencil and made a large tick upon it, and passed it back to us. It was all settled in less time than it takes to set down . . . After this there was a long silence. The pencilled paper lay in the centre of the table. At length I said, 'Might it not be thought rather cynical if it seemed we had disposed of those issues, so fateful to millions of people, in such an offhand manner? Let us burn the paper'. 'No, you keep it', said Stalin.   (Quotation from Westoby, 1981, p. 6.)

Although the Russians have always denied that Stalin agreed to Churchill's proposals, they did use this as a basis for their activities after the war. Indeed, in their desire to show how strictly they were observing it, they helped to ensure that Greece did not come under communist power; had it not been for the Soviets, Greece may well have been the ninth communist state of Eastern Europe by the mid or late 1940s (for details see Kousoulas, 1975). As for the West, it was never very clear what Churchill meant by 'predominance'—how long this was to last, whether it referred to military and/or economic and/or political and/or some other form of predominance, etc. Suffice it to say that this document served as a basis for the Soviet belief that the West would do little to prevent Russia from exerting its influence in much of Eastern Europe after the war.

The percentages agreement did not cover *all* of the countries that came under communist control in the 1940s, and a quotation from another document—an interview Stalin gave to a *Pravda* correspondent in 1946—may help us to understand some of the mentality behind Soviet involvement in other East European countries:

. . . The following circumstances should not be forgotten. The Germans made their invasion of the USSR through Finland, Poland, Rumania, Bulgaria and Hungary. The Germans were able to make their invasion through these countries because, at the time, governments hostile to the Soviet Union existed in these countries. As a result of the German invasion the Soviet Union has lost irretrievably in the fighting against the Germans, and also through the German occupation and the deportation of Soviet citizens to German servitude, a total of about seven million people.* In other words the Soviet Union's loss of life has been several times greater than that of Britain and the USA put together. Possibly in some quarters an inclination is felt to forget about these colossal sacrifices of the Soviet people which secured the liberation of Europe from the Hitlerite yoke. But the Soviet Union cannot forget about them. And so what can there be surprising about the fact that the Soviet Union, anxious for its future safety, is trying to see to it that governments loyal in their attitude to the Soviet Union should exist in these countries? How can anyone who has not taken leave of his senses describe these peaceful aspirations of the Soviet Union as expansionist tendencies on the part of our State? *Subsequently estimated at 20 million. (Cited in Churchward, 1975, pp. 253–4.)

It would be extremely naïve to suppose that this represents the *sole* reason for Stalin's moves to bring more and more countries into the Soviet sphere of influence. Despite his denials of 'expansionism', he had always been interested in increasing Soviet influence in the world *if* he believed he could get away with it; this approach accorded well with his desire optimally to blend traditional Russian attitudes, 'socialism in one country' and Marxist notions of 'socialist internationalism'. Nevertheless, it would be equally absurd to dismiss completely Soviet fears of attack, 'capitalist encirclement', etc., given the country's recent experiences in two world wars.

If the percentages agreement, plus a mixture of fear and expansionist aims, help to explain Soviet involvement in Eastern Europe after the war, we need to ask why the West did not do more to counter Soviet activity. Again this is a complex question to answer, but one major reason was that most citizens in the West were war-weary and wanted security and peace; the success of the

Labour Party in the 1945 British elections was one indication of this. In these circumstances, there emerged a 'Cold War'—a war of words rather than actions—in which Western politicians could criticize the communists (and vice versa), but ordinary citizens did not have to return to the fronts.

Against the general backcloth of deteriorating East–West relations, the actual path to communist power in each European state varied, just as their inter-war histories, levels of economic development, and social composition varied (politically, however, there was greater similarity, in that only one country, Czechoslovakia, had established anything like a liberal democratic tradition before the war). Let us now consider two countries in depth—one in which Soviet involvement was minimal, and one in which it was decisive.

Of all the East European states to be taken over by the communists after the Second World War, in only two—Albania and Yugoslavia—can the native communists be seen to have taken power more or less on their own. Neither country bordered directly on to the USSR or was in the corridor between the Soviet Union and Germany. Moreover, Albania had not been mentioned in the percentage agreement, while Yugoslavia was to have been equally under Soviet and Western influence. With this in mind, let us consider Yugoslavia in more detail.

Yugoslavia was one of the many 'new' European states created in the aftermath of the First World War, and emerged from the ashes of both the Ottoman and Habsburg Empires. In December 1918, Serbia, Croatia, Bosnia, Hercegovina, Slovenia, and Montenegro were united under the Serbian King, Alexander, to form the Kingdom of Slovenes, Croats, and Serbs. Although the Kingdom initially had a form of liberal democracy under a monarchy, the King became a virtual dictator from 1929, following an incident in parliament in which the leader of the Croatian Peasant Party was assassinated. Assassination was to be the fate of the King himself in 1934, when a Croatian nationalist murdered him in Marseilles. Alexander was succeeded by Peter II. However, he was still a minor (14 years of age), so that Yugoslavia—as it had been renamed in October 1929—was ruled by a regent, Prince Paul. Paul and his government became increasingly pro-Nazi, a stance which was unpopular with many Yugoslavs. A military group strongly opposed to the Germans eventually overthrew this government in a *coup d'état* in March 1941. Only ten days after the new, pro-Western government under General Simovic had installed itself, the Germans (together with the Italians, Hungarians, and Bulgarians) invaded Yugoslavia. The Simovic government, as well as King Peter and Prince Paul, went into exile in London; control of Yugoslavia was up for grabs. Parts of the country were annexed by neighbours, the rest was under Axis occupation. Various movements emerged in Yugoslavia, most of which essentially identified with and tried to rule a particular part of the country. In Croatia, for instance, there were the pro-Nazi Ustashi, and in Serbia the initially anti-Nazi and pro-monarchy Chetniks. By the autumn of 1941, two main resistance movements had emerged in Yugoslavia—the Serbian-based Chetniks under Mihailovic, and a communist guerilla movement under Tito which tried to get support from virtually all of the rest of Yugoslavia.

The communist party was by no means a new phenomenon in Yugoslavia. Indeed, it dated from the earliest days of the new state; it was established in 1919 as the Socialist Workers' Party of Yugoslavia, changing its name to Communist Party of Yugoslavia in 1920. The communists soon proved to be quite popular, securing considerable peasant support in some areas (especially Macedonia and Montenegro) and by the time of the November 1920 elections had emerged as the third largest party in the country. However, the communists were virtually outlawed in 1921, following the murder of a former interior minister by a communist. Along with all other political parties, they became fully illegal under the dictatorship introduced at the end of the 1920s. Although the party continued its theoretical debates about Yugoslavia's future, it did not in practice play a major role in Yugoslav politics again until the 1940s.

Once the communists had again become heavily involved in real politics, the leadership initially explicitly played down their revolutionary aims, emphasizing instead that they represented the only group organized on a pan-Yugoslav scale to be resisting the Germans. In fact, when communists in Montenegro and Hercegovina stressed the revolutionary aspects of the movement, they were censured by the Central Committee. Although the Chetniks and the communists collaborated for a brief time, ideological and personality differences led to a major clash between them late in 1941, after which Tito refused to allow communists to work with the Chetniks. Instead, a network of 'National Liberation Committees' was established in as many parts of Yugoslavia as the communists could take control of. These committees served both to help the resistance efforts, and to administer and govern at the local level; they also performed a very useful role in spreading communist propaganda. Central government was still in a state of chaos, but the communists did claim that a National Liberation Front and, from 1942, AVNOJ (the Anti-Fascist Council of National Liberation of Yugoslavia) not only existed but constituted the *de facto* government of the country. Initially, the communists did not push this claim in the outside world; the western allies still officially recognized the Simovic government (by this time headed by Subasic), and the Soviets did not rush to recognize Tito's regime, since they were still at this stage anxious not to upset the Western powers.

The situation changed dramatically in 1943, when it was discovered that many of the Chetniks were collaborating with the Germans. Whereas the allies had been supporting Mihailovic until then, support now switched to Tito and his partisans. The communists felt that the time was ripe to intensify their bid for power, and in November AVNOJ claimed that it represented the sole legal government in Yugoslavia. A government organization of sorts was established in Jajce (Bosnia), and it was decreed that King Peter II would not be permitted to return to Yugoslavia until the Yugoslav people had been given an opportunity to decide for themselves what kind of political system they wanted.

Thus by the end of 1943, such central government as there was within Yugoslavia was very much under the influence of Tito and the communist partisans. Moreover, Tito's movement had swelled and become considerably more popular since the discovery that the Chetniks had been working with the Germans. There remained the question of the government-in-exile. Largely through British efforts, the two governments in fact reached agreement on several key constitutional issues (e.g. on the principle of a federalized state in June 1944). When the allies met at Yalta in February 1945, they agreed to urge the government-in-exile and AVNOJ to merge. This wish was realized in March 1945 when a provisional government of 'Democratic Federal Yugoslavia' was formed by merging the two governments. At first, this really did appear to be a compromise government. Subasic occupied the important post of foreign minister and—as long as their representatives had not collaborated with the occupation forces—various political parties were not only allowed to exist but to be represented in the so-called 'Temporary Assembly'. This state of affairs was short-lived, however, and by the summer of 1945, it was becoming clear that the communists were harassing non-communist politicians. Many of the latter fled Yugoslavia (e.g Subasic in October 1945). In the November 1945 elections to a new Constituent Assembly the official list of candidates put up by the communist-dominated 'National Front' went uncontested. The first act of the assembly was to abolish the monarchy (November 1945) and establish the Federal People's Republic of Yugoslavia. In January 1946, a new constitution was promulgated; Yugoslavia was officially under communist control.

Although Soviet troops entered Yugoslavia in the closing stages of the war, the evidence strongly suggests that the native Yugoslav communists would have taken power on their own anyway. All the Soviet troops did was to clear the vestiges of the occupation forces; this could equally well have been done by the Western allies, and the only reason it was not was because of an agreement between Moscow and the Western capitals. Thus, the communists in Yugoslavia owed little to the Soviets, and most of their achievement in taking power was attributable to their own organization (both political and military), their rapidly increasing popularity amongst the largest section of the population (the peasantry), and the fact that they were the only organization that stood for the whole of Yugoslavia rather than just one or other area. This last fact meant that the West, which was committed to the continued existence of a united Yugoslav state, also supported the Tito partisans—which is yet another factor helping to explain the communist success in Yugoslavia. This relatively popular and indigenously led revolution is in marked contrast to the other East European takeover to be considered, the Polish.

Like Yugoslavia, Poland had only been a sovereign state since the end of the First World War. Before that, it had been divided up between the Prussians, the Austrians, and the Russians. In the first years following the ending of World War One, Poland, like many countries in Eastern Europe, had experimented with a form of liberal democratic government. But this foundered in 1926 when Marshal Jozef Pilsudski—a socialist and a nationalist—led a military coup, following which Poland was essentially under a dictatorship. After Pilsudski's death in May 1935, the government of Poland was taken over by officers loyal to his cause.

A communist party had existed in Poland since December 1918. However, a number of factors served to ensure that it did not become a major and/or popular force in the inter-war period. First, there was the fact that the Pilsudski regime clamped down on all political parties. Second, as an adjunct to the USSR's own 'Great Terror', Stalin himself dissolved the Polish Communist Party in 1938, and imprisoned or executed many of its members. Third—and most important—the Polish communists were incapable of distinguishing themselves in the popular mind from the Soviet communists; for most Poles, communism meant Russia. Russia had played a major role in dividing up Poland in the eighteenth and nineteenth centuries. Even following the First World War, the Bolsheviks had unsuccessfully attempted to overrun Poland (1919–20); and at the outbreak of the Second World War, the Nazi–Soviet pact had led to Poland being divided up yet again by the Germans and Russians, in what is often called the 'fifth partition' of Poland. Finally, to most Poles communism meant atheism—and most Poles were devout Catholics. It is abundantly clear why Polish attitudes towards the Russians and communism were anything but amicable.

With the overthrow of the Polish regime by the Germans (1939) and the subsequent German invasion of Russia (1941) there was a revival of the Polish communist party. Nevertheless, the native communists still played a very minor role in the Polish resistance movement, providing only about 5 per cent of the movement's fighters. Indeed, most of the resistance fighters (the 'Home Army') were as much anti-communist as they were anti-fascist, and the so-called 'Underground State' (a form of government) in Poland during the war did not involve communists.

However, the Red Army had been moving further and further into Poland since the beginning of the decade, and what in retrospect must seem to have been the last chance for the non-communist Poles to run their country after the war was lost by October 1944. By the summer of 1943, the Soviet (Red) Army looked as if it would soon be entering Warsaw. As in the Yugoslav case, so Poland too had a government-in-exile in London, headed by the leader of the Peasant Party, Mikolajczyk; he ordered one of his close companions, General Bor-Komorowski, to take over the Warsaw area resistance movement (the Home Army) in July 1943, to ensure that once the Germans *were* ousted, Poland would not simply be under Russian occupation instead

of German. By the beginning of August 1944, Bor-Komorowski had sufficient power in Warsaw to attempt to oust the Germans. However, the attempt eventually failed and many resistance workers were taken prisoner—
partially because of lack of help from the Soviets and because the Soviets prevented the Western allies from landing in Warsaw and helping the Home
Army. The reasons for the Soviet stance are several, but apart from the fact
that Moscow did not recognize the government-in-exile, which the West did,
Anglo-Soviet relations *vis-à-vis* Poland had been soured in 1943 because of
London's allegations of Soviet involvement in the massacre of over 10,000
Polish officers in the Katyn Forest (for details see Zawodny 1962). Thus the
Germans succeeded in resisting the Polish Home Army, which meant that
when the Soviets pushed back the Germans and entered Warsaw in January
1945, they did not have a powerful Polish resistance movement to contend
with. Having considered briefly the failure of the Polish resistance movement
to form a government, let us consider how the unpopular communists
managed to do this.

One major reason was the fact that the Soviets had planned the takeover
very carefully. As the Red Army gradually took over more and more of
Poland, so Comintern-trained agents were brought in to organize party units
and to oversee the establishment of local government. As control of local
government was consolidated, so policies likely to make the communists
more popular with the peasant majority of the population—notably land reforms—were implemented. Indeed, the communists had by this time learnt
the symbolic disadvantages of calling themselves communists; the party was
renamed the Polish Workers' Party from the beginning of 1942. However,
the leading lights of the party were split. On the one hand, there were the
communists *within* Poland, who in December 1943 established a 'National
Council for the Homeland' in Warsaw; although this included representatives of other parties (e.g. the Peasant Party and the Socialist Party), it was
dominated by communists and headed by Boleslaw Bierut. This Council proclaimed itself the sole legitimate representative of the Polish nation. On the
other hand, there were the Poles in the Soviet Union, most of whom were
members of the 'Union of Polish Patriots'. These people, too, wanted to govern Poland once the Germans had been ousted. By January 1944, they had
formed themselves into the Central Bureau of Polish Communists in the
USSR, and requested the Soviet government for permission to begin preparing
to take over the administration of Polish territory 'liberated' by the Soviet
Army. By the summer of 1944, it was clear that there was a potential clash
between the two groups, so that representatives of both met with Soviet officials to discuss the future of Poland. Eventually, the Soviet-based communists agreed to work with and subordinate themselves to the National
Council in Warsaw. When the Red Army crossed the Polish–Soviet frontier
in July 1944, the National Council announced the creation of a Polish Committee of National Liberation. This committee was based in Lublin, which

was proclaimed the temporary capital of Poland. This wartime government, known best as the Lublin Committee, consisted solely of communists or communist sympathizers. Within a couple of days, it had signed agreements with the USSR on the new Polish boundaries. It then set about implementing various nationalization measures and other socialist policies.

Following the failure of the Home Army and the Underground State to take over Warsaw, the Lublin Committee in December 1944 declared itself the Provisional Government of Poland, and Gomulka, (General) Secretary of the Polish Workers' Party, was named one of the new government's two deputy-premiers. In January 1945, the USSR officially recognized the Lublin Committee as Poland's Provisional Government. The Western allies, who still officially supported the Mikolajczyk government in London, protested; but Churchill himself had publicly accepted Stalin's demands that any future Polish government should be 'friendly to the Soviet Union'. Moreover, at this point Stalin maintained that the new Provisional Government would form only the *nucleus* of a proper government, to which could and should be added 'democratic' leaders both from within Poland and from abroad.

In fact, such additions were carefully controlled by the Soviet authorities and various groups were harassed. In March 1945, for instance, leading members of the Home Army and Underground State were arrested for alleged collaboration with the Germans. But the West was not in a good position to counter such actions. For all this, *some* inclusion of non-communists *was* tolerated. In June 1945, negotiations for the inclusion of non-communists in the Provisional Government were concluded, and a new government was formed in July. Nominally, five parties were to be involved; but the National Democratic Party was completely excluded, and the Peasant Party—Poland's largest in terms of support—was to be allocated no more than one third of the posts. In fact, an analysis of the composition of this government reveals that virtually two thirds of all the posts (14 out of 22) went to members of the Lublin Committee (Lotarski 1975, p. 352). Mikolajczyk, now back in Poland, was made second deputy-premier and, appropriately in a predominantly peasant country, Minister of Agriculture.

The Peasant Party, still under Mikolajczyk, now started to become increasingly critical of the way the communist-dominated political system was being run, almost certainly justifiably alleging that communist proposals for the organization of the forthcoming election would lead to severe under-representation of the non-communist parties. Faced with such criticism, the communists delayed the elections, and instead instituted a referendum on three constitutional issues. The Peasant Party in fact supported the three proposals, but in order to distinguish themselves from the communists, urged their supporters to vote against one of them. This led to the arrest of many members of the Peasant Party and general harassment.

A few months later, in January 1947, Poland had its first post-war elections to parliament (*Sejm*). During the electoral campaign, many more members of the Peasant Party were arrested, including 142 of the parliamentary candidates. The official results of the election were, at the very least, highly questionable. But the communists claimed that 80 per cent of the votes had been cast for the communist front, so that there was no constitutional reason for involving the Peasant Party (who were attributed with a mere 10 per cent of the votes) in the government. By February 1947, Bierut had become President, and the pro-communist socialist leader Josef Cyrankiewicz was appointed Prime Minister.

There were increasing arrests throughout 1947, and in October Mikolajczyk fled to London; what many believed to have been the most popular political party in Poland had been broken. Many more of its leaders fled, whilst others felt that the best way to deal with the communists was to remain and to work with them. They therefore created a new Polish Peasant Party (Left), which soon merged with the communist-sponsored People's Will Peasant Party to form the United Peasant Party; this party recognized communist hegemony.

Having brought the Peasant Party under control, the communists now concentrated on bringing the socialists even further into their fold. The left-wing socialists had been sympathetic to the communists anyway for some time, so that it came as no real surprise when, in December 1948, the Polish Workers' Party and the left wing of the Polish Socialist Party merged to form the Polish United Workers' Party. The communists had consolidated power.

Although the Polish communists acquired power both through massive support from the Soviets and through various unconstitutional measures, the picture so far painted would be less than complete were we not to include certain details on the growth of the Polish Workers' Party. Membership grew from 4,000 in June 1942 to 30,000 in June 1945, 364,000 in July 1945, 820,000 in December 1947 and over a million just before the unification at the end of 1948 (this is all out of a total of approximately 25 million people—figures from Sanford 1981, p. 558 and Lotarski 1975, p. 347). Whilst many people were probably opportunists and/or wanted the extra rations that membership entailed, we must allow for the fact that some joined because they genuinely supported the communist cause. The balance of the two kinds of members will never be ascertained; but post-war Polish history strongly suggests that large numbers of Poles never overcame their pre-war hostility to communism.

CHINA

It is interesting that the demise of the Romanov dynasty occurred within just a few years of the fall of the Qing (Manchu) dynasty in China (1911). But the period between the ending of monarchy and the takeover by communists took almost forty years in China, in contrast to the few months in Russia. Despite this, China did not undergo a proper bourgeois liberal-democratic stage or a major industrialization process following the collapse of the monarchy, and indeed was even more of a peasant society in 1949 than was Russia in 1917.

China had been ruled by the Qing dynasty since 1644. But by the beginning of the twentieth century this was considered anachronistic by many Chinese intellectuals. A political reform movement emerged in 1898, designed to promote the interests of a very small, nascent capitalist class which felt that China's industrialization, such as it was, was too much in foreign hands. Even the emperor himself felt that some economic modernization was necessary, and from 1901 on tried to emulate the Japanese, who had managed to modernize economically whilst retaining much of their traditional culture. Subsequently, he accepted that political modernization was also needed, and by 1910 a new constitution had been introduced, the first elections had been held and a National Assembly (i.e., a parliament) formed. However, many progressive intellectuals felt that the reforms were too few and too modest, and a lot more lost faith in the Qing dynasty's commitment to parliamentarianism when it overruled the National Assembly's policy on railways, introducing instead a policy which favoured foreign investors.

The dissatisfaction with the Qing dynasty, particularly its over-sympathetic policies towards foreigners, burst in October 1911, when an uprising took place in Wuhan. This spread rapidly to other areas. Fifteen of the twenty-one Provincial Assemblies that had been established in 1909 declared their independence of the central government. The old order was breaking down. In November, two rival regimes were established—those of Yuan Shikai in Beijing and of Sun Yat-sen in Nanjing. By February 1912, the boy-emperor Pu Yi had abdicated, and Sun Yat-sen agreed to a compromise proposal made to him by Yuan. In return for Sun renouncing much of his power, Yuan had to agree to a constitutional government along lines laid down by Sun. It soon became clear, however, that the central government was far from being in control anyway, and there followed a period in which most of China was effectively run by local warlords. In the eyes of many intellectuals (see, e.g. Lu Xun's 'The True Story of Ah Q'), the 1911 revolution had brought no significant improvement in China.

Nationalism had been an important factor in Chinese politics since the nineteenth century, largely because of foreign (especially British, German, Russian, and Japanese) interference in and exploitation of China. But its flames were spread after the First World War. At the Paris Peace Conference (1919), the delegates agreed to strengthen Japan's position in China, which led to nationwide protests by groups (the so-called May Fourth Movement) from all social classes in China. As a result, the Chinese delegates refused to sign the Paris Peace Treaty. This led many Chinese intellectuals to believe that action could get them somewhere, and they decided to organize themselves. At this stage, the most promising party seemed to be the Nationalists (Guomindang or GMD) under Sun Yat-sen. Sun looked for foreign support, and this came almost exclusively from the new Soviet government. This fact encouraged some of the intellectuals to look more closely at the ideas of both Marx and Lenin, and they were particularly impressed by Lenin's analysis of imperialism. For them, such views accorded well with their own ideas of national autonomy, and they broke away from the GMD to form communist groups. The first such group was founded in 1920 under Chen Duxiu; in the same year, many agents from Comintern went to China to help spread communist ideas. All this resulted in the formation of the Chinese Communist Party (CCP) in Shanghai in July 1921. But the CCP was not the only group to be influenced by and attracted to Soviet ideas. The Guomindang, still under Sun, co-operated increasingly with Soviet advisors, and in 1923 the GMD and the CCP joined together to form a United Front. By the following year, the GMD had modified its policies and doctrines to such an extent that many communists actually went over to it as a larger and potentially more powerful organization than the CCP.

But this co-operation was relatively short-lived. Sun's death in March 1925 led to a dispute between the GMD and the CCP as to who were Sun's rightful heirs. The new head of the GMD, Chiang Kai-shek, was far less sympathetic towards the communists than Sun had been, and relations worsened to such an extent that in April 1927 the United Front collapsed completely. This was followed by massacres of communists by members of the GMD—notably in Shanghai in April 1927, but also in other cities. Many intellectuals were horrified by the Guomindang's 'white terror', as these massacres are known, and turned towards the CCP. But the CCP was not yet in a position to mount a real counter-attack. Although the communists were able to make some sort of a comeback in certain major towns, the majority had by the end of the year been forced to flee to the mountains. Much of the country was now being run by the GMD under Chiang, based in Nanjing. It was from this point on that Mao Zedong emerges as a major communist leader—though his position was not yet fully secure even within the communist movement.

Between 1927 and 1931, Mao managed to set up various local soviets along the Russian pattern in various parts of southern China. Although the GMD continued to harass the communists, they were unable to break them, and when Japan invaded Manchuria in 1931, the GMD was too occupied in resisting the foreign invaders in the North to worry much about the communists in the South. It was in this climate that a 'Chinese Soviet Republic' was established in November 1931, principally in the south-eastern province of Jiangxi; Mao was elected to head this. The communists soon introduced a land reform, and peasant support increased. But the urban communists now moved from the towns to the Chinese Soviet Republic and challenged Mao. Not only did they claim that Mao's understanding of Marxism was poor—a fact reflected in his apparent greater interest in peasants than urban workers—but they also argued that his methods of warfare were basically unsound. They were able to wean the bulk of the CCP away from guerilla tactics towards more conventional warfare. Largely because of this, the earlier successes of the communists in rebutting attacks by the GMD were turned into failures, and by the end of 1934, the Chinese Soviet Republic had collapsed. Mao's guerilla tactics, which had been condemned and mocked by the urban communists, now seemed to have proved to be the superior approach to warfare. But this realization came too late to save the Jiangxi Soviet. Mao and his followers had to flee. They headed North, on the famous 'Long March' to Yan'an, to consolidate and to plan ways to continue the struggle.

Despite the attacks on the communists, many nationalist members of the GMD felt that there was still a lot of common ground between themselves and Mao's followers. Most of the communists also felt that it would be better for the GMD and the CCP to work together rather than against each other, and for a short while in 1936 and 1937, an informal United Front operated. In July 1937, a new Sino-Japanese war broke out, and both communists and nationalists decided that their remaining differences were less important than their common interest in defending China; a formal United Front once again came into existence. For a couple of years, the CCP and the GMD worked together to fight the Japanese. But differences kept emerging, and by the beginning of 1941, the two parties were again in conflict. The communists now virtually withdrew from the Sino-Japanese War—which fully occupied the GMD until 1945. This period was a very fruitful one for the CCP in terms of being able to spread its message amongst the peasantry whilst the GMD was otherwise engaged. It managed to persuade large numbers of Chinese either to join the party and/or its own Chinese Red Army. By 1945, the latter numbered some 900,000 soldiers, whilst party membership had grown from about 40,000 in 1937 to over 1.2 million; by January 1947, the membership had almost doubled again to over 2.2 million (figs. from Schurmann, 1968, p. 129).

The war with Japan ended in August 1945, and within a couple of months the GMD and the CCP were again fighting each other, despite the fact that the Americans had succeeded in getting both sides to agree to co-operate. The Americans continued to press for a coalition government in China, as a result of which they refused to provide the GMD with the arms and munitions requested. The Soviets, on the other hand, whilst not officially supporting the CCP against the GMD, gave the former very real help by preventing GMD troops from moving into Manchuria until they, the Soviets, left it in 1946. Upon the Soviet departure, fighting between the CCP and the GMD broke out again, this time in north-east China. By the beginning of 1947, most of China was in a state of civil war, with an increasing number of peasants favouring the communists following the latter's implementation of a land reform in various parts of China from May 1946. The Americans, under General Marshall, admitted that the US policy of reconciling the CCP and GMD had failed, and promptly left China. Over the next two to three years, the communists were able to take all the key Chinese towns from the nationalists. In September 1949, at a CCP conference in Beijing, the communists elected a

'Central People's Government'. In the following month, the communists proclaimed the People's Republic of China, and in November, the GMD fled to Taiwan to continue the Republic of China there.

Although the CCP had received indirect help from the Soviets in the early stages of their final struggle with the GMD, this had declined over time. Indeed, once Stalin had suggested to Mao in March 1949 that the CCP should consolidate its gains but make no further bids for control in other parts of China, the Chinese communists went very much their own way. The Soviet role in the communist takeover in China should therefore not be overemphasized. On the other hand, like Lenin's in Russia and Tito's in Yugoslavia, Mao's role in the Chinese revolution was very important. He could be highly pragmatic when this seemed appropriate, and had attracted many peasants—the bulk of the Chinese population—with his land reforms and hostility to the landlord class. The GMD, in contrast, seemed increasingly to put the interests of the wealthy before all else. Moreover—and this is important—Maoist ideology was almost as nationalist in content as that of the GMD itself; this, too, helps to explain the success of the Chinese communists.

CUBA

The communist path to power in Cuba was quite different from the takeovers we have so far considered. Not only did it not take place during or in the confused aftermath of a war, but Castro was not even a communist when he took power in 1959.

Although at the time of the takeover Cuba was still predominantly an agrarian country, it was not a particularly impoverished one, especially in comparison with Russia or China at the time of their revolutions. In some branches of production, wages were almost as high as in Western Europe or Canada, and there were more cars and television sets per capita than anywhere in Latin America (O'Connor 1970, p. 1). It was also basically a capitalist society, but of a very peculiar sort. The economy had not diversified like most countries undergoing capitalist development, being highly dependent on one product, sugar. Although much of the sugar industry was run on capitalist lines, the nature of the product is such that most Cubans were rural rather than urban dwellers, working on the land rather than in factories. Moreover, the country was highly dependent on foreign investment, and there was only a small indigenous bourgeois class. Once again, therefore, we have a unique case, but one which exhibits *some* similarities with other countries being analysed. Let us now examine the buildup to communist power.

From the sixteenth century to the end of the nineteenth, Cuba was a Spanish colony. But in 1898, war broke out between the Americans and the Spaniards; the US won, and occupied Cuba until 1902, when the island became relatively independent. The one major limitation on Cuban sovereignty now was a clause—the Platt amendment—in the 1901 constitution which granted the USA the right to intervene in Cuba if the political system appeared to be under serious threat. Several such instances did in fact occur between 1902 and 1934, when the amendment was dropped and a trade agreement signed. To no small extent, the anti-US dimension of Cuban nationalism, which formed a major plank of Castro's propaganda in the 1950s, was derived from these incursions into Cuban domestic affairs in the early twentieth century.

It was also during these years that the Cuban Communist Party emerged. It was founded in 1925, and was soon one of the largest in Latin America. It played an important role in overthrowing the Machado dictatorship in August 1933, although Machado was replaced by the reformist nationalist Professor Grau San Martin rather than by the communists. Grau was himself overthrown in January 1934, and for the next decade or so, Cuba was effectively run by Fulgencio Batista. Although Batista is sometimes seen as a right-wing dictator, he was not clearly so at this period; for instance, he permitted rival political parties. Largely because the communists had earlier criticized other left-wing parties for taking what they (the communists) saw as a nationalist line in the Grau era, they were unable to join with these socialist parties—notably the 'Cuban Revolutionary Party' (better known as the *Autenticos*) headed by Grau—in the late 1930s. Instead, they aligned with Batista, who was eager to gain support, and in 1939 renamed themselves the Revolutionary Communist Union (RCU). The RCU played a major role in securing Batista's presidency in 1940; the communists were rewarded for their support by being given two ministerial posts in Batista's cabinet.

But in 1944, Grau was elected President. The old rivalry between the communists (now renamed the Popular Socialist Party or PSP) and the Autenticos prevented collaboration; indeed, Grau mounted a campaign against the PSP in 1947.

Grau was succeeded as president by another Autentico, Carlos Prio, in 1948. The PSP attempted to improve relations with the Autenticos, but to no real avail; they were now destined to play a relatively minor role in Cuban politics until the late 1950s.

Meanwhile, troubles developed *within* the Autentico party. A breakaway group called the *Ortodoxos* formed under Eduardo Chibas. This party accused the Autenticos of having betrayed democracy and condoned corruption; a leading member of the Ortodoxos was one Fidel Castro.

In 1952, before Castro could run for parliament as an Ortodoxo candidate, the democratic regime in Cuba was overthrown in a *coup d'état* led by Batista. It might be imagined that the Batista dictatorship would have brought the Autenticos, the Ortodoxos, and the PSP (i.e., the communists) together in a common fight against him. This did not in fact happen, largely because the Autenticos and the Ortodoxos did not trust the communists, given the latters' earlier involvement with Batista.

Early in 1953, Castro tried to use the courts to have the Batista regime declared illegal. His attempt failed, and he decided to use force. On 26 July 1953, Castro led just a couple of hundred men in an armed attack on the huge Moncada barracks in Santiago. The attack was a miserable failure, with many of Castro's followers being killed. Castro himself was arrested and sentenced to fifteen years' imprisonment; sixty-eight of his fellow Moncadists were executed (Gonzalez 1974, p. 84). However, the event itself and Castro's speech at his trial served to inspire a movement which was later to play the major role in the eventual overthrow of the Batista regime—the *July 26 Movement*. Castro's supporters were not the only ones to suffer because of the July 26 affair. The communist PSP was also banned, and, in Leninist fashion, verbally attacked the spontaneity, opportunism, and adventurism of Castro.

In an endeavour to defuse the growing opposition to his regime, Batista granted a general amnesty in May 1955. Castro was freed, and soon made his way to Mexico, where he set up the July 26 Movement; in March 1956, he formally left the Ortodoxos. At the end of 1956, Castro and his followers arrived back in Cuba aboard the boat *Granma*; they came under heavy attack from Batista's forces. The few survivors of the July 26 Movement eventually came together in the Sierra Maestra mountains, where, for about a year, they fought as a guerilla movement. But their successes were few, and they secured little support from fellow Cubans. Indeed, the most successful sections of the July 26 Movement were operating in the towns, and Castro was not directly involved in this. But the situation was changing rapidly. Both the urban sections of the July 26 Movement and other anti-Batista groups had tried to organize various demonstrations (including a general strike) against the increasing repressiveness of the Batista regime; these attempts had failed, which had the dual effects of leading various oppositionists to look towards Castro once again, and further intensifying Batista's repression. The dictatorship now became so draconian that even the USA protested and cut off arms supplies to Cuba.

By the late spring of 1958, Castro and his brother, Raul, were making various successful attacks on government forces. Batista launched a major attack on the Sierra Maestra guerillas in May 1958, but with little success. Indeed, by August, not only had the July 26 Movement pushed back government forces, but it was launching counter-offensives; one of the leading figures in these was the Argentinian, Ernesto Che Guevara, who had been with Castro since the latter's stay in Mexico.

The guerillas—the 'Rebel Army'—were scoring many successes, to no small extent because Batista's harshness and corruption had lost him support even amongst many of his own military officers and government officials. Castro, in contrast, preached radical democracy—he wanted a return to the spirit of the 1940 liberal-democratic constitution—as well as a nationalism based principally on criticism of US imperialism. Cities and towns fell rapidly to the Rebel Army, and Batista's military support collapsed. On 1 January

1959, Batista fled to the Dominican Republic and the Rebel Army entered Havana. Castro was now in power.

Castro had led a tiny guerilla army (never more than a few hundred men) against a full-sized army and won. He had been broadcasting regularly, and was an impressive speaker. Other groups fighting the Batista regime had either failed miserably and/or had committed atrocities which made them unpopular with ordinary Cubans. So Castro became a popular revolutionary hero by taking power in a coup that had involved only a minute section of the population directly and which, as yet, was not socialist. The Soviets had in no way been involved. Castro's conversion to communism was to come gradually, largely as a result both of his differences with the USA and because of the injustices he saw as leader of Cuba. He set about trying to improve the lot of the poor (e.g. in housing)—something he felt the economy could well stand—only to find that private entrepreneurs were largely unwilling to reduce their profits to satisfy his sense of justice. There was wealth in the country, but the people who had it were not willing to allow a redistribution. It was this kind of reaction, plus the excessive zeal of some of those implementing Castro's policies (especially in the case of land reforms) that led to a greater polarization in society than Castro had expected. Faced with the decision whether to ease off or push ahead, Castro chose the latter. At the same time, he deposed the President—whom he had himself installed—and various other ministers (July 1959) on the grounds that they were excessively sympathetic towards the USA and American attitudes towards the creation and distribution of wealth.

By 1960, relations between the USA and Cuba had hit a new low, as Castro nationalized first the US oil companies (June 1960) and then all other American enterprises. This was followed by a nationalization of most of the large, indigenously owned enterprises.

As relations with the USA worsened, so those with the USSR improved. Mikoyan (Soviet first deputy-premier) visited Havana in February 1960, and promised a modest amount of aid to the new regime. Castro was moving closer to communism. Another major impetus came in April 1961, when a number of ex-Cubans living in the USA, believing they had the support of the US government, mounted a badly planned invasion of Cuba (the Bay of Pigs incident). Castro had no problem in rebutting the invasion, upon which he established diplomatic relations with Moscow and proclaimed a socialist revolution in Cuba. In December 1961, Castro went further still and stated publicly that he was now a Marxist–Leninist, although he admitted that he had read very little Marxist or Leninist literature. He described himself and his followers as 'sentimental Marxists, emotional Marxists' (Gonzalez 1974, p. 146), and in September 1964 again made it clear that he had not come to power as a 'scientific Marxist' with some long-term strategy.

What of the development of the communist party? It will be recalled that the communist party (PSP) and Castro had been on basically bad terms for most of the 1950s. But by 1957, one section of the PSP had become supportive of Castro, and, after he seized power, the new Cuban leader made extensive use of the PSP for implementing his policies. After all, Castro had very little organization of his own. Signs that he was becoming more sympathetic towards the communists were visible already in 1959. In October, for example, a former leading member of the July 26 Movement, Hubert Matos, was arrested and charged with 'anti-communist' treason and 'representing powerful interests at home and abroad'; he was subsequently sentenced to 20 years' imprisonment. However, at this stage such defence of communism should be seen primarily as defending whatever the Americans most disliked rather than as very positive support for communism or the PSP. But Castro became increasingly aware that an organization was necessary for implementing policy, helping to resocialize the population, etc. In 1961, this awareness led to the merger of the PSP and the July 26 Movement into the new 'Integrated Revolutionary Organization' (ORI). However, this became an effective organ only from March 1962, after Castro had attacked various PSP leaders and barred the most important of them, Anibal Escalante, from any high-ranking office, on the grounds that he had tried to take over the ORI. Even so, the ORI was short-lived. In February 1963, Castro dissolved it and created in its place a United Party of the Socialist Revolution (PURS); one of the reasons for the change was to ensure that the 'old communists' (i.e., former PSP members) did not become dominant. Eventually, in October 1965, the Communist Party of Cuba (CPC) emerged from the PURS. But even now it played a minor role in Cuban politics; not until the 1970s did the CPC begin to play its 'leading role' in Cuba.

AFGHANISTAN

When Soviet troops entered Afghanistan in December 1979, some of the Western media gave the impression that the USSR was imposing communist rule on an unwilling neighbour. This is not strictly accurate; Afghanistan had already been under communist rule since April 1978, and the Soviets were merely helping to bring in a potentially less terroristic and less unpopular communist ruler.

Unlike some of the other Asian communist states, Afghanistan has not been fully colonized in the past two centuries. Indeed, during the eighteenth century, when Afghanistan came into existence as a state, she was herself an aggressor, overrunning parts of Northern India. As the Russian and British empires spread in the nineteenth century, Afghanistan's expansionist role declined. Instead, she became a buffer state between the Russian empire and the British colony of India. British claims that Russia was attempting to infiltrate Afghanistan led to no less than three major wars between the Afghans and the British during the nineteenth century.

In 1919, following fighting within Afghanistan, Britain and the Afghans were again briefly at war. This resulted in what many believed would be the end of British involvement in Afghan politics, since the UK officially recognized Afghan independence. From 1919 to 1929, Afghanistan was ruled by the very anti-British but progressive King Amanullah. But in his later years, Amanullah attempted to modernize Afghanistan too quickly, along the lines taken by Ataturk in Turkey. This led to a revolt by the Muslim clergy (the mullahs), who overthrew the monarch. This was followed by fighting and confusion, and the British once again became involved in Afghan politics, helping to put General Nadir Shah into power; he was a distant cousin of the deposed monarch and was soon crowned as the new king. But even Nadir Shah's more moderate reforms alienated many of the very conservative mullahs, and he was assassinated in 1933. His nineteen-year-old son, Mohammed Zahir Shah, came to the throne—although power was more in the hands of three of Zahir Shah's uncles, who effectively ran the government for almost twenty years. Zahir Shah formally remained in power until 1973, when a *coup d'état* led by his cousin and brother-in-law General Daoud, led to the abolition of the monarchy.

In the last twenty-five or so years of his reign, King Zahir Shah made a number of faltering steps towards major political reform, and also began to move closer to the USSR. Let us examine these two points more closely.

In 1949, there were relatively free and open elections to a new 'Liberal Parliament'; almost half of the deputies elected to this were seen as left-wingers of one sort of another. This led to nervousness among some members of the royal family; the Liberal Parliament was dissolved in 1952, and the more progressive political forces harassed. The new government that came in was headed by General Daoud. During the 1950s and early 1960s, Daoud began to steer Afghanistan away from its traditional Western allies towards the USSR, largely because of the latter's sympathetic attitudes towards the Afghan position in its territorial disputes with Pakistan. Soviet aid to Afghanistan was nothing new, having started in 1919; but its scale increased dramatically under Daoud. Afghan dependency on the USSR increased still further after September 1961, when the dispute with Pakistan led to the closure of Afghanistan's links to its Indian Ocean outlets. This meant that Afghanistan had to conduct most of its trade via the USSR, especially since the Shah of Iran, in agreement with President Kennedy, refused to help the Afghans build a new road outlet via Iran (Halliday 1978, p. 18).

But many Afghans, including the king, became increasingly uneasy at the growing dependence on the USSR; because of this, and a feeling that the tensions with Pakistan would be lessened were the Prime Minister to go, Daoud was prevailed upon to resign in 1963. He accepted the push gracefully (see Dupree 1980, pp. 554–8). The new government was more prepared to compromise with Pakistan—which itself was more willing to negotiate now that Daoud had gone—and within two months, the Afghan-Pakistani border was open again. As a consequence, Afghanistan was able to become less dependent on Moscow.

The mid-1960s also saw renewed attempts by King Zahir Shah to modernize the political system. A new constitution was promulgated in October 1964, and introduced a period known as the 'New Democracy'. There was a new bicameral legislature—most of the members of which were elected, rather than appointed—greater freedom of the press, and political parties were once again tolerated. It was in these circumstances that the present communist party, the People's Democratic Party of Afghanistan (PDPA), was established, holding its first congress in January 1965. Before examining its development, we need to see how the Afghan monarchy fell and was replaced by a republic.

Although King Zahir Shah himself permitted a liberalization of the political system in 1964, both he and other members of the royal family soon became uneasy about developments, just as they had after the 1949 liberalization. By 1966, he was clamping down on political parties once again, believing them to be either anti-monarchy or anti-Islam or both; his conservative reaction was supported by the powerful mullahs. Despite this, he felt it would have been unwise to ban parties outright, so he played a cat-and-mouse game with them. This led to growing dissatisfaction among most of the more politically aware citizens (mainly the intelligentsia) in Afghanistan. The King's legitimacy was further undermined when, during the severe drought of 1969–72—in which up to half a million died—it was discovered that Afghanistan was supplying water to Iran in return for oil; many felt the King had his priorities all wrong. The drought led to a rapidly deteriorating economic situation in Afghanistan, which only added fuel to the general discontent. While the King was away in Europe, General Daoud and the military mounted a successful and almost bloodless *coup d'état* in July 1973. So ended almost 230 years rule by the Durrani dynasty.

Daoud immediately proclaimed Afghanistan a republic, and became both President and Prime Minister. As he consolidated power, so he introduced more political reforms; expectations among the radical intelligentsia were running high. But doubts began to creep in by 1977. In that year, what looked like a potentially progressive new constitution was promulgated; but when the new Cabinet it envisaged was announced, it became obvious that Daoud had filled it with friends and relatives (including members of the former royal family), and had refused to include any left-wing representatives. He then personally appointed the Central Committee of the new 'National Revolutionary Party', the only political party explicitly permitted under the new constitution. Whatever the name of the new party, Daoud's practice looked increasingly despotic. At this juncture, we need to consider what had been happening to the PDPA.

The PDPA was founded by Nur Mohammed Taraki as a party 'guided by the scientific ideology of the working class'—in other words, as a Marxist-

Leninist party. But the industrial proletariat proper was minute in Afghanistan, so that the party programme (1965) called for an alliance of workers, peasants (the bulk of the population), intellectuals, and even the bourgeoisie—almost everyone, in fact, with the notable exception of the Muslim clergy. This led the government to argue that the PDPA was hostile to Islam and, despite the PDPA's protestations to the contrary, the party came under severe pressure from the authorities from May 1966. Disagreements on the way forward, the conflict with Pakistan, the nature of the party—plus personality clashes and ethnic differences—led to a split in the PDPA in the summer of 1967. The two major factions to emerge were the Khalq (meaning 'the people') under Taraki, and the Parcham (meaning 'the banner'), under Babrak Karmal. On the question of the party, the Khalqi wanted a party based principally on the working class and adhering to strict Leninist organizational principles, whereas the Parchami favoured a much broader party in the initial stages of the revolutionary process. There is thus some similarity between this split and that between the Bolsheviks and Mensheviks in Russia decades before. One practical ramification of this difference was that the Parchami agitated amongst the military in the last days of the monarchy, whereas the Khalqi did not.

It is therefore hardly surprising that when Daoud—with military support—took power in July 1973, the Parchami supported him, and were in turn rewarded. In the first months of the new republic, the Parchami were represented in the central government, and also played an important role in providing administrators for local government. But as Daoud's rule became more personalized, so the Parcham's role in the republic declined; many of the Parchami ministers, for example, were sent abroad as ambassadors (Halliday 1978, p. 29). At the same time, Daoud became increasingly anti-Soviet, and moved towards the pro-US Shah of Iran. Such developments led the leaders of the Khalq and the Parcham to overcome their former differences, and in July 1977 they were formally reunited; their principle aim was to oppose and undermine Daoud's increasingly repressive regime.

The communists were not alone in their growing antipathy to Daoud. Many peasants, for example, were bitterly disappointed when a land reform promised in 1977 failed to materialize, and many felt that Daoud had been far too conciliatory towards Pakistan on the age-old territorial disputes. The growing discontent was reflected in the fact that there were no less than seven unsuccessful attempts to overthrow the Daoud government before the communists finally succeeded, in April 1978. In that month, a leading Parchami, Professor Mir Akbar Khyber, was murdered in Kabul. Many believed that the Daoud government had been behind this, and mass demonstrations broke out at Akbar Khyber's funeral. The demonstrators shouted anti-US, anti-Iranian, and anti-Daoud slogans. Daoud responded by arresting leading left-wingers, including both Taraki and Karmal, on 26 April. At this, Hafizullah Amin (a leading member of the Khalq), who was initially only put under house arrest, contacted PDPA sympathizers in the military. Many of these officers had at one time been sympathetic to the Parcham. But many had recently switched their allegiance to the Khalq, believing it to be committed to more rapid and radical change; moreover, rather like the Mensheviks in 1917, the Parcham was tainted with having worked with the old order. The left-wingers in the military attacked Daoud's palace on the morning of 27 April, killing the President and most of his family. By the evening, they had taken power and released those arrested the previous day. A new Revolutionary Council, headed by Taraki, was rapidly formed. At the beginning of May, this body ratified the composition of a new Cabinet, comprising solely Khalqi and Parchami politicians, for the government of Afghanistan. There was some resistance from Daoud loyalists, but this was brought under control within a few days. The PDPA had in essence consolidated power with, it seems, the loss of about a thousand lives (Dupree 1980, p. 771 and 1979, p. 34).

There is considerable agreement among Western analysts that neither the Soviets nor any other foreign power played any significant role in the Afghan revolution of April 1978 (see, e.g., Dupree 1979, pp. 46–7 and Stern 1980, pp. 141–2). Rather, the communists came to power amid growing dissatisfaction with a relatively new government that had promised much but had done little and which became increasingly personalized and repressive. Yet the communists could not have succeeded without the support of the military. The takeover was virtually spontaneous, and spokespersons for the new regime admitted subsequently that the PDPA had not expected a revolutionary situation to develop so soon. Like so many other countries in which the communists have come to power, capitalism had barely begun; both the bourgeoisie and the industrial proletariat formed a tiny proportion of the population. Indeed, not only was Afghanistan a poor, underdeveloped, agricultural country, but some 15 per cent of Afghans were nomads, who do not fit properly into any Marxist class analysis.

CONCLUSIONS

Although it has been emphasized that the way the communists come to power is in each case unique, it will also be clear by now that certain factors are common to many or all takeovers.

(i) *The socio-economic setting.* With the notable exceptions of the GDR and Czechoslovakia, and contrary to what one might expect from the writings of Marx, communists have taken power in relatively underdeveloped, predominantly agrarian societies. Typically, not only is there a small industrial proletariat, but also a very small indigenous bourgeoisie. Both the economy and the social structure are generally very much less diverse than in the advanced liberal democracies.

(ii) *The political conditions.* Communists have so far not taken power in a country with a well-established liberal democratic political tradition (i.e., with a proper bi- or multi-party system, largely autonomous mass media, etc.). Czechoslovakia is to some extent an exception to this, but it seems that many citizens there lost faith in liberal democracy when other liberal democracies forced the country to cede territory to Nazi Germany in September 1938 (the Munich Agreement). Most of the countries have had dictatorships and/or colonial rulers—some more enlightened than others—in the years preceding the communist takeover. In several states, the old system had collapsed—perhaps through being corrupt and/or excessively repressive and/or for having promised much but done little (in short, through being out of touch with what the masses wanted). Many states had also been relatively recently established (e.g. Czechoslovakia, Yugoslavia) and the new governments had not invariably been able to build up widespread and solid support. Moreover, the old regime has frequently collapsed largely as a result of war. Indeed, recent involvement in a major war is a feature common to the majority of countries that have come under communist rule. In some cases—particularly those of the newer communist states—the war was closely related to the end of colonial rule. For instance, Angola and Mozambique became communist states following the ending of Portugese rule.

(iii) *The geographical factor*. Several states now under communist rule are so partially because they are situated next to the USSR, which has wanted 'buffer' states along as much of its border as possible; this leads on to the next point.

(iv) *The role of external powers*. It is far from clear that countries now under communist rule would be so had it not been for the policies of other countries. This is not quite as simple a point as is sometimes suggested, by which I mean that it is not merely a question of whether or not the Soviets have actively intervened to help native communists. Obviously, several countries are now communist because the Red (Soviet) Army helped to install them. However, as is evident from the case of Eastern Europe, the situation might have been otherwise had the Western allies been determined not to let these countries come under communist rule. Likewise, many of the countries which came under communist control in the mid-1970s (such as Laos, the southern part of Vietnam, Angola, Mozambique) did so partially because of Soviet support—which was in most cases of an indirect kind—and partially because the US, in particular, lost its determination to prevent the communists coming to power. Similarly, had several West European powers not accepted the inevitability of decolonization, the political voids in which communists have sometimes come to power would not have been created. In other countries (e.g. North Korea, Afghanistan), the communists might have been overthrown themselves, either by indigenous and/or outside forces, had it not been for support from other communist powers.

This all works in the opposite direction too. Several countries might now be communist had it not been for the deliberate actions—or inaction—of major foreign powers. Greece is one example that has already been mentioned; others include Northern Iran in the mid-1940s, Burma (late 1940s), Malaya (late 1940s and the 1950s), South Korea, and Guatemala (1951–4); for further details see Hammond 1975c, pp. 30–7. South Vietnam would almost certainly have fallen to the communists sooner than it did had it not been for US and Australian military aid.

(v) *The role of the military*. Although the role of foreign armies has often been crucial to the success or failure of a bid by native communists to take power, the role of the indigenous military is frequently also of major importance. Sometimes, the fact that the army of the old regime has virtually disintegrated means the communists have met with little armed resistance. In some cases, the military (or a substantial part of it) merely refuses to defend the old regime, but does not lend much support to the communists. In other cases, the military actively supports the communist bid (e.g. Afghanistan). And in yet other cases (e.g. China, Yugoslavia), the communists themselves create new armies—usually guerilla ones—to fight the incumbent regime's army and/or an occupying force.

(vi) *The role of the communist party*. Communist parties are frequently much better organized than their opponents, which is one of the factors contributing to their success. Often, they have not collaborated with the old regime, which in some cases distinguishes them from other parties and increases their support. In countries where they have come to power gradually, over a period of months or years, it has often been the case that other political parties were popular, so that the communists have had to undermine the position of their opponents by what is usually called 'salami tactics'. This frequently pertains to countries in which the communists were heavily dependent on outside assistance, although it is also to some extent true of the USSR, where the Bolsheviks reluctantly permitted other parties to exist until 1921. The *gradual* accession to power in indigenous takeovers can help the communists to build up popular support—for instance, by implementing land reforms—in those parts of the country in which they have defeated opposition forces, and news of this can spread to other areas, thus increasing support still further (e.g. China). Although formally committed to Marxism–Leninism, several communist parties have included at least as much nationalism in their ideology and propaganda as Marxist rhetoric; this, too, has often added to their popularity.

(vii) *The role of individual leaders*. In several states, the communists owe some of their success to the fact that they had determined, able, and charismatic leaders—Lenin, Mao, Tito, Castro, and Ho Chi Minh are good examples. This factor particularly pertains to those countries which had little or no outside help in their bid for power. Another point about leadership is that communist leaders are typically intellectuals—highly educated, intelligent, and well travelled. Indeed, the masses' role in communist takeovers is frequently essentially a background one; it is often their misery and discontent that inspire communists to attempt a revolution on their behalf.

Even from this brief survey, the reader will realize that—the problems of typologization notwithstanding—there are definite patterns to communist takeovers. In the following chapters, we shall see that there are also discernible patterns to the methods used by communists to consolidate and maintain power.

Basic Further Reading

W. H. Chamberlin, 1965.
L. Dupree, 1979, 1980.
E. Gonzalez, 1974.
J. Guillermaz, 1972.
F. Halliday, 1978, 1980.

T. Hammond (ed.), 1975a.
M. McCauley (ed.), 1977.
H. Seton-Watson, 1956.
B. Szajkowski, 1982.

3

TERROR AND COERCION

IN the next two chapters, we shall look at two very different ways in which communists try to ensure compliance with their aims—one based on fear, the other on changing the way people think.

For a long period following the Second World War—probably at least until the early-to-mid-1960s—many political scientists rather unquestioningly used the term 'totalitarian' to describe the nature and system of communist states. For many, the single most important feature of totalitarianism was a regime's use of terror; indeed, terror has been called the 'linchpin' of totalitarianism (Fainsod 1954, p. 354). It is certainly the case that what US President Jimmy Carter argued will probably prove to be the most terroristic regime of the twentieth century ('most' in the sense of the terror affecting the greatest proportion of the population) has been a communist one, Kampuchea under Pol Pot. And a leading writer on communist affairs, Chalmers Johnson, has written, 'Very possibly the most damning criticism of Communism in power is that its practitioners have been unable to think of any way other than terror to bring about the changes they desire' (in Dallin and Breslauer 1970, p. vi). Such a statement is sweeping, and far from wholly accurate. But it does serve as justification for devoting a whole chapter to the question of extreme coercion and terror.

The first part of the chapter is concerned with definitions of terror. Following this, we shall consider examples of its use in the communist world, suggest why it is used, and the advantages and disadvantages of such use. Finally, it will be argued that its use tends to decline over time, and that—contrary to what Johnson argues—communists *do* try to use methods other than terror for bringing about change.

THE CONCEPTS OF COERCION AND TERROR

All states have some apparatus—the police, intelligence services, etc.—for helping to ensure that citizens abide to the maximum extent by the state's official code of conduct as laid down in laws. But the levels and nature of coercion (i.e., forcing citizens to comply with the state's rules) vary considerably from one society to another. These differences depend on a large number of factors, including the types and scale of cleavages that exist between the state and the citizens, between the citizens themselves, the dominant attitudes on how to deal with social deviance, etc. Even allowing for such differences, there comes a point at which quantitative differences in levels of coercion become a qualitative difference between a 'highly coercive' and a 'terroristic' regime. Although the point of transition is often difficult to pinpoint in the real world, a number of relatively specific indicators can be identified. Let us begin our search for these by considering two rather different definitions of terror. In a 1972 review article, Robert Slusser is content to use the definition given in Webster's *New Collegiate Dictionary*—'. . . the systematic use of violent means by a party or faction to maintain itself in power (Slusser 1972, p. 428)'—which, given the point made above about high levels of coercion (which can involve 'violent means') is not very enlightening. Moreover, the use of the word 'systematic' is potentially misleading, for reasons that will emerge shortly. Let us therefore consider a second definition.

The single most important work on political terror in communist states is that by Dallin and Breslauer, who define the subject of their study as follows: 'By "political terror" we mean the arbitrary use, by organs of political authority, of severe coercion against individuals or groups, the credible threat of such use, or the arbitrary extermination of such individuals or groups (1970, p. 1).' This is a far more satisfactory definition than that used by Slusser for a number of reasons. First, it distinguishes more clearly between terror by the state and terror by groups or individuals. The latter is called, in common parlance, 'terrorism', and does not concern us here; we are concerned only with terror used by the state against citizens. Second, and far more importantly, Dallin and Breslauer's definition includes (twice) the all-important word 'arbitrary'. One of the features that distinguishes terror from other forms of coercion is that those affected by it are unaware of the 'rules of the game'; there are a number of ramifications to this. As a general point, the state must be operating overwhelmingly according to the 'rule of law' if it is to avoid being labelled 'terroristic'. Rules must be specific, widely publicized, widely known, and consistently applied by the state. Citizens must be able to predict whether or not their actions or words (or non-actions and silence) will bring them into conflict with the state authorities; when they cannot, terror is present. There may well have been some pattern to Stalin's purges of the 1930s, for instance, as Conquest, Moore, and others suggest, but if the people *affected* by the purges cannot see why they are being arrested, and if others live in fear because of the apparently indiscriminatory nature of such arrests, then the regime has become one of terror. This is certainly true of the USSR during the 1930s, for instance. At the end of the 1940s and the beginning of the 1950s, Harvard University's Russian Research Center interviewed a large number of Russian *émigrés*; these interviews made it quite clear that many Soviet citizens were unaware of the logic of the 1930s purges—

. . . one gains the clear impression that a large portion of the population fails to sense any clear connection between a specific act and the dreaded descent of the secret police. Particularly during the *Yezhovshchina*, as the great purge of the latter thirties became known after Yezhov, then head of the police, quite a number of people were certain that their arrest had been a mistake—a stupid slip on some part of the bureaucracy that would soon be put to rights by getting in touch with the responsible officials. Convinced of their own essential loyalty, they could not understand why they found themselves in jail. This kind of reaction appears to have been rather frequent among educated people.   (Moore 1966, p. 157.)

Even if one considers the purge of 'wealthy' Soviet peasants (the kulaks) at the end of the 1920s and early 1930s, it will be found that many peasants were unclear as to whether they would be considered a kulak or not because of *vague* definitions given by the leadership. Moreover, since the Soviet leaders had appeared tacitly to accept a plea by Bukharin in the mid-1920s to the peasants to 'get rich', it was incomprehensible to many peasants why, within four or five years, any attempt to get rich could lead to their being labelled a traitor. Thus there were elements of terror at this earlier stage too.

Another important component of the rule of law is that citizens must be guaranteed practicable means for complying with the state laws. For instance, a government might declare it illegal for citizens to own factories; this might be seen as arbitrary and even silly (economically) by many citizens, but at least owners can hand their factories over to the state. They have, in other words, the possibility of conforming with the new law. If one is Jewish, or has a black skin, then arbitrary maltreatment of Jews (as in Nazi Germany) or blacks (as in South Africa) by a state is an example of terror, since the people 'breaking' the new rules have little or no realistic possibility for conforming with them.

A related point is that a regime is also terroristic if sections of the population are treated as *potential* enemies, solely because of their past economic and/or social status. If a revolution has led to a change in the society's rules, one should surely be treated as deviant only when and if one actually breaks the new rules. This point was explicitly acknowledged in Mao's concept of 'class enemy'; he rejected many European communist regimes' concepts of class enemy based on former position, preferring to see how people actually behaved following the revolution.

From the above points, it can be further argued that laws should be rational and reasonable by most ethical standards if the state is to avoid charges of being terroristic. This is, of course, a highly subjective matter, but I would argue that an unreasonable law is that which exists in some communist states whereby it is either *de jure* (e.g. Vietnam) and/or *de facto* (e.g. the USSR since the February 1984 law on passing information to foreigners) forbidden for natives of a given country to meet foreigners—especially those from non-communist states—on any sort of a social basis. The state's intention is usually reasonably clear—to minimize the chances of its own citizens being 'tainted' by or even fully aware of alternative value-systems, and to restrict the amount of information about the given society that reaches the outside world. This law is not only morally questionable and often arbitrarily applied, but is based on dubious assumptions. Foreign visitors can easily exchange ideas with hotel-receptionists, shop-assistants, waiters, etc.—with whom they have to and are permitted to communicate—as well as by talking to natives sitting at the same table at a café or restaurant.

The 'rule of law' also implies that citizens must be guaranteed a fair trial if they fall foul of the authorities. They must not be detained indefinitely without being charged, and they must be entitled to proper defence facilities (i.e., defence lawyers must genuinely try to represent the interests of the defendant rather than those of the state). The outcome of trials should not be pre-ordained, and defendants should be assumed innocent until proven guilty.

The final point about the 'rule of law' is that it is basically incompatible with any kind of police state. Several aspects of the police state, such as the points about trials, have already been mentioned; but there are two others to be elaborated. The first is that the agents of coercion should be answerable to the public—even if indirectly, via elected state representatives and/or members of the vanguard party. Where the powers of the police and courts are not in any meaningful sense regulated by other branches of the state, we can talk of a police state. Second, the vast majority of the agents of state coercion should be readily identifiable (notably through being uniformed), and the population at large should more or less accept the necessity for both the existence of the secret police force and the uses to which the force is put. For example, many citizens might accept the use of undercover police officers for tracking down child-molesters, drug-traffickers, or terrorists. On the other hand, they might not accept the state's use of such officers for listening to political conversations in cafés and making arrests on the basis of such eavesdropping, especially if such conversations have no tangible action-consequences.

The above points lead us to a third major component of Dallin and Breslauer's definition, viz. the notion of a *threat* of severe and arbitrary coercion as well as *actual* arbitrary coercion. Some, such as Carl Friedrich (1969, p. 145), maintain that communist states are still totalitarian because, even though actual arbitrary coercion has in most cases ceased, the *potential* is still there; such an argument goes too far. If a child is told it will be punished if it plays on the street, but in fact is not penalized when it does, then the threat will gradually lose its power as a deterrent. Every so often, punishment (i.e., *actual* coercion) must be administered to endorse the threat. On the other hand, if one does even occasionally punish the child, then the mere threat of this will usually be sufficient to restrain him or her from playing on the street. This, in simplified form, is what is meant by the credible threat of severe arbitrary coercion. If there are genuine *acts* of arbitrary coercion every few years, then the *threat* of action will encourage most people to do and say as little as possible of anything they suspect might one day be interpreted by the regime as anti-statist. Hence, whilst Friedrich's concept of 'psychological terror'—which for him does *not* have to be backed up by relatively frequent violent purges, and exists simply if a state has a secret police force—is too broad, Dallin and Breslauer's inclusion of a 'credible threat' is acceptable. Once again, Slusser's definition, with its reference to the 'use of violent means' is too narrow, since a regime may be described at a given point in time as terroristic even though no violent acts have been performed by it for two or three years.

We have seen that there are a number of different aspects of terror, and that the 'rule of law' concept is a complex one. Not every terroristic regime will display all the elements of terror listed, just as some non-terroristic regimes may sometimes display terroristic features. Similarly, there are degrees of terror, even between countries which display all or most of the characteristics listed. As mentioned earlier, the borderline between a highly coercive and a terroristic regime is often hazy in the real world, and analysts may well disagree on whether a given country is terroristic or not. But we also know that terror does exist in the real world, and we have seen that it can be defined reasonably clearly in terms of a number of components. As a general rule of thumb, a terroristic state is one in which a substantial proportion of the citizenry lives in fear and uncertainty because of the behaviour of the state's agents.

Having defined the concept of terror in general terms, it is useful to distinguish between terror that is deliberately initiated by the senior political leadership (described by Dallin and Breslauer as 'purposive terror') and terror which is instituted by lower level cadres, often in their zeal to display loyalty to the regime and/or feel that they have an important role to play in the building of communism ('situational terror'). This distinction can be of importance, as we shall see.

THE USE OF TERROR IN COMMUNIST REGIMES

Most communist states have employed terror at one time or another, although the extent and nature of such usage has varied considerably. In this section, the emphasis will be on the more extreme cases of terror in the communist world, those in which the state takes the lives of citizens for political reasons. This is the form of terror that most clearly declines over time, and that is morally the most unacceptable. Let us start by considering the oldest communist state, the USSR; this country has to some extent acted as a test-bed for many political methods employed in communist states, including the use of terror.

Lenin came to power in a country which, from several angles, was not yet ready for many of the communists' ideas and policies. The proletariat—here, in the commonly accepted sense of the manual urban workers—constituted only a tiny percentage of the population, most of whom were peasants. Elections to the Constituent Assembly late in 1917 suggested that most Russians, whilst supportive of a government committed to change, envisaged such change as being in the direction of more distribution of land to the peasants, rather than a 'dictatorship of the proletariat'. The fact of the Civil War between 1918 and 1920 showed beyond doubt that there were substantial numbers of Soviet citizens who opposed the Bolsheviks. Under such circumstances, a high level of coercion by the new regime was, if not necessarily pardonable, at least predictable and by some criteria necessary. Not only was the regime highly coercive, but it also established a security police force—a key element in any terroristic regime—in the form of the Cheka.

There were unquestionably several aspects of terror in the Lenin era, and Lenin made it clear that he was not opposed to the use of terror if it helped the Bolshevik cause (see McClosky and Turner 1960, pp. 444–5). On the other hand, most people who were arrested and executed would know that this was because they had shown some form of real resistance to the new Bolshevik regime. In terms of both scale and nature, the Lenin era was not nearly as terroristic as the one which followed it.

Lenin's death (January 1924) was followed by a power struggle, in which Stalin was victorious by about 1929. Stalin believed that the economy would have to be developed very rapidly and under centralized direction, which led to the introduction of the USSR's first five-year plan in 1928. Although this was initially primarily concerned with industry, it very soon became clear that industry could only develop if there was investment. Investment needs money, of which there was relatively little spare in the Russia of the late 1920s. Moreover, given both the refusal of the Bolshevik regime to compensate foreign companies whose factories were nationalized after the revolution, and the fact that the Western economies were heading towards economic crisis anyway, foreign sources could not be relied upon to produce the necessary funds. Hence, the buildup or accumulation of capital would have to come from within. Largely for this reason, the original Bolshevik (Leninist) aim of encouraging peasants to join collectives voluntarily— through seeing for themselves the advantages of such organizations in 'model collectives' set up around the country—was changed by Stalin into a policy of compulsion. Such a policy was bound to lead to a major reaction, and it was largely because of this negative response to collectivization that the so-called 'dekulakization' policy of 1929–31 was implemented. 'Kulaks' were defined as the wealthy peasants who owned their land and employed others; the campaign was officially aimed at ridding Soviet society of such capitalist-minded elements—through deportation, dispatch to labour camps and even execution. In fact, the policy was to no small extent also mounted in order to show all peasants what would happen if they did not accept the government's policy. The policy did represent terror. On the one hand, the classification of a given peasant as a kulak was often at the discretion of some local official. On the other, the policy of collectivization itself was very vague—both in its timing and in the definition of a collective farm—so that to expect peasants, sometimes on pain of death, to accept something so ill defined was in itself highly arbitrary. This all said, it would appear that much of the terror at this stage was 'situational'—caused by over-zealous local officials; in a famous article of 1930 ('Dizzy with Success'), Stalin argued that local party officials had gone further than the leadership had intended in forcing collectivization and dealing with kulaks. Whilst this undoubtedly represented on one level a scapegoat argument, it probably also contained an element of truth.

According to most analyses, the late 1920s/early 1930s was not as terroristic a period in terms of apparent arbitrariness as that from the end of 1934 to 1939, even though Hough estimates that $3\frac{1}{2}$ million people died as a result of the collectivization policy (Hough and Fainsod 1979, p. 152). What is usually called the 'Great Terror', began to emerge at the end of 1934. In December of that year, a young man called Nikolaev assassinated the head of the Leningrad party organization, Kirov. There is still much debate as to whether Nikolaev was self-motivated, or whether he was in fact working on Stalin's orders. Whatever the truth of the matter, the important point is that, just as Hitler had used the burning of the Reichstag in 1933 as justification for a clampdown on political activity, so Stalin used Kirov's assassination as an excuse for introducing a new wave of terror. Stalin told the security police (by now called the NKVD) that they were behind in their duties, changed their leadership, and instructed them to be more vigilant. But this was clearly insufficient for Stalin. Following a telegram from him to Molotov, the great purge of 1936–8 was inaugurated. Show trials—trials which are widely publicized and used by a regime for propaganda purposes rather than the pursuit of justice—became a familiar feature of Soviet life. Although the arrests, trials, etc. appeared arbitrary to those affected by them, there does seem to have been a pattern to the authorities' actions, as was pointed out earlier. Without elaborating the details, suffice it to say that the further up the social, economic, and political hierarchy one was, the greater the likelihood of arrest. We shall probably never know the exact scale of the Great Terror. Andrei Sakharov, a Soviet physicist and dissident, estimates that between ten and fifteen million people lost their lives as a result of both the collectivization campaign of the late 1920s/early 1930s and the subsequent 'Great Terror' (Sakharov 1968, p. 52). At the other end of the spectrum, Jerry Hough estimates the number of those who died as a direct result of the Great Terror at 'a figure in the low hundreds of thousands' (Hough and Fainsod 1979, p. 177); this is, of course, in addition to the three and a half million of the earlier period. Whichever figures one adopts, what is abundantly clear is that a very large number of Soviet citizens—many of them leading communists—fell victim to the Stalin terror of the 1930s. Shortly after the Great Terror, in 1941, the Soviet Union was forcibly brought into the Second World War; in such a situation, terror was even more inappropriate than before, and subsided. But examples of it occurred again after the War, in the shape of the so-called 'Leningrad Affair' of 1948–9 and the 'Doctors' Plot' of 1952–3. Fortunately, neither of these led to terror on anything like the scale of that of the 1930s, and in March 1953 Stalin died. Millions were still in the labour camps, but the new leadership very soon revealed its intention dramatically to change the situation regarding terror. One of its first acts was to execute the head of the security police, Beria. This was followed by a substantial reduction in the powers of the security police, and eventually condemnation of the Stalinist terror and the release and rehabilitation of many of the labour camp internees. Since the mid-1950s, there has been a substantial reduction in the scale and range of terror in the USSR. It is certainly true that dissidents are often badly treated—and cannot necessarily expect even a trial (many simply disappear into psychiatric hospitals). But such people will in almost all cases know why they have fallen foul of the authorities, and will in most cases survive their ordeals; in this sense their treatment is not directly comparable with that meted out in the 1930s. Let us now turn to consider China.

China, too, has had its terroristic periods, though these appear to have led to far fewer deaths than in the USSR. In the decade following the communist takeover, there was no civil war to speak of. Nevertheless, many parts of China had not yet shown support for the communists, and 'controlled class warfare', exercised by the party and the army, was exercised against many Chinese citizens. In particular, there was an attack by the regime on the rich peasants, a policy of 'liquidating the landlords as a class'—somewhat reminiscent of the dekulakization policy of the Soviets. Two important differences, however, were that the Chinese communists had not initially *encouraged* peasants to get rich, and that the authorities allowed former landlords to recant and declare themselves loyal to the new regime. Moreover, there were far less deaths than in the Soviet dekulakization. In these senses, the period was less terroristic than the late 1920s/early 1930s in the USSR. At this time, there were no major purges of leading party members in China. It is true that in the mid-1950s, Gao Gang and Rao Shushi were tried and found guilty of anti-party activity; but neither was executed, and the charges against them were essentially true anyway, unlike most of the charges against leading Bolsheviks in the period 1936–8.

The most wide-scale purge and terror in China since the consolidation of communist power began in 1966. In that year, the Great Proletarian Cultural Revolution (hereafter, GPCR) openly revealed a major clash of personalities and policies in Chinese politics. On the one hand was Mao Zedong, committed to constant revolutionary change and what might be described as a somewhat purist approach to the building of communism. He strongly disapproved of what he perceived to be a growing bureaucratization in Chinese society, not unlike that of which he was so critical in the USSR. On the other hand there was Liu Shaoqi, a more pragmatic politician who felt that hierarchy and professionalism were necessary if Chinese society was to progress. The Cultural Revolution brought the conflict between these two 'lines', as they are usually called, into the open. During this period, Mao used the Red Guards to break down hierarchy and bureaucracy within Chinese society. There was certainly terror—not only purposive, but also situational—in this period, a fact which comes out nicely in the following quotation from the head of the Institute of Sociology attached to the Chinese Academy of Social Sciences:

But beginning in 1966, during the 'Cultural Revolution', when nothing was allowed to remain intact, the rule of law was also demolished and lawlessness prevailed.... During those ten years of the 'Cultural Revolution' the Constitution was ignored and the country's laws and decrees were blithely discarded and people were detained and tortured and their homes sacked.   (Fei Xiaotong, 1981, p. 8.)

In 1980, it was officially stated by the Chinese authorities that 729,511 people were framed and persecuted during the Cultural Revolution, of whom 34,800 died as a result (*A Great Trial in Chinese History*, 1981, p. 20). More 'ordinary' citizens were affected than in the Soviet case, mainly in the form of harassment by Red Guards. This all said, relatively fewer people were arrested, let alone exterminated, than in Stalin's 'Great Terror'. Indeed, several of those who suffered during the GPCR have made comebacks in the post-Mao period; the most striking example is the current *de facto* leader of China, Deng Xiaoping. This, too, is quite different from the earlier situation in Russia.

Mao died in September 1976, and there have been show trials of sorts since then—notably of the 'Gang of Four'. This was a group of radical leaders responsible for many of the atrocities of the GPCR. Although the trial of the 'Gang of Four' was a show trial and in one sense an act of terror, certain points should be borne in mind. Most importantly, the defendants were allowed defence lawyers (although these in fact said little at the trial), and it is not clear that they were forced to accuse themselves of acts of which they had not been guilty (though see Bonavia, 1982, pp. 120–2). Nor were they executed, despite having been found guilty. Finally, they had indeed been involved in the perpetration of many crimes against humanity—so that one can hardly compare the Chinese 'Great Trial' of 1980 with the similarly named event in the USSR in 1938.

Eastern Europe has also experienced extreme terror. In the late 1940s and early 1950s, there were a number of show trials of people who, just a few years before, had themselves played major roles in the communist leaderships. The trials of Rajk in Hungary, Slansky in Czechoslovakia, Kostov in Bulgaria, Pauker and Patrascanu in Romania, Xoxe in Albania—these and others testified to the highly arbitrary nature of many of these regimes at that time. Trumped-up charges of 'Titoism', 'Trotskyism', nationalism and being in the pay of Western intelligence agencies (all of which in essence meant not being sufficiently loyal and sycophantic towards Stalin) were made against these party functionaries, and many of them were subsequently executed. Many lower-ranking party members and ordinary citizens were also affected; it has been estimated that between 125,000 and 250,000 people were imprisoned for 'political crimes' between 1947 and 1953 (Fejtö, cited in Westoby 1981, p. 73). To no small extent, the terror was an extension of Stalin's terror and paranoia to Eastern Europe—which is one reason why Yugoslavia, which was largely independent of the USSR from 1948, experienced less terror than most of its neighbours. There was also a strong element of anti-Semitism in these purges. In Eastern Europe generally, as in the USSR, terror has declined dramatically since the mid-1950s. Let us now turn to look at other parts of the communist world.

From April 1975 to January 1979, Kampuchea was ruled by one of the most fanatical political leaders in modern times—Pol Pot. Although some writers, such as Laura Summers (1981, esp. pp. 420–6) have played down the horrors of the Pol Pot regime, the admittedly tenuous evidence we have strongly suggests that it created human misery on an unprecedented scale; in recent years, only Amin's regime in Uganda comes close to having perpetrated such heinous crimes against the population. When the Khmer Rouge took power in Phnom Penh in April 1975, they immediately ordered the capital's inhabitants (approximately $2\frac{1}{2}$ million, or one third of the total population) to leave their homes and go to the countryside. The initial justification given for this was that the country was critically short of food, and that the leaders had no intention of applying to the Americans for help. Indeed, despite its official rejection of the Chinese model, the Pol Pot regime was in many ways similar to the Maoist, North Korean, and Albanian regimes in its emphasis on self-reliance and independence of all foreign agencies. However, food shortages were not the only reasons for the radical movement of population. In September 1977, Pol Pot stated publicly at a rally in Phnom Penh that the cities had been considered potential centres of counter-revolution—full of foreigners, petty bourgeoisie, etc.—and that this political motive was a very important one in the decision to evacuate the cities (Zasloff and Brown 1979, p. 34).

Unlike its Indochinese neighbours, Vietnam and Laos—which do not appear to have had widescale systematic executions, although they have experienced some aspects of terror—there are many reports of executions in Kampuchea in the mid-1970s. The first to be shot were senior government and military officials of the previous regime; such people had been warned to leave, but do not appear to have done so on any meaningful scale. Following these executions, virtually the whole of the professional and bourgeois classes became 'fair game' for the new regime, and vast numbers of their ranks were exterminated. However, as in other communist regimes, it was not merely citizens who were, by communist criteria, 'objective enemies' of communism who suffered in all this. Very soon, many communist revolutionaries who had in the past worked closely with the Vietnamese—the latter being hated by the Pol Pot regime—were now liable for arrest and execution. Moreover, in the Spring of 1977, there appear to have been several purges at lower levels of the party. The reasons for this are not entirely clear. One hypothesis is that local officials were actually concerned at the level of alienation to the regime of the people in their regions. This led many of these lower-level party members not to implement harsh central policies—suggesting that there are sometimes clashes between the agents of 'purposive' and 'situational' terror. Another reason seems to have been that there were many clashes between different factions within the Communist Party of Kampuchea; even at the top of this party, there were at least three major groupings—the Pol Pot radicals; the Khmer Viet Minh, who were sympathetic towards the Vietnamese communists; and a group of intellectuals who wanted a moderate but also internationally independent path towards socialism.

The scale of the Kampuchean terror is difficult to assess. In his September 1977 speech, Pol Pot estimated that between 1 and 2 per cent of the population were enemies of the revolution and needed to be dealt with as such; this produces a figure of 50–100,000 as a *minimum* number. Although Pol Pot maintained that there should be 'neutralization' and 'eradication' of the smallest possible number of this 1 to 2 per cent, reports that have reached the West suggest that at least the total number estimated above suffered under this most radical of communist regimes. Western estimates of deaths during the first year to eighteen months following the takeover by the Khmer Rouge go as high as 1.2 million; of these, however, many were deaths due to illness and starvation. But R. Shaplen estimated in 1977 that about 200,000 Kampucheans had been executed since Pol Pot came to power (cited by Zasloff and Brown 1979, p. 41). In 1976, the Kampuchean head of state, Khieu Samphan, seemed to acknowledge that the population had declined by about a million in the period April 1975 to September 1976, although some of this decline is attributable to people fleeing Kampuchea, as well as to deaths. In May 1977, Ieng Sary (Kampuchean Deputy Prime Minister, responsible for Foreign Affairs) stated that between 4,000 and 6,000 people died as a result of state actions in the early days of the new regime—which, at least, represents a minimum figure. The present Kampuchean government announced in mid-1983 that the number of 'genocide victims' of the Pol Pot regime was 3.3 million; this figure is, however, from a government with a vested interest in discrediting its predecessor to the utmost. Finally, in one of the most thorough analyses of this question, Vickery (1984, esp. p. 187) concludes that the total number of above-normal deaths (including starvation, exhaustion, etc.) in Kampuchea from April 1975 to January 1979 was about 740,000, of which up to 2–300,000 were the result of executions by the Pol Pot government. At the end of the day, we cannot produce any conclusive figures on the number of deaths directly or indirectly attributable to the Pol Pot regime; but it is absolutely clear that a great deal of suffering was caused by arbitrary decisions of a very radical leadership, anxious to settle old scores, to eradicate other communists who disagreed with their way of reaching socialism, and to force ordinary citizens to do all sorts of things those citizens did not want to do (e.g. move to the countryside, collectivize, etc.).

Afghanistan, too, experienced a great deal of political terror in the first eighteen months or so following the revolution of 1978. Officials of the overthrown government and officers of the pre-communist armed forces were the first major groups to suffer. But very soon, the dominant communist faction—the Khalq communists—were directing some of their terror against the smaller Parcham faction. Many people were arrested and executed without trial. The Pul-e-Charki prison outside Kabul soon gained a reputation as a house of horror, and the head of the secret police was nicknamed 'King Kong'. According to unconfirmed reports, trenches for burying up to a hundred executed prisoners at a time were dug around the prison, and filled in up to three or four times a week at the peak of the terror. Once again, definitive figures on the number of people killed as a result of this terror are not available. However, many Afghans believe that approximately 25,000 citizens lost their lives as a result of the communist regime's terror in the period from April 1978 to January 1980 (Hyman 1982, p. 9). When Karmal took power at the end of 1979, the situation seems to have improved, and the regime made serious attempts to muster support rather than terrorize the population. However, it appears that terror is increasing again at present, as the policy of blending communism and Islam proves increasingly to be a failure.

The African communist states have certainly had purges and other forms of terror too. In the Congo, for instance, the very small but powerful Communist Party almost disappeared in 1972, after a series of violent purges had been instituted by the then Congolese leader, Ngouabi, to purify its ranks. A similar purge was carried out in 1975–6, after Ngouabi had denounced the entire party membership. In Angola, there was a violent purge of Nito Alves and his supporters (the so-called Nitista faction) in 1977. And terror has played a major role in the history of communist rule in Ethiopia—indeed more than in any other African communist state. The main period of the so-called 'revolutionary red terror' was from April 1977 to June 1978. It was above all the result of a struggle between the dominant communist group (under Mengistu) and other political groups, both Marxist and non-Marxist. Estimates of the number killed range from 3,000 to 10,000, whilst thousands more were arrested and tortured (D. and M. Ottaway, 1981, pp. 152–4).

WHY IS TERROR EMPLOYED?

A study of the use of terror in communist regimes reveals that there are certain patterns to it. There is often a need for coercion, at least, which can soon turn into terror (particularly of the situational kind) in the takeover period. Usually, there are genuine enemies of the regime, so that coercion and terror are here used for defence of the regime. However differences between approaches and/or a desire to settle old scores can lead to one group of communists using terror against another group. This was true in Eastern Europe in the late 1940s and early 1950s, when many Moscow-oriented communists in these countries set out to purge the more nationalistic communists in the country. A similar phenomenon occurred in Afghanistan—in terms of the relationship between the Khalq and Parcham factions of the party—in Ethiopia, Angola and elsewhere. Sometimes, this in-fighting and terror by one group against another group may take years to emerge into public view; it constitutes part of the explanation for the terror in the USSR in the 1930s, and during the GPCR in China from 1966.

Once the communists have essentially consolidated power, they are committed to a rapid and wide-ranging transformation of society; this is partially a function of the fact that most communists take power in societies which are not, by most classical Marxist standards, ready to move to socialism. Such rapid change, directed from above, is often called the 'mobilization' stage of societal development. Radical change can rarely, if ever, be accepted gracefully by all sections of society; typically, collectivization of agriculture leads to much hostility from the peasantry, for instance. In order to overcome active resistance from some members of society and to serve as a warning to other potentially resistive members, the regime introduces a campaign of terror. But this is not necessarily the end of the terror. Later in the mobilization phase, the chances are that the leaders will feel the need to make excuses for the fact that certain expectations they themselves have raised amongst the population have at best been only partially fulfilled. This comes out nicely in the following quotation from Vyshinsky (chief prosecutor during the Soviet Great Terror) at the so-called Great Trial of March 1938, in which he blamed Bukharin and other leading Bolsheviks for the shortages that still existed almost a decade after the five-year plans had first become operational, about twenty years after the Bolshevik revolution, and at a time when Stalin had recently claimed that socialism had at last been achieved:

In our country, rich in resources of all kinds, there could not have been and cannot be a situation in which a shortage of any product should exist . . .
It is now clear why there are interruptions of supplies here and there, why, with our riches and abundance of products, there is a shortage first of one thing, then of another. It is these traitors who are responsible for it.   (Conquest, 1971, p. 563.)

In other words, the regime was blaming some of its erstwhile best sons and daughters in an attempt to retain or strengthen legitimacy in the eyes of the population. Thus terror can be used to perform what we might call a 'scapegoat' function, as well as to force people to abide by a policy. Looking at this from a slightly different angle, we would argue that terror can sometimes play an important role in an individual leader's attempt to acquire popularity and legitimacy, in that he or she can blame and punish other leaders for any major problems that society is experiencing.

Another function of terror is the provision of cheap labour. A state that is attempting to modernize the economy rapidly using only its own resources (i.e., as distinct from borrowing from abroad) needs to accumulate funds in any way possible. Excessive exploitation of the peasantry has, empirically, often led them to destroy their produce rather than give it to the state, so that the kinds of force used against the peasantry in the early years of a regime can become self-defeating. On the other hand, the more qualified people in industry and the technically advanced branches of the economy may not give of their best if they feel that differentials are too low—and yet the regime cannot afford to pay them large salaries. Hence, by creaming off some of the most skilled people in society and sending them to labour camps, the regime can acquire their services for no more than it costs to keep them fed and housed. Not only the USSR, but also many of the East European regimes, China, and elsewhere have arbitrarily arrested specialists and sent them to labour camps partially for this reason.

The use of terror to back up, in various ways, policies of enormous change may help to eliminate incongruent value-systems and instil new ones. In other words, if people are forced, for instance, to collectivize, they will probably initially react negatively; over time, however, they *may* see the advantages of the organizational form that has been imposed, quite irrespective of any propaganda that may accompany the forced collectivization.

Atomization is another function of terror; people become too scared to form subgroups in society which might otherwise have constituted some form of threat to the leadership. Moreover, lack of discussion means that, other things being equal, all but the most thinking and critical individuals are likely to be persuaded by the regime's propaganda more than might be the case if opposition views were allowed to be disseminated freely.

Finally, it should be noted that organizations associated with the implementation of terror—notably the security police—can find the terror functional in the sense of justifying their self-aggrandizement, overfulfilling quotas, promotion, etc. Perhaps it even fulfils a psychological need for some authoritarian and/or revengeful personalities—although, in the case of local officials, their ability to satisfy this need is dependent on there being a terroristic atmosphere in a given country in the first place.

THE DYSFUNCTIONS OF TERROR

Although we have outlined a number of advantages, from the regime's point of view, of terror, there are also many disadvantages to this form of political rule.

It is sometimes argued that terror performs a useful function in keeping upward (vertical) channels of social mobility much more open than in other systems. There are two flaws in this argument. First, upward channels are very open anyway in the mobilization phase. A society trying to modernize needs lots of new skills, including managerial ones, which ensure this. Second, if people at the top are being removed by the terror machine, their subordinates will very soon learn the inherent dangers of accepting a senior position of responsibility. In other words, channels might remain open, but this is of little use to a developing state if one major reason for such openness discourages people from moving upwards. Hence this particular 'function' is not in fact useful; it is dysfunctional, discouraging both initiative and leadership. Indeed, in the case of the Stalinist terror, the removal of many leaders from the upper echelons of the military meant that Russia suffered more during the Second World War than would almost undoubtedly have been the case had Stalin not disposed of most of his generals. It can also be argued that Pol Pot might still have been in power had he not alienated so many military officials and other communists. And China is now experiencing far more problems in implementing its modernization programme (the so-called 'Four Modernizations') than would have been the case had Mao and his supporters not shut down so many of China's educational institutions during the GPCR, which has resulted in a serious shortfall of skills and experience now.

Closely related to the above point is the fact that fear of the consequences by managers etc. of underfulfilling plans can lead them to make false returns to the central planners and/or ensure fulfilment through illegal means. Both kinds of action are ultimately dysfunctional to the regime. In the first case, false data that are included in official descriptions of economic performance and future plans give a distorted picture of the actual state of the economy— which can over time lead to scepticism amongst the citizenry about the regime's claims, and thus a lessening of any legitimacy the regime may have. In the second case, the emergence of a 'black' or illegal economy similarly leads to an undermining of the legitimacy of the regime and its communist goals, since it encourages many people to look after their own interests above society's, can lead to corruption, etc.

A third dysfunction of terror is brought out clearly in Solzhenitsyn's *The First Circle*. In the novel, inmates of a labour camp are forced to use their skills to develop a new kind of scrambling device for telephones. This they do, but their lack of enthusiasm means they take far longer to do it than would have been the case if they had done it willingly. If speed is an important factor in the usual communist approach to development, then a frequent resort to terror—unjustified prison sentences for skilled people etc.—can be dysfunctional.

Finally, we should not forget that it is not only *within* a given communist state that communism can acquire a bad reputation through excessive use of terror. This, too, can be dysfunctional to a leadership, in that it can be used by outsiders to justify an invasion. One of the many reasons why the Soviets helped to bring Karmal to power in Afghanistan was precisely the fact that Taraki and Amin had been giving communism a bad name amongst Muslims, not only in Afghanistan, but in the Middle East generally. It was a period when many Arab states—Iran above all—had been turning increasingly anti-Western, and the Soviets were hoping to capitalize on this.

If Amin's terror was hindering such a political improvement in communist–Islamic relations, then he would have to be replaced by a more tolerant, less repressive leader. The Vietnamese invasion of Kampuchea has also been justified on one level in essentially similar terms (i.e., to end a communist terror). At a more general level, it could well be the case that socialism would be more popular in both the first and third worlds nowadays had it not been for many of the atrocities that have been committed by communists in the twentieth century.

THE DECLINE OF TERROR

We have seen that high levels of coercion and particularly terror are frequently characteristics of the early years of a communist regime. There are two, closely related reasons for this. The first is that there is typically a large gap between the conditions pertaining at the time of communist takeover and the level of development from which Marx envisaged socialism proceeding. As we have seen, communists have yet to take power in an advanced industrial state in which a highly politicized and numerically dominant proletariat is ready and keen to move to socialism; because of this, communists feel the need to bridge this gap themselves. This leads us to our second explanatory factor—the political approach and personality of revolutionary leaders. Such people are prepared to 'force' the pace of historical development—they are voluntarists—in order to reach a stage *from* which socialism can proceed. They are prepared to deal harshly with all the hostilities and problems that arise from this approach. For them, the ends justify the means. In those countries where the leaders have in essence been installed, the leaders may pursue such hard-line policies not only—or even *necessarily*—because they themselves are excessively tough-minded, but perhaps because they are scared of the consequences to themselves of not rooting out alleged enemies within their societies. This would help to explain some of the actions of various East European leaders in the late 1940s and early 1950s, before Stalin's death.

However, although traces of it may well remain, terror typically declines once a communist regime has undergone its consolidation and mobilization phases. In other words, terror ceases to be a salient feature of the regime. There are a number of reasons for this. In many cases, new leaders, with different ideas and approaches, will eventually replace the people who implemented the terror. The new leaders may well have been affected by the terror themselves in some way and will have seen how it can become self-perpetuating unless decisively stopped. They will want to ensure that the revolution is not going to continue to devour its best sons and daughters—themselves possibly included! This helps to explain the execution of Beria, the trial and imprisonment of the Gang of Four, and the political demise of many East European Stalinists in the 1950s. But the new leaders are not only interested in saving their own necks. Typically, they will feel that it is time for the regime to move away from power based on fear towards power based on authority; they will, in short, be seeking more solid bases for what we call 'legitimacy'. Whereas the revolutionary leaders may claim their right to rule (which is what is meant by legitimacy) from an abstract ideology, subsequent leaders may well prefer to acquire their legitimacy less from Marxism–Leninism than from the support of the masses. Although they will not go so far as to introduce a Western-style political system in their search for greater legitimacy, they will try to base their right to rule primarily on the fact that they are governing well. In short, they seek legitimacy through the good performance of the system. This in itself helps to explain the decline of terror; the leaders will now accept that the disadvantages of this form of rule are clearly outweighing any advantages. At the same time, particularly if the mobilization phase has been a fairly lengthy one, the society will have become more complex. As Karl Deutsch, Samuel Huntington, and others have argued, the more complex a society becomes, the greater the need for a certain amount of decentralization of decision-making and a secure, predictable climate in which people can act more rationally. If such a situation is not allowed to develop, the system will be unable to make any significant moves forward, since excessively centralized control of a large-scale and highly complex economy and polity is unrealistic, even in the age of the computer. Expressing all this crudely, a more sophisticated society needs a more sophisticated form of political rule. At the same time, economic modernization means that greater wealth is generated. Greater wealth means that investment in industry can continue, but also that the state will have more and better resources for achieving its ends—both through greater use of material incentives to citizens and the use of more sophisticated socialization processes. Typically, there will be a greater stress on socialist legality at this stage. This greater emphasis on both normative and material forms of power means that there can be a lessening of coercive forms of power. Normative and material forms of power are superior to coercive power in the long term, since they will, if implemented properly, tend to give the regime greater popular support—and power based on mass acceptance is both more attractive and probably more enduring than power based above all on fear. Thus communist regimes do *tend* to move away from terror over time, preferring and being better able to place more emphasis on incentives, socialization, and non-terroristic coercion for ensuring compliance and bringing about change.

CONCLUSION

Even allowing for the problems in obtaining reliable data, it should by now be abundantly clear that communists in power have made extensive use of terror. Although many twentieth-century communist leaders have attempted to justify the use of terror, it should be noted that Marx himself seems to have opposed it. He did accept the need for state coercion during the 'dictatorship of the proletariat', but condemned the terror that followed the French Revolution. According to McLellan (1980, p. 229):

He [i.e. Marx—LTH] strongly criticised the use of terror by the Jacobins in the French Revolution; its use was for him a sign of the weakness and immaturity of that revolution which had to try to impose by sheer force what was not yet inherent in society.

As has been emphasized (and will be again at various points in this book), the argument about 'immature' revolutions is extremely germane to an understanding of much that has happened in the communist world, including terror. This said, it has also been argued that the more extreme dimensions of terror usually decline over time, even though there are still aspects of it in most communist states—indeed, in most countries of the world. One of the most effective ways of keeping state terror in check is to allow genuine freedom of speech and media that are both independent of the state and able to investigate important aspects of the state's activities. Unfortunately, these freedoms are not yet a feature of the communist world. Until they are, there are still too few safeguards against a resurgence of terror—even though both a dialectical, Marxist approach and a cost–benefit approach suggest that such a resurgence on a major scale is unlikely in most of the older communist states.

Basic further reading

Amnesty International, 1984a
F. Beck and W. Godin, 1951.
R. Conquest, 1971.
A. Dallin and G. Breslauer, 1970.
F. Fejtö, 1974, pp. 14–25.
A. Hyman, 1982.
G. Leggett, 1981.
B. Moore, 1966.
J. Pelikan (ed.), 1971.
F. Teiwes, 1979.
C. Thayer, 1981.
A. Westoby, 1981, pp. 72–6

4

POLITICAL CULTURE AND
SOCIALIZATION

In the last chapter, we saw one way in which communists seek to ensure citizen compliance. In this chapter, we shall consider a rather different approach, and one that is usually more pervasive and long lasting—namely attempts to change people's basic beliefs and values. These attempts are, supposedly, not made only to ensure compliance, but also to produce better, more socially minded citizens. Although Marx himself did not actually use the term 'political culture' (Meyer 1983a, p. 5), his notion that the ideas of the ruling class permeate society—and hence that our values and attitudes are malleable rather than innate—can be seen as the starting-point for the emphasis twentieth-century communists have placed on the need to transform people's outlooks, to remould 'political culture'. The term itself was used by Lenin (White 1977, p. 58), although it does not appear to have been used in English until Sidney and Beatrice Webb employed the term in the 1930s (Brown 1974, p. 100); we can note parenthetically that the term 'political culture' in its *modern* sense is much more recent, having first been used by Gabriel Almond in a 1956 article (Brown 1977, p. 3). Most communists in power have placed considerable emphasis on the importance of propaganda, political education, etc. as a way of changing the citizenry's political outlook. Even the arts have been subjected to communist control and have been consciously used to try to instil new values; in 1934, when 'socialist realism' was being formally adopted in the USSR as the approach to be used by all artists, Zhdanov declared that Stalin had described Soviet artistic writers as 'engineers of human souls'. Given the great emphasis communists themselves place on culture and socialization, then, a study of their attempts at creating a new political culture should—in theory—tell us much about the malleability of the human mind.

Unfortunately, the study of political culture is one of the most contentious areas in comparative communism—indeed in comparative politics generally. There is considerable disagreement among scholars on the definition of culture, the way it interacts with the political process, how we should study it, how important it is, etc. Some see culture as a dependent variable (i.e., something to be explained). Others see it as an independent variable (i.e., something to explain other variables). A third group sees it as simultaneously a dependent and an independent variable, whilst still others see it as an 'intervening' variable (i.e., coming between dependent and independent vari-

ables—see Dittmer 1983). Some analysts would even question the very existence of political culture. As with certain other phenomena considered in this
book, I would argue that political culture does exist if people believe it exists
and act accordingly; this certainly pertains to the communist world. Moreover, the circumstantial evidence on the existence of political culture is in my
opinion overwhelming—so many communist states profess to adhere to the
same ideology, have similar institutions, and similar levels of development
that we need concepts which will help us to understand why there are still important differences between them. Culture is one such concept. Thus culture
is a very controversial subject, and political scientists are still at a relatively
elementary stage in their understanding of it—but it is also an important and
interesting concept, and it is necessary to be aware of the phenomenon and of
the stage analysts have reached in their understanding of it.

A final introductory comment is that there is considerable overlap between
the concepts and content of ideology and 'official culture'. The two concepts
have been separated here solely because both culture and ideology are relatively large topics, and a single chapter on them both would have been unacceptably long. Ideally, the reader interested in the role of ideas and
propaganda in communist societies will read both this and the next chapter
together, since they are intimately related.

SOME DEFINITIONS

As Mary McAuley (1984a, pp. 14–15) has pointed out, most definitions of
political culture fall into one of two main categories, either the 'subjectivist'
or one that explicitly includes political behaviour. Adherents of the latter
would argue that political culture is concerned not only with what people
think, but also how they behave, with Fagen's definition (1969, p. 16—see
too pp. 5–6) being fairly typical: 'Political culture is here understood to include patterns of action as well as states of mind'. Other supporters of this
approach include Tucker (1973, esp. pp. 176–83) and White (1979, esp. pp. 1
and 16–18). Such an approach is considered unsatisfactory by the subjectivists. They argue that we are interested in what people think and believe partially because we want to understand why they behave in particular ways. In
other words, they are interested in explaining actions in terms of what is in
people's minds, using culture as an independent variable. For this reason,
they reject the notion that political culture should include political behaviour
on the grounds that such an approach is circular; one cannot explain X in
terms of Y if X and Y are one and the same thing. In the field of comparative
communism, the best-known exponent of the subjectivist approach is Archie
Brown, who defines culture as

. . . the subjective perception of history and politics, the fundamental beliefs and values, the foci of identification and loyalty, and the political knowledge and expectations which are the product of the specific historical experience of nations and groups (1977, p. 1—for other subjectivist definitions see Kavanagh, 1972, esp. pp. 10–14 and Bertsch, 1982, p. 64).

It is not only the subjectivists' wish to avoid circularity of argument that has led them to focus on the narrow conception of culture. There is also the problem, particularly acute in the case of communist states, that citizens may act in a particular way less because they *want* to (i.e., in line with their values and beliefs) than because they *feel obliged* to. For instance, if participation by ordinary citizens at meetings or in elections is largely the result of pressure from political activists, then inferences about citizen beliefs and attitudes in such societies may be even more questionable than they are when made about societies in which such behaviour is to a much greater extent a matter of individual choice. In other words, there are sound reasons why the subjectivists have their doubts about the behaviourist approach.

However, the subjectivists themselves face problems when they move beyond abstract conceptualization to more concrete analysis of political culture—and in fact finish up including *some* types of behaviour themselves. In order to understand this problem, it is necessary to distinguish firstly between *definitions* and *approaches to the study* of political culture and secondly between what people think, what they say, and how they act. In their endeavour to ascertain people's values, beliefs, and knowledge of the political system (i.e., in their *approach to the study* of culture), most 'subjectivists' look at what people say (e.g. in surveys) and write. In doing so, they are actually looking at one form of action or behaviour. Just as there may well be a gap between citizens' attitudes towards communist elections and how they actually behave when it comes to election time, so there may also be a gap between citizens' attitudes and what they *say* or even *appear* to say about the system. On the latter point, for instance, it is quite feasible that an outside observer will misinterpret cryptic comments, erroneously 'read between the lines', etc. Conversely, it seems to me that there are occasions when, in seeking to ascertain what people 'really' think, actions may well speak louder than words.

In sum, neither definition or approach to the study of culture is fully convincing; both have strengths and weaknesses, and a definition or approach that explicitly includes behaviour can sometimes give insights the narrower subjectivist approach cannot. Some of the problems of approaches to the study of political culture will be considered in more detail later in the chapter. At this point, the concern is primarily with definitions; of these, the fact that there are times when it is necessary to draw a clear distinction between what is in people's minds and how they behave means that the subjectivist ones are in general more satisfactory.

In one of the pioneering comparative studies of political culture, Almond and Verba (1963, esp. p. 15) suggest that attitudes, beliefs, etc. can be described as 'patterns of orientation toward political objects', and that these orientations can be classified into three 'modes'—'cognitive', 'affective', and 'evaluational'. 'Cognitive' orientations are what people *know* and *believe* about the political system (here referring to institutions, political actors, policies, etc.); 'affective' orientations are what people *feel* about the system; whilst 'evaluational' orientations are *judgements* and *opinions*. Based largely on these three kinds of orientations, Almond and Verba define three ideal-types (see chapter fifteen) of political culture—parochial, subject, and participant. In the first of these, citizens know little about the political system and hardly relate to it; instead, the ties are mainly to the family, the tribe, etc. Such a culture is said to be typical of traditional—what are sometimes called 'underdeveloped'—societies. In a subject culture, citizens possess a good knowledge of the political system, have well-developed affective orientations towards it, but are essentially passive. In a participant culture, citizens not only know a lot about the system and its component parts, and have views on it, but also believe that they can and should play an active role in it (i.e., participate in a meaningful way in the political process). This threefold classification of ideal-types is not intended merely to make analysis easier, but is also normative and hierarchic (i.e., a participant culture is seen as superior to a subject culture, which in turn is better than a parochial culture). Of course, no real society fits properly into any of these three categories; in any country, some citizens will be more politically aware than others and will have different *strengths* of orientation, partially reflective of their own personalities. Moreover, as Almond and Verba acknowledge, countries appear to move between categories over time. Almond and Verba also acknowledge that too much participation might not actually be very desirable, in that it could be highly inefficient for all or most citizens to be involved in all or most major areas of politics (e.g. decision-making, administration, etc.). Hence, they devised the concept of a 'civic' culture, in which citizens are not all politically active but at least feel that they have the right and the opportunities to participate should they so desire. This is seen by them as the optimal political culture, both in normative terms and in terms of helping to maintain political stability. Of relevance to us is not only the notion that there are different kinds of political culture, but also that the communist states are said by some to be closest to the subject culture ideal-type (and thus inferior to and less developed than the liberal democracies), whilst others claim that they are rapidly becoming participant or even civic cultures. We shall see that it is in fact very difficult to obtain a satisfactory image of a given country's political culture (always assuming there is such a thing), so that this particular debate has to remain largely in the realm of speculation. But this does not mean that the debate itself is irrelevant or pointless, any more than the inability to prove or disprove the existence of 'false consciousness' (see chapter ten) means that we should not be aware of this concept.

So far in this discussion, we have focused on what might be called 'macro'-

cultures—that is, the overall political climate in a given country. In fact, when we come to study 'the' political culture of a given country, it soon becomes clear that we need to distinguish, conceptually at least, between various subdivisions of a given culture. For analytical purposes, four such subdivisions are usually recognized. The first is the *official culture*, by which is meant the set of values, beliefs, etc. that the regime claims it wants the citizenry to hold. In communist states, this can be inferred from a number of sources, including communist party programs, ideological statements at congresses and Central Committee plena, books of 'the' leader's sayings, constitutions, and official analyses of the 'new socialist person'. Then there are the attitudes etc. prevalent amongst the political élite, which is called the *élite culture*. Theoretically, it may be supposed that this is the same as the official culture. In practice however, there may well be a perceptible gap between what the élite claims it believes in and what cultural approaches that explicitly incorporate behaviour will suggest it actually believes in. Third, there is the *dominant culture*—namely the culture of the mass of the population. The notion of a dominant culture does not imply that everyone has exactly the same views, values, etc. as everyone else; rather, the idea is that a majority of citizens share the same *basic* values. For instance, most people in Britain, the USA, or Australia appear to accept the basics of the political system, even though they may vote for different parties, disagree on particular policies, etc. In some societies, there does not appear to be such an overall consensus on basic values. Instead, there is among the citizenry a range of conflicting *subcultures*, which is our fourth analytical category. Some would argue that there is no dominant culture in Yugoslavia, for instance, but rather a number of subcultures, based largely on ethnic affiliation. Ethnicity is only one possible base for a subculture; among the many others are religion, class, and gender. It seems reasonable to infer that the degree of compatibility between different subcultures will be one major factor influencing the political stability of a given country. Of course, in the real world, even countries with a dominant culture will have a range of subcultures; there are always some people in any society who disagree with the majority on really fundamental political issues. Similarly, to distinguish analytically between a dominant culture and an élite culture does not mean that they are necessarily very distinct in the real world. Indeed, it is allegedly an aim of communists in power to merge all cultures and subcultures, so that they do not stress differences themselves.

If political culture refers to beliefs, knowledge, etc., the *process* whereby individuals acquire their political orientations is called *political socialization*. The socialization process starts from earliest childhood. However, and contrary to what is sometimes maintained, socialization does not suddenly stop when the child becomes an adult—the process continues throughout adult life. Certain events—perhaps a war, a major economic depression, or a revolution—can radically alter people's political orientations. Conversely, an individual's basic childhood values may remain throughout adult life; this does not mean that socialization has stopped, merely that the individual is constantly being resocialized in the original values.

Once again, it is useful for analytical purposes to distinguish two main types of socialization. On the one hand, there is what Kavanagh (1972, p. 30) calls *purposive* socialization, in which a particular agency consciously and openly strives to instil particular orientations. This form of socialization is very prevalent in the communist world where—in contrast to the situation in liberal democracies—the official culture holds that it is desirable and proper for the party and state to inculcate particular orientations. Thus the concepts of agitation and propaganda have a positive connotation in official communist culture, in marked contrast to the situation in the West; the negative reaction of most Westerners to the concept of propaganda is itself a product of our own socialization. On the other hand, there is *latent* socialization. In this case, there is no overt, deliberate, and organized attempt to inculcate values, yet they are transmitted nevertheless. For instance, parents often transmit political orientations to their children—by the way they react to news broadcasts, in the way they talk about authority, etc.—even though they may not consciously be attempting to inculcate values.

There are a number of socialization *agencies* in any society; those most frequently singled out in analyses of communist societies are the family, peer groups (e.g. at school or at work), the educational system, the media, and mass organizations (here, this includes the communist party). In most cases, the first two of these are latent socializing agencies (which is not to say that parents, for instance, do not sometimes attempt to socialize children purposively), whereas the latter three are predominantly purposive agencies, working for the state in its broad sense.

WHAT FACTORS INFLUENCE POLITICAL CULTURE?

In this section, we shall consider some of the factors other than purposive socialization agencies that affect political culture. The number of such factors is enormous, so that all that can be done here is to mention a few; the main reasons for listing them are to give the reader some idea of the complexity of analysing a particular political culture, and to show, in a very generalized way, why the dominant culture in one communist state can differ so much from that in another.

One of the most frequently cited influences on culture is past political traditions and experiences. For example, one would probably expect attitudes towards involvement in another country's affairs to be different in a country with a long expansionist tradition (e.g. Russia) from those in a country which has for much of its past been occupied by foreign invaders (e.g. former colonies, such as Angola or most of South Yemen). Pre-communist political traditions of leadership may also influence orientations. For example, it is often suggested that Castro found it easier to dominate the Cuban political system because of the widely accepted tradition of the wise and strong individual leader (the *caudillo*) in that country than would have been the case in Czechoslovakia, with its pre-communist tradition of basically liberal-democratic institutions and ideas on leadership. Even the geography of a country may have contributed to the development of certain political traditions. For instance, citizens in relatively small mountainous countries (e.g. Afghanistan, Yugoslavia) may be more prepared to put up a fight against an invader—even a major power—than citizens in a similarly small but flattish country, where the attitude that it is futile to resist may well have become dominant.

Communists take power in countries with very different religious and philosophical traditions. Among the many one could cite are Islam (Albania, Afghanistan, etc.), Confucianism (China, Korea, etc.), Roman Catholicism (Poland), Protestantism (East Germany), etc. In many countries, there was a large variety of widely supported religions and/or philosophical traditions before the communists took power—for example Catholicism, Orthodoxy, and Islam in Yugoslavia. Other things being equal, one would expect the socialization process to be even more complex in such societies than where the communists have only one or two main value-systems to understand, overcome, and replace.

Of course, 'the past' is not only pre-communist; events that have happened since the communists came to power can also affect current political orientations. For example, the way in which the communists come to power may well affect popular attitudes; other things being equal, one would expect citizens to be more positively disposed towards the communist political system if this was established by native communists (especially if they were popular before taking power) than where communism is seen primarily as a form of government imposed by a foreign army. Experiences of wars, major political events (e.g. Stalinism, the 1968 invasion of Czechoslovakia) are also likely to affect current attitudes.

But political culture is affected by ongoing developments too. For instance, a regime which had little support when it took power can acquire more by performing well. Impressive economic growth over many years, coupled with rising standards of living, marked improvements in educational and health facilities for the masses—these sorts of factors can help to build up more positive support for the system.

The list of factors could extend for many pages yet. But two main points should already be clear. First, communists have a wide range of pre-communist traditions to understand and deal with if socialization and resocialization methods are to stand a chance of success. Second, culture is a complex and dynamic phenomenon; it is never static, and present experiences can affect attitudes just as much as knowledge of the past.

AGENCIES AND METHODS OF PURPOSIVE SOCIALIZATION

Communists use a number of methods for trying to inculcate new values. In some—particularly in Asia—citizens are often subject to mass overt indoctrination campaigns (e.g. some of the Chinese 'rectification' campaigns) and 'thought reform' programmes. In these, citizens may be taken to camps and made to study the new official culture (this was common in southern Vietnam after 1975), or party activists will come to the villages and explain the new system and the desired values. Such methods tend to be most common in the early stages of communist rule, although this is by no means always the case; many would see the Chinese GPCR of 1966–76 as being, on one level, another example of campaign indoctrination. Usually, such campaigns are very crude, and ordinary citizens can usually survive them intact merely by formally declaring loyalty to the new values; those who do not may be deported (this was common in Cuba) or unofficially permitted to flee the country (e.g. Vietnam). But such campaigns are often directed even more at party members than at ordinary citizens—and these 'vanguardists' must display much greater knowledge of and commitment to the new values.

Most purposive socialization methods are rather more subtle and continuous than those just outlined. In the schools, in addition to obvious methods such as compulsory study of Marxism–Leninism, even 'non-political' subjects such as mathematics (see Volgyes 1974, p. 49) and biology will be taught in a way that is designed to bring existing cultures closer to the official culture. An example from a foreign-language textbook will highlight this point. A 1974 East German textbook for the study of the English language included a section on 'some parties and organizations', in which various political bodies in the GDR, the UK, and the USA were listed. The only British 'parties and organizations' listed were the Communist Party of Great Britain, the Labour Party, the Young Communist League, and Trade Unions. Similarly, the only three American 'parties and organizations' referred to were the Communist Party of the United States, the Young Workers' Liberation League, and the Civil Rights Movement (Klug 1974, p. 72). There were no references to the Conservative Party, the Liberal Party, or the small parties (e.g. nationalist ones) in the UK, or to the Democrats and Republicans in the USA. By almost any objective criteria, these were serious omissions, and one does not have to be a 'cold warrior' to argue that if this list of organizations were to be used as the basis of an English-language class on the political systems of the UK and USA, then the students would in all probability receive a very distorted image. School children are also encouraged to be much more conscious of the collective than they are in Western states (see Bronfenbrenner 1970). They are taught to reprimand each other for misbehaviour, and a 'bulletin board' in most classrooms will frequently name not only students who have been meritorious in the past week, month, or whatever, but also those who have not been living up to socialist standards. The curricula in schools are very much more standardized and under central (i.e. ministry) control than in liberal-democratic countries, and children are usually encouraged to learn facts and figures rather than to question. On the odd occasions when children have been encouraged to criticize—as in the GPCR—this has been temporary and connected with a particular political aim of the leadership. The educational system is, in sum, geared to producing unquestioning conformity to official values.

Even after they have left school, young people are subject to attempts by the authorities to mould their political orientations. The most obvious agencies are the youth leagues in all communist countries, which have a major socialization role to play along with their other roles. The communist party, the trade unions, and other mass organizations are partially responsible for socializing and resocializing the adult population.

The media are under strict control in the communist world and are also geared to purposive socialization. A Westerner who has watched and understood a news broadcast in almost any communist state will have been struck by the way it differs from news broadcasts in most Western media. In communist countries, news broadcasts are generally far less sensationalist and—unless there is a political campaign against a particular negative phenomenon under way at the time—will contain much less 'bad' news than is the norm in Western countries. News is largely intended to help with the socialization process, showing how well the particular regime is doing; in other words, most domestic news is positive. Indeed, whereas Western media concentrate on specific events that have just occurred, much of what appears in the press or on television in communist countries tells of general, long-term developments that would hardly be considered news at all in liberal democracies. Alternative sources of values, such as Western newspapers, are generally very difficult to obtain, with Yugoslavia being the most liberal communist state in this regard.

THEMES OF THE OFFICIAL CULTURE

Despite all the methodological problems in studying culture (see especially the next two sections), it is possible, through an analysis of various official documents, to obtain an image of the culture the political élite alleges it wants citizens to internalize. From these, we can, for instance, produce a picture of the ideal 'new socialist person'. A typical image is that contained in the 1961 CPSU Party Program, where the 'moral code of the builder of communism' (i.e., initially party members, but eventually everybody) is spelt out:

> devotion to the communist cause; love of the socialist motherland and of the other socialist countries;
> conscientious labour for the good of society—he who does not work, neither shall he eat;

concern on the part of everyone for the preservation and growth of public wealth;

a high sense of public duty; intolerance of actions harmful to the public interest;

collectivism and comradely mutual assistance: one for all and all for one;

humane relations and mutual respect between individuals—man is to man a friend, comrade and brother;

honesty and truthfulness, moral purity, modesty, and unpretentiousness in social and private life;

mutual respect in the family, and concern for the upbringing of children;

an uncompromising attitude to injustice, parasitism, dishonesty, careerism and money-grubbing;

friendship and brotherhood among all peoples of the USSR; intolerance of national and racial hatred;

an uncompromising attitude to the enemies of communism, peace and the freedom of nations;

fraternal solidarity with the working people of all communist countries, and with all peoples.

(pp. 108–9.)

The above definition is typical in that it contains not only *general* moral tenets but also specific references (namely to friendship and brotherhood in the USSR). An analysis of such descriptions in official documents, the media, etc. from various communist states reveals that the relative emphasis on both general points and specifics varies from country to country and over time. In the early 1970s, Ivan Volgyes ran a content-analysis of the major newspapers of the eight East European communist states over a six-month period, and concluded that 'emphasis on creating the ideal Communist "new man" has tended to diminish somewhat' (1974, p. 51), but that the regimes still worked hard at creating loyal and dedicated citizens. In other words, the stress on *general* aspects of the better person has, according to Volgyes's research, declined while specific themes have increased. Volgyes isolated eight themes that were particularly emphasized, but discovered that the frequency of individual themes varied considerably. Overall in Eastern Europe the rank-order of themes (number one being the most frequently stressed, number eight the least) was as follows.

  (i) building of socialism
  (ii) anti-imperialism
  (iii) socialist morality
  (iv) patriotism
  (v) anti-individualism
  (vi) socialist commonwealth
  (vii) anti-nationalism
  (viii) anti-Stalinism.

Within individual countries, the rank-order would deviate quite substantially from the norm, often in line with what anyone knowing a little about the politics of a given country would expect. Hence, the theme most stressed in the main Yugoslav newspaper (*Borba*) in the early 1970s was anti-national-ism, followed by patriotism; this reflects the problems the central authorities were having with the various ethnic groups in Yugoslavia at the time, and the endeavour to create among the citizenry an identity with Yugoslavia as a whole rather than with Croatia or Macedonia or wherever. On the other hand, anti-nationalism was the least emphasized of the eight themes in Poland, where ethnic problems have not been a major issue. In Albania, the least stressed theme was the socialist commonwealth—which again is under-standable in view of the fact that Albania had left the Soviet 'fold' at the be-ginning of the 1960s. Some of the findings are less readily comprehensible. Thus Romania had (and still has) a reputation for very personalized and authoritarian leadership, and is sometimes described as the second most Stalinist (after Albania) of the East European regimes. Yet the second emphasized theme in Romania's leading newspaper (*Scinteia*) in the period of Volgyes's research was anti-Stalinism. This is probably explained by the fact that Romania has a reputation for wanting to maximize its independence of Moscow; hence anti-Stalinism is more of a criticism of the Soviet Union than of the type of leadership and political configurations associated with Stalin.

The relative weighting of themes can and does vary over time even within a given country. In the early 1970s, 'patriotism' was the least stressed of the eight variables in the leading East German newspaper (*Neues Deutschland*). This was at a time when the East Germans were anxious to play down the no-tion of 'Germanness' as they sought to differentiate the GDR ever more from the FRG (West Germany). By the late 1970s, however, the leadership was de-veloping a new image of 'East Germanness', and was trying to instil in the citizenry a stronger identification with just that part of Germany that now constitutes the GDR. Although I am unaware of any content-analysis that proves this point, my own reading of the East German press leads me to believe that 'patriotism' would have moved well up the East German rank-ings table by the late 1970s. The reader who is interested in following up the themes of communist socialization is urged to look at the next chapter.

This cursory examination of the agencies, methods, and themes of sociali-zation in the communist world tells us nothing at all about how *well* they work. As we shall now see, measuring the success of socialization—as part of the overall process of investigating culture in the communist states—is an extraordinarily hazardous business.

HOW DO WE STUDY POLITICAL CULTURE?

The ways in which we set about actually studying political culture and the success rate of purposive socialization in a given country depends to a large extent on which of the two basic definitions of culture we have adopted. It has already been argued that there are severe problems in trying to determine attitudes and beliefs through political behaviour in countries in which most overt political activity is very much under party and state control rather than voluntary and spontaneous. The nature and scale of such control is dealt with at some length in a number of subsequent chapters, so that all we need do here is note that the study of overt political behaviour in communist countries in non-crisis situations will tell us little about basic beliefs and values.

The approach of the subjectivists is far more interesting and potentially fruitful. Archie Brown is widely acknowledged to be the leading figure in this field *vis-à-vis* communist states, and an analysis of his approach to the study of political culture will reveal both the concrete suggestions that have been made for studying such culture, and some of the problems associated with these. The most elaborate proposal for an analysis of political culture based on the subjectivist definition is contained in the introduction to the Brown and Gray collection that appeared in 1977; a second edition appeared in 1979, but contained only minor amendments to the first, and references here are to the 1977 edition. In this, Brown expands upon a proposal made in one of his earlier books (1974, pp. 96–100) and elaborated an analytical framework for the study, in the form of four component parts of political culture to be researched by each of the contributors. These four components were previous political experience (i.e., people's subjective interpretations of their country's pre-communist history); values and fundamental political beliefs (deeply held beliefs about concepts such as egalitarianism, paternalism, and liberty; these *may* be reflected in orientations towards current political issues); foci of identification and loyalty (e.g. ethnic group, social class, village, political party, nation; also 'symbols', such as past leaders or flags); political knowledge and expectations (citizens' knowledge not only of their own political system but also of alternatives, which can affect expectations). Brown's intention was for the contributors to discover as much as they could about these four components of culture in each of the seven countries studied in the volume (China, Cuba, Czechoslovakia, Hungary, Poland, the USSR, and Yugoslavia), in order then to deal tentatively with four important questions. These questions were:

(i) What is the relationship between the process of political socialization and political culture? Here, the emphasis is on the relationship between the dominant and the official political culture. Brown was particularly interested in the success of communists at *changing* political culture and creating the 'new socialist person'.

(ii) What is the relationship between the dominant political culture and political subcultures? Brown also raised the interesting but difficult question of why a particular culture should dominate and why it (and certain subcultures) should persist.

(iii) What is the relationship between levels of socio-economic development and political culture? Here, Brown pointed to the enormous problem of obtaining full and/or reliable and/or comparable data, and emphasized that no more than a very generalized picture of levels of socio-economic development could be drawn.

(iv) What is the relationship between political culture and political change? This relationship was described by Brown as 'the major subject of our enquiry' (p. 19); the concern was with culture on the one hand and change in political institutions, political processes, and—to a lesser extent—particular policies on the other.

The contributors to the Brown and Gray volume were aware that the testing of values, beliefs, and attitudes in communist states is extremely difficult for Western observers. We cannot, for example, conduct independent opinion surveys in the way we can in our own societies. Even if we could, there is always the problem that respondents will answer survey questions in the way they believe they ought to answer them rather than as they want to answer them; this problem pertains in Western societies too, of course, but it seems safe to assume that it is a less serious difficulty in a more open society. Because such opinion testing was not possible, Brown had to devise a method that *was* feasible, and proposed the use of seven sources for the study of communist political cultures. The sources suggested were survey data collected within communist states themselves by citizens of those states; systematic interviewing of *émigrés*; creative literature; memoirs; accounts by long-term foreign residents; historiography (the writing of history); and literature within communist states on the problems of creating the 'new socialist person' and a communist consciousness. Brown stressed that the methods chosen were subjective and impressionistic, but concluded that if a wide range of methods and a variety of sources were used and seemed to produce similar results, then one might be in a position to start generalizing about the political culture of a given country or type of socio-political system. In theory, this sounds very reasonable. Yet if we examine the seven sources closely, it becomes clear that none of them, except perhaps the last, is without dangers. This is not the place for an in-depth critique of the various sources, so that I shall confine my discussion to just two examples of such problems.

The first relates to the use of survey data from the communist states themselves. Several communist states do not conduct surveys that would be of relevance to a cultural study (e.g. Angola). Others do, but publish few, if any, of the findings (e.g. the GDR). Even when they do, the survey methods used are not always properly elaborated, so that the value of the findings is in some doubt. But let us concentrate on those countries that do publish lots of survey data and where the methodology appears to be at least acceptable for the time being. The reader may well expect such surveys to be propaganda exercises; if communists believe that 'facts' *should* be presented in a particular light in order to assist in the socialization process, then surely data that are published (in contrast to data that are intended for the eyes of the decision-makers only) may well be presented in a deliberately misleading way. Brown countered this suggestion by arguing that 'many surveys have produced data which deviate too much from the official values and ideals for them to be dismissed as propaganda' (p. 10), a view which he still seems to hold (see Brown, 1984b, p. 191). At first sight, this argument seems eminently plausible; if surveys reveal high levels of disaffection or low levels of political knowledge, for instance, then they surely cannot be propagandistic, since they portray the regime's socialization process in a bad light. Brown himself seemed to subscribe to this viewpoint in assuming that propaganda must always be 'flattering' (his word) to the regime. This may well be true. But it may also be the case that data are—at least sometimes—presented in a way that is designed to give the regime justification for mounting a new ideological clampdown and/or for discrediting a previous regime. I know of no firm evidence to support this hypothesis; but at least we should be aware of this possibility when we are considering the results of such surveys.

The second example relates to the accounts by long-term foreign residents. Here one needs to ask what sort of people such residents are; since Brown does not specify them (he does give three examples in the 1974 book, but these are problematic—for reasons that are too complex to be elaborated here), we shall have to speculate. Some will be Western journalists, whose job anywhere is to report on 'interesting' events, developments, etc.; the more mundane aspects of the lives of the masses do not often provide material for the reporter. To be sure, journalists working for serious newspapers such as *Le Monde* or *The Times* or *The Washington Post* are not generally as sensationalist as their counterparts on the more popular newspapers. But one can still question the notion that Western journalists have a sound grasp of what 'the masses' in communist states know, believe, etc. about the political system. Another type of foreign long-term resident is the diplomat, who is discouraged from mixing excessively with the natives in communist states, since this can be risky. This is not to say that diplomats have no contact with natives of communist states—they do. But often these will be mainly government officials and domestic staff who have been closely vetted by (and may even be working for) the security organs. The Western diplomat may be fed a particular and distorted image of the mass culture by the host government's officials, and/or he or she may be very selective in what he or she believes and remembers of what he or she is told, again possibly remembering only negative points that endorse existing prejudices. After all, diplomats are representatives of their own government, and are not necessarily the least subjective observers of systems ideologically hostile to their own. Academics do not usually spend more than a few months at a time researching in communist states; a few do, and are probably among the most useful examples of long-term foreign residents. Westerners actually working for communist states (e.g. as translators) are less subject to the kinds of criticism that journalists and diplomats are. However, not only are their numbers small, but many are either communists or fellow-travellers, whose judgement might be as coloured—albeit in a different direction—as the other groups mentioned.

Without going any further, it should be clear that the subjectivist approach has its limitations. To his credit, Brown is explicitly aware of many of the problems, and argued that the 1977 work was only a 'preliminary essay' (p. 20) in the field. He certainly urged caution and diffidence, and stressed that sources must be used with discrimination. Unfortunately, such a 'discriminating' reading of our sources contains the risk that we will select only those findings that endorse our existing prejudices, and reject as atypical or 'mere propaganda' views that run counter to our expectations. Moreover, as Skilling (1984, pp. 118–19) has suggested, we may obtain a quite different picture of the culture of a given country according to whether we use subjectivist definitions and approaches or more explicitly behaviouralist ones; since we have suggested that both definitions and approaches have strengths and weaknesses, it will not invariably be obvious which image of the political culture seems to be more convincing. No one has yet been able to provide a fully satisfactory solution to this particular problem, although Brown's most recent (1984a) edited collection on culture shows that our understanding of both definitional problems and approaches is—because of a very lively, scholarly debate—becoming more sophisticated.

Whatever the methodological problems involved in the subjectivist approach, and however conflicting our interpretations of such findings may be, no one can deny that it has yielded a great deal of both fascinating and valuable information (e.g. from opinion surveys) that was not previously accessible to many scholars.

A KEY PROBLEM—SELECTION OF ORIENTATIONS

One of the most difficult problems facing analysts is to decide how and why people choose between the multitude of factors that can affect political culture. If East Germans are discontent with their present government and look for alternatives, are they more likely to yearn for what they perceive to have been better periods in their past, or to look enviously at contemporary West Germany, or both? If they look at the pre-communist past, will they look to Wilhelmine Germany, the Weimar Republic, or even the best years of the Nazi regime? A good example of this problem is provided by Jack Gray in his analysis of the Confucianist tradition in China. He argues (1977, pp. 199–200) that Confucianism represents a compromise between the two main traditional strands of Chinese political thought, namely Legalism and Daoism. According to the former, humans are motivated solely by self-interest (a view not dissimilar from Hobbes's); based on this assumption, it is further argued that harmony in society can only be achieved with an all-powerful government. Daoism, in contrast, is based on a more optimistic view of humanity; if left alone by central government, people will organize themselves into harmonious social relationships. Clearly, the two approaches are diametrically opposed, and it is far from obvious what a compromise position would be.

Gray does produce one—based on the notion that government is needed to educate people, who can then organize themselves 'harmoniously'— although the fact that some people will always deviate from the accepted and acceptable patterns of behaviour means that a powerful state machinery is still required as a 'stand-by'. This may sound like an optimal blend of two principles, but putting it into practice and ensuring that the central government does not become over-powerful is another matter altogether. Gray then proceeds to list seven major sets of contradictions (pp. 202–4) within Confucianism, arguing that 'Imperial China handed down to modern times not one consistent set of ideas and attitudes, but a range of choice' (p. 202). From this, it becomes clear that to argue that pre-communist traditions affect contemporary political orientations in China tells us very little. One could perform a similar exercise with any communist state and come up with conflicting ideas and traditions from the past, so that we are back with the problem of how and why citizens choose their values, beliefs, etc. This problem applies to all societies, of course—there are wealthy, public-school educated Britons with socialist views and conservative blue-collar workers, for instance—but the problem is sometimes glossed over by writers who want to argue that values from the pre-communist period are swamping attempts by the communists to change political culture. Sometimes, one could cite a different set of pre-communist traditions from those referred to and produce a quite different conclusion. The problem is not peculiar to Western analysts; communists in power also have to try to maximize their understanding of the reasons why citizens select some values and reject others if the purposive socialization process is to be maximally effective.

DOES COMMUNIST SOCIALIZATION WORK?

We have seen that communists themselves seem to believe that it is important and possible to inculcate new values and attitudes, and we have briefly considered how they set about this. We have also seen how difficult it is to ascertain exactly what the mass of the population thinks and knows about politics. Our problems in this area are such that we cannot properly answer the question 'does communist socialization work?'. But this does not prevent us from making a few general comments, or from at least considering the findings of researchers into political culture.

Let us start by considering the sort of evidence that would suggest that socialization has not been a success. One might look in this instance for evidence of anti-social and/or overtly anti-state (i.e. 'deviant') behaviour. Mass unrest of the sort considered in chapter twelve could be seen as one important symbol of failed socialization. It could be argued that if citizens are not actually trying to overthrow a regime or system, then socialization has been sufficiently successful. This is what we can call a minimalist approach. But communists themselves argue that such minimal levels of success are insufficient, and that they are striving for something more than this. Moreover, such events as Hungary 1956 or Poland 1980–1 are few and far between, and there are many other forms of anti-social behaviour to be considered—and which cause communist leaderships concern—including the committing of crimes, alcoholism (currently seen by some Soviet analysts as a greater real threat to the USSR than a nuclear war—see *The Age* of Melbourne, 1 January 1985, p. 1), absenteeism, or even engaging in activities of which the leadership officially disapproves (e.g. listening to Western pop music in some communist states). How significant are such forms of anti-social behaviour? There are, in fact, severe problems in obtaining statistics on such forms of 'deviant' behaviour for most communist states. Even assuming we had reliable and verifiable data, however, there would still be the problem of interpreting these. If the data showed widespread disaffection, it seems safe to assume that the socialization programme has not worked (though see below, on official and élite cultures). But if the data showed that such forms of behaviour were *not* widespread, this only tells us that socialization *might* have been successful. Many people may be conforming more through fear than because they have internalized the values of the 'new socialist person'; certainly the punishments for committing many crimes are far more severe in communist states than in liberal democracies. Let us now consider the evidence the subjectivists have collected.

Several surveys conducted in the communist states suggest that a lack of knowledge of the 'basics' of Marxism–Leninism, communist history, and the present political system is a widespread problem. For example, a 1976–7 survey of over 800 Hungarian communist youth leaders—whose knowledge should, of course, be well above the average for young people—revealed that

> ... some of those interviewed thought Josef Stalin was commander-in-chief of the German Army while others said the former Soviet leader was governor of Hungary during the 1950s ... 17 per cent knew nothing about Lenin ... only 13 per cent of those questioned were able to go beyond the fact that he was a 'revolutionary and a famous statesman'.... (Cited in McAuley, 1984a, p. 38.)

A survey of Belgrade secondary students published in 1972 revealed that a staggering 70 per cent of teenagers did not know who the founders of Marxism were (Dyker 1977, p. 81).

It would seem that cognitive orientations are by no means the only problems—affective and evaluational orientations are also causing concern. One of the most serious problems seems to be that many citizens have a cynical attitude towards the communist party. For instance, according to a 1980 poll of students at Fudan University (Shanghai), 55 per cent of the respondents saw the special privileges of communist party cadres as the biggest social problem in contemporary China; this was more than double the percentage (23 per cent) who saw unemployment as the biggest problem (figures from Liu 1983, p. 618), despite the fact that Shanghai has long been the worst area in China for unemployment. Cynicism towards party members is readily explained when we look at some of the findings of opinion surveys amongst communists themselves. The results of a Polish poll taken in major industrial enterprises and published in 1971 suggested that 52 per cent of party members had only a 'passing interest' in politics, with 8 per cent declaring they had no interest whatsoever (Kolankiewicz and Taras 1977, p. 113). Another Polish survey revealed that only 10 per cent of the interviewees thought that other people joined the communist party for ideological reasons whereas 60 per cent thought that careerism was the main reason for joining (ibid., p. 114). Possibly even more worrying—for the communist authorities, at least—is the result of a 1960 Yugoslav survey amongst students, which revealed that 11.3 per cent of those students interviewed who were party members were not prepared to call themselves Marxists (Dyker 1977, p. 80); evidence of similar problems of cognitive, affective, and evaluational orientations can be found in communist youth leagues (see Schwartz 1973 and Montaperto, 1973). If this is the case amongst the allegedly politically most aware, it is perhaps less surprising that the results of a Polish survey published in 1971 suggested that the majority of people (71 per cent) in all social groups either had no interest or else only a slight interest in politics and ideology (Kolankiewicz and Taras 1977, p. 113). Even allowing for the fact that the Polish population has a reputation for being more anti-communist than most in the communist world, such figures give a disturbing picture of the capacity of communists to change political culture, and have been more or less replicated in other states (see the results of a survey of young Hungarian workers that was published in 1972—in Schöpflin 1977, p. 147). But perhaps most distressing of all—for the communists—was the result of an East German survey conducted by the Central Committee's Institute of Public Opinion in the early 1970s, which showed that 94 per cent of those polled wanted to emigrate to the FRG (cited in McCauley 1981, p. 18).

Having considered evidence and arguments to suggest that communists are not very successful in their socialization attempts, let us now look at the counter-arguments. The first point is that socialization success is a relative concept (i.e., we cannot say it is either a total failure or a total success) and that it takes time to change political culture; on the time-scale of world history, most communist states are very young. Moreover, since the scale of desired change is so great, we would expect the new culture to take longer to emerge than where there is a smaller gap between the dominant existing values and the new values the leadership may want the citizenry to hold. The task involves not only resocializing ordinary citizens, but also—and prior to this—training political activists in the new values and in the optimal methods for transmitting these. None of this can be achieved overnight.

Another point is that the socialization process may have been more successful than surveys reveal because the questions asked would in most cases give only a partial reflection of citizen orientations. The term 'politics', for instance, means different things to different people; in some of the surveys cited, respondents did appear to be interested and involved in politics at the workplace and local level, but appear to have thought that they were really being asked about 'politics at the top' (this point is partially endorsed by Kolankiewicz and Taras 1977, pp. 113–14). Moreover, some analysts have argued that many *basic* tenets of socialism have been well internalized—in Eastern Europe, at least (see Volgyes 1974, p. 54 and Hanhardt 1975, p. 87); if citizens were to be asked whether they would prefer an improved, less éli-tist socialist system or a full-blooded capitalist one (with its competition, insecurity, etc.), it is by no means clear that the majority would opt for the latter.

Assuming for a moment that the survey data available are a fairly accurate reflection of orientations, it is possible to interpret them from a radically different perspective from the most obvious one. Let us suppose for the sake of argument that most communist regimes are not actually very anxious to create the 'new socialist person'. After all, a society full of such people would mean that there was little justification any longer for a vanguard party and a coercive state—and hence a political élite. If socialization were to work too well, the political élite would lose its *raison d'être*. This is a major reason why a sharp distinction was drawn earlier between 'official' and 'élite' cultures, and why the word 'allegedly' has frequently been used in discussing the official culture. It is possible that many members of the political élite are not actually as concerned by the survey data as we might suppose they should be. If their main concern were the maintenance of the system and the distribution of power much as it is, then a low level of interest in politics is precisely what many members of the élite would want. Moreover, these people may well be aware that one of the major reasons why socialization has not been more effective is almost certainly because of the gap ordinary citizens perceive between what the political élite claims it believes in and how it actually behaves; if it is a matter of 'don't do what I do, do what I say', is it surprising that there appears to be widespread cynicism? If it is the case that the basics of socialism have been largely accepted and that the élite is in most cases also able to maintain its position without too much overt unrest, then it could be argued that socialization has been highly successful. I am not arguing that this is the case. For one thing, any congruence between the dominant culture and what the élite wants might be less the result of purposive socialization than of economic development policies (i.e., rapid industrialization and urbanization tends to undermine old values and lead to new ones in any kind of political system); this would all be in line with classical Marxist notions that the economic base ultimately determines the superstructure, including the political culture. Nevertheless, it seems to me important to provide radically different interpretations to those which see socialization as having been a failure, if such alternative arguments are plausible.

If the above hypothesis about élite intentions is correct, the reader might wonder why élites bother to continue to perpetrate the myth of the 'new socialist person'. The answer is simple. By claiming that the system is working to create this new being—a person who is very superior to most ordinary humans, with all their complexities and failings—the élite can claim that society still needs the vanguard (i.e., themselves) to ensure that this new person eventually materializes. Thus the need to create the elusive 'new socialist person' can be seen as a means of élite legitimation. Conversely, an abandonment of the concept would undermine the élite's position, one of its main reasons for existence. In short, there is no obvious reason why the concept of the new socialist person should be abandoned at present—the political élite would have more to lose than to gain in doing so.

SUMMARY AND CONCLUSIONS

It has been argued that the study of political culture and socialization is a very important but particularly problematic area of comparative communism. There are advantages and disadvantages to both the major definitions and approaches to political culture that have been outlined, and neither is fully right or wrong. It has further been argued that various results of opinion surveys—assuming these are reliable and valid—do not have to be interpreted in the most obvious ways. Alternative interpretations are not necessarily any more convincing, but at least they give us a much wider perspective on the topic.

One point to stress in these concluding remarks is that political culture is a constantly changing phenomenon. The dominant culture, the subcultures, the élite culture, and the official culture are all constantly interacting with each other and with political institutions, policies, etc. To suggest that one component always dominates another in some unidirectional manner would be naïve; the influences are multi-directional.

Clearly, there is still much work to be done in the fields of culture and socialization, both in terms of conceptualization and empirical research. If the communist regimes were more prepared to permit independent survey research, some but not all of these problems would be overcome.

Basic further reading

G. Bertsch, 1982, ch. 3.
A. Brown (ed), 1984a.
A. Brown and J. Gray (eds.), 1979.
R. Fagen, 1969.
D. Kavanagh, 1972.
R. Montaperto, 1973.

J. Schwartz, 1973.
R. Solomon, 1971.
Studies in Comparative Communism,
  Autumn 1977 and Spring/Summer 1983.
I. Volgyes, 1974, 1975.

5

OFFICIAL IDEOLOGY AND LEGITIMACY

OFFICIAL ideology (that is, the ideology of the party–state complex) is sometimes taken to be one of the principal features distinguishing the advanced industrial communist states from the liberal democracies (e.g. Brzezinski and Huntington 1964, and Westoby 1981, p. 313). It is also often seen as one of the major factors distinguishing the socialist states of Africa—Nyerere's Tanzania or Kaunda's Zambia—from the communist ones such as Angola or Ethiopia, even though the political structures and the policies in both types of country may well be very similar (or equally underdeveloped—see Löwenthal 1970). And communist states themselves frequently stress the importance of ideology to the overall system. It should be clear, therefore, why ideology is important. Despite this, relatively little has been written on the subject. There are a number of reasons for this. One is that many contemporary western scholars feel that ideology is essentially 'icing on the cake'—that official ideology exists for the sake of appearances, but that it does not in fact play any very significant role in day-to-day politics. A related point is that it is a highly abstract concept, and many feel that the amount of effort required in any attempt to convey the nature of communist ideology is disproportionate to what this tells us about the real world. And finally, there are those (e.g. Kautsky 1973, esp. pp. 148–70) who do not believe that communist ideology is a distinct phenomenon anyway.

For all this, any general study of politics in the communist world would be seriously deficient were there to be no inclusion of the concept, nature, and role of the official ideology. Thus, although this chapter is not one of the longer ones—to no small extent because we considered much of the content of what we shall in this chapter call 'pure' ideology in chapter one, and much of the way in which it is disseminated in chapter four—this does not in any way suggest that ideology is of less importance than topics to which more pages have been devoted. Much of the discussion must be even more speculative than other parts of this book; but by now the reader should have realized that many of the most important aspects of the phenomenon we call communism can be neither neatly defined, nor easily explained, nor quantified.

THE CONCEPT OF IDEOLOGY

Basically, a political ideology is a set of related ideas about the individual, society, and the political system; but such a definition tells us little, and is only a starting-point. For instance, it does not explain the difference between a political theory and an ideology. We need therefore to consider a number of definitions, so as to produce a more detailed and meaningful picture.

In 1966, a debate on the concept of Soviet ideology began in the pages of *Soviet Studies*; many of the points raised can be generalized to ideology in the communist world as a whole, so that the polemic serves as a useful springboard. In the first contribution to the debate, Alfred Meyer defined Soviet ideology as 'the body of doctrine which the Communist Party teaches all Soviet citizens, from school children to the higher party leadership' (Meyer 1966, p. 273).

One problem with this definition is that it defines ideology in terms of 'doctrine' (i.e., what is taught, instruction). This tends to imply a basically static and unidirectional phenomenon, something that is transmitted downwards and that has to be learnt. At best, this gives us only a partial picture of what ideology is and does. The second criticism of this definition is that it contains a highly abstract conception of the communist party. If this party teaches everyone, including the 'higher party leadership', then who exactly is defining the 'body of doctrine' and teaching it? It should be clear that this definition is both too narrow and conceptually problematic to be very useful.

These and other weaknesses in Meyer's argument led David Joravsky to produce his own alternative definition of ideology. This starts with a consideration of ideological beliefs:

When we call a belief ideological, we are saying at least three things about it. Although it is unverified or unverifiable, it is accepted as verified by a particular group because it performs social functions for that group. 'Group' is used loosely to indicate such aggregations as parties, professions, classes or nations. 'Because' is also used loosely, to indicate a functional correlation rather than a strictly causal connection between acceptance of a belief and other social processes. (Joravsky, 1966, p. 3.)

In this definition, we are made aware of two of the most important aspects of ideology. First, it is a set of beliefs, many of which cannot be proven either true or false; in other words, they are based on commitment and subjective choice, much as religious beliefs are. Second, the ideology serves a purpose for a group, such as a social class or a political élite. Although, as Mannheim has pointed out, we do sometimes talk of an individual's ideology, most social scientists are normally referring to the ideas of a group and/or an historical period (Mannheim calls this a 'total' ideology—see 1936, pp. 49–53), not an individual, when they discuss ideology and I shall follow that practice here. This 'collective' and practical dimension of ideology is very important, and is the most significant feature distinguishing an ideology from a political theory. A political theory is an attempt to explain what is (empirical theory) and/or what should be (normative theory), but does not necessarily relate to any particular group or activity; only if a theory is *used* by a group to guide it and to defend its actions does it become an ideology. Joravsky later summarizes all this as follows: 'Ideology, then, is unacknowledged dogma that serves social functions' (Joravsky 1966, p. 4). This definition is still not entirely satisfactory, since the use of the term 'dogma' can suffer from the same problems as the term 'doctrine' (i.e., it can imply an essentially static phenomenon); however, Joravsky's is much closer to an acceptable definition than was Meyer's.

Other commentators have made the point explicitly that the group must be aware of itself and have organized or be organizing itself. Thus Schurmann, writing on the PRC, defines ideology (specifically the ideology of an organization) as 'a manner of thinking characteristic of an organization . . . a systematic set of ideas with action consequences serving the purpose of creating and using organization' (Schurmann 1968, p. 18).

Communists themselves would doubtless agree with much that is contained in the latter definitions. An official Soviet definition, for instance, looks remarkably similar to some of those already cited: '. . . a system of definite views, ideas, conceptions, and notions adhered to by some class or political party' (quoted by Dawisha 1972, p. 158). This said, they would also want to follow Lenin and emphasize that communist ideology differs markedly from bourgeois (liberal democratic) ideology, not only in its content, but even in its nature. For them, communist ideology is 'scientific', whereas bourgeois ideology is highly subjective. In other words, many communists would take issue with Joravsky's point that ideology—any ideology—is 'unverified or unverifiable', since they believe that much of communist ideology is both verified and verifiable. This is not in fact the case; Marxism–Leninism, as the communists call their ideology, is postulated on a materialist conception of history, and it is logically impossible to prove that a materialist conception is correct, an idealist one incorrect. Given that the basic premiss of Marxism–Leninism is subjective, it follows that the ideology as a whole must be.

Although communists usually argue that their ideology is scientific, this does not mean that they do not recognize that the content of ideology can and does change. Indeed, this would be difficult for them to do, given that their whole approach to the world—a dialectical approach—emphasizes change and dynamism. How is this apparent contradiction explained? Although it is in fact never fully resolved, communists in power do provide some sort of answer in more or less overtly recognizing two levels of ideology—what Seliger has called 'fundamental' and 'operative' ideology, Barrington Moore the 'ideology of ends' and the 'ideology of means', and Schurmann 'pure' and 'practical' ideology (see Seliger 1976, esp. p. 109; Moore 1950, pp. 402–3; and Schurmann 1968, esp. pp. 21–45); Schurmann's is as useful a terminology as any, and will be used for the rest of this chapter. The Chinese overtly recognize these two forms, calling the former 'theory' and the latter 'thought'. The Russians make a less clear-cut distinction, but recognition of it is implied in various ways, such as in the following extract from a speech Yuri Andropov made in April 1982:

The socialist system in this or that country arises as a result of the application of the *basic* principles of communism, *correctly modified*—as Lenin taught—*in their details* with reference to national and nation-state differences. (Andropov, in *Pravda*, 23 April 1982, p. 2—original emphasis.)

In other words, Andropov's 'basic principles' are essentially pure ideology, his modifications and details practical. Although the distinction between the pure and the practical ideology is often difficult to draw in practice, this theoretical distinction is of use when attempting, for instance, to understand how two communist parties, both allegedly committed to the same ideology, can be highly critical of each other. In fact, the common allegiance is really only to a method of analysis (dialectical and historical materialism) and a few general principles (the end-goal of communism, democratic centralism, etc.); it is, expressed differently, only the pure ideology that is common. The practical ideology, as might be inferred from the Andropov quotation, contains much that relates to the specifics of a particular country at a particular time, and the interests of that country may well be in conflict with those of another communist country despite common end-goals and a common long-term commitment to socialist internationalism.

Following on from this, the practical ideology—even though we may call it, as well as the pure ideology, Marxism–Leninism—may contain many elements which have little or nothing to do with the ideas of Marx and Lenin, and which may indeed be in conflict with some of them; professed long-term aims may clash with present interests, leading to contradictions and problems in communist ideology.

One final point is that the positive attitudes communists have towards their own ideology is in marked contrast to Marx's views on ideology. As Chambre (1967, pp. 314–15) points out, the concept of ideology had a largely negative or pejorative connotation in the nineteenth century, and Marx's writings are invariably critical of the falsificatory nature of ideology.

THE FUNCTIONS OF IDEOLOGY

The following seven-point analysis of the functions of ideology is based on what is in many ways still the most useful analysis of ideology for the beginner, Karen Dawisha's (1972), although it has been modified to suit present purposes; the functions to be considered are legitimation, justification, motivation, activation, communication, socialization, and limitation.

(*i*) *Legitimation*

In chapter three, it was argued that naked power is usually a brittle form of rule, and that, sooner or later, states and their leaders almost always seek to gain acceptance by, and preferably the support of those over whom they rule. They also need to convince themselves of their right to make decisions on behalf of society. In short, they seek the authority to rule, which we call 'legitimacy'. Legitimation (i.e., the acquisition and maintenance of legitimacy) is a—often the—major function of ideology in communist states. In the Western world, system legitimation is acquired not only by socialization methods, but also by a number of other channels, such as contested and relatively open elections, comparatively free media that can question politicians and their actions, the rule of law, etc. In the partial or total absence of many such legitimating mechanisms, communists make greater use of ideology in their attempt to acquire authority, both in their own eyes and in the eyes of the populace (despite the fact that it can be argued that a truly socialist political system, as envisaged by Marx, should not *have* to strive to legitimate itself—see Berki 1982). Many communist leaders, for instance, will cite the writings of Marx and Lenin in their endeavours to gain public support and authority for their actions. In other words, pure ideology is being used here as a legitimation agent; this is basically what Rigby (1982, esp. pp. 10–15) has called 'goal-rational' (i.e., related to the end-goal of communism) legitimation. However, the pure ideology is often vague and/or contradictory and/or difficult to get across to the masses. Moreover, much of it refers to a situation still many years off, and many communist leaders come to feel that this pure ideology is either making insufficient contribution to the legitimacy of the regime, or that it is positively hindering it by raising people's expectations above what the system can provide in the short term. For this reason, practical ideology comes to dominate pure ideology, and to incorporate values and ideas which may have more in common with some of the particular country's traditional values, or with Western values, or merely with what the government thinks is realistic in the foreseeable future, than with the ideas of Marx or Lenin. An example of this is the reference many communists in the older states have been making in recent years to 'real' (sometimes 'realistic' or 'actually existing') socialism.

The basis of this argument is that socialist governments can only move society towards communism at a rate determined by the availability of resources; citizens, for instance, cannot expect an abundance of goods if they are not themselves producing those goods. Thus, leaders might try to explain why there are still shortages, despite the fact that socialism has been officially proclaimed, by reference to 'real' socialism. A typical analysis of the concept was provided in 1979 by the head of the Central Committee's Academy of Social Sciences in the GDR:

Real socialism means above all that the communist parties of the socialist countries are led in their policies by the laws of social development and their objective requirements. It is not idealistic hopes which determine developments in the economy, in politics, in the social and spiritual-cultural life, but the objective necessities confirmed by historical experience.   (Cited in Holmes, 1981d, pp. 131–2.)

This pragmatic approach to socialism can be seen as being out of line with classical Marxism (part of pure ideology), which is implicitly criticized—or at least seen as a distant goal—in the reference to 'idealistic hopes'.

Such statements, then, are designed to give the population a realistic view of their leaders and the system, which is intended in turn to give the system greater legitimacy. The logic of this is perhaps not immediately obvious, and needs to be explained. What the ideologists are basically attempting to do is to bring official descriptions of what is happening and what can realistically be achieved in the near future more in line with what the population perceives in its everyday life; if the ideologists' claims appeared to be totally unrealistic and out of line with the ordinary citizens' own experiences of the system and its performance, there would be a credibility gap that would undermine legitimacy.

Of course, communists claim to represent the vanguard of society, and to be building a much better society. Therefore, excessive pragmatism and emphasis on the limitations of the government could also lead to legitimacy problems; if communists are limited in their ability to change existing situations, then support for and faith in their long-term goals will wane. Partially for this reason, communists usually place great emphasis on economic growth and the achievements of the system (including sporting achievements) at the same time as they are tempering people's expectations. The idea is to show that although Utopia cannot be created overnight, nevertheless real progress on the long hard path *is* being made. Let us look briefly at the question of economic growth.

Some see the emphasis in communist practical ideology on economic growth—which often, as a corollary, stresses the need for material incentives—as clashing with Marxist ideals. Some Western Marxists, for instance, argue that the great emphasis placed by communists in power on boosting production is making the citizens of those countries more competitive and consumer goods oriented. According to these Western critics, this in turn diverts attention away from the finer ideals of communism, and makes aspirations increasingly materialistic (in its non-philosophical, everyday sense), and similar to those of citizens in the bourgeois democracies. Whether such developments are desirable or not, it is certainly the case that many communist ideologists place extraordinary emphasis on the importance of raising productivity, increasing efficiency, and generally producing more of everything. A fairly typical statement is this one by a member of the East German Politburo and head of the East German Trade Union movement: 'Communism without economic growth would not be another form of communism, but rather no communism at all.' (Harry Nick, cited in *Deutschland Archiv*, no. 1, 1982, p. 40.) Such developments have led some commentators to see the economic reforms that were introduced in many communist states in the 1960s and 1970s partially as legitimation exercises, and the media coverage of these reforms as ideology (see, e.g. Baylis, 1971 and 1972). It is certainly the case that economic performance statistics are often presented in a deliberately

misleading fashion in the communist mass media, and this must surely be
to give both citizens and foreigners the impression that the government is
running the economy rather better than is actually the case (i.e., for legitimation purposes). Once again, the GDR provides a good example of this. In recent years, industry in that country has generally performed better than
agriculture; whilst the leaders must acknowledge that there are problems in
the agricultural sector in order to encourage greater efforts, too great an emphasis on problems could lead to dissatisfaction and uncertainty, which in
turn can have detrimental effects on the rest of the economy. In time, this
could become serious, and undermine the legitimacy of the regime. Thus,
figures on agricultural production have sometimes been presented in such a
way in *Neues Deutschland* (the GDR's main newspaper) that an unwary reader
would gain the impression that performance has been better than is actually
the case. The method is a clever one, and involves the presentation of data in
what looks like but is not an identical format. For instance, there were shortages of meat and other foods in the GDR in 1982. When figures on the fulfilment of the 1982 plan were published in *Neues Deutschland* in January 1983,
nearly all the statistics were presented in terms of 'percentage fulfilment of
the 1982 plan'; since the plan-targets for 1982 were higher for almost all commodities than they had been in 1981, a 100 per cent fulfilment figure for a
given product meant that more of it had been produced in 1982 than in 1981.
But the figures on the availability of food items were an exception—they were
presented in terms of levels achieved in 1981 rather than percentage fulfilment of the 1982 plan. This made the 1982 figures look better than they
would have done had the East German Statistics Office presented the data on
food in the same format as the other data. It takes a very observant reader to
notice such jiggery-pokery. As indicated above, however, a regime must be
very careful not to mislead too blatantly; if agricultural figures look good, yet
there are serious shortages of food in the shops, the legitimizing function of
an ideologically based presentation of statistics can backfire, and the regime
actually lose rather than strengthen its support.

If a regime does have to acknowledge failures, a common ploy is to blame
individual leaders (often agricultural ministers) for the shortcomings and replace them. Just occasionally, as in Poland in recent years, the scale of the
problem is so large that even such scapegoat measures are insufficient, and
the regime loses much, even most, of its legitimacy. In fact, some communists
seem to have recognized the possible dangers of placing too much emphasis
on economic performance. The Chinese, for instance, while promoting an
economic growth ideology in the form of the 'Four Modernizations' campaign (this basically calls for the development of industry, agriculture,
defence, and science and technology) also stress that China's economic problems are such that the average per capita income will continue to be below
that of the developed countries for many years to come, so that communist

ideology must be used to defend the system against the 'corrosive influence' of Western ideas (see Hu 1982, p. 15).

Some regimes, it must be acknowledged, seem to have been more success-ful in legitimizing themselves on the grounds of economic performance than on pure Marxism–Leninism. Hungary is a good example. When he came to power following the 1956 uprising, Janos Kadar faced potentially severe problems in legitimizing his rule. Over the next few years, however, he showed that he was prepared to tolerate criticism, even of some rather basic aspects of Marxism (such as the class approach to social divisions) if this helped to improve his popularity (Toma and Volgyes 1977, p. 47–8). His sup-port seems to have grown in particular as the economic reforms Hungary introduced in the late 1960s (known as the New Economic Mechanism) led to higher living standards and greater economic freedom for many Hungarian citizens. However, like many Western Marxists, some Hungarian citizens have clearly been upset as what they consider to be basic tenets of the pure ideology, such as the commitment to egalitarianism, have been sacrificed for the benefit of strengthening regime support (Toma and Volgyes 1977, pp. 133–4), and even Hungary may experience increasing problems with such a performance-based form of legitimation.

One final but important point about communist emphasis on economic growth is that it would be wrong to see this only in terms of system legitima-tion. In line with the pure ideology, many communist leaders genuinely seek to bring up the level of less developed areas of the country to that of the lead-ing parts. In order to do this without encouraging excessive resentment in the wealthy areas, a healthy overall growth situation is necessary.

In addition to the emphasis on growth, communist leaders often try to prove that society really is progressing—even if slowly—towards the distant goal of communism by claiming that their society has reached a new stage of development. This is seen in the sometimes highly elaborate systems of label-ling used to describe the various periods of a given country's history under communist rule. As was pointed out in chapter one, Marx used the terms socialism and communism virtually interchangeably, whereas Lenin made a much clearer distinction between them. Late in life, Lenin did make some sort of distinction between 'building socialism' following a revolution and 'socialism' proper; but there was never any further subdivision. Only in re-cent years have the Soviets decided that there is yet another stage, so-called 'developed' (or 'mature') socialism; whereas the building of socialism is now said to have lasted from 1917 to 1936, and socialism proper from 1936 to the early 1960s, 'developed socialism' has been in existence since the early 1960s, and is a concept particularly associated with Brezhnev (for further details see Evans 1977). The GDR has an even more elaborate analysis of the stages of socialism. In the latter half of the 1940s, the East Germans were not yet officially building socialism; rather, they were primarily concerned with destroying the vestiges of the Nazi period, and therefore described the political arrangements as an 'anti-fascist democratic revolution'. From that period on, the East Germans have been so slippery in their own analyses that Western scholars cannot reach agreement on the precise periodization. Some see the beginning of socialism as dating from 1950, for example, whereas others maintain that this stage was not embarked upon until the Second Party Conference in July 1952 (see Rilling 1979 and Fischer and Weber 1979). At present, the most authoritative analysis of this question is the SED's own official history (published in 1978), according to which the stages are as follows—anti-fascist democratic revolution, 1945–9; beginning of the socialist transformation of society, 1949–52; construction of the basis of socialism 1952–8; struggle for the victory of socialist production relations, 1958–61; comprehensive construction of socialism, 1961–70; formation of developed socialist society, 1971 to the present. According to one's perspective, this can all be seen as reflecting an awareness that significant changes in society have been made—or, viewing it more cynically, as an attempt by an entrenched élite to acquire greater legitimacy by giving the impression that things really are changing, and for the better, contrary to most people's perception.

In addition to all the above legitimation techniques, there is another weapon in the arsenal of communist ideologists that is potentially at least as powerful as any of the methods mentioned so far. That weapon is *official (state-sponsored) nationalism.* The concept of nationalism is dealt with at length in chapter 13, but at this point we should note that in communist states as in others, nationalism is frequently an important part of the state's ideology. It serves a number of different purposes. First, there is the task of nation-building, of encouraging the population to identify with a new or relatively new political unit. This is because many communist parties—with some notable exceptions (e.g. China)—take power either in young states and/or in countries which had been governed for many years as colonies of imperialist powers and in which there had not developed a strong identity with the central authorities. Let us briefly consider both types of case. The first type applies to much of Eastern Europe where, for instance, Albania, Czechoslovakia, Hungary, Poland, and Yugoslavia were all either formed or else reconstituted as sovereign states after World War One. Poland, for instance, became a sovereign state again at that time—although it had been a state in its own right up to the eighteenth century. The GDR is even newer, in that Germany (i.e., what is now both East and West) had been a single country from 1871 to the end of the Second World War, at which point it was first informally, and in 1949 formally divided into two German states. The Indo-Chinese and most African communist states are typical of the second type.

But communists can never be satisfied with just creating a new national identity; they also want to develop a socialist consciousness and jump what many analysts believe are necessary stages of economic and political development. The point about the speed at which communists usually want to develop their country leads us to official nationalism's second function—to gain popular support for radical development policies. Such policies—seen, for instance, in communist drives to collectivize agriculture—frequently lead to hostility from many citizens, and the use of nationalism (often based on traditional nationalism) is one way in which communist ideologists attempt to counter this. Stalin started this with 'socialism in one country' in the 1920s. In China, Mao really began to emphasize the concept of 'self-reliance' from about 1960 on, when the Sino-Soviet split meant that China could no longer look to the USSR and had to develop using its own resources and skills; the concept of 'self-reliance' was not new, but it was not a major plank of Chinese communist ideology until the 1960s. North Korea, too, has a similar concept in the Juche doctrine, which was defined by Kim Il Sung in 1965 as 'the principle of solving for oneself all problems of the revolution and construction in conformity with the actual conditions of one's country, and mainly by one's own efforts' (quoted in Cumings 1974, p. 34). Numerous other examples could be cited.

In the past, two factors have often served to delay or retard the development of this form of official nationalism in communist states. The first is Marx's own emphasis on the desirability of socialist internationalism, which seeks to minimize feelings of national identity. The second—which the Russians themselves would see as a corollary of the last point—is the loyalty to Moscow that has been expected of new communist states; this was particularly true while Stalin was alive (i.e., until 1953). This second factor, however, tends to play ever less of a role, as most new communist leaderships realize that the problems of acquiring regime legitimacy can be compounded if they devote too much time and effort to eulogizing the 'home of the first socialist revolution'. This problem was experienced by many East European states in the first few years following the Second World War, especially since the citizens in many of these countries felt that communism had been imposed by outsiders anyway (Poland being a prime example). At that stage, however, those states were heavily dependent on and partially under the control of the USSR, so that Stalin had little difficulty in securing compliance from the new communist leaderships. Nowadays, the situation is in most cases very different. Of the new communist states, Afghanistan is the one most heavily dependent on the USSR, and the constant declarations of loyalty to Moscow are presenting the Karmal regime with extraordinary problems of legitimation. But neither the Indo-Chinese nor the African communist states have failed to learn the lesson of the East European states, and the communist leaderships there have made strenuous efforts not to identify with the Soviet leaders more than with their own populations. In Africa, the Soviets have been rebuffed in a number of ways—for instance, in not being allowed to establish permanent military bases—by the Angolan, Mozambican, Ethiopian, and other regimes, on one level because the respective leaderships do not want to appear to be toadying to a foreign government. Although Ethiopia—alone amongst all the African states—has never been colonized, the other communist states of Africa have, and the leaders want to ensure that their populations do not see their country merely exchanging one group of foreign rulers (usually Portuguese or French) for another (Soviet or Cuban). Indeed, there are currently signs that the leaders of several of these countries are looking to the West for more support and trade—not so much as a replacement for Soviet support as a counterweight to it, to avoid excessive dependency on any one country.

The third function of official nationalism—which may sometimes coexist with the other forms—is to bolster support for the regime when other sources of legitimation, such as economic growth, are faltering. Unfortunately, since this form of nationalism is generally invoked when the regime is performing poorly, it will often seek scapegoats for problems that have arisen and/or try to force a common identity on all groups in the country, which can lead to ethnic tensions. The search for scapegoats can even involve racism (e.g. anti-Semitism in Poland in the late 1960s), and/or a form of xenophobia (in the sense of blaming foreigners or other countries for problems in one's own country), as the ideologists attempt to divert the mass's attention away from the failings of their own leaders. Although such xenophobia may be directed against the capitalist world—for example Korea's frequent attacks on 'Japanese imperialism'—it can also be directed against other communist states (e.g. Yugoslav and Chinese attacks on Soviet 'social imperialism'). All this is hardly conducive to the creation of a conflictless communist world—which is also true of a fourth and final possible role of communist nationalist ideology, the acquisition of public support for an expansionist foreign policy in the name of both traditional national interests and alleged socialist internationalism.

Since official nationalism is such an important component of ideology, let us now consider three case studies; Romania, Vietnam, and Angola between them incorporate many of the aspects of nationalism we have referred to.

When the communists took power in Romania, there was initially a power struggle between two main factions. Although some writers have seen this struggle in terms of a 'pro-Moscow' group versus a more nationalistic group, the majority view nowadays is that both groups were vying for the Soviet Union's support. It is certainly the case that the group around Gheorghiu-Dej which eventually won was seen as the more nationalist of the two factions (the other being led by Ana Pauker). However, having consolidated power, Gheorghiu-Dej proved throughout the 1950s to be a very loyal ally of the USSR, and emulated the Soviet system in a number of ways. In other words, the communist leadership at this stage clearly put loyalty to the Soviet Union above any nationalistic inclinations. Indeed, they dealt harshly with the many intellectuals who were preaching an anti-Soviet nationalism—and rewrote Romanian history to emphasize the long tradition of friendship with

Russia. Ideology at this stage then was emphasizing 'socialist internationalism' (here meaning loyalty to the USSR) rather than Romanian nationalism.

The situation began to change dramatically at the end of the 1950s beginning of the 1960s. At that time, the Soviets—backed, most vocally, by the East Germans—started pushing hard for an international division of labour within Comecon (see chapter 14). For now, all we need to note is that the plan would have meant that Romania would have been one of the breadbaskets of Comecon—that is, it would have remained a predominantly agricultural country and provided the industrial countries such as Czechoslovakia and the GDR with much of their food. Gheorghiu-Dej and the rest of the Romanian leadership were bitterly opposed to this, and accused the Soviets of wanting to retard their economic development. They argued that the Soviet and East German plan was very un-Marxist, and that *all* countries wanting to build socialism and communism had to have a well-developed industrial base. The Romanian leader decided that he would learn from the Soviets themselves—and began to develop his own version of 'socialism in one country'; given the somewhat different conditions of the Romanian case, however, this eventually led to the formulation of 'independence within interdependence'. This meant that Romania was not only to become less dependent on the Soviets as a source of investment for economic development, but also that it began to develop an overt official nationalism. Thus the communist party began to reassess history, playing down the friendship with the Soviet Union, and emphasizing the essential continuity between the contemporary leadership and past leaders. As a leading analyst of Romanian politics points out, not only did this seem a good way of improving the regime's image in the eyes of the ordinary Romanian people, but, 'Discontentment and political dissent, instead of being channelled into the system as inputs, were successfully deflected by the regime to external (Soviet) targets' (Shafir 1981, p. 606). The campaign started with a 're-Romanization' of place-names and a reassessment of historical figures who had earlier been criticized by the communists. The liberation of 1944, too, was now reinterpreted, to play down the role of the Red (Soviet) Army and enhance the part played by the Romanian communists. Then, in 1964, a tract allegedly written by Karl Marx and previously unknown was published in Bucharest. This was the 'Notes on the Romanians', in which the author condemned Russia's incursions into Romania in the nineteenth century. A strongly chauvinistic official nationalism was being developed rapidly.

Gheorghiu-Dej died in 1965, and was replaced by Ceausescu—who has over time developed and encouraged Romanian official nationalism. Indeed, he has now gone further than his predecessor, in that whereas Gheorghiu-Dej emphasized the links between the *party* and earlier Romanian leaderships, Ceausescu has emphasized the continuities between earlier leaders—such as Michael the Brave, Stephen the Great, Vlad the Impaler, and Dimitri

Cantemir—and himself personally. All this has been done at a time when Romanian economic performance has been deteriorating, and is an example of official nationalism being linked with yet another legitimation mechanism, the *personality cult* (see Gill 1982, and chapter eight).

However, in emphasizing historical tradition, Romanian official nationalism has sometimes led to tension between the dominant ethnic group (the Romanians) and the ethnic minorities (notably Hungarians, Germans, and Jews). For example, Romanian historians have been encouraged to 'prove' that Romanians inhabited Transylvania long before the Hungarians did, which many Hungarians living in Romania have found offensive. The German minority, too, has expressed concern on occasions that official Romanian nationalism might become a threat to them (see Gilberg 1981, pp. 200 and 210). Although Ceausescu and official spokespersons have tried to emphasize that the new nationalism is to bring all Romanians—of whatever ethnic origin—together, sharing a common set of values in which they can take pride, there are many Romanian citizens who respond to the official nationalism in a way quite different from that intended by the leadership. Thus the Romanian leaders will have to show some sensitivity in their official nationalism if they are not to trigger hostile unofficial nationalism.

While there were two Vietnams, the Vietnamese communists had a somewhat similar problem to the East Germans, the North Koreans, and to a lesser extent the South Yemenis, in that there had been widespread feeling, both amongst many of the country's own people and among other states, that it was an artificial unit, part of a larger 'natural' whole. By the summer of 1954, following a war with the French, the Vietnamese communists had control of one part of the country (the North), whilst a new republic eventually emerged in the South. For many years both prior to and following this, while they were fighting either the French or (verbally) the South Vietnamese regime, the communists had linked nationalism and communism, by emphasizing the progressive nature of anti-colonialism. In the period from 1945, the communists continued to emphasize the close relationship between patriotism and communism, arguing somewhat sophistically that 'Genuine patriotism is . . . part and parcel of internationalism', and, 'In our country, to be a patriot means to love socialism, patriotism is closely linked with socialism, and the communist is the most genuine patriot' (Ho Chi Minh in 1951 and Pham Van Dong in 1960 respectively, cited in Turner 1975, pp. 111–12).

Of course, this was an attempt to harness traditional attitudes to the new communist regime's values, and in so doing distance them from the values of either the French colonizers or 'the other Vietnam'. This policy continued throughout the period of the Vietnamese War, when the communists used nationalism as part of their propaganda campaign against the Americans.

The situation and tasks changed quantitatively if not clearly qualitatively following the *de facto* reunification of Vietnam in 1975 (formal reunification came in 1976). The communists now had to start an indoctrination campaign amongst the South Vietnamese, show how they were not only the same nation as the North Vietnamese but also that they should therefore accept the same politico-economic system as the North Vietnamese had had for decades. Moreover, the Vietnamese leadership has been encouraging chauvinism—bellicose nationalism—among its own people since the late 1970s, as the Vietnamese ousted Pol Pot in Kampuchea and installed a new communist regime; not only the French, but the Soviets and some Vietnamese themselves have long seen Laos and Kampuchea as essentially part of one 'natural' political unit in which the Vietnamese would play the dominant role. Thus the Vietnamese communists have not only the problem of developing an identity with the state among their own citizens, but are to some extent sharing with the Heng Samrin government the problems of creating an identity between people and regime in Kampuchea. Nationalist tensions between Kampuchea and Vietnam will continue for the foreseeable future, and the ideologists in both countries have a major integration and legitimation task ahead of them.

Although Angola comprises approximately one hundred ethnic groups, three are dominant: the Ovimbundu, Mbundu, and the Bakongo. In the years preceding Angola's independence from Portugal, there was often considerable struggle between the three main liberation forces—which to no small extent reflected their different ethnic bases. Thus the group which was eventually victorious—the MPLA—drew its support principally from the Mbundu, the Mesticos (half-castes) and Assimilados (black Africans who had officially registered as Portuguese citizens). In contrast, UNITA found its supporters principally amongst the Ovimbundu of Eastern Angola, whilst the FNLA was most popular among the Bakongo of Northern Angola. It is hardly surprising, therefore, that once the MPLA had secured power, it was going to face problems of unifying the Angolan people and creating a single nation. There have indeed been many indications of such difficulties. On the one hand, UNITA has continued to operate and to be a serious thorn in the Angolan regime's flesh. On the other, there have been several instances of ethnic tension within the MPLA, indicative of the major problems the leadership faces in trying to overcome traditional national rivalries. Thus in May 1977 one of the MPLA's top leaders, Nito Alves, was expelled from the Central Committee, accused amongst other things of being a 'black racist' and spreading racism (notably against Mesticos and the Portuguese still in Angola). When the MPLA held it first congress in December 1977, it was decided to admit to the MPLA 'Party of Labour' formed at that date only dedicated Marxist–Leninists free from tribal and racial prejudices; the latter prerequisite testified to the severe ethnic tensions that still existed not only within society but within the party itself.

However, the regime has done more than simply spout rhetoric in its endeavours to integrate the various tribes of Angola and legitimate its rule. For instance, having decided that the original intention to establish state farms as the principal unit of agriculture was not going to work for the fore-seeable future, the leadership decided to allow various groups to become small-scale farmers on what had been Portuguese, then Angolan state-run estates; one major ramification of this was that the Ovimbundu were encouraged to take over the coffee-growing estates, which was seen as having the important political advantage of weaning this tribe away from UNITA and towards the MPLA regime.

There have been various other ethnic conflicts within the MPLA—there was another major outburst in 1980, for example—showing that the regime is still at an early stage of nation-building and encouraging official nationalism; if the leaders themselves cannot transcend traditional rivalries, they are not going to be very successful at eradicating this in society at large.

Two final points about the legitimating function of ideology need to be made. The first is that communists can benefit from a phenomenon that is advantageous to all types of government—namely, that some citizens will accept that a government is legitimate simply because a group of leaders claims to constitute the legitimate government and has ruled the country for some time. For such citizens, 'might is right'. In one sense, the ideologists might appear to have relatively little to do in terms of legitimizing the regime in the eyes of such people, other than to keep letting them know of its existence and of its continuing claim to the right to rule. However, this form of legitimacy has its drawbacks. The principal one is that, were the communists to be overthrown, such citizen support can readily be transferred to a new group; this probably pertains to many Poles, which helps to explain why the imposition of martial law did not lead to even greater public outcry, but also why the Polish regime currently almost certainly enjoys a very limited and frail form of legitimacy. The second point is that the sheer scale of involvement in society by communist governments creates greater problems of legitimation than most liberal democracies experience. Expressed another way, citizens can blame communist governments for a wider range of the problems that inevitably arise in any kind of society since the political system assumes responsibility for so much. Although, in theory, the converse also pertains (i.e., there is more to praise the government for when things go well), it seems to be generally true that most people are quicker to criticize governments than to praise them.

(ii) Justification

Whereas legitimation is concerned with a system as a whole, and the people who run it (i.e., the regime), justification relates to specific policies. For instance, at the end of the 1920s, Soviet ideologists had to explain why it was now considered improper for peasants to attempt to enrich themselves (much as Chinese peasants have recently been called upon to do), in marked contrast to what they had been told by Bukharin in the mid-1920s.

(*iii*) Motivation

Reference is often made in the literature to the *teleological* or *chiliastic* dimension of communist ideology. By this is meant that communist ideology serves as a guide to some distant end-goal of a society of plenty. In other words, ideology can act as a motivator to a better future. This is particularly true for communists before they come to power and in the early stages after having taken power, when the ideas of Marx and Lenin, and just a desire to improve the world around them, inspires them to action. In other words, it is largely the pure ideology—plus the realities of a given situation—that motivates at this stage. For instance, it is the ideology as much as anything that inspires communists to nationalize banks and factories or collectivize farms, in the belief that such structural change is a necessary prerequisite to the changes in people's consciousness needed for the attainment of communism; what the Ottaways have written of the African communist states—'Ideology has determined the choice of institutions, the thrust of foreign relations, the direction of major policy decisions . . .' (D. and M. Ottaway 1981, p. 195)—is widely applicable. As communist power becomes consolidated, the pure ideology probably plays ever less of a role in motivating communists, as the concrete problems of governing come to dominate. However, the pure ideology has yet to be totally abandoned in any communist state, and it seems reasonable to suppose that the long-term aims of the classical theorists of communism are at the backs of the minds of many communist leaders.

(*iv*) Activation

If the pure ideology can serve to motivate communists themselves, the vanguard must then use both pure and practical ideology to activate, inspire—or, to use Joravsky's term, 'energise' (1966, p. 2)—the masses, to encourage participation in the building of a communist society. This function tends to be most visible at the 'mobilization phase' (i.e., when power has been consolidated and the communists wish to introduce a series of radical changes in society), but lasts well beyond that.

(*v*) Communication

Like all ideologies, communist ideology has a particular set of phrases and a particular conception of certain key words, which virtually constitute a language; indeed, Michael Waller has written a book with the title *The Language of Communism*. This language 'acts as a kind of "social cement" by providing the terminology through which social reality is expressed' (Dawisha, 1972, p. 162). Thus terms such as capitalism, imperialism, liberalism, individualism, bourgeois, fascism, etc. almost invariably have negative connotations in the communist world, whereas agitation, propaganda, collectivism, vanguard, planning, the dictatorship of the proletariat and socialist internationalism all have positive connotations; it should be obvious that the evaluation of some of these concepts would be quite different in the language of liberal democracy. It should be noted, however, that some communist concepts change their connotations from positive to negative or vice versa according to the time and place—pluralism and Stalinism are two good examples.

As with other functions, the communication function of ideology can be problematic. One problem is that although key terms might become familiar enough to ordinary citizens, the actual meaning of such terms is often not properly understood. Thus more than sixty-five years after the October Revolution, Soviet leaders still feel that

There has arisen a clear need for the preparation of a book that both sets out in a simple way the basic principles of Marxism–Leninism and also provides a lively narrative of the heroic path taken by our party and people.   (Chernenko, in *Pravda*, 15 June 1983, p. 2.)

At other times, the terms may be understood, but the constant repetition of slogans as a shorthand way of describing real enough problems in the world can make people indifferent to these problems.

(*vi*) *Socialization*

The communication function, and particularly the ascription of positive and negative evaluations to key concepts, is closely linked to the general socialization or integrating function of ideology. Since this was explored in the last chapter, it need detain us no further.

(*vii*) *Limitation*

The limiting function is often seen as one of the major aspects of ideology in the more advanced communist states; by this is meant that pure Marxism–Leninism creates certain boundaries or constraints—limits—which communist leaders feel they cannot really transgress. One might suppose, for instance, that the Cuban leadership secretly feels that the economy would benefit enormously from a major injection of US capital, or that the Angolans may feel similarly about South African capital. However, the two leaderships have spent so much time and energy criticizing 'Yankee imperialism' and South African racism respectively that it would be difficult to justify the policy of inviting investment from these countries. This said, we should be very careful not to overestimate the limiting function of ideology; there are numerous examples in the communist world where leaders have chosen a policy one may well not have expected. This process was already under way in Lenin's time, but really intensified under Stalin, whose criticism of egalitarianism as a bourgeois concept, for instance, is seen by many (e.g. Zaslavsky 1982, chapter 4) as the rejection of a basic tenet of classical Marxism (i.e., of pure ideology). Indeed, Lenin (e.g. in the 1899 essay 'Our Programme'),

Stalin and many subsequent communist leaders have emphasized that Marxism should always be adapted to changing situations, and that nothing in it is sacred. In line with this argument, for example, Stalin introduced fee-paying schools, much bigger wage differentials in industry, etc. Once this principle had been firmly established by the Soviets, a precedent had been set which has been utilized time and again in the communist world; Pandora's Box had been opened. For instance, the Yugoslavs, Chinese, and some other communist states are prepared to tolerate unemployment; Yugoslavia and Poland have in the past both permitted widescale decollectivization; the private plot in agriculture has become increasingly encouraged in many communist states in recent years (Albania and, to a lesser extent, Cuba being notable exceptions); Cuba, China, Poland, Mozambique, and other communist states are now encouraging foreign (capitalist) investment in their economies, while many other countries (e.g. the GDR) have made it clear that they are keen to co-operate with capitalist firms on projects in third countries; Mozambique has expressed its willingness to trade with South Africa; China has permitted private schools since 1979; and so the list goes on. Such moves are often justified on the grounds of *temporary* necessity, and the old Stalinist argument that whatever helps the development of a given economy towards high levels of industrialization and plenty—as long as it is under the control of a communist government—is compatible with long-term Marxist aims. Moreover, new ideological terms have been developed to show that the communists are fully aware of the possible dangers of some of their actions. For instance, the more contact the GDR has had with West Germany, the more clearly it has distinguished between economic co-operation and ideology. It was in this context that the concept of *Abgrenzung* (delimitation)—which emphasizes the significant differences between bourgeois and socialist ideologies and systems, and has its origins in the Soviet conception of 'peaceful coexistence'— was developed at a time when contacts between East and West Germany were being intensified.

It should by now be clear why the limiting factor should not be overemphasized. At best, the pure and past practical ideology can be seen as a fence around a field; if the field needs to be expanded, modifications and expansions are made to the fence accordingly. If parts of the fence seem to be no longer necessary—if they rot—they are replaced by new fencing. There is precious little of the fence that is truly permanent.

SUMMARY AND CONCLUSIONS

It has been argued in this chapter that in its most common usage ideology is a set of ideas, many of which are unverifiable, that both guides and helps to legitimate a group and its policies; when we talk of communist ideology in this book, we mean the official ideology of the regime in communist countries. It has further been argued that there are two basic types of ideology—

pure, based on the ideas and methods of Marx, Engels, and Lenin, and practical, designed principally to integrate society and the political system—although the two are closely interrelated and often difficult to distinguish in the real world.

Some commentators believe that ideology is of essentially marginal and declining significance. Having considered the arguments and evidence in this chapter, does this point of view seem convincing? By now, the reader will probably have realized that what such writers are usually referring to is *pure* ideology; once we are aware that the term ideology is being used by such authors in this narrow sense, we will have a much clearer understanding of why it is that other writers do not see ideology as being in decline. If we use the broad conception of Marxism–Leninism—that is, to include both the pure and the practical forms—then it surely becomes obvious that ideology is still very important. Although pure ideology might be in decline, practical ideology is not. Looked at from another angle, we would argue that the relative weight of the various functions of ideology changes over time, which is quite different from saying that ideology as a whole is dead or dying. Indeed, there is a strong argument that as communist regimes move away from the more coercive forms of rule so typical in the early stages following a revolution towards more normative forms of power, so the legitimating role of ideology comes to assume greater importance. And some contemporary Marxists have argued that ideology *always* plays a major role in society, even a fully communist one (see Althusser 1979, p. 232).

We have seen that ideology, partially because of the constant interaction of the pure and practical components, is simultaneously flexible and complex. This flexibility and complexity has both advantages and disadvantages in terms of legitimating the system and the political élite. One of the advantages is that different parts of the ideology can appeal to different sections of the population, and thus help to gain the support of such groups. For example, some of the major components of practical ideology, such as nationalism and the stress on economic and sporting achievements, will appeal to many ordinary workers and peasants, to many of whom pure Marxism–Leninism will probably be of little interest or attraction. On the other hand, many progressive intellectuals could well find the nationalism or personality cults distasteful, but will be attracted to various aspects of pure Marxism–Leninism. Another advantage of the flexibility is that some components which are basically irrelevant in a particular country can be downplayed. For instance, Marx's emphasis on the role of the industrial workers in a socialist revolution is of little relevance to many predominantly agrarian communist states; if the ideology were too rigid, this sort of incongruity could lead to serious questioning of the élite's right to rule. Some commentators prefer to call the communist ideology 'malleable' or even 'corruptible' rather than flexible; such terms clearly have more pejorative overtones than the latter word. The choice of descriptive term—flexible, malleable, adaptable, etc.—depends on one's perceptions of the reasons for change in ideology. But what is clear is that Marx himself would not have wanted his ideas to have been treated as sacrosanct and immutable. His whole approach was dynamic, and he believed that theory and practice are in constant interaction; this interaction is called 'revolutionary *praxis*' by Marxists.

Nevertheless, there comes a point at which the flexibility of ideology starts to become dysfunctional. For instance, various leaders can disagree amongst themselves—sometimes profoundly, as with Stalin and Trotsky, or Rakosi and Nagy—on ideology and its implications for policy. One group that wants to emphasize the pure ideology might accuse another that is more concerned with practical ideology of being *revisionists* (i.e., guilty of unjustifiably revising basic tenets of the ideology). Conversely, the second group might accuse the first of being *dogmatists*, of sticking too rigidly to ideas and policies that are now outdated. Lane (1976, p. 20) has pointed out that in communist states there is an assumption that only the communist party can correctly interpret the ideas of Marx and Lenin and apply them to the contemporary situation; if the leaders of this party cannot agree amongst themselves on the ideas, then the validity of both the ideas and the leaders' claims to a right to rule comes into question. Such leadership disagreements make the allegedly 'scientific' nature of Marxism–Leninism begin to look decidedly subjective and hence to lose some of its authority.

In most cases, where there is a clash between pure and practical ideology, the latter takes precedent. This, too, has inherent dangers for the legitimacy of the system and élite, however, As classical Marxism and Leninism are increasingly put into the background, and ever greater stress is placed on nationalism, economic growth, personality cults, etc., the danger arises that if any of these becomes counter-productive as a legitimizing agent, then regime legitimacy becomes that much more fragile. Too much stress on official nationalism, for instance, can encourage unofficial nationalism, which in turn can lead to political instability. Too much emphasis on economic performance is dangerous if the economy begins to perform poorly; the Polish leadership learnt this the hard way. And one wonders how many stages of socialism and communism the communists are capable of devising; it is quite possible that many peoples' faith in communist leadership actually declines a little each time some new stage is 'revealed', especially since many of the older states are now explicitly saying that the higher stages of socialism (developed socialism) will last for 'an historically prolonged stage' (both Andropov and Chernenko argued this). In its 1961 Programme, the Soviet communist party actually promised the population that communism would in the main be achieved by 1980; this promise has quietly been forgotten by the leadership since Khrushchev's removal, but one suspects that many Soviet citizens remembered it with cynicism as 1980 came and went.

Another problem of ideological flexibility is that communists sometimes find they have to rank-order and choose between their enemies and aims—in a sense, between their slogans—and in the process adopt policies that are unsocialist by almost any criteria. The pure ideology suggests that there is always a 'scientific' method to enable communists to make a choice between two options, but, of course, this cannot provide the actual answer to a specific dilemma. Thus, during the Falklands/Malvinas conflict Cuba had to decide whether Argentinian 'fascism' or British 'imperialism' was the worse evil, and chose the latter—thereby lending some support to an extremely reactionary regime. China, too, has on occasions recognized highly oppressive, right-wing regimes (e.g. Pinochet's Chile) largely because the USSR has refused to do so. In this case, Soviet 'social imperialism' is seen as an even worse evil than a reactionary military dictatorship.

Despite its flexibility, ideology can on occasions lead communists to a very imperfect understanding of problems in their own societies. For instance, excessive emphasis on class analysis as the basis of conflict in society has led some regimes to underestimate the significance of other cleavages and sources of dissatisfaction, such as ethnic tensions or the alienating effect of overcrowded and inadequate housing. In other words, there are times when Marxism–Leninism is, for all its flexibility, still too rigid, and it can give communists blind spots about certain phenomena.

But many such problems are extreme cases, and one must be careful not to assume that the flexibility of ideology is constantly leading communist leaderships into these sorts of dilemmas or blind alleys. Many 'temporary expedients' that have been criticized by Westerners as 'unsocialist' or as being incompatible with long-term aims—which represent tensions in the ideology—may in fact be based on sound judgements that are much less clearly at odds with the intended end-goals than the critics imply. A good example is communist attitudes towards Western transnational corporations. As mentioned above, several communist states are now positively encouraging such corporations to set up plants in their country, and even to take profits out of the country. Although many Western Marxists have accused communists in power of a 'sell-out' for doing so, on the grounds that such corporations represent a form of neo-imperialism, this is only one way of looking at such policies. The communists can and do argue that this is a good way of bringing rapid industrialization, high technology, and employment to an underdeveloped country, so that the corporations are helping to bring a country closer to the economic levels necessary for socialism and communism. They further argue that as long as the corporations abide by regulations laid down by themselves (i.e., are under some sort of communist control) then there is little to worry about. And of course, in decades to come, there is nothing to stop communist governments from nationalizing the corporations' factories and equipment. This case demonstrates well why there are times when we should be cautious about overemphasizing tensions between pure and practical ideology, or between long-term goals and short-term expedients.

This leads us to the final question, concerning the effectiveness of ideology in legitimating communist systems. Let us first consider the issue of regime legitimacy amongst ordinary citizens. It was argued in the last chapter that we are still at an elementary stage in terms of knowing what the masses in the communist world really think and know about their political systems, so that we cannot yet provide a satisfactory answer to the question 'how effective is ideology?'; as Alfred Meyer once pointed out, it is often only when a regime has fallen or is under overt threat from the masses that we can be certain it has had a low level of legitimacy amongst the ordinary citizenry. Despite this, we can certainly make the point that there are *degrees* of legitimacy; no political system is either fully supported or totally rejected by the populace. For analytical purposes, we can divide attitudes towards a regime into four basic categories—positive support (a citizen is basically enthusiastic about the political system and its rulers), positive acceptance (a citizen does not wish to see the system replaced, but may be critical of some aspects of it, including perhaps some of its politicians, and therefore demonstrates limited enthusiasm for it), negative acceptance (a citizen would prefer a different political system, or at least a different set of leaders, but is not prepared to do anything to bring about such change), and active rejection (a citizen is prepared to engage in activities that could help to bring about the collapse of a regime and/or system). In the real world, of course, many citizens will move between categories—to no small extent as a reflection of the efficacy of the ideology. What is important is that communist systems—like other political systems—do not *need* positive support from all or most of the citizens, a point recognized by the Hungarian leader Kadar when, in 1961, he changed the traditional communist adage (actually based on a similar line in St Luke's gospel) of 'whoever is not with us is against us' to 'whoever is not against us is with us'. In other words, if the majority of the population falls into the first three categories (especially the first two) mentioned above, then a system can be seen as enjoying popular legitimacy, which in turn means that the ideology has been sufficiently effective. The limited evidence available suggests that ideology *has* been sufficiently effective—in this specific sense—in a majority of the older communist states at least.

But what of the people disseminating the ideology? Do they believe in it? Generally speaking, people asking this question are referring to *pure* ideology—and the most convincing answer is that some communists believe in it more than others. Although there are undoubtedly large numbers of careerists and opportunists in the ranks of every communist party in power, one has only to study the writings of some of the Hungarian, Yugoslav, and other communist theoreticians (e.g. the late Edvard Kardelj) to realize that some of these people genuinely believe in Marxist goals, and are attempting to make a serious and creative contribution to the pure ideology. Moreover, one does not have to agree with everything Marx or Lenin wrote to be a 'genuine' communist, any more than one has to believe and agree with everything in the New Testament to be a true Christian. Even those communists who may have lost faith in the pure ideology will often realize the importance of the practical ideology to their own position and the political system, and in this sense see ideology as important. This said, Lewis (in Lewis 1984, 1–41; see too Rigby 1982, p. 16) has argued convincingly that there are times when leadership élites lose faith in themselves, which undermines their own legitimacy. The most common problem is that lower- and middle-ranking party and state officials sometimes start to question the legitimacy of a regime if there are serious rifts amongst the senior politicians and/or if important policies seem to be failing. In fact, Lewis even argues that political crises in Eastern Europe are more likely to occur when the regime has lost legitimacy amongst this group—which he calls 'intermediate cadres'—than amongst the population at large, and relates this to several of the major revolts we shall be considering in chapter 12.

It should thus be clear that the regime's ability to legitimate itself both to the population and to itself is very important. It is not only a matter of avoiding political crises, however. Another point is that the greater the legitimacy of the regime, the easier it is for communists to introduce wide-ranging changes rapidly. For these reasons, it is in the interests of communist leaderships to minimize tensions and contradictions both within Marxism–Leninism in its broadest sense, and between this ideology and perceived reality.

Basic further reading

G. Bertsch and T. Ganschow (eds.), 1976, section 4.
K. Dawisha, 1972.
D. Joravsky, 1966.
P. Lewis (ed.), 1984.
R. Macridis, 1983, esp. Part 2.

T. Oleszczuk, 1980.
T. H. Rigby and F. Feher (eds.), 1982.
F. Schurmann, 1968, Ch. 1.
M. Seliger, 1976.
A. Zinoviev, 1984, esp. pp. 216–38.
P. Zwick, 1983.

6

THE PARTY

In the communist world, the communist party is usually the single most important and powerful political agency. This has led some commentators to refer to communist countries as 'partocracies'—i.e., societies ruled by the party (see e.g. Avtorkhanov 1967, esp. 369–76). Similarly, one commentator has argued that the party, in Eastern Europe at least, is 'polymorphic'—i.e., it assumes many shapes, and even 'the state' is in fact just one of the forms the party adopts (T. Lowit, cited in White, Gardner, and Schöpflin 1982, p. 148). I would argue that this somewhat overstates the case; for one thing, other institutions do occasionally usurp the party (e.g. the army in Poland from December 1981), or else vie with it for power (e.g. in Stalin's Russia); further details on party–state relations can be found in the next chapter. Moreover, the statement could not be applied to the communist world as a whole, since, for instance, Cuba had a Marxist–Leninist leadership before a communist party had been properly established, and indeed the party played a minor role there until the 1970s. A similar situation pertains in Ethiopia, where there was no properly constituted communist party until September 1984. But these are the exceptions, and it is generally true that one cannot begin to understand politics in the communist world without a solid grasp of the nature, structure, and role of the party.

In this chapter, we shall examine the structures and functions of the party, and then the question of the party as an élite. Before doing any of these things, however, we need to consider what the communist parties actually call themselves.

NAMES OF PARTIES

Many communist parties do not in fact feature the word 'communist' in their titles; this is usually for historical reasons. In nearly all such cases, what we now consider to be the communist party actually started as a merger between the former communist party and some other—usually socialist—party. Thus the Socialist Unity Party in the GDR was formed by merging the Communist Party and the Socialist Party in April 1946; the Korean Workers' Party was formed by merging the Communist Party and the New People's Party in 1946; and the Hungarian Workers' Party was formed by merging the Hungarian Communist Party and the Social Democratic Party in June 1948. This point about mergers is not always the sole explanation however. Although the 'united' part of the Polish communist party's official title—the Polish

United Workers' Party—does refer to the merging of the communists with the Polish Socialist Party in December 1948, there had already been a Polish Workers Party since January 1942. There are a number of reasons why it was called this rather than the Polish Communist Party; most of these relate to Polish attitudes towards the Soviet Union. First, there had been a Polish Communist Party in the inter-war years which had been suppressed by Comintern (see chapter 14) in 1938 for being 'contaminated by hostile elements' (Leslie 1980, p. 228), and most of its leaders had been executed in the Soviet purges of the 1930s. It would thus have been unwise to remind people of this fact by using the same name when a new organization was established, and indeed the Polish Workers' Party stressed that it was not a member of Comintern. Second, Poland had just been partitioned by Russia yet again, as a result of the Nazi–Soviet Pact of 1939. Third, most Poles were Catholics, and were therefore hostile to what they saw as the atheism of Soviet communism. Finally, the Polish Communist Party had had a reputation for constant infighting. The leaders of the party now wanted to create a new image, of a party which was not torn by inner strife and which could work with other political parties to defeat the Nazis and create a democratic state.

Although most of the parties which adopted these hybrid and/or 'new image' titles have retained them, not all have. Thus the Romanian Communist Party merged with the Social Democratic Party in February 1948, forming a new Romanian Workers' Party; soon after the present leader, Ceausescu, took power in 1965, it was decided to rename the party the Romanian Communist Party.

In one case—Yugoslavia—the party is not even called a party, but a league. The decision to change from the original name—Communist Party of Yugoslavia—to the new name was adopted by the 6th Congress in 1952, ostensibly on the grounds that the party should now become the main arbiter in the political system, rather than be directly involved in the day-to-day running of it. Expressed another way, the party was to become more clearly distinguished from the state (see Singleton 1976, p. 134), and was not to claim to be either totally infallible or devoid of internal disagreements. To no small extent, however, the change can also be seen as a symbol of Yugoslavia's rejection of the Soviet system and as an attempt to create its own distinctive brand of socialism. After all, the traditional conception of a communist party was and is based on the ideas of Lenin: 'league', on the other hand, was a term more associated with Marx—although, at the time of the change of name, the Yugoslavs did not explicitly recognize Marx's influence (Rusinow 1977, p. 75).

STRUCTURE OF THE PARTY

In line with Lenin's conception of the party, all communist parties (including those not in power—even the allegedly more liberal 'Eurocommunist' ones) are organised on the basis of *democratic centralism*. According to an official East German definition, democratic centralism consists of the following:

(1) Leadership of the party by an elected centre.

(2) Periodic elections of all leading party organs from bottom to top.

(3) Collective leadership.

(4) Periodic accountability of the party organs to the organizations that elected them.

(5) Strict party discipline and subordination of the minority to the majority.

(6) The absolute binding force of the decisions of the higher organs for the lower organs and the members.

(7) Active participation of the party members in their organizations through the implementation of decisions, utilizing criticism and self-criticism as a guaranteed method of eliminating shortcomings and for improving work. (Ehlert *et al.* 1973, p. 197.)

The first part of the definition of democratic centralism contained in the 1982 statute of the CCP reveals even more clearly the basically centralist direction—

Individual party members are subordinate to the party organization, the minority is subordinate to the majority, the lower party organizations are subordinate to the higher party organizations, and all the constituent organizations and members of the party are subordinate to the National Congress and the Central Committee of the party.

A very important point that needs to be noted about this concept is that the *noun* is centralism, the *adjective* democratic. In other words, the basic tenet is centralism, not democracy. The implications of this for discussion and decision-making are surely clear enough.

Let us now consider how this organizational principle is reflected in the actual structure of communist parties. In most cases, communist parties are structured in a pyramid fashion according to the territorial-production principle. This is to say that the lowest levels of the party—usually called *primary* or *base* party organizations—are most commonly organized in work-places (factories, schools, hospitals, farms, etc.), whilst all higher levels are organized on a geographical basis—the village, the town, the province, the region, etc. In larger base level organizations, members meet to elect a committee, which in turn elects a bureau and a secretariat; in smaller base organizations, the members themselves elect the bureau and/or secretariat (or just a secretary, if the unit is *very* small), since there will be no committee. The base organization also elects representatives to the next level of the party—probably the village or town conference. These representatives in turn vote representatives to the next tier—perhaps a regional or district conference—and their own committee, which elects a bureau and secretariat. And so it goes on; the same basic pattern is repeated at all levels up to and including the centre.

There, the conference is called a Congress, the committee becomes the Central Committee, and the bureau generally becomes the Politburo or Presidium. This whole structure is probably most readily grasped from figure (i).

From fig. (i), the essential similarity of each tier of the party becomes obvious. The indirect nature of elections should also be clear; thus the ordinary rank-and-file members have no direct say in who is elected to the Party Congress, let alone the Central Committee or Politburo.

As might be expected given the large number of countries considered in this study, the 'typical' pattern is not adhered to in every detail by every communist party; a number of peculiarities will emerge in the next few sections. Nevertheless, if the logic of the diagram is grasped, then the essentials of party structure will have been understood. Let us now look in a little more detail at each of the central organs.

(i) The Party Congress

In every communist party, the Congress is formally the highest organ; in none of them does it in practice play a very important role. The Congress is usually scheduled to meet every four or five years—though in practice, this rule can be rudely broken. For instance, there was a gap of ten years between the 5th and 6th Congresses of the Korean Workers' Party, of eleven years between the end of the 8th and the start of the 9th Congress of the CCP, of some thirteen years between the 18th and the 19th Congresses of the CPSU, and no less than sixteen years between the 3rd and 4th Congresses of the Vietnamese communist party. Increasingly, however, the meetings of Congresses are being regularized.

The Congress brings together elected representatives from all over the country. It includes top politicians, representatives of key functional and territorial groups, and always has a smattering of shop-floor workers and farmhands to make it look like a genuine organ of people's power. It is a relatively large body; the 26th Congress of the CPSU (1981) had 4,994 delegates, the 12th CCP Congress (1982) had 1,690 delegates, the 2nd Congress of the Cuban Communist Party (1980) had 1,772 delegates and there were over 600 delegates to the 4th Congress of the Mozambican communist party (Frelimo).

The Congress usually meets for approximately a week at a time and has a number of items on the agenda. It will listen to and be expected to approve a report—usually from the General Secretary—of the ways the country and party have developed in recent years, and how they are going to develop in the next four or five years. There will be some discussion—usually very formalized—of this report, and its recommendations will then be codified into Congress resolutions and adopted. In other words, the general policies for short- and sometimes long-term development have to be ratified by Congress.

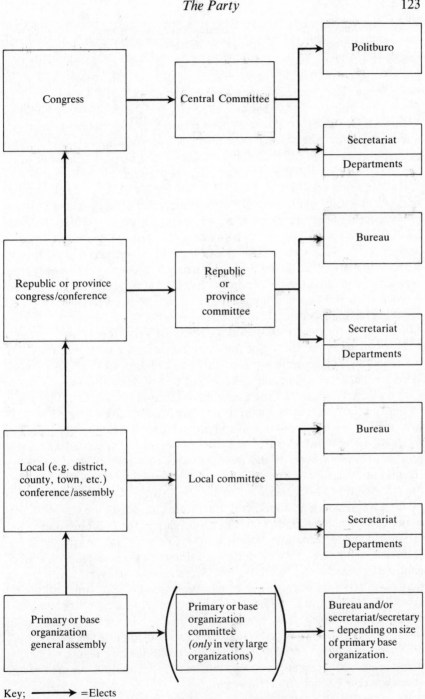

Key; ——→ =Elects

Fig. (i) A Typical Communist Party Structure (simplified)

Another item on the agenda is the selection of a number of smaller, central organs—most notably the Central Committee.

Sometimes, the Congress will also change the rules of the party (usually known as the party statute) and might even ratify for publication a new party programme. The programme is a lengthy but often vague document which sets out the long-term goals for both the party and the country as a whole.

Apart from these formal tasks, attendance at the Congress can be seen as a reward for many long-serving party loyalists—people who will never make it to the inner sanctums of power, but whom senior party officials want to re-pay in some way for all the devoted service they have given to the party.

Although the majority of Congresses are rather dull, with speech after speech all basically agreeing with and/or elaborating upon the General Secretary's speech, not all are. Sometimes, a General Secretary will himself decide to drop a bombshell. The best-known example of this is Khrushchev's 'Secret Speech' at the 20th Congress of the CPSU, held in February 1956. In this, Khrushchev openly criticized Stalin, referring to the many errors his predecessor had committed. At other times, the General Secretary may be pressed to go further than he had intended and/or the floor speeches will be outspoken, even highly critical. Two good examples of this are the extraordinary 14th Congress of the Czechoslovak Communist Party (CPCS) on 22 August 1968 (often known as the Vysocany Congress, after the suburb of Prague in which it was held) and the extraordinary 9th Congress of the Polish United Workers' Party (PUWP) in July 1981. At the first of these, there was condemnation of the Warsaw Pact invasion, and many more conservative members of the Central Committee—who at one time could have expected to have been re-elected with no discussion and no problem—found that they had lost their seats. The Polish Congress was no less interesting. It started with a dispute between the bulk of the delegates and the then General Secretary (Kania) and his supporters about the way in which the elections to the key organs should be conducted. Eventually, the Central Committee was elected by the Congress in a genuinely free vote, following which the Central Committee considered the candidates for membership of the Politburo and Secretariat and made recommendations to the Congress; previously, both the Congress and the Central Committee had simply been presented with a list of names prepared by the Politburo and Secretariat themselves, which meant that these last two bodies were in practice essentially self-appointing and appointed the Central Committee (this practice is typical of most communist parties, but contravenes the regulations as laid down in the party statutes). In short, Congress delegates (as well as the Central Committee members) were now asserting their formal right to select the leadership. Kania was eventually re-elected General Secretary; but he only secured 68 per cent of the votes, whereas 100 per cent is the norm.

As a concluding point to our analysis of the party Congress, it should be noted that Lenin himself originally believed in much more regular and lively

Congresses, at which real differences of opinion could be heard. In many ways, he started the rot himself when he banned factionalism (i.e., the formation of and conflict between subgroupings within the party) at the 10th Congress of the Soviet communist party in 1921. Nevertheless, the process was greatly accelerated by Stalin, whose interpretation of the role of the Congress is probably closer to the practice in most communist states than is Lenin's original conception.

(ii) The Party Conference

As mentioned earlier, the meetings of party representatives at the local levels are often called party conferences. Somewhat confusingly, there are also central conferences in some communist states. Yet again, the trend for this was set by the Soviets, who held a number of conferences—as well as congresses—in the early years after the Bolshevik revolution.

The Soviets have long since ceased holding central party conferences; the last was in 1941. But in many other states—among them China, Korea, Laos, Poland, and Romania—conferences are both allowed for in the party statute and held in practice. In Bulgaria, for instance, conferences were held in 1950, 1974, and 1978.

The conferences are not central organs as such—which is one reason why they do not appear in figure (i) above—but rather special meetings held at any time the leadership feels it is necessary to discuss with a wider audience a particularly serious problem or series of problems that has to be resolved. In contrast to the situation at party Congresses, elections are not normally held at conferences.

(iii) The Central Committee

In every party statute, the Central Committee is the highest party organ between meetings of the Congress. It is normally convened twice or three times each year—though, as with the Congress, this pattern can be severely disrupted. Meetings usually last only a day or two, although—as usual—there have been major exceptions to this. Thus a meeting of the Vietnamese Central Committee held in late 1981 lasted twenty five days. Central Committees are much smaller than Congresses; they range in size from less than thirty (27 in the 1976 Beninois Central Committee) to several hundred (348 in the 1982 Chinese Central Committee).

Full meetings of the Central Committee are called plenary sessions or plena. At these plena, there is often a dominant theme—such as the state of the economy, foreign relations, educational reform—though this is not invariably the case. One pattern that is emerging in the Soviet Union and Eastern Europe, and which may well develop elsewhere as time passes, is that the last plenum of the year is devoted principally to a consideration of the one-year economic plan for the following year.

The usual pattern for a plenum is for a Politburo member to deliver a report, following which there is a discussion. At the end, a conclusion will be drawn—again, usually by a member of the Politburo, often the General Secretary himself. It is usually at Central Committee plena that promotions to or demotions from the Politburo and/or Secretariat are announced, since such moves need the ratification of the Central Committee. Although these changes are usually mere formalities, this is not invariably the case, and the Central Committee can sometimes act as an arbiter between warring factions in the Politburo. One example of this is the June 1981 plenum of the PUWP's Central Committee, at which the members were required to express their confidence (or lack of it) in each individual member of the Politburo. But the best-known instance of the Central Committee being called upon to act as an arbiter is a Soviet one. In 1957, a group of Politburo members—subsequently to become known as the 'anti-party group'—tried to remove Khrushchev from his position of First Secretary. Although there was a majority against Khrushchev in the Politburo, the leader was not prepared to step down. He argued—correctly—that Politburo members cannot force other members to resign unless this has the formal support of the Central Committee. He then rapidly and selectively convened the Central Committee—many members of which were new and owed their position to Khrushchev—which formally gave its backing not to the 'anti-party group' but to Khrushchev. It should be noted in parentheses, however, that senior Soviet politicians learnt their lesson from this episode; when the majority of Politburo members again wished to remove Khrushchev in 1964, they made sure that the Central Committee was convened and supported their actions before the leader himself could try to counter them. Such precedents will no doubt have taught both ordinary Politburo members and General Secretaries in other communist states much about the mechanics of maintaining or taking power by use of the Central Committee!

(iv) The Secretariat

One of the most powerful institutions in the communist world is the Central Committee Secretariat. Despite this, the importance of the Secretariat is not always sufficiently strongly emphasized in textbooks. Although there have been occasions on which the Secretariat has been down-graded and even abolished (in China between 1966 and February 1980, for instance), it is surely of great symbolic importance that in most communist states the person considered to be the number one politician is head of the Secretariat, the General (in some countries First—the two titles are for our purposes synonymous)

Secretary; exceptions to this include China, where the top party post was for a long time the party chairmanship, and Angola, where there is a party President.

The Secretariat is formally elected by the Central Committee, although in practice the Politburo—and especially the General Secretary—has most say in these elections. The number of secretaries is usually low—never exceeding twenty—but below them is a large and complex system of *departments*.

The Secretariat is responsible for providing information to the Politburo (some of the members of which, of course, will be the senior secretaries themselves); for checking that party policy is carried out, both by party functionaries at lower levels and central state organs such as the ministries; and for personnel policies, which is considered in more detail in the section on party functions. Although the Politburo would appear to take all the final decisions on major issues, it is clear that the Secretariat plays a key role in this process at times. This is suggested by a reference the former General Secretary of the CPSU, Chernenko, made in a Soviet book published in 1980, in which it is revealed (p. 367) that the draft of the 1977 Soviet constitution was discussed twice by the Central Committee, five times by the Politburo, and no less than eighteen times by the Secretariat. Whilst the fact that the Politburo discussed it several times indicates that that body did not play merely a rubber-stamping role in the decision-making process, it does seem likely that the Secretariat was highly influential in the overall process. For all these reasons, McAuley's definition of the Soviet Secretariat—'the party's civil service' (1977, p. 200)—is an apt one. Most of the Secretariats about which we have any information seem to meet on average once a week.

As in any political system, so in the communist world knowledge is a source of power. Thus the Secretariat, as provider of much of the detailed information used by the senior decision-makers for reaching their decisions, has a tremendous capacity for influencing the outcome of discussions; anyone wishing to see how this general point applies in liberal democracies should read the sections of the Crossman diaries concerned with the relationship between a cabinet minister and his or her civil servants.

(v) *The Politburo*

In practice, the topmost organ of power in almost all communist states is the Political Buro, usually abbreviated to 'Politburo' though sometimes called the Presidium (as in Czechoslovakia and Yugoslavia). Despite this, the Politburo is also one of the most mysterious bodies, for the simple reason that communist parties generally provide very little publicly available information on it. Indeed, if one compares the amount of detail given in party statutes on each of the central organs, one soon discovers a very interesting correlation—namely that the more important the body, the less detail given on it, and vice versa. Although Western scholars have gleaned a reasonably detailed picture of some of the formal aspects of various Politburos over the years—how many members they have, how frequently and when they meet— our understanding of the way they work, how much real debate goes on in them, etc. is still very limited given their importance. It is a telling comment that, in contrast to the US Presidency or the British Cabinet—on both of which there is sufficient literature for year-long specialized courses on them to be taught in British universities—there has not yet appeared either a comparative or a really comprehensive single-country, book-length analysis of the Politburo (though see Löwenhardt 1982 on the CPSU Politburo and Lieberthal 1978 on the CCP's). But all is not lost. Some hard information, and even more intelligent and knowledgeable speculation, can provide us with a partial picture of this body.

The Politburo is usually composed of anything between five and up to fifty members, with fifteen to thirty being the norm. As in the Central Committee, there are full and candidate (or 'alternate') members; the salient difference between these is that full members have voting rights, candidate members do not. We have details of the frequency of meetings from only a few communist states. Thus the Soviet Politburo normally meets once a week, on Thursdays. If the week's business is not completed, then a second session may be held on the following Tuesday. This second meeting does not appear to be needed very often, since it was revealed at the 26th Congress of the CPSU that the Politburo had met 236 times between the 25th and the 26th Congresses; this was over a five-year period, which means that there was an average of slightly less than one meeting a week. Following Andropov's promotion to the post of General Secretary in November 1982, the Soviet press began to publish brief reports on Politburo meetings, a practice which continued under Chernenko and Gorbachev; indeed, even Politburo speeches are now occasionally published (see *Pravda*, 16 Nov. 1984, pp. 1–2). This reporting of meetings was not a total innovation in the communist world—Bulgaria and Romania, for instance, had already been publishing brief reports of some Politburo meetings—but it was a new departure for the Soviets, and could mean that the reporting of politics at the top, including on the frequency of Politburo meetings, in many of the Soviet-oriented communist states could now become more open. At present, we know that the Polish Politburo meets, in normal times, about as often as its Soviet counterpart, as does the Standing Committee (see below) of the Chinese Politburo. The Hungarian Politburo meets only half as frequently, however (i.e., once a fortnight on average), whilst the Vietnamese Politburo convenes—to quote a Vietnamese academic I questioned on this—'rather infrequently'.

Although the composition of Politburos varies from case to case, there is a clear pattern that the Politburo becomes increasingly representative of key functional and territorially based groups over time; in the early years, the body is more likely to be made up of people who played a major role in the revolution than of representatives of key groups. Another salient feature of Politburos is that they are even more overwhelmingly male-dominated than other central party organs (for further details see Jancar, 1978, esp. pp. 88–105).

We can only speculate on the way the Politburo functions. It seems highly possible that when one leader is very dominant in the political system—a Castro, Ceausescu, or King Il Sung—then there will be less real discussion than in a communist state where the power and status of the General Secretary relative to other Politburo members is less. Indeed, certain inferences about the power of the Politburo members *vis-à-vis* the leader can be drawn from various formal and informal variations that exist in the actual structures and operating patterns of the Politburos. Thus we know that Stalin rarely consulted the whole of the Politburo (see Khrushchev 1970). Rather, he would selectively convoke perhaps four, five, or six members of the Politburo—the actual combination of members kept changing—if he wanted to discuss a particular policy. In doing so, he minimized the chances of the Politburo ganging up on him and removing him. Nowadays, in contrast, there appears to be some real division of labour within the Soviet Politburo; further details on all this can be found in chapter eight.

The structure and operation of the Chinese Politburo is somewhat different. As the Politburo grew (from 11 in 1949 to 23 in 1980), an inner core was created, the Standing Committee of the Politburo. At present, this has six members, and it seems reasonable to infer that it meets more frequently and has more power within the Politburo than the rest of the membership of the Politburo.

A somewhat similar arrangement is to be found in Romania, Korea, and elsewhere, although Romania does not have a body actually called the Politburo. There, the top body is called the Political Executive Committee; this 47-member body has an inner core, the 15-member Permanent Bureau. Of the two bodies, the Permanent Bureau is much closer to the Politburo of other countries, a fact borne out by a brief analysis of its history. The Romanians had a Politburo until 1965, when it was replaced by a Standing Presidium. This Presidium was in turn replaced by the Permanent Bureau in 1974. One important way in which this Permanent Bureau differs from other Politburos is that it is elected not by the Central Committee, but by the Political Executive Committee (i.e., by a much smaller body). The most feasible explanation for this is that Ceausescu feels he can keep a tighter control over a smaller body than a larger one, whilst at the same time he can argue that the Permanent Bureau is subject to outside control in the sense of being elected by another body rather than appointing itself. However, it should be noted that the Political Executive Committee can only choose the members of the Permanent Bureau from among its own ranks.

Details on the Politburo's relationship with the Secretariat in communist countries are, like most aspects of politics at the top, rarely revealed by communists themselves. However, we saw above that the Secretariat does play an important role in some key areas of Soviet decision-making. Moreover, a recent statement by Chinese Secretary, Wang Renzhong, tells us two things about the relationship in China. First, he revealed that real differences of opinion sometimes arise between the Secretariat and the Politburo; this fits poorly with the monolithic image of communist parties sometimes presented by Western commentators. Second, he also made it clear that when such differences arise, the Politburo invariably overrides the Secretariat (1982, p. 17). Hopefully, we will one day have a much more detailed picture of the relationship between Politburo and Secretariat in the communist world generally. For now, we can only assume that the Soviet and Chinese relationships are fairly typical of many communist states.

ROLE AND FUNCTIONS OF THE PARTY

The role of the party in all communist states is to act as a vanguard, to lead and direct the rest of society. This is very much a Leninist conception of the party, and is one of the key features distinguishing communist parties from socialist ones. While the Yugoslavs did modify this general role-description in the 1950s—the party was only to guide, rather than lead—even Yugoslavia has now reinstated the leading role concept. Although this leading role is now generally accepted, it was some time before it was as overtly recognized as it is now. For instance, the concept did not appear in any of the early constitutions of the older communist states. The new trend—to state explicitly in the constitution that the party leads the state and society—was started by Czechoslovakia in 1960, and has subsequently been followed by the majority of countries.

But how is this overall role translated into specific functions? So far, we have tended to consider only the functions of specific agencies within the party relative to each other; we now need to look more generally at the party's role in society.

For most purposes, the party (together with the state) can be said to have three general tasks:
—defence of the system
—allocation and adjudication
—socialist and ultimately communist construction
These general tasks are a little abstract, however, so that for analytical purposes it is preferable to talk of five principal party functions:
(1) Goal-setting
(2) Goal-attainment
(3) Socialization
(4) Recruitment
(5) Linkage
Let us consider each of these in turn.

Goal-setting

In any society, goals have to be specified—even if these are essentially oriented towards maintenance of the status quo. In societies which are formally committed to a long-term goal—the building of communism—the party must not only tell the citizens where they are going but also what route they are to take. It sets the general guidelines—the overall direction and balance of the economy for the next five or ten years, the level of education that the population can look forward to, etc.; the state machinery is then supposed to work out the details of these policies, and is responsible for their implementation.

The impetus for such general goal-setting normally comes from the Politburo, and is then approved by the Central Committee and, every so often, the Congress.

Goal-attainment

As mentioned above, the elaboration of detail of policies, and their implementation, is in theory the task of the state machinery rather than of the party. In fact, there have often been criticisms of party officials—either from party leaders and/or from the press—for trying to substitute themselves for state officials. Only very rarely—for instance during the Chinese Great Leap Forward of 1958–60 and to some extent in Khrushchev's Russia—has the party been encouraged directly to implement policy itself. Although Romania now seems to have decided that it makes little sense to try to separate party and state too clearly, most other communist countries have in recent years been trying to distinguish party and state more visibly. In theory, then, the party is in most cases not meant to be directly involved in implementing policy. Rather, it is to exercise *kontrol*—a Russian word meaning 'checking on' or 'supervision'. This *kontrol* function is one of the party's most important. If things go wrong—factories are under-fulfilling their plans, building programmes fall behind schedule, etc.—it is ultimately up to the party to find out why and take measures to see that the problems are overcome. It is in this sense that the party is responsible for goal attainment.

Socialization

Political socialization was considered in detail in chapter 4, so that all that needs to be done here is to include the function in our list.

Recruitment

The recruitment function of parties can be divided into two main areas:
   (*a*) recruitment into the party itself;
   (*b*) recruitment to all important posts in society.

Most parties in the liberal democracies are remarkably easy to join; indeed, in some states of the USA, one can call oneself a member of a party simply by registering to vote in a presidential primary. Membership of communist parties is not nearly so easy—those already in it ensure this.

The normal method for joining the party is that an adult wishing to join will submit an application to the primary or base party organization where he or she works; this request to join must be accompanied by recommendations from, typically, three members of the party, of at least two to five years' standing, who have known the applicant for some time (at least a year). Sometimes, for younger applicants, one or more of the referees can be committee members of the communist youth league rather than party members. If the base organization approves the application, it then goes to the committee at the next level of the party for ratification. If this committee ratifies the base organization's recommendation, the applicant is admitted to the party on payment of his/her membership dues. In most communist states, the new member becomes a candidate or probationary member; this means he or she does not have voting rights nor can he or she be elected to any party organs. Some states (e.g. Bulgaria, Hungary, Romania, and Yugoslavia) grant full membership right from the moment of joining. But in most, the candidate is carefully assessed during this probationary period (usually one year) to see that he or she is paying dues in full and on time, attending meetings regularly, not indulging in excessive consumption of alcohol or other anti-social behaviour. Assuming the candidate passes muster, full membership will be ratified by the base organization and the committee at the next level.

One interesting variant of the above method of joining is the Cuban. Until 1975, candidates for membership of the party there had to be nominated by the 'workers' assemblies' (i.e., by workforces in a given production unit). The idea behind this was that it would ensure that party members were really the best workers, and seen as such by their work-peers (i.e., it would help to give party members legitimacy amongst their fellow Cubans). However, this system was modified in 1975, so that new individuals can apply for membership themselves in a similar fashion to that used in other parties, as described above. One reason for this is that individual Cubans who were not directly part of a 'workers' assembly' (e.g. housewives) had no proper channels for joining the party. In addition to individual applications, the Cuban Central Committee, its Secretariat, or even the Politburo itself can invite individuals to join the party, though even these pople must normally be approved by the base organization and the next highest party level (except where 'security considerations' preclude this). Given these modifications to membership rules, the way has been opened for the more self-selective recruitment typical of other communist parties, although it should be noted that at least two commentators believed that the original method (i.e., where workers choose from amongst themselves who can join the party) was not being de-emphasized through to the end of the 1970s (Casal and Perez-Stable 1981, p. 85).

It should not be assumed that, once in the party, a member automatically stays in for life. Communist parties have periodic 'exchanges of party cards', whereby the behaviour of party members is scrutinized, and less than satisfactory members will either not be issued with a new card or else might be reduced to candidate status for a trial period. In 1980, 30,000 members of the Romanian Communist Party were not issued with new cards following such an exchange. More dramatically, the 1970 exchange of party cards in Czechoslovakia was clearly used as an excuse for ridding the party of anyone considered to be over-sympathetic to the ideas of the 'Prague Spring'; nearly half a million members (almost a third of the total membership) were not readmitted to the CPCS. In addition to such exchanges of cards, particularly unsatisfactory members can be reprimanded at any time by their local base organization; if this body recommends expulsion, it will normally be ratified by higher levels.

One of the most interesting questions is whether the members of the communist parties are essentially self-motivated or—rather like more exclusive organizations in the West, such as the Masonic lodges— are approached and asked to join. Unfortunately, this is not a question that can be answered with any degree of exactitude. However, there is much evidence to suggest that many members are approached. Two pointers to this are the statements of party leaders about the social composition of parties, and the analyses that have been undertaken of 'party saturation' among different occupational groups; these two points need some elaboration.

At the end of the 1960s and into the early 1970s, most of the East European countries, Cuba, China, and some other states were publicly calling for a 'reproletarianization' of the communist parties. In the aftermath of the events in Czechoslovakia in 1968–9 (and, in the Chinese case, the GPCR) many leaderships seem to have wanted to show that they were not becoming too remote from the mass of the workers, the people supposedly constituting the most important group in society. At the same time, the party leaderships seemed anxious to counter what they perceived to be the growing political power of the technical intelligentsia—engineers, managers, etc.—over party functionaries. Therefore, by pursuing—or at least appearing to pursue—a policy of encouraging more blue-collar workers to join the party, they were killing two birds with one stone. In fact, some communist parties—e.g. the Czechoslovak—were much more successful in implementing this policy than others (e.g. the Bulgarian and Cuban); but the point is that such a policy implies that some individuals are more likely to be encouraged to join than others.

The second point—'party saturation'—is connected to the first, but has never been stated as policy quite as overtly. In other words, it has long been understood in many communist states (certainly the older and more stable ones) that some occupations imply party membership. As a general guideline, the further up the social hierarchy one is (in terms of income and status), the more likely it is that one's job implies party membership. In the USSR, for example, over 99 per cent of industrial managers are members of the CPSU—a far higher proportion than blue-collar workers. Although the party is supposed to be composed of the 'best' members of society, the term 'best' is subjective, and we saw in the discussion of reproletarianization that leaderships sometimes become sensitive to the charge that the party is becoming too élitist and detached from the group it claims to favour.

There is, of course, some contradiction between points one and two. This can partially be explained away in terms of changing emphases in recruitment policy. However, it should also be borne in mind that the reproletarianization policy was not particularly vigorously pursued in some countries, which suggests that it was more for show than a serious intention. Moreover, many parties base their social composition figures on the social standing of a person *at the time of joining the party*, not current occupation. Hence, if many 'proletarians' who joined the party in the 1970s were actually top workers who were likely to be promoted to managerial posts at some future stage (the GDR calls such people 'black employees'), then one's image of the 'reproletarianization' might be rather different. One final point is that some parties now admit quite openly that they are not primarily interested in recruiting ordinary workers. This seems to be borne out by the following statement on the CCP's current recruitment policy:

Since the fall of the Gang of Four [i.e., since the late 1970s—LTH] the emphasis of recruitment policy has been on cadres, intellectuals and those who possess technical skills . . . One of the most frequently mentioned problems is the lack of trained cadres in the Party. . . . (Saich 1981, p. 114.)

—a policy that is reminiscent of some earlier periods in the CCP's history, such as the early 1960s.

The recruitment function is not restricted to new party members. At least as important is the role the party plays in ensuring that every key position in society is held by a person basically acceptable to the party. We have now reached the point at which we can discuss what can be called the party's 'trump-card'—the *nomenklatura* system.

Unfortunately, the point made earlier about central party organs—that the more important they are, the less is revealed about them by communist states—also applies to some extent to the functions of the party. In other words, there has been remarkably little official documentation published on the *nomenklatura* system. Nevertheless, a mixture of hard evidence, circumstantial evidence, and hearsay provides a reasonably detailed picture of the system. Since there appears to be more information on the Soviet and Polish systems than on others, we shall concentrate on them; until more evidence becomes available, we can only surmise that they are fairly typical of other countries.

The basis of the Soviet system is quite simple. At every level of the party, the committee has two lists of posts and the people filling them. The first—

the so-called *basic nomenklatura*—is a list of the posts considered to be the most important ones at that level; these include key party posts, but also state posts, posts in the media, education, etc. In one of the very rare instances of the Soviets publishing anything on the *nomenklatura* system, the following general information and details on the Novosibirsk town committee's lists were given:

The communist party directs the selection and placing of leading cadres not only of party, but also of state and social organizations. Party organs determine the *nomenklatura* of posts, the filling of which is confirmed by the party committee. Such a system permits the avoidance of subjectivism, and provides the correct use of employees. The party committee itself decides which posts to include in the *nomenklatura*. For instance, nearly 800 posts are on the *nomenklatura* of Novosibirsk town committee. Included on it are the secretaries and heads of departments of the committees at the next level down of the party; chairpersons and deputy chairpersons of the executive committees of the soviets [councils—see next chapter]; the directors, chief engineers and secretaries of party committees of large industrial enterprises and building-sites; the heads of higher educational institutions; and other employees with a high level of responsibility (*Lektsii* . . . , 1971, p. 329.)

It is the task of the party to ensure that these key posts are filled by the most suitable candidates. The meaning of 'suitability' will vary according to the particular job. Thus it seems clear that anyone who wants to be a party secretary or the editor of a party newspaper is going to have to be extremely reliable and loyal politically—and, of course, a member of the party. A chief engineer in a factory, or a chief agronomist on a collective farm, in contrast, is going to have to be above all a technical specialist; although the town committee would prefer him or her to be a party member, this is not absolutely necessary. In other words, not everyone who is appointed to a post on the basic *nomenklatura* is a member of the party. In Chinese terminology, the selectors must look for the optimal blend between 'redness' (i.e., political reliability) and 'expertness', according to the particular job; one suspects that the latter quality becomes increasingly important as communist states become more industrialized and technologically advanced.

The second list held by the committee at each level is the so-called 'registration and supervision *nomenklatura*'. This, too, is a list of posts and the people filling them—but the posts are of a lower status than those included on the basic *nomenklatura*. Although a full official list of these does not appear to be available, it seems reasonable to infer that included on it will be deputy-headteachers, deputy-editors, directors of smaller factories, etc. In this case, the party is not so directly involved in the appointing of people to the posts. But departments of a party committee will have to be informed of and agree to appointments made to these posts; in doing so, it has a good idea of the up-and-coming people, from amongst whom it will one day want to pick appointees to its basic *nomenklatura*. This comes out clearly in the source cited earlier:

Apart from the basic *nomenklatura* there is also the registration and supervision *nomenklatura*; on it are included posts, the filling of which is agreed with departments of the party committee. The registration and supervision *nomenklatura* is a kind of reserve of cadres for promotion to leading posts. (Ibid., p. 329.)

The Soviet list cited above only refers to a town-level *nomenklatura*. It is thus of interest to look at what is alleged to be an official *nomenklatura* guideline (i.e., a list of what posts should be included) for all levels, which was smuggled out of Poland (see pp. 138–9). It is unfortunately not clear whether this covers both kinds of *nomenklatura*, or only the basic one (assuming, of course, that the Poles make the same kind of distinction as the Soviets— which might not be the case).

The *nomenklatura* lists include details of the people whom the party has singled out as leaders or potential leaders. In the language of communism, such people are called 'cadres', who can be defined as people holding leadership positions of one kind or another in any party, state, economic, or social organization. But where does the process of cadre identification and selection start? At the primary/base level, the party is required to keep its eyes and ears open for new talent, people who rise above the crowd in terms both of their political qualities and their work. In doing so, the party may well be guided by reports from the communist youth leagues and/or schools, telling it that comrade x was a particularly worthy student who may well turn out to be the kind of superior individual the party is looking for to fill *nomenklatura* posts. Moreover, any person appointed to one of the posts on the registration and supervision *nomenklatura* is formally entered on to the party's list of cadres and investigated by the party. Once an individual is promoted to a post in the basic *nomenklatura*, he or she may well come under the scrutiny of a higher-level party organ. This is because many posts in the Soviet Union are on the basic *nomenklatura* of one party committee and the registration and supervision *nomenklatura* of another. For instance, a factory director may simultaneously be on the basic *nomenklatura* of a town party committee and the registration and supervision *nomenklatura* of a regional party committee (Hough 1969, p. 116).

According to the very limited evidence available, the size of *nomenklaturas* (both kinds) seems to vary quite considerably. Thus, according to figures provided by White, Gardner, and Schöpflin (1982 pp. 135 and 148), the USSR's *nomenklatura* currently covers approximately three million posts; the Polish *nomenklatura* increased from approximately 100,000 posts in the early 1970s to about 180,000 in 1980; Czechoslovakia's *nomenklatura* at the end of the 1970s was approximately 100,000; whereas Hungary's was perhaps as low as 10,000 (there is very little information on the Chinese *nomenklatura* system—see Schurmann 1968, pp. 162–3 and 186). Even allowing for differences in population, it becomes clear that, for example, the Polish party was by 1980 feeling a greater need for control of posts than was Hungary—

although, of course, even this control was not absolute, since it could not prevent the eruption of major societal tensions.

A relatively large amount of space has been devoted to the *nomenklatura* system which, it will be recalled, has been called the party's 'trump-card'. The importance of the system is not merely a Western perception, but is acknowledged by communists themselves. Stalin claimed that 'cadres decide everything', and the Soviet passage quoted from above makes the importance of this system abundantly clear—'. . . Work with cadres—this is the key aspect of the party's work, its chief task' (p. 330).

Thus the party is involved in the filling of all important posts in society; indeed, this applies to elected posts as well as to appointed posts, since the choice of candidates in communist elections has in the final analysis to be approved by the communist party.

To many Westerners, this system appears unacceptably controlled. In many ways it is, since individuals who 'blot their copy-book' will find it much more difficult to have a second chance in such a monopolistic system than in a more pluralistic, less centralized system. On the other hand, two points should not be overlooked. The first is that the stress on individual privacy—and on individual rights more generally—is much more a tradition of Western societies than of most of the societies considered in this book; many of the latter were oriented towards the collective, and the rights of the collective over those of the individual, even before the communists came to power than is sometimes acknowledged. Second, the system must be seen in a realistic perspective. As the division of labour within societies deepens, so the notion that the party has absolute power over appointments becomes an ever less tenable proposition. There is nothing to suggest that there is an infinite supply of nuclear physicists or computer programmers, for instance. In other words, the party is limited to some extent in its recruitment work, and it would be naïve to suppose that all the people who fill posts on the *nomenklatura* have identical political or technical views. This does not require detailed elaboration. Suffice it to point out that political differences often emerge at the very top of communist party structures, in the Politburo; if this elaborate and rigorous process of selection cannot produce harmony and unity in such a relatively small body, then it would seem absurd to suppose that it will in a system covering in some cases millions of posts. Indeed, one party committee's interpretation of a suitable individual may differ from another's, which adds more variety and colour to the initially grey and uniform picture of the *nomenklatura* system. Thus the party's recruitment system gives it enormous powers—more than any other organization—but not absolute power.

Linkage

The fifth and final function is linkage. The totalitarian image of a party

NOMENKLATURA OF THE POLISH UNITED WORKERS PARTY

Source: *Labour Focus on Eastern Europe*, vol. iv, nos. 4–6, p. 55.

List of posts falling under the nomenklatura of the Party Central Committee, regional committees and district (town and neighbourhood) committees

A. *Nomenklatura posts of the Party Central Committee*

I. Party functions: personnel politically responsible for Party bodies and publications; secretaries of Party committees

1. Heads of Central Committee departments, their deputies, the inspectors, main instructors, and political reporters of the Central Committee.
2. The first secretaries and zonal secretaries of regional Party committees.
3. The rector, vice-rectors, institute (group) directors, and scientific workers at the Academy of Social Sciences.
4. The chief and deputy editors of *Trybuna Ludu*, *Nowe Drogi*, *Życie Partii*, and *Chłopska Droga*.
5. The directors of the Bydgoszcz and Katowice Party schools.
6. The first secretaries of Party committees in the ministries and central state administration.

II. High state functions: the administration of state and economy

1. The president and vice-presidents of the Diet of the People's Republic of Poland.
2. The president and deputy-presidents, the secretary and members of the Council of State.
3. The president and vice-presidents of the Council of Ministers.
4. The president and vice-presidents of the Supreme Chamber of Control.
5. The president and vice-presidents of the Council of Ministers Planning Commission.
6. Ministers, vice-ministers, and directors-general.
7. Chairmen of the presidia of regional people's councils.
8. Ambassadors and plenipotentiaries, embassy and legation advisors, consuls-general.
9. The presidents of the Supreme Court and regional tribunals.
10. The public prosecutor of the People's Republic of Poland, his deputies, and regional public prosecutors.
11. The president and vice-presidents of the Polish Academy of Sciences, the administrative secretary and his assistants.
12. The head of the Diet Chancellory and the Council of State Chancellory.
13. The commander-in-chief of the police force, and his deputy.
14. Regional commanders, their first deputies charged with state security, the first deputies charged with the police.
15. The chairman and vice-chairmen of the National Raw Materials Board.
16. The chairman of the National Mining Board.
17. The presidents and vice-presidents of the State Administration.
18. The president and vice-presidents of the National Bank of Poland, and the directors of central banks.
19. Delegates of the government of the People's Republic of Poland.
20. The chairmen and vice-chairmen of the central, regional, and sectional boards of the Co-operative Unions.
21. Members of the secretariat of artisan organizations.
22. The directors-general of nationwide industrial unions and of the central management and offices of domestic trade.
23. The regional directors-general of the Polish Railways and of National Telecommunications.
24. The directors-general of the regional unions of Public Works.
25. The commander-in-chief of the Fire Brigade.
26. The director-general of public institutions (Lot, Orbis, Wars, etc.).
27. The deputy to the permanent Comecon representative of the People's Republic of Poland, the deputy to the Comecon secretary-general nominated by the People's Republic of Poland.
28. Directors of the various Polish offices abroad: the departmental heads of the Comecon Secretariat and UN Secretariat nominated by the People's Republic of Poland.

III. Functions in social organizations

1. The president, vice-president and secretary of the Polish Committee of the National Unity Front.
2. The presidents, vice-presidents, and secretaries of the Central Trade Union Council; the presidents, vice-presidents, and secretaries of the Trade Union Federations.
3. The president, secretary-general, and secretaries of the Association of Fighters for Freedom and Democracy.
4. The presidents, vice-presidents, and secretaries of the youth organizations.
5. The president of the National Women's Council, and the president of the League of Women.
6. The presidents and secretaries-general of the Higher Technical Organization and the Polish Economic Society.
7. The chairman of the Higher Council of Co-operatives.
8. The president, *ex officio* vice-presidents, and secretaries of the Polish–Soviet Friendship Association.
9. The president and secretary-general of the Society of Polish Journalists.
10. The president and secretary-general of the Union of Polish Writers.
11. The president and secretary-general of the Association of Polish Jurists.
12. The president of the Higher Lawyers Council.
13. The president and vice-presidents of the Union of Agricultural Circles.
14. The president and vice-presidents of the Union of Agricultural Producer Co-operatives.
15. Full-time presidents, vice-presidents, and secretaries of social and cultural associations.
16. The president of the National Defence League.
17. The president and vice-presidents of the Volunteer Firemens Association.

IV. Functions in the Army

1. The head and deputy-head of the General Staff.
2. The head and deputy-heads of the political directorate of the Army.
3. The inspector-general of Home Defence.
4. The inspector-general of (military) instruction.
5. The Senior Commissariat officer.
6. The inspector-general of the Engineering Corps.
7. The commanders of military regions and their assistants responsible for political matters.
8. Commanders of the Armed Forces and their deputies responsible for political matters in: (*a*) the air force, (*b*) the navy, (*c*) aerial defence, and (*d*) military defence of the frontiers.
9. The head of the Internal Military Corps.
10. The head of the personnel department at the Ministry of National Defence.
11. The head of the (Military) Instruction Inspectorate.
12. The head of the Home Defence Inspectorate.
13. The head of the directorate of the Second General Staff.
14. Persons proposed for the rank of general.

V. Functions in the mass media, publishing houses, and scientific institutions

1. The chairman, deputies, and directors-general of the Radio and Television Board.
2. The chairman, vice-chairmen, and directors of the 'RSW–Prasa' Board.
3. The chief and deputy editors and the directors of: the Polish Press Agency, the Polish 'Interpress' Agency, the Central Photographic Agency, Artistic and Graphic Publications, the Society for Documentary Film Production, and Polish Film News.
4. The director of the publishing co-operative *Książka i Wiedza*.

NOMENKLATURA OF THE POLISH UNITED WORKERS PARTY

continued

. The chief editors of *Ideologia i Poliyka* and *Zagadnienia i Materialy*.

. The directors and chief editors of scientific and literary publishing houses.

. The chief editors of national circulation dailies, weeklies, and monthlies.

. The directors-general of Polish Radio and Television.

. The directors of specialized national institutes of scientific research.

. The directors of the foreign broadcasting service of the Polish Academy of Sciences.

. Departmental secretaries and assistant secretaries, as well as directors of the Bureau of the Polish Academy of Sciences.

Nomenklatura posts of regional Party committees

Party functions: personnel politically responsible for arty bodies and publications; the secretaries of Party ommittees

. The first secretary and the secretaries of various sections of the district, town, and neighbourhood committees.

. Personnel politically responsible for the regional Party committees.

. The chief and deputy editors and the secretaries of the regional committee press.

. The first secretaries of Party committees in higher education; the first secretary of Party committees in the presidia of regional people's councils; the first secretary in the regional police directorate.

. Full-time secretaries of Party committees in enterprises and combines falling under the regional committee nomenklatura, including all those placed under Central Committee management.

Functions in government bodies, regional administration, and the economic apparatus

. The vice-chairmen and secretaries of the presidia of regional people's councils.

. The chairman of the Regional Economic Planning Commission, and regional school inspectors.

. Heads of departments of the regional people's council presidia (as estimated by the executive committees of the regional Party committee).

. Deputy regional commanders (except the first deputies responsible for State Security and for the Police).

. Heads of departments of the regional police force (as estimated by the executive committees of the regional Party committee).

. The vice-presidents of regional tribunals.

. Deputy regional public prosecutors.

. The directors of regional penal institutions.

. The chairmen of (regional) delegations to the Supreme Chamber of Control, the regional inspectors of PIH and OKR.

. The presidium chairmen of district, town, and neighbourhood people's councils.

. District police commanders and their deputies responsible for State Security.

. The presidents of district tribunals.

. District public prosecutors.

. The presidents of regional administrative tribunals for social insurance.

. The chairmen of regional arbitration commissions.

. The directors (presidents) of regional economic organizations, industry unions, regional organs, and regionally administered cooperatives and enterprises (except the chief director of the regional union of Public Works).

. Regional branch directors of the National Bank of Poland, the Agricultural Bank, the Polish Savings Bank, the State Insurance House, and the Social Insurance Department.

18. The directors-general of key combines and enterprises (and deputy directors if so decided by the regional Party committee).

19. Regional commanders of the Fire Brigade.

20. Directors of medical establishments and of the social services.

21. Leaders of the regional delegations of the General Office for the Supervision of Press, Publications, and Public Performances.

III. Functions in social organizations

1. The presidents, vice-presidents, and secretaries of regional committees of the National Front.

2. The presidents, vice-presidents, and secretaries of the regional trade-union councils.

3. The presidents, vice-presidents, and secretaries of the regional leaderships of youth organizations.

4. The president and (full-time) members of the regional leadership of the Association of Fighters for Freedom and Democracy.

5. The chairmen, vice-chairmen, and secretaries of the regional leadership of the Union of Agricultural Circles.

6. The presidents of the regional womens council and of the regional League of Women leadership.

7. The presidents, vice-presidents, and secretaries of the regional leadership of the Trade Union Federations.

8. The regional presidents and full-time leaders of artistic, social, cultural, sporting, and paramilitary associations', as well as professional bodies such as the Higher Technical Organization and the Association of Polish Jurists.

IV. Functions in the mass media, publishing houses, and scientific institutions

1. The chief and deputy directors of Polish Radio broadcasting stations and of Polish Television centres.

2. The chief and deputy editors of the main local dailies and cultural and social magazines.

3. The chief and deputy editors of regional press and book publishing houses.

4. The rectors and vice-rectors of higher education establishments.

5. Theatre managers and artistic directors.

6. The directors of (regional) museums.

C. *Nomenklatura posts of district (town and neighbourhood) Party committees*

I. Functions in the Party: personnel politically responsible for Party bodies; secretaries of Party committees

1. Those politically responsible for district (town and neighbourhood) committees.

2. The first secretaries of town committees (not integrated into a district) and of rural communes.

3. The (full-time) secretaries of Party base committees and organizations in enterprises coming under the district nomenklatura.

II. Functions in government bodies, local administration and the economic apparatus

1. The vice-presidents and secretaries of the presidia of district, town, and neighbourhood people's councils.

2. The chairman of the District Economic Planning Commission, and the departmental heads of the district people's council presidia (as estimated by the executive committee of the district Party committee).

3. Primary and secondary school inspectors, the heads of secondary technical colleges.

4. The vice-presidents of district tribunals.

5. Deputy district public prosecutors.

sending orders downwards to an atomized society had some validity in Stalin's Russia, at times in Mao's China, more recently in Pol Pot's Kampuchea, and elsewhere. But as time passes, this picture tends to change. In the early days of a regime, the party has to consolidate, and to mobilize the population for major change; in many cases, the country is still led at this stage by the man who guided the revolutionary takeover, and who can inspire many to work hard and not think too much about political participation. But as the years pass, the regime slows down and changes. Although much has been achieved in terms of economic development, growth rates slacken and people begin to wonder when all their previous endeavour will really pay off to them as consumers, etc. The revolutionary leader may by now be in his grave. The regime becomes increasingly aware that it must introduce tangible changes if it is to retain the support of those who earlier basically favoured it, and to obtain the support of younger generations and people still hostile to it. In such a situation, it makes sense for the party to operate more in a bi- than in its former essentially uni-directional manner. It still needs to convey slogans from the leadership to the people, explain policies, encourage workers to produce more. But it also often demonstrates a greater willingness to listen to the people than before. It may feel a need to discover what is making citizens dissatisfied—which can have a threefold spin-off for its legitimacy. First, the mere act of listening to people who want to complain or make suggestions for improvement will tend to make those people more favourably disposed towards the regime. Second, if it acts on these complaints and suggestions, then the regime might find its problem areas become less difficult. Third, as a result of points one and two, people might work harder, which leads to higher output, better satisfaction of consumer demands, etc.

The above is, of course, an idealized picture. But reality can and often does work along these lines. The point certainly seems to have been recognized by many of the older communist states of Europe. Many of these now encourage the primary organizations to listen more closely not only to their members, but to all the employees in a factory or on a farm or in a school. Some communist parties even see themselves as having to integrate the interests of different groups in society (e.g. Hungary and Yugoslavia, see chapter nine)—a very overt statement that the party must respond to subdivisions in society, as well as guide society. An even more tangible manifestation of this is the establishment of centres for the testing of public opinion—centres which are in most cases very much under party control. Of course, some parties have claimed they have always performed such a linkage function. The CCP's 'mass-line' approach to policy-making was based on the notion that the masses' views should at least be heard before a final decision on policy was made; once made, the masses should be involved in implementing it. In this particular case, however, the evidence nowadays suggests that the masses' involvement was often only in implementation, rarely in discussion. Moreover, we must be wary of being over-deterministic about this; Czechoslovakia and

Poland are two good examples of the fact that communist parties sometimes follow zig-zag patterns in terms of their policies on linkage.

In concluding this section on party functions, a point that has so far been implied but not overtly stated is that the *balance* of functions will vary according to time and place. For instance, a relatively new communist regime will seek to nationalize industry and collectivize agriculture; once this has been done, the party will be more concerned with seeing that the economy functions smoothly than with making major changes in the ownership pattern in society. Similarly, the party's role in foreign policy will be much more complex and involved in a superpower like the Soviet Union than it is in a small, essentially inward-looking country like Albania, North Korea, or Benin.

THE PARTY AS AN ÉLITE

It is often argued in the West that the communist parties—as the key element in communist states—are highly élitist. Thus Bottomore writes—

The political system of Communist countries seems to me to approach the pure type of a 'power elite', that is, a group which, having come to power with the support or acquiescence of particular classes in the population, maintains itself in power chiefly by virtue of being an organised minority confronting the unorganised majority... (1966, p. 42).

It has already been shown that communist parties are in most cases comparatively difficult to join; in this sense, they are exclusive organizations. Now let us consider other ways in which communist parties might be considered élitist. Clearly, it will be necessary to consider whether or not they constitute 'power élites'; but let us begin by briefly considering them as social and economic élites.

The CCP is the world's largest political party, having over forty million members. In this sense, it could be called a 'mass party'. On the other hand, the population of the PRC is over one billion, so that only approximately 4 per cent of Chinese are members of the communist party. Even allowing for the fact that only adults can join the party, so that the figure of forty million should more properly be taken as a percentage only of the adult population (producing a figure of over 7 per cent), party members are still only a tiny minority of the population. Viewed from this perspective, the term 'mass' seems rather misleading; élitist might be more appropriate. In fact, membership of the communist party in China is low in comparison with many other countries. Since many of these do not provide a breakdown of the population into adults and minors, we are forced to look at party membership as a percentage of the total population; this fact should be borne in mind when considering the following statistics—the percentage of citizens in the communist party—since it means that they are invariably lower than would be the case if party membership were expressed as a percentage only of the adult population.

Table 1. *Membership of the Party as a Percentage of the Total Population*

1	Korea (North)	16.0
2	Romania	14.6
3	Germany (East)	13.1
4	Czechoslovakia	10.4
5	Bulgaria	9.7
6	Yugoslavia	9.6
7	Hungary	8.0
8	Soviet Union	6.7
9	Poland	6.3
10	Albania Cuba	4.4
12	Mongolia	4.2
13	China	4.0
14	Vietnam	3.0
15	Laos	1.0
16	Yemen (South)	0.9
17	Mozambique	0.8
18	Afghanistan	0.6
19	Angola Congo	0.4
21	Kampuchea	0.01
22	Ethiopia	0.006
23	Benin	0.005

Source: Calculated by the author on the basis of figures in R. F. Staar, 'Checklist of Communist Parties in 1983', *Problems of Communism*, March–April 1984, pp. 43–51 (however, the figure for Mozambique is based on Isaacman 1983, p. 124).

From Table 1, it is clear that the front-runners in the communist world (i.e., the countries with the highest proportion of party members) are the DPRK, Romania, and the GDR. At the other end of the spectrum are most of the communist parties of South-East Asia and Africa. Three points can be made about the table. First, party members are a small proportion of the total population even in those countries at the top of the league. Second, it is not the case that communist states with formal multi-party systems (see chapter 9) therefore have a lower proportion of citizens in the communist party. Finally, there is a definite tendency for the more economically developed countries to have higher proportions of members, although this general pattern is not without important exceptions (compare North Korea and Hungary, for instance). Research shows that membership usually rises the longer the communists are in power, though purges and/or mass unrest can temporarily reverse the general trend.

There are other ways in which the party constitutes a social élite. Thus the average educational level of party members is invariably much higher than the average level in the population at large. Moreover, empirical analyses have shown that the social composition of communist parties does not accurately reflect the overall social composition of society; white-collar workers, managers, etc. are heavily over-represented in comparison with blue-collar workers, peasants, etc. (see appendix and White, Gardner and Schöpflin p. 141). In terms of gender discrimination, communist parties are still male-dominated, especially in the higher party organs (see again Jancar 1978, pp. 88–105).

There are strong grounds for supposing that the party membership as a whole constitutes an *economic* élite, in the sense that the average income of party members is well above that of the mean average for the population as a whole. Precise details on this cannot be given, largely because of the relative paucity of material on income distribution in the communist world. But from what we know of distribution in the Soviet Union and the PRC, for instance (i.e., from two major states which have for most of their histories approached communism from rather different angles), it is clear that this point about mean average income is valid; it can be noted parenthetically that income distribution is becoming increasingly unequal in China at present. But income alone is only one way in which the party membership constitutes an economic (and social) élite. Another very important one is that many party members enjoy a number of privileges which are either not available at all, or else less readily available to ordinary citizens. These privileges include access to special shops, exclusive hospitals, and in some cases the right to travel abroad and to obtain hard currency.

Most importantly of all, the party membership can be seen as a political— or power—élite. It has, for instance, far more say in the making of important decisions than any other group. This is partially a function of the *nomenklatura* system discussed above, which means that the key decision-making bodies at all levels of society are either staffed by party members and/or very much under party influence. As Raymond Aron, discussing the USSR, has written, 'Politicians, trade union leaders, public officials, generals and managers all belong to one party . . . (quoted in Haralambos 1980, p. 113).

The domination is also a function of the self-recruiting nature of communist parties, and of the fact that both the electoral and socialization systems are very much under party control. Finally, there are special 'party groups' in virtually all important decision-making bodies in most communist countries. These groups often hold additional meetings separate from the rest of the body, and frequently come to the full meeting with a party line that has already been worked out and agreed upon by the group members. In practice, it will be difficult for the rest of the decision-making body to override the wishes of the party group.

In the analysis of élitism to this point, we have talked of 'the party' or 'the party membership', almost as if thousands or even millions of people in a given country constitute a homogeneous grouping. Of course, to suppose that they do—or even that this is possible—would be highly ingenuous. All party members wear other hats—as workers, farmers, husbands, mothers, consumers, etc. Some members have been in the party for years and are serving on one or more important committees, whilst others are newcomers, who enjoy considerably less power and status. These differences of role and status both within the party and in society at large can lead to conflicts of interest between party members and even within one individual. This makes 'the party' a very much more complex—and interesting—phenomenon than a formal and aggregated analysis of its role and position can ever reveal. Unfortunately, the very complexity and constantly changing nature of the phenomenon makes it difficult to analyse in any depth. However, there is one division within the party that can and must be identified in any consideration of the party as an élite—that between the full-time professional party functionaries (usually called the *apparatchiki*, a Russian word meaning members of the apparatus) and the rest of the membership, the rank-and-file. The *apparatchiki* occupy all the key posts within the party—they staff the secretariats, and all committees and bureaux (certainly above the primary level) will include several of these functionaries. They are paid by the party, usually make a career in the party organization (though often switching from party apparatus to state apparatus as they climb the social and political ladder), and will as a group have vastly more influence in the party than the ordinary party members.

By now, the attentive reader will probably be expecting the next point—namely, that the very importance of the *apparatchiki* means we do not have very much information on them. Analysts of Soviet politics disagree on the exact scale of the Soviet party apparatus, although most accept that a figure of between 100,000 and 200,000 is about right; this makes the Soviet party apparatus a very tiny group relative to the membership as a whole. The Chinese revealed in 1984 that there were approximately nine million party cadres; but this figure will include part-time party officials (e.g. members of party committees who have full-time jobs outside the party), so that the membership of the apparatus proper will be considerably smaller than this.

The *apparatchiki* enjoy the greatest privileges of all the party members—certainly in terms of status, access to scarce commodities, etc. Moreover, they have far more knowledge about society at large, the party in particular, and other specific briefs—industry, education, or whatever—at the level at which they work, and, as pointed out earlier, knowledge is power. Above all, perhaps, the available evidence strongly suggests that it is the *apparatchiki* who dominate the process whereby the *nomenklatura* posts are filled. Although the *nomenklatura* lists formally belong to the committee at each level, the secretariat actually holds them, administers them—and in all probability has most say in who occupies the *nomenklatura* posts.

Thus when we are talking of the party as an élite, it makes sense to distinguish between the ordinary members—many of whom will not be so noticeably better off either economically or in terms of status than the people they work with—and the *apparatchiki*. The latter are really the élite within the élite in a political, social, and economic sense, and some rank-and-file party members will identify more closely with the non-party people around them than with the *apparatchiki*. For these reasons, to describe communist political systems as 'partocracies' is potentially misleading; if jargon is to be used at all, then 'apparatocracies' would be a more accurate term (though, admittedly, a dreadful word, and still subject to the caveats made at the beginning of this chapter).

Some attempts have been made in a number of communist countries to reduce the gap that can and does arise between ordinary party members, those who sit on party committees and the party *apparatchiki*. One of the most visible ways in which this has been done is through the introduction of a system of rotation of office-holders within the party. In 1961 for instance, Khrushchev introduced a compulsory turnover system into the committees of the CPSU. The principle was that between one quarter and one half of members should be replaced every time a new committee was elected. The system had an escape clause, however, which allowed for 'outstanding comrades' to be exempted from this requirement. Had it been properly implemented, this system could in one real sense have rendered the committees even more élitist in that, whilst the majority of members could not expect to stay for more than a few years, a small core could stay on indefinitely. However, the Soviets abandoned the principle in 1966. Albania has had a form of rotation principle since 1966, whilst both Romania and Yugoslavia also have one (for a brief analysis of the Romanian system see Shafir 1981, p. 610). It would, however, be grossly unfair not to point out that Yugoslavia has taken the rotation principle far more seriously than either Albania or Romania, particularly since Tito's death (for details on its implementation at the highest level see chapter 8). But even in Yugoslavia, analyses over time of the top party and state offices reveal that whilst most individuals do not occupy the same senior post nowadays for more than a year or two, they may well be moving from one top position to another rather than making way completely at the top.

Two concluding remarks about the party as an élite need to be made. The first is that it should never be forgotten that—in Leninism, if not clearly in Marxism—the party is *supposed* to be an élite of sorts; the whole notion of a 'vanguard' is based on such an assumption. This said, the original conception of such a vanguard was of a group of the politically most enlightened people, not of a social and economic élite, or even of a power élite in the somewhat pejorative sense this term is commonly used in the West. Certainly, communists themselves sometimes reveal extreme sensitivity to charges that they constitute an élite. For instance, a recent article in the principal Romanian newspaper criticized Western attempts to apply élite theories to communist societies, and argued that the cadres in such societies are leading on behalf of the masses rather than in their own interests (Zapirtan, cited in *BBC Summary of World Broadcasts*, 1982, p. EE/7201/i). Readers can judge for themselves how convincing such an argument is.

Second, in addition to the various kinds of concrete evidence available on the party and its *apparatchiki* as an élite, surveys cited in the last chapter suggest that there is probably widespread feeling in many communist countries that the party is unjustifiably élitist (for further evidence, see e.g. Pravda 1979, *passim* and esp. 214, 227, 233).

SUMMARY AND CONCLUSIONS

It has been argued that the party is in the vast majority of communist countries the most powerful political agency, and that its power derives from a number of sources. These include its organizational principles, its role in the selection and election of personnel to all leading posts in society, its involvement in the socialization process, the fact that it does not have to compete against other parties (see chapters 7 and 9), etc. It has further been argued that the party membership constitutes an élite, although one needs to distinguish, at the very least, between the *apparatchiki* and the ordinary members of the party; the former have considerably more power and prestige than the latter. The party is not a homogeneous group; differences of opinion and interest can and do arise within it—frequently on relatively minor issues, sometimes on major issues.

Communist parties try to incorporate methods into their work style that will ensure that individual party members who do not match up to expectations are brought into line. For example, the need for criticism and self-criticism is frequently emphasized. In practice, however, the party is often less successful at self-monitoring than it should be, either by its own criteria or those inherent in most conceptions of democracy. Thus 'bureaucratism' in the work of the party apparatus is frequently criticized by senior politicians, but the success rate in combatting this problem is in most cases low. In short, there is insufficient answerability in communist parties, and when careerism, corruption, and bureaucratism become salient aspects of a given party, there is precious little external pressure that can be brought to bear in order to rectify the situation. This shortage of inbuilt safeguards is a major weakness of Leninist organizational principles.

Many of the points made above will be more fully appreciated once the role and nature of the state has been analysed; this is done in the next chapter. As with chapters 4 and 5, so chapters 6 and 7 should be read together if the reader is to obtain a reasonably comprehensive picture of the major political organs in the communist world.

Basic further reading

G. Bertsch, 1982, ch. 4.
S. Fischer-Galati (ed.), 1979.
M. Gehlen, 1969.
R. Hill and P. Frank, 1983.
L. Holmes (ed.), 1981b.

W. Simons and S. White (eds.), 1984.
M. Waller, 1981.
S. White, J. Gardner, and G. Schöpflin, 1982, ch. 4.

7

THE STATE AND ELECTIONS

In this chapter, we begin by considering the concept of the state, and communist (both classical and contemporary) views on it. This is followed by an examination of the structure and functions of the various parts of the state in communist countries, and the nature and role of elections and other forms of popular control. The discussion then focuses on the relationship between the communist party and the state, following which some concluding remarks are made.

WHAT IS THE STATE?

Many Western analysts, both Marxist and non-Marxist, would broadly accept as a starting-point Weber's definition of a state as that organization which can 'successfully claim the monopoly of the legitimate use of physical force within a given territory' (quoted in Miliband 1973, p. 47). The notion of force or coercion has to be understood here in a broad sense, to include not only the police and other overtly coercive bodies, but also those state organs which make, implement, and adjudicate the rules binding on society, viz. legislatures, executives, state administrations (bureaucracy), and the judiciary. Even if one accepts that the state's primary role is to keep order in the broad sense just defined, the modern state takes upon itself many additional tasks. Most notably, in both liberal democracies and communist countries the state increasingly assumes responsibility for the welfare of citizens. It provides health services, educational facilities, social security systems, etc., so that many of the bodies listed above are designed to assist as well as to coerce citizens. The state also assumes responsibility for protecting citizens from outside forces, so that another part of the state machinery is the military. Finally, the state is meant to represent the best interests of society; if officers of the state are to coerce citizens, they should seek the authority to do so. In the modern world, as the 'divine right of kings' and other somewhat antiquated forms of legitimacy disappear, an increasing number of states accept that the most important source is public approval, and one of the ways to acquire this is to make leading state officials accountable—particularly by presenting them to the public for acceptance or rejection in elections. As shall be shown, communists tend to have a rather different view of elections from that held by most Westerners, and they certainly organize them in a different way. Nevertheless, they do generally accept that elections help to legitimate the rulers, and they see elections as an important link between the state and society.

CLASSICAL MARXIST THEORIES OF THE STATE

For the classic theoreticians of Marxism, the contemporary Western (capitalist) state was an instrument through which the ruling class oppressed the rest of society. But the nature of the state *following* a socialist revolution was not examined in much detail by either Marx or Engels or Lenin. Certainly, all three accepted that the new order would need to protect itself from the remnants of the old; not everyone would welcome the moves to take the means of production into social ownership, for example. For this reason, they accepted that there would be a need for a new type of state—the 'revolutionary dictatorship of the proletariat'—in the immediate aftermath of a revolution. But Marx only referred explicitly to this concept on a few occasions, and never gave any details on it—how long it would last, how it would be structured, etc. Nor is it clear what would follow this. Nevertheless, Marx did stipulate that there would no longer be a separate state 'caste' standing above the rest of society as at present; the state would gradually be subordinated to society, and hence no longer superior to it. Marx also wrote that there were several aspects of the Paris Commune (1871) which he felt would be features of a state following a socialist revolution. These features included full revocability of elected deputies, the payment of such deputies at workers' wages, and the replacement of the professional army by a people's militia. But here we encounter another of the ambiguities in Marx. Not only did he say that the Commune's policies were not socialist, but it is also unclear as to whether or not those aspects of the Commune which did appeal to him were to be a feature merely of socialism or also of communism proper since, as was pointed out in chapter one, he tended to use these terms interchangeably. Some would want to argue that Marx must have meant the lower stage of communism (socialism), since both money relations and government would disappear at the higher stage. But the latter point in particular is open to question. Marx (and Lenin) argued that the state always has a class nature, from which one might infer that in a classless society (i.e., communism), there will be no state. Engels certainly gives this impression, when he argued in 'Anti-Dühring' (1878) that the state will 'wither away' in the transition from the lower to the higher stage of communism. Marx, too, referred at various points to the 'abolition' of the State, and Lenin believed that 'Marx's and Engels' views on the state and its withering away were completely identical' (in Tucker 1975, p. 370). Despite this, Marx did argue that in a classless (communist) society, 'governmental functions will be transformed into simple administrative functions' (cited in McLellan 1981, p. 22), which Engels later reworded as 'the government of persons is replaced by the administration of things and the direction of the process of production' (ibid., p. 24). Although one might infer that 'government' here implies some coercion of individuals by the state, whereas 'administration' is more of a technical exercise, neither Marx nor Engels ever properly explained the difference, and the longer one thinks about the two terms, the hazier the distinction between them becomes. This ambiguity is only compounded by the point Marx made in a discussion with the anarchist Bakunin in 1875: '. . . when class rule has disappeared, there will no longer be any state *in the present political sense of the word*' (McLellan 1980, p. 222; emphasis added). In other words, and contrary to what many people believe, Marx did not necessarily argue that the state would disappear under communism proper; his views are unclear. What he seems to be arguing is that an oppressive state would disappear, and ordinary citizens would have the minimal state machinery necessary for the smooth running of society very much under their control. Unfortunately, there is a logical contradiction in this, in that one of the salient features of communism for Marx is that people would no longer be alienated from each other, their labour process, and the world around them—including the state. But if *A* gives decision-making powers to *B*—for instance, to make decisions about the 'process of production'—then *A* is in fact externalizing his or her own powers, and there is still some form of alienation. Revocability might be seen by some as the answer to this problem, but in practice, as various communist states have discovered, it is extremely difficult to optimalize a recall system.

Was Lenin able to clear up these theoretical problems? In short, the answer is no. He too saw the state as an organ used by the ruling class to keep other classes suppressed, and argued that in the early stages after a socialist revolution, the vestiges of the bourgeois state machinery would have to continue to exist. However, the state machinery would now be under the control of the proletariat or its party, so that his conception of the 'dictatorship of the proletariat' is in essence an old state system run by the new and temporary ruling class. Lenin argued that the division of labour would essentially disappear in the higher stage of communism, and that all the major functions of the state (such as accounting) would be performed by ordinary citizens in a rota system. He does not seem to have accepted that the growing complexity of both society and technology might render this extremely difficult.

Towards the end of his life, Lenin began to acknowledge that the 'new' Soviet state was becoming increasingly autonomous, not only of society and the proletariat but even of the communist party itself. However, he had no satisfactory solution to this problem; indeed classical Marxist theory does not provide a satisfactory solution to the problem of how to overcome the potential tendency of a new socialist state to develop its own identity and rise above society, alienating ordinary citizens in much the same way as previous states have done.

CONTEMPORARY COMMUNIST THEORIES OF THE STATE

From the above analysis, it becomes clear that the continued existence of some form of state machinery in communist countries *is* compatible with a particular interpretation of what little Marx, Engels, and Lenin wrote on the nature of the state following a socialist revolution. No communist leadership yet claims to have achieved communism proper (the 'higher stage'), and the need for a temporary dictatorship of the proletariat—whatever that might mean—was accepted by the classical theoreticians of Marxism.

This said, there are some theoretical problems with the justification of the state put forward by many communist leaderships in power. The most obvious one relates to the class analysis communists apply to their own societies. It was argued above that Marx, Engels, and Lenin accepted that the state always represents the interests of a particular class; this pertains to the dictatorship of the proletariat as much as it does to the bourgeois state, the salient difference being that the latter serves the interest of a minority whereas the former represents a majority. Although, as has been argued, Marx may have envisaged some sort of state existing under communism, it was most certainly to have been quite different from any hitherto existing state, whilst Engels wrote that 'When at last it [the state] becomes the real representative of the whole of society it renders itself unnecessary' (cited in Holmes 1981c, p. 258). Lenin also accepted the notion that the state invariably has a class dimension. No communist regime yet claims to have created a classless society; it is argued instead that classes in the communist countries are 'non-antagonistic'. But if class relationships are no longer antagonistic it becomes unclear why a state, formed after a revolutionary takeover to suppress hostile elements in society, is still needed and indeed lives on in an essentially similar format. The illogicality of this position comes out most obviously in the Soviet notion of a 'state of the whole people', a concept which is spreading in the Soviet-oriented communist states. The concept arose in the early 1960s, when Khrushchev claimed that the state no longer needed to represent just the proletariat and the poor peasantry, but could act on behalf of all groups/ classes in society. Such a concept was explicitly rejected by Lenin as an illogicality; he argued that the *whole* transitional period between capitalism and communism must be the 'dictatorship of the proletariat'. The Chinese certainly accepted the Leninist argument, and have been highly critical of the Soviets for their new conception of the socialist state (although their own concept of a 'people's democratic dictatorship' is also not without problems). Not only is the Soviet state to represent the whole people—it is actually to be strengthened, something which is, for once, unquestionably out of line with classical Marxist theories. Indeed, most communist states nowadays claim that the state must be strengthened in the foreseeable future and only one, Mongolia, has included in the constitution a requirement that the state will eventually disappear.

What kind of argument is put forward to justify the continued existence of the state? There are several components to this, broadly corresponding to the major wings of the state. First, communists have to cope with hostility both at home and abroad. Stalin's view that the class struggle would actually intensify under socialism is not widely held in the contemporary communist world; but even when it is claimed that antagonistic class differences have been overcome, it is argued that there are people in the country working for hostile foreign powers, which necessitates a security police force. Then there is the need for a military force to protect the citizens from foreign attack. Marx's notion of an armed people's militia is not rejected in principle, and some countries have made serious attempts to set one up; but it is argued that modern methods of warfare are so sophisticated that a highly trained, full-time and professional military is also necessary. Nowadays, the external threat is not necessarily only from capitalist states; as Kampuchea, Vietnam and other countries have learnt, it may well be from another communist state. The external threat is not merely military, however. As communication media have become more sophisticated, it has become easier for non-communist countries to beam both anti-communist propaganda and uncensored information into communist countries (what can be called 'ideological encirclement'), which can be used as an argument for an ideological apparatus, as well as giving further justification for the security police.

In addition to *defending the system*, the state is responsible, under guidance from the party, for *allocating resources* in society and *adjudicating conflicts* that might arise from such allocation. Since communists believe more in conscious, directed allocation than in the 'invisible hand' of the market, and since one needs to be at the centre of a system to see what is available in society and whose needs are greatest, a centralized state bureaucracy (e.g. planners) can be justified. Moreover, a judiciary is needed to ensure socialist justice when a conflict over resource allocation arises.

A third general function of the state (again in conjunction with the party) is to build a better society. This involves making decisions for change, and ensuring that the consciousness of the masses is raised and altered to prepare them for the higher stage of communism. These tasks, too, are used to justify the continued existence of the state. All this is encapsulated in the following statement by Peng Zhen, a member of the Chinese Politburo, when he introduced the new Chinese Constitution for approval by the National People's Congress in November 1982: 'With the establishment of the socialist system . . . the task of our state power . . . became primarily to safeguard the socialist system and to guide and organise socialist construction.' (*Beijing Review*, 13 December, 1982, p. 12.)

In one sense, it could be argued that a functional analysis of the state reveals that the classical Marxist–Leninist notion of the state as an instrument of class rule is too simplistic, and that there are times when the state clearly stands above classes. For instance, not *all* laws—even in a 'bourgeois' state—are class-based (e.g. traffic regulations, laws on rape, murder, theft of public property, etc.). Given this, it becomes clearer why the state might continue to exist even when fundamental class antagonisms have, allegedly, disappeared. A Marxist may well retort that the classical theoreticians did realize this, as revealed in the references to government being replaced by administration. But even if one were to accept that there can be administration without political power—which, as was argued above, is highly questionable—there are some developments in the theory and practice of the state in communist countries which are out of line with Marxist predictions and even the long-term aspirations of Lenin as revealed in *The State and Revolution*. The most important point here is the *concentration* of power in the hands of the state (and party) apparatuses. There are four interrelated factors which can be and are sometimes used to justify this. First, there is the argument that the *scale* of modern societies precludes direct participation in important decision-making, so that the masses have to elect representatives to make decisions on their behalf; these representatives in turn appoint the administrators. The second is that tasks are constantly becoming more specialized, that the division of labour—in communist societies as well as liberal-democratic—makes it difficult for people to participate in numerous different aspects of the work of the state. Present developments are thus quite different from Lenin's predictions. Third, most communists believe in attempting to reach communism as rapidly and efficiently as possible, which can also be used as an argument for restricting mass involvement in the running of the state (i.e., because the more discussion there is of problems, the longer decisions can be delayed). Finally, Lenin's notion of a political vanguard can be used to justify the concentration of powers into the hands of a party and state élite. These arguments are not incontrovertible (for further details, and an analysis of the flaws in these propositions, see Holmes 1981c, pp. 265–72), but they do help to explain how communists justify both the continued existence of the state and even its strengthening, and why the structure of the state bears a marked resemblance to that in liberal democracies.

THE STRUCTURE AND FUNCTIONS OF THE COMMUNIST STATE

As with the party, so state structures in the communist world are generally based on the principle of democratic centralism. Thus, according to article three of the 1977 Soviet Constitution:

The Soviet state is organized and functions on the principles of democratic centralism, namely the electiveness of all bodies of state authority from the lowest to the highest, their accountability to the people, and the obligation of lower bodies to observe the decisions of the higher ones. Democratic centralism combines central leadership with local initiative and creative activity and with the responsibility of each state body and official for the work entrusted to them.

Despite this common framework, the detailed application of the principles of democratic centralism, as reflected in the organization of the state, differs from country to country; all that can be done here is to highlight the main patterns.

One of the most basic divisions is between the federal and the unitary communist states. The former (i.e., the USSR, Yugoslavia, and Czechoslovakia) are subdivided into republics, each of which has a set of institutions—a constitution, a legislative assembly, an executive, ministries, etc.—which are structurally similar to the central (federal) bodies, but which obviously have less power and jurisdiction than their central counterparts. The democratic centralism principle means that republics can only pass laws or administer themselves in a way that is compatible with federal legislation. Because of this, and the fact that all state organs are formally subordinate to the (centralized) party, the republics have in general considerably less autonomy in the communist states than do their counterparts in Western federal states. The exception to this is Yugoslavia, where the republics' powers relative to the central authorities are comparatively high. The republics in the federal communist states are supposed to have equal rights, and in theory are conjoined voluntarily. In practice, however, any attempt at secession in any of these countries would be met by strong resistance from the centre. Contrary to what might be expected, it is not simply larger states that are federal, and smaller ones that are unitary. Rather, the federal states are the ones with the greatest actual or potential tension between different ethnic groups.

Let us now examine the various central state organs in communist countries; following this there is a brief analysis of local state politics.

(i) The Representative Assemblies

In the three federalized communist states, the central state representative assemblies are bicameral. Thus the Supreme Soviet in the USSR comprises the Soviet of Nationalities, to which each of the fifteen republics sends thirty-two deputies (many national groups which are not large enough to qualify for their own republic have autonomous regions, etc. and also send deputies to the Soviet of Nationalities) and the Soviet of the Union; the Czechoslovak Federal Assembly consists of the Chamber of Nations (75 Czech deputies; 75 Slovak deputies) and the Chamber of the People; while the Yugoslav Federal Assembly is made up of the Chamber of Republics and Provinces (twelve delegates from each of the six republics, eight from each of the two autonomous provinces) and the Federal Chamber. In the unitary states, the assemblies are unicameral. Most are actually called assemblies (often the National Assembly or the People's Assembly); exceptions include the USSR, the National People's Congress in China, the Sejm (or Diet) in Poland, and the Great People's Khural in Mongolia. The size of the legislatures varies considerably, as would be expected given the enormous differences in the size of population of individual countries. Thus the Chinese National People's Congress tops the list, with just under three thousand deputies, whilst the

Supreme People's Council in the People's Democratic Republic of Yemen has only one hundred and eleven deputies. The assemblies are in most cases elected once every three to five years.

Most assemblies are scheduled to meet between two (e.g. USSR, Czechoslovakia) and four (e.g. Hungary) times per annum. But, as with party congresses, this rule is sometimes broken quite dramatically. For instance, the Chinese National People's Congress was not convened for a decade after its January 1965 session. When they are convened, assemblies generally sit for less than a week at a time. This gives some indication of the relatively minor role most of them play in their respective political systems, despite the fact that they are constitutionally the highest organs of state. Although we have less empirical information on most of them than we would like, most assemblies appear to play a 'rubber-stamping' role much of the time, formally giving approval to laws and decrees (the legislative function), one and five-year plans, annual budgets, etc., which have really been drawn up and decided upon elsewhere in the political system. Votes of approval (e.g. of new laws) are commonly unanimous, although recent studies suggest that such votes are being preceded by increasingly open discussions in many states. This frankness of discussion seems to have gone furthest in the case of Yugoslavia; the Polish Sejm has also witnessed comparatively open debate and divided votes on various occasions in the past. Even in these two countries, however, there is much less significant and open debate than there is in, for instance, the British Parliament or the US Congress. The presence of a formal multi-party system in some communist states appears to make little difference to the functioning of the legislatures. For example, the frank debates in the Yugoslav Federal Assembly take place despite the fact that only one political party is represented there, whereas debates and votes in the GDR's People's Chamber—in which five political parties are represented—are so controlled that it has only once experienced a less than totally unanimous vote. This was in 1972, when a few members of one East German party, the Christian Democratic Union, either voted against the proposed new law on abortion or else abstained.

Although the assemblies themselves in most cases play an essentially ceremonial and legitimating role in the legislative and debating process, recent research suggests that various committees and commissions attached to the legislatures are playing an increasingly prominent role in drafting legislation and/or scrutinizing legislative proposals, certainly in the older states (see e.g. Minagawa 1975 and Nelson and White 1982).

The formal legislative function is not the only one performed by communist assemblies. Another is to represent the various sections of the community—the different parts of a given country, and, increasingly, different ethnic, gender, and functional groups. At present, many groups (including women and workers) are still heavily under-represented, whilst others (notably male members of the intelligentsia) are clearly over-represented. But the situation is improving, and is in several cases better than in comparable Western institutions (White 1982, *passim*, and esp. p. 193).

Although most assemblies seem to play a relatively insignificant role in the policy process, communists do seem to feel the need that liberal democrats feel to give the appearance that elected representatives of the people are acting as watchdogs on other parts of the state. This 'watchdog' role, then, is a third function of assemblies. They are formally superior to the executive wings of the state, which conversely are answerable to the elected assemblies. For instance, the legislatures in theory elect the state's chief executive officials—although in practice, this too seems to be essentially a rubber-stamping exercise much of the time. Indeed, important changes in senior state personnel (e.g. membership of the Council of Ministers) which formally require ratification by the assembly sometimes occur without its direct involvement at all (e.g. in Cuba in December 1979 and January 1980—see Dominguez 1982b, pp. 28–9). Individual deputies also have the right to challenge state bureaucrats; indeed, in several states they are now required to do this if they have been 'mandated' by their electorate (see below). However, not only are such mandates usually few and vague (see e.g. Hill 1980, pp. 95–100), but the deputies have little real power to do anything if they receive unsatisfactory (or even no) answers from ministry officials, etc. Once again, however, the various committees attached to the national assemblies do seem to be playing a more meaningful role in exercising *kontrol* over the state bureaucrats in several countries than was once the case.

(ii) The Executive and Administrative Organs

Although formally subordinate to the assembly, the executive organs of the state—those entrusted with the implementation of policy—generally have considerably more real power than the elected assemblies. At the highest levels, we can distinguish between the government and the office of the head of state (presidency). In most communist countries, the government is called the Council of Ministers; exceptions include China (the State Council), the DPRK (Administrative Council), Yugoslavia (Federal Executive Council), and Czechoslovakia (simply 'the Government'). The government is formally elected by the national assemblies, although in practice this usually means simply endorsing the list supplied to the deputies by the presidium of the assembly. The Council of Ministers comprises the ministers, state secretaries, and, in federal states, senior state officials from the republics (and autonomous provinces in Yugoslavia). This means that the Council of Ministers is often considered to be too large for effective government, so that an inner core—the presidium—is formed. The chairperson of this presidium is often referred to in Western literature as the 'prime minister' or 'premier'.

The government is responsible for ensuring that the legislation emanating from the assembly, which is in turn usually based on general guidelines laid down by the party, is implemented. In practice, government officials frequently play a greater role in drafting legislation than the members of the assembly themselves, and are certainly involved in more decision-making—even if this is often of an essentially day-to-day nature—than the deputies. In addition, although most countries still accept that only the assembly should pass 'laws', an increasing amount of legislation is in the form of 'decrees', 'statutes', etc. which do not need ratification by the national assemblies, but which in practice are often as binding and widely applicable as laws themselves. These 'lesser' forms of legislation usually emanate from the Council of Ministers, and its legislative role is growing in many communist states at the expense of the assemblies.

The government supervises the work of the ministries and state committees below it. These bodies are responsible for the administration of policies in their respective branches of industry or other areas of competence (e.g. wage setting, compiling economic plans, schools, culture, etc.). When we refer to 'the state bureaucracy', we are primarily talking about the full-time professional functionaries in these state administrative organs.

Although the term 'government' has been applied here to the Councils of Ministers (or their functional equivalents), it should be emphasized that this has been done merely because such bodies are described in such terms by the communist states themselves. In practice, these organs usually have considerably less power than, for instance, the British government. The reader must constantly bear in mind that the whole state structure is subject to guidance from the communist party, and the party Politburo is in many ways more like a government (and certainly a cabinet) than is the Council of Ministers. There have been, almost inevitably, exceptions to this. Thus the Cuban Council of Ministers had far more real power in the 1960s than did the Politburo (Casal and Perez-Stable 1981, pp. 81–4), and the Ethiopian state organs have necessarily had more power than the party (i.e., because the latter has only just come into existence). Moreover, some governments are considerably more autonomous of the party than others. There was a marked political liberalization in Hungary in the years 1968–73, for instance (coinciding with the major liberal reform of the economy known as the New Economic Mechanism), which was accompanied by a major increase in government autonomy of the party (see White, Gardner and Schöpflin 1982, pp. 103–4). But such exceptions are rare, and a high level of government subordination to the party is still the norm in the communist world. This is not to say that government ministers do not disagree with, for example, their approximate counterparts in the Secretariat of the Central Committee; obviously they sometimes do. But these disagreements are usually well hidden from public view, and the limited evidence we have suggests that the party will 'win' any such dispute in the vast majority of cases.

In addition to the government, there is the office of the head of state.

Several communist countries formally have a state president (e.g. Mozambique, Czechoslovakia, China). In some other countries (e.g. the USSR, Mongolia), the chairperson of the presidium of the national assembly is in practice the head of state. A third group of communist countries has created Councils of State (e.g. Cuba, Bulgaria, GDR) or a Presidential Council (Hungary, PDRY), which are bodies designed to act as a collective presidency; in practice, however, even these collective presidencies do have a chairperson who is the real head of state. These bodies are generally small, rarely exceeding twenty members. They are to represent the assembly when it is not in session, convene sessions of the assembly, and in many cases exercise some control over the government. A major function of the presidency is to represent the state in foreign relations (e.g. sign foreign treaties, accredit ambassadors, formally declare war, etc.). They are also frequently formally responsible for appointing senior state officials (including the highest military and judicial officers), and they award state honours (e.g. medals). Occasionally, they are called upon to interpret the laws of the country. A collective presidency may even be formed in order to create more jobs at senior levels; the latter may have been the case in Vietnam (see Kershaw 1982, p. 339). The president can initiate legislation, and in some communist countries (e.g. Romania) has the right to pass laws and make important decisions without requiring formal ratification by the elected assembly.

As in some Western countries, such as France, the constitutional description of the roles of the head of state and the head of the government are vague, so that the actual relationship between the two can fluctuate. For instance, Podgorny (Soviet president, or Chairman of the Presidium of the Supreme Soviet, 1965–77) seems to have strengthened the office *vis-à-vis* other state bodies, a trend which continued when Brezhnev replaced Podgorny in 1977; the Soviet presidency was probably further strengthened *vis-à-vis* the premiership when Kosygin was replaced by Tikhonov as prime minister in 1980. Very occasionally, the presidency can be the most powerful organ in the political system (e.g. in Yemen—see Ismael 1981, p. 768). In most cases, however, the presidency—like the government—is ultimately very much under party control.

(iii) Local State Organs

Although the local level was virtually ignored in Western studies of communist politics for many years, there has been a marked improvement in this area recently, although the USSR, Yugoslavia and perhaps China still tend to receive much more attention than most other countries. This lack of interest was partially because of Western perceptions that all meaningful politics occurs at the top in communist countries, and partially because the communist states themselves were sometimes slow to form local state bodies and/or were not very forthcoming in providing information on them. Fortunately, this imbalance is now being rectified; after all, it is at the local level that many people come into their most direct and frequent contact with the state.

In most communist countries there are now representative assemblies, executives, and administrators at the various local (e.g. village, town, province, region, republic, etc.) levels. The representative assemblies—local soviets in the USSR, national committees in Czechoslovakia, organs of people's power in Cuba, etc.—are elected, and are to deliberate on local issues, such as the local budget, construction plans, etc. As with central organs, it is usually the executive and administrative bodies which have most real power at this level, despite the fact that the officers to the executive are elected by and formally answerable to the assembly. Although local assemblies generally meet more frequently than their central counterparts (e.g. town soviets are supposed to meet six times per year in the USSR), the fact that the executives meet far more frequently and are entrusted with the day-to-day responsibility of running a given administrative unit obviously confers considerable power. The executives have below them full-time, professional state administrators (the local state bureaucracy) for administering the party and state decisions handed to them; many members of the executives will in fact also be from the ranks of the state administrators, which adds to the power of the executive over the ordinary deputies to the local assemblies. Most of the latter are part-time, working on the local assembly in addition to their regular jobs in a factory, on a farm, or whatever. Moreover, the full-time local state functionaries are answerable not only to the local elected assemblies, but also to the higher levels of the state administrative machine; if local administrators were to receive conflicting orders, they would almost always follow those from their administrative superiors rather than the local elected deputies.

Turnover of deputies in most countries is relatively high, which can be seen as a way of involving a large number of citizens in the work of the state. The evidence available also suggests that local state bodies are becoming increasingly active. This must be seen as a positive development in terms of democracy and adherence to Marxist ideals. On the other hand, one must also keep such developments in perspective. As we shall see, the communist party exerts enormous influence on the selection of deputies (as well as full-time state administrators, via the *nomenklatura* system), and the methods by which ordinary citizens can exercise some control over the state are in practice severely limited. We need also to ask *why* more citizens are being involved; in some cases, it seems that this is being done primarily in order to find a (cheap) method of easing the load on the professional administrators, a point partially endorsed by the following quotation from Friedgut's study of local soviets:

... there has been an increase in the number of citizens involved in the administration of local soviets. Their relations to the administrators have, however, changed. They are now subordinates working for the administrators rather than replacing them in government. (Friedgut 1979, p. 219.)

Of course, there could be a dynamic to this, by which I mean that experience in the more mundane administrative tasks might act as a school for ordinary citizens, who will then demand more responsible involvement, in the way the classical Marxist theoreticians would have wanted. But this still seems to be a long way off, and it is far from clear that it would not be successfully resisted by the professional administrators anyway.

(iv) *The Military*

Although both Marx and Lenin were primarily concerned in their writings on the state with the representative bodies and the state bureaucracies, they did appreciate the important role played by the military, police, and judiciary.

Increasingly, the military in communist countries is structured along essentially similar lines to those of the armed forces in the West. China did formally abolish the distinction between officers and ordinary soldiers in the GPCR, but this distinction—and ranks—have now returned. Armies are professional for the most part, although compulsory conscription means that there is always a substantial number of soldiers, sailors, and airpersons who are not highly trained or experienced. Some countries (e.g. Yugoslavia, Cuba) have supplemented their armed forces with people's militias; but in no case have these replaced the professional armed forces.

For the most part, the professional military plays an essentially similar role in the East European states (including the USSR) to that played by the military in most liberal democracies. It exists to defend the country, and acts as a sort of pressure group for much of the time, seeking to gain as high a proportion of the state's budget as the politicians will allow. This said, the politicians and bureaucrats are usually well aware of the importance of the military, and of the fact that it is potentially the most powerful group in society, so that they will be rather more careful to nurture the military than other groups. For the most part—though see below—the military does not abuse its special position too much, to some extent because most military personnel in the more developed communist states seem to accept the basic social hierarchy and division of labour. As long as the politicians treat the generals with respect and run the country reasonably efficiently, then the generals will tend not to interfere excessively in civilian affairs. However, there is another side to this relationship between the civilians and military. This is that the communist politicians have increasingly sought ways further to integrate the military into the main bodies of the political system. For instance, the military often has representatives in the Politburo itself, as well as the top state organs (e.g. Council of Ministers). In addition, several communist leaders have had themselves awarded the status of Marshal (e.g. Brezhnev in 1976), which is presumably intended to give an impression of citizen interest in military affairs.

Although the military does not appear to play a dominant political role in the domestic politics of most industrially advanced communist states (the reference here is to involvement in the politics of its own country, not the military's role in suppressing political movements in other countries), there has been one major exception to this in recent times. This exception is Poland, where a general (Jaruzelski) assumed first the premiership (February 1981) and then the position of head of the party (October 1981). Shortly thereafter, he declared martial law in the country, and Poland was effectively being run by the military. This form of rule, previously unknown in communist East Europe (Marshal Tito made it clear he was first and foremost a civilian politician rather than a military man), has set a precedent which could be emulated in other communist states in future if civilian politicians seem to have lost control of a given country or perhaps because the military feel that the civilian politicians are denigrating the nation through excessive obsequiousness to a foreign power. This point is not merely speculative. In 1965, a group of nine men—all with close party and/or military connections—were charged with conspiracy in Bulgaria. It seems that many of the military men involved felt that the Bulgarian leader, Zhivkov, had been too subservient to the Soviets, which they felt offended Bulgarian national pride (for fuller details see J. Brown 1970, pp. 173–85). There was also an attempted military coup in Albania in 1960.

The military has tended to play a greater role in politics and society in the non-European communist states than in Eastern Europe or the USSR. In China, for example, the People's Liberation Army (PLA), the state bureaucracy and the CCP never enjoyed a clear division of labour under Mao. Military personnel could be involved in administration, harvesting, and other kinds of work that Westerners would not normally expect soldiers to perform. The GPCR saw a marked increase in the role of the military in politics, as Mao used the PLA (together with the newly formed 'Red Guards', young Maoist activists) to counter what he perceived as excessive bureaucratism in both the CCP and the state administrative organs. It was perhaps Mao's gratitude to the military that led him to nominate the head of this, Lin Biao, as his successor in October 1968 (Hinton 1978, p. 72); Mao subsequently seems to have changed his mind on this. But the post-Mao leadership has sought more clearly to delineate the functions of the various bodies of the party and state, so that the Chinese military is now playing a role more similar to that of the military in Eastern Europe.

The same is broadly true of the Cuban military. In the early days following his accession to power, Castro—who even now always appears in public in military uniform—used the army to perform many administrative functions. With the increasing institutionalization in Cuba, which has become particularly visible since the mid-1970s, the military appears to be performing more conventional tasks. The Chinese and Cuban pattern may well gradually spread to the newer communist states of Asia and Africa.

(v) *The Police*

Theft, rape, murder, vandalism, etc. are problems in communist states just as
they are elsewhere, even if some countries are not as open in acknowledging
this as they might be. The USSR, for instance, publishes very few statistics on
crime. The nature, rate, and reasons for crime are more the concern of the
sociologist than the political scientist; the primary concern here is with the
position and power of those that fight it.

Broadly speaking, a distinction can be drawn between those branches of
the police that deal primarily with non-political crimes, and those that are
concerned with political misdemeanours (popularly known as the secret police, although security police is a more appropriate term). The former is in
most cases staffed by full-time professionals, the latter invariably is. It would
seem, both a priori and empirically, that the security police also have rather
more say in the political system than do the regular police. Some indication
of just how powerful the security police can be is suggested by the case of
Rankovic in Yugoslavia. He was the organizational secretary of the LCY, and
was seen by some as Tito's closest ally until 1966 when it was revealed that he
had amongst other things been using the security police (UDBa) to exert considerable control over the Yugoslav populace. With his fall, the powers of the
security police declined, and the political atmosphere in Yugoslavia changed
almost overnight.

At one time, Western observers felt that the authoritarian and somewhat
sinister aspects of the security police were such that the head of such an organization would never become a leader of a country allegedly building communism. This assumption was disproved in November 1982, when
Andropov, who had been head of the USSR's KGB from 1967 to May 1982
became the Soviet leader. Certainly, like the military, the security police tend
to be represented at the highest levels of both party and state in communist
countries. And, despite Zinoviev's suggestion in 1918 that the Soviet security
police might soon be able to wither away (Barghoorn 1971. p. 101), security
police forces in the USSR and elsewhere, like the other wings of the state, are in
most cases being strengthened at present.

(vi) *The Judiciary*

Although a detailed analysis of the administration of law falls outside
the scope of this book, no chapter on the state would be complete without
some reference to the legal system. Let us first consider the main criminal
courts.

In virtually all communist states, there is a tiered system of courts. At the
top is the Supreme Court; below this there are usually courts at each administrative level. There are both full-time, professionally trained judges and lay
('people's') assessors in most local courts, although most constitutions allow

for some cases to be conducted solely by the professionals. Both the specialist judges and the people's assessors are formally elected in the majority of communist countries; exceptions include Romania, where both judges and assessors are appointed, and Poland, where the professional judges are appointed. The nature of the election varies. For instance, most judges of the Supreme Court are elected by the deputies to the national assembly, often on the proposal of the head of state. In many countries, the local judges and assessors are also elected by the representatives to the local assemblies (e.g. Cuba, North Korea). In other countries, some of the judges and assessors at the lower levels are elected directly by the citizens (e.g. Albania, GDR, Mongolia, USSR). However, in all this talk of elections, the point should never be forgotten that the communist party will insist on approving all or nearly all candidates for office before they are presented to the electors, be they the citizens themselves or the elected assemblies.

In addition to the regular courts, there exist in many countries local courts run by the people themselves with minimal involvement by the state. For instance, there are the 'self-management' courts in Yugoslavia, and the 'comrades' courts' in the USSR. Such courts tend to deal with minor infringements within a work-place or community; the regular state courts deal with all the more serious criminal cases.

The powers of the courts in most communist states are considerable. Individuals often do not have the right to choose their defence lawyer, and the vast majority of communist constitutions allow for some cases to be held out of public view. The latter cases will mostly be concerned with political dissidence, and the system means that there is no popular control—in the simple sense of justice being seen to be done by ordinary members of the public—in some of the most sensitive political cases. In contrast to the trend observable in most liberal democracies, the death penalty is still considered a perfectly acceptable form of punishment in most communist states. Not only murderers, but also rapists, corrupt officials, black-marketeers and others are relatively frequently executed.

A final point is that most communist states do not have special courts for deliberating on the constitutionality of legislation and other constitutional issues—bodies which would approximate to the US Supreme Court or the Federal Constitutional Court in West Germany, for example. The two exceptions to this are two of the federal states, Yugoslavia (which established a constitutional court in 1963) and Czechoslovakia (1968). Although relatively little is known about these courts, it would seem that one of their major tasks is to resolve potential conflicts between federal and republic-level legislation.

ELECTIONS

The reader will by now be aware that some officials in the communist world (notably the state bureaucrats) are appointed, whilst others are elected; it is with the procedures for selecting the latter that we are primarily concerned here. Ultimately, the party exerts considerable influence over virtually all elections in the communist world, and it could be argued that this factor produces a basic uniformity. Nevertheless, there are some important differences between the electoral processes in the various communist states, and these cannot be totally dismissed. In this section, we shall consider methods of election and the question of choice; the nomination procedure; the questions of secrecy and suffrage; electoral results; and the functions of elections.

The methods of electing deputies to both local and national assemblies vary quite considerably in the communist world. For instance, elections are direct in many communist states, that is, ordinary citizens themselves elect representatives to all local assemblies (e.g. at the level of the village, the town, the region, etc.) and to the national assembly. In some communist states, however (e.g. China, Cuba, Hungary, Kampuchea, Mozambique, and Yugoslavia), the system is a mixture of direct and indirect elections. Citizens directly elect deputies to some levels (invariably to the most immediate local level), whilst deputies to many or all other levels are elected only by the deputies of the assemblies at the level immediately below them (a useful starting-point for further details is Simons, 1980).

Another way in which elections differ from one country to the next is in the matter of electoral choice. In several communist states—e.g. the USSR, Albania, Bulgaria, North Korea, and Czechoslovakia—there is no real choice for the voters, unless one includes their right to strike out the name of the one official candidate on the ballot paper. This essentially 'no choice' situation has been changing in recent years, as an increasing number of the communist states have rejected the Soviet approach and introduced an element of choice into elections. These states include East Germany, Hungary, Poland, Romania, Yugoslavia, Cuba, Vietnam, Kampuchea, and China. However, the 'choice' in communist elections is very limited. To start with, some countries ensure that certain candidates start with a much better chance of being elected than others. A good example is the GDR, where constituencies are large and have several deputies (i.e., they are multi-member constituencies). When the voter receives the list of potential deputies, there will be two groups of candidates' names. The first is of the so-called 'seat' candidates; these are the candidates whom the authorities organizing the election prefer and are urging the electorate to endorse. The second group is of 'surplus' candidates; voters may express a preference for a particular 'surplus' candidate over a 'seat' candidate. But in order for a 'surplus' candidate actually to be elected in place of a 'seat' candidate, there must not only be a large majority of votes for the particular 'surplus' candidate—which is difficult, given the multi-member nature of East German constituencies, and hence the fact that electors may well vote for different 'surplus' candidates—but there must also be a concrete rejection of a particular 'seat' candidate; the point just made about multi-member constituencies is equally pertinent here. In other words, a 'seat' candidate must receive less than 50 per cent of votes to be rejected and replaced by a 'surplus' candidate. Given that many East Germans do not mark their ballot papers at all, and that this is taken to represent acceptance of the official list in the rank-order in which it is presented, it should be clear why, despite formal claims that the electors have a choice, the electoral system is geared to ensuring that the authorities' preferred candidates are elected. Indeed, the 'surplus' list exists less to give the electors real choice than to acquire popular endorsement for 'reserve' candidates. Hence, if a 'seat' candidate dies or for some other reason can no longer perform his/her duties as a deputy, then he/she is automatically replaced by a 'surplus' candidate. Such a system avoids the need to hold by-elections.

Not all 'limited-choice' elections are quite as controlled as the East German. In both Hungary and Yugoslavia, for example, there is some real choice for electors, and there is no distinction between 'seat' and 'surplus' candidates. Indeed, even if there were, the fact that these countries have single-member constituencies means that it would be very much more difficult for the authorities to control voting preferences than it is in the GDR.

Some communist states—notably Cuba and Vietnam—now include a provision for a 'run-off' system. There, as in other countries, it is insufficient for a candidate to come first in a contested election; he or she must also receive over 50 per cent of the vote. If no candidate receives this in the first round of elections, a second round is held, usually a week later, in which the least popular candidates are dropped from the list. Given the relatively low numbers of competing candidates, this has so far always ensured that one candidate does receive the necessary support in the second (or run-off) round. In practice, Cuba uses the second round more than Vietnam does. In the April 1984 Cuban municipal elections, 23,099 candidates stood for 10,966 seats. In the first round, held on 15 April, 10,494 candidates were elected. A second round was held a week later in the 472 wards ('circumscriptions') in which no candidate had received a majority vote.

For all these variations, electoral choice in the communist states is still very restricted, in two main ways. First, there is no choice in many—often a majority of—constituencies, particularly for national assemblies. For instance, in the April 1971 Hungarian national elections, there was only one candidate in 303 out of the 352 constituencies; this figure increased to 318 out of 352 in the June 1975 elections and to 337 in the 1980 elections. In other words, the trend was for less and less constituencies to offer any choice. It is not entirely clear why this happened, although one suggestion put forward by a Hungarian Central Committee Secretary is that the lack of democratic traditions in his country meant that some people who might have run for office did not do so out of fear of the possible social ignominy of losing (Korom 1983, pp. 28–9). It should be noted that, in this particular case, the Hungarian authorities themselves were concerned about this trend and passed legislation in December 1983 designed to encourage more competition in elections. Second, as pointed out earlier, the whole electoral process is very much under the control of the communist party. It exerts influence largely through the supervision of and involvement in the work of the so-called *blocs* or *fronts* (e.g. the National Front in the GDR and Czechoslovakia, the Fatherland Front in Bulgaria and Vietnam; the Chinese People's Political Consultative Conference, which has been reactivated since 1978, plays an essentially similar role in the PRC). These bodies are designed to act as a linchpin between the communist parties and mass organizations (and minor parties, where these exist), and one of their main practical tasks is to organize elections. This involves establishing electoral committees or commissions— which must have a core of communist members—producing ballot-forms, organizing vote-counting, etc. The fronts ensure that no candidates stand in opposition to the communist party or its policies; in fact, many non-communists in both one-party and formally multi-party states are elected even to the national assemblies, but they will have been scrutinized and passed by the front on the basis of instructions from the communist party. When it is further borne in mind that communists appear to feel obliged to make representative assemblies increasingly reflective of the major subdivisions (e.g. territorial, functional, sexual, etc.) in society it becomes clear why the notion of too much choice or 'spontaneity' in elections would not be acceptable to the authorities.

If voters are not allowed to choose between different political platforms, what official justification can there be for the minimal electoral choice available in some countries? The general answer is that voters are offered a choice between different kinds of personality. Some voters may prefer an older person, whom they have known as their deputy for years, and whom they have come to trust; such a person may not be particularly dynamic, but the electors know his/her strengths and weaknesses. Other voters may prefer a younger, more dynamic deputy, someone who may be less well known but who gives the impression that he/she will get more done. There are partial exceptions to this line of argument; in Yugoslavia, for instance, it is accepted that society comprises different interests, which can be reflected in different electoral preferences (see e.g. Cohen 1977, pp. 183–4). But even in the Yugoslav case, such interests will not be officially recognized if they are in any way 'anti-socialist'.

We have seen that there are severe limitations on electoral choice even in those communist countries that offer it, let alone those that do not. This would seem to be very undemocratic to many Westerners, yet communists will reply that this is because we tend to place too much emphasis on the election itself. They themselves tend to place at least as much emphasis on citizen involvement at the pre-election stages, particularly the nomination stage. But just how great is the say of ordinary citizens at this point in the electoral process? Once again, we see that there are differences between communist states but that—at the end of the day—the communist-dominated blocs will ensure that acceptable nominations are made, particularly for higher level assemblies. In order to demonstrate some of these differences, let us consider the nomination process in two states, the USSR and Hungary.

In the Soviet Union, only *organizations*, not individuals, can nominate people as candidates to elected offices. Usually, a number of work-collectives in a given constituency will choose one nominee each. Representatives from the collectives will then meet under the guidance of the electoral commission to decide which of the numerous nominees will become the candidate (i.e., whose name will appear on the ballot paper). In fact, the instructions the electoral commission has received from above on the kind of candidates sought, plus the presence of the party core in the commission, mean that there is heavy pressure on the various representatives to allow themselves to be 'guided'. Moreover, given that the nominations from each organization will themselves frequently have been heavily influenced by the party (e.g. the primary party organization in a factory), it becomes clear why Western observers are rarely persuaded that the Soviet masses have very much say even at the nomination stage. Indeed, some Soviet political scientists have themselves pointed out that the emphasis on nomination by place of work seriously disadvantages many citizens, such as housewives and pensioners, who have little or no right to the formalistic participation enjoyed by others at the nomination meetings (see Hill 1980, pp. 34–8).

The Hungarian system is somewhat less controlled, and does have a potential solution to the problem just mentioned. In Hungary, not only organizations but also individuals have the right to nominate candidates. This has to be done at the 'nominating convention'; at such a meeting an individual can propose another individual and this can be accepted by the electoral authorities as long as at least one third of the people present at the convention endorse this nomination by a show of hands. But such a nominee must still accept the basic principles of socialism, and the notion of anyone who is fundamentally opposed to the system's values standing for election is explicitly rejected. Moreover, such theoretical 'spontaneity' from the floor occurs very rarely in practice, which may be because some potential nominators fear that they will be seen as troublemakers if they engage in such activity. In sum, the Hungarian system is by most criteria more democratic than the Soviet, but it too is far from optimal; the December 1983 electoral law only overcomes *some* of the undemocratic aspects of past practice.

In liberal democracies, much is made of the notion of secrecy at election time. In the communist world, elections are occasionally explicitly public. For instance, in the Mozambican elections of 1977, the electors cast their votes at large public meetings through a show of hands. It was argued that the high rate of illiteracy meant that many electors would not have been able to read names on a ballot-sheet in a private booth; although there is obviously much to this argument, it seems difficult to believe that it would not have been possible to devise ballot papers that used colours to represent different candidates if the authorities had had the will to ensure genuine secrecy of voting. But such low levels of literacy and openly admitted lack of secrecy are typical only of a few, new communist states, and the clear trend nowadays is for communist countries to claim that balloting is done in secret. For this reason, most communist states now provide individual polling booths at polling stations. However, even the provision of such booths does not ensure the secrecy of the vote in practice. Only a few states, including Yugoslavia and Hungary, stipulate that ballot papers must actually be marked, which means that the voters have to use the booths; of course, this is rather an academic exercise in those constituencies where there is no choice of candidate, but at least it does ensure a modicum of secrecy. But in most states, voters who accept the official candidate or list of candidates—and its priorities where there is the 'seat'/'surplus' distinction—merely enter at one end of the polling station, have their name ticked off, walk through the station and drop their unmarked card (admittedly often in an envelope) in the box at the other end. In short, they do not use the polling booths, which means that the authorities can easily ascertain which citizens have definitely accepted the official list, and which might not have done. For this reason, Western commentators have argued that the typical communist election is not really secret, since some citizens may fear the consequences of exercising their right to use the polling booth. There is little concrete evidence that using the polling booths does disadvantage citizens. But perception is what really matters, and if people *believe* that they will suffer in some way (e.g. in terms of job promotions) by exercising their right, then formal claims to secrecy become meaningless. If most communists really believed in secret voting they would follow the Hungarian and Yugoslav examples.

There is a growing tendency for suffrage in communist states to be universal, though many countries have in the past disenfranchised former bourgeois elements and several, including China, still do not permit a few 'politically non-reformed' citizens to vote. In most communist countries, all sane, non-criminal citizens have the vote at 18 years of age; in Angola it is 17, and in Cuba only 16 (also 16 in Yugoslavia if one is employed rather than at school).

Voting is not formally compulsory in most communist states, Kampuchea being a rare exception to this. Nevertheless, there is considerable pressure on citizens to cast their votes. Not only are elections usually held on Sundays and/or public holidays, and provision made on trains and other forms of transport (including even space ships in the case of the USSR!) to ensure maximum turnout, but the communist party and the mass organizations will send canvassers around to homes to encourage people to cast their vote. Moreover, inasmuch as citizens have their names ticked off when they vote, it appears that some fear the consequences of not turning out on election day. Partially because of such pressures, and in some cases because of falsification of election returns (see Zaslavsky and Brym 1978, pp. 369–70), turnouts at elections in the communist world appear to be very high. Official statistics suggest that over 98 per cent of electors cast their votes in most communist states, particularly for the national assemblies; Yugoslavia is usually bottom of the list, but still reports over 90 per cent turnout for most elections. Turnout is often less for local elections; in the June 1984 Polish local elections, for instance, the figure was reported to have been 74.95 per cent. But even this is high in comparison with many Western local elections, and is in any case in a country with a higher level of tension between the regime and the people than many communist states.

Not only is turnout high, but acceptance of the official candidates is also usually above 95 per cent. Once again, there is some variation here between national and local elections; whereas candidates are hardly ever rejected at the former level, this does happen (i.e., candidates receive less than 50 per cent of the vote) at local levels. Albania and North Korea are perhaps the bizarrest communist states in terms of electoral turnout and results. According to official Albanian reports, in the latest (November 1982) elections to the People's Assembly, 1,627,968 citizens (i.e., all those eligible) cast their vote, of whom only one voted against the official list, and eight returned invalid papers; this represented a deterioration in comparison with the 1978 election, when only one voter abstained and no one voted against the official list. In the most recent North Korean elections (February 1982), it was claimed that all electors other than those abroad had voted by noon, and that every single vote had been cast for the official candidates. Such results cannot be treated seriously.

It has been shown that electoral choice is either essentially non-existent or else very limited in the communist world; that secrecy is not in practice a feature of most communist elections; that several countries have essentially indirect electoral systems; and that in most countries the communist party exerts enormous influence at all stages of the electoral process anyway. Given all this, the reader might well wonder why communists bother with elections at all. In fact, elections serve a number of functions for the authorities. First, particularly at the local level, they do give the electorate *some* opportunity to express political preferences, if only within a narrow framework. Closely connected to this is the fact that elections serve to increase information flows between the regime and the electorate. In the newer and/or more controlled communist states, the information flow is largely one way, from leaders to led. During the overall electoral process (i.e., including the nomination stage, door-to-door canvassing, meetings of the electorate with the candidate, etc.), the authorities have a good opportunity to explain current policies and political structures, for instance. But in the more advanced communist states, such contact can increasingly be seen as a form of public opinion survey, where local officials can discover what it is that is particularly upsetting the electorate—on local issues, if not national ones. To a limited extent, then, the electoral process may give the voters some influence on public policy.

A third function is to educate the masses in a particular form of political participation. As was pointed out in chapter two, communist states have not generally had very democratic (here in the sense of participatory) pre-communist traditions, yet they are committed to the long-term encouragement of mass participation in public administration. Such participation is still very much under party control, but no communist party has actually rejected this as a distant goal. Therefore, the mobilization of the masses and involvement of them in some form of collective political activity at election time is a way of giving them experience in politics and administration. For instance, it seems that over seventeen million Soviet citizens (many of them members of the CPSU) were involved in electoral commissions, canvassing, etc. during the 1975 Soviet election (Friedgut 1979, pp. 78 and 98–9).

Fourth, and leading on from this, communist states need to change their deputies from time to time—to give some people more significant political experience, to bring in new blood, etc. Several states now have electoral rules that require minimum levels of deputy turnover at each election. For example, under the 1980 Vietnamese electoral law, only one third of existing members of the National Assembly may stand again for election. A few states that have had such a rotation principle for some time, such as Hungary, have now decided that too much turnover is dysfunctional, since there is insufficient continuity and the advantages of experience can be wasted; they have therefore reduced it. But the basic point remains that changes of deputies in almost all countries require elections.

Finally, elections are intended to help legitimize the political system; this is one of their major functions. All the theoreticians of classical Marxism argued that in a socialist democracy the masses would have to have some control over the state via elections, and it would be difficult and probably pointless for communist leaderships to refute this. From what little empirical evidence we have, however, such legitimation attempts enjoy limited success. A survey taken in Czechoslovakia in 1968—when, presumably, people were more open in expressing their opinions than usual (see chapter twelve)—revealed that only one per cent of the respondents felt that the country's electoral system was the best one 'for the "democratic" expression of the people's will' (Pravda 1978, p. 189). Evidently, even in the countries in which electoral reform has gone furthest (i.e., Yugoslavia and Hungary), there is widespread cynicism (ibid., p. 189).

In short, elections perform several functions in the communist world, even if these are not identical—certainly in their relative weightings—to those in liberal democracies.

OTHER FORMS OF POPULAR CONTROL OF THE STATE

Elections are only one way in which the masses, formally at least, exercise control over 'their' state. Another method is by having and using the right of recall (revocation) of deputies. Once again, this relates back to Marx and to Lenin, who emphasized the importance of revocability in a socialist democracy. Unfortunately, this aspect of politics in the communist world has not been researched very much, to no small extent because many communist states themselves treat the matter as an essentially marginal one. Certainly, many constitutions formally grant voters the right to recall deputies if these prove unsatisfactory. But the details of how this actually works are rarely spelt out, for reasons which emerge from the following quotation from a Polish source, which gives details on Poland but also says that this pattern is widespread:

... electoral law and Seym regulations reflect the constitutional principle that the Seym has the right to demand that the electorate revokes the mandate of a deputy who fails in the exercise of his parliamentary duties.

The constitutions of other socialist states provide analogous possibilities. It is characteristic, however, that these constitutional decisions are not accompanied by practical possibilities of implementation. This is the case in the Polish People's Republic, where no executive law exists to specify which bodies are entitled to demand revocation of a deputy's mandate and determine the procedure to be followed in such cases. It may be assumed that the postulate requiring that parliamentary mandates should be revocable had greater practical significance during the revolution ...

This necessity seldom arises nowadays in the period of peaceful construction of socialism ... (emphasis added).

The author goes on to make it clear that it would be the party, together with the mass organizations—not the electorate as a whole—that would in practice deal with a deviant deputy: 'In drastic cases, party discipline and the influence exercised by massive social organisations, proves sufficiently effective' (Burda 1978, pp. 77–8).

Not all communist states have been quite as cavalier as this on the issue of revocation. For instance, we know that in the USSR the organization that nominated him or her is to instigate an investigation of an allegedly unsatisfactory deputy. The executive body of the assembly of which he or she is a deputy is then required to mount an investigation. If this executive feels that there is a case against the deputy, then the electorate which originally voted him/her on to the assembly is called upon to decide, by a show of hands, whether or not the deputy is to be recalled (Pravda 1978, p. 177). As will be obvious from this description, the executive usually plays the most significant role in the whole recall process. This said, it should be noted that an average of four hundred deputies per year at all levels were revoked in the decade to 1980 (figs. from Vinogradov 1980, p. 180). This represented a huge decline in comparison with, for instance, the 1930s; moreover, the figures are out of a total of over two million soviet deputies, and thus represent only a tiny proportion. The most frequent reason given for the recall of Soviet deputies is their failure to fulfil the mandates given them by their electorate (for further details on the Soviet revocation system see Friedgut 1979, pp. 132–7). The mandate has been defined by one Soviet writer as 'the trust placed by the voters of an electoral district in the person they nominate as member of a representative organ to express their wishes and interests as far as the law allows him to act on their behalf' (Bezuglov 1973, p. 22). This general mandate, however, usually includes specific instructions, such as a demand for a new road to be built in the locality. The deputy might not in fact succeed in getting the road built, which may seem to be reason enough for recalling him or her. However, it is difficult in practice to say that a given deputy has broken his/her mandate, for at least two reasons. First, the deputy may not fulfil *all* instructions, but may well carry out a majority; this would be seen by most Soviet theoreticians as satisfactory. The reasons for non-fulfilment of some instructions may well include being outvoted at a soviet meeting, and cannot always be put down to mere inefficiency or deliberate thwarting of the electorate's wishes. Second, the deputy may attend a soviet meeting and realize that the demand for the new road runs counter to the interests of other localities. Although he/she is primarily to represent his/her electorate, the deputy must take broader Soviet interests into consideration and not fall into parochialism, as pointed out by Soviet writers such as Ilyinsky (quoted in Bezuglov 1973, p. 27). It thus becomes clear why the system of revocation in the USSR is rather more difficult to implement than might be obvious at first glance, which in turn helps to explain the relatively low number of recalls. On the other hand, the careful screening of candidates before they are elected also helps to explain why so few are found to be unsatisfactory.

The Yugoslavs have taken the concept of mandating much further than anybody else with their 'delegate' system. Under the terms of the 1974 constitution, the Yugoslavs explicitly reject the notion of 'representative' democracy, arguing that all too often the elected deputies can and do vote in conformity either with instructions from above or their own will, without taking sufficient note of the wishes of the electorate. Under the delegate system, in contrast, groups of citizens elect delegations, who then elect from their own numbers delegates to higher assemblies. These delegates are instructed on the positions to be adopted in debates at the meetings of these higher assemblies. The delegates are obliged to vote in the way the delegation has instructed them to—unless they are persuaded by a better argument at the assembly meeting. If this happens, they are required to report back to the delegation; if the delegation is dissatisfied with the reasons given, they can suggest to the electorate that chose the delegation that the particular delegate(s) be recalled. Conversely, they can recall the delegates themselves and send other delegates to future meetings of the higher level assemblies. This is therefore a variation on the mandate system rather than a totally new system, and the delegations have in practice considerably more say than the ordinary voters. But the Yugoslavs do at least appear to be trying harder than anyone else at present to make the relationship between mass involvement and efficiency in the work of the assemblies more meaningful.

Yet another way in which citizens can attempt to influence and exert control over the state machinery is via the media, especially the press. Letters do appear in newspapers in which ordinary citizens will criticize the work (or lack of it) of a given ministry, for example. The newspaper will then try to gain some response from the minister. Sometimes, no response is forthcoming. On other occasions, the minister will promise to deal with the source of dissatisfaction—but follow-up letters months or even years later will reveal that nothing has in fact been done in many cases. Many communist states—and some Western observers—have made much of the increasing numbers of letters to the press in recent years. However, we should keep this form of citizen participation in perspective, for reasons which are more appropriately analysed in chapter ten.

PARTY–STATE RELATIONS

The relationship between the party and the state in communist countries is a complex one, both in theory and in practice. As pointed out in chapter 6, many constitutions have in recent years and for the first time referred explicitly to the 'leading', 'directing', or 'guiding' role of the party in the political system (e.g. Czechoslovakia 1960, Romania 1965, Cuba 1976, USSR 1977), an extraordinary fact given the predominant role of the party in the vast majority of countries. This 'leading' or 'guiding' role is crystallizing in most countries—in theory, and to some extent in practice—into a division of labour between the party and the state as follows:

(i) General policy guidelines—the party.
(ii) Detailed legislation, based on general guidelines—the state.
(iii) Administration of implementation—the state.
(iv) Checking on implementation and those responsible for it (*kontrol* and *nomenklatura*)—the party.

In other words, party and state are meant to complement each other, and party *apparatchiki* are sometimes rebuked by senior party politicians for attempting to 'substitute' themselves for state officials (i.e., for attempting to perform the latters' tasks).

One major exception to this general trend of separating party and state is Albania, where the two are officially ever more closely merged. However, the distinction in other countries between party and state is in practice often hazy, as can be inferred from the communists' own criticisms of 'substitution'. A major reason for this is personnel overlap. For instance, at the top of the political system there has emerged a pattern whereby the head of the party is frequently also the head of state. In the USSR, Brezhnev waited approximately thirteen years before becoming *de facto* president (i.e., he became First/General Secretary in 1964, and Chairman of the Presidium of the Supreme Soviet in 1977), whereas Andropov waited only about seven months (November 1982 to June 1983) and Chernenko a mere two months;

the Soviets recently explicitly stated that it will in future be normal Soviet practice to combine both posts (speech by M. Gorbachev in *Pravda*, 12 April 1984, p. 1), although they broke this pattern themselves in July 1985 when Gromyko, rather than General Secretary Gorbachev, became the new head of state. In some countries, the party leader is head of the government rather than head of state (e.g. Kaysone Phomvihane in Laos), whilst in Cuba, Fidel Castro is in practice the head of the party, head of state, and head of the government. The head of the party is also in many countries the *de facto* and/or *de jure* head of the armed forces, perhaps as chairperson of the state's 'Defence Council' and/or Commander-in-Chief of the military. In fact, some constitutions (e.g. the Albanian) even stipulate that it is to be the head of the party who is also head of the armed forces. In Cuba, the constitution requires that the head of state is the Commander-in-Chief of the armed forces; this gives Castro yet another formal office.

This overlap of party and state personnel is found not only at the apex of the political system, but at all levels. There is invariably considerable overlap between the Politburo, the Central Committee Secretariat, the Presidium of the Council of Ministers and the collective presidency; between the Central Committee and the Council of Ministers; between the republic-level party and state executives, etc. To take just one example, of the 16 members of the 1980 Cuban Politburo, 11 were also members of the Council of Ministers and 14 were on the Council of State. Over 90 per cent of the members of the Cuban National Assembly at the beginning of this decade were also members of the party. This particular aspect of party–state merging has gone furthest in Romania. There, the members of a local party bureau occupy the vast majority of the posts in the executive ('permanent bureau') of the 'people's councils' (the Romanian local assemblies). Moreover, since 1975 the first party secretary at each level is also the chairperson of the local branch of the state front (the Socialist Unity Front). Finally, it should be remembered that the vast majority of state bureaucrats, military officers, senior police officials and professional judges in communist countries are members of the communist party; in most cases, where there is a formal multi-party system, military officers are not permitted to join any party other than the communist.

There are also important functional reasons for the blurring of the distinctions between party and state. For instance, if party officials are to supervise (*kontrol*) the work of state officials properly, they need to understand the latter's work. This has meant in practice that they often become as narrowly specialized as the people to whom they are supposed to be giving general political guidance.

It is largely because of such functional and personnel interpenetration and overlap that scholars such as Mary McAuley (1977, p. 186) and Michael Waller have argued that the party and state are essentially inseparable, and that they should really be seen as *jointly* constituting the state as we understand it in the West. McAuley argues that to do this will confuse the newcomer to communist politics less than if one makes a clear distinction between, in the case of the USSR, the party and soviet institutions. My own teaching experience does not confirm this view. Nevertheless, the basic point that McAuley and Waller are arguing does make a lot of sense in some contexts, as long as we clarify one or two issues. Most fundamentally, we need to make the distinction—as we did with ideology—between the narrow and broad conceptions of 'the state'. Up to this point, I have generally referred to the state in its narrow sense—that is, I have distinguished it from the party. However, if one believes—and this *is* a subjective matter—that the party–state complex in communist countries has a *basically* similar relationship to the rest of society as the state in bourgeois countries (i.e., that it stands above it, rather than being subordinated to it as Marx would have wanted), then we can call this complex 'the state', using this term in a broad sense. This implies that the party is not the politically organized wing of the masses for keeping the state under control on behalf of the masses, but, instead, also stands above society. Once the reader is aware of these two conceptions of the state, many apparent contradictions in the literature on communist politics can be resolved. For instance, it can then be pointed out that communists themselves almost always use the term 'state' in the narrow sense. They do this both for theoretical and practical reasons. For example, it often makes sense for party leaders to draw clear distinctions between 'the party' and 'the state' when an unpopular policy is being implemented or when a policy has failed. At such times, the party can use 'the state' as a scapegoat. Another example is when communists claim that the state has begun to 'wither away', as Soviet leader Khrushchev did in the late 1950s/early 1960s. If we examine the Khrushchev era, we find that although there were concrete signs of a 'withering away' of the state in the narrow sense (e.g. the abolition of most ministries, the revitalization of the soviets), there was also a visible strengthening of the party, which took over many of the functions that had formerly been performed by state bodies. It was in the interests of the Soviet leadership to use the term 'state' in its narrow sense, since the USSR could then be argued to be developing in conformity with the prognosis of Marx and Lenin. On the other hand, many Westerners (including Marxists) felt that power in the Khrushchev era was still highly centralized, and that a small political élite still ruled the USSR. In other words, they felt that the Soviet claims were superficial and cosmetic. They could therefore argue that the state in the narrow sense might appear to be withering away, but that in its broad sense—which is almost certainly how Marx himself would have used it in this context—it was not. All that had happened was a shift of balance between the two major components of the state in its broad sense. For a meaningful 'withering away of the state' to occur, we would have to see a transfer to the masses of the powers and position not only of the state bureaucrats, the military, etc., but also of the communist party *apparatchiki*. In sum, I would argue that it is sometimes better to see the state in its narrow sense, and at other times in its broad sense, depending on the context. One final point is that the term 'state' is used in its narrow sense in the rest of this book; if reference is made to the broader concept, the term 'party–state complex' is employed.

SOME CONCLUDING REMARKS

We have now examined the major formal political institutions in the communist world. We have seen how citizens are encouraged to participate, but mainly in the representative state bodies and election to these. State bureaucrats are still overwhelmingly appointed rather than elected. For this reason, changes in the electoral and revocation laws in recent years should be noted but kept in perspective. Within the state, the elected officers are not the most powerful ones. And in any case, the state is in most countries under the control of the party, which is not answerable to the masses in any meaningful sense and membership of which is still very low relative to the population (or even the proletariat). For the so-called 'dictatorship of the proletariat' or 'state of the whole people' to become what they are claimed to be, leading executive officials in both the party and state would need to be far closer and more responsible to the masses. One thing is fairly certain—if Marx were alive today, he would be bitterly disappointed to see political systems which claim to be on the threshold of communism being led by generals or former security police chiefs.

Basic further reading

G. Bertsch, 1982, ch. 5.

N. Harding (ed.), 1984.

L. Holmes (ed.), 1981b.

D. Nelson and S. White (eds.), 1982.

A. Pravda, 1978.

W. Simons (ed.), 1980.

S. White, J. Gardner & G. Schöpflin, 1982, ch. 3.

8

LEADERSHIP AND SUCCESSION

HAVING examined the party and state, we can now focus upon the apex of the political system, the senior leadership; for our purposes, this can be defined as the membership of the Politburo (or its equivalent). In particular, we shall be looking at the *de facto* head of the party (in most cases the General Secretary of the Central Committee), who is usually portrayed in the Western media as 'the' leader of a given communist country and the single most powerful person in the system. However, it shall be shown why such an image can be misleading; it glosses over the fact that there is a variety of leadership configurations in the communist world and that the position of 'the' leader can sometimes be highly precarious.

It was announced on Friday, 10 February 1984 that the General Secretary of the Central Committee of the CPSU) and Chairperson of the Presidium of the Supreme Soviet (i.e., president) of the USSR, Yuri Andropov, had died at 4.50 pm the previous day. On 11 February, Melbourne's leading newspaper *The Age*, speculated on the identity of the future new Soviet leader, naming three men as the front runners (Vorotnikov, Romanov, and Gorbachev). The CPSU Central Committee announced on 13 February that it had elected a new General Secretary; the name of this person, Konstantin Chernenko, had not been among those suggested by *The Age*.

In November 1982, about a fortnight after the death of Leonid Brezhnev (who had been the General Secretary of the CPSU's Central Committee since October 1964 and president since 1977), Western commentators were taken by surprise when the USSR's Supreme Soviet did not name a new Soviet president; the post was not filled until 16 June 1983, when Yuri Andropov, the then General Secretary, was elected. And in July 1985 the world's media were again surprised when Gromyko, rather than Gorbachev, was named Soviet president.

The purpose of relating these three stories is not to criticize the media (some of which, such as *The Times*, correctly predicted Chernenko's appointment), but rather to highlight the fact that despite years of 'Kremlin-watching', 'Beijing-watching', etc. we still know remarkably little about leadership, and particularly leadership change, in most of the communist world. In this chapter, we shall consider the reasons for the unpredictability of leadership succession, after having examined the different types of leadership configuration and change. Some of the most interesting questions that have been raised in the literature on communist leadership in recent years will also be addressed. Let us begin though by considering why leadership is still not properly institutionalized.

WHY IS LEADERSHIP NOT INSTITUTIONALIZED IN MOST COMMUNIST COUNTRIES?

It is perhaps an irony of communist politics that while most communist states have a reputation for strong leadership and leadership powers far in excess of those in liberal democracies, the position and powers of leaders are generally ill defined in official documents such as constitutions. For instance, with the notable exception of Yugoslavia, there is no mechanism in the communist world for the regular replacement of 'the' leader. Some states other than Yugoslavia have regularized *parts* of the leadership change mechanism—China, for instance, now limits the tenure of both the president and the prime minister to a maximum of ten years (i.e., two five-year terms of office). But this is quite different from limiting the tenure of the General Secretary.

Indeed, China highlights another problem of leadership in the communist world, namely that it is sometimes unclear which post represents 'the' leadership position in a given country. There is certainly a clear trend nowadays for the General Secretary of a given Central Committee to be seen as 'the' leader, a trend which has received a legitimating boost as an increasing number of constitutions have specified that the party guides or directs the state. In some countries, where there has been both a party Chairperson and a General Secretary, the former has been seen as the real head of the party—one thinks of Chairman rather than Secretary Mao, for example. However, the clear trend nowadays is for the post of Chairperson either to be abolished or else converted into an essentially honorary post carrying few powers. Another observable trend, referred to in an earlier chapter, is for the General Secretary to be simultaneously head of state. But the latter practice is still relatively new, and has in most cases not been constitutionally endorsed. In any case, constitutions in the communist world are frequently modified or replaced to suit changed political circumstances, so that there is no guarantee that what a constitution stipulates today will not be changed tomorrow if a new leadership feels the constitution is obstructing some change it wishes to introduce; in general, constitutions are far more subject to political whim in the communist world than they are in the liberal democracies. Despite these trends, the leadership configuration in China reveals not only that the relative position of posts can fluctuate, but even that it cannot always be assumed that a particular post carries with it the notion that its incumbent will be 'the' leader. Thus, most Western analysts agree that the most powerful politician in Beijing is Deng Xiaoping, who is neither the head of the party (Hu Yaobang), nor head of state (Li Xiannian), nor head of the government (Zhao Ziyang). Deng does occupy a variety of formal posts (for details see below), but seems to exert his influence more through his own personality and the respect accorded to him by other leaders than through any of these offices. Even in the oldest communist state, the picture is not entirely clear. In 1953, immediately following Stalin's death, Georgii Malenkov became premier whilst at the same time retaining his post of Central Committee Secretary. Until September 1953, there was no number one secretary in formal terms; despite this, Malenkov seemed to be 'the' secretary for a few days. But on 21 March 1953, Malenkov was prevailed upon to choose between his two main posts. He chose to give up the secretaryship and retain the premiership, which strongly suggests that he perceived the latter as the potentially more powerful of the two offices (Rush 1968, pp. 60–1 argues this). In fact, since about the mid-1950s, the General (or First as it was called 1953–66) Secretaryship has, as in so many other countries, emerged as the most important post. However, there is some evidence to suggest that in recent times, the General Secretary has sometimes been so ill that he has not played a major role in decision-making. This may well have been the case in Brezhnev's later years, in the last six months or so of the Andropov era, and from early on in the Chernenko 'reign'; in late 1984, there was much speculation in the media that Gromyko (the then foreign minister) and possibly Ustinov (the then defence minister, who in fact died in December 1984) were the most powerful politicians in Moscow. If all this is indeed the case, it could suggest that the role of the General Secretary in the USSR is not always as great as is often assumed. Unfortunately, this is not the only—or necessarily the most convincing—way of looking at recent developments. It can equally well be argued that the election of aged and infirm leaders (Andropov, and particularly Chernenko, both fit this description) to the post of General Secretary suggests that the other leaders do perceive the General Secretaryship as potentially the most powerful office, and have therefore on occasions elected people to it who are unlikely to be able to exploit the powers of the office to the maximum extent. Why they should do this is not the concern here. Nor does it matter which of these two very different interpretations of recent developments in the General Secretaryship is adopted. The important point is that even in the Soviet case—which is generally seen as one of the most clear cut—it is not always completely obvious who the leader is. Let us now examine the reasons for this confusion.

One major reason often put forward is the nature of Marxist-Leninist ideology. It is argued that the classical theorists' emphasis on the collective—in marked contrast to liberal democratic theorists' stress on the individual, which can handle the concept of 'the' leader—is such that the notion of 'the' leader, or even 'leaders' is difficult to legitimate. In fact, as with so much in Marxism, the picture is not entirely clear. As already pointed out, their writings on the Paris Commune suggest that Marx and Engels were opposed to the notion of leaders developing into a class or caste above society, rather than to leadership *per se*; as long as decision-makers were subject to recall and genuinely accountable to the masses, then Marx and Engels appeared to have accepted them as necessary, at least in what we nowadays call the social-ist phase. This might suggest that communist states could and should institu-tionalize leadership in line with Marxist precepts. But here we return to the problem of 'who are the leaders?' It could be argued that Marx and Engels were concerned with *state* leaders, rather than party leaders; they did not really deal with the latter. This said, it was argued in chapter 7 that Marx and Engels would almost certainly see the modern party-state complex as 'the state' in the broad sense, from which it follows that they would argue for mass control of both state (narrow sense) *and* party leaders. Lenin's views are more complex. He certainly accepted the notion of leadership for both state and party; by stressing the need for 'collective leadership', he produced a for-mula which, theoretically, could overcome the dichotomy between the indi-vidual and the collective. However, as Trotsky (cited in McLellan 1980, p. 79) pointed out, Lenin's views on the vanguard party and democratic cen-tralism were such that the *logic* of his organizational principles gravitated to-wards the single, powerful leader; indeed, Trotsky used the term 'dictator'. Moreover, various concrete measures introduced by Lenin endorsed the no-tion that he was not averse to the single leader. In 1921 (i.e., *after* the revol-utionary takeover), he introduced the concept of 'one-person responsibility (*edinolichie*) plus collegiality' as the managerial principle for running indus-trial enterprises; if he could favour such a blending of individual leadership and collectivity at the workplace, then there is no obvious reason why the principle could not or should not apply to the political system as a whole. Any suggestion that Lenin believed the vanguard and leadership were neces-sary only *before* the revolution is absurd.

Marxism–Leninism is thus less of a hindrance to leadership institutionali-zation than is sometimes maintained. Even the suggestion that such institu-tionalization is out of line with the dynamism of Marxism–Leninism and its commitment to an eventual 'withering away of the state' is unconvincing; there is at least as much potential for phasing out leaders in a situation in which such people have limits on their tenure of office as there is in the actual situation pertaining in most of the communist countries. Certainly, Marx and Engels (and probably Lenin) would be averse to the long tenures, per-sonality cults, policy and personnel immobilism, etc. that are both possible and more likely to occur in a situation where leadership is not properly defined and/or regulated.

In addition to the ideological factor, there are at least three other impor-tant reasons for the non-institutionalization of leadership in the communist world. The first is that leaders of a revolutionary take-over often feel that they need to 'see the revolution through'—i.e., to consolidate following the takeover, and to create the foundations of the new, better society. This pro-cess takes time—many years—and a limitation on their term of office would obviously be seen as a hindrance by many revolutionary leaders. Thus in the

vast majority of cases, the person who played the leading role in the communist takeover will stay on as leader until his death; this is particularly so in the
case of genuinely indigenous takeovers.

Secondly, and closely related to the last point, both 'the' leader and other
members of the leadership will, following the revolutionary takeover, often
perceive the need for some semblance of stability in a period of great flux.
The communist regime is new and its policies involve great change, so that
the leadership as a whole may well feel that the mass population will need
some symbol of continuity in the form of the same leader over a number of
years.

Third, there is the democratic centralist nature of communist systems,
coupled with the desire of most leaders in all kinds of political systems to stay
in power. Even in the West, genuinely voluntary resignations by top leaders
are a rare occurrence, the cases of Harold Wilson (British prime minister) in
April 1976 and Pierre Trudeau (Canada, 1984) being notable exceptions. In
the West however, the existence of a genuine multi-party system means that
the electorate can change 'the' leader at regular intervals. This does not only
apply to countries where the president (if he/she is the number one politician)
is directly or almost directly elected by the mass of the population, as in
France or the USA; even in the UK, voters can remove a party in power, the
members of which themselves will often then pressure their leader to resign
for having led the party to defeat. Moreover, the concept of a 'separation of
powers' in the USA and some other Western states means that one section of
the political leadership can introduce limitations on another; the introduction by Congress and the majority of the states of Amendment 22 to the US
Constitution in 1951 (this limits the term of office of any one individual as US
President to a maximum of ten years, or two-and-a-half terms of office) is a
prime example. 'Democratic centralism' does not recognize such a separation
of powers principle, and it is unclear where a formal challenge to the indefi-
nite tenure of General Secretaries would come from. Indeed, in the one case
where a limit on the tenure of office *has* been introduced (Yugoslavia) the formal regulations were introduced by the leader himself, mostly to become
operative *after* his own death.

Given that leadership arrangements are still essentially non-institutionalized, let us now consider what kinds of leadership configurations can exist.

TYPES OF LEADERSHIP

Most people would accept that Khrushchev's position as 'the' leader was not
identical to Stalin's, or indeed to Brezhnev's; in other words, whilst the list of
top offices may stay essentially the same in a given country, the relative positions of people occupying those posts may well vary over time. For analytical
purposes, we can distinguish between four main leadership configurations—
supreme leader; first amongst equals; oligarchy within collectivism (a term

devised by Gill 1984, p. 24); and collective leadership. Two important points about this typology need to be noted. First, the typology is based on the perceived *power* of leaders, not their public image. Thus a given leader may appear to be 'the' leader for public consumption (i.e., as a *symbol* of leadership), whereas the circumstantial evidence we have suggests that that person has in fact little more power in decision-making than some of his peers (students of British politics may recognize some similarity between this distinction and that drawn by Bagehot in the nineteenth century between the 'dignified' and 'efficient' elements of the British constitution). The second point is that these are ideal types; in the real world, leaderships can and do fall between categories and even move between them over time.

The supreme leader is in most cases a charismatic leader, someone to whom others attribute very special qualities—in most cases because he led the revolutionary takeover. The latter is not invariably so, however, as the cases of Stalin and Ceausescu (Romanian leader since 1965) show. Such a leader has considerably more power than the other members of the Politburo (or its equivalent). A full-blooded 'personality cult' may well develop around him. In other words, not only does such a leader usually accrue more of the top offices in the party–state complex and have considerably more say in the decisions than anyone else, but he also claims—or allows it to be claimed on his behalf—that he is the ultimate interpreter of Marxism–Leninism, and even that he has made a substantial contribution to the ideology. Moreover, he may have history rewritten to emphasize his past role in the revolutionary struggle, and will permit or even encourage exuberant public displays of love and loyalty to himself; this may include an insistence that public buildings carry his portrait, that towns be named after him, etc. In fact; the supreme leader may well permit or encourage an image of himself as someone possessing superhuman, even godlike qualities, to such an extent that he may appear to stand far above even the party itself (on all this see Gill 1982, pp. 95–103). At present, the two most overt personality cults in the communist world are those surrounding Kim Il Sung (North Korea) and Ceausescu, with the former being the more extreme example. Two extracts from a book on Kim's ideas will give the reader some idea of the remarkable claims that can be made. The first is to be found on the dedication page at the beginning of the book:

Dedicated most humbly and respectfully to the greatest philosopher of the world, the respected and beloved leader, President Kim Il Sung, the shining sun illuminating the road for millions of people in the world for independence, and a Messiah whom the world people hold in high esteem.

Further on in the book we read how Kim Il Sung has allegedly made a greater contribution to socialist ideology, methodology, and practice even than Marx or Lenin:

It is possible that the leader of one socialist country may be far superior to the leader of another socialist country in terms of ideology, theory and ability of leadership . . . Comrade Kim Il Sung is the greatest theoretician of modern times, he has given an original ideology to the world, he has a unique position in the history of mankind, he has not only given an original theory of revolution and construction, but also laid down the methodology for realising the idea. . . . he is the most distinguished and prominent leader ever known to mankind . . . It may be said that by his Juche philosophy and by his outstanding leadership, Kim Il Sung has fulfilled the unfulfilled tasks of Marx, Engels, Lenin and Stalin. (Both quotations from Mukherjee 1983, introduction and pp. 116–18.)

It should not be supposed that only writers in developing countries can provide such adulation of a communist leader. On Stalin's death, the British communist newspaper *The Daily Worker* wrote: 'Long live the immortal memory of the greatest working-class leader, genius and creative thinker that the world has ever known.' And the leader of the British communist party described Stalin as the man 'whose miracles of communist construction are of a character that even Marx would never have dared to believe possible' (both quotations from Westoby 1981, p. 111). There is no need to pass much comment on this sort of writing. Suffice it to make two general points. The first is that the communist leaders and/or propagandists involved in such writing are often very sensitive to criticisms of a personality cult (see Mukherjee 1983, pp. 107–8; for a refutation by the Chinese that the recent call to read and study the works of Deng Xiaoping represents a move towards a personality cult, see *Beijing Review*, 8 August 1983, p. 4). Second, Marx was clearly opposed to such cultism/deification; in a letter he wrote in 1877 he made clear his opposition to anything that tends to encourage 'superstitious belief in authority' (in Tucker 1978, p. 521). Unfortunately, as Meyer (1970a, p. 11) points out, it is an irony that the major political movement of the twentieth century that most emphasizes the power of the 'nameless historical forces' is the only one to be known by its founder's name. In other words, a cult has built up around Marx himself and his works—even among highly educated intellectuals in advanced industrial countries—and once a precedent has been set, it can all too easily get out of hand.

In the first amongst equals configuration, one person dominates most areas of decision-making, but to a lesser extent than the supreme leader does. There may be aspects of a personality cult about the first amongst equals leader, but far less than there are around the supreme leader. Other leaders do not venerate, let alone fear, the 'first amongst equals' in the way they often do the supreme leader. Examples of such leaders in the communist world include Khrushchev in the period 1957–64 and Kadar.

The oligarchy within collectivism arrangement is one in which a group of usually three to five individuals (typically the General Secretary and the premier, plus perhaps the head of state and one or two others) have far more say in decision-making than other members of the senior leadership, and work together as an inner core of the Politburo. There is usually a broad division of labour between the members of such an oligarchy. Thus in the late 1960s and into the 1970s, there appeared to be a quadrumvirate in the Soviet Politburo (Brezhnev, Kosygin, Podgorny, and Suslov), while the current Standing Committee—itself an inner core—of the Chinese Politburo appears to be dominated by Deng, Zhao, and Hu.

Finally, there is what most communist parties claim is their ideal leadership formation—collective leadership. This can assume various forms. In what we can call 'pure collectivism', all members of the collective leadership deliberate as equals in all major areas of decision-making. But this can be dysfunctional, in that it is quite likely that no one will have a particularly deep knowledge of any given policy-area. Therefore, in practice it may well be considered more desirable to have a division of labour between various leaders—one concentrating on relations with the West, another on industry, the third on ideology, etc. We can call this 'selective collectivism'. Finally, there is the arrangement which *probably*—remembering that we still have relatively little hard information on politics at the very top—most typifies actual collective leaderships in the communist world, which we can call 'mixed collectivism'. In this configuration, individual leaders will tend to specialize in one area or another, and will bring their specialized knowledge to the leadership team. But the team as a whole will deliberate on major decisions for a given problem area. This said, in the real world factions may well form around different policy proposals or sets of policy proposals. These subgroupings within the collective leadership may centre on two or more leading politicians, thus implying some sort of hierarchy of leaders within an allegedly collective framework. This might appear at first sight to be essentially the same as oligarchy within collectivism. However, whereas oligarchy within collectivism implies *horizontal* stratification within the collective and a relatively unified inner core of leaders, the configuration just described implies *vertical* division (i.e., two or more top leaders conflict with each other, and each of them has a coterie of 'second-rank' leaders as supporters). The USSR between 1953 and 1957 would be an example of this last sort of collective leadership.

Having considered types of leadership configuration, the reader is reminded that even where there is collective leadership, Western analysts—perhaps because of our own orientation towards the notion of individual leadership—writing on 'leaders' mostly focus on the General Secretary and assume that his removal, or the appointment of a new one, is of major political importance. Whether or not this is the case will be considered later in the chapter; for now, let us examine how 'the' leader is replaced in communist countries.

ON INCUMBENT PARTY LEADERS DEPARTING

An introductory comment on leaders departing in the communist world is that several communist states—among them Cuba and Laos—still have their original leader; it is possible that we shall see new modes of leadership change in some of these countries, on which we can at present only speculate. Potentially the most interesting case of this sort is North Korea. The Democratic People's Republic of Korea has been under the leadership of Kim Il Sung since its establishment in September 1948; Kim is both General Secretary of the Korean Workers' Party and President of the Republic. Kim is now a relatively old man (born 1912) and we can expect to see him succeeded in the 1980s. It is conceivable that he may even become the first communist leader to resign voluntarily. Whether he does or not, he has nominated his own son, Kim Jong Il, to succeed him. Although nepotism is rife in the communist world, there has not yet been a case of the top position passing from father to son; if this does happen in North Korea, we will witness a unique case of a communist dynasty. It should be noted that something similar is also happening in Cuba, where Castro has nominated his own brother to succeed him. Let us now move from speculation to fact, and typologize the ways in which leaders are replaced in communist countries.

(i) Death

Still the most common reason why a leader, particularly a supreme one, goes is because nature takes him; all Soviet General/First Secretaries other than Khrushchev have left by this door. In most cases, death is through natural causes. However, there has been speculation that both Taraki and Amin (both Afghanistan) and Ngouabi (Congo) were assassinated on the instructions of other leaders, and Rush (1968, p. 56) even raises doubts about Stalin's death. Interestingly, assassination of top leaders by ordinary citizens is not, so far, a feature of communist politics; there have certainly been attempts on the lives of 'the' leader by ordinary citizens (including Lenin in August 1918—for details see Shub 1966, pp. 361–3—and, apparently, Honecker in December 1982), but none has succeeded.

Following the death of a supreme leader, the personality cult typically fades too. Indeed, within three to five years of the death of the former leader, there is often criticism of some aspects of his personality and rule, the amount of such criticism varying considerably. The demystification of Stalin is most associated with Khrushchev; of Mao with Deng; and of Tito with Dedijer (see Rigby 1968a; Chiang Hsin-li 1981; Stankovic 1982, p. 497, and Dragnich 1983, p. 372).

(ii) Forced resignation

Over the years, a number of communist leaders have been forced to resign. The pressure has most frequently come from peers (usually the Politburo), although the evidence available strongly suggests that the main pressure has sometimes come from the leaders of another country, usually the USSR. Let us consider examples of both types of case.

(*a*) *Peer pressure*

The most common reason for other members of the senior leadership group to pressure a General Secretary to resign is the failure of policies. Such failures are often highly visible, in the form of mass demonstrations. Most Polish leaders (Ochab in 1956, Gomulka in 1970, Gierek in 1980, and Kania in 1981), for example, have been urged to transfer power to another man following mass unrest.

Not all such cases are related to such overt signs of dissatisfaction. In October 1964, Nikita Khrushchev (USSR) was forced to resign, although he was officially reported—as is so often the case in these sorts of removals—to have resigned because of old age and poor health. In fact, Khrushchev had a string of policy failures to his name. In foreign policy, for instance, there was the Cuban missile fiasco of October 1962 which, it was widely felt, had humiliated the USSR in the eyes of the world; there was also the emergence of the Sino–Soviet dispute, which appeared for a while in the early 1960s to have weakened the Soviets' hold over the smaller communist states. At least as important was the failure of key domestic policies, particularly in agriculture. In the 1950s, Khrushchev had appeared to have solutions to many of the economic problems of the countryside. But the failure of such policies, notably the so-called Virgin Lands campaign, was symbolized by the fact that in 1963 the harvest was so poor that Khrushchev felt obliged to import grain from the West—including the USA—for the first time in decades, and just months after Washington had humiliated Moscow over the missile incident. Although policy failures were a major factor in Khrushchev's demise, they were not the only one. Another was his *style* of leadership. Khrushchev was subsequently criticized for being too impetuous and for taking insufficient note of specialist knowledge. His penchant for nepotism (particularly in using his son-in-law for important diplomatic assignments) also irritated the other leaders. Finally, as Tatu (1970, pp. 396–8) emphasizes, Khrushchev appears to have been planning to make individual members of the Politburo responsible for technical areas of agriculture, a plan which was quite unacceptable to his fellow leaders. Khrushchev's peers had tried once before to remove him, in June 1957. On that occasion, the majority of the Politburo had attempted to vote Khrushchev out of his office of First Secretary; Khrushchev outmanœuvred them, arguing formalistically but correctly that only the Central Committee of the party had the right to revoke a First Secretary. He was able selectively to convene the Central Committee, many members of which were protégés of Khrushchev; the Central Committee overturned the Politburo decision, and reaffirmed Khrushchev in his post. The Politburo plotters had lost. Khrushchev then had them dubbed as hostile to the party (which is why the plotters were called the 'anti-party group'), and their powers were rapidly reduced. This incident was not lost on the 1964 plotters, who ensured that the Central Committee was ready to vote Khrushchev out of office. Support was not difficult to obtain, since so many Soviet party and state administrators had suffered in one way or another (predominantly as regards their careers) under Khrushchev. Moreover, they too were disillusioned by the many policy failures. This, plus the fact that various factions within the Soviet Politburo overcame their differences in order to close ranks against Khrushchev, helps to explain why he was removed so relatively easily in October 1964. Other examples of leaders being forced to resign because of personal and policy failings include Novotny (Czechoslovakia, 1968) and Chervenkov (Bulgaria, over a two-year period 1954–6).

(b) Outside pressure

There are a number of reasons why the Soviet Union and sometimes other communist states (such as Vietnam) will interfere in the domestic leadership arrangements of another country. A common one is that a domestic leader seems to be losing control to such an extent that the communist system appears to be endangered. A prime example of this is Hungary in 1956, when Gero was removed. A variation of this theme is where a leader is being so harsh with his own subjects, allegedly in the name of communist radicalism, that he is giving communism a bad reputation. If allowed to continue, this might provoke overt mass unrest and in any case will make communism unpopular in neighbouring states that *might* otherwise be becoming more sympathetic to it. Examples of this sort of involvement include the removal of Pol Pot in Kampuchea (1979) and, possibly, Amin in Afghanistan (also 1979).

Yet another reason why the Soviets might intervene is because they feel that a particular leader is pursuing goals which are widely at odds with Soviet aims. For instance, there is considerable circumstantial evidence to suggest that Walter Ulbricht was forced to resign with Soviet connivance in May 1971, partially because he had been trying to create an alternative model of socialist development to the Soviet one and, even more importantly, because he was placing obstacles in the way of an improvement in relations between Moscow and Bonn (i.e., his policies were having an adverse effect on Soviet strategic interests). The notion of an alternative model of socialism, unacceptable to the Soviets, also helps to explain Soviet involvement in the removal of Dubcek in Czechoslovakia in 1969.

Finally, it needs to be appreciated that 'peer pressure' and 'outside pressure' frequently go hand-in-hand; the one often endorses the other.

(iii) Regularized change

As mentioned earlier, Yugoslavia is the only communist state to have fully regularized leadership change, not only in the leading state organs but also in the communist party (LCY). The process of institutionalization began in the 1969–71 period, when regular turnover of both party and state leaders—

excluding Tito himself—was introduced. Since then, there have been so many marginal changes that it would be confusing and of little value to elaborate them; instead, I shall focus on the situation since Tito's death. Tito himself was both head of the party and of the state until his death in May 1980, upon which the acting deputy leader of the party, S. Doronjski, became the President of the LCY Presidium (i.e. the *de facto* head of the politburo) and L. Kolisevski became the new head of state. Under the party rules, Doronjski was to be replaced in October 1980; he was, by L. Mojsov. The rules at that time stated that the President of the Presidium was to stay in office for one year, changing each October; once again, the change-over went according to plan in October 1981. At its Twelfth Congress in June 1982, the LCY reconfirmed the notion of annual turnover of party leaders, but altered the change-over date from October to June. Rather than give the then President, D. Dragosavac an extension of his office to June 1983 (which would have given him a twenty-month tenure), he was replaced by M. Ribicic, who in turn was replaced by D. Markovic in June 1983. In short, the notion of a one-year term of office has so far been strictly observed. Although less powerful than the General Secretary in other countries, the Presidium of the LCY does have its own Secretary; for the record, the Secretary is changed every two years. The point about strict observance of regular change applies also to the offices of head of state (changed annually) and the premiership (changed every four years—currently held by Yugoslavia's first female prime minister, Milka Planinc).

Although Yugoslavia has kept very much to its stated intention of regular leadership change, there are some signs that change may be afoot. In November and December 1982, the then head of the LCY, Ribicic, argued that Tito himself had said that one year was insufficient for a person in a leadership position to become fully familiar with the job (in *BBC Summary of World Broadcasts—Eastern Europe*, 7802/B/22). If this argument were to gain widespread acceptance, we might see the head of the party and/or the state in Yugoslavia staying in office for more than a year, perhaps three or four years. The argument does make some sense, and a move in this direction would not necessarily undermine the general principle of regular change of leader. However, inasmuch as the reason for such frequent turnover of leaders is to give each of the republics and the autonomous provinces a bite of the 'top position' cherry, it is possible that there will be a feeling that individual republics etc. will have to wait too long to occupy the top positions, so that it is at present unclear whether or not Yugoslav leadership positions will in future be refilled less frequently than at present.

HOW DO NEW LEADERS EMERGE?

As with so many aspects of comparative communism, *Soviet* succession patterns tended for many years to be seen as the norm in the communist world.

Therefore, because there really were power struggles following the deaths of Lenin (1924) and Stalin (1953), it was widely assumed that such struggles were typical of the period following the departure of the head of the party. Nowadays, this image has justifiably been questioned. In addition to the Yugoslavs, the Vietnamese, and even the Soviets themselves have experienced smooth leadership transitions. In short, it has become obvious over time that an overt and prolonged struggle between contesting factions is *not* an inevitable feature of communist systems following a leader's death, even though such struggles are still common enough.

It might be assumed that one way in which the smooth succession could be ensured is for an ageing leader to nominate a successor. This certainly happens, and examples will be cited in some of the following case-studies. However, there are dangers in doing this, which is one of the reasons why incumbents nominate successors ever less nowadays. Even where successors are nominated, this by no means ensures a smooth succession. What are the problems? One is that the successor may become impatient and thus try to accelerate the removal of the incumbent leader. Another is that other members of the senior leadership group may become envious of the nominee, and in fact make life more difficult for him once the former leader has gone than might otherwise have been the case. Given that what might initially have appeared to be an obvious solution to a change of leaders is in fact problematic, and given that it rarely overtly occurs in the communist world anyway, let us now consider examples of both 'smooth transitions' and 'succession struggles', following which we shall examine the factors that turn leadership change into one or other of these. First, however, a definition of what constitutes a 'smooth transition' and a 'succession struggle' is required. In order to do this, we need to create a framework for analysing leadership at times of succession; a useful one is what can be called the '3 Ps + X' approach, so called because it focuses on power-bases, personalities, policies, and 'special features'. An elaboration of these will make the framework clearer.

(1) *Power-bases.* There are in fact three additional 'Ps' to be incorporated into the analytical framework as subdivisions of power-bases—viz. posts, patronage, and politicking. In the case of the first of these, it is necessary to examine the kinds of offices contestants for the top leadership position occupy at the time of the former leader's departure, which new ones they fight for, and what power such offices seem to confer. 'Patronage' (or 'clientelism') refers to the practice adopted by many leadership contestants of promoting people in various parts of the party and/or state machinery over which these individual contestants are particularly influential (e.g. the party apparatus, the security police, a particular region, etc.) to powerful party organs, particularly the Central Committee, the Secretariat, and even the Politburo. The individual leadership contestant hopes that the people he has thus promoted—his 'protégés'—will support him in any struggle with other contestants; such support often is forthcoming, although protégés do sometimes

turn against their patron if they perceive it as being in their own interests to do so. In the present context, 'politicking' refers to the practice of
some individuals in a leadership succession struggle to form alliances with
other senior leaders either to strengthen their own position and/or in order to
weaken the position of another contestant. The latter case has been emphasized by Alfred Meyer (1983b), who argues provocatively that we should
look at succession struggles less in terms of a struggle *for* power than as a
struggle *against* power. Whilst Meyer may have gone too far in the opposite
direction from the 'struggle for power' school—succession struggles often include *both* individuals who are striving for power *and* others who are mainly
concerned with preventing a certain individual from becoming top dog—his
corrective is a very useful one.

(2) *Personalities*. Here, one is looking at the personal characteristics of individuals in the leadership, both as they appear to an outside observer and, if
this seems to be different, as they appear to other members of the leadership.
For instance, do people who 'win' succession struggles appear to be the most
able, the most ambitious, the most ruthless, the most experienced, or the
most compromising? Do they need to be popular with the masses? Do they
have to be 'revolutionaries', or are bureaucratic types more likely to succeed?

(3) *Policies*. Finally, we need to see if there are major differences of policy
between contestants for power and, if so, who wins and why. Do policies
have to appeal to the masses, or is it more important that they appeal to
other leaders? Is there in fact any conflict here (i.e., between public support
and leadership support)?

(4) *The 'X'-factor*. It would be foolish to suggest that all leadership
changes can be analysed solely in terms of the three factors just outlined. As
is so often the case in comparisons, there are *special circumstances* in individual cases which make each leadership change unique; these circumstances
can be called the 'X'-factor. This might include foreign involvement, and
even what can only be described as fate. The 'three P's' approach is designed
to maximize the possibilities for comparison; once these factors have been
exhausted, we have to look at the peculiarities of each case. As Beck *et al.*
(1976, p. 61) have argued, there is a limit to how far we can draw general patterns of leadership change.

With the above framework in mind, we can now define 'smooth transition'
and 'succession struggles'. In a *smooth transition*, the major political posts are
rapidly filled, and the new leadership configuration quickly stabilizes itself.
There are no subsequent major leadership changes (other than through
death) for, let us say somewhat arbitrarily, five years. Outsiders are not aware
of serious policy disagreements and/or personality clashes within the Politburo. In a *succession struggle*, the senior posts may or may not be filled
rapidly; if they are, the incumbents' positions are perceived as insecure, and
we may see several changes of leaders in the top three posts (head of the
party, head of the government, head of state) in the five years or so following

the departure of 'the' leader. There are major alternative policy proposals, possibly overt personality clashes, and in all probability signs of major attempts by the leading contestants to build up patronage bases.

Finally, one difficulty the reader will encounter in reading several detailed studies of individual succession struggles is that analysts often disagree on when a given leader 'won' the competition; this is yet another of the problems encountered in studying leadership succession.

(i) Smooth transitions

A good example of just how smooth leadership succession can be is provided by Vietnam. The leader of the communist revolution there and the undisputed leader since the 1940s, Ho Chi Minh, died in September 1969. His former position of Chairman of the Party was not filled, probably because there was a widespread feeling that this post was an honorific one for the leader of the revolution, and that it was rather unnecessary, inappropriate, and politically unwise (i.e., in terms of making other leaders suspicious) to fill it. Rather, the Vietnamese communists fell into line with most communist parties, having only a First Secretary; this was Le Duan, who had occupied the post since 1960. The other most important members of the senior leadership were the *de facto* head of state Truong Chinh (his formal title was Chairman of the Standing Committee of the National Assembly which, unfortunately, cannot properly be described as the Vietnamese equivalent of the post of president since the *formal* office of head of state—a purely honorary post at that time—was occupied following Ho's death by the 81-year-old Ton Duc Thang) and the prime minister, Pham Van Dong. Le Duan, Truong Chinh, and Pham Von Dong—plus perhaps the military chief, General Giap—had been the most powerful politicians after Ho himself until 1969; following Ho's death, none of them changed their formal position. Moreover, the limited evidence available suggests that none of them indulged to any notable extent in either patronage or factionalism following Ho's death (Elliott 1975, p. 42).

According to Pike (1978, p. 128) and some other commentators, none of the leaders had particularly strong, assertive personalities (although Rogers 1976, p. 128 disagrees). Whether or not they did have strong personalities, all the leading politicians appeared to be able to compromise—in marked contrast to the situation in many other countries. This is perhaps one of the reasons why the Vietnamese leadership group has been described as 'the most durable ruling communist group anywhere' (Pike 1978, p. 66).

There certainly were some policy disagreements over priorities, with some commentators even referring to this as the Vietnamese 'Great Debate'. The main issue of contention in the period following Ho's death was whether North Vietnam should devote most of its energies to the war with the South (Le Duan's position) or to socialist construction in the North (the line taken by Truong Chinh). However, the notion that this was a 'great debate' is misleading if not erroneous, in that both Le Duan and Truong Chinh accepted that *both* goals were necessary. Thus the differences were ultimately ones of emphasis, not of fundamentals.

The most obvious peculiarity of the Vietnamese case is the fact that the country had been fighting foreign forces on and off for a quarter of a century at the time of Ho's death; the fact that Vietnam was still fighting a major war until the mid-1970s, and minor ones even after that, is a major reason for leadership continuity and a lack of signs of overt struggle. War efforts—in any country—require unity at all levels, so that it is not surprising that the Vietnamese leadership held together. At the time of writing, the leading trio in 1969 was still in power.

The successful removal of Khrushchev in October 1964 has been attributed largely to the fact that senior politicians of different persuasions were able to overcome their differences in order to remove a common embarrassment; Leonhard (1968, pp. 69–70), for instance, refers to a coalition of 'conservatives' and 'moderate modernisers'. This thesis is supported by the fact that there was a stable coalition—in communist terms a 'collective leadership'—for years following Khrushchev's ouster; the leading figures in this leadership were Brezhnev, Kosygin, Podgorny, and Suslov. The notion of collective leadership was not new, of course, but the term received renewed emphasis from the senior Soviet politicians in the autumn of 1964, and they took concrete measures to ensure adherence to the principle. Most notably, they argued that no one individual should in future fill more than one of the top leadership posts. Thus, whereas Khrushchev was both head of the party and prime minister at the time of his ouster, Brezhnev became the new head of the party, whilst Kosygin was the new premier. In 1965, Mikoyan was replaced as head of state by Podgorny. Suslov did not occupy any of the top three offices, but was chief ideologist and, from all the available evidence, appears to have played a major role in policy making. This configuration remained unchanged until 1977, when Brezhnev finally replaced Podgorny as president. Rigby's research (1970) suggests that there was very little in the way of a build up of patronage around the senior leaders for several years after 1964. Nor was there any very obvious alliance-formation; if anything, the top leaders aligned with each other in the early years, rather than with lesser leaders against each other.

Although Brezhnev had a much more dominating, emotional, and forceful personality than Kosygin, neither man was as volatile, spontaneous—indeed, hot-headed—as Khrushchev, nor as charismatic as some of the people who occupied the senior positions in the Bolshevik party in the first years after the October Revolution. Suslov was a rather stern, conservative communist. Podgorny was livelier than Suslov, but not to a marked degree. In short, the evidence suggests that the differences of personality in the leadership team were insufficient to upset the overall balance most of the time (although

Brezhnev and Podgorny do appear to have eventually fallen out with each other).

The evidence suggests that there were no really fundamental policy disagreements in the early years. There appears to have been common agreement that the *de facto* process of merging party and state institutions and tasks that characterized the Khrushchev era was to be reversed, that the economy was to be strengthened, and that Russia was not to be humiliated in international politics again—which meant more expenditure on defence. One of the reasons why there was relatively so little disagreement was that there emerged a sort of division of labour between the leaders; Brezhnev was concerned primarily with foreign policy and, to some extent, agriculture, while Kosygin was responsible for industry. Podgorny was responsible for the soviets, whilst Suslov was in charge of ideology and relations with other communist parties. The first major conflict seems to have come in August 1968, when the Soviets—as the heads of the Warsaw Pact—had to decide how to deal with the 'problem' (as they saw it) of Czechoslovakia. But despite apparent major differences amongst the leaders on this issue, the collective leadership survived intact, and indeed there were no major changes in the Politburo until 1973.

Probably the single most important 'X'-factor in the Khrushchev succession was the fact that most senior politicians in the USSR were anxious to avoid the one-man dominance typified by both Stalin and Khrushchev. If another Stalin were to have emerged, their very lives would have been in danger, whilst another Khrushchev could have humiliated both themselves and the country once again and could have forced through even more 'harebrained' schemes (i.e., radical policies that were not properly evaluated and which ultimately failed). This particular case therefore fits to some extent with Meyer's notion of a 'struggle against power'—apart from the fact that there was no struggle!

(ii) Succession struggles

The first succession struggle in the communist world began in January 1924 following Lenin's death. Stalin eventually won—according to some by 1929 and to others by 1934. How did this all come about?

It was far from clear in the Soviet Union of the 1920s which leadership post was the most important. In fact, Stalin was the one who transformed the post of General Secretary of the Central Committee into the all-important leadership post. He was appointed as the first General Secretary in 1922 (Lenin never occupied this post). At the time, the office was seen by most as an essentially administrative one. But over the years, Stalin developed the post, exploiting the powers it conferred for influencing problem-perception, agendas, the selection of key personnel throughout the political system, etc. Lenin had been head of the Soviet government (i.e., prime minister), and it is to some extent testimony to the fluidity of Soviet institutions at the time and the fact that it was still personalities rather than posts that were dominant in the power structure that the fact that Rykov succeeded Lenin as premier has all but been forgotten by history. This all said, Lenin himself recognized already by the end of 1922 that Stalin had 'concentrated enormous power in his hands' as General Secretary, and the leader of the revolution was fairly clearly aware that Stalin might make much of his new post. Stalin had certainly made full use of other important offices he had occupied, notably as Commissar of Nationalities (1917–23) and Commissar of the Workers' and Peasants' Inspectorate (1919–22). Stalin did eventually (1941) become premier too, but this was long after his power had been consolidated. None of the other major contestants for power occupied what we nowadays think of as the key offices. Trotsky had control over the military, but was urged to resign his post in January 1925. On the other hand, the seven-person Politburo was by now clearly the key political organ, and its membership remained remarkably stable in the period 1922–6; only Lenin 'left' (i.e., through death), and he was replaced by Bukharin. But from 1926–30, as Stalin consolidated power, so the composition of the Politburo changed dramatically.

Stalin used his position as General Secretary to promote a number of protégés. He had made many contacts in the provinces in his capacity as Commissar of Nationalities and Commissar of the Workers' and Peasants' Inspectorate. He was able to promote many people to various party organs at all levels, including the Central Committee.

Stalin was a master of politicking. In 1923, he formed an alliance with Zinoviev and Kamenev (the so-called 'Triumvirate') within the Politburo, largely in order to run the Politburo and to undermine Trotsky. Having succeeded in the latter, Stalin then turned on his former colleagues (1925) and undermined them. Zinoviev and Kamenev subsequently joined forces with Trotsky to form the so-called 'Joint Opposition'; but they could not gain much support or credibility after having been so critical of Trotsky in the recent past. Meanwhile, Stalin sided with Bukharin and the 'rightists' against Trotsky, Zinoviev, and Kamenev; having defeated the latter, Stalin then turned on Bukharin, Rykov, and Tomsky (who now formed the 'Right Opposition'), thus having in essence consolidated power by the late 1920s. The General Secretary used his massive power in the 1930s to ensure that former contestants in the leadership struggle were removed once and for all.

Far from nominating a successor, Lenin had in 1922–3 dictated a series of notes—known collectively as his 'Testament'—in which he evaluated the other members of the senior leadership; none of them was above criticism. Trotsky and Stalin were seen as the most capable members of the leadership team, and were dealt with in most detail; however, Bukharin, Zinoviev, Kamenev and others were also assessed by Lenin. Although Trotsky was seen as the *most* able member of the leadership (Deutscher 1966, pp. 250–1), Lenin also felt that the Commissar of War was often too self-confident, and—interestingly, given Trotsky's later criticisms of Soviet bureaucracy—that he was too attracted to the 'purely administrative side of things'. There is insufficient space here to go through Lenin's evaluations of the other leaders, although it is interesting to note that Bukharin was seen as the leading theoretician and the best-loved party leader. Stalin was described as very able, but Lenin also felt that he had too much power and that he did not always exercise this wisely. The leader of the revolution feared Stalin's impulsiveness and rudeness, and in January 1923 suggested in a letter that Stalin be removed as General Secretary; it was many years before the contents of this letter became widely known. If we add to this 'Testament' other insights into the personalities of the leading contestants for power, we form a picture of a situation which is once again in line with Meyer's notion of a struggle against power. In other words, Trotsky was feared by many of his peers; he was both ruthless and brilliant, and there is much evidence to suggest that others were anxious to keep such a man under control. Given his subsequent actions, it is ironic that Stalin was not generally seen in this light, despite Lenin's warning. Rather, he was seen as a somewhat dull but dependable and competent administrator, someone upon whom other more intellectual and creative leaders would foist the mundane tasks of party administration which they themselves were loath to accept. Moreover, Stalin appeared to many to be a compromiser and conciliator—what Deutscher calls 'the man of the golden mean' (1966, p. 297). For instance, Stalin and Trotsky had frequent disagreements, and it was almost always the former who made the first gesture for resolving their differences. One other feature of Stalin's personality deserves mention, since some psychology-oriented approaches to the Stalin phenomenon have made much of it. This is that Stalin was something of an outsider *vis-à-vis* the rest of the leadership group—less highly educated, less well-travelled, still in some ways a relatively crude Georgian peasant type. According to such psychological interpretations, this made Stalin feel inferior to the others, which fuelled his ambition to beat them in the power struggle. Probably the most likely alternative to either Trotsky or Stalin was Bukharin; but he was generally seen as too volatile to be a good leader, both in terms of his own personality and, probably as a corollary, his political views. This can be inferred from the fact that he was known as one of the 'ultra-leftists' at the time of the revolution, but was the leader of the 'Right Opposition' by the late 1920s.

Turning now to the question of policies, Stalin's most successful was 'socialism in one country'. This policy was a general one, concerned with the overall direction to be taken by the USSR in the coming years. As such, the main alternative in the mid-1920s was Trotsky's 'theory of permanent revolution' (see chapter one for further details on these policies). Since Trotsky's policy implied further revolutionary upheaval at home and probably warfare abroad, it is hardly surprising that it did not appeal to many Russians, most of whom were war-weary and of the opinion that the policy was unrealistic anyway given the failure of attempted socialist revolutions in Hungary (1919) and Germany (1918–19). Stalin's policy, on the other hand, was initially sufficiently vague for most people not to have realized that it too implied major social upheaval. Moreover, it appealed to traditional patriotic and messianic values in many Russians; Stalin seemed to be saying that the Soviet Union could show the rest of the world the way to a higher level of civilization without necessarily being involved with other countries. Not only was Stalin's policy more popular than Trotsky's with the masses, but also—and to some extent as a corollary—rank-and-file party members and party *apparatchiki*.

The main 'X'-factor in Stalin's rise to power is probably the fact that Lenin's 'Testament' was not made known either to the party or to the public at large in the mid-1920s; had it been, it is possible that there would have been a concerted effort to undermine Stalin and to remove him from his office of General Secretary. That the 'Testament' was kept within a small circle is explained by the fact that all of the senior leaders were criticized to a greater or lesser extent in it, and because some of them felt that Lenin had been over-harsh in his judgement of Stalin anyway. Unfortunately, history proved Lenin correct.

Like the USSR, China was led from the time of its revolution by a charismatic man. Unlike Lenin, however, Mao lived long enough not only to ensure the consolidation of communist power, but also to oversee the first stages of the transformation of Chinese society, the economy and the polity. In some ways then, he was both the Lenin and the Stalin of the Chinese revolution, although one must be careful not to take this analogy too far; having the authority of a Lenin, he did not feel the need to purge his rivals to anything like the same extent or in the same way as Stalin did. Nor did he industrialize his country to the same extent as Stalin.

Mao appears to have either formally or informally nominated three possible successors over the years. The first was Liu Shaoqi, who finally fell out of favour in the mid-1960s for what Mao perceived as Liu's overly bureaucratic and hierarchical approach. The second was Lin Biao, who was officially confirmed by the party as Mao's successor in 1969. However, Lin's activities following the end of the most extreme period of the GPCR (i.e. 1969) represent a good example of the danger mentioned earlier that a named successor will become impatient. There is considerable evidence to suggest that Lin became anxious to wear the mantle of supreme leader, that Mao realized this, and that Lin was consequently 'removed'; he died in a mysterious air crash over the Mongolian People's Republic in September 1971. After this, Mao was careful not to raise the expectations of any of his fellow leaders too far, although he did make it clear at the end of his life that he would be happy to see Hua Guofeng succeed him; allegedly, Mao had told Hua 'with you in charge, I am at ease' (Chang 1981, p. 19).

In fact, the period immediately following Mao's death in September 1976 was marked by a power struggle—initially between the so-called Gang of

Four (a group of four radical leaders that included Mao's widow Jiang Qing) and a group around Hua Guofeng. This struggle was in essence terminated about a month after Mao's death, when the members of the Gang of Four were arrested. They were subsequently (four years later!) sent to trial, found guilty and two of them were sentenced to death; the death sentence was later commuted to life imprisonment.

With the Gang of Four out of the running, a struggle developed between a coalition around Hua (this has been called the 'Third Force'—see Ting Wang 1977, pp. 5–6) and another, known either as the 'bureaucratic clique' or, more commonly nowadays, the 'pragmatists'. Following his rehabilitation in July 1977, Deng Xiaoping emerged as the leader of the latter group, although Hu Yaobang and Zhao Ziyang also became increasingly important within it. The 'pragmatist' group seemed clearly to be in the ascendancy by the time of the 3rd Central Committee plenum in December 1978; however, as various authors (see e.g. Nethercut 1983, p. 30) have pointed out, the pragmatists did not *finally* defeat Hua and the 'Third Force' until September 1982, at the Twelfth Congress of the CCP. Let us now examine the struggle in terms of the '3 Ps + X' framework.

Looking at the power bases, we see that Hua (like Malenkov in the USSR following Stalin's death) started out with the best opportunities for becoming the new leader in the sense that he occupied the two top posts after Mao's death. Hua had been made acting premier in January 1976; following the death of Zhou Enlai in April 1976, he formally became the prime minister, and number two in the communist party (First Vice-Chairman of the CCP). Following the overthrow of the Gang of Four, Hua became Chairman of the CCP (technically, of the Central Committee), thus taking over Mao's formal office; in fact, Hua was the first person to be both head of the party and of the government. However, Hua's position as both head of government and head of the party was slowly but surely eroded. In September 1980, he was urged to resign as premier, being replaced by the current prime minister, Zhao. The weakening of Hua's party position was more subtle and prolonged. In February 1980, the Central Committee re-established the Secretariat, and appointed Hu Yaobang General Secretary of this; the post had not in fact been filled since Deng had lost it at the beginning of the GPCR, having held it since 1954. The Secretariat became responsible for the running of the party, and, in doing so, undermined Hua's position as Chairman. In June 1981, Hu took over as Chairman from Hua, although Hu himself lost the post in September 1982, when the office of Chairperson of the CCP was abolished. Since that time, the General Secretaryship has been widely perceived as the most important party office, and is still occupied by Hu. Interestingly, Deng has not in recent years occupied any of what are in most communist countries seen as the top positions (though see below). This *might* reflect his sensitivity to charges of concentrating too much power in his hands. Alternatively, and in my opinion more persuasively, it is indicative of his desire to see his policies continued after his death. By this I mean that by appointing younger men than himself to the top positions (at the end of 1984, Deng was 80 years of age, compared with Hu's 69 and Zhao's 66), men who appear to have a basically similar approach to China's future development, Deng probably hopes to ensure some continuity of his policies after his own death. In one sense then, this is a novel approach to the problem of succession—although there is no absolute guarantee that Hu and Zhao *will* continue with Deng-type policies following the latter's death, or even that they will be able to retain their posts. It should not be assumed that Deng has not occupied any important posts in recent years, however. He has held several, particularly in the military; he was Chief-of-Staff of the military from 1977–80 and is currently Chairman of both the party and state military commissions. In September 1982, Deng was elected Chairman of the newly created 'Central Advisory Commission'. This body is a sort of 'council of elders'; members must have been in the CCP for at least forty years and have made a major contribution to the party. Its primary *raison d'être* seems to be to permit promotion of younger people to the Central Committee by absorbing older members from that committee into the new body. However, it also ensures that the 'wise old men' are formally organized into an organ which can guide and advise the Central Committee. Although Yugoslavia has an outwardly similar body (the Council of the Federation), the Chinese organ appears to be more powerful. Finally, Deng is a member of the Standing Committee of the Politburo; Hu and Zhao also became members of this body in February 1980.

Although Hua occupied more important posts than Deng or Hu or Zhao in the early days of the struggle, Deng was far more assiduous than the party chairman in building up support at various levels of the party and state—particularly in the CCP and the PLA (military) at the provincial level. Hua did have a potential power base, particularly in the security organs. However, he did not use this to any obvious advantage, other than to purge supporters of the Gang of Four.

Finally, there is the question of politicking at the top. As Chang (1981, pp. 4–8) has pointed out, once the Gang of Four was out of the way, Hua was supported by two main factions—the leftist 'whatever' faction (so called because they basically argued that 'whatever' Mao had said or done must be correct and defended) and the 'petroleum' faction (a group of economists and technical specialists who had been responsible for running the economy when Zhou Enlai was premier). The 'pragmatists' comprised three main groups, centring on Deng, Chen Yun, and Peng Zhen; these worked together to oppose the Hua group.

Turning now to personalities, the members of the Gang of Four were in at least one sense analogous to Trotsky—other leaders feared them and what they stood for. They were ruthless, radical extremists. Hua was different. Although a Maoist to some extent, he was more in line with Mao's less radical periods than with the Mao of the GPCR. He was also a rather grey bureau-cratic type with little personal attraction. He was relatively inexperienced at political intrigue at the top, and this aspect of his personal qualities played very much against him in the power struggle. In contrast, Deng was a sea-soned political intriguer, who had learnt much from two periods of disgrace under Mao (1966–73 and from April 1976); perhaps these periods of dis-grace, which Hua had not suffered, gave Deng's desire for power an ad-ditional cutting edge. Deng has a reputation for being shrewd but approachable. Above all, he is seen as a pragmatist, in marked contrast to the radical extremism of the Gang of Four and even the less radical Maoism of Hua. Therefore, although he has a strong personality, Deng has not generally been feared by other leaders, in contrast to Trotsky. Indeed, following the de-cline of the Gang of Four, it was Hua—with his connections to the security forces and his involvement in the suppression of the Tiananmen Square inci-dent (see chapter 11)—who seemed more of a potential threat. The other members of the 'winning team'—Hu and Zhao—are also both very pragma-tic politicians. Hu had been Deng's closest aide for years, and had a repu-tation for an imaginative approach to problems. Zhao did not have a history of closeness to Deng, but impressed Deng with his leadership of China's most populous province, Sichuan.

The policy differences between the Hua and Deng groups were not initially as great as those between Trotsky and Stalin or between the main contestants following Stalin's death. Basically, Hua took what might be called a 'moder-ate Maoist' line, with more emphasis on ideology than Deng. But *both* Hua and Deng supported Zhou's policy of the 'four modernizations' (first referred to by Zhou in January 1975). In the early stages, then, it appeared that the policy differences between Hua and Deng were more of degree and political style than of major substance; only subsequently did the substantial differ-ences become clear to all. Deng's pragmatism was epitomized in his famous dictum (in fact taken from Mao) 'seek truth from facts' (i.e., as distinct from abstract theory), and he was overall less ideologically oriented than Hua. Deng also placed much more emphasis on the importance of material incen-tives, and was less concerned about the essentially anti-egalitarian thrust of his policies.

The 'X'-factor in this struggle is less obvious than in the Vietnamese or Soviet cases. However, I would argue that the factor beyond Deng's control that helped him and his team to power was Mao's own vagaries and radical-ism. Many members of the political élite, at both central and local levels, had suffered in one way or another under the GPCR and/or felt that this period had done enormous harm to China's development. This helps to explain the rapid demise of the Gang of Four. But Hua, too, was in a sense also damned in having been unofficially chosen by Mao—whereas Deng, who was in the tradition of Liu Shaoqi and Zhou Enlai, and who had suffered so much under Mao, thereby gained an advantage over his rivals. In short, it would seem that the post-Mao succession struggle accords reasonably well with Meyer's notion of a 'struggle against power'. Many influential people were primarily concerned with ensuring there would be no new Mao—although it must be acknowledged that many others positively supported Deng's approach.

WHAT LEADS TO SUCCESSION STRUGGLES?

We have seen that there is no set pattern to leadership change in the communist world, there being smooth transitions as well as succession struggles. We now need to consider why leadership change varies so much. Adherents of the 'psycho-politics' approach will argue that it depends very much on the personalities of the leaders involved; this is almost certainly one factor, but it is probably a marginal one in most cases, since ambition and a desire for more power is a feature of most leading politicians in most societies. Another possible explanation has been put forward by the ever-stimulating Alfred Meyer, who suggests that the smooth transition may reflect fundamental problems in the political system, whereas the succession struggle reflects a basically healthy system (1983b, p. 165). Unfortunately, Meyer does not elaborate this thesis. But the implication seems to be that leaders will close ranks and cover up differences if the system is under serious threat (external and/or internal), whereas they will be prepared to reveal their disagreements if they perceive no such threat. The hypothesis is an appealing one, and could certainly be applied both to the Vietnamese case (i.e., divisions within the leadership could have led to conflict over tactics and strategy in the war against the South, which in turn could have had disastrous consequences for the Hanoi leadership) and the Khrushchev succession (i.e., the new leadership was very anxious to restore the USSR's international status and the image of strong and competent leadership at home). It can even be argued that the regularization of the Yugoslav system was designed to ensure an absence of major leadership conflict in the post-Tito era, since conflict could have been exploited both by elements within Yugoslavia who wished to see the country broken up and perhaps even foreign powers, notably the USSR (see Zaninovich 1983, p. 185). As with any neat correlation in the social sciences, however, we must be careful not to place too much faith in this hypothesis. Some would dispute the notion that the Soviet system was healthy and under no serious threat in the mid-1920s, for instance, while others would question the notion that there was such a threat to the system in the mid-1960s. Nevertheless, the Meyer thesis does provide us with a new and interesting perspective on leadership succession, which basically suggests that struggles are 'normal' given the absence of institutionalized change.

One other argument to consider is that put forward by Esherick and Perry (1983, p. 172) that 'A succession which involves one *type* of leadership to another is likely to be more prolonged and difficult than a simple transfer of power from one group of leaders to another.' A comparison of several successions leads one to question this. Stalin was as much a supreme leader—albeit of a different nature and personality—as Lenin, and the way in which he came to power was at least as 'prolonged and difficult' as any of the subsequent Soviet successions. Conversely, the transitions from Khrushchev, Ulbricht, Tito, and Ho went remarkably smoothly.

SUCCESSION STRUGGLE OR SUCCESSION CRISIS?

Closely related to Meyer's thesis just mentioned is the suggestion by Valerie Bunce (1981, esp, pp. 11 and 236–40) that succession struggles are actually functional to communist systems. During such struggles, the argument goes, policy innovations are more likely and there may well be an unblocking of upward mobility channels as changes are made in party and state apparatuses. In short, the population can see signs of change and will usually assume that this will be for the better. This goes against the traditional view, which is that succession struggles represent political crises and lead to instability. Once again, the evidence is conflicting. Many of the troubles in Eastern Europe in 1956 *can* be related to mass perceptions of leadership differences and struggles—both within the individual East European states and the USSR—whilst many other struggles have not been accompanied by mass unrest or other overt signs of political crisis. In short, Bunce has provided a useful corrective to the traditional view, although her own argument is not watertight; at least it must now be accepted that a succession struggle does not necessarily represent and/or fuel a political crisis—sometimes it does, but at other times it does not.

IS THERE A TREND TOWARDS SMOOTHER LEADERSHIP CHANGE?

Some observers of the Soviet scene have recently been suggesting that the last four changes of General Secretary there suggest that the whole process is becoming more systematized and smooth, and that this may set a pattern for the communist world. They point to the speed both at which the General Secretaries have been appointed, and at which Andropov and Chernenko became head of state, as evidence of smooth and *de facto* more institutionalized leadership change. Such assumptions *may* be correct, but cannot go unchallenged. A comparative analysis of succession struggles reveals that they often take months to emerge, and that rapid filling of the office of head of party and head of government or state is not in itself proof that a succession struggle will be avoided. Hence the fact that there was no very visible struggle in the Andropov era could relate to the fact that the General Secretary soon became very ill and looked certain to die in the not-too-distant future; other leaders may well have been prepared to hide their differences given the impending departure of Andropov. A similar argument might apply to Chernenko, although there were *some* signs of a power struggle within the Kremlin (for a speculative, kremlinological—but fascinating—analysis of this see Zlotnik 1984). On the other hand, Gorbachev was much younger and fitter when he took office, and may well stay in office long enough for the hypothesis to be properly tested. The evidence for other countries is also conflicting, and we should once again be wary of 'cosy' assumptions.

IS THERE A TREND TOWARDS COLLECTIVE LEADERSHIP?

Yet another widely held assumption is that there is a trend away from the supreme leader and even the 'first amongst equals' towards collective leadership (see, e.g. Korbonski 1976, pp. 8–10). This has been disputed by some, such as Myron Rush (1974 and 1976, p. 25) who see the pattern as being from individual rule to collective rule and back to individual rule; the return to individual rule will be in the form of the gradual emergence of one leader from within a given collective leadership. Which of these conflicting views is more persuasive? Using our earlier classification of leaderships, I would argue that there *is* a perceptible trend away from the supreme leader—which is not to say that one supreme leader is never followed by another, as the Lenin to Stalin or Gheorghiu-Dej to Ceausescu cases reveal—but that once the notion of the supreme leader has been effectively rejected, there is unlikely to be a move back towards it. One major reason for this is that many leaders will have had direct negative experience of the supreme leader configuration, and will want to ensure that the levels of whimsicality of such rule—under which their very lives might be at risk—cannot recur. This said, there is much less reason to assume that there is an 'irreversible' trend (the term is from Korbonski 1976, p. 10) from the first amongst equals (i.e., a form of individual leadership) configuration to the more collective forms of leadership. In some cases this pattern is perceptible, in others it is more open to question. There is much to suggest, for instance, that Andropov had considerably more say as General Secretary, at least while he was well, than Brezhnev did for most if not all of his period in office; if this is an accurate assessment—and we again face the problem of reliable information—then the arguments of *both* Korbonski and Rush come into question. This is not to say that there is no change or dynamism to leadership arrangements; clearly there is. But I would argue that there can just as well be moves away from collective leadership over time as moves towards it. I would further suggest that this relates both to the personalities of the new leaders and, more importantly, their perceptions of the previous leadership arrangements. If collective leadership has been accompanied by political stagnation, a new leadership team or even an existing one may take the opportunity of, say, a General Secretary's death to promote or allow to emerge a new 'first amongst equals', someone whom they feel will be able to push through much needed reform. The Andropov and Gorbachev eras *could* be interpreted from this perspective. This is not to argue that other leaders will not keep some sort of control over 'the' leader, including the capacity to remove him if major initiatives fail. But this notion of 'some control' is quite different from either oligarchy within collectivism or collective leadership as these terms have been defined.

HOW DO LEADERS MAINTAIN POWER?

The relative non-institutionalization of the position of top leaders not only affects leadership change, but also means that leaders have constantly to work at maintaining their position once they have 'consolidated'. Indeed, the notion of 'consolidation' of power by communist leaders is a relative rather than an absolute one, and even supreme leaders' powers can fluctuate quite considerably over time (a prime example is Mao).

In more collective leaderships, the head of the party maintains power largely subject to the approval of his peers. To a large extent, the maintenance of power by a supreme leader or first amongst equals is achieved through the kinds of mechanisms visible at the succession stage, notably the maintaining of power bases; this can include demoting protégés who become too independent and promoting new ones, demoting other leaders, etc. There are some important differences, however, between coming to power and staying in power. The most important one relates to policies. In a succession struggle, it is policy *proposals*, and possibly successful implementation of the first stages of the policy, that can help a given leader to 'win' the contest. But over time, it may be insufficient merely to have attractive ideas for improvement—ideas must usually be seen to be working. This said, there are—in addition to the power-bases—two major reasons why an incumbent leader can often survive policy failures. The first is that a clever leader may see problems developing at an early stage and make some lesser leader(s) responsible for the policy area (e.g. agriculture); if the policy is later perceived to have failed, the top leader has a scapegoat and can often maintain his position. Second, there is the question of alternatives and the possibilities for removing the leader. Other leaders may have doubts as to whether the situaton would be markedly improved under some other leader or leadership configuration. Even if they do agree on the need for leadership change, they may disagree on the direction of change, and will therefore acknowledge that it will have to be resolved by a succession struggle. They may feel that such a struggle following the removal of the incumbent will endanger the regime more than one or two policy failures—particularly bearing in mind the fact that policies rarely *totally* fail anyway, but are, rather, less successful than had been anticipated. Moreover, it should not be forgotten that the supreme leader or the first amongst equals is often in the number one position largely because of his superior skills at politicking, and this relationship *vis-à-vis* the other leaders may last indefinitely. In sum, leaders maintain power partially through their own skills and actions and partially because of the perceptions, attitudes, and actions of others.

DO NEW LEADERS MAKE A DIFFERENCE?

The title of the 1981 book by Valerie Bunce referred to above is *Do New Leaders Make a Difference?* In this, Bunce concludes that in both liberal-democratic and communist states 'new leaders mean new policies and old leaders mean the continuation of old priorities—it is almost as simple as that' (p. 255). But is it really so simple? Bunce has been criticized from a number of angles, some of which are important but rather technical for the novice (see, for example, Bahry 1983). Other criticisms and doubts are easily elaborated, however. For instance, there is the notion of 'difference'. It is surely a truism to say that new leaders will make *some* difference and introduce *some* changes. But Bunce is saying more than this—that new leaders make bigger policy changes than leaders who have been in office for some time. The argument is, then, that the differences under new leaders are *significant*. Unfortunately, what looks like a major policy change to one observer looks to another like minor 'tinkering with the works'. Bunce attempts to overcome this by taking a largely quantitative approach, analysing changes in budget priorities. One problem with this is that budgetary priorities may be seen as less significant policy changes by many citizens than, say, the relaxation of censorship. Even if we disregard this, however, there are not only the problems of obtaining reliable and complete budgetary data and interpreting them in a generally acceptable way, but also of proving that such changes are the result of initiatives by new leaderships. For instance, were the Soviet economic reforms of 1965 an 'initiative' of the new leadership, when in fact there had been major experimentation from at least 1962? Is the 'Four Modernizations' in China a major initiative of the current leadership when Zhou had proposed the policy in 1975? What seems to have been the case in both these examples is that new leaderships gave the general go-ahead for ideas that had already emerged under the previous leadership. This does, of course, represent some sort of leadership initiative; but one would want to distinguish this from a situation in which new leaders actually have new ideas themselves and introduce them. The examples might also suggest that there was policy stagnation in the late Khrushchev and late Mao eras; even though a convincing argument to this effect might be made *vis-à-vis* the economy (although my own view is that there were significant attempts at changing economic priorities in the later Khrushchev period, at least), there were certainly initiatives in other areas, such as culture, party organization, etc. In fact, there are often plenty of policy initiatives even under leaders who have been in power for many years; the sorts of factors prompting this—major policy failures, pressure from abroad, etc.—are analysed in chapter 10. For now, three main points can be made. First, the scope for initiative will vary considerably according to the type of leadership and the general political cli-mate in which the new leader(s) come(s) to power. Second, stagnation is a feature of some—but not *all*—long-standing communist leaderships. Third, whilst new leaderships obviously make *some* difference, some make consider-ably more than others (depending to some extent on the imaginativeness of new leaders) and it is far from clear that there are always more significant policy changes under new leaders than there are under leaders who have been in office for some time.

ARE OLD LEADERS A PROBLEM IN THE COMMUNIST WORLD?

Another ramification of the largely non-institutionalized nature of commu-nist leadership is that some leaders have—by liberal-democratic standards—remarkably long tenures. Several leaders—among them Tito, Zhivkov, Hoxha, Kadar, Kim Il Sung, and Tsedenbal—have been or were in power for more than a quarter of a century, for instance. Related to this is the fact that the average age of many communist leaderships is high—either because the team in power has grown old through being in office for many years or because others have had to wait so long to take over. It is sometimes assumed that this is a problem. In analysing this assumption, it is useful to distinguish clearly between old leaders (in terms of years) and leaders who have been in power for many years. Usually, there is a close correlation between these two. But the cases of Chernenko and Castro reveal that this is not invariably so, and that we therefore need to treat them separately. Considering first the question of age, it is often maintained that old leaders—let us say of sixty-five and over—are more conservative and less able than younger ones. This is a generalization, and one that does not stand up particularly well. There have been many energetic and innovative older leaders in both the communist and liberal democratic states; not only the Chinese and the Yugoslavs, but also the Americans know this from first-hand experience. This said, it is certainly the case that the older leaders are, the greater the likelihood of illness that will interfere with their work. This often *is* a problem, since important de-cisions that need to be made may be delayed. But there are other ways of looking at this. For instance, it can be argued that some leadership suc-cessions may actually have been smoother precisely because the outgoing/dying leader was ill for some time before 'departure', which meant that ar-rangements for the transfer of power could be made in a more orderly way than where an apparently healthy leader dies suddenly (see, e.g. the com-ments on the Tito succession in Zaninovich 1983, p. 185). Moreover, if top leaders are old and in poor health when they take office, they may not stay in power very long—which has distinct advantages both in terms of giving a few more individuals the opportunity of a taste of politics at the top and prevent-ing new over-personalized leaderships.

Let us now turn to the question of long tenure. Where a leader or small group of leaders stays in office for many years, frustration may develop among younger potential leaders—that is, officials of the party-state complex who feel that their access to the higher levels is being blocked. This certainly can be a problem, with the 'stability of cadres' policy adopted in the Brezhnev era (see Rigby 1970, pp. 179 and 191) being a prime example. The problem can be alleviated through the expansion of existing leadership bodies, the creation of new bodies, and by ensuring the relatively frequent turnover of ministers, republican party bosses, etc. Such measures can overcome much of the frustration, although some individuals will still be disappointed that they cannot reach the summit of power; the relatively small number of posts at that level in any system means that this will always be a problem, however.

It has already been argued that even leaders who have been in office for many years can have significant new policies. Sometimes, this is based on the fact that 'the' leader himself has a bold imagination. Even if he lacks this, he can change either the small team of personal advisers that heads of party at least seem to have in many communist states and/or even the membership of the Politburo (see Frank 1978, p. 113). In this way, new ideas can circulate at the top.

In short 'old' leadership can be but is not necessarily a problem in communist states.

IS KREMLINOLOGY RELEVANT?

'Kremlinology' (or its equivalent for communist states other than the USSR) is the study of the fine detail of leadership practice—who signs obituaries in the press, the order in which leaders stand at a May Day parade, who meets visiting foreign dignitaries, which leading politicians served with which others in their early careers, etc.—and the drawing of inferences, based on such study, about the relative powers and the policy stances of individuals within the leadership. In many ways, it is an unsatisfactory form of analysis. On the other hand, the secrecy that surrounds so many communist leaderships forces us to adopt what many analysts realize is a questionable method if we are to try to understand 'politics at the top'. Kremlinology *can* be relevant, as long as we are fully aware of its limitations. For instance, as we saw at the beginning of this chapter, it does not have an impressive track-record for predicting new leaders; this is widely accepted, and need not detain us. Rather less generally appreciated is the fact that an analysis of a given politician's career and allegiances is often of little value in predicting that politician's behaviour, policy-orientations, etc. once he/she becomes a member of the Politburo or even 'the' leader. Several analysts (e.g. Hough 1979 and 1980) have, for instance, argued that there are 'generations' of Soviet politicians, relating to their experience—or lack of it—of Stalinism, the 'Great Patriotic War' (i.e., World War Two) etc., and that this gives politicians of a given age-cohort a similar view of the world which is distinguishable from that of politicians from another age-cohort. The evidence on this is, to say the least, questionable. Without repeating details given earlier in this chapter, the point could be made that the history of succession struggles, for example, reveals that people of similar age and background can support very different policies, change long-standing political allegiances, etc. both during and after a change of leadership period. It also reveals that a new General/First Secretary may have appeared in the past to have had policy orientations similar to those of his predecessor, but that once in power these may change dramatically; he may have given the impression of sharing the predecessor's approach merely in order to stay at the top, in the hope that he will later be able to make a bid for power. Even assuming one appears to have a good grasp of a given individual's personality, political style, and policy orientations, and that the given individual seems to be adhering to traditional priorities, etc. during the struggle, he may be subject to so many constraints from other leaders that, once again, our knowledge is not particularly useful in terms of predicting policy outcomes. Thus, it *is* of interest to know about the order of line-ups at parades, etc. It is even more useful to know about career backgrounds, which are of particular value if we want to create a sociological portrait of communist leaderships/political élites. But we must also be careful not to get these out of perspective, and to realize that even the most sophisticated kremlinology is not a reliable guide to future actions by leaders.

CONCLUSIONS

A wide range of topics has been covered in this chapter, which is already so long that it makes little sense to reiterate every argument. Rather, certain key points will be emphasized. The first is that leadership could be institutionalized much more than it is in the communist world without contradicting Marxism–Leninism. The Yugoslav arrangements would not necessarily suit every country (in particular, it would be much more difficult in the unitarist states to determine who should become the new head of party and head of state each year, and annual turnover is in any case perhaps *too* frequent), but they do show that regularization is possible; as the saying goes, 'where there's a will, there's a way'. Second, many widely held assumptions about leadership succession are now out of date or do not apply on a comparative basis; many allegedly 'comparative' hypotheses were in fact based on a study of only one country (often the USSR) which is always dangerous. Third, it is clear that there is no set leadership configuration in the communist world, although there are patterns; many alleged 'trends' from one leadership arrangement to another must be questioned, and our analyses refined. Fourth, it has been suggested that reality and appearance are not always identical in leadership configurations. This comes out most clearly in the distinction drawn earlier between the symbolism and actual power of 'the' leader's position. Finally, there is no perfect leadership arrangement. Genuinely collective leadership can lead to slow and compromising decision-making, which is not always in the general interest, whereas one-person dominated leadership can be highly arbitrary and based on inadequate awareness of the many aspects of any given problem. Personalized leadership by one leader over a long period *may* lead to stagnation—but this can also apply to collective leadership, especially if the individual members stay in office for many years. In the latter case, an imaginative leader could introduce more changes over time than a collective leadership. For these sorts of reasons, we can expect to see constant movement between the more individualized and the more collective forms of leaderships, as politicians at the top seek to improve on whatever went before.

Basic further reading

C. Beck *et al.*, 1973.

A. Brown, 1980.

V. Bunce, 1981.

P. Chang, 1981.

R. B. Farrell (ed.), 1970.

G. Gill, 1982.

A. Korbonski, 1976.

M. Rush, 1968, 1974.

Studies in Comparative Communism,
    Autumn 1983.

9

MINOR PARTIES, MASS ORGANIZATIONS, AND GROUP POLITICS

In this chapter we shall consider various political organizations other than the communist party itself or the state organs proper. We begin by looking at minor parties and mass organizations, following which the polemical issue of interest and pressure groups in the communist world will be examined.

MINOR PARTIES

It comes as a surprise to many, reared on media which refer to the 'one-party communist states', to discover that a large number of these in fact have bi- or multi-party systems, *formally* at least. In fact, for our purposes we can distinguish between three basic types of party-system in the communist world—
1. Formal multi-party systems.
2. Formal one-party systems, in which other parties operate illegally.
3. One-party systems proper.

In type one there is in addition to the communist party one or more minor parties, which are represented in elections, have seats in the assemblies, etc. This kind of arrangement can be found for instance in Bulgaria, China, Czechoslovakia, the GDR, North Korea, Poland, and Vietnam.

A second group of communist states—mainly the newer ones—does not formally tolerate and/or incorporate parties other than the ruling communist party, but has been unable finally to crush all opposition parties. This is particularly true of the communist states of Africa. In Angola, for example, the MPLA has as yet been unable finally to eradicate UNITA. Until the late 1970s Ethiopia represented a hybrid of types one and two in that it formally recognized some (five) political parties, whilst there were other groups claiming to be parties, but which were not officially recognized and which were struggling against the governing group. Although some of these were clearly anti-Marxist (e.g. the Ethiopian Democratic Union), others were Marxist but had a different orientation from the group in power. Thus the Ethiopian People's Revolutionary Party, composed principally of urban-based members of the intelligentsia, was a Maoist group, while the main aim of the basically Marxist Tigre Popular Liberation Front was to ensure the secession of Tigre from the rest of Ethiopia. Some, but not all, of these illegal groups continue to operate. In Asia, there is the peculiar situation of Kampuchea. From 1975 to 1979, the country was ruled by the ultra-radical—even by communist standards—Communist Party of Kampuchea (CPK) led by Pol Pot. This was replaced in January 1979 by the National United Front for the Salvation of Kampuchea, led by Heng Samrin and given considerable support, both at the takeover stage and subsequently, by the Vietnamese. At the time of writing, the CPK had recently dissolved itself; but this is presumably to make it more difficult for the official Kampuchean regime to track down this party, rather than a sign that the CPK leaders have given up their original aims.

It should be noted that although reference has been made to 'parties' in this second kind of arrangement, many of these organizations are as much underground armies as they are political organizations. But inasmuch as they do represent ideologies and want to take power on the basis of popular support (i.e., as distinct from merely through military force), the term 'party' seems to be as appropriate as any.

Even amongst the third group of communist states—those which do have only one political party (e.g. Albania, Cuba, Hungary, Mongolia, Romania, USSR, Yugoslavia)—some did initially experiment with the multi-party system. The best example is the USSR itself, in which the Bolsheviks (eventually to become the CPSU) more or less tolerated other political parties until 1921. It was not until the year of the Kronstadt uprising (see chapter 12)—and Lenin's perception that the regime was in danger—that the Bolsheviks finally decided that not only was discipline within their own ranks to be tightened, but also that the continued existence of alternative organizations and ideologies was dysfunctional to their (i.e., the Bolsheviks') consolidation of power.

Whom do the Minor Parties Represent?

In classical Marxism, the 'dictatorship of the proletariat' was to be a political system in which the majority group in the population would exercise a dictatorship over those elements hostile to socialism. As has been argued in earlier chapters, the exact nature of this dictatorship was never spelt out by the classical theorists. What is clear, however, is that they realized that not everyone would have a fundamentally similar attitude towards the new political system. Yet it would be erroneous to suppose that the minor parties which exist legally in so many communist states are to represent the interests of the minority that may be opposed to socialism. The assumption that these parties represent a formal opposition, by classes basically antagonistic to the proletariat and its dictatorship, is a false one. Before going any further, we need to say something about the concept of class and other social cleavages as perceived by communists in power.

Contrary to popular belief, none of the communist states claims to have eradicated classes altogether. In most, it is argued that there exist two classes (proletariat, collective peasantry) and a stratum (intelligentsia). Since workers in the factories do not personally own the means of production, whereas peasants do usually have their own private plot and collectively own the farms they work, it is argued that the relationship of peasants and workers to the means of production is different. However, since peasants are not generally allowed to employ—and thus exploit—others, the antagonistic dimension of class relationships is held not to exist. The position of the intelligentsia—broadly defined in the communist world as those who earn their living by mental as distinct from manual labour—is not different from the blue-collar workers in terms of their relationship to the means of production; formally, they are proletarians in the strict sense (i.e., people who earn their living by selling their labour rather than from their property). But communists themselves see a fundamental distinction between mental and manual labour, which is why the intelligentsia is distinguished from the manual proletariat, yet is described as a stratum rather than as a class. It could be argued—and has been, by writers such as Djilas (1966), Konrad and Szelenyi (1979)—that although the members of the intelligentsia do not formally *own* the means of production, they *do* control it (i.e., in being managers, planners, politicians) and in this sense do constitute a class separate from the ordinary workers. Whatever the validity of such an argument, it is not subscribed to by the communist states themselves, and therefore is not used as a way of explaining the existence of multi-party systems.

However, some of the explanation for the continued existence of non-communist parties is already beginning to emerge from the above. Although most of the communist states other than the very newest ones claim to have eradicated *antagonistic* class relationships, they do not claim to have abolished all basic divisions in society. Given that their formal analyses tend to refer to at least three basic groups, only one of which is the proletariat proper, it becomes clear that the 'dictatorship of the proletariat' might not give proper representation to other groups. Of these other groups, the largest is invariably the peasantry, and it is therefore hardly surprising that peasant (sometimes 'agrarian') parties figure prominently among the lists of minor parties in communist states. In many countries, the communists are aware that they do not yet have the full support of the peasantry. Therefore, rather than try to suppress political organizations representing this class, they have in many cases decided to retain a peasant party—but have succeeded in keeping this very much under communist control. Many of the other parties are to represent the intellectuals, the petty bourgeoisie (e.g. private shopkeepers) and even some former capitalists; this is particularly true in China and the GDR.

But not all of the minor parties are intended to represent groups of people united principally by economic criteria. In Czechoslovakia, some of the minor parties exist primarily as representatives of particular national groups. Even representation of religious groups via political 'parties' is tolerated in some communist states. In the GDR, for instance, the CDU is meant to represent primarily the interests of Christians, whilst the Chongu party in North Korea also represents a religious sect. And in Poland, many Catholics have been represented in the Sejm by the 'neo-Znak' and 'Pax' groups of deputies.

One final point is that the minor parties are mostly small in terms of membership numbers. For example, the four minor parties in the GDR have only about 400,000 members between them, compared with over 2.2 million members of the Socialist Unity Party. The total membership of China's eight minor parties is only 120,000, a very small figure relative to the Chinese population. However, their memberships often include large numbers of people in important posts, particularly academicians, so that data on the size of minor parties do not necessarily reflect the perceived status of such organizations in society.

Why Were the Minor Parties Originally Permitted, and Why do They Still Exist?

If we look for reasons for the existence of minor parties in some of the communist states, we find that official explanations frequently emphasize the fact that these parties are to represent different groups, in the way described above. For instance, a Soviet theoretician has written: 'The objective conditions of the existence of the multi-party system under socialism consist in the social heterogeneity of society, which is retained not only in the transitional period, but at the subsequent stages as well' (Petrenko 1981, p. 84). Such an official definition does not explain, however, why some communist states have multi-party systems while others do not. In order to understand the reasons for the existence of such parties, we have to look at both historical and international dimensions of the politics of individual countries.

As we saw in the early part of this book, communist parties have often taken power in the vacuum following a major war, and in many cases have in essence been installed by a foreign power. It was also shown how the division of Eastern Europe after World War II was largely the outcome of negotiations between and differing interpretations by the victorious allies. Out of these negotiations—and the realities of Eastern Europe, in terms of social and economic structures—emerged the concept of a People's Democracy. This term seems to have first been used by Tito in 1945 (Brzezinski 1967, p. 25), although it was in some ways related to Mao's 1930s concept of a 'new democracy' and the still earlier notion of a People's Republic (the first of which were Tannu Tuva in 1921 and Mongolia in 1924). The concept of a People's Democracy seemed to represent nicely the hybrid or compromise system that was necessitated by the negotiations. The Western allies insisted on some form of multi-party, parliamentary system; the Soviets were equally adamant that they were not prepared to accept political systems in the countries on their European borders that could allow the emergence of fascist regimes or even Western-type liberal democracies that would be intolerant of communism. Thus the People's Democracies would be neither liberal democracies nor one-party states. This said, a number of right-wing (though by no means exclusively fascist) parties were banned, leaving essentially only centrist and left-wing parties in the 'multi-party' systems. For example, the fascist Slovak Populist Party in Czechoslovakia was banned, but so too was the right-wing but not fascist Agrarian Party.

In addition to this factor, it should be noted that other parties had helped the communists either take and/or consolidate power in several countries of Eastern Europe, and the communists were aware that large sections of the population might turn against them (i.e., the communists) were they to show their gratitude to these other parties by abolishing them.

Closely related to the last point is the fact that the communists were unpopular and/or did not represent the majority of the population in any of these countries. It therefore made more sense to attempt to integrate parties representing other groups (other than extreme right-wing ones) than to ban them, which could lead to further hostility and might undermine the communists' own position. Although one way of integrating them was, as we saw in chapter six, to incorporate them into the communist party itself, the multi-party system was another way of achieving a similar goal. Indeed, a multi-party system meant that there was less risk that the 'vanguard party' would be diluted by former members of other parties who did not really accept Leninist organizational principles.

It should thus be clear why there gradually emerged the notion of a formal—but already restricted—multi-party system in some communist states. By the end of the 1940s, it had become clear that this system was one in which the communists would always hold the trump card. The balance of seats in parliament, the kind of propaganda that could appear in the non-communist party newspapers, the *nomenklatura* system for all important posts in society—these and other crucial matters were always to be ultimately in the hands of the communists. Once this system was established, and the communists could see how they could always keep the other parties under control, the disadvantages of trying to abolish the minor parties came to outweigh any possible advantages. As other communist parties saw how the multi-party system could be accommodated to Leninist political principles, some of them (e.g. Vietnam) decided to follow the example of the East Europeans.

Although historical circumstances provide the bulk of the explanation for the existence of multi-party systems in most communist states, it should not be supposed that such systems have now outlived themselves. The advantages to the communists of such a formal multi-party system are several. First, there is the propaganda and regime-legitimizing value of having what looks like a multi-party system. The regime's leaders can argue both at home and abroad that they are as democratic as other systems having multi-party arrangements, and it is far easier for critics of the communist countries to condemn the *absolute* absence of a multi-party system than it is to criticize the particular conception of a multi-party system adopted by communists. Moreover, the Yugoslav theorist Vracar argued in 1966 that since a multi-party arrangement actually seems to strengthen capitalist systems, then there is no inherent reason why this should not equally be the case in a socialist country. His argument rested on the premiss that the main parties in capitalist societies are all *basically* supportive of the existing system, whether it be Democrats and Republicans in the USA, Labour and Conservative in the UK, or Liberals and Labor in Australia. If, therefore, one had a multi-party system in a communist state, in which the parties differed only on marginals rather than on the fundamental commitment to socialism, then by analogy socialism would be strengthened (cited in Fejto 1974, p. 354). Although his own country's politicians have not adopted this argument (though they do seem to have considered it—see Rusinow 1977, p. 374, fn. 59), others clearly have.

This leads us to the next point, which is that communist states can generally keep their eye on nascent oppositionists more easily if these people are given organizations which allegedly represent their interests than where no such organizations exist. Although the minor parties do not act in any meaningful sense as opposition parties, they can serve a very useful function in giving the communists a particular viewpoint on a given issue, and providing the country's leaders with some idea of the likely reactions of particular groups to a proposed piece of legislation. In other words, they serve to widen the perspectives of communists on important questions via the feedback role they play.

A third function also relates to feedback—this time from foreign political parties. For instance, when the Korean Democratic Party renamed itself the Korean Social Democratic Party in January 1981, a South Korean expert interpreted this as being aimed at establishing ties with socialist parties of the non-communist world (cited in *1982 Yearbook on International Communist Affairs*, p. 201). Similarly, David Childs (1969, p. 104) has argued that one of the reasons for the continued existence of minor parties in the GDR is to act as a bridgehead to similarly named parties in West Germany and elsewhere. Although this bridgehead role can fluctuate as East–West relations improve or deteriorate, the receiving of foreign delegates to the minor parties' congresses can be a useful source of inside information on other states—a form of information-gathering—for the communist leaderships.

Fourth, there is the point that Leninist parties themselves are not supposed to tolerate factionalism (i.e., subgroupings within the party). This is not to say that factionalism does not exist in the ruling communist parties—it frequently overtly does. But by allowing other parties formally to represent the interests and views of people who do not wish to follow the leadership's views too closely, communist regimes are creating a release valve and minimizing the chances of factionalism, particularly at the lower levels.

In sum, the minor parties perform a number of functions in communist regimes. To argue that they are irrelevant is both factually questionable and culturally biased. The important point to remember is that one should not attempt to understand their position as being essentially the same as that of opposition and/or minor parties in the liberal democracies, and that they are not intended to serve as alternative sources of government. Such an arrangement was aptly described in the 1960s by one of the leading official Polish theoreticians, Jerzy Wiatr, as a 'hegemonic party system', in which the communist party leads all the others (see Ionescu 1967, p. 248). In practice, this means that the minor parties have never mounted any really serious challenge to the communist party, a point which applies to all the established communist states permitting minor parties. This 'hegemonic' conception of leadership by the communist party means that by having a formal multi-party system, the communists can virtually have their cake and eat it.

The Future of the Minor Parties

Communist states disagree amongst themselves on the future of the minor parties. For instance, Albania seems to be strongly opposed to any consideration even of the question of a multi-party system, criticizing the 'opportunist justification of pluralism of political parties in the socialist system' (Szajkowski 1981b, p. 43). An equally firm line—if expressed in less extreme terms—is taken by most Soviet theoreticians. Petrenko writes as follows:

... the return to a multi-party system in the USSR and other socialist countries where a one-party system has been established would undoubtedly be a step backward ... The tendency to social homogeneity, and consequently to a one-party system, is natural for socialist society ... (1981, p. 110).

Certainly, as the communist states become 'developed socialist', and start talking of moving on to the early stages of communism, so it *could* be argued that organizations intended, at one level, to represent different groups and interests should disappear; in a communist society, people are not to be divided in any meaningful sense by their position in the economic system, race, creed, etc.

Yet if we look at even the oldest and most economically developed of the communist states, we see that at present neither the division of labour nor nationalist tensions nor religious dissidence show any signs of disappearing. Indeed, the division of labour is at present deepening, as the industrialization process leads to the same complication of the labour process as it does in the liberal democracies. Thus some communist states more or less overtly recognize that communism is still such a long way off that the minor parties will continue to play a role for the foreseeable future. For example, Mao is alleged to have said that he did not envisage the eventual abolition of the united front (of political parties), whilst the post-Mao leadership has stated that, 'It is our desire as well as our policy to exist side by side with the democratic parties for a long time to come, exercise mutual supervision and bring their initiative into play to serve socialism!' (*Peking Review*, 6 January 1978, p. 14). At the 11th Congress of the Bulgarian Communist Party (1977), First

Secretary Zhivkov argued that the Bulgarian Agrarian People's Union will also continue to exist for the foreseeable future, whilst the Czechoslovak leader Husak made a similar statement about Czechoslovakia's minor parties in the same year.

Not only such statements, but the trends in the practice of communist states in recent years also suggest that such regimes have been moving away from some of the more radical aspects of building communism in recent years. Such developments suggest that there should be little theoretical problem in justifying the continuation of a multi-party system in communist states for many years to come. Even in those countries which formally have one-party systems, recent developments have tended to be in the direction of the spirit, if not yet the letter, of a multi-party arrangement. This is seen in both the theory and practice of elections, for example. Thus despite the statements by Soviet and Albanian theoreticians, it is not entirely beyond the bounds of possibility that even the USSR itself might in years to come allow the emergence of what is, in practice at least, a form of multi-party system. It is certainly the case that there is no stipulation—in their constitutions or in the communist party rules or in any other such documents—that one-party states are so for reasons of principle; rather, as we have seen, it is generally a matter of historical tradition.

Before moving on to the next section, one very important point needs to be made. Despite all the rhetoric of those communist states which formally do have a multi-party system, it cannot be said that the minor parties play more than a marginal role in any of these countries. Therefore, the really interesting question in the future will not be whether a given communist state abolishes or introduces a multi-party system, but rather how multi-party systems actually operate. We need to look for signs of a real upgrading of the minor parties if we are to talk of a genuine multi-party system. Communist proposals in the assemblies will have to be overturned by minor parties; the newspapers of such parties will have to represent views genuinely at odds with those of the communist newspapers; elections will have to be far more genuinely contested than in the past; etc. Until such developments occur, it would probably be most accurate to describe those communist states which have formal multi-party systems as 'modified one-party systems'. Such countries have learnt the advantages—in terms of legitimacy and feedback—of allowing minor parties to exist.

MASS ORGANIZATIONS

In terms of sheer numbers of members, political parties—including the communist parties themselves—are small relative to the so-called mass organizations in communist countries. These organizations can between them include over 80 per cent of the adult population (e.g. the Committees for the Defence of the Revolution in Cuba) and in some countries are eventually to embrace virtually everybody. There are a wide range of such bodies, including organizations to represent national minorities (e.g. the Council of Workers of Hungarian Nationality in Romania), cultural groups, hobby groups, groups for improving relations with other countries, and farmers' organizations. But the most significant in the communist world as a whole are the women's movements, the youth movements, and the trade unions. All of these have some tasks in common—notably to explain communist party policies to their members, to encourage members both to support these policies and to participate actively in their implementation—but each also has specific tasks. Let us now consider these.

Women are supposed to have equal rights to men in communist states, and much has been done to bring about such equality. Nevertheless, it is perhaps testimony to the fact that still more needs to be done—and certainly that women are seen as in some sense constituting a special group—that organizations exclusively for them exist in virtually all the communist countries. One of the tasks of these organizations is to look after the interests of women; although few such bodies do very much in terms of pressing the politicians on behalf of women (though there is some evidence that this has been happening in Cuba in recent years, for example), several are seen as a form of training ground, in which women can become more aware of politics and the society in which they live prior to playing a more active role in politics. Another task of some women's organizations is to encourage more females to enter the work-force; this is particularly true in countries where there is an overall labour shortage (e.g. Mongolia, the GDR). In some of the newer communist states, the women's organizations also try to encourage more women to fight against 'class enemies'; this may well involve the formation of women's militias to take on groups that have not accepted the new communist regime and are mounting attacks against it (e.g. in Mozambique).

The youth movements in the communist world similarly act as training grounds for future administrators and politicians. The organizations are usually divided into at least two main wings—one for children up to their mid-teens (often called the 'Pioneers'), and another for teenagers and young adults. The overwhelming majority of children in most countries join the Pioneers or its equivalent. This organization arranges camps, teaches skills in cooking, tying knots, etc. and is in some ways similar to boy scout and girl guide organizations in the West—except that boys and girls are not usually separated. However, there are also important differences between these organizations and their approximate Western equivalents. The most significant is that the communist children's organizations are much more overtly political, indoctrination being seen as one of their positive and necessary functions; this may well include elementary military training, to prepare youngsters to defend the motherland. The proportion of young people in the youth leagues (e.g. the Komsomol in the USSR, the Ho Chi Minh Youth League in Vietnam, the Communist Youth Federation in Hungary, etc.) is usually lower than in the children's organizations, with about 75 per cent of young people being the maximum membership in most countries. There is an increasing tendency for the membership of these leagues to be highest amongst students and lowest amongst young unskilled workers. This largely reflects the fact that the youth league is the single most important stepping-stone into the communist party, and young people who are anxious to 'get on' in society will be aware of this. But not all members of the youth leagues will be able or will want to join the communist party later in their lives, and there are other functions performed by these organizations. In the less developed communist states, such as Mozambique or Yemen, youth leagues play an important role in raising literacy rates amongst young people. And in many communist states, the youth leagues are often a source of extra cheap labour, for harvesting, heavy construction work, and even for resettling the adult population (notably in Pol Pot's Kampuchea).

In order to understand the position of trade unions in the communist world, one must start by appreciating that their role is fundamentally different from that of similarly named bodies in the liberal democracies. The Bolsheviks—in particular, Trotsky—argued in the early days of Soviet rule that the notion of groups of workers organizing themselves into mass unions to defend themselves against the state made sense in a capitalist, bourgeois democracy, but was an illogicality in a workers' state. This might or might not be a convincing argument, but in any case it is postulated on the assumption that there really is a workers' state; this is not the place to deal with this important question, but suffice it to say that this line of argument has served as the basis of official policies on trade unions in almost all the communist world ever since. If the trade unions are not to defend groups of workers against the state—certainly in the sense of organizing strikes—what *is* their role? In fact, they perform several functions, in addition to the general ones performed by virtually all mass organizations and outlined earlier.

First, although they are not intended to defend groups of workers against a fundamentally antagonistic state, they are to look after the interests of individual workers against insensitive or corrupt bureaucrats, managers, etc. In most communist countries, for instance, a worker who has been dismissed from work—e.g. for repeatedly turning up late, alcoholism, etc.—has the right to appeal to the union. If the factory union committee thinks the dismissal unfair, it can raise this with the management; if no agreement is reached, the union can then insist on a tribunal, or that higher state/party/ trade union bodies be called in to investigate and adjudicate. A second function of trade unions in most communist states—and one that sometimes conflicts with the first function—is to assist management in various ways. Not only do the unions play a major role in ensuring that workers meet production schedules, observe labour discipline, etc., but they also often play *some* role in enterprise decision-making. The amount varies from time to time and place to place, but in most of the Soviet-oriented communist states, major decisions are supposed to be made according to the principle of 'one-person management and collegiality'. According to this, the manager of an enterprise has overall responsibility for the running of that enterprise, but is obliged to consult with the enterprise trade union and party committees on key issues. The notion of 'key issues' is in practice often highly subjective, and trade union members often criticize management for not having consulted them. In some countries, notably Hungary, attempts have been made to overcome this via the unions' 'suspensory veto' right; this means that, in theory at least, decisions with which the trade union fundamentally disagrees can be vetoed temporarily, until some compromise is reached. The possibility that trade union committees will find they have split loyalties (i.e., between workers and management) is enhanced by the fact that senior managers will themselves often be members of the trade union committee. Unlike the situation in most Western countries, trade unions in the communist world are typically organized on the basis of one union for a whole branch or sector of the economy; one ramification of this is that everyone working in a given factory, from the top director to the cleaners, will be eligible to join only one and the same trade union. Given all this, it may come as a surprise to learn that trade union membership rates amongst industrial workers is 95 per cent plus in many countries. The reason for this is relatively simple to explain: in addition to the functions already outlined, communist trade unions play a major role in administering social welfare. Maternity benefits, sickness benefits, social insurance, etc. are primarily organized and distributed by trade unions. Moreover, the trade unions often have the best holiday hostels to which workers are likely to have access, and thus act as a sort of package-tour operator.

Unions play various other roles—for instance, they often have a formal right to propose legislation to the national assembly, although this right is not generally exercised to any significant extent. They can also play a major role in the retraining and/or redeployment of workers necessitated by technological change. In sum, they have several functions to perform, without being involved in the organization of strikes.

Although most citizens in communist states are members of at least one mass organization, it should by now be clear that the reasons for joining these can be very diverse, and high membership levels are by no means necessarily a sign that the masses are highly politicized and supportive of the system; some people will be, others will not. Now and again, there are complaints that the mass organizations are working too much in the interests of the party–state complex, helping the authorities to direct and control the masses rather than representing the latter's interests in the higher organs of party and state. Dissatisfaction can lead to occasional attempts to establish 'free' (i.e., independent of the party and state) trade unions, such as has occurred in the USSR since 1977 (see Haynes and Semyonova, 1979 or Ziegler 1983) and in Cuba in 1983 (see *Communist Affairs*, January 1984, p. 12). The fact that the organizers of these are usually subjected to harassment of one kind or another—even though they may only be calling for rights formally granted in the constitution, not Western-style trade union rights (see Ruble 1981, p. 103)—shows how little autonomy the state-sponsored mass organizations have. When the official mass organizations do start to become more autonomous of the party–state complex, they may well be disbanded, and re-established under greater control; this happened to the Czechoslovak youth league (The Union of Youth) in 1970. The rights of trade unions and other mass organizations vary quite considerably, from Yugoslavia and Hungary at one end of the spectrum to Albania at the other. But it remains the case that communist parties have the right to be involved in the selection of all leading officials in unions, youth leagues, etc. (via the *nomenklatura* system), and indeed exert considerable control over them. Does all this mean that there is essentially no independent political activity or group politics in the communist world? This is one of the questions to which we must now address ourselves.

GROUP POLITICS

Some definitional problems

Social scientists use the term 'group' in all sorts of different ways. For instance, political sociologists may refer to a collection of individuals as a group merely because those individuals share common attributes (e.g. levels of education, income, status, etc.) and/or occupy a similar position in the division of labour (i.e., they have similar jobs). But the members of such groups—which we call *social* and *functional* respectively—may not actually perceive themselves as members of the group. Even if they do, they may do nothing to further their collective interests. If, on the other hand, such individuals *are* aware of their collective interests and do organize themselves so as to promote and/or defend these interests, they constitute an *interest group*. Often, such groups will be based on social or functional groups; trade unions and professional associations are good examples. But there are other kinds of interest groups. For instance, a government might announce that it intends to build an airport near a quiet village, which may lead all or most of the villagers—professional people, farm labourers, shopkeepers, etc.—to join forces, usually only temporarily, to resist the proposal. This, then, is an example of an interest group not based on similarity of social characteristics or position in the division of labour, but on a common interest in a specific issue. For this reason, we often call such groupings *issue-oriented* interest groups. This term is not entirely watertight, since in the real world functional interest groups may be very issue-oriented; but the term is useful for distinguishing different kinds of groups.

Another definitional problem is that individuals might form a group on the basis of shared beliefs in a common ongoing cause. For instance, they might attempt to influence decision-makers *on behalf of* some disadvantaged group that would find it either difficult or impossible to promote/defend its own interests (e.g. children, the sick, animals, etc.). Conversely they may organize themselves around a somewhat more abstract cause, such as protection of the environment. Clearly, the notion of 'group interests' is quite different in these sorts of cases from the kinds referred to above, such *cause-oriented* groups having less to gain *personally* from their group actions. For this reason, the use of the term interest group is potentially misleading. Moreover, a group may be self-aware and organized, but is not in any meaningful sense attempting to influence decision-makers. A good example is the trade unions in communist countries which, as we have seen, often devote much of their energy to administering welfare benefits, arranging holidays, etc. When they are performing such functions, they are looking after the interests of their members, even though they may not be very involved in the policy process. A third point is that a group might indeed be attempting to influence the decision-makers—by making its views known to these people—but has little or no power to force these decision-makers to take heed of the group's interests. Expressed another way, the group has essentially no *bargaining power*, no *pressure* which it can exert on the decision-makers. For all these sorts .of reasons, analysts sometimes make a distinction between interest groups and *pressure groups*. The distinction cannot always be sustained in the real world; politically active interest groups are frequently pressure groups, for instance. But at least the reader should now be aware of some of the reasons why analysts sometimes want to use different terms, and also why there are limitations on our ability conceptually to differentiate between different kinds of groups. Let us now draw all these points together, and specify the conditions that must be fulfilled in order for a group of people to constitute an interest and/or pressure group.

First, as mentioned briefly earlier, the group must have developed or be developing a self-awareness of itself as a group; interests must be consciously *aggregated*, not merely inferred by outsiders on the basis of the perceived common interests of a number of individuals. It is easy to overlook this point if one lives in a society in which communications are highly developed, the media relatively open, and where the biggest problem of organizing a conference is often the chore of working out all the fine administrative details. In the communist states, the development of a group consciousness is not always so easy. In some of the newer states, communication channels are still at a relatively low level of development. This is less of a problem in the more industrially developed communist states, but even in these, the channels of communication are rarely as open as they are in the West. Journals and newspapers—through which individuals can communicate with each other and develop a group consciousness—are subject to varying levels of censorship, although it is a fact that specialized, functional groups increasingly have their own journals which are less prone to censorship than more publicly available media. The convening of conferences, too, in communist states is usually subject to official scrutiny (see Holmes 1981a, pp. 88–9 and 93). This is not to say that all conferences are manipulated by the central authorities in some totalitarian way; some are and have been, but—certainly in the more advanced communist states—conferences of specialists appear to be increasingly autonomous of central political interference.

Assuming that a group awareness of common interests has developed, the second precondition arises. This is that there should exist channels through which the group can *articulate* its views to the decision-makers, and there must be some evidence that the group is able to use these. To some extent, this overlaps with point one; a representative of a functional group writing in a national newspaper may very well be simultaneously appealing to others with a similar functional position and/or opinion (i.e., in order to develop an awareness of common interests and views) *and* attempting to influence decision-makers. Another way in which the group may articulate its interests is for members of it to be elected to various decision-making bodies, at which individuals can act as spokespersons. Alternatively, the group might be able to bend the ear of someone who is on, say, the Central Committee or even the Politburo, who will then articulate the group's interests.

A third precondition—which must apply if we are to talk of a pressure group, but does not necessarily pertain if we are referring only to interest groups—is that groups should have some means whereby pressure can be exerted (i.e., they must have some form of bargaining power). In the liberal democracies, many groups have various forms of sanctions which they can use against decision-makers whom, they feel, are not paying sufficient attention to their case. The best-known of such sanctions, particularly for pressure groups based on the division of labour, is the withdrawal of labour or strike. A strike can seriously affect the economic interests of a state or of a company; in both cases, decision-makers will be forced to take serious heed of the demands of the group, and probably reach some compromise. Strikes do occur in the communist world, and not only in a major crisis situation such as Poland experienced in the early 1980s. Indeed, a few communist states have on occasions constitutionally permitted workers to strike, although this has always tended to be more of a right on paper than in practice, and nowadays strikes are in most countries treated as illegitimate and symptomatic of a major flaw in society. They are usually spontaneous and seldom involve the official trade unions; workers organize themselves on a temporary basis, usually to remove a specific grievance. It is an interesting point that—in Eastern Europe at least—strikers are generally very successful. As Alex Pravda notes, 'Yugoslav evidence shows that strikes are a highly successful and effective form of protest, and this is borne out generally by East European experience' (1979, p. 225). But the very success of these is largely because they represent significant tensions in society which the authorities wish to lessen. The disincentives to strike are usually so great—upward mobility chances can be substantially reduced, there are no strike funds or social security benefits, strikers can be imprisoned or even shot—that the authorities know that workers will not disregard these lightly. For these reasons, strikes cannot generally be considered as part of normal group politics; rather, as suggested by Pravda (1979), they should in most cases be seen as a form of essentially illegitimate protest politics. So what other forms of sanction or bargaining power do groups have?

One of the most important is a refusal to co-operate to the maximum extent with the decision-makers. In communist states, as anywhere else, the deepening of the division of labour tends to strengthen the political position of various groups upon which the party–state complex becomes increasingly dependent. The most frequently cited example is that of the technical specialists. For instance, if the specialists feel that their interests are not receiving sufficient attention from the decision-makers, they can become less co-operative, which can in turn lead to less efficiency, more problems, and hence less regime legitimacy. It follows that it is in the interests of the decision-makers to satisfy the interests of specialists, to a degree compatible with what are perceived as more general interests. Thus the technical specialists may be seen to have *some* sort of bargaining power *vis-à-vis* the decision-makers, although this power is usually limited and indirect by Western standards. In addition to this form of pressure, it is possible for groups to bribe officials as a way of attempting to influence decision-making. Corruption certainly occurs in communist states (see e.g. Staats 1972, esp. pp. 46–7; Liu 1983; Schöpflin 1984), although the evidence available so far is insufficient for us to be able to ascertain whether or not self-aware groups—as distinct from individuals—attempt to bribe officials to any significant extent. Then there are appeals to public opinion, in the hope that the decision-makers will take heed of this; such appeals do occur in the communist world, albeit on a very limited scale in comparison with the West.

Some other forms of pressure common in liberal democracies are *not* generally a feature of the communist world, largely because of the nature of the political system. These include contributions to party funds; organized and legitimate lobbying of parliamentarians; and various forms of essentially legitimate civil disobedience (e.g. open and tolerated protests, withholding rates, etc.). But, of course, to say that there are far *fewer* possibilities for groups to exert pressure in the communist world is quite different from saying that there are *no* possibilities; some form of bargaining does occur.

Finally, it should by now be clear why minor parties are in many ways more like interest or pressure groups than political parties as we normally understand them, in spite of the fact that they do meet one of the main criteria for distinguishing parties from groups—namely, the putting up of candidates for elections.

Western Views on Interests and Groups

The so-called group theory of politics is generally agreed to have been first elaborated by Arthur Bentley in a book published in 1908. According to this theory, all political decisions can be seen as the result of group interactions. In one sense, this is a truism, in that Bentley's notion of groups was very broad, and would include a small leadership group, the aggregate effect of large numbers of unorganized individuals (e.g. a class), etc. At the time, however, the concept seemed revolutionary, and represented a new way of looking at the political process. By the 1950s and 1960s, Western (mainly American) political scientists began to refine the approach, and to make a clear distinction between the group theory of politics and theories of groups in politics. The latter differs from the former mainly in that it is concerned almost exclusively with the role of interest and pressure groups in the political system; its concern is thus narrower and more specific than that of group theory, which has few adherents nowadays. It was and is argued by many political scientists that freely constituted groups representing specific interests in society are and should be an integral part of a true democracy, along with a genuine multi-party system, a free press, etc. Interest and pressure groups thus form an important component of the so-called 'pluralist' conception of democracy, in which power is spread among many organizations. Variants of the pluralist conception of democracy underpin most Western governments' approaches to politics, which in turn means that interest and pressure groups are, by and large, held to be both legitimate and indeed desirable. In fact, there is sometimes a gap between what is in theory and in practice acceptable in the way of group politics in the West; but that is not our concern here, and we need now to compare this view of the role of interests and groups with that in the communist world.

Communist Attitudes Towards Interests and Groups

In recent years, many communist states have increasingly acknowledged not only that there are different interests in their societies—within as well as between classes and strata—but also that these can sometimes clash in significant ways both with each other and with the public interest generally. Even the Soviets, who are often slower than some of their East European colleagues in recognizing cleavage potentialities in society, have overtly accepted this. As academician G. M. Gak acknowledged as early as 1955, various types of interest exist in socialist society; by the late 1960s/early 1970s, Soviet writers were openly recognizing that such interests can be in 'collision' with each other (see Hill 1980, esp. pp. 85–95). However, the Soviets still do not accept that there might be *fundamental* clashes of interest between groups and/or between a group and the state. Other countries have gone further than the Soviets. For instance, two Polish political scientists have acknowledged that conflicts of interest in Poland may sometimes be linked to basic class antagonisms (see Triska 1977, p. 167).

Although an increasing number of communist states recognize the existence of conflicts of interest under socialism, their attitudes towards organized interest groups and pluralism vary quite considerably. For some, such as the Soviets, the very word pluralism denotes something negative and Western, and both interest and pressure groups are officially anathema. Others take a less rigid view, and see some form of pluralism as healthy and compatible with socialism. This does not mean encouragement and acceptance of competition—especially among political parties—but does entail a recognition of the rights of groups to form and to express their interests to the decision-makers. Skilling (1966, pp. 442–8), for instance, cites two communist theoreticians (the Yugoslav Djordjevic and the Slovak Lakatos) who by the 1950s and 1960s respectively were arguing that interest groups are inevitable in every kind of political system, including socialist ones.

Of all the communist states, the ones that have gone furthest along these lines over time are Hungary and Yugoslavia (Czechoslovakia in 1968 and Poland between August 1980 and December 1981 represent special and ultimately short-lived cases). Thus a leading Yugoslav theoretician has written:

The self-managing socialist society therefore postulates a certain form of political pluralism ... this pluralism appears primarily as a form of pluralism of interests and organisations on the basis of these interests ... These organisations do not appear— or, more exactly, are appearing to a lesser extent—as the expression of general political differences. They are formed for the purpose of pursuing specific shared interests of self-managers, or rather they express specific forms of self-management interests. (Kardelj, 1978, pp. 133–5.)

And in Hungary, the communist party not only officially recognizes the existence of group interests, but actually encourages groups to make their interests known. According to the former Minister of Culture, Imre Poszgay,

Amidst present socio-political conditions the HSWP [the communist party], in addition to developing its organising abilities, can fulfil its interest-integrating functions only if the different group interests can manifest themselves openly and come into conflict with one another ... (quoted in Huber and Heinrich 1981, p. 154.)

Does all this mean that these communist states are closer to Western attitudes than to the more conservative communist states? This is a matter of opinion, but I would argue that there remain two very important points distinguishing even the most liberal communist states from the West. The first is their attitude towards the notions of pressure and bargaining. At the end of the day, all communist parties in power still seem to agree that it is the party's role to make major decisions in line with general societal interests, and that it is not to yield to pressure from groups; the observant reader will have noticed that the Hungarian source cited above refers to groups being in conflict only with each other, not with the party–state complex. For communists, the encouragement of interest aggregation and articulation should be seen both as a way of reaching optimal decisions on the basis of the maximum inflow of information, and as a way of justifying policies on the grounds that group interests were explicitly acknowledged and incorporated into the final decision, rather than as an acknowledgement that the party and state decision-makers are obliged to compromise with groups. Indeed, communist theoreticians make it clear that the party–state complex is not to yield to pressure from the strongest and/or the most selfish groups, which is how many communists see pluralism—and particularly group politics—functioning in liberal democracies. The second point is that Western pluralist theorists argue that any group of individuals should be able to form an interest or pressure group *on their own initiative*, and should not be subject to 'control' by government authorities. Even in those communist countries in which interest groups are officially recognized, high levels of group autonomy of the party–state complex are not tolerated, let alone encouraged.

The Nature of Group Politics in the Communist World

We have seen that some communist states are more prepared than others to recognize the legitimacy of interests and groups, although the notion of groups pressuring the party–state complex is universally condemned. But just because a phenomenon is not officially recognized does not necessarily mean that it does not exist. Conversely, official recognition does not automatically signify that groups play a very important role in practice. On the limited evidence available, the nature and scope of group politics is somewhat different from that in the West; let us examine this.

It has already been explained why strikes in the communist world cannot be accepted as group politics in the normal sense of this term. A similar argument applies to various attempts at forming genuinely autonomous issue- or cause-oriented groups, such as unofficial peace or environmentalist movements; the fact that one can be arrested merely for expressing a view means that such activity should more accurately be described as illegitimate protest politics. In fact, there is in my opinion little if any conclusive evidence of full-blooded (i.e., overt, autonomous, self-motivated, and legitimate) interest or pressure group activity in the communist world other than in non-normal situations (i.e. as a temporary phenomenon in a crisis situation); Yugoslavia would be the only possible and partial exception to this. It is true that there is evidence of some real bargaining in communist states, and it is almost certain that groups do sometimes attempt to use threats or sanctions. But even allowing for this, the nature of politics in the communist world is such that the interaction between groups and decision-makers differs in some important respects from such interactions in the West; the similarities and differences require further elaboration.

The first point relates to the near absence of autonomous, self-motivated and self-organized group activity. Most interest/pressure groups arise from already existing functional and/or social groups, rather than because a few individuals have independently made great efforts to join forces with others of similar persuasion. Examples of issue- and cause-oriented groups which have not been harassed by the authorities are rare, although the case of the 1958 Educational Reform Act in the USSR suggests that such activity may sometimes occur (see Schwartz and Keech 1968). However, even in this case, it does look as if a common group awareness (i.e., amongst all individuals opposed to Khrushchev's proposals, not merely discrete sets of individuals in different functional groupings)—if it formed at all—did so only *after* the leadership had published proposals and called for comments. This seems to be a feature of much of the group politics in the communist world; increasingly, leaders will *consult* with groups, ask their opinions and proposals, etc. and in this sense give the groups some form of potential influence. But such *co-optation*, as it is often called, represents a very restricted form of group politics, and constitutes only a part of what Westerners generally understand by the term. It appears that groups rarely *initiate* a debate themselves in the communist world, and instead have to wait for the go-ahead from the authorities. Moreover, it is possible that one of the reasons why leaderships consult with groups is to secure their support for some new policy (i.e., to influence the group rather than be influenced by it); this can happen in liberal democracies too.

Another feature of group politics in communist countries, as in the West, is that some groups have potentially more influence (in terms of access to decision-makers, status of the group, etc.) than others. One division often mentioned in the literature on group politics is that between *insider* (or institutional) and *outsider* (or associational) groups. The former are in a sense part of the party–state complex (e.g. the military, ministerial bureaucrats, local party *apparatchiki*, etc.), whereas the latter (e.g. peasants, workers) are not. Expressing this differently, the insider groups are the sorts of groups which themselves often take important decisions on behalf of others, whereas the outsider groups do not. This leads us to the problem of *boundaries*. Not only must we never forget about communist party involvement in almost all groups (including minor parties), but it is also sometimes difficult to say whether a particular organization is an interest/pressure group or in fact a decision-maker. A good example is the ministries. Sometimes, ministries take important decisions which are binding on units below them. At other times, ministries try to promote or defend their own interests in the higher decision-making bodies, such as the Council of Ministers or the Politburo. This problem notwithstanding, let us focus on those occasions when such organizations do seem to be acting primarily as interest groups. It is widely accepted that insider groups play a much greater role in politics and are more likely to be able to make their views known to and to influence the decision-makers than are outsider groups. Yet there even appears to be some pecking order among the insider groups, relating to the prestige, functional role and other aspects of a given group. Thus, on the evidence available, generals and academicians seem to have more potential influence than senior trade union or women's organization officials. For this reason, the former are sometimes referred to as the 'élite' groups. However, here we encounter another aspect of the boundaries problem. Some of these élite groups are *so* 'inside' that one wonders whether they qualify as interest groups at all, as distinct from part of 'the élite'. As Brown (1974, pp. 71–2) has pointed out, three of the seven groups analysed in the Skilling and Griffiths volume on Soviet interest groups (1971) are official apparatuses (the party *apparatchiki*, the security police, and the military), and are therefore in a different league from the other four (industrial managers, economists, writers, and jurists). Pressure from and conflict between the former set of groups is usually described as *bureaucratic politics* rather than interest/pressure group politics. This dimension of the boundary problem notwithstanding, it is important to realize that most analysts would accept that at least *some* of the functional groups in this and other studies sometimes act as interest/pressure groups.

A pecking order of sorts can be found too among the outsider groups, where there is also an élite (e.g. artists); this, too, often relates to the social status of the group. Some social and functional outsider groups find it difficult, because of their nature, to organize themselves into interest/pressure groups. Peasants, for example, are usually spread over huge areas, and therefore face enormous problems in developing an awareness of themselves as a group and in aggregating their interests. This does not mean that leaders take no notice of such social functional groups' interests. In fact they often do, since they are usually aware that the cumulative effect of lots of individuals being opposed to a policy can be just as damaging as a negative response from a highly organized group. Thus interests and groups can be influential in communist politics without those groups' interests being properly aggregated and articulated or the groups being self-aware and highly organized. But few would call this phenomenon an example of group politics (though see Oksenberg 1974, esp. pp. 336–7), which for most analysts implies more active involvement by groups.

One final point—this time common to both liberal democracies and communist states—is that we must be wary of over-generalization when making inferences about social or functional groups that appear to be acting as interest/pressure groups. Often, the latter are more fluid than the former. Thus 'managers', 'economists' or 'women' may actually be very divided—for instance, along regional or generational lines—on one given issue and largely united on another. Thus, one has always to specify the particular issue when arguing that a given social or functional group is acting as an interest/pressure group; this point is sometimes overlooked by analysts (see e.g. Hardt and Frankel 1971, p. 173).

SUMMARY AND CONCLUSIONS

The available evidence suggests that there is an increasing amount of a *limited* form of group politics—consultations, etc.—in the communist world, and this is linked to several factors (the decline of terror; the increasing complexity of both the division of labour and technology; the growing sophistication of citizens and leaders alike, etc.). But we have also seen that both attitudes towards and the nature of minor parties, mass organizations, interest and group politics in the communist world differ in significant ways from what we normally understand by these terms in Western societies—even allowing for the fact that none of these terms can be defined in totally satisfactory, unambiguous ways. We have seen too that some—perhaps much—of what is described as interest group politics is more accurately described as bureaucratic politics.

In conclusion, we would broadly agree with Skilling's analysis of the role of groups in communist politics, particularly as his position has become clearer (see his 1983 article). Basically, the argument is that groups play some role in the political process, but that we should be careful not to overemphasize their role and influence, especially *vis-à-vis* the party–state complex. Skilling actually uses the term 'qualified pluralism' (1983, p. 8) to describe the nature of group politics in communist countries; as long as we, like Skilling, constantly bear in mind that the level of qualification varies considerably from one communist country to another, this term is a valid one. However, in order to enhance the descriptive qualities of the term, it would be useful to expand it to 'qualified and controlled pluralism'. With this in mind, let us now attempt to gain some overall perspective on the political process.

Basic further reading

T. Baylis, 1974.

G. Bertsch and T. Ganschow (eds.), 1976, section 6.

L. Cohen and J. Shapiro (eds.), 1974, pp. 317–78.

D. Goodman (ed.), 1984.

R. Gripp, 1973, pp. 126–39.

D. Lane and G. Kolankiewicz (eds.), 1973.

F. Petrenko, 1981.

B. Ruble, 1981.

H. G. Skilling, 1966, 1983.

H. G. Skilling and F. Griffiths (eds.), 1971.

S. G. Solomon (ed.), 1983.

J. Triska and C. Gati (eds.), 1981.

10

THE POLICY PROCESS AND POLITICAL PARTICIPATION

AT various points in this book, we have touched upon the policy process; having considered the major agencies that are involved in this, we are now in a position to draw all these strands together and focus explicitly on the process itself. Although this subject may be less attractive to some readers than, say, terror or dissidence, an analysis of the policy process is in fact a singularly important topic, since a better understanding of it will place us in a stronger position for a discussion of some of the really big questions of communist politics, such as 'how democratic are communist states?' or 'how close are the communist states to the situation in which the government of persons has been replaced by the administration of things?' or 'have these countries really achieved socialism?' These are all enormous questions, and it is beyond the scope of this book to attempt to cover them—one major reason being that terms such as 'democracy' mean quite different things to different people. For example, is democracy possible only if it is direct, or is an indirect system (i.e., where citizens entrust most of the decision-making to politicians) an acceptable form of democracy? If the latter is the case, is democracy mainly concerned with citizen input, involvement in the administration of policies, a fairly equal balance of both, or perhaps something else altogether? Without labouring the point, it should already be clear that there is a wide range of contentious issues here.

But definitional problems are not the only reason why we cannot yet proceed as far as we would like in our assessment of communist political systems as reflected in the policy process. Another is a familiar one in the study of the communist world—a shortage of data. Certainly there has been an enormous growth in the study of the policy process and mass participation in recent years—so much so that the latter has been called a vogue (e.g. Unger 1981, p. 121, and Hill 1983, p. 275). Much of this, however, has to remain speculative, since it is often based either on intelligent and informed guesswork and/or questionable sources of information. Even where we do have what looks like reliable data, Western analysts can differ in their interpretations of these; this point is elaborated later in the chapter. In sum, both data deficiencies and disagreements on interpretations mean there is still a long way to go in our understanding of the policy process in the communist world; nevertheless, we are building up an increasingly detailed picture.

Of course, in one sense it would be impossible to produce anything like a comprehensive picture that accurately portrays 'the' policy process in all communist states, at all times, and in all areas of policy—one very major reason being that there *is* no single policy process. The defence policy process is likely to look rather different from the education policy process, for instance, and both these will probably be rather different in Czechoslovakia than in Angola. However, it is possible to produce a common framework for analysing policy processes, and to incorporate into this all the variables that seem to have played a role in the processes already studied by Western analysts in different policy areas, countries, and periods. All this is elaborated below, when we consider the analytical model. Before this, however, we need once again to spend a little time considering the meaning(s) of the key terms to be used in the discussion.

SOME DEFINITIONS AND THE MODEL

In every society, decisions have to be made; a decision can be defined as 'a choice made by a person or collective for one of several alternative ways of acting' (Löwenhardt 1981, p. 13). Although many writers use the words 'policy' and 'decision' interchangeably, there are times when it is useful to distinguish them. For example, a political party may produce a manifesto during an election campaign in which it claims that it is party 'policy' to reduce unemployment; one would not usually use the term 'decision' in this context. When that party comes to power, the decisions it takes on economic policy may actually lead to higher unemployment, despite its alleged policy. Here, then, policy is used in the sense of a formal commitment of a party to something, which may or may not be compatible with the decisions that party takes in power. Another example of the distinction that can sometimes be drawn is that a group of politicians may deliberately avoid discussing a particular problem, so that policy—here, in the somewhat different sense of government attitudes towards any given social issue—emerges as a result of what are sometimes called 'non-decisions'. For instance, a stranger arrives in a new country, to find that a particular ethnic minority is being seriously discriminated against. As an outsider, he or she can see that, according to most moral codes of conduct, the government ought to be doing something about the plight of this minority. But the underprivileged group is so weak that it cannot pressure the government—which prefers to sweep the problem under the carpet. Although a few government spokespersons may try to claim that the government has *no* policy on this question, this is basically deceitful. A policy exists, but does so as a result of a (possibly tacit) agreement amongst the society's top decision-makers *not* to make any decision. A decision overtly to approve the situation of the minority would appear to many politicians to be unwise; better, then, to keep the whole problem off any agenda. Finally, 'policy' is seen by some writers as the sum total of a number of specific decisions. In other words, the concept of 'a' decision in this context is of something which is part of a larger entity, 'a' policy. In sum, 'political decisions' and 'policies' are often used interchangeably—but there are times when it is useful to draw distinctions between the two.

What of the term 'policy *process*'? Decision-making or policy-making (unless otherwise specified, these two will be used interchangeably from now on) is only one part of a much bigger phenomenon in society. For instance, a group of politicians might take what looks like an important decision, but if they are unable to ensure its implementation, then the decision itself becomes much less significant. For this reason, decision-making and all the stages leading up to it constitute only one part of a series of activities, which can therefore be called a process. For analytical purposes, the process can be seen as a system comprising six stages; these are explained shortly.

Let us now turn to consider the use of the term 'model'. What follows is an *analytical* model—that is, a structured framework for analysing a particular phenomenon. It is *not* a descriptive model (i.e., a systematized picture of an already observed phenomenon) of *the* policy process in communist states, for reasons already given.

In the discussion of the analytical model, I have sought to clarify where mass participation might fit in, since this is still all too often divorced from the policy process as a whole. For instance, several recent studies of 'mass participation' have concentrated either on the work-place (e.g. Sawer 1978; Triska and Gati 1981) or on local politics (e.g. Nelson 1980a; Friedgut 1979; Blecher and White 1979; Schulz and Adams 1981), without in every case making the point sufficiently forcefully that this is all part of the bigger phenomenon of the policy process. The model can distinguish between direct and indirect *influence*, and at different stages of the process. Following Dahl, manifest or direct influence is defined as follows:

If A wants outcome X; if A acts with the intention of causing B to bring about X; and if as a result of A's actions, B attempts to bring about X, then A exercises *manifest* influence over B . . .

whereas implicit or indirect influence is explained thus:

If A wants outcome X; then although A does not act with the intention of causing B to bring about X, if A's desire for X causes B to attempt to bring about X, then A exercises implicit influence over B . . . (Dahl, 1976, pp. 30–1.)

Reference is made in the discussion of the model to 'potential' influence (whether manifest or implicit), since it is usually even more difficult to prove a causal relationship between proposals or demands for change and the taking of a particular decision in the communist world than it is in the liberal democracies. Various other definitions are considered at appropriate points in the discussion of the component parts of the model; for now, let us consider the model in diagrammatic form (fig. (ii)).

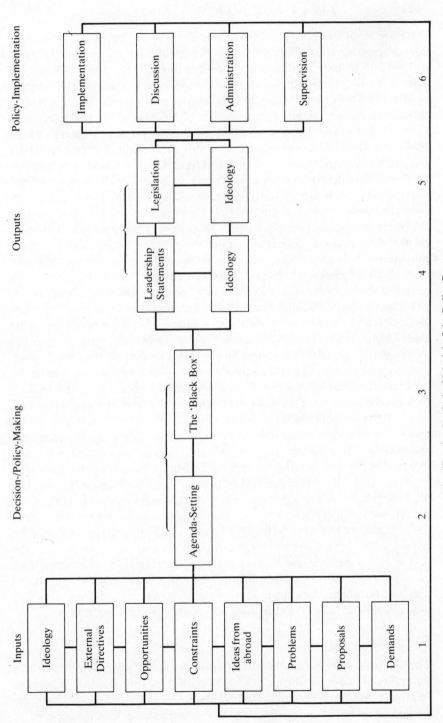

Fig. (ii)   An Analytical Model of the Policy Process

Before considering each of the component parts of the model, certain important points need to be emphasized. First, although the process has been divided into six parts, it should be noted that this has been done solely for the sake of clarity. In the real world, the process is never as neat as the diagram might suggest. For instance, it must be appreciated that this process is continually in motion; poor implementation of the policy, for example, eventually leads to the decision-makers' perception of another 'problem', which leads to a new round of policy outputs. For this reason, Easton and others have referred to the 'feedback loop', and have linked the final stage back to the first. I have deliberately refrained from the use of this term, since I believe that it can be taken to imply a set sequence of stages which does not necessarily accord well with reality. For precisely the same reason, I have not adopted the common practice (see, e.g. Lane 1978, p. 204) of using arrows to indicate relationships between different stages of the policy process; this too gives a potentially misleading impression of a set sequence of events and unidirectionality. This somewhat abstract point can be illustrated by an example. A group of leaders—decision-makers—might perceive a problem, and ask for proposals to overcome this. Here, the sequence will be one (perceived problem); two and three (a *minor* decision, simply to call for advice); four (the leadership call for proposals); one (the proposals); two and three (a *major* decision on policy); four (the leadership statement on policy); five (legislation); six (implementation). Thus the stages are not moving neatly from one to the next, but are moving backwards and forwards. This leads to the second, closely related caveat. This is that it should not be assumed that the development of a given policy will necessarily proceed through all six stages. Sometimes, for example, there is little or no obvious follow-up to leadership statements; this is particularly true when leaders are in conflict with each other, so that lower ranking officials are not sure which set of instructions to heed. Occasionally, a demand will be realized (i.e., implemented) before the leadership has made any decision about it (this happened in the case of the amalgamation of factories in the Ukraine and Leningrad in the early 1960s, for instance: see Holmes, 1981a, pp. 54 and 266–73). Finally, not only can the sequence vary, but different stages can be happening *simultaneously*; in the real world, stages one and six may well be occurring at the same time. This pertains also to *different* components within the *same* stage; several inputs may well be influencing agenda-makers simultaneously.

Let us now consider the individual parts of the model in some detail.

Stage One—Inputs

The first part of the process is usually called the 'input' stage. In other words, we are looking here at the kinds of factors that lead the decision-makers to feel that a decision is needed in the first place. One such is *ideology*. Given the alleged commitment to the building of communism—which is supposed to inspire communist leaders to constant improvement of society—ideology can be seen on one level as an input; the significance of this variable is considered in greater detail later in this chapter. Second, there are *external directives*. At the national level these might be instructions from Comecon, the Warsaw Pact, or another communist state, for example. At the local level, they might take the form of a general directive (either a leadership statement or a piece of legislation) that requires disaggregation by a local council or enterprise (for instance a five-year development plan). Here, then, is an example of the points made above about sequence and multidirectionality. By *opportunities* is meant that technological advances, changes in international alignments, increased taxes, etc. may give the leadership new opportunities for investment, peace initiatives, or whatever; indeed, a change of the top leadership may itself generate new possibilities and lead to a wide range of new policies. Yet decision-makers also work within *constraints* of some kind, and these too can play a major role in the decision-making process; financial constraints are an obvious example, international opinion a less obvious one. '*Ideas from abroad*' refers to the fact that decision-makers often explicitly study experience in other countries before reaching a decision. For instance, Andropov is known to have looked closely at the East German, Hungarian, and Bulgarian economic systems and to have urged others to do so in the months preceding the July 1983 announcement of a policy aimed at the partial decentralization of the Soviet economic system. Sixth, the leaders might be worried about what they see as a *problem* in society, such as high labour turnover rates in industry. This is another example of where stages can overlap or intertwine, in that poor implementation of a previous decision (here, a decision to improve productivity and output by reducing labour turnover) has become such a problem that it leads to a new decision. It is also an example of where the implicit or indirect influence defined earlier may operate. Thus Nelson has argued that the Romanian leadership's decision to raise the status of workers' councils at the beginning of 1978 was *partially* a response to that leadership's perception of dissatisfaction at the work-place, dissatisfaction that was having a negative effect on turnover and hence productivity (Nelson 1980b, p. 545). In other words, a decision designed to give greater job satisfaction to the workers can be taken, even though these workers have not made any overt attempts to influence the decision-makers. The seventh component is *proposals*; specialists or ordinary members of the public may write letters to the press, for example, suggesting ways in which a given situation might be improved. Finally, there are *demands*; here, people attempt manifestly to influence the decision-makers to take a decision which favours those people. If several individuals join together to press their demands collectively and openly (interest aggregation and articulation) they constitute a pressure group (subject to the limitations of pressure group politics analysed in chapter nine); but demands can be made by individuals too. It should be noted that proposals can sometimes become demands, in the sense that they get out of hand and acquire a momentum of their own, undesired by the leadership. A good example is the use of wall posters in China in both 1957 and 1978–80; in both instances, the leadership wanted to allow the Chinese people to let off steam and to suggest moderate proposals for improving the system, but the movements rapidly got out of control and had to be suppressed.

Stage Two—Agenda-Setting

Modern societies are so complex and engender so many problems that a filtering process has to occur between the input stage and the stage at which final decisions are made. At the highest decision-making level in communist societies, this filtering process—the prioritization of inputs—is usually performed by Central Committee secretariats, which play a major role in deciding which items should appear on the agenda of the Politburo (or its equivalent). In this sense, the agenda-setters have considerable influence. Not only do they decide which issues to include and which not, and the order in which these issues are to be discussed, but they will often provide the decision-makers with much of the information that is used in reaching a final decision. Both the choice of information and the way in which it is presented will affect the decision-makers' perception of the issue and thus their decision. Finally, it should not be forgotten that the top secretaries will actually be in the Politburo (or its equivalent) anyway, and thus play a very direct role in the decision-making process.

However, secretariats are not the only 'filtering' bodies. *Censorship* is another form of filtration, and will also affect the way the decision-makers (and others) perceive problems, proposals, etc. Thus the mass media in communist countries can simultaneously play a role as a channel for proposals (stage one) and as a censor (as part of stage two)—in addition to other roles at later stages.

Stage Three—The 'Black Box'

The final decisions on a given issue are made in what is often called the 'black box'. At the central level, this will normally be the Politburo (or its functional equivalent) if the decision is a very important one, but might also be the Council of State, the Council of Ministers, etc. At lower levels, it could be the executive committee of a local council, a local party bureau, an enterprise production committee, etc. Particularly at the highest levels, this stage of the process is usually very secretive (in liberal democracies as well as communist states), which is why it is referred to as the 'black box'. Many writers would agree that this is the real heart of the policy process, and that all of the other components are highly dependent on this one.

Stage Four—Leadership Statements

The leaders (decision-makers) have now reached a decision and give the public a general idea of what the new/modified policy is to be. This will often be in the form of a policy *statement* which is relayed in the media, though at the lowest level it might be simply a speech by the chairperson of a collective farm to the farmers; such statements are a form of 'output'. Speeches made by leaders for public consumption are not only included to communicate information, however; they are also designed to justify a particular decision, and can thus be seen as *ideological*.

Stage Five—Legislation

General pronouncements on a policy are not normally sufficient if a decision is to be properly implemented. The 'fine print' now has to be worked out, so that *legislation*—here understood in a relatively broad sense, to include the production and issuance of directives, decrees, detailed plan targets, etc., as well as formal laws—is the next stage. The legislation will often contain dates by which the new policy is to be implemented, detailed definitions of some general concept contained in the leadership statements, etc. Often, there will be articles in the press, perhaps even programmes on the radio and television, explaining and justifying the legislation; this is why *ideology* is included at this stage too. This refinement of stage four is also an output.

Stage Six—Implementation

Basically, implementation is that stage at which decisions are carried out—or not, as the case may be. In addition to the act of *implementation* itself—sowing wheat, restructuring a school curriculum, etc.—there are a number of ways in which ordinary citizens can be involved at stage six. Often, there will be some *discussion* of the policy—for instance of the best ways to achieve a particular goal that has been set. The people actually involved in turning the policy into reality might also have questions or doubts about the policy, and will therefore wish to discuss these with someone who has been telling them what the policy is; here, then, stages four and six can be simultaneous. *Administration* is also an integral part of the implementation process, and can—indeed should, according to most communist ideologies—involve the masses; Khrushchev encouraged this very much from the late 1950s, and even developed his concept of the 'state of the whole people' in 1961 to encapsulate the essence of the changes he was introducing. There must also be some *supervision* of the implementation—the checking or *kontrol* function. This is often primarily the responsibility of the party, but ordinary citizens are frequently encouraged to keep an eye on each other's performance, either as individuals or via mass organizations. As mentioned in chapter 7, two communist states do have constitutional courts. In one sense, these could warrant a separate box ('adjudication') in the analytical model; in practice, however, their role is so small in the communist world as a whole that it makes more sense just to mention them here and include them under 'supervision'.

SOME OF THE PROBLEMS OF RESEARCHING THE POLICY PROCESS AND MASS PARTICIPATION

Difficulties in obtaining and assessing the value of data constitute only a few of an enormous number of problems we face in trying to research and analyse the policy process and the significance of popular participation in this. One of the biggest problems is to prove causal relationships. For instance, we might be able to show that a group of educationalists made proposals to the leaders without having first been asked, and that a policy later ensued that was very close to what the educationalists had been arguing for. But it is usually extremely difficult to *prove* that the decision-makers were responding in any direct sense to the proposals. It could be that *both* the leaders *and* the educationalists perceived a problem at about the same time, and that the leaders came up with similar ideas to those of the specialists because of having studied foreign experience, or the writings of Marx, or some other factor.

This leads to the next point, which is that it is also rarely possible to rank-order possible influences and inputs. Taking the example cited earlier of the upgrading of workers' councils in Romania, Nelson pointed out that the Romanian leadership was probably *also* responding to the serious strikes by miners (i.e., a demand input) in the Jiu Valley in 1977 (1980b, p. 545). What we do not know is whether the long-term or the short-term factor was more influential on the Romanian leadership (i.e., does the leadership seem to respond more to manifest or to implicit influence?), whether they played an almost equal role, or indeed whether there were other factors of which we are simply unaware.

Another major problem is that it is often difficult to distinguish between what is usually called on the one hand 'volitional' (i.e., self-motivated) and on the other 'guided' participation. In other words, do people participate in discussions or write letters to the press purely of their own accord, or are they encouraged to do so by local party activists, for example? This is a very important question to answer if we are to consider the really big questions of democracy, socialism, etc.—or even if we want to make valid comparisons between communist states and liberal democratic ones. An example of the kind of situation that can be encountered is provided by Falkenheim; if the views of Chinese *émigrés* he interviewed are at all typical, it would seem that many Chinese in the immediate post-GPCR period attended political meetings not because they genuinely wanted to participate but because of fears of the consequences of not attending. This is not to say that people feared for their lives, but, more usually, for their job prospects, housing prospects, etc. Apparently, many Chinese attend political meetings in order both to show willing (i.e., be at least marginally involved in politics), and to find out what official policy on a given issue is, so that they do not inadvertently criticize it in their day-to-day living (Falkenheim 1978, p. 22). Moreover, although Falkenheim's respondents seemed to be generally aware of their rights to criticize local leaders, few did, for fear of retaliation (e.g. in terms of promotion, welfare benefits, educational opportunities—see 1978, pp. 26–7). Without going into a long theoretical discussion, there are few who would consider this kind of political participation 'democratic' and/or 'socialist'. An attempt has been made to lessen this problem in the analytical model by distinguishing between proposals, demands, and discussion. Discussion is used here as something to do with decisions already taken, whereas proposals and demands are held to occur before the major decision has been reached. This means that a clear conceptual distinction is made between a discussion which *results* in suggestions going upwards (e.g. from a town to the central party/ state authorities, and from stage six to stage one) and one which has purely informational and/or propagandistic and/or disaggregative functions (i.e. which stays at stage six). But this only solves a part of the problem—and the distinction may well be difficult to draw in the real world anyway.

The problem of volitional versus guided participation is linked to the problem we face in attempting to make a meaningful distinction between the scale and the nature of participation in the policy process. Put even more crudely, we really want to distinguish clearly between quantity and quality. Communist analyses of their own levels of democracy usually place far more emphasis on the *numbers* of those participating than on the *nature* of such participation. Even some Western analysts have a tendency to do this (e.g. Hough)—although, to be fair, such writers do usually stress somewhere in their article or book that they are aware of the limitations of the predominantly quantitative approach.

There are many more problems that one could list. If one wants to start answering the big questions, listed at the beginning of this chapter, then one would have to introduce a number of explicit assumptions about priorities. First, one would have to prioritize the component parts of the analytical model. For example, one would have to say that one considers one form of participation in the policy process (say self-initiated demands) more important than another (such as discussion or administration). Some would even want to omit stage six altogether—although if they did and were using the model, then they would have to do so for all to see and therefore for all to judge. Second, not only would one have to prioritize the individual parts of the model, but also policy areas. Using the *analytical* model one might create *descriptive* models of a range of policies in one country, and would have to stipulate which were considered more significant and which less. For instance, someone might wish to argue that evidence of meaningful mass participation in the drawing up of a constitution—assuming one could obtain this—is not very convincing proof that a particular country is highly democratic if that constitution in fact seems to play very little role in the real politics of that country. Conversely, even a slight increase in the role of ordinary citizens in the defence policy process might be seen as highly progressive and democratic if we then compare the new situation with the situation in other countries.

In sum, we still have a long way to go in our analysis of the policy process, especially in terms of making comparative judgements. But one point of consolation is that at least some of the problems listed above pertain to other kinds of political system too; communist studies specialists can share *some* of their burdens and theoretical hurdles.

FACTORS AFFECTING PARTICIPATION IN THE POLICY PROCESS

Although it would be dishonest not to make the reader aware of many of the problems we face in analysing politics in the communist world, it would be equally wrong to give the impression that we know very little. In this section, I shall briefly consider the sorts of factors which seem to lead to more or less participation in the policy process—which lead, in other words, to shifting balances between the component units of the model from policy to policy, country to country, period to period. Some of the points are borne out by empirical evidence; others are assumptions based on logic, knowledge of other systems, and experience more generally. It must be emphasized that none of the factors can be taken in isolation; each is constantly interacting with the others. The following analysis took as its starting-point Archie Brown's list of variables for a cross-polity examination of the structure of decision-making (1971, esp. pp. 127–48), but has been modified and considerably expanded where this seemed appropriate. Thus, it would seem that the following are the most important factors affecting levels and types of participation in the policy process:

    (i) The political culture and ideology
    (ii) The policy area
   (iii) The spatial dimension of a policy
   (iv) The technicality of a policy
    (v) Level of development and stability
   (vi) Group interest in the policy
  (vii) Forums for participation
 (viii) Public interest in the policy
   (ix) The cost of a policy
    (x) The urgency of a decision
   (xi) The international aspects of a policy
  (xii) The coherence of a policy
 (xiii) The nature of the leadership.

Let us consider these in turn.

(i) *The political culture and ideology*

Although political culture is difficult to analyse, we have to allow for the possibility that traditions of what is acceptable and what is not have a place in any comprehensive attempt to explain the policy process. By this, we are not referring *only* to pre-communist traditions. Research on participation in various communist countries shows that some citizens *seem* to have little interest in politics, and are quite happy to leave decision-making to others (e.g. for a detailed study of Yugoslavia, see Triska and Barbic 1980), while Ronald Hill has suggested that the Soviet authorities often feel they have to *teach* citizens how to participate (1980, *passim* and esp. pp. 172–6). This apparent indifference may be genuine in the case of some citizens; in others, it may be that people do not wish to lend legitimacy to a system they have never accepted and/or because they feel their views will not be listened to and/or because they remember the recent past (for instance, the communist 'mobilization' phase), when it could have been positively dangerous to air one's political opinion. In other words, the communists themselves may be largely to blame for citizen reticence to participate. The example of Spain following Franco's death shows that many citizens can rapidly 'learn' to play a meaningful participatory role if they believe there is some point—if they feel that they can air these views openly and that these views will be listened to.

One other aspect of culture is what we can call the culture of bureaucratic conservativism. By this is meant that local officials may be used to administering in a particular way, and are slow to respond to leadership calls for a change in political style and greater participation. This is one possible explanation for the kinds of problems Cuba, for instance, has faced in increasing participation at the work-place. In 1978, workers in 34 per cent of Cuban enterprises were offered no opportunity to discuss the 1979 plan, while the suggestions of the work-force in another 58 per cent were completely ignored. Consequently, only about 8 per cent of enterprises had anything like meaningful participation (Dominguez 1982b, p. 39). Even allowing for the possibility that this 8 per cent happened to be the largest enterprises—which would mean that a higher percentage of the work-force had a say in their plan than the figures we have might suggest—the situation is clearly far from satisfactory. Although it is feasible that top leaders complain about such situations primarily in order to give themselves greater legitimacy, a balanced assessment would also allow for the possibility that some leaders really are concerned that moves towards communism are being delayed by local party and state officials loath to change their attitudes and style.

The role of ideology is also difficult to analyse, but—equally—must be included. For the sake of a clearer exposition, the distinction drawn in chapter 5 between pure and practical ideology (or theory and thought) can be used. Given the vagueness in the writings of Marx, Engels, and Lenin on the exact nature of communism, the 'pure' ideology provides primarily a methodological approach to policy-makers, rather than a blueprint of what is to be achieved. This said, it is not clear that this 'dialectical' methodology is so very different from Western approaches in terms of actual application. In both cases, change is brought about as a reaction to the existing situation, and it makes little practical difference whether we describe this as 'dialectics' or 'problem-responsiveness'. In sum, this aspect of 'pure' ideology is not nearly as clear a distinguishing feature of the communist policy process as might initially be supposed. Practical ideology is really part of the policy itself (i.e. part of the model) rather than a factor explaining it, so that it should be excluded from this part of the analysis.

(ii) The policy-area

In communist states—as in others—some areas of policy are considered more sensitive than others. For instance, the public is not generally encouraged to discuss—even in the sense of criticize or question—defence, foreign policy, security, censorship, or the role of the party in the communist world. On the other hand, citizens are frequently encouraged to discuss draft constitutions (e.g. GDR 1968, Bulgaria 1971, USSR 1977) some aspects of economic and social policy (e.g. family policy in Vietnam in the early 1970s), the mistakes of past leaders (e.g. of Mao and the Gang of Four in China). local issues, etc. Indeed, some communist constitutions even explicitly state that important issues have to be discussed by the population at large, though it is usually up to the party to decide what these issues are.

(iii) The spatial dimension of a policy

Closely related to point two is what is sometimes called the spatial dimension of a policy. By this is meant that mass participation tends to be more significant (i.e., less guided, involving more open debate) on a wider range of local issues than of national ones. It is largely for this reason that most of the studies of mass participation that have appeared in recent years have focused on the work-place, village, or town. Such studies also suggest that there are some perceptible differences in the nature of public participation in local politics in town and country. A study of Poland in the late 1960s/early 1970s suggests that rural citizens know their local representatives (deputies) much better and contact them more often than urban citizens—although urban deputies tend to be more responsive to the demands made by their constituents, and generally more efficient than their rural counterparts (Triska 1977, pp. 166–75). In other words, if the Polish findings are at all typical—and at present we have insufficient data to know whether they are or not—then the trend is away from the more personalized participation of the village to a more impersonal situation, in which citizens make demands on their local politicians less frequently (i.e., in one sense the rate of participation decreases) but can expect a greater response when they do (i.e., at another level the participation is more meaningful).

(iv) The technicality of a policy

Other things being equal, politicians will tend to consult with specialists more on technical issues than on general, non-specialized ones. This said, it should not be overlooked that in communist states, as in liberal democracies, specialists often disagree amongst themselves. Thus, even in areas of technical complexity (e.g. nuclear energy) the decision-makers might consult specialists, but will still, at the end of the day, have to make a political decision. Expressed another way, it is not *necessarily* the case that the technicalization of society dramatically increases the power of the specialists (either manifestly or implicitly) to influence decisions. One final point about the technicality of a policy, and one that is often overlooked, is that although increasing technicalization might give *specialists* a greater say in the policy process— which can be seen in some ways as a democratization of the process—ordinary citizens are likely to find it more difficult to participate in some discussions. Thus, greater opportunities and 'democracy' for one group does not necessarily lead to an *overall* increase in democratization.

(v) *Level of development and stability*

In a 1967 article, Sharlet argued that communist systems develop through three overlapping phases, which he calls 'preindustrialization', 'industrialization', and 'postindustrialization'. He goes on to argue that the level and nature of participation in the policy process varies from stage to stage (pp. 248–50). Without elaborating the argument, it does seem sensible to argue that the decline of terror, the slowdown in revolutionary change, and the deepening of the division of labour as communist states grow older are *likely* to increase opportunities for participation by both specialists and ordinary citizens—a point endorsed by various recent empirical studies. However, the point cannot be pushed too far, for various reasons. First, two of the most economically developed states, the GDR and Czechoslovakia, seem to have less meaningful participation than some less economically developed ones. Second, some explicit reference to stability and legitimacy must be included, since leadership perception of potential instability can lead to a general clampdown politically, which will affect opportunities for participation. Of course, if the instability erupts into a virtual breakdown of the system, such as happened in Poland from August 1980 to December 1981, then meaningful participation may well increase dramatically—though usually only temporarily.

(vi) *Group interest in the policy*

Different policies will affect different groups in society in different ways. Therefore, two factors affecting the policy process are the extent to which a group is affected by it, and how powerful that group is within society. For example, politicians have to be more careful not to upset the military than university teachers of foreign languages, for rather obvious reasons.

(*vii*) *Forums for participation*

The range and nature of forums for participation are going to have an effect on the policy process. For instance, it is easier for individual specialists to realize they have interests and approaches in common with others if they can get together with their peers at conferences, where they can discuss their views and possibly aggregate them. If there are no conferences, or if such conferences are so much under control that specialists cannot discuss issues freely, then the awareness of common views and/or interests is less likely to develop. Looking at a concrete example of the importance of forums, this time relating to mass participation at the local level, the Cubans did not have any municipal councils until the Matanzas experiment of 1974—which meant that there simply were no bodies at that level in which local inhabitants could participate.

A final dimension of this factor is that citizens in communist states—as in other kinds of political system—will often be more willing to participate in forums if access to these is relatively easy. For instance, many more Yugoslav citizens attend pre-electoral voters' meetings or serve on workers' councils than stand for election to communal assemblies, one reason being that the latter involve more commitment (e.g. travelling time to meetings, attending regularly over a long period of time, etc.) and more initiative (see Triska and Barbic 1980, pp. 60–1).

(*viii*) *Public interest in the policy*

Senior communist politicians are not required to be responsive to what they perceive to be the majority opinion in society (or amongst the people whose support they want) in quite the same way as politicians in the West, for the simple reason that they do not have to seek electoral support in such free and competitive elections.

Nevertheless, communist politicians do have to bear public opinion in mind when they are making policies, since the adoption of too unpopular a policy can lead to the kinds of mass unrest that occurred in the GDR in 1953, Novocherkassk (USSR) in 1962, etc. Not only are individual politicians under threat in such a situation, but the political system itself might be endangered. Therefore, politicians have to be aware of the likely reactions of the public when reaching decisions, particularly decisions which directly affect the everyday lives of ordinary citizens (e.g. pricing policies, productivity norms, etc.). This is an example of the implicit influence of the masses. That the communist states themselves are aware of the significance of public opinion is implied by the growth of public opinion surveying in many of them in recent years (particularly Hungary, Yugoslavia, and Poland).

(*ix*) *The cost of a policy*

As Archie Brown points out, it seems safe to assume that the greater the potential cost of a policy (notably investment policy), the greater the chances that the highest decision-makers will want to be directly involved in the final decision. He also argues convincingly that, in the Soviet case at least, 'the possibility of radical change in the allocation of resources is very limited in cases where extremely large investment is involved (1971, p. 145).

At present, we have insufficient empirical evidence to know whether this is generally true of the policy process in the communist world—but it is a persuasive hypothesis.

(*x*) *The urgency of a decision*

As in other political systems, so in communist states there are times when a decision has to be made very quickly. An obvious example is in wartime, when a regime must respond as rapidly as possible to the actions of the enemy. But there are other times too, such as following a natural disaster (floods in China, earthquakes in Yugoslavia, drought in Mozambique, etc.), when it is far from clear that it would be more 'democratic' to discuss policy alternatives with the masses than it would be for a small leadership group or even one leader to decide on emergency measures for dealing with the crisis and which might save thousands of lives.

(*xi*) *The international aspects of a policy*

As with ideology, so international considerations can simultaneously be seen as a part of the policy process and a factor affecting it. Put simply, the less external constraints on the policy process, the greater the potential scope for internal debate and participation. This does not, of course, mean that such potential will always be realized; from what little is known about Albania (which does not align with any state, communist or otherwise), there seems to be little scope for real debate or meaningful participation.

(*xii*) *The coherence of a policy*

The less ambiguous a policy, the less room there is for those involved in implementing it to exploit loopholes and distort (if they are opposed to it) and/or merely disaggregate in their own way the intentions of the decision-makers. This is another potential area for indirect influence on the policy process, in that poor implementation leads to new problems for decision-makers to solve; the policy process is constantly in motion. However, it should also be noted that a policy might be poorly implemented less because those responsible for implementation are opposed to it than because they are not sure exactly what is wanted; when in doubt, many people will simply do nothing or stick to methods they know. Thus incoherent and/or insufficiently detailed policy-making can affect the overall policy process, even though there might be no obvious clash of interests involved.

(*xiii*) *The nature of the leadership*

The nature of the leadership in a given communist state will have a profound effect on the policy process. For instance, where there is a supreme leader who likes to dominate the policy process, the opportunities for meaningful sub-leadership participation will be much less than where there is a collective leadership, the members of which seek legitimacy on one level by basing decisions on a balanced analysis of well-researched and evaluated information. Power struggles between leaders will also often lead to an increase in sub-leadership participation, as individual contestants seek support for their own policy orientations.

The *personalities* of leaders also have some effect on the policy process; while this is fairly obvious at the national level, recent empirical analyses suggest that this factor also plays some role at the local level. Put simply, citizens feel that there is more point in discussing issues with some local officials (party secretaries, elected councillors, etc.) than with others, because some officials are more approachable and/or get more done for their local population than others.

CONCLUSION

Many comparative analysts of the policy process argue that the communist states are nearer to the 'rational-synoptic' (or 'teleological') ideal-type of policy process than they are to the 'disjointed incrementalist' one. What do these rather awesome terms actually mean, and how convincing is this argument?

The 'ideal-type' is considered in detail in chapter 15; for now, we can say that it is an abstract idea, based on a phenomenon observed in the real world, but pushed to its extreme or pure form. What of the other terms? In the 'rational-synoptic' or 'teleological' ideal-type, the policy process is, as might be expected, highly rational, in the sense that decisions are not made in a random way (e.g. simply as a response to a particular problem that has just arisen) but rather in a planned way, geared to some distant goal. This is where the 'synoptic' or 'teleological' dimension comes in; synoptic means comprehensive while teleological means, in this context, linked to some final goal. As mentioned above, it is often maintained that the communist policy process is much nearer to this ideal type than the liberal democratic policy process. The basis of this argument is that communists have an end-goal (communism), and, given the nature of the political and economic system (democratic centralism, state ownership of the means of production, the five-year and one-year plans, etc.) the means to ensure a more integrated and orderly policy process. The second ideal type, in contrast, is less orderly. Policies are made in an *ad hoc* manner, as a response to a particular problem or pressure group. There is no clear end-goal, and the nature of the political and economic system is such that it would not be possible to integrate policies fully even if this were desired. Whereas the 'rational-synoptic' approach will be typified by bold, clear-cut policies, which are carefully thought out and related to other policies, the 'disjointed incrementalist' approach is typified by slight or marginal changes to existing policies. The latter is what is meant by incrementalism. At the same time, the policy process is disjointed—in two senses. First, policy areas are not explicitly related to each other. If politicians decide that more funds are needed in one area, they will find them somehow (possibly by printing more money), without going into a thorough analysis of how they could be acquired through cutting in other areas. So this first meaning of 'disjointed' is that policy areas are not explicitly related to each other or to some end-goal. The second meaning is that neither decision-making nor the administration of policy is concentrated in one place. The American political system, for instance, is based on the concept of a separation of powers—both among central agencies (Presidency; Congress; Supreme Court) and between the centre and the fifty component states (which also have their own approximate equivalents of the three central agencies just listed). This is quite different from the theory of democratic centralism.

Do recent empirical analyses endorse the notion that the communist states are nearer to the 'rational-synoptic' end of the policy process spectrum? Overall, the answer would be yes—but such a brief answer is potentially misleading, and a more satisfactory one requires more detail.

There is little doubt that the policy process (here meaning the sum total of the myriad of policy processes going on at all levels all the time in each communist state) is under greater control in communist states than in the West. There are a number of reasons for this. One that is often mentioned in Western literature is touched upon above in the discussion of the ideal-types—the fact that communists reject spontaneity, believe in the conscious and planned construction of a better society and the vanguard role of the party. Although mass participation is a desirable and necessary goal if a truly socialist or communist society is to exist, such participation must be 'of the right sort', as communists see this. In other words, it must be constructive, not destructive, and play a positive role in the building of socialism. This is one reason why there is so much 'guided' participation in communist states (in the form of expecting citizens to vote, to be involved in administration, to march in May Day parades, etc.); at one level, citizens are being taught what the authorities expect of them as the transition to self-administration takes place. Communists have always rejected anarchy, and believe that people can only govern themselves once they have learnt the correct way to do things and to work by the same basic code. This leads to another point—often omitted in Western analyses. This is that communists never start with a clean slate—i.e., when they take power, they inevitably inherit traditions, prejudices, and problems from the previous society. Usually, there will be ethnic tensions, sexist attitudes, great inequalities between regions, and a host of other problems to be overcome. The communists do not want free speech and other forms of political participation to perpetuate these kinds of prejudices and patterns. If we also remember that the scale of change from an existing society to a truly communist one is enormous, and that communists are usually impatient to implement this change as quickly as possible, then we may begin to see communist attitudes towards mass participation, and the fact that there is still so much guidance, in a somewhat different light. An example of all this is provided by Albania. In 1967, Albania underwent the second stage of its own version of a cultural revolution. According to one leading analyst of Albanian politics, a major aim of this was to involve women more in (guided) politics, and, in doing so, to break down their traditional conservatism (Pano 1968, p. 180). This conservatism was closely related to the Albanians' traditional adherence to Islam, which accords women second-class status; it was partially for this reason that Islam (and indeed all religion) was banned in Albania in 1967.

Of course, a desire to keep the transformation of society 'on the straight and narrow' is not the only reason communists display such a penchant for guided participation. Another is that such participation serves a number of functions designed to add legitimacy to the regime—by mobilizing people behind new policies, informing them of the reason for policies, making the system more efficient (by taking trivial tasks away from professional administrators), showing the world at large how many citizens play a part in politics, etc. And one should never forget that many communists enjoy their élitist, privileged position in society, and feel that by encouraging participation over which they then exert considerable control, they can *appear* to be moving towards communism and self-administration without, in fact, undermining their position to any great extent.

Overall, then, there is still considerable control of the policy process and mass participation, and the absence of genuinely competitive elections for the really important political posts means that politicians are under less pressure to respond to citizen demands than politicians in the West. Even steps in the direction of more participation are typically faltering; if local politicians and/ or local citizens seem to be becoming too powerful from the centre's point of view, they may well have some of their powers reduced (a good example is the reorganization of Polish local political structures in the early 1970s). And when local organs *are* upgraded (e.g. local soviets in the USSR, the organs of popular power in Cuba), it seems to be invariably the case that they are dominated by local party members—many of whom will be as concerned with their own careers as with the problems and interests of ordinary citizens—and that non-party people tend to play a more passive role.

In spite of all these reservations, the fact remains that there are 'real politics'—open conflicts—in the communist world, not only at the top, but at all levels of the system. Generally speaking, the evidence suggests that more ordinary citizens and more specialists are exerting more influence on the policy process than ever before, even if this is limited. Local politicians are more frequently in open disagreement with each other and with their superiors, and are subject to greater demands from local citizens, than ever.

Although it still seems to be comparatively rare that ordinary citizens can block or substantially alter major policy proposals (e.g. of national significance) of senior politicians, such cases do occur. One example in Khrushchev's proposal for educational reform in 1958; and in the late 1970s, Yugoslav citizens in Zadar (Croatia) were able to block a proposal to build a nuclear power plant (Dobbs 1979). The reader can find many more examples in the literature cited at the end of this chapter. Thus, despite the many methodological problems cited in this chapter, the impression is that—in contrast to the picture so often conveyed in the Western media—citizens in the communist world generally do have *some* say in decision-making and the policy process, even though this varies enormously from one country to another, is limited by Western standards, and there is much less scope for the organizing of pressure groups. There appears also to be a mixture of 'guided' and 'self-motivated' participation, and a dynamism to such participation. In fact, the dynamism is such that we shall probably witness an increasing amount of self-motivated participation, as guided participation raises the level both of people's political knowledge and their expectations. Such developments will almost certainly lead to tension between the communists' élitist tendencies and their professed long-term aims; but such, in their own terms, is the dialectic of political development.

Despite the signs of greater participation in the policy process, these are still clearly inadequate for some observers. Various Marxist critics of the communist states, for instance, argue that citizens there (as in the West) are suffering from 'false consciousness', or what the non-Marxist Steven Lukes has called the 'third dimension' of power (Lukes 1974; see too Ritvo 1960). These concepts are complex, but the basic argument is that many citizens think they are having more say in the system, but in fact are not in any meaningful sense. Using the Dahlian approach employed earlier, the argument is that although A may make demands on B to which B responds, A has been indoctrinated by the system (over which B has enormous control, especially via the socialization process) to couch demands in such a way that B's power position is not fundamentally undermined. A is unaware of his/her 'real' interests, and only sees his/her interests in terms of what can realistically be expected within the existing power structures. There is still enormous power inequality between A and B, which for some Marxists is not proper socialism, and for Lukes is not proper democracy. The argument is a very interesting one, although it is impossible to prove (or disprove) conclusively that people have 'real' interests of which they are unaware, or that what looks like political apathy is in fact a sign of a more sinister malaise. Whatever the truth of the matter, what is clear is that some citizens in the communist world are profoundly dissatisfied with the various channels of participation permitted by the authorities, and find that they cannot influence the policy process to the extent and/or in the way they would prefer. Some of these people simply 'switch off' from politics. But others are less quiescent. Their frustration leads many of them to go beyond the official channels and engage in what can be called 'illegitimate' (i.e. not sanctioned by the party–state complex) forms of politics. This activity forms the subject-matter of the next three chapters.

Basic further reading

A. Brown, 1971; 1978.
V. Falkenheim, 1978.
T. Friedgut, 1979.
L. Holmes, 1981a.
J. Hough, 1976.
P. Juviler and H. Morton (eds.), 1967.

J. Löwenhardt, 1981.
D. Nelson (ed.), 1980a.
M. Oksenberg, 1982.
D. Schulz and J. Adams (eds.), 1981.
R. Sharlet, 1967.
J. R. Townsend, 1969.

11

DISSIDENCE

HAVING examined politics 'at the top' and within the official channels in communist states, the next three chapters will be devoted to various illegitimate—from the standpoint of the party–state complex, at least—forms of politics. In some cases, such political activity diverges only marginally from what is acceptable; in other cases, those engaged in such activity are questioning the basics of the political system itself. In this chapter, the focus is on the dissidents, of whom the Western media have made so much in recent years. As in other parts of the book, however, so here a distinction has been drawn—in this case between dissidence, nationalism, and popular unrest— primarily in order to make the analysis of this kind of politics clearer and more manageable; in the real world, as will become obvious, there is a great deal of overlap between the various forms of illegitimate politics.

A DEFINITION OF DISSIDENCE

The word dissidence derives from the Latin words *dis*, meaning apart, and *sedere*, to sit, so that a dissident is someone who sits apart from the regime, and possibly even from the mass of the population. But such a definition is very vague, and one produced by the Soviet dissident Roy Medvedev provides a clearer picture of what a dissident is:

... a dissident is someone who disagrees in some measure with the ideological, political, economic, or moral foundation that every society rests on ... But he does more than simply disagree and think differently; he openly proclaims his dissent and demonstrates it in one way or another to his compatriots and the state. In other words, he doesn't just complain in private to his wife or close friends. (Medvedev 1980, p. 1.)

A distinction has been drawn by Reddaway between dissent—which, in this chapter, is used interchangeably with dissidence—and opposition. According to this approach, opposition goes further than dissidence, in that it not only questions official actions, policies, etc., but also consciously seeks to replace them with another set and 'implies an aspiration to rule in place of the existing rulers' (Reddaway 1978, p. 122). Like so many other concepts, the distinction is clearer in theory than in practice, since many dissidents imply opposition in the criticisms they make. Since they cannot in most cases organize an opposition movement, however, and since it would be absurd to suppose that one person could overthrow a regime, we can see why there is sometimes a useful distinction to be drawn, even in the real world, between the dissident and the oppositionist.

In this section of the chapter, we shall be seeing what it is that dissidents criticize and/or advocate, how dissidents disagree amongst themselves, the scale of dissidence in various countries, etc. Since Soviet dissidents are the best-known and most widely analysed ones in the West, we begin by examining them. Thereafter, we shall consider East German, Czechoslovak, and Chinese dissidence.

Dissidence in the USSR

There have, of course, been people who fundamentally disagree with the values and goals of the Soviet regime ever since the Bolsheviks took power in 1917. But the 'dissident movement', as it is often called, is primarily a phenomenon that has existed since the mid-1960s. Let us begin the analysis with a brief historical overview.

Following Stalin's death in 1953, there was a 'thaw' in Soviet intellectual life. Literature, art, music—all became more honest and free than they had been during Stalin's period. 'Socialist realism'—according to which art should play a positive role in building socialism, not a negative and/or critical one—was still officially the approach to be adopted in novels, paintings, symphonies, etc., but the concept was open to a much wider range of interpretations and applications than before.

To some extent, the 'thaw' of the mid-1950s was an outcome of the leadership struggle going on in the Soviet political system. Whilst there was a contest between liberals, conservatives, and middle-of-the-roaders, no one was able or willing either to produce a clear-cut policy on censorship or to enforce it.

Once Khrushchev had consolidated power—by the early summer of 1957—he began to give a little guidance on what was and was not expected of artists and intellectuals in the building of communism. Many commentators have pointed to Khrushchev's ambivalence in his attitudes towards art and intellectual freedom generally. To some extent, this was because of his own personality; he was by nature a volatile and impulsive man, and this helps to explain the changes in his attitudes. One minute he would seem to be a progressive (e.g. by allowing the publication of both Yevtushenko's poem 'Stalin's Heirs' and Solzhenitsyn's *One Day in the Life of Ivan Denisovich* in October and November 1962), the next a reactionary (for instance in December 1962, when he ordered the closure of a modern art exhibition). But Khrushchev's own personality is only part of the explanation for the volatility of official attitudes towards intellectual and artistic freedom in the Khrushchev era. Another important factor was leadership politics. Basically, much of Khrushchev's liberalism was a direct reaction to Stalinism. Indeed, the fact that he allowed publication of *One Day in the Life of Ivan Denisovich* should be understood not so much as an example of Khrushchev's progressiveness, but rather as part of his own policy of de-Stalinization. Solzhenitsyn's criticism of Stalin was well in line with Khrushchev's own, and Khrushchev probably believed that his own position would be enhanced if he permitted this fairly overt criticism of his predecessor. Sometimes, though, Khrushchev's *apparently* liberal attitude towards intellectuals—which, as has been argued, was often so primarily because of his own interests—came in for criticism from colleagues. At such times, and if he felt at all endangered by such leaders' criticisms, he would tighten up his policy. This argument provides a better understanding of the changeability of Khrushchev's policies.

Following Khrushchev's ouster in 1964, the new leadership emphasized that the sudden changes of policy typical of the Khrushchev years would not characterize their own approach. This was comforting to many progressive intellectuals—although, of course, they wanted to ensure that the stable policy was in line with their own attitudes; they had experienced relative freedom of expression, and they wanted to retain it. Unfortunately for them, the new leadership soon made clear that it had no intention of encouraging further criticism of Stalin. Brezhnev and Kosygin were more conservative than Khrushchev, and felt that too much emphasis on the failings of previous leaders might have an adverse effect on the public's perception of the present leadership (i.e., themselves). This had serious implications for censorship and the freedom of intellectuals to criticize. Solzhenitsyn's *One Day in the Life of Ivan Denisovich* was banned, and there was criticism in the newspapers of excessively negative analyses of Soviet society.

The new leadership very soon demonstrated its resolve to halt what it saw as a liberal rot. Already in 1965 there were a number of arrests of critical intellectuals in Moscow and the Ukraine. A major controversy erupted in February 1966 when two writers, Daniel and Sinyavskii, were tried for 'defamation of the Soviet system' by smuggling manuscripts abroad pseudonymously. They received harsh sentences of five and seven years' imprisonment respectively. The controversy flared up still further at the time of the CPSU's 23rd Congress in March 1966, when the novelist Sholokhov (winner of the Nobel Prize for Literature the previous year) not only added his own condemnation of Daniel and Sinyavskii, but went so far as to say that their prison sentences were too mild. The tensions between the liberal intelligentsia and the authorities were increasing.

A new wave of arrests in 1967 was followed by another highly controversial trial at the beginning of 1968, this time of Galanskov and Ginzburg. They were accused and found guilty of circulating details on the Daniel–Sinyavskii trial, and received harsh prison sentences; Galanskov later died in prison. The attack on the intellectuals led a number of them to decide to print their own underground journal, aimed primarily at informing others of the harassment to which many intellectuals were being subjected. This 'self-publishing'—or *samizdat* as it is better known—was seen primarily in the *Chronicle of Current Events*, which first appeared in April 1968. The journal was committed to freedom of expression, and included in its heading Article 19 of the Universal Declaration on Human Rights:

Everyone has the right to freedom of expression; this right includes the freedom to hold opinions without interference and to seek, receive and impart information and ideas through any media and regardless of frontiers . . .

Despite this, it was not concerned primarily with giving alternative interpretations or political programmes to those of the Soviet authorities. Rather, it was mainly a diary of the repression of intellectuals and others who believed in the right of free speech in the USSR. It provided details on arrests, trials, prison sentences, and prison conditions.

Although the chronicle itself did not act as an overtly political journal, the more people read of the authorities' harsh and often arbitrary treatment of others who were only asserting what they believed the USSR had promised them in the constitution, the more overtly political critiques of the Soviet system appeared. One of the most famous of these was published in *samizdat* form in 1969—Amalrik's 'Will the Soviet Union survive until 1984?'. Amalrik argued in this that the Soviet working class was no longer the repository of revolutionary ideas, and that any hope for change must be based on a section of the intelligentsia, whom he also called the Soviet Union's 'middle class'. He argued that an actual political movement—the 'Democratic Movement'—was emerging amongst members of this group, even though he also acknowledged that this 'movement' lacked organization or even a clear ideology (Amalrik 1969, esp. pp. 52–4). Despite its analytical imprecision, Amalrik's document constituted a damning critique of both the Soviet system and the bulk of the Soviet citizenry, and in 1970 Amalrik was tried, sentenced, and imprisoned.

In that same year (1970) a Soviet 'Human Rights Committee' was formed, with the aim of defending human rights in the USSR. Two of its leaders subsequently became well known in the West as leading Soviet dissidents: Valery Chalidze and Andrei Sakharov. The latter—at one time a leading nuclear physicist—had already made his mark with a long essay entitled *Progress, Coexistence and Intellectual Freedom*, which was published in the West in 1968, and which is considered later in this section.

Although the number of dissidents—people prepared to write critically about aspects of the Soviet system—was growing, the security police (KGB) were also mustering their forces against the intellectuals. In November 1971, they launched an all-out attack on the *Chronicle of Current Events*, and by 1972 the publication had been silenced. It was not long before a new version—*A Chronicle of Human Rights in the USSR*—was being printed, but this time it was based abroad, in New York.

By the late summer of 1973, the regime seemed to be adopting a new line in its war on the dissidents. Instead of trying to keep their existence and ideas as little known as possible, they tried to mobilize public opinion against them. It would seem that the regime decided that one of the most effective ways of undermining the prestigious dissidents such as the mathematician-novelist Solzhenitsyn or Sakharov was to publish criticisms of them from other, equally distinguished Soviet intellectuals and artists. Thus letters critical of the dissidents appeared in the press, signed by such leading figures as the composers Khachaturian and Shostakovich, the film actor and director Bondarchuk, and the violinist Oistrakh. This was happening at the same time as yet another important trial of dissidents—this time of the historian Yakir and the economist Krasin—was being held in Moscow. The trial was used partially to mount a major campaign against both Sakharov and Solzhenitsyn. But if the intention had been to silence these men, the attempt was to no avail. In January 1974, Solzhenitsyn's possibly most damning criticism of Stalin's prison-camp system—the *Gulag Archipelago*—was published in Paris. Very soon after its publication, Solzhenitsyn was arrested, stripped of Soviet citizenship, and expelled from the USSR; after spending some time in Western Europe, he now lives in the USA.

But expelling one leading dissident could not crush the spirit of others; in the same year that Solzhenitsyn was expelled, the *Chronicle* began circulating again within Russia itself.

For many Soviet intellectuals, the high point of 1975 was the Helsinki agreement on co-operation in Europe. The Soviet Union was a signatory to this, and was therefore formally committed to respect a wide range of human rights specified in the third section (or 'basket') of the agreement. Shortly after the full text of the document had been published in the Soviet press, an eleven-person Helsinki monitoring committee was established under the leadership of physicist Yuri Orlov; another leading member of the committee was Ginzburg, by now out of prison. The group was encouraged by the statements of Jimmy Carter who, on becoming President of the USA in January 1977, stated publicly that the defence of human rights throughout the world would be one of his administration's main concerns. Although this proved to be bolder in the saying than in the enacting, Carter's words acted as a major boost to the dissidents within the USSR. However, the authorities soon clamped down, and there were a number of arrests in 1977. It was not long before the leading lights of this group were arrested, tried, and sentenced; some were subsequently deported. Thus Ginzburg was tried and imprisoned in July 1978, then released in April 1979 and deported to the USA; Orlov was sentenced in May 1978 to seven years' imprisonment followed by five years' exile.

In an endeavour to assert and test his rights as a Soviet citizen, Roy

Medvedev (a dissident historian) attempted to stand in the March 1978 Soviet elections; needless to say, he did not receive the nomination for candidacy. But by this time, as Roy Medvedev himself openly acknowledges, the Soviet dissident 'movement' had temporarily collapsed (Medvedev 1979, p. 26). This low point of Soviet dissidence has by and large continued into the 1980s. In January 1980—at a time when he started criticizing the Soviet intervention in Afghanistan—one of the longest standing thorns in the Soviet authorities' flesh, Sakharov, was sent into internal exile in the closed city of Gorkii. Later that year, several dissidents were sent out of Moscow whilst the Olympic Games were being held, in order to minimize their chances of conveying complaints to foreign visitors. Moreover, most of the remaining members of the Moscow Helsinki monitoring group were arrested and imprisoned or exiled in 1980 and 1981; the group was finally disbanded in September 1982.

It should be noted that the intensity of repression since 1979 has not succeeded in silencing the dissidents altogether. In the summer of 1982, for instance, a new group—the Group for Establishing Trust between the USSR and the USA—was established in Moscow, with the aim of pressuring the Soviet authorities into a nuclear disarmament programme with the Americans. This peace group—led by Sergei Batovrin—was only just managing to survive at the time of writing, and several leading members have been either encouraged to leave the country (e.g. Batovrin himself, and Oleg Popov) or interned in psychiatric hospitals and/or in prison (e.g. Oleg Radzinskii). Thus the short-term future of the USSR's peace movement—like Soviet dissidence more generally—does not appear to be very bright, and there were still many arrests and heavy sentences being passed at the time of writing.

Having given a brief historical survey, let us now try to analyse what has sometimes been called in the past the dissident 'movement'. In fact, one of the points that emerges very clearly from reading the ideas and criticisms of various Soviet dissidents is that the only factor linking many of them has been the feeling that there is something wrong with the Soviet system and its policies. But the analyses of what is wrong, and what corrective measures should be taken, differ considerably. To illustrate this point, the views of Solzhenitsyn, Sakharov, and Roy Medvedev can be compared and contrasted.

As Michael Cox points out, many Westerners misinterpreted Solzhenitsyn in the 1960s and early 1970s, thinking him to be a progressive revolutionary (Cox 1975, p. 5). In fact, by the mid-1970s it was clear that Solzhenitsyn was a rather reactionary nationalist, whose intellectual roots can be found in nineteenth-century Russian Slavophile thinkers such as Khomyakov and the Aksakov brothers. One of Solzhenitsyn's prime targets is Marxism–Leninism; he himself is a very religious man, and he deplores an ideology based on a humanistic and materialistic conception of the world. His hostility to Marxism–Leninism makes Solzhenitsyn critical of the political system based on it. He sees the Soviet government as terroristic and lawless, élitist, and lacking national pride (a cardinal sin for Solzhenitsyn). But Solzhenitsyn has been critical of the Russian *people* too, for what he sees as their dishonesty in not standing up to a repressive regime. At one time, Solzhenitsyn seemed to believe that the West was a far better place than the USSR in the particular senses that it was freer, and that both people and leaders had more real commitment to their political system. But since coming to the West Solzhenitsyn has become increasingly disillusioned; he now thinks that the West is as morally decadent as his homeland, and he lives an unhappy life in Vermont.

Sakharov (like Solzhenitsyn) was at one time a Marxist, although his brand of Marxism was always of the liberal, humane sort, rather than the more austere 'scientific' type. But by the mid-to-late 1960s, Sakharov had concluded that many of the problems of the Soviet Union derived from Marxist ideas, and he abandoned Marxism. Since then, he has been what might be called a progressive liberal or a democratic, non-Marxist socialist. Whereas Solzhenitsyn has now become almost as critical of the West as of the USSR, Sakharov's intellectual development has virtually been in the opposite direction. Thus in one of his most famous early writings—*Progress, Coexistence and Intellectual Freedom*—Sakharov criticized *both* the USSR and USA (the latter for, among other things, its treatment of blacks and its involvement in Vietnam). In the early 1970s, however, his views changed dramatically, and he became so anti-Soviet (and anti-Marxist) and pro-Western that he even argued General Pinochet's regime in Chile was an improvement on Allende's. Somewhat ironically for someone who played a major role in developing the Soviet hydrogen bomb, Sakharov has long been a major campaigner for nuclear disarmament. However, he now accepts the view of many Western governments that such disarmament is most likely to come about if the West can negotiate with the Soviets from a position of strength. He thus supported the deployment of new NATO missiles in Western Europe in 1983. The final point is that Sakharov's pleas for more freedom of expression have tended to be based on more instrumental or pragmatic arguments than Solzhenitsyn's. Thus he has argued that the only way the Soviets' technological and economic levels can be raised to those of the West—which he sees as one way of reducing East–West tension—is by allowing scientists and others to work independently of state ideology and control.

The third example, Roy Medvedev, was and remains a Marxist. He was one of those intellectuals who were encouraged by developments under Khrushchev—he joined the CPSU in 1956, shortly after Khrushchev's strong criticism of Stalin at the 20th Congress—and who became disillusioned with the way the post-Khrushchev leadership has tried to play down the errors of the past. His criticisms of the Soviet system are very similar to some of the East German dissidents to be considered later in this chapter, in that he believes that Marxism provides a humane approach to life, and that too many Leninists have turned Marxism into a rigid, dead dogma. He criticizes the practical implementation of democratic centralism, arguing that there is little democracy and far too much centralism. In one of his best-known works, *On Socialist Democracy*, he argues that the Soviet bureaucracy (he means here the party *apparatchiki* as well as the state functionaries) is actually hindering the development of the USSR towards real socialism. This is because it suppresses lively exchange of constructive criticism and views, leading to a 'them and us' attitude in society which has little to do with socialism. Like the late Robert Havemann (see below), Medvedev believes that change can and should come from the party itself—with prompting and pressure from intellectuals. Although he believes that the West can exercise some influence over the Soviet leaders, he sees this as being of marginal relevance; change in the Soviet Union has got to come from within.

It should be clear even from this cursory glance at the views of three leading dissidents that there has been a wide range of views among the Soviet intellectual critics. For this reason, I would argue that the term 'movement' should be used very cautiously when talking of the Soviet dissidents. Indeed, if there had been greater homogeneity of views, and thus something closer to an actual movement, the Soviet dissidents might not have been in quite as sorry a state as they are at present. It remains to be seen whether attempts to link dissidents around narrow—if important—issues, such as a campaign for disarmament, will give them greater strength in the future; at present, the short-term outlook is grim.

Dissidence in the GDR

One of the biggest differences between dissidents in the USSR and those in the GDR is that the leading East German critics have all been Marxists. There is no East German equivalent of Solzhenitsyn—one possible reason being that most East Germans, for fairly obvious reasons, do not look to the past with the longing and romanticism that some Russians do.

The first really overt dissident voices in the GDR were heard in the mid-1950s, after the brutal suppression of rioting citizens in June 1953. By 1956, with both this and the Soviet leadership's condemnation of Stalin and Stalinism in mind, a number of intellectuals felt that the time had come to speak out. Some of these voices were calling for relatively specific reforms. For instance, Werner Dorst was concerned that the educational system should promote the most intelligent and gifted students, not those showing the most overt political loyalty. Fritz Behrens and Arne Benary were concerned primarily with making the economy perform more efficiently—although their suggestions as to how this should be achieved, especially their calls for industrial organization along the lines of Yugoslav 'self-management', had profound implications for the distribution of power in society and were therefore political. But the most overtly critical and significant voices were those of a group centred on Wolfgang Harich. Harich, a lecturer in philosophy at the Humboldt University in East Berlin, was the chief author of a document which appeared in 1956 and which came to be known as the 'Harich Programme'. Some indication of the importance of this is seen in the fact that as late as 1970, one Western commentator described it as 'the only consistent formulation of East German reform communism that has come to be known outside the GDR' (Lippmann 1970, p. 16). Amongst the many proposals made by Harich were that there should be a real choice in elections; the state legislature (*Volkskammer*) should be a genuine discussion forum and independent of party control; forced collectivization of agriculture should be stopped; and that workers' self-management in industry, along the Yugoslav lines, should be introduced. However, Harich and his co-authors did not stop at changes in the organization of the state and society—they also advocated major change within the party itself. For instance, they called for the expulsion of all Stalinists—who were seen as essentially 'fascist'—from the party, and for more power to the rank-and-file membership at the expense of the party *apparatchiki*. Moreover, in line with similar aspirations in other parts of Eastern Europe in 1956, the Harich programme called for a specifically German road to socialism; the time for blind and often inappropriate emulation of Soviet theory and practice was over. Given that the communist leadership in the GDR has never been very liberal even in comparison with some other communist leaderships, it was hardly surprising that Harich was arrested in November 1956; the following March he received a ten-year prison sentence, of which he served seven years before being released. He continues to criticize the East German regime from what he sees as a more humane Marxist viewpoint. However, he does not advocate a self-managing society, let alone an anarchistic one. He believes that a centralized state machinery *is* necessary, and will become increasingly so as large-scale problems (e.g. environmental pollution) proliferate and require implemented and enforced solutions. This said, state officials must be uncorrupt and properly answerable to the people.

Several supporters of Harich were also tried and imprisoned in 1957, and this clampdown led to a relatively quiet period in the history of East German dissidence. At this stage (late 1950s), those who felt too strongly about the system could in any case always leave it without too much difficulty. But in August 1961, and only a few weeks after Ulbricht had publicly promised that one would not be built, East German soldiers erected a wall along the frontier between East and West Berlin, making it very much more difficult to excape from the GDR. Perhaps ironically, the East German leadership appeared to become slightly more liberal following the construction of the Berlin Wall. This was most obvious in the introduction of the New Economic System in January 1963. This called for a certain amount of decentralization of decision-making in industry, and was interpreted by some as a sign that the leadership—feeling more self-assured now that skilled workers and peasants could no longer flee—was prepared to place more confidence in the citizenry. It was in this atmosphere that the man who was to become one of the best known of all the East German dissidents, the chemist Professor Robert Havemann, produced a trenchant (but again Marxist) critique of the regime in a series of lectures given at the Humboldt University in the 1963–4 academic year. In these lectures, Havemann called for a more humane form of socialism, in which people would be free to make constructive criticisms aimed at building a better society. He criticized the authoritarian nature of the regime, and was particularly harsh and open about interference of what he saw as party dogma in the development of natural science; in this, his views were somewhat akin to those of Sakharov in the USSR.

The view that the East German leadership had become more tolerant of criticism was dispelled soon after Havemann's lectures. The chemist lost his chair at the university and his party membership. Admittedly, he was not sent to prison; but his enforced retirement was a serious blow. Nevertheless, Havemann continued to criticize what he saw as the authoritarian—even Stalinist—aspects of the GDR's political system, usually in articles or books smuggled into and published in West Germany. Havemann praised the political experimentation of the Prague reforms in 1968, and later argued that East Berlin would one day have its 'Spring' too.

One of Havemann's most frequent criticisms was that the political leaders did not recognize that most East Germans had accepted the basic tenets of socialism, so that they (the leaders) should now place more faith in the masses and allow them a greater role in the running of their own society. A typical article was one which appeared in the West German newspaper *Frankfurter Rundschau* in December 1973 entitled 'The government should show confidence in its own people'. In it, he argued that there was no dictatorship of the proletariat in the GDR, only a 'dictatorship of a clique of party functionaries'. In line with his view that most East Germans basically accepted socialism, he argued that, 'The sole threat to socialism is the present form of the state which rules here' (Havemann 1974, p. 47). However, like Harich, he also believed that change—away from 'bureaucratic' socialism and towards a humane variant—should come from above; he reasoned that such change would be more secure than one induced by rioting mobs.

In the autumn of 1976 the GDR authorities took their lead from the Soviet Union and decided to clamp down on the dissidents before they gained too much steam in the wake of the Helsinki agreement. The balladeer, Wolfgang Biermann, who has described the GDR's political and social system as 'computer Stalinism', was expelled to West Germany—and Havemann was placed under house arrest. Eighteen months later, a relatively new, but highly influential dissident, Rudolf Bahro, was also imprisoned; subsequently, he too was expelled. Bahro's analysis, though Marxist, calls for a much more liberal and decentralized communist society than, most notably, Harich's. Bahro in his book *The Alternative in Eastern Europe* (published in West Ger-

many in 1977) accepted that an authoritarian state is necessary in the immediate aftermath of a revolution, but felt that the party–state complexes in
Eastern Europe had outlived this justification for their role, and should start
transferring more power to the ordinary people (i.e., very much in line with
Havemann's ideas). He maintained that the events in Czechoslovakia in 1968
showed very clearly the validity of his argument that the East European
party–states had become reactionary and were hindering the development of
genuine socialism and communism in that part of the world.

Despite the large number of expulsions in the late 1970s, the 'grand old
man' of East German dissidence, Havemann, stayed in his native country
and continued to criticize the regime, despite harassment. Towards the end of
his life (he died in April 1982), Havemann became closely involved in what
has since 1981 become the most sensitive domestic issue in East German politics, the unofficial peace movement. The background to this is that the intensified repression of the late 1970s was accompanied by a marked increase in
the militarization of East German life. In particular, school children were
compelled to undergo elementary weapons training, which led to tensions
between the church (predominantly evangelical in the GDR) and the communist authorities. By 1981—encouraged by the peace movement in the West—
Havemann and various church leaders (such as Pastor Eppelmann) were
becoming increasingly critical of the militarization in their society. They
called for a 'social peace service', whereby young people should be given the
option to perform peaceful social work for two years rather than the eighteen-
month military duties required by existing laws. Towards the end of 1981,
Havemann and others actually sent a letter to Brezhnev in the USSR, calling
on the Soviet leader to work harder for peace. This movement thus has
narrower aims than many of the earlier dissidents (including Havemann himself) had. On the other hand, this more specific and tangible target seems to
have attracted a large number of followers, particularly young people, in the
GDR. Although the authorities have tried to clamp down on this, they are in a
very embarrassing and ambivalent position, since it is the official policy of the
GDR to work for peace. At the time of writing, this peace movement—though
coming under strong pressure from the authorities—is the most important
political movement ever to have emerged in the GDR, and it might be that the
dissenting intellectuals have learnt the same lesson as their Soviet colleagues.
This is that abstract criticism of 'bureaucratic socialism' or distortions of
Marxism or party interference in science is not likely to attract many followers, even supposing there were many citizens basically sympathetic to the
criticisms. But by focusing on a specific issue that both directly affects ordinary people (in this case the requirement that young people perform military
service for the state) and appears to be closely in line with official policy, previously isolated dissident intellectuals might actually be able to create a
popular movement. The progress of the 'peace movement' in the GDR and
elsewhere—it is also strong in Hungary—should be watched with interest

(for further details on the GDR see Mushaben 1984 and Ramet 1984; on Hungary see Kosegi and Thompson, n.d.).

Dissidence in Czechoslovakia

The recent history of dissidence in Czechoslovakia bears some similarity to that of the USSR and the GDR. In all three, for instance, intellectuals have been the principal source of criticism of the regime. In all three, the Helsinki agreement of 1975 gave added impetus to the dissidents. As in the Soviet Union and East Germany, the Czechoslovak dissidents have tended to move away from general critiques towards more specific complaints/issues in recent years. Czechoslovakia, like the GDR, also provides us with an example of what can be seen as the most extreme and horrific form of political protest by dissident intellectuals. In January 1969, the student Jan Palach publicly set fire to himself; he died clutching a note calling for the abolition of censorship and the closure of a Soviet propaganda broadsheet published in the Czech language (East German examples of self-immolation as a form of political protest include Pastors Oskar Brusewitz in 1976 and Gerhard Fischer in 1978). Self-immolation is a sobering testimony to the strength of commitment of some dissidents. But there are also differences between the nature of dissidence in these three states. For instance, Czechoslovakia stands approximately midway between the GDR and the USSR in terms of the range of political orientations of the dissidents. Whereas there has been a very wide range in the USSR and a very narrow one (virtually exclusively Marxist) in the GDR, the leading Czechoslovak dissidents have nearly all been socialists of one kind or another (there have been no right-wing dissidents of note) but by no means all Marxists. Another important point is that some former leading politicians (e.g. Josef Smrkovsky and Jiri Hajek) have been amongst the most outspoken critics of the regime.

There had been dissidence in Czechoslovakia prior to 1968, but the harsh Novotny regime had seen to it that this never got out of hand. However, when the Communist Party itself inaugurated a major liberalization in 1968, it opened a Pandora's Box which has never been entirely closed since, despite the present conservative regime's attempts. As the events of 1968–9 will be considered in the next chapter we shall concentrate here on dissidence since that time, leaning heavily on Kusin's analysis (Kusin, 1979).

In the immediate aftermath of 1968, there was an uneasy coalition of hard-line conservatives (e.g. Bilak, Indra) and more reformist politicians (including Dubcek himself until September 1969, when he was expelled from the party presidium) running Czechoslovakia. At this stage, only those perceived as dangerous radicals were suppressed by the regime. Thus the economist Ota Sik and the Prague television chief Jiri Pelikan were forced to emigrate, and organizations such as KAN (the Club of Non-Party Committed) and

K-231 (a group of former political prisoners) were shut down. But there was still hope among many that real change could be brought about, that the spirit of 1968 could be rekindled. There was even a new left 'Revolutionary Socialist Party' set up—although its membership amounted to only nineteen, all of whom were tried early in 1971, and most of whom were sent to prison for opposition to the Czechoslovak Communist Party and subversion of the Czechoslovak Republic. More importantly, an unofficial 'Ten Points Manifesto' was drawn up on the first anniversary of the Warsaw Pact invasion of Czechoslovakia (21 August 1969) and widely circulated. This criticized the invasion, the new high level of censorship, and called for the ratification of two international covenants on human rights that some members of the Czechoslovak government had signed in October 1968. The last of these demands was to remain very much in the minds of the dissidents over the coming years, as shall be seen.

By 1970, the reformists at the top of the party had all either been removed or encouraged to change their views, and a widespread purge of the party in the summer of that year meant that reform-oriented individuals in Czechoslovakia would now have to operate outside the party itself. Despite this, former party-members were still by far the most significant group of dissidents. Some of these formed themselves into a Socialist Movement of Czechoslovakia, which produced and disseminated a number of important documents in 1970 and 1971. Of these, two merit particular attention. The first was the '28 October Manifesto', so called because it was issued on the 52nd anniversary of the establishment of an independent Czechoslovak state (i.e., October 1970). The implication was clear; Czechoslovakia should not allow others to limit its sovereignty. In addition to this point, the manifesto reiterated the signatories' commitment to most of the reforms discussed in 1968. In February 1971, the second major document—the 'Short Action Programme of the Socialist Opposition'—began to circulate. Like earlier documents, the programme revealed that the authors were not only socialists, but even accepted a Leninist approach to political organization. But this did not mean they accepted the official Communist Party—they did not, and they made this clear. The authorities, who were by now becoming increasingly repressive, finally decided that the Socialist Movement of Czechoslovakia had gone too far when it circulated an 'election appeal' shortly before the November 1971 elections. Approximately 200 members of the movement were arrested between December 1971 and January 1972—of whom 47 were imprisoned following trials in July and August 1972.

The trials of the summer of 1972 led to a rapid decline in attempts by former party members to take on the authorities. From now on, the majority of leading dissidents were not former politicians but intellectuals—writers, historians, etc. Until now, the intellectuals had often been divided by their general political positions—pro-Lenin Marxists, anti-Lenin Marxists, non-Marxist socialists—but they gradually began to realize that their common interests in relatively specific issues, such as the treatment of political prisoners, outweighed their political differences.

By the mid-1970s, two important developments abroad gave Czechoslovak dissidents new hope and determination to keep up their pressure on the authorities. The first was the emergence of the Eurocommunists, whom people such as Zdenek Mlynar initially believed would give dissidents in Eastern Europe support in their struggle. In fact, the support was lukewarm; but, given what subsequently happened in Czechoslovakia, the disappointing response seems to have given the dissidents even more determination not to give up. The other factor was the growing formal commitment of the Czechoslovak authorities to respect human rights. The Helsinki agreement was one sign of this. But at least as important in Czechoslovakia was the not unrelated fact that the government finally formally ratified the two international covenants on human rights which had been signed back in October 1968. The covenants officially came into force in March 1976, but were not published until November of that year. Their publication gave a new incentive to the dissidents—who produced what must be seen as one of the most important unofficial documents of the 1970s, Charter 77.

Charter 77 appeared at the very beginning of 1977. There were originally 242 signatories—but many others (including the former party leader Dubcek) very soon gave it their support, and by the end of the year the number had increased to almost 900. Although most of the signatories were intellectuals, approximately one-third were factory workers. The main concern of the authors and signatories was to ensure that the Czechoslovak regime abided by both its commitments to respect human rights and its own constitution and legal code. In other words, it was less general than early programmes and manifestos, and concentrated on keeping the authorities to their own promises; as one of the main spokespersons for the Charter, Jan Patocka, put it, the goal of the movement was 'a certain moral dignity' (cited in *Time*, 21 February 1977, p. 10).

It was not long before the authorities reacted to the Charter—and they did so negatively. One of the three spokespersons for Charter 77, the playwright Vaclav Havel, was arrested in January, and kept in prison until May; he was tried in October, but received the relatively light punishment of a suspended prison sentence. He was not prepared to give up his involvement in Charter 77, however, and has subsequently spent several long periods in prison. The second, former Foreign Minister Jiri Hajek, was harassed. The third, the philosopher Jan Patocka died in March 1977—allegedly as a result of the harsh treatment he received during interrogation by the security police. Many other signatories were encouraged to leave their homeland for good; although some did, many decided they would prefer to stay in Czechoslovakia to continue the struggle. This led to many of them losing their jobs.

Although many of its supporters were harassed, Charter 77 gave new life to the dissident movement in Czechoslovakia. New, independent journals began to appear in 1978 (e.g. *Economic Review* and *Historical Studies*). An informal university arrangement—called by some the 'anti-university', by others the 'Patocka university' (in honour of the dead ringleader of the Charter 77 movement)—emerged in 1978, whereby former university teachers who had lost their jobs gave seminars to young people who were prevented from attending university for political reasons. Although this eventually collapsed (one of its main driving forces, Julius Tomin, was deprived of his citizenship in 1981 and now lives in the West), it showed very clearly that many intellectuals were prepared to defy the regime's attempts to stop their activities. In December 1980, a massive biography of the liberal philosopher who founded the Czechoslovak republic, Thomas Masaryk, was illegally published in *samizdat* form; it represented the determination of many intellectuals to keep hopes alive that Czechoslovakia would one day be a liberal democracy again.

Harassment of the dissidents continues. In May 1981, for example, twenty-six human rights activists were arrested, eight of whom were charged with 'subversion of the Republic', and there have been many more arrests and trials since. But the spirit of the dissidents has not been broken. There is still a Charter 77 group, and it continues to send appeals to the government (see e.g. *Communist Affairs*, October 1982, pp. 836–7 and April 1984, p. 144).

Following the 1968 invasion of Czechoslovakia, there has been what the authorities call a 'normalization' of political life. In essence, this means a return to many of the repressive aspects of the pre-1968 regime, plus a reassertion by the Czechoslovak leadership of its loyalty to Moscow. But this repressive regime has not been able to crush the dissidents completely. The latter have become more specific in their demands over time, and are a continuing embarrassment to the regime—above all, because they highlight the hypocrisy of a leadership which often does not abide by rules it has itself laid down.

Dissidence in China

The available evidence suggests that there has been far less self-motivated dissidence in the PRC than in most of the European communist states. Moreover, contemporary Chinese dissidents are not typically members of the intelligentsia, at least in terms of their occupation. These are just two of the ways in which Chinese dissidence differs from that in the other countries we have considered. Let us now look a little more closely at this Asian example.

At one level, dissent in the PRC is not a new phenomenon. In Mao's time, for instance, there were two major periods of what some would call dissidence. In 1957 Chinese citizens were urged to 'let a hundred flowers bloom, let a hundred schools of thought contend'; in other words, they were encouraged to express themselves freely on political issues. This 'Hundred Flowers

Campaign' was intended on one level to prevent the emergence of the political tensions that had arisen in other communist states in the aftermath of the USSR's de-Stalinization (1956); Mao did not want a Chinese version of the Hungarian uprising. But the movement very soon got out of hand, and thousands of Chinese (mainly intellectuals) finished up in labour camps for having been *too* critical of the regime; in that the authorities were punishing people for their political views, such people can be seen as dissenters of sorts. Although the regime very soon and very forcefully made it clear that only criticism of specifics, not the political system generally, would be tolerated, one of the methods encouraged during the 'Hundred Flowers Campaign' survived. This was the wall-poster, which lasted until 1980 as a medium for expressing political sentiments. For much of the Mao period, the kinds of views expressed were usually either in support of official policies or else of highly specific and ultimately marginal complaints. However, during the GPCR a second wave of open dissidence occurred, in the sense that wall-posters often criticized named leaders. But here again, the dissenters were being encouraged—if not by all the top leadership, then by one faction or another. Many Red Guards, for instance, would put up wall-posters criticizing opponents of Mao amongst the leadership—most notably the 'Liuists'. It is for this reason that one must be careful when talking of dissidence under Mao; much of what came to be treated as dissent was not self-motivated but occurred after the 'green light' had been given from leaders. If it overstepped the mark, the authorities clamped down, and the criticism essentially ceased.

To some extent, this is true of much of the 'dissidence' in the post-Mao period. For instance, there was a major outburst of criticism of aspects of the regime by ordinary citizens from November 1978 to late 1979. The reason we can be so specific about the starting-point is that, once again, the leadership gave the signal for the criticism to commence. The background to this can be traced to 1976. On 5 April 1976, there was a mass, spontaneous protest in the heart of Beijing, Tiananmen Square. The demonstrators—thousands of them—were protesting against the radicals in the leadership for having tried to suppress many ordinary citizens' attempts to mourn publicly for the late premier Zhou Enlai. Many of the protestors also expressed their support for the man who had taken over Zhou's mantle of moderation and pragmatism, Deng Xiaoping. As a result, Deng was blamed for the incident and dismissed from office. After Mao's death (September 1976), Deng gradually worked his way back to the top. Following the arrest of the Gang of Four, Deng began to turn his attention to his main competitor, Hua Guofeng; though not a radical, Hua was closer to Mao's position than Deng himself was (see chapter 8 for further details). It was in this context that the Central Committee, on Deng's prompting, decided to review the Tiananmen Square incident on 15 November 1978; the committee resolved that the riot had been a 'completely revolutionary event', and Mao and the pro-Maoist leaders were implicitly criticized. This acted as a catalyst to many Chinese citizens, who wanted to let off steam after the oppression of Mao's last decade. The wall-poster received a major boost, with new critical posters appearing daily; the most famous site for such posters was the so-called 'Democracy Wall' near the centre of Beijing. Most of the posters, it must be said, were very specific in nature, asking why a particular individual had not yet been allowed to return to urban life, etc.

But wall-posters were not the only medium through which Chinese citizens expressed themselves politically, and they were certainly not the most interesting phenomenon in terms of their depth of criticism and analysis. Thus a large number of unofficial journals started to appear, of which the most famous were the *5 April Forum, Beijing Spring, Voice of the People*, and *Exploration*. Unlike their counterparts in the USSR or Eastern Europe, these journals were sold openly on the streets and for a while there was no attempt by the authorities to suppress them. One reason was that many of them were basically positive about Deng and the new leadership's policies, directing most of their criticism to the Maoist period; this was particularly true of *5 April Forum* and *Beijing Spring*.

Unfortunately, as in 1957, it was not very long before the leadership decided that the situation was getting out of hand. Possibly encouraged by the critical writing, many citizens—ordinary workers and peasants—began to express their dissatisfaction even more overtly, by staging protests and sit-ins. For instance, there was a peasant demonstration in Tiananmen Square in January 1979, and a sit-in at Shanghai railway station in the following month. Moreover, *some* of the journal articles and wall-posters were very critical of the contemporary leadership. It was in this situation that Deng and the other leaders decided to clamp down in March 1979. The number of areas where wall-posters were permitted was dramatically reduced. In addition, there was a wave of arrests; according to one analyst, up to 2,000 arrests were made in Beijing and Shanghai alone (Benton 1980, p. 76). Amongst those affected was the leading critic of Deng, the editor of *Exploration*, Wei Jingsheng. He had been arguing that the new Chinese leaders were not essentially different from their predecessors, and that what China needed at least as much of the official policy of the 'Four Modernizations' was the 'fifth modernization' of real democracy. Though a socialist of sorts, Wei was not a Marxist—seeing Marxism as the root of totalitarianism—and he argued that there was more freedom and democracy in the capitalist states than in his own country, an argument which did not endear him to the Chinese leadership.

Following the mass arrests of late March, there was a lull. But by May–June 1979, the unofficial journals began to reappear, as did more critical wall-posters; dissatisfied citizens had not yet had their say.

By the autumn of 1979, the Chinese leadership had decided to put the lid more firmly on the criticism. Wei himself was put on trial in October. He was accused of having passed military secrets to foreigners (he had made some critical comments to foreign journalists about China's invasion of Vietnam in early 1979 and had released statistics on Chinese losses) and of agitating for the overthrow of socialism; he was sentenced to fifteen years' imprisonment. Protests about Wei's sentence and dissemination of the transcript of his trial led to more arrests in November. In December, the number of walls officially available for wall-posters was further reduced; Beijing's 'Democracy Wall' was cleaned up and left blank, to be replaced by a smaller wall in a park well away from the city centre. Moreover, a new law stated that *all* posters had to be signed and registered. But this was not all. Many of the unofficial journals were now proscribed (e.g. in Guangzhou). Finally, in February 1980, the Central Committee decided to 'recommend' (i.e. instruct) the National People's Congress to rescind parts of Article 45 of the 1978 Constitution in such a way as to remove the right of Chinese citizens to 'speak out freely, air their views fully, hold great debates, and write big-character posters'; the latest Constitution makes no reference to the rights of citizens to put up wall-posters, and emphasizes that citizens must respect public order and the interests of the state and motherland (see chapter two of the 1982 Constitution, especially arts. 35, 51–54).

Since February 1980, there have been more trials of dissidents, and more prison sentences. For example, in July 1980, the co-founder of the *5 April Forum*, Liu Qing, was sentenced to three years in a labour camp for participating in the January 1979 peasant demonstration in Beijing and, more importantly, for disseminating a transcript of Wei Jingsheng's trial. There was another wave of arrests in the spring of 1981 affecting, among others, the radical Marxist dissidents Wang Xizhe and Xu Wenli; in 1982, they were sentenced to fourteen and fifteen years' imprisonment respectively for 'counter-revolutionary activities'.

We have seen that the post-1978 wave of criticism was largely leadership inspired. On the other hand, the so-called Democracy Movement of 1978–9 rapidly got out of hand, and the leaders responded with arrests by March 1979. Given this, the re-emergence of critical wall-posters and journals in May–June can be seen as self-motivated on the part of the critics; in other words, it constitutes real dissidence, and is from most points of view a new development.

Although the dissidents are currently in a sorry state—many of the leaders being in prison—it is clear that the Chinese leadership is beginning to experience some of the problems of its European counterparts. The dissidents did show signs that they were beginning to create a real movement in 1980 (see Benton 1982b, pp. 10–11), which suggests that under certain conditions the Chinese dissidents could be sufficiently organized to develop as a reasonably coherent whole. This said, it should not be overlooked that there have been significant political and philosophical differences amongst the Chinese, as amongst the dissidents in many other countries; a comparison of the views of

Wang and Wei, for example, will endorse this point (see e.g. Benton 1982a; Wang Xizhe 1980 and 1982). Moreover, it has been pointed out that the criticisms from many of the authors of the wall-posters were of a highly specific nature rather than being general political analyses. For these reasons, the term 'political movement' should be used very sparingly with regard to the Chinese dissidents. Neither was the number of dissidents ever very large; whether one accepts Gardner's figure of 'two or three hundred activists' (White, Gardner and Schöpflin 1982, p. 262) or Benton's reference to up to 2,000 arrests in Beijing and Shanghai alone in the crackdown following Wei's trial, one is talking about a tiny percentage of the Chinese population. The available information suggests that most of the dissidents also come from a similar background and are to a large extent time-specific, in that they represent a backlash to the GPCR. Many joined the Red Guards during the GPCR, but subsequently lost faith in what they were doing. Following official criticism of the GPCR in the late 1970s, these people felt betrayed. They had missed the tertiary education they would normally have expected to have received, and are therefore not qualified for the better jobs in contemporary Chinese society. They are mostly in their thirties by now, and it would be very difficult for them to acquire a university education at this stage. They have thus usually been doing jobs of far lower status than their social background would suggest, and feel bitter. They are the 'lost generation' (for biographical sketches on many of them see Amnesty International 1984b, pp. 19–51). Older members of the intelligentsia have not generally figured amongst the dissidents; the new leadership is emphasizing the importance of the intellectuals—at least those with practical expertise—to the Four Modernizations, and is treating them reasonably well. Whether or not younger Chinese will feel as hostile to the regime as the 'lost generation' remains to be seen. On the one hand, the younger generation is now able to enjoy the educational privileges that will later give them access to the better jobs. On the other, the general political climate in China is now such that many young people are becoming more outspoken about shortcomings, as seen in the various campus demonstrations in Beijing and elsewhere that were reported in the Western media in late 1984. In sum, although it seems that there is little momentum at present to the Chinese dissident 'movement' that emerged at the end of the 1970s, it is possible that a new generation of intellectuals who are not afraid to speak out could make dissidence a more salient aspect of Chinese politics in the future.

We have now considered dissidence in four communist states, and have highlighted both similarities and differences. Many more examples could be cited—the Praxis group in Yugoslavia, Paul Goma in Romania, Nguyen Chi Thien in Vietnam, etc.—but we already have sufficient material to permit a comparative analysis of the phenomenon of dissidence in the communist world.

A COMPARATIVE OVERVIEW

Having looked in a little detail at just a few of the many examples of dissidence to be found in the communist world, let us now address the following
questions from a comparative perspective:

    (i) Who are the dissidents?
   (ii) What do they criticize?
  (iii) What do they advocate?
  (iv) Why is there more criticism at some periods than at others?
   (v) How are they treated by the authorities?
  (vi) Why do the authorities react in the ways they do?
 (vii) How politically significant are the dissidents?

(i) Who are the dissidents?

Generally speaking, the dissidents in the communist world come from the
intelligentsia—in the broad sense of being better educated people who earn
their living from mental rather than manual labour. Although this is not
invariably the case—most of the leading Chinese dissidents are workers, despite the fact that some of them are the children of cadres—most of the
people considered in this chapter are academics, artists, religious leaders,
scientists, etc. This is hardly surprising; their very work leads and enables
many members of the intelligentsia to consider the societies they live in (and
others) in more depth than people who have to spend much of their lives
operating machines in factories or working in the fields. Of course, most
members of the intelligentsia are *not* dissidents—in fact, many are themselves
part of the party–state complex so frequently criticized by the dissidents.
Thus the term 'intelligentsia' can be narrowed down to 'the intellectuals'—
here meaning members of that section of the intelligentsia which on its own
initiative considers the world around it from a more critical standpoint than
others and/or people for whom ideas are all important. Here again, it would
be erroneous to suggest that all—or even most—intellectuals become dissidents. Many look more critically than others at the world around them, but
learn to live with it; and again, there are many intellectuals in the party–state
complex who, having examined their system critically, still find it preferable
to other kinds of system and do not want fundamental change.

    Another interesting point is that a large number of dissidents are socialists
of one kind or another. They are opposed to many aspects of the economic
system of capitalism—especially large-scale private ownership of the means
of production, job insecurity, and the wastefulness of resources many believe
is typical of capitalism. Many—although by no means all—of these socialists
even accept a basically Marxist analysis of the world, and in this sense are
Marxists; what they abhor is an over-dogmatic and narrow interpretation of
Marx's views, and many are highly critical of the élitist aspects of Leninism.
How is it that so many leading dissidents are socialist and some even Marxist

if they are so alienated from an allegedly Marxist–Leninist system? This is a complex question, and limits of space mean that all that can be done here is to provide some tentative answers; for the most part, the reasons elaborated are not mutually exclusive. One possible explanation is that purposive social-ization processes in the communist states may be relatively effective on many citizens, including many intellectuals. The latter may well criticize aspects of a particular regime, but basically accept that the system is heading in the right direction and is better than capitalism. Just as there are regime critics within liberal democratic states who nevertheless accept the basic tenets of liberal democracy, so there are also critical socialists within communist states. Second, many intellectuals will adopt some form of socialism less because of the purposive socialization process than because of their own reading, discussions, etc.—just as many intellectuals do in the West. Whether intellectuals are socialists primarily because of purposive socialization suc-cesses or their own study, they will often criticize acts of their government which they genuinely believe go against socialist tenets. Third, many critical intellectuals may feel that the most effective way to criticize the regime is to do so from within its own frame of reference, using its ideological parameters and language. Such dissidents may or may not be genuine in their alleged commitment to Marxism or merely socialism; but they feel that the best way to secure greater freedom of speech, etc. is to couch their criticisms within the terms officially accepted by the party–state complex. Finally, it is possible that most basically left-wing dissidents are more optimistic that the authori-ties and/or the masses will eventually listen to them than are most of the non-socialist critics. Many of the latter will simply keep relatively quiet (i.e., they will complain just to their family and friends, rather than publicly), believing that to criticize openly is certainly pointless and probably dangerous. More-over, many will not wish to compromise themselves by couching criticisms within the regime's own frame of reference and language. As has been shown, there are always *some* non-socialists who feel they must speak out whatever the consequences. There are other non-socialists who will feel that they can speak out when the society is in turmoil and the authorities seem to have lost control—as in Poland at the turn of this decade and in many of the newer communist states. But this brief analysis will, I hope, explain why it is that there can be and are so many socialist dissidents in allegedly socialist states.

(ii) What do the dissidents criticize?

It has been shown that there are sometimes big differences between dissi-dents; this is more the case of the Soviet dissidents than of dissidents else-where. At a very general level, the vast majority of dissidents criticize, either explicitly or implicitly, the way in which their societies are ruled. This is not invariably so; it would be going too far to suggest that all members of the un-official peace movement in the GDR are fundamentally opposed to the system of rule there, just as it would be to suggest this of the CND (Campaign for

Nuclear Disarmament) movement in Britain. Because some dissidents criticize fundamentals and others criticize specifics, it is not possible to produce a list of criticisms that summarize the views of all dissidents in the communist world. However, it is possible and useful to produce a list of those more general features of communist systems that are most frequently attacked by the dissidents, even though not all dissidents will agree with some of the points.

(a) The élite position of party and state officials

In the past, writers such as Djilas have criticized the emergence of a 'new class' in the communist world. Although many contemporary dissidents sympathize with the sorts of criticisms made by Djilas, many feel that the concept of class is too problematic in existing communist societies—and indeed too vaguely defined in Djilas' own writings—to use the term 'new class'; Konrad and Szelenyi, for example, have explicitly argued that the Marxist concept of class is very difficult to apply at all to the states of Eastern Europe (1979, passim and esp. pp. 42–4). Thus, although the concept of a 'new' and 'ruling' class is not common amongst the dissidents, the latter do criticize the privileges and élitism of party and state officials. They criticize the concentration of power and the lack of answerability to the masses—which can result, for instance, in corruption going unchecked for long periods of time and on a large scale.

(b) The unresponsiveness of party and state officials to popular demands

As Oleszczuk has pointed out (1982, pp. 530–1), dissidents frequently cite examples of mass unrest to show how unresponsive party and state officials are to popular demands; frustration with the formal channels of complaint or discussion is one of the factors that can lead people to take to the streets. Dissidents often argue that this could be avoided if party and state officials would listen more to ordinary citizens.

(c) Lack of constitutionalism and legality

One of the most interesting aspects of much of the dissident writing is that it often calls not for radical change (in the short term, at least), but merely for the regime to adhere to rules of political conduct which that regime itself has produced or agreed to. This will often mean a call for proper observance of the state constitution, and perhaps of international documents, such as the Helsinki agreement. Dissidents often criticize the arbitrariness of the security police and the courts, contrasting this with the pledges to uphold the rule of law made in various state and party documents.

(d) Distortion or betrayal of socialist ideas and ideals

As mentioned earlier, many dissidents are socialists. These critics complain that the political élite is not implementing policies designed to perfect socialism and eventually usher in communism. Even worse, the dissidents maintain that the élite often *claims* it is pursuing socialist policies when it is not; this, it is argued, alienates sections of the population and gives socialism a bad reputation.

(e) Soviet domination

Particularly among the East European (i.e., excluding the Soviet) dissidents, a frequent criticism is that their own and others' countries are too much under Soviet influence. This was—as would be expected—fuelled by the Warsaw Pact invasion, under Soviet direction, of Czechoslovakia in 1968. It received another boost at the end of 1979, when the Soviets intervened in Afghanistan. Although these were very highly visible examples of Soviet interference, many dissidents feel that the Soviets play a continuing role in both the domestic and the foreign policies of their own governments— and they resent this.

Although this criticism has tended to be heard most often from the East European dissidents, some of the Soviet dissidents themselves have criticized what they see as the imperialism or superpowerism of their own state. In his letter to the Soviet leadership of 5 September 1973, for instance, Solzhenitsyn wrote:

In fact, we have only *one tenth* of the military obligations we pretend to have, or rather that we intensively and assiduously create for ourselves by inventing interests in the Atlantic or Indian oceans (p. 35.)

and

The whole of world history demonstrates that the people who created empires have always suffered spiritually as a result. The aims of a great empire and the moral health of the people are incompatible. We should not presume to invent international tasks and bear the costs of them . . . (p. 36.)

(f) Poor performance

Although most dissidents do not advocate the consumer-oriented society, many do argue that the regime should provide the citizens with what those citizens have a right to expect in terms of living standards. Consumer goods industries should be encouraged to fulfil their plans just as much as heavy industry. The argument is usually that this is the *minimum* the regime should be doing, very much as a second best to allowing greater political freedom. As Liehm and others have argued, it is assumed in many communist states that there is a social contract (sometimes called a social compact) between leaders and led, whereby the political freedoms of the latter are kept well in check, in return for which the leaders are expected to ensure a constant rise in the standard of living (cited by Oleszczuk 1982, p. 536).

However, given the not inconsiderable differences in living standards within the communist world, it is hardly surprising that some dissidents take a different view. Thus Havemann did on occasion criticize the East German regime precisely for making the population too interested in their standard of living, arguing that this undermined the development of the political consciousness he saw as being necessary for true socialism.

(iii) *What do the dissidents advocate?*

Most generally, the dissidents advocate change in their political systems. But there is little common ground on the questions of the nature and pace of such change, or who should bring it about. Many dissidents refer to some essentially vague 'third way', according to which there is a political system somewhat akin to Western concepts of democracy, but in which the economy is either socialist or perhaps mixed (i.e., in which there is some, small-scale capitalism). Even some of the Marxist dissidents call for the mixed economy, realizing that the sort of political pluralism they are advocating necessitates *some* form of mixed economy in the short-to-medium term. This emerges from the following statement made at the end of 1980 by Wang Xizhe:

Although a gradual reform of the economic base is now underway [in China], we still have a system of state ownership under the rule of the Centre; a multi-party system, however, can only be built on an economic base in which all kinds of ownership systems are developing together: collective ownership, cooperatives, self-management and petty capitalism. Should China, then, restore free capitalism? This too would be impossible. The only development possible for China is towards what I have all along envisaged the order of New Democracy as being . . . China should develop a further period of New Democracy, comprising a variety of constituent economies. (1982, pp. 65–8.)

The more pluralistic society will, according to most dissidents, include trade unions that are autonomous of the party–state complex. Moreover, many want a form of multi-party system; the precise nature of this is not always clear, especially given the limited variety of forms of economic ownership advocated by most. There is universal agreement, however, that the state must be less arbitrary in its treatment of citizens—the rule of law must dominate, the powers of the security police be curtailed, and the courts must be as autonomous of politics as is realistically possible.

There is no clear pattern as to which section of society the dissidents look to for change. Many of the East German dissidents have tended to look to the communist party itself, on the grounds that any attempt to change the society from below will probably lead to counter-measures and reactionary moves from the leadership, which will hinder society's development. The Soviet dissident, the late Andrei Amalrik, looked primarily to the middle-class intellectuals, arguing that the working-class has neither the will nor the political know-how to challenge the political authorities. Wang Xizhe, in contrast, sees young workers and students as the source of future democratization in China, and argues that it is un-Marxist to look to party leaders or the middle class for revolutionary change.

(iv) *Factors affecting the emergence and scale of dissidence*

It might appear to many Western liberals, brought up to expect a wide range of freedoms, that there should be much more dissidence in the communist world than there appears to be. Moreover, some periods in the history of individual communist countries have been so repressive that Westerners might expect to see powerful underground movements opposed to such state activity. In fact, an analysis of dissidence suggests that the mere existence of an oppressive regime is not what normally leads to the emergence of widespread dissidence and dissident movements. Ironic as it may initially seem, there is a high correlation between the liberalization of a regime and the emergence of widescale dissidence. This point needs elaboration.

During periods of terror and/or high levels of coercion, the disincentives to engage in dissident activity are so strong that all but the most committed individuals will prefer to keep a low profile. In such situations, dissidence is in any case unlikely to lead to anything but imprisonment and probably execution for those who engage in it. There are, of course, always a few who will speak out against the most terroristic regime; but these are almost always voices in the wilderness. Once a terroristic regime has been officially denounced by a new leadership, however, the tensions that have built up over the years will often explode into the open. Very often, the criticisms the dissidents wish to make of the past, and the ideas for improvement, will be similar to those the new leaders are making, and individuals will feel encouraged to speak openly. It would be inappropriate to call all those who speak out at this period 'dissidents', however, since, although they are critical, their views are so close to those of the leadership. However, there comes a point at which criticism of the past begins to become dysfunctional, and the new leaders try to curb the excesses of criticism and to slow down the process of change. It is at this point that dissidence emerges. Intellectuals in particular have tasted the freedom to criticize, and they disagree with leadership attempts to limit discussion. They feel that the new leadership has now let them down—in a word, they feel betrayed. They have acquired the taste for relatively free discussion, and they are loath to give it up. Conversely, the leadership—whilst wanting to repress dissidence—is usually sufficiently aware of the dangers and dysfunctions of returning to full terror that it feels restrained from launching an all-out, long-term attack on the dissidents. Moreover, moves towards more collective leadership can lead to less clear guidelines being handed down to the security forces on how they should deal with dissidents, which can further restrain these forces' zeal. Reddaway might be correct when he argues that the security police become bureaucratized over time, which also helps to explain why the clampdown on dissidents is less than total. Rather, there emerges a sort of cat-and-mouse game between the authorities and the dissidents. Ironically—to a certain point at least—the more individuals the leadership picks on, the more new individuals will stand up and be counted. This is what Sharlet (1978) refers to as the 'dialectic' of dissent and repression.

Specific developments will also encourage or discourage dissidents. In recent years, factors encouraging them have included *détente* and the emergence of Eurocommunism, while discouraging factors include the harsh treatment meted out by the authorities.

Although the dissident 'movements' in the Soviet Union, Eastern Europe, and China are, on the whole, at a low ebb at present, it would be wrong to suppose that dissidence has been crushed. What Medvedev wrote of the Soviet Union in 1978 surely has far more general validity:

The dissident movement, today weakened, will sooner or later revive with new vigour. This is inevitable, for without it there can be no effective solution to the most important and most complex problems of social and public life in a country like the USSR. (1979, p. 31.)

(v) Treatment by the authorities

The authorities in the communist world have used a wide variety of methods to repress and weaken the dissidents; these can be summarized as follows.

(a) Imprisonment

At some point or other, all the communist states have sentenced dissidents to prison sentences. The length and type of sentence varies, as does the charge. But the principle is the same—dissidents are less dangerous behind prison bars. The trials are sometimes widely reported show-trials—designed to act as a deterrent to others, as well as to give the official media an opportunity to tarnish the image of individuals—and at other times hardly reported at all. For instance, Alexander Ginzburg was in 1978 once again tried for dissident activity; his trial was not reported in the national Soviet press, only in a local newspaper, and even then some two weeks after the trial had finished.

(b) Internal exile

One method of dealing with better-known political dissidents in recent years has been to send them into exile within their own country. Without doubt, the most famous example is Sakharov, who is now in internal exile in the closed city of Gorkii.

(c) Exile abroad

A number of communist states have evidently decided that one of the simplest, cheapest and most effective ways to limit the influence of dissidents on the rest of the population is to expel them. It should be emphasized that not all dissidents know they are about to be exiled. In some cases (e.g. the East

German Wolfgang Biermann, the Soviet Alexander Zinoviev), individuals are permitted to go abroad and, once there, are stripped of their citizenship.

(d) House arrest

An increasingly popular method of dealing with dissidents since the late 1970s has been to put them under house-arrest (i.e., they live at home, but under constant police surveillance, and with very limited movement outside their home). Examples include Havemann in the GDR and Havel in Czecho-slovakia.

(e) Psychiatric hospitalization

The Soviet authorities are probably the best-known users in the communist world of psychiatric hospitals as a means of dealing with dissidents. In 1961, whilst Khrushchev was still in power, the Soviet authorities ratified a statute entitled 'On the immediate hospitalization of mentally ill people representing a social danger', and it is basically this law which the authorities, especially when Brezhnev came to power, used as one of the main weapons for combatting dissidence. The most famous—or infamous—centre for the use of psychiatric treatment against dissidents is the Serbskii Institute in Moscow. In the late 1960s and early 1970s, a number of leading dissidents—including Grigorenko and Zhores Medvedev—were declared insane, and subjected to often highly questionable 'medical' treatment. However, starting with the Canadian Psychiatric Association in 1971, a number of Western specialists criticized the use by the Soviets of mental hospitalization for dissidents. Since then, it has tended to be less well-known dissidents (i.e., less well-known to the West) who are most likely to be hospitalized, although the Soviets, Bulgarians, and Czechoslovaks have become so sensitive to Western charges of using psychiatric hospitals for political reasons that they have withdrawn from the World Psychiatric Association in the 1980s.

From the authorities' point of view, the advantages of hospitalization over imprisonment are several. There is no need for a trial, which can lead to excessive publicity, and possibly even a form of martyrdom for some dissidents. Nor is there a set term of internment. Psychiatrists can experiment (e.g. with conditioning drugs) on dissenters. Finally, it is often more difficult for friends of a hospitalized dissident to prove that he/she is sane—sanity and insanity being highly subjective concepts—than that the charges against an individual dissident are trumped up. In short, there is less problem of answerability on the authorities' part if they declare a dissident mentally imbalanced than if they have to go through the whole process of a trial and sentencing (for details on Soviet use of psychiatric hospitals for political reasons see Bloch and Reddaway 1978).

(f) Media campaigns

One of the ways in which communist leaderships attempt to deal with dissidents is to discredit them and their ideas through media campaigns. Such campaigns will often sow doubts in ordinary citizens' minds about the dissidents' long-term aims. In particular, dissidents will often have their names linked to specified or unspecified foreign agencies. Even if such charges—or merely hints—are pure fabrications, such implied treason will often discredit dissidents amongst many citizens who might otherwise have been more sympathetic towards them; although citizens might not be fully convinced that an individual dissident is in the pay of foreign enemies, once the seeds of suspicion have been sown they are very difficult to remove. It should be borne in mind that this method of dealing with dissidents usually accompanies some other method—for example, exile or a trial and imprisonment—and is rarely considered sufficient in its own right.

(g) Execution—overt and covert

Nowadays, dissidents are rarely sentenced to death for their alleged crimes in the older communist states, although there have certainly been cases of this in China in the relatively recent past (for details see Amnesty International 1984b, esp. pp. 74–5 and 116). Most of these states now appear to feel that this would necessitate too blatant a disregard for criminal codes, or else an unpopular rewriting of them, and that they might turn dissidents into martyrs.

However, there has been a disturbing number of deaths of dissidents under very mysterious circumstances even in the older states. For instance, Konstantin Bogatyrev died in Moscow in 1976, allegedly from head injuries received when attacked by a gang of hooligans. Although it is not possible to prove or disprove their allegations, many of Bogatyrev's friends, both within the USSR and in the West, believe that he was murdered by the KGB.

Dissidents are not necessarily safe even when they have left their native country and settled in the West. In recent years, a number of Bulgarian and Romanian dissidents have either died in curious circumstances or else have narrowly escaped fairly unambiguous attempts on their lives; the Bulgarian, Georgi Markov, died in London in September 1978 after having been stabbed with a poisonous umbrella—very possibly by the Bulgarian security police.

(h) General harassment

All the methods listed so far are the more extreme ones. But for many dissidents, their treatment is less dramatic. Such people will find that they lose their jobs and cannot find another, that their children cannot enter university despite having the necessary qualifications, that they are unable to obtain a better apartment, etc. Although less severe than most of the other measures listed, such tactics are also reprehensible—and probably even more widespread.

(*vi*) *Reasons for the authorities' reactions*

There is no single explanation for the hostile ways in which communist regimes react to the dissidents. At any given point in time in any particular country, however, the explanation is likely to involve a complex amalgam of some or all of the factors elaborated below.

(*a*) *Historical traditions*

In none of the countries examined in this volume, with the sole exception of Czechoslovakia, were liberal-democratic values firmly established in the period preceding the accession to power of the communists. Although the communists came to power professing very different aims from those of their predecessors, their actual methods are often similar. Allegedly 'for the good of the cause', communists will often revert to traditions of dealing with political dissenters that are embedded in the culture of their particular country and which would seem far less unacceptable to most ordinary citizens in those countries than—it is to be hoped—they would be to most citizens of the established liberal democracies.

Another aspect of historical tradition that should not be overlooked or underplayed is that communist leaders themselves—or their communist predecessors—were once dissidents (i.e., before they came to power). Hence they are acutely aware of the potential dangers to a regime of political dissidents. Although it is not generally the case that contemporary dissenters have in fact organized themselves to nearly the same level as the communist dissidents of earlier years, the long-term possibilities undoubtedly cause concern to the present party and state leaders.

(*b*) *Marxist–Leninist Ideology*

It has been argued in this book that communists in general derive at least as much from the ideas of Lenin as from Marx; this point helps to make an understanding of communist leadership reactions towards dissidents easier. The Leninist conception of the communist party as a vanguard means that it can be argued that it is a logical nonsense for people who are not members of the vanguard to criticize the party and suggest alternative policies. This argument is not watertight, of course. Not only are some dissidents themselves party members, but the nature of party recruitment—particularly in the more established communist regimes—is such that opportunists and careerists are at least as likely to join and make their way to the top as the 'politically most conscious'. Another aspect of Leninist party organization is democratic centralism, according to which there can be no further discussion of a topic once a decision on it has been taken. This, too, can give ideological justification for a clampdown on dissidents.

Finally, freedom of criticism is not an absolute right but a subjective concept in Marxist–Leninist ideology, something to be interpreted according to an analysis of existing conditions. This, too, can be used by leaderships to justify a clampdown. Criticism is only tolerable when it is constructive—as defined by the vanguard—and should help with the building of a better, socialist/communist future. Hence, although many dissidents argue that civil rights guaranteed in state constitutions are not being granted by the authorities, such rights are in fact not claimed to be absolute in most of the communist world. This comes out clearly from the following extracts from two communist constitutions. According to article 50 of the 1977 Soviet constitution:

In accordance with the interests of the people and in order to strengthen and develop the socialist system, citizens of the USSR are guaranteed freedom of speech, of the press, of assembly, of meetings and of street marches, and demonstrations. [Emphasis added.]

Similarly, article 64 of the present Hungarian constitution states that:

The Hungarian People's Republic, *consistent with the interests of socialism and the people*, shall guarantee freedom of speech, freedom of the press, and freedom of assembly. [Emphasis added.]

(c) Bureaucratic Conservatism

Western leftists who resent criticism of the communist world often seem to forget that the people governing the older states are by no means necessarily 'revolutionaries', and must not be confused with the Lenins, Ho Chi Minhs, and Che Guevaras of the past. Many are professional politicians and administrators who may well prefer orderliness and incrementalism to constant revolutionary upheaval. For such people, the Marxist dissidents represent an embarrassment, for a number of reasons. On the one hand, the dissidents criticize aspects of the present—usually including the leadership itself—and highlight failings of the regime. On the other hand, the Marxist dissidents in particular undermine the position and legitimacy of the leaders in a more long-term way, not only by highlighting the slowdown in the transition to communism, but also in arguing that the slowdown may well be largely a result of the continued existence of a self-appointed party–state élite. By criticizing the élite *immanently* (i.e. from what is, allegedly at least, largely the same theoretical standpoint), the criticism is that much more poignant than criticism from non-Marxists, whom the leaders can dismiss as reactionaries.

In this context, it is useful to refer to Weber's analysis of advanced industrialism. In talking about bureaucracy—principally in the capitalist context—Weber argued that 'the sure instincts of the bureaucracy for the conditions of maintaining its power in its own state (and through it, in opposition to other states) are inseparably fused with the canonization of the abstract and "objective" idea of "reasons of state"' (in Gerth and Wright Mills, 1970, p. 220). State bureaucracies in any system display a distinct tendency to self-justification on the grounds of 'reasons of state'. Although Weber himself did not explicitly deal with this question, I would argue that the tendency is even greater in states where the underlying ideology is of maximal state involvement (i.e., communist states). Moreover, Weber further argued that the 'mass party', as well as the 'great state', is an ideal breeding ground for bureaucracy; as argued in chapter 6, the communist states do, on a comparative basis and in one sense, have 'mass' parties.

(d) Leadership fears

On the basis of official statements, it appears that some leaders fear that the dissidents might be working for foreign, anti-communist forces. In the 1960s and 1970s, for instance, Polish and Soviet leaders on occasion referred to the Zionist threat to the world, whilst the demise of East–West *détente* led a number of Soviet and East European leaders to talk about threats from the hawkish West. In many cases, such expressions of fear—as related to dissidents—should be taken with a pinch of salt; leaders in all kinds of political system have learnt the potential advantages of referring to a foreign threat in order to gain greater popular support. On the other hand, the West's involvement in Russia in 1918, Cuba in 1961, or Vietnam in the 1960s and 1970s, and its support for rebel forces in Afghanistan, Angola, and elsewhere mean that some fears are well founded, and help create an atmosphere in which anyone speaking out against the system may genuinely be suspected of working for hostile foreign agencies.

(e) Response to particular events and developments

In addition to the more general reasons already given, specific events can cause leaderships to become even less tolerant of dissidents than usual; the holding of the Olympic Games in Moscow in 1980 and the concomitant influx of foreigners is a prime example. Any generally tense period in a given communist state (e.g. Czechoslovakia 1968, Poland at the turn of the decade) can lead to a clampdown on dissidents not only in that country but also in others (i.e., in case there is a spillover or reaction in them).

(vii) The political significance of the dissidents

There is some justification for the charge that the Western media tended in the 1970s to focus too much on dissidents in the communist world at the expense of other aspects of politics. Even now, the names of Sakharov or Solzhenitsyn are probably better known to the average Westerner than the names of Tikhonov, Zhao, or Le Duan. To no small extent, this reflects two of the aims of the media—to highlight political tensions in the communist world (and, by implication, enhance the image of liberal democracy) and to concentrate on the more sensational dimensions of the communist world rather than the more mundane aspects (they tend to do this of the rest of the world, too, of course). But it would be unwise to go to the opposite extreme and argue that the dissidents are politically irrelevant. There are a number of reasons why, despite the fact that the political significance of the dissidents should be kept in perspective, a study of them should nevertheless be considered an important and integral part of any study of politics in the communist world.

One reason is the rather obvious—but often overlooked—point that the dissidents are dissidents largely because the authorities have chosen to label them as such. An awareness of them thus tells us much about the nature of the political system more generally. In most liberal-democratic states, the closest equivalents of the dissidents in the communist world (i.e., people who want and publicly advocate a radical change in the political system) are usually relatively free to go about their business as long as they are only propagating views; if—as in the case of terrorists—their views lead them to kill and maim others, then the authorities in any kind of system will attempt to suppress them.

Numerically, the active dissidents in the communist world are of negligible significance. In the USSR, one is talking of a couple of thousand at the height of overt dissidence (i.e., late 1960s and early 1970s), out of a population of some 240 million. The membership of the Polish dissident organization KOR was 34 in 1979; the low Chinese figures and the number of signatories to Charter 77 were given earlier. But such relatively small numbers do not necessarily mean that the dissidents are unimportant. As has been pointed out, the establishment of many communist regimes was the result of work by a relatively small number of political activists—the USSR and Cuba are prime examples.

At present, the intellectual dissidents in the communist world are, in general, poorly organized—and given that the communist dissidents of former times adopted Leninist organizational principles, which have been retained, it is in one sense more difficult for today's dissidents to organize themselves than it was for the communists in the pre-revolutionary period. In short, the communist regimes are generally better organized and have greater control than earlier regimes. This higher level of control is partially the result of the development of technology. Yet the spread of technology, especially in communications, can also help the dissidents. They can discover—e.g. via the US-sponsored 'Radio Liberty', 'Radio Free Europe', 'Radio Marti', and the 'Voice of America', or the BBC's 'World Service', for instance—what dissidents elsewhere are doing, which can inspire them. The increased tourism encouraged by many communist regimes in recent years—partially to bring in more hard currency—has made it easier to smuggle dissident documents in and out of the communist countries, which helps to spread ideas and makes individual dissidents feel less isolated. This can in turn encourage them to persevere in their activities in the face of severe harassment. There are certainly examples of mutual support, understanding and even contact between many of the dissidents in different countries. For example, Hungarian dissidents sent a letter of support to Czechoslovakian and Polish dissidents in March 1984, and some of the Chinese dissidents wrote to Solidarity leaders in Poland expressing their support. Whilst it would be naïve to suppose that—in the foreseeable future at least—there is going to be any sort of international uprising in several countries of the communist world simultaneously, such internationalization of ideas is important for two main reasons. First, individual dissidents can refine their own analyses and tactics by becoming involved in direct or indirect dialogue with dissidents elsewhere. In particular, they can learn the benefits of joining forces with other dissidents within their own country and refine their organization. Second, the level of repression against dissidents is never uniform throughout the communist world. Thus dissidents in a country in which the security forces are being particularly harsh can receive moral support and encouragement from dissidents in countries enjoying a more liberal phase. The implication is that individual dissidents will keep up their morale and continue their criticism in a country in the grip of a clampdown, whereas if they do not feel they are part of a bigger phenomenon, they might be more ready to abandon their activities altogether.

In sum, the small numbers of dissidents do not necessarily tell us very much about future potential. It would be premature to argue that the dissidents in general are a major political force in the communist world, although it is conceivable that they will become better organized and more significant in the future. Much depends on the environment within which they operate. The world has already seen that dissident intellectuals in the communist world *can* sometimes have a major impact if they reflect a widespread feeling of discontent. Thus the Polish dissident organization KOR played an important role in the years 1976–81 in both spreading and reflecting popular discontent in Poland, which led to the emergence of Solidarity and, for a while, a kind of politics hitherto unknown in the communist world. Whilst the gap between regime and population is wider in Poland than in many communist states, the growing economic problems in much of the communist world during the 1980s could increase popular dissatisfction. As—and if—the gap between regime promises and performances widens to an intolerable level, so the role of the dissidents could become extremely important; discontent, even if it is widespread, needs leadership and alternative ideas if it is to stand a realistic chance of leading to meaningful political change. Let us now consider examples of widespread discontent manifesting itself openly in the communist world.

Basic further reading

R. Bahro, 1978.
G. Benton (ed.), 1982a.
W. Connor, 1980.
R. Medvedev, 1980.
T. Oleszczuk, 1982.
P. Reddaway, 1978, 1980.

G. Sher, 1977.
H. G. Skilling, 1981.
Studies in Comparative Communism,
    Summer/Autumn, 1979.
R. L. Tökes (ed.), 1979.
Wang Xizhe, 1980.

12

MASS UNREST

PERHAPS the most important sign that control can never be total even in societies which some Western scholars still wish to call totalitarian is the fact that under certain conditions, large sections of the populations of these countries are prepared to demonstrate on the streets their extreme dissatisfaction with the regime's policies, the regime itself, or—most frequently—both.

There have been large numbers of strikes and riots in the communist world—far more than is generally known. But limits of space mean that we have once again to be selective in our coverage. The examples chosen for reasonably detailed analysis in this chapter have been singled out because they represented really serious threats to the communist regime in each case, often leading at least to a change of the top leadership. Thus, although other examples of mass unrest are mentioned, the ones concentrated upon are Kronstadt 1921 (USSR); GDR 1953; Hungary and Poland 1956; and Poland since 1968. Also included here is Czechoslovakia 1968. In fact, it differs from all the other cases (with the partial exception of Hungary 1956) in that calls for and attempts at major change did not initially come from below; the masses only became involved in a major way once Czechoslovakia had been invaded. But since huge numbers of people eventually demonstrated on the streets, it is appropriate to include the 'Prague Spring' in this chapter.

THE KRONSTADT REVOLT—1921

When talking of popular uprisings under communism, many people refer to the East German uprising of 1953 as the first. This is not strictly accurate, since there were, for instance, significant revolts in the USSR even under Lenin. The reference here is not to the immediate consolidation period—notably the Civil War from 1918–20—but rather to those incidents which occurred once it seemed that the communists had consolidated power. The most important early example of such dissatisfaction was the Kronstadt Revolt in 1921, which was probably the politically most embarrassing event for the Bolsheviks in the first decade after the Revolution. Whereas earlier opposition to the Bolsheviks had emanated from sections of the population that could—to varying degrees—be seen to be anti-Bolshevik and, more importantly, anti-socialist, the Kronstadt rebellion included many who were basically committed to socialism and had been Bolshevik supporters.

Towards the end of February 1921, there was a series of strikes and demonstrations in Petrograd, at which workers expressed their dissatisfaction with their lot. As a result of the Civil War and the hostility of many peasants to the Bolsheviks, there were food shortages in many towns. The government had been sending out detachments to seize produce from the peasants, but this was only leading to greater hostility in the countryside; there were a number of peasant revolts at the end of 1920 and in early 1921, of which the Tambov rebellion was the most violent. Thus, food was not reaching the towns in sufficient quantities. To avoid starvation, many urban workers had been going out to the countryside in gangs to seize food for themselves from the peasants. The government realized that such action would only antago-nize the peasants still further, and therefore sent out armed detachments to stop the food expeditions. Although the armed detachments usually found little difficulty in stopping the gangs of workers, the latter could still strike in the towns. The dissatisfaction of the proletariat—in whose name the revolu-tion had allegedly been staged—was causing concern to the Bolsheviks. Consequently, whilst dealing with the problem of strikes by declaring martial law in Petrograd, the Bolsheviks also saw to it that food supplies to Petrograd were improved, and became more tolerant of the food expeditions. Although this seems to have placated many of the workers, there were signs of a grow-ing feeling of solidarity between them and the peasants; many workers now felt that it was the Bolsheviks rather than the peasants who were causing the biggest problems in Russia. The sailors on Kronstadt island near Petrograd, who had a reputation for being political radicals, decided that the time was ripe to show the Bolsheviks that their erstwhile supporters were far from satisfied with developments. At the end of February, the crew of the *Petro-pavlovsk* voted in favour of a set of demands to be made of the Bolsheviks. The demands were highly political—including ones for the release of political prisoners; free trade unions and political parties; soviets run by and for the workers and peasants rather than Bolshevik functionaries; freedom for peasants to grow what they want; and the ending of special privileges for communist party members. Indeed, the sailors charged the communists with having betrayed the revolution. On the following day, the sailors organized a mass meeting in the main square of Kronstadt; it was attended by approxi-mately 15,000 people. A senior party official was sent to talk to the crowd and was heckled; the crowd endorsed the *Petropavlovsk* demands. Following this, a Provisional Revolutionary Committee was set up to negotiate with the central government. The committee lasted for fifteen days, despite demands from the Bolsheviks that it should surrender. Eventually, in early March, Trotsky sent a special detachment to storm Kronstadt; the local (Petrograd) garrison had been disarmed, for fear that the soldiers might decide to join the Kronstadt sailors. By 17 March, the Kronstadt sailors had been defeated. Not only were thousands killed in the fighting, but large numbers of soldiers died *en route* to Kronstadt; in order to reach the island, they had had to cross the thin sheet of ice in the channel separating it from the mainland, and many had fallen through and drowned. Several of the sailors who survived the fighting were subsequently captured and executed by firing squads.

Although the insurrection did not spread to Petrograd proper, and despite the victory of the Red Army, the Bolsheviks were visibly shaken by the Kronstadt revolt. They described it publicly as a 'counter-revolution'; but many, including Lenin himself, realized that the events had shown how tenuous support for the Bolsheviks was, even amongst people who had once been ardently pro-Bolshevik. In this context, the 10th Congress of the communist party decided to clamp down politically—but also to liberalize economically, so as to remove what was perceived as the underlying cause of much of the dissatisfaction. In fact, an analysis of the demands of the Kronstadt rebels (and the Petrograd strikers of late February) reveals that political dissatisfaction—the feeling that ordinary people were not having enough say in the new state—was as great as economic dissatisfaction. But the Bolsheviks probably correctly judged that most ordinary Russians would not protest too much about lack of political freedom as long as their bellies were full. Thus, at the same time as other political parties—and even factions within the communist party—were being banned, the Bolsheviks decided to adopt the New Economic Policy. Some concessions had been made. The Kronstadt revolt was not a complete failure.

RIOTS FOLLOWING STALIN'S DEATH—SPRING 1953

There were three important instances of revolt in the immediate aftermath of Stalin's death (March 1953)—one in Bulgaria, one in Czechoslovakia and one in the GDR.

In the Bulgarian case, several hundred tobacco workers in Plovdiv rioted against their work conditions in May 1953. From the little information available, the riot appears to have been spontaneous and linked only to specific economic grievances (see J. Brown 1970, pp. 25–6). The Bulgarian leadership responded by sending Politburo-member Anton Yugov to placate the workers; this he succeeded in doing. The Yugoslavs later claimed that eight ring-leaders of the Plovdiv riots had been executed, but the accuracy of this report is in some doubt.

Rioting also occurred in Czechoslovakia at the beginning of June. On 30 May, the government announced the end of most rationing—but also a currency reform which, in practice, meant that many ordinary workers lost most of the value of their savings. Although the move was explained principally in terms of needing to strengthen the economy, another reason was in fact to soak up much of the spending power of Czechoslovak citizens and thus virtually break the black market (i.e., a black market can only exist if people have money to spend in it). Thus an economic grievance led to riots and demonstrations in a number of towns, including Prague. But the most serious troubles were in Pilsen, Western Bohemia. Approximately 5,000 workers went on strike and occupied the Town Hall. It soon became clear that the specific economic grievance had only acted as a trigger to the workers, who now made overtly political demands. They called for free elections, and revealed their attitudes towards the Soviet Union by destroying Soviet flags and portraits of Stalin. The communists organized a counter-demonstration, and the rioters were soon dispersed. President Zapotocky appeared on television, and admitted that some mistakes had been made in the implementation of the reform. Although he said the government would nevertheless retain it, promises of wage increases were also made. For the time being, all was peaceful again.

Neither the Czechoslovak nor the Bulgarian troubles can be seen as being of nationwide significance—that is, they did not trigger off riots or demonstrations throughout the country. In contrast, the East German uprising of June 1953 *was* nationwide, and can thus be seen as the first of the great displays of popular dissatisfaction with the communist regimes after the Second World War.

The East German communists had been consolidating power ever since 1945. In 1946, for a number of reasons too complex to elaborate here, the socialists agreed to merge with the communists to form a new 'Socialist Unity Party'. By 1948, the communists had made it clear that this party was to be a Marxist–Leninist one, organized along the lines of democratic centralism; this led many former socialists to criticize the way the 'new' party was developing. Moreover, the promise of a 'German road to socialism'—made in 1946 by Anton Ackermann—was abandoned, and the communist leaders now seemed bent on emulating the Soviet Union as closely as possible. Given that most Germans had a long-standing hatred of the Russians—a feeling that was not tempered by the fact that the Soviets had extracted enormous reparations from their zone of Germany after the war—such developments did not bode well for the future. But East Germany was at that stage still occupied by Soviet troops, and there was little the disgruntled socialists could do; indeed, there was little any ordinary German could do about the presence of the Soviets. Likewise, many Germans were deeply opposed to the division of their former country into two states in 1949 (the Federal Republic of Germany and the German Democratic Republic); but again they had little say in the matter, since both the Eastern and Western parts of Germany were under military occupation by the victors of the war. So the GDR was largely forced upon its citizens, many of whom were anti-communist. But in the early years of its existence, the GDR authorities, backed by the continuing Soviet presence, had little problem in keeping the population under control.

In 1952, however, the GDR authorities decided to push ahead with the building and consolidation of socialism. Amongst other things, this meant the collectivization of agriculture. This was too much for many farmers, who reacted either by fleeing to West Germany or by producing less. As would be expected, this led to food shortages by the winter and early spring of 1953. As skilled workers began to read the writing on the wall, many of them also fled to the West. In addition to these problems, Stalin had proposed to the three

Mass Unrest

Western powers in the Federal Republic (USA, UK, France) that Germany be reunited; this raised expectations and, when it came to naught, led to frustration in the GDR.

Hence, the situation was tense by the spring of 1953. Furthermore, Stalin's death had led initially to confusion at the top of the Soviet political system, followed by the emergence of a premier, Malenkov, who seemed to want to liberalize the USSR. Soon after the new leadership had emerged in the Soviet Union, the East German leader, Ulbricht, approached the Soviets, informed them of the worsening economic situation in his country, and requested economic assistance. The new Soviet leaders said they were unable to help, and suggested that the programme of building socialism be slowed down, so as not to alienate the population. Ulbricht was not prepared to accept what he perceived as the new 'soft' line in Moscow—he himself having long revered Stalin. Thus, far from relaxing the pressure, Ulbricht announced measures designed to increase industrial output; the implication of the proposed measures was that East German workers would have to work harder if they were to maintain their levels of income. The Soviets told Ulbricht early in June to ease off. Ulbricht, hearing rumours that the Soviets were prepared to support a bid by two somewhat more liberal Politburo-members (Zaisser and Herrnstadt) if he did not toe the line, did so—temporarily. An official statement appeared in the leading East German newspaper on 11 June 1953 which promised to correct many of the government's mistakes (e.g. its handling of the peasants) and raise the living standards of all. Despite this, the new rules on increased output remained, and were to come into effect on 16 June. On that day, building workers in East Berlin came out on strike; although many of their demands were essentially narrow and economic, some were more political (e.g. for free elections). By the evening of 16 June, Ulbricht declared that the party had been wrong—but it was too late.

News of the Berlin building workers' strike spread very rapidly, and on 17 June, there were strikes and demonstrations throughout the GDR. Although the Soviet occupying forces had initially maintained a low profile, and urged the East German security forces to do the same, the situation appeared to be getting out of control. By the afternoon, Soviet troops and East German police were tackling the demonstrators, and by the end of the day, the uprising was over.

No completely reliable figures on the deaths and imprisonments resulting from the suppression of the revolt are available, but most analysts are prepared to accept the official West German figures of at least 25 killed during the revolt, 42 executed subsequently, and 25,000 people arrested. The vast majority of these were workers.

Subsequently, the Soviets blamed one of their own leaders, Beria, for urging the GDR to abandon its building of socialism. Ulbricht, too, claimed that there were elements in the East German leadership prepared to work with Beria to bring about the end of socialist construction in Germany. A decade later, Khrushchev added the name of the Soviet premier, Malenkov, to that of Beria as being to blame for the June troubles. But the East Germans have always also maintained that the June 1953 uprising was partially the work of foreign agents, working on behalf of Western governments to overthrow the East German regime. Even if it were true that the West had plans to reunite Germany as a liberal democracy (i.e., as distinct from Stalin's proposals for reunification, which implied a GDR-type system throughout), it is absurd to suppose that the West could have actually *caused* all the strikes and demonstrations throughout East Germany in June 1953. The most that can be said is that the West did play some role in publicizing the Berlin events—which other East German citizens will soon have learnt about and from which they took their lead. A lighted match put to a wet powder keg will not cause an explosion; in the GDR, the powder was very dry indeed. People were thoroughly dissatisfied; this, added to the confusion at the top and the apparently more liberal leadership in the USSR, seemed to be an optimal mixture for mass revolt. The attempt to introduce new work-norms, not Western infiltration, was the lighted match.

A number of concessions were made by the regime following the revolt. To no small extent, these were made possible because the Soviet Union now decided that it would be able to assist the GDR economically after all. Moreover, the leadership had learnt much about defusing a tense situation; this experience was to serve them well in 1956, when other East European regimes were experiencing even worse riots than the June 1953 ones.

THE 1956 TROUBLES

For a number of related reasons, 1956 can be seen as a watershed year in the history of world communism. Nowadays, the first event that comes to many peoples' mind is the Hungarian uprising; in fact, this was but the culmination of a complex series of developments which at one stage gave some analysts reason to believe that the peoples of Eastern Europe would overthrow their communist rulers.

Dissatisfaction was rife in Eastern Europe. It was argued in chapter 2 that many of the new regimes had been in essence installed; not one had come to power as a result of the majority of the population freely expressing its desire for such a system. We have seen too that, following the establishment of the communist regime, the communists had introduced widespread terror and coercion in all the states. Millions of peasants had been collectivized, in many cases against their will; industrial workers were expected to work hard for relatively little return as economies were rebuilt and/or modernized; many intellectuals and workers wanted a freer political system. And in addition to all this, many ordinary citizens abhorred the sycophancy of their leaders towards the Soviet Union.

Thus, if the right trigger were to be squeezed, the gun in Eastern Europe was ready to go off. Ironically, the finger on the trigger was the Soviet Union's own. In 1955 and early 1956, four developments occurred which must be grasped if the East European troubles of 1956 are to be properly understood.

First, the Soviet leadership denounced Stalin. Following a number of veiled criticisms of Stalin that had been made from the moment of the former leader's death, Khrushchev delivered a major attack on his predecessor at a closed session of the 20th Congress of the CPSU. In the so-called Secret Speech—though it did not remain secret for very long—Khrushchev criticized many of the 'errors' (in 1961, he called them 'crimes') perpetrated by Stalin. Many East Europeans now began to ask themselves why they should tolerate their own Stalinist leaders; if the Soviet Union could have more liberal leaders and policies (Malenkov had been ousted, but Khrushchev's policies were increasingly similar to the former premier's) then why could not they also have a 'New Course'?

Second, the Soviets—especially Khrushchev—gave the impression that they were prepared to tolerate some variety in the paths towards communism taken by the various East European states. Stalin had censured the Yugoslavs in the late 1940s, to the extent of having them expelled from Cominform, largely because Tito was not prepared to subordinate Yugoslav interests to Soviet ones. Subsequently, Tito and other leaders devised Yugoslavia's own autonomous road to socialism. In 1955, the new Soviet leadership made conciliatory gestures towards Tito; although Yugoslavia never fully returned to the Soviet fold, relations between Moscow and Belgrade improved dramatically. In June 1956, Tito and Khrushchev signed a declaration on future co-operation between the USSR and Yugoslavia. Of particular interest to many East Europeans was the following statement—

... the parties hold the view that the paths of socialist development vary according to the country and conditions that prevail there. They agree that the diversity of forms of development of socialism is a positive factor. Both parties are opposed to any attempts to determine the paths and forms of socialist development of others ... (cited in Fejtö 1974, p. 76.)

Another symbolically very important gesture in this connection was the announcement carried in all Soviet-bloc newspapers in April 1956 that Cominform had been dissolved. And at about the same time as all this was happening, the Italian communist leader Togliatti started openly advocating what he called 'polycentrism'. By this he meant that there should be several centres directing the building of communism—in other words, each country should find its own path. This concept, too, did not go unremarked in Eastern Europe.

Closely related to the second point is the fact that the Kremlin's recognition of Yugoslavia's right to follow its own path to communism meant for many East Europeans that the Yugoslav 'model' had received the seal of approval from Moscow. As Fejtö points out (1974, p. 78), there were three dimensions of the Yugoslav approach which particularly interested reformers in other East European countries—de-collectivization; decentralization and the struggle against bureaucracy; workers' councils. In other words, it was the *details* of the Yugoslav system, as well as the fact that Yugoslavia had been given approval to pursue its own path, that interested many in Eastern Europe.

The fourth factor, one very much stressed by Ionescu (1965, pp. 47–9), was the establishment of a neutral Austria in 1955. Like Germany, Austria had been occupied by the victors after World War II; however, unlike the German situation, the occupying forces agreed to withdraw from Austria as long as it was universally understood that the country would remain neutral. This meant above all that Austria was not to join either NATO or the Warsaw Pact.

Having elaborated these four 'framework' points, let us now examine the two countries in which there were the worst outbursts of popular discontent, Poland and Hungary.

Poland had been led by an arch-Stalinist, Boleslaw Bierut, since the late 1940s. Bierut died in Moscow shortly after the 20th Congress of the CPSU, and was succeeded by a more liberal leader, Edward Ochab. But Ochab was unable to suppress a growing tide of unrest, which first burst into the open at the end of June, in Poznan. Workers at the Zispo factory had been complaining for months that they were being expected to work more and be paid less. A delegation was sent to Warsaw to complain, but was told that nothing could be done, and that the workers should get on with their jobs. This was too much for the Zispo workers and on 28 June they decided to march on Poznan town hall with a list of economic demands. As the workers marched through the streets, they were joined by thousands of other workers, and in a very short time the slogans became more overtly political. The demonstrators called on the state to allow the Roman Catholic church to exist and operate freely, and made their hatred of the USSR very plain. Within hours, the army and the security police had arrived, and by evening the demonstration had been crushed. According to Fejtö (1974, p. 96), 54 people were killed and 300 wounded. The mood throughout Poland very soon turned bitter.

The Ochab regime tried to ease the tensions by a variety of means. They announced new elections, to be held in December. They reduced the powers of the police. Although the alleged ringleaders of the Poznan demonstration were put on trial and found guilty, the sentences passed were considered relatively mild. Most important of all, the government did recognize that many of the workers' grievances—not just in Poznan, but more generally—were valid. As part of its attempt to approve the economic situation, the Polish government secured new credits and better trading terms from the USSR.

At this stage, the Stalinists (*Natolinians*) within the Polish party attacked the 'New Coursers'; the disagreement flared up violently at the seventh plenum of the Central Committee, held in late July. The Soviets sent their prime minister, Bulganin, to Warsaw—ostensibly to attend the Polish national celebrations; Bulganin was not permitted to attend the plenum. Nevertheless, the Natolinians made several demands which were largely in line with Soviet interests. It can also be noted in parenthesis that the Natolinians called for a purge, which was to be directed largely against the Jews; in the event, the anti-Semitic element in the Polish leadership had to wait until 1968 for an opportunity to pursue their anti-Semitic aims.

The Stalinists constituted a minority in the Central Committee, and the plenum produced a programme which promised a much better life for Poland's workers, both economically and in terms of participation in the running of their factories. But this was all vague. The people's political awareness was now at a high level, and they wanted action and a new leader. There were some signs that a new leader might be installed; the former head of the Polish communist party, Gomulka—who had been imprisoned under Bierut and had called for an independent Polish path to socialism in the 1940s—was now fully rehabilitated and readmitted to the party.

On 13 October, the Polish Politburo met; Gomulka was present. Major changes were agreed upon, but it was acknowledged that such policy changes had to be ratified by the Central Committee. A meeting of this body was therefore scheduled for 19 October. But before the Central Committee met, there were signs that a *coup d'état* by the Stalinist Natolinians and some of the top army generals might be mounted. Gomulka and the reformers urged the Polish population to stay calm and not to do anything that could justify action by the military (e.g. there were to be no demonstrations). The population conformed with the request, thus depriving the Stalinist politicians and the military of any justification for declaring a state of emergency.

In this tense situation, Khrushchev and a number of top Soviet politicians and military officers arrived unexpectedly in Poland on 19 October, the day of the Central Committee plenum. Undaunted, the Central Committee met, and announced that Gomulka was standing for the post of First Secretary of the party. Only after the meeting did Gomulka, Ochab, and other Polish leaders deign to discuss the Polish situation with the Soviet leaders.

The negotiations between the Soviets and the Poles through the night of 19–20 October were tough. The Soviets were able to threaten military intervention; the Poles made it quite clear that such an act would unite the Polish people even more fiercely against the Soviets, and that a blood-bath would ensue. Both Gomulka and Ochab steered a careful but firm line, emphasizing that the Poles had no intention of renouncing communism or internationalism (i.e., they would not withdraw from the Warsaw Pact) and that the Soviets had no right to interfere in leadership politics within Poland. This line seems to have been accepted by the Soviets, who returned to Moscow later that day (20 October). On the following day, Gomulka announced a programme for Polish development; this combined economic liberalization (e.g. decollectivization if peasants wanted this) with 'democratization'—which was not, however, to endanger socialism. This ambiguity in his approach was further reflected in the fact that Gomulka called for a Polish path to communism at the same time as he was stressing that Poland would be a loyal member of the communist bloc.

The programme was less radical than many Poles had hoped for. Moreover, many felt that Gomulka was still being sycophantic towards the USSR. But the Central Committee was broadly satisfied that it was the best path to be trodden in the circumstances and elected Gomulka First Secretary. There were various demonstrations over the next few days, especially when the Soviets intervened in Hungary. But, ironically, it was largely *because* the Soviets forcibly put down the Hungarian rioters that the Poles were not invaded. Most Poles now realized that they should take what they could whilst it was on offer; Gomulka had promised considerable liberalization, a Polish path to socialism and, if the people were willing to accept this, he could virtually guarantee no Soviet intervention. Furthermore, in mid-November Gomulka induced the USSR to cancel Poland's outstanding debt and to supply a major new injection of credit. Although Soviet troops remained on Polish soil, they had not been used against the population—who now showed that they were prepared to accept a bird in the hand for the time being, rather than hope for two in the bush; the Poles did not want to suffer the humiliating defeat the Hungarian masses had just experienced. Over the next few months, much of the liberalization programme was indeed implemented. Of greatest importance to the greatest number of people was the decollectivization that was tolerated; by the end of the year, the number of collectives had dropped substantially, from 10,600 to 1,700. In the factories, workers' councils were established to give the shop-floor workers more say in management; although these soon lost any powers they had had, the wind had been taken out of the revolutionary sail of October and November.

The strikes in Poznan can be seen as one of the many inspirations to action in Hungary. The Hungarian events—described by a French commentator as 'the first anti-totalitarian revolution', and one which was simultaneously anti-capitalist and anti-bureaucratic (Lefort 1977, esp. p. 18)—were even more traumatic for the people involved than the Polish. The story deserves a reasonably full narrative.

Following Stalin's death, there was a struggle in the Hungarian leadership between the liberal 'New Courser' Nagy and the arch-Stalinist Rakosi. Nagy replaced Rakosi as Prime Minister in the summer of 1953 (with some Soviet connivance, it seems); Rakosi stayed on as First Secretary of the party. Like Malenkov in the Soviet Union, Nagy favoured more investment in light industry at the expense of heavy industry. Even more importantly, in the view of the peasants, was the fact that Nagy announced that not only would collectivization in the countryside slow down, but that existing collective farms could be dissolved if a majority of their members wished it. Rakosi—and the predominantly conservative party *apparatchiki*—were bitterly opposed to this New Course, and acted to counter the decollectivization. For almost two years—before Nagy was removed from his premiership in March 1955—there was a tug-of-war between those who supported Nagy and those who preferred the hard-line approach of Rakosi.

Rakosi was now in the ascendancy over Nagy. In April 1955, Nagy was expelled from the Politburo and the Central Committee; by the end of the year, he had even been deprived of his membership of the party. But Rakosi's victory was a pyrrhic one. Nagy now produced his own alternative model for building communism within Hungary, free of the need to keep within the bounds set by the rest of the party and Moscow. Many intellectuals were excited by Nagy's views, and a number of discussion groups—including the Petofi Circle—discussed and spread Nagy's ideas.

Meanwhile, the criticisms of Stalin and Stalinism made at the 20th Congress meant that Rakosi had to temper his own hard-line approach, an approach that had led to renewed terror in the year or so since Nagy's ouster. He began to introduce a very moderate version of the New Course, thus reversing many of his own previous policies. The volte-face did not go unnoticed amongst the general public, whose confidence in and support for Rakosi reached an all-time low. In a last-minute attempt to undermine the opposition, Rakosi managed to secure Central Committee support for an all-out attack on Nagy. In June and July 1956 there was official condemnation and the arrest of Nagy and about four hundred 'conspirators'; the Petofi Circle also came under attack. At this stage, the situation in Hungary was getting seriously out of control, and some members of the Hungarian Central Committee appealed to the Soviets for help. In mid-July, Soviet Politburo-member Mikoyan arrived in Budapest; on the day following his arrival, Rakosi resigned, allegedly because of hypertension.

However, Rakosi was not replaced by Nagy. Rather, the new party chief was Gero—a man closer to Rakosi than Nagy, even if he was less of a hard-liner than his predecessor. Thus his appointment did not satisfy the many Hungarians who wanted a more radical change, along the lines of those proposed by Nagy. That both the Soviets and the Hungarian leadership itself soon realized that people wanted more than just the removal of Rakosi soon became evident; not only were more and more concessions made, but Nagy himself was reinstated in the party. But this was still insufficient; people wanted Nagy as their leader. One of the last concessions made by Gero proved to be one of the most dangerous. In October, he had the former Minister of Defence—the hated hard-liner Farkas—arrested, at the same time as many more nationalistic and/or liberal army officers were released from prison. Many of these soon made it clear that they, too, were attracted by Nagy's view of Hungary's future. The regime no longer had a reliable military machine.

On 22 October, the Petofi Circle adopted a ten-point programme of reform, very much along the lines of Nagy's proposals of early 1956. One very interesting point is that it called for the establishment of 'even closer links with the USSR on the basis of the Leninist principle of absolute equality'. Meanwhile, university students went further, calling for the evacuation of Soviet troops, a genuine multi-party system and a demonstration of solidarity with the Poles, to be held the following day. On 23 October, the Hungarian regime reluctantly agreed to permit the demonstration the students had organized. It began in the afternoon—peacefully at first—but soon the streets of Budapest were full of citizens venting their hostility to Gero (and Rakosi) and the existing political situation. They called for free and secret elections, and the installation of Nagy as their leader. By the evening, the situation was tense—and the Hungarian security police started shooting at demonstrators outside the Budapest radio station. The tensions had reached crisis point. Events now moved swiftly, and in various directions. On the one hand, Nagy was re-elected to his former post of prime minister. On the other, the Soviets—some say on the request of Hungarian Politburo-member Marosan—intervened militarily to quell the riots; Soviet troops were garrisoned in and around Budapest, and there was no problem in deploying them rapidly. It soon became clear that Gero was unable to handle the situation, and he was replaced on 25 October by the man who is still the party chief in Hungary, Janos Kadar. Kadar enjoyed the twin advantages of being known as a nationalist (like Gomulka in Poland) as well as a communist, and of having been imprisoned under the hated Rakosi. This gave him considerably more authority in the eyes of the dissatisfied masses than Gero could ever have acquired.

By the end of October, then, Hungary had a new party leader, and a new prime minister who negotiated a cease-fire with the Soviet troops; the latter began to withdraw from Budapest. Nagy at this stage (late October) introduced various political reforms which, although they did not please the Soviets, were nevertheless tolerated by them largely because of the ambiguity of their nature (e.g. Nagy's new government included several well-known non-communists, but also many who could be regarded as communist hardliners). At the end of the month (30 October) the Soviets published a declaration in which they not only referred to a 'socialist commonwealth' (i.e., implying sovereignty within a loose confederation) but also offered to consider withdrawing both economic advisers and troops from any member-state of the Warsaw Pact which indicated such a wish.

However, on the very same day that this declaration was made, Nagy announced the restoration of a multi-party system in Hungary; the implication was that this would not be the mere façade of a multi-party system that existed in some other East European states, but something more akin to the kind of system that existed in the liberal democracies. This, at least, was how many Hungarians *wanted* to interpret it, even if this was going further than Nagy himself actually intended. As if this was not enough to raise Moscow's eyebrows, Nagy announced on 31 October that he would begin negotiations for Hungary's withdrawal from the Warsaw Pact; once again, this was largely under pressure from the demonstrators. On the following day (1 November), presumably in order to show that Hungary was quite prepared to accept the kind of neutrality that Austria had accepted the previous year, Nagy's government officially proclaimed Hungary's neutrality; this was going much further than the Soviets had in mind in their 30 October declaration.

After some deliberation, the Soviets decided that Nagy had gone too far. At dawn on 4 November, Soviet troops once again moved on the demonstrators in Budapest. Despite the resistance put up—mainly by workers—the demonstrators simply did not have either the organization or the equipment to counter the Soviet tanks. More than 20,000 people were killed in the fighting (Harman 1983, p. 160). That very same morning, Kadar announced that Nagy's government had been too slack in dealing with counter-revolutionary elements, and that he (Kadar) had supported the Soviet army's moves to fight reaction. He now effectively took power. Nagy fled to the Yugoslav embassy, thinking that the Yugoslavs would support him and the Hungarian rebels. In fact, Yugoslavia eventually decided to support the second Soviet intervention, on the grounds that socialism really did appear to have been under threat. Once Tito supported Soviet intervention, Nagy realized it was pointless staying in the Yugoslav embassy and left on 21 November. He was arrested and eventually executed.

It would be a mistake to suggest that the Hungarian uprising depended on one man alone. Nagy *represented* a popular mood, and this was not destroyed either by Nagy's effective defeat early in November or by the Soviet tanks. Following the Soviet actions, there was a general strike in Hungary, and even a sort of alternative government, in the form of the Greater Budapest Central Workers' Council (established 14 November) which was active until its leader was arrested early in December. Workers' councils were not confined to Budapest but were springing up all over Hungary by late October. The arrest of the leader of the Budapest Central Workers' Council signified a clamp-down, and 'workers' militias' were established to eradicate workers' councils and other potential sources of opposition to Kadar's regime.

But this is not the end of the story. It is true that working-class power had been crushed by the Hungarian communist party and Soviet tanks. Yet once Kadar had regained control, he slowly began to liberalize Hungary, along some of the lines Nagy had advocated. The most obvious differences from Nagy's policies were that there was no multi-party system and no neutrality. Nevertheless, over the years Kadar has quietly moved Hungary further and further away from the Soviet model, and most observers now agree that he is one of the most popular leaders in the communist world. Whereas Gomulka came in as a liberal, only to become increasingly repressive, Kadar started on a bad note and became steadily better.

CZECHOSLOVAKIA 1968–9

As has been shown, many of the East European states acquired less Stalinist leaders in the years following Stalin's death. Even in the GDR, where there was no such change, the one-time hard-liner Ulbricht had mellowed considerably by the early 1960s. One clear exception to this general trend was Czechoslovakia, where the Stalinist Novotny had actually *come* to power in 1953, and was still in power at the beginning of 1968. It is true that Czechoslovakia had introduced some form of economic reform in the mid-1960s (following a near crisis in the economy in 1962–3), which was to have led to some decentralization of power. But the reform had even less real impact than outwardly similar ones in other countries of Eastern Europe. Power was still highly centralized, and dissatisfaction was growing. The Slovaks wanted greater equality *vis-à-vis* the Czechs; intellectuals wanted greater freedom; workers wanted more say in the running of industry. The growing general discontent—which, ironically, was flamed partly because Novotny did not clamp down as tightly as he might have done on dissidents—burst in the form of a student demonstration in Prague in November 1967. The demonstration was in fact about a relatively minor issue—the living conditions in university dormitories—but the violent police reaction to it incensed large numbers of Czechoslovaks. Many students were injured, and their leaders were conscripted into the military.

Despite this, the actual trigger for what was to become known as 'the Prague Spring' did not come from below. Behind the scenes, senior people in the communist party itself were becoming increasingly dissatisfied with Novotny's style of leadership—especially the concentration of power, and the arbitrary nature of much of his decision-making. A party debate along these lines began in October 1967, and culminated in the removal of Novotny from his post of First Secretary on 5 January 1968. The man who replaced him, Alexander Dubcek, was the head of the Slovak wing of the party and, according to Skilling, had led the attack against Novotny in the preceding weeks (Skilling 1972, p. 46 and 1976, p. 166). Evidently, Novotny had seen the writing on the wall and in November 1967 had appealed to the Soviet leadership for support; it was not forthcoming.

The implications of the January change of leadership were not immediately obvious. Dubcek was known within the party less as a radical than as a moderate reformer. No other major changes of leadership were made. Moreover, Novotny was still the Czechoslovak president and a member of the party Presidium (i.e. politburo). All that did seem likely at this stage was that the position of the Slovaks *vis-à-vis* the Czechs would improve. The ambiguity—and caution—of Dubcek came out clearly in a speech he made towards the end of January to the Slovak Central Committee. In this, the new leader said that the 'general line' of party policy would not be changed; rather, the party would have to be adapted somewhat to fit the changes that had occurred and were occurring in Czechoslovak society.

However, news of the recognition by its leader of a need to adapt the party soon spread, and kindled hopes in many people of major change. Intellectuals in particular began discussing ideas for political reform, both by establishing new discussion groups (e.g. KAN—the Club of the Non-Party Committed, and K231—the club of former political prisoners), and by conducting debates in the mass media, which suddenly became very much more open. Despite growing fears amongst the conservatives within it, even the party was becoming a supporter of reform, if somewhat moderate in comparison with the more radical intellectuals. One of the first major symbols of this was the publication of a new short-term party programme, known as the *Action Programme*, at the beginning of April. This was made public on 10 April, and further raised expectations of significant political change. Although it still emphasized the leading role of the communist party and gave no details on future changes in the electoral law, it also called for a revitalization of Czechoslovakia's minor parties, some sort of political pluralism (i.e., the right of groups in society to form and to apply pressure for their interests to be heeded), workers' councils in industry, more power to the local state representative organs, and religious freedom. Of particular symbolic importance was the fact that the powers of the security police were to be dramatically curtailed and that Czechoslovakia was to become a federal state. Some of the proposals being put forward in the spring of 1968 pertained to the real 'sacred cows' of communist rule; even what has been described as the 'trump card' of the party, the *nomenklatura* system, was criticized—and indeed for a short while was actually *abolished* (Skilling 1976, p. 349).

Despite all this, party documents such as the *Action Programme* did emphasize that Czechoslovakia was *not* intending to leave the Soviet bloc; even the more radical reformers in the leadership had learnt the lesson from Hungary that one of the limits not to be transgressed in any reform period is that of loyalty to the Soviet Union and the Warsaw Pact.

The reform movement was gaining momentum. At the same time as the *Action Programme* was adopted, Novotny lost his post as President of Czechoslovakia, a further nail in the Stalinists' coffin. Although conservatives such as Indra and Bilak were expressing concern, the moderate reformers were still in the ascendancy at this stage. Their position was strengthened still further at the end of May, when the Central Committee decided to vote Novotny off its ranks and to convene an extraordinary congress by the end of September. It was widely believed that the Congress would give formal party consent to the reform measures being advocated by some of the leaders.

But the tensions between the conservatives and the reformers in the party were growing. At the end of June, a group of the most radical reformers published a manifesto known as the *2000 Words*. The authors expressed their fears that the reform movement—even along what they saw as the relatively moderate lines of the *Action Programme*—was losing its drive. Dubcek, trying as ever to steer a middle course, criticized aspects of the manifesto. In particular, he was critical of the suggestion that mass pressure should be exerted, for instance in the form of strikes, to remove less popular party and state officials; this he saw as political anarchy, something anathema to all communists. Nevertheless, his criticism and actions were insufficient for the conservatives within the party leadership, who by now were seriously worried that the situation was getting out of control.

Indeed, they were not the only ones who were viewing developments with increasing alarm. Party leaders in Moscow, East Berlin, Warsaw, and elsewhere made their private doubts very clear to the public at large in the middle of July, when the so-called 'Warsaw Letter' was published in most of the major newspapers of the Soviet bloc. In this, the parties of the communist states around Czechoslovakia not only urged the Czechoslovak leaders to ensure that the party kept full control of the situation, but also warned that they felt that socialism *generally* was under threat, which rendered the Czechoslovak developments of concern to all in Eastern Europe. This was a clear warning to the Czechoslovaks that the other East European countries felt they would have a right to interfere in Czechoslovakia's internal affairs if the CPCS leadership allowed 'anti-socialist' forces too much rein.

Dubcek and other Czechoslovak leaders met with their Soviet and East European counterparts on a number of occasions between late July and the middle of August, and assured them both that there was nothing to cause concern and that, anyway, it was a matter for the Czechoslovaks themselves to deal with. Dubcek assured them that the party would maintain its leading role, and that his version of socialism—sometimes called 'socialism with a human face'—was perfectly compatible with accepted communist norms. At the same time, however, a new draft statute for the communist party appeared in the middle of August which included some very radical proposals by communist standards. For instance, ever since Lenin had banned it in the Soviet communist party in 1921, factionalism (i.e., struggles between formal subgroupings within the party) in communist parties had been seen as a cardinal sin; one of the major principles of democratic centralism is that once a decision has been taken, there is to be no further disagreement and the minority is to obey the majority. The draft statute envisaged legitimizing the right of minorities within the party to express their disagreement with majority decisions. This was intolerable to conservatives, both within Czechoslovakia and beyond. Developments such as this led Czechoslovak conservatives to come out even more openly in their criticisms of what was happening within their country. They warned the Presidium (politburo)—the last time on 20 August—that the situation was getting out of control; their warnings were rejected. Learning of this, and fearing that the proposed forth-coming Congress would at least endorse all the recent proposed changes if not make even more, the Soviets—seemingly encouraged by Ulbricht and Gomulka—decided to send in Warsaw Pact troops to 'normalize' the situa-tion and 'save socialism'. The details of the decision cannot be known for sure; but Valenta produces a strong argument to suggest that the Soviets had decided on 17 August that an invasion would eventually be necessary. The 20 August decision in the Czechoslovak Presidium no doubt acted as the imme-diate precipitatory factor (Valenta 1979, esp. pp. 123–53). According to the Soviets, Warsaw Pact 'assistance' had actually been requested by some mem-bers of the Czechoslovak Communist Party itself. There is circumstantial evi-dence to suggest that leading conservatives (including Indra, Bilak, and Kolder) *might* have given the nod to the Soviets; but they—and the man who was eventually to replace Dubcek, Gustav Husak—denied this in the post-invasion period (Skilling 1976, pp. 716–18).

Late on 20 August 1968, Warsaw Pact troops (from the USSR, GDR, Poland, Hungary, and Bulgaria) entered Czechoslovakia. On the morning of 21 August, Pact aircraft landed in Prague; later in the day, in came the tanks and other military hardware. The exact number of troops is not known, but the *lowest* estimate is a quarter of a million; the Warsaw Pact was taking no chances. Even if the Czechoslovak army had retaliated—an unlikely occur-rence anyway—its troops numbered no more than 175,000.

At the same time as Prague was being occupied, the Soviets arrested a number of the reformers—both moderates (of whom Dubcek himself was the most important) and more radical leaders (such as Smrkovsky and Kriegel) and flew them off to Moscow. The immediate response to all this of the Czechoslovak leadership left—notably President Svoboda—was to tell both the military and the people not to resist; to have done so would undoubtedly have led to massive bloodshed, and it is doubtful whether anything positive would have been achieved. Throughout the whole occupation the numbers of Czechoslovak citizens injured appears to have been in the 50 to 100 range.

The term 'Prague Spring' is in some ways misleading, in that it can give the impression that the progressive movement in Czechoslovakia was stopped by the summer invasion. This is not the case. As has already been noted, the leadership sparked off a wide-ranging debate in the media that went well be-yond the party. But until the summer, ordinary Czechoslovak workers had played a relatively minor role in the democratization process. Although pub-lic opinion polls indicated that there was widespread support among them for political reform, few played a very active role in this reform. However, their political awareness was growing, and was considerably enhanced in July, when the 'Warsaw Letter' touched nationalistic strings in the hearts of ordinary Czech and Slovak citizens. As would be expected, this awareness, and a desire to participate actively, grew enormously from the time of the in-vasion. Nationalism was not the only aspect of political awareness that bloomed; the workers now took a much greater interest in the democratization debate and indeed took over the leading role in defence of greater democracy. From September 1968, workers' councils began to spread and become much more active throughout Czechoslovakia.

Nor did developments suddenly cease in the party. On the day following the invasion, the promised extraordinary (14th) Congress was convened in a Prague factory; the congress is usually known as the Vysocany Congress, after the suburb in which it was held. Although many of the top leaders were not present—an acting First Secretary, the relatively unknown Silhan, was elected—those who did attend were quite prepared to condemn the Soviet-led invasion claiming that it broke international law.

Six days after their arrest by the Soviets, leading politicians such as Dubcek were back in command in Prague. The Soviets had evidently realized that they could not rule by force indefinitely; some sort of *modus vivendi* with people whom the Czechoslovak citizenry would more or less accept was necessary. On the other hand, Dubcek's hands were also tied to some extent, and on his return he called for 'normalization' and endorsed Svoboda's argument that resistance would only be counter-productive.

From the time of Dubcek's return until his formal resignation in April 1969, the tensions between the conservatives and the progressives continued. Typical of the ambiguity of the period were the decisions of the Central Committee plenum held at the end of August. On the one hand, the Vysocany Congress—held just days before—was declared invalid and the reformer Kriegel was dropped from the Presidium (i.e., this was a victory for the conservatives). On the other hand, two of the leading conservatives—Kolder and Svestka—were also dropped. The new member of the Presidium was Husak, who, at the time, seemed to many to be one of Dubcek's close supporters. Two quotations from him at about this time endorse this point. Husak was reported in the Czechoslovak press as saying on 20 August that—

I am firmly convinced that the new course represented by comrade Alexander Dubcek is so strong among the Czech and Slovak people that there is no longer any force able to close the door, to bring us back and block our future development.

Shortly after the invasion he persisted in his support of the Dubcek line—

The question is the following: either give firm support to Dubcek and the others or have no confidence in them. There is no third way. I stand firmly behind Dubcek's conception. I was its co-author and I will support him entirely; *either I will stay with him or I will leave with him.* (Cited in Rupnik 1981, pp. 111–12.)

Although there was this struggle between the conservatives and the liberals after August, it was always highly probable that the former would eventually win. Freedoms were increasingly curtailed; political discussion clubs such as KAN were banned, and there was ever more censorship in the press. Ordinary citizens protested—sometimes in their hundreds of thousands (e.g. after the student Jan Palach publicly burnt himself to death in January 1969). But such demonstrations grew less frequent as it became clear that the 'normalization' was there to stay. Hopes for genuine change slowly faded, particularly from the late spring of 1969. At the end of March, an ice hockey match between the USSR and Czechoslovakia was played in Stockholm. Czechoslovakia won. This led initially to rejoicing throughout the smaller country—but once out on the streets, many in the crowds turned violent, and vented their wrath against anything Soviet they could find (e.g. Aeroflot offices). The anti-Soviet feeling was intense. But rumours soon spread that high-ranking military officers, tired of all the 'anarchy', were preparing to stage a *coup d'état*. It was in this crisis situation that Dubcek, at a Central Committee plenum in the middle of April, formally resigned. He suggested as his successor the man whom, as we saw above, had appeared even after the Warsaw Pact invasion to have had a basically similar attitude towards change in Czechoslovakia, Husak. Dubcek remained on the party Presidium; but his fate was sealed. The few demonstrations there were about the change of leadership were half-hearted; after all, Dubcek himself had nominated Husak.

Although Husak argued that there was to be no fundamental change in the general line of the party or state, merely differences in the way the goals would be reached, it became clear over the following months that the spirit of the Prague Spring was rapidly dying. The citizenry made one last major show of defiance, on the first anniversary of the Warsaw Pact invasion. It was crushed violently by the police, and used as an excuse for introducing a near state-of-emergency. A few days later, Dubcek was removed from the party Presidium, while some of the more radical leaders were forced off the Central Committee. The Workers' Councils were disbanded by the end of 1969. In January 1970, Dubcek lost his seat in the Central Committee. Prime Minister Cernik was replaced by the conservative Strougal, whilst Bilak became very much more influential in the senior echelons of the party. With Dubcek out of the way, a massive (non-violent) purge of the party—organized in terms of a formal exchange of party cards—was set in motion. Almost a third of the membership (nearly half a million people) were dismissed.

By the summer of 1970, the ideas of 1968 had almost all become mere memories. Even the one concrete change—federalization—was not as significant as it might have been, for the simple reason that the federalization of the *party* that had been called for had not materialized. Given that the leading role of the party over the state was now very much asserted again, the federalization of only the state representative organs was at best a half-measure.

In May 1971, the official 14th Congress was held. This adopted new party statutes which tightened still further the party's control over the state and society. The most exciting experiment to date in communist democratization was over. Since that time, Czechoslovakia has been one of the most orthodox, hard-line of all the Soviet-oriented communist states.

POLAND 1968, 1970, 1976, 1980 ON

The optimism that many Poles felt with the accession to power of Gomulka in 1956 had largely turned sour by the mid-1960s, as the new leader became increasingly authoritarian. As early as 1957, the progressive journal *Po Prostu* was shut down. Another example was the forcible closure of the intellectual discussion club, the 'Club of the Crooked Circle' in February 1962; this had been a club for discussing politics, and was clearly becoming too critical for Gomulka's regime to tolerate. The increasing pressure on intellectuals led to an open letter being sent in 1965 by two of the leading dissident intellectuals, Kuron and Modzelewski, to the party and youth organizations in Warsaw University. The two were arrested and imprisoned.

At first, ordinary Poles showed little interest in the struggles going on between the authorities and these intellectuals. But events in 1968 made many ordinary citizens begin to realize that the regime's increasing intolerance might one day affect them as well as the intellectuals. In March 1968, two students were expelled from Warsaw University for allegedly leading a protest movement. There had been a lot of tension and unrest at the university at least since Kuron and Modzelewski's arrest and imprisonment; but the most immediate cause of the protest was the authorities' decision to ban a popular Polish play, Mickiewicz's *Forefather's Eve*. The two students had been gathering signatures protesting against this ban. The expulsions led to demonstrations at Warsaw University, which in turn led to a violent reaction by the riot police. As news of this spread, so student demonstrations—some of them supported by non-students—mushroomed throughout Poland (e.g. in Krakow, Wroclaw). The troubles lasted about three weeks, and remained concentrated in higher education institutions. Indeed, the authorities consciously attempted to drive a wedge between students and workers; the 12 March issue of the Polish party newspaper *Tribuna Ludu* carried a front-page report on a counter-demonstration by workers at the Zeran car factory: 'Above a crowd of more than six thousand workers, who came here directly from their individual workplaces, we read banners with such admonitions as "Students to their studies, writers to their pens"' (Karpinski 1982, p. 120). But even if this division between workers and intellectuals was genuine—and there is much to suggest that the Zeran workers were not necessarily typical—the repression that followed upset many ordinary Poles. Not only were students punished, but many leading professors (e.g. Leszek Kolakowski, Wlodzimierz Brus) lost their posts. There were changes, too, in the senior organs of both party and state (e.g. Ochab lost his post on the Politburo). Of particular concern was the anti-Semitism of the authorities that emerged clearly at this time. During 1967, the Warsaw Pact countries had supported the Arabs in the Arab–Israeli War. In Poland in 1968, the leadership kept referring to Zionists at work in Polish society, operating on behalf of the imperialists to undermine the communist regime. As a result, and largely under the supervision of the hated security chief Moczar, about half of Poland's Jews felt compelled to leave the country—to the obvious pleasure and relief of the party leadership. Although some Polish citizens were themselves anti-Semitic, the whole affair left a nasty taste in many people's mouths.

The events in Czechoslovakia at this time were watched with interest in Poland. But the crushing of the Prague movement by Warsaw Pact troops, plus the increase in police powers after March, led to a mood of despondency amongst many Poles. Ironically though, just as it had become clear that the Prague Spring was essentially dead, so major unrest again erupted in Poland; the March 1968 events had evidently only been a relatively minor foretaste of things to come.

Like so many mass riots in the communist world, the trigger for the 1970/1 troubles was basically economic. On 12 December 1970, Gomulka announced large price increases (up to 20 per cent) on a lot of basic commodities—notably food—which he tried to cushion with a reduction in the prices of several luxury goods, such as televisions and vacuum cleaners. At the same time, a new incentive wage system was announced, which for many would mean more work for less pay. The economy was in a sorry state, and the leaders were trying to solve their problems by forcing a regime of austerity on ordinary Poles. Not only were the moves themselves unpopular, but Gomulka had timed its announcement very badly. To announce food price rises just before Christmas was an act of extreme political insensitivity in a country of so many Catholics.

On 14 December, when they should have gone back to work after the weekend, shipyard workers in the Three Towns (Gdansk, Gdynia, and Sopot) went out on strike and demonstrated against the price rises. They also tried to burn down the local party headquarters. The police counter-attacked. Next day, the strikers and demonstrators were back, and this time were successful in their attempt to burn down the regional party headquarters. The police again reacted violently, killing a number of demonstrators (the authorities acknowledged six dead, but this must be seen as a minimum figure). News of the troubles spread rapidly, and shipyard workers in Szczecin emulated their comrades in the Three Towns. They too set fire to the local party headquarters, and they too were shot at; Gierek later acknowledged 17 killed in Szczecin (Harman 1974, p. 247). By the weekend, factory workers in many parts of Poland were either on strike or had threatened to come out on strike the following week.

The authorities realized that the mood in the country was one of extreme anger; something had to be done. Strikers had been shot and killed, and this had not deterred other workers from continuing their struggle.

The major change came on 20 December, when an extraordinary plenum of the Central Committee announced that the new First Secretary was to be Edward Gierek; the deposed Gomulka was not even present at the meeting.

There were a number of other changes at the top of the PUWP—including the promotion to full membership of the Politburo of two men who had a reputation for being hard-liners, Moczar and Olszowski.

Despite the promotion of hard-liners, Gierek started on a relatively conciliatory tone. The same evening (20 December), he broadcast to the nation on both television and radio. He admitted that a gap had developed between the party and the people, and said that this would have to be bridged. He also promised that prices would be frozen for two years—although he did not rescind the rises of the previous weekend.

Poland was relatively quiet over Christmas and New Year. But as workers began to return to work after the holiday, a new wave of strikes, again centred on the shipyards, began to spread. The demands of the strikers were mostly relatively specific—revocation of the new work norms, release of people arrested in the pre-Christmas troubles, and a return to the pre-12 December price levels for food. The strikers were particularly militant in Szczecin, following the publication of an article in the local press which stated that workers had volunteered to make up for time lost through strike action in December. The workers had made no such offer, and were very bitter that the media were so blatantly propagating lies about them. This turned them into the most vociferous of the January strikers. Gierek realized that if something was not done, he might be following Gomulka into the political wilderness in the very near future. He therefore went to Szczecin to speak to the strikers personally and explain the problems of the Polish economy. He appears to have made a relatively good impression—his image was of someone who was honest, acknowledged the errors of his predecessors, and really did have the interests of Poland at heart. Although a minority of workers wanted to continue the strike, the majority in Szczecin now accepted that the new leader should be given a chance to nurse the economy back to health. The strike was called off.

There was just one more act in the 1970/1 Polish play. A few weeks after the Szczecin workers had returned to work, there was a strike by workers (mostly women) in the city of Lodz. This time, the authorities evidently decided that the December/January troubles must not be allowed to continue indefinitely. They were devising plans anyway for improving the situation, so that they now finally decided to rescind the 12 December price increases.

The main thrust of the new leadership's economic policy in the early 1970s was allegedly to develop Polish industry by borrowing money from the West (this was the heyday of *détente*) and investing it in industry. Unfortunately, this policy eventually went horribly wrong, for a number of reasons. First, much of the money borrowed was actually used to pay the workers more. Real living standards in Poland improved markedly in the early 1970s. Clearly, this meant that there was less to invest; buying the workers off in the short run was quite likely to lead to problems in the long term. Second, the oil crisis of 1973 led Western creditors either to request repayment of their credits—the West itself was in problems, and needed all the cash it could get—and/or not to make new loans to the Poles. Hence, before the Polish investment programmes had gone far enough to start yielding returns, the Poles were being asked to repay much of the money they had borrowed. The crisis in the Western economies eventually began to affect prices within Comecon too; a change in pricing procedures within the CMEA in 1975 further exacerbated Poland's economic problems.

By 1976, then, Polish workers had had real increases in their incomes. But in an endeavour to pay off their Western debts, the Polish authorities had since about 1974 been anxious to sell anything they could to their creditors. Since the investment programme had faltered before it had ever really got off the ground, it was not sophisticated industrial products that the Poles could sell. Instead, they were selling basics—in particular, agricultural products (e.g. meat). There was thus a situation in which Polish workers had the money to buy goods, but the authorities preferred to sell these to the West. In order to reduce home demand, the party began to consider a price restructuring. Gierek had hinted at possible food price increases at the 7th Congress of the PUWP (December 1975); but this remained hypothetical and vague at this point.

The concrete suggestions for price rises came in June 1976. On 24 June the Polish prime minister presented government proposals for price increases; they were to be effective from 28 June. On the day following the announcement, workers in many parts of Poland came out on strike. This time, the heart of the resistance was not the Baltic shipyards but Warsaw (especially the Ursus tractor factory) and the town of Radom. In the latter, the well-established tradition of burning down local party headquarters was repeated. In both Warsaw and Radom, the police were again brutal, although no shootings were reported this time (two rioters were killed, but allegedly in an accident with a tractor).

Unlike 1970, the authorities immediately gave in and agreed not to introduce the price rises. But that was by no means the end of the story. The ringleaders of the rioting workers were tried and given relatively severe sentences (up to ten years' imprisonment). Although they were all released by the summer of 1977, there was one very significant long-term outcome of the Radom and Ursus affair. For the first time, dissatisfied workers and intellectuals began to make serious contact with each other. Although there was still often mutual suspicion and different views on the world, representatives of these two groups now explored their common interests. At the end of September 1976, an organization known as KOR (the Polish initials for Committee for the Defence of Workers) was established. Though small, KOR represented an important link organization between two key groups in Polish society. This linkage was to become all important over the next few years. In September 1977, shortly after the release of the last of the 1976 rioters in July,

KOR modified its name to KSS-KOR (the first three initials standing for the Committee for Social Self-Defence) and spelt out its aims:

(1) The struggle against political, ideological, religious, or racial repression and help for those suffering from such persecution.

(2) The struggle against breaking the rule of law and help for the victims of illegality.

(3) The struggle for institutional guarantees of civil rights and freedoms.

(4) The support and defence of all social institutions aimed at the realization of human and civil rights. (Karpinski 1982, p. 199.)

Following this, a number of independently published critical books, journals, and newspapers began to appear and to keep Polish citizens abreast of important political, social, and economic developments. The election of a Pole—Cardinal Wojtyla—as Pope in October 1978 gave a great boost to ordinary Polish citizens; the Catholic Church was now looked on by many even more than before as a powerful alternative organization to the communist party-state.

The growth of criticism and aspirations in Poland in the years 1976–80 was not confined only to disaffected workers and intellectuals. Senior members of the party and state were becoming increasingly open in their acknowledgement that something was seriously wrong in Poland. In the summer of 1979, a leading economist (Bratkowski) publicly attacked the government, arguing that one of the major reasons that the Polish economy was in such a mess was the existing political situation. According to him, this was outdated; the kind of political system he advocated was one in which the media and trade unions were independent of the political authorities and the communist party was separate from the state machinery. This was followed in October 1979 by the circulation of a document written by, among others, certain leading members of the party. This also criticized the party structure and argued in a rather similar vein that the political structure was a major hindrance to the development of the economy. This document was tacitly criticized at the end of October, in a draft report prepared for the forthcoming Eighth Congress of the party. However, although the draft criticized the 'enemies of socialism' in Poland, it did call on the party to conduct a lively discussion with the Polish citizenry, in order to find a way forward.

Towards the end of 1979, disagreements amongst the senior politicians became very visible. While the party chief—still Gierek—acknowledged that there were serious problems in the economy, the prime minister (Jaroszewicz) defended his government's performance and refused to accept any blame for the Polish situation. This led to his replacement in February 1980 by Babiuch; Jaroszewicz also lost his seat on the Politburo at this time. But the Polish people were showing an increasing hostility towards many of their leaders. For instance, in the March 1980 elections, the security chief (Kowalczyk) received a symbolically significant blow when the electors moved him from first to sixth position in the prioritized list of parliamentary candidates.

The following month (April), prime minister Babiuch announced a reorganization of the Council of Ministers, and a number of policies designed to improve the state of Poland's economy. One of the proposed measures was the withdrawal of subsidies on foodstuffs; the leadership was again playing with fire.

There were a number of relatively minor strikes in Poland in the first few months of 1980. But the trigger that led to what has since become known as 'the Polish August' was, as so often before, the announcement of increases in the price of food. On 1 July, the prices of meat in the food shops attached to factories was raised by 40 to 60 per cent. Gierek went on television and emphasized that the state simply could not afford to rescind these price increases. However, an interesting new phenomenon now emerged. Instead of most workers going out on strike, they elected leaders to negotiate wage increases (i.e., to compensate for the price increases) on their behalf with enterprise managers. The novelty in this was that previously all negotiations had had to be conducted through trade union and party bodies, both of which could be seen to represent the interests of the state as much as those of the workers. To the surprise of many, the central authorities permitted management to negotiate with these independently elected workers' leaders. It soon became clear, however, that the general idea behind the government's tolerance of all this 'free' collective bargaining was one of 'divide and rule'. The proposed increases for workers varied quite considerably from region to region, factory to factory; as so often happens in the West, the workers with the most industrial muscle were to receive the biggest increases.

As news of this unequal treatment approach spread—KSS-KOR playing a major role in disseminating the information—more and more workers decided to strike. They were not prepared to allow the government to introduce divisions in their ranks. On 14 August the workers in the Lenin shipyard in Gdansk—scene of so much unrest in 1970—came out on strike following the sacking of one of their best-known leaders, Anna Walentynowicz. The workers not only demanded Ms Walentynowicz's reinstatement, but also stipulated a number of conditions relating to their pay. A deal on the latter was worked out between management and the strike leaders—but was rejected by the rank-and-file. A couple of days later, on 17 August, strike leaders in the Three Towns co-ordinated their activities and produced a list of 21 demands. Of equal importance, they established an 'Inter-Factory Strike Committee' (MKS) to co-ordinate struggles in different factories. Thus were sown the seeds of what was to become the world's most famous workers' organization—Solidarity. Poland was at the beginning of what Leszek Kolakowski has called 'the world's first workers' revolution' (Kolakowski, 1981).

The events in Poland since August 1980 cannot be dealt with in depth here;

all we can do is to look at a selection of what seem to me to have been the most significant highlights.

Following the issuance of the 21 demands and Gierek's rejection of them in a television broadcast on 18 August, strikes spread across Poland. Very soon, the Inter-Factory Strike Committee network covered all the major industrial centres. Gierek tried to calm the situation down by the time-honoured method of blaming the head of the government for the situation. On 24 August, prime minister Babiuch was replaced by Pinkowski. At the same time, Gierek admitted that he had made mistakes, and announced that a number of changes would be made. For instance, the law on trade unions was to be modified. But the Polish leaders now seemed to take contradictory paths yet again. On the one hand, the party agreed to negotiate with the Inter-Factory Strike Committee; this was important, since it recognized the workers' demands to be treated as a whole rather than on the previous, divisive, factory-by-factory basis. On the other hand, strong hints were also dropped that the Soviet Union might intervene militarily, and a number of KSS-KOR activists were arrested; this threatening approach only brought even more workers out on strike. The Politburo took a vote on 29 August as to whether the Polish military should be used to break the Gdansk strikes (it being felt that that was the centre of the whole movement). It seems that a majority (8 to 5) voted in favour of military action. But the Polish military and security police chiefs appear to have argued that they would not be able to guarantee the loyalty of their men; the party chiefs would have to find some alternative solution to the crisis.

It was in this context that one of the most important events in the history of the communist world—the signing of the so-called 'Gdansk Agreement'— took place on 31 August 1980. The agreement was signed by four representatives of the Polish authorities, including the deputy-premier, Jagielski, and nineteen representatives of the Inter-Factory Strike Committee, including the man whose droopy moustache soon became known to millions of television viewers in the West, Lech Walesa. Although the types of demand being made were in most cases similar to demands that had been made on earlier occasions (e.g. in a 1979 document entitled 'A Charter of Workers' Rights'—see *Labour Focus on Eastern Europe*, vol. iii, no. 4, Sept–Oct 1979), the fact that the authorities now publicly agreed to most of the demands, with some modifications, made the Gdansk agreement a document of singular historical importance.

For a few days, there was a feeling of euphoria in Poland. The struggles of 1956, 1968, 1970, and 1976 now seemed to have been worth the blood and conflict. The strikes were called off. But the elation was short-lived.

On 6 September, Gierek resigned, allegedly because of ill health. He was replaced by Stanislaw Kania, the party leader responsible for security and the military since 1971. There were also other important changes at the top. For

instance, the man responsible for pressuring so many Jews in the late 1960s—
Moczar—seemed to be in the ascendancy, in that he was the first leader to
speak in favour of Kania at the Central Committee meeting that approved
the appointment of the new First Secretary. Thus the leadership change
looked as if it would probably usher in a tougher approach from the top—
although the early statements of these new leaders in fact gave a rather contradictory picture of what could be expected. On the one hand, the new union
arrangements and agreements were endorsed. On the other, Kania promised
to clamp down on 'anti-socialist' elements, notably KSS-KOR. The latter statement of intent was rejected by the Inter-Factory Strike Committee; indeed it
strengthened its resolve not to let the newly won concessions flitter away in
the way they had following previous riots and strikes. On 22 September, delegates from different branches of industry and regions met and agreed the
statutes of a new, independent trade union. 'Solidarity' had been born.
Within days—and following further harassment from the authorities, Solidarity had called a general strike. It was to be the first of many over the next
fourteen or fifteen months.

There were numerous clashes between Solidarity and the authorities in the
period from October 1980 to December 1981. There were problems of recognition, harassment of members, charges that Solidarity had become a political opposition force, attempts to raise food prices and strikes against these,
then progress followed by reversals again. The Soviet Union and Warsaw
Pact forces threatened to intervene on more than one occasion. But Solidarity continued to grow; its membership topped 10 million, which made it some
three to four times bigger than the communist party (PUWP), and meant that
almost 60 per cent of the work-force were members of the new union.

As Solidarity grew and achieved more of its aims, so it began to have a
major divisive impact on the communist party itself. This emerged most
clearly in July 1981, when the PUWP held an extraordinary Congress. For the
first time, and following demands for a revitalization of the concept of
democratic centralism from rank-and-file party members in Torun in April,
delegates to the Congress were elected in what seems to have been real
secrecy. There was also competition between candidates for the Central
Committee and the Politburo (for details see Ascherson 1981, pp. 271–2),
and this demonstrated clearly the divisions in the higher echelons of the
PUWP. One symbol of this was the results of the elections to the Politburo.
Whilst progressives such as Solidarity-member Zofia Grzyb were voted on,
so too were hard-liners such as Olszowski and Siwak. Moreover, the Congress saw a big rise in the number of military officers being elected onto the
Central Committee; the significance of this was not as obvious at the time as
it subsequently became.

The divisions within the PUWP were mirrored in Solidarity. There were
those (such as Rulewski) who called for a more radical leadership than that
being given by Walesa, whilst others, such as the intellectual Kuron, believed

that Solidarity should proceed on a step-by-step basis. In addition to the PUWP and Solidarity, the other major organization involved in the negotiations in this almost anarchic period was the Catholic Church. On the whole, the church tended to urge moderation—particularly after the death of the Polish primate, Cardinal Wyszynski, in May 1981 and his replacement in July by Glemp.

In sum, the period from August 1980 to December 1981 cannot be understood simply in terms of the party-state complex versus Solidarity. There were subgroupings within each of these, and the church was involved. There were, in other words, struggles for power at all levels and in all parts of society.

It is not easy to explain precisely why the Polish authorities finally decided that things had gone far enough. In September–October 1981, Solidarity held its first national congress, at which several radicals were elected to senior leadership positions. A draft programme was put forward which was far more overtly political than many earlier documents; it called for free elections and a multi-party system, plus union control over the economy. Moreover, the leaders of KSS-KOR now argued that there was no longer any need for their organization as a separate entity, so that they dissolved it voluntarily. Solidarity was now representing intellectuals as well as workers—a dangerous mixture for the communist regime. A clear sign that major change could be in the offing came in October 1981 when Kania was replaced as party chief by the man who had been prime minister since February, General Wojciech Jaruzelski. Though a military man, many Poles seemed to have believed that Jaruzelski was fair, if firm. For historical reasons, the military in Poland was still treated with some respect by most Poles, and even though Jaruzelski had been involved in suppressing Polish workers in the past (e.g. in 1970/1), many were prepared to accept that he was at that time only carrying out the orders of the politicians.

Hence it would be incorrect to suppose that most Poles immediately felt that Jaruzelski's accession to power was a sinister development. Indeed by this stage—with the economy in an appalling and constantly worsening state, and winter coming on—many Poles felt that the near anarchy could not and should not continue. The squabbles within Solidarity were beginning to irritate many—particularly since the workers' leaders often seemed to be much better at criticizing than at suggesting concrete ways to rescue Poland from its plight.

For a couple of months, Jaruzelski showed some willingness to try to work with both Solidarity and the church to find a solution to Poland's ills, though his attitudes were not unambiguous. On the one hand, he was ordering the arrests of more militant members of Solidarity, and even introduced a diluted form of martial law in the sense that troops were dispersed throughout Poland, allegedly to ensure that goods in short supply were distributed in a fair and orderly manner. On the other hand, he did convene a meeting between himself, Walesa, and Glemp, in which he tried to work out some sort of compromise with Solidarity. Perhaps the most serious item to be discussed was the question of restoring Poland's economy. Ultimately, it was disagreements about this—plus, perhaps, pressure from the Soviets—that led to the imposition of martial law in December. Basically, the Polish authorities argued that if Solidarity believed it should have some control over the economy, then it would have to participate in a 'mixed commission'. In other words, Solidarity would share with the party-state complex the responsibility of running the economy. But the Solidarity leaders rejected this offer. In their opinion, this meant that they would become part of the system and would have to bear responsibility for the accumulated errors committed over the years. Whilst Jaruzelski was offering 'participation', the fact that he was having Solidarity members arrested seemed to show that he would not tolerate much divergence from the regime's approach to problems. Many workers' leaders felt that Solidarity's involvement would probably be a facade, designed primarily to give legitimacy to the party's policies. Solidarity's leadership's position was thus understandable. Its own proposal was that a National Economic Council should be set up which would be quite independent of the party and state authorities. The Council would have the right to examine all policy proposals, and to comment on them. In this way, Solidarity argued, the work-force would have some say in economic policy-making without seeing its leaders merely become part of the establishment. Jaruzelski would not accept this line of argument.

So the meeting between Jaruzelski, Walesa, and Archbishop Glemp in the late autumn of 1981 ultimately came to naught; neither side would make sufficient concessions to the other. Eventually, Jaruzelski's (and possibly the Soviets') patience ran out. With the threat of yet another general strike looming, plus Solidarity stating on 3 December that 'the government has destroyed the chances of arriving at a national *entente*' and on 7 December that radical action was necessary, Jaruzelski appeared on television at 6.00 a.m. on Sunday 13 December and declared a 'state of war' and martial law in Poland. Within days, universities and schools were shut down, leading Solidarity activists were arrested, communications were cut, various key industries were put under direct military control, and the six-day week was brought back. Pockets of resistance remained, but the military had in essence taken control. Indeed, Poland was now run not by the Politburo but by a 'Military Council of National Salvation'.

In October 1982, Solidarity was finally declared to be an illegal organization. In November, Walesa was released; initially, he kept a low profile. Martial law was suspended in December 1982 and formally lifted in July 1983. Since that time, Solidarity has continued to operate as an underground organization and Walesa is once again a major critic of the regime. However, a new, official trade union movement has come into being; at the same time of writing, the membership of this was growing slowly, but looked set to increase when some of its leaders made it quite clear that they were *not* mere mouthpieces of the government and were quite prepared to criticize the party-state complex openly. The country is slowly moving back to 'normalcy'—whatever that is in the Polish context. But the future is far from clear. Poles have learnt how free they can be, and that even the PUWP can be changed. They know, too, that the detested Soviet Union itself was highly embarrassed by the picture of a so-called workers' state being ruled by men in jackboots, and will seek to keep such a form of rule to a minimum. But ordinary Poles have also seen that there are limits to their freedom to protest. Perhaps there cannot be an enduring solution to the Polish troubles. But one thing is certain—the communists have no better solutions to this kind of social situation than anybody else.

A COMPARATIVE OVERVIEW

Having considered a number of examples of mass challenge to authority, let us now attempt to answer the following questions from a comparative perspective.
  (i) Who demonstrates?
 (ii) What form do demonstrations take?
(iii) How do the authorities react?
(iv) Why do such demonstrations occur?
 (v) What factors lead to external intervention?
(vi) How successful are demonstrations?
(vii) Are the demonstrations 'political'?
In answering these questions, I shall lean on the comparative analysis made by J. M. Montias (1981), but modifying and adding as seems appropriate. For example, Montias excludes Czechoslovakia 1968, which will be included here.

(i) Who demonstrates?

One of the most interesting features about the strikes and riots is that peasants and unskilled workers rarely play a major role. In fact, peasants only rarely become involved at all, probably largely because they are territorially so dispersed; urban workers, in contrast, tend to be concentrated in large factories and/or suburbs of a city. Unskilled workers often feel more insecure in society and *vis-à-vis* the regime than do skilled workers; their very lack of skill often makes them more deferential than skilled blue-collar workers, who may well feel that their expertise is as useful and difficult to acquire as that of the white-collar managers, administrators, and party-state officials. Montias has also pointed out that there is more likelihood of a strike amongst workers in a highly labour-intensive and labour-paced industry than elsewhere; by 'labour-paced', he means that skilled workers rather than machines tend to set the pace of work. Typical 'labour-paced' industries include mining, ship-building, and construction; it is certainly the case in many of our examples that the initial impetus for strikes and riots has started in these branches. One other point noted by Montias is that women do not normally play a very significant role. The reasons for this require further research. But some of the factors that would be included are that women do not traditionally go into many of the branches of skilled, labour-intensive, and labour-paced industry that were listed above and that, despite much legislation on sexual equality passed in the communist states, many women still appear to have a predominantly deferential attitude towards men and authority. This factor is changing, of course, and some women have played major roles in strikes (such as Anna Walentynowicz in Poland and Fu Yueha in China—on the latter see Amnesty International 1984b, pp. 21–3); as more women perform skilled, labour-paced work, one would expect Montias' observation on what might be called the 'sexual division of rioting' to become ever less valid. Intellectuals, especially students, can also play a role in riots and demonstrations; but, contrary to what people such as Wright Mills (see Triska and Gati 1981, p. 1) or Marcuse have argued, they are not necessarily the sole repository of hope for major change. Workers, too, can play a major role in social and political change.

(ii) *The nature of demonstrations*

Demonstrations of dissatisfaction take a number of forms. Typically, conflicts start with a strike. This might well then go beyond the work- or study-place and on to the streets, where there will be speeches, placards, etc. Often, the demonstrators will single out a target for attack. Such targets are often buildings associated with party-state repression—police stations, party headquarters, military installations.

(iii) *The reactions of the authorities*

The authorities react to mass unrest in different ways. Sometimes—as in Kronstadt 1921 and the GDR 1953—the basic response is to counter with force; some concessions may be made, but these are mostly short-term and given with bad grace. Sometimes, a group of leaders will decide that the top leader must be replaced if the regime is to stand any chance of reaching a *modus vivendi* again with the population. This was the case in Poland in 1956, 1970, and 1980. The new leader will in some cases be a popular politician; at other times he will be a compromise between what most people seem to want and what the USSR will tolerate (examples of both can be found in Hungary 1956). The response to change in Czechoslovakia in August 1968 came from an outside agency, not the indigenous leadership. Later, when the masses became significantly involved, the Czechoslovak leadership responded in a similar way to the Hungarians in late 1956; in 1969, Husak could have appeared to many of the other senior politicians as a potential Kadar, and it only emerged over the months and years following April 1969 that the new

Czechoslovak leader was really very different from his Hungarian counterpart. A third method—and none of these are mutually exclusive—is to negotiate with the workers to reach some compromise solution. This was basically the case in Poland in June 1976 (in addition to coercion) and Romania 1977 (Jiu Valley miners' strike).

(*iv*) *Reasons for unrest*

The reasons for such demonstrations can be divided into long-term dissatisfaction and immediate triggers. The dissatisfaction may well have historical roots—people may feel either that their leaders were imposed on them or that these leaders imposed themselves. If the regime then terrorizes the population, ordinary citizens are unlikely to identify in any meaningful way with their leaders. But whilst this terror is still operating, the disincentives to demonstrate will far outweigh the incentives for most people. When the leadership itself renounces terror, however—or seems to be under instruction from above (i.e., Moscow) to do so, as happened in the mid-1950s—then citizens will in many cases reassess their attitudes towards displays of disaffection. But the contemporary performance of a regime can be an alternative or additional source of general dissatisfaction. The very nature of communist rule—the vanguard concept of leadership, the planned and largely state-owned economy—means that when things go wrong, notably when the economy performs badly, the authorities are bound to be blamed by ordinary citizens. Even so, it normally takes a specific event—the announcement of a price rise, the raising of work norms and foreign intervention are the most common ones—to turn long-term dissatisfaction into overt demonstrations. Czechoslovakia 1968 was a somewhat different case. Here, the reform started at the top, and there were no major disturbances for a long period. This does not, of course, mean that the Czechoslovak people were not disaffected from the Novotny regime; there is much empirical evidence to show that many people were. But if the new leadership itself seems to be introducing changes broadly in the direction most people want, then there seems to be little purpose in striking or demonstrating dissatisfaction in some other way. Ordinary citizens *did* come out on the streets in 1968—but only when the Soviet and other Warsaw Pact forces intervened. The riots did not last long, partially because many Czechoslovaks believed their more popular new leaders' arguments that it would be counter-productive and that anything gained between January and August 1968 would be endangered if the invaders were excessively provoked, and partially because many felt that it was pointless anyway.

Of course, we could turn this question on its head and ask why there are not more demonstrations. There are several reasons. One is that many citizens are politically apathetic much of the time. Another is that there are strong disincentives to rebel—demotion in one's job, imprisonment, even death. A third is that strikes and demonstrations are at best semi-legal.

Whereas the right to strike and demonstrate is understood as a basic right in the liberal democracies, the status of such activities is ambiguous in most communist states. The cynic may explain this quite simply in terms of a power élite wanting to minimize the threats to its position. Whilst there is certainly much truth in this interpretation, the reasons for ambiguous attitudes towards public displays of dissatisfaction are more complex than just this. These states claim to be workers' states, so that official recognition of the rights of groups of workers to strike against them raises all sorts of theoretical problems. One ramification of this ambiguity of official attitudes towards strikes and demonstrations is that many citizens, even if they do not fully accept the legitimacy of their regime, are nevertheless loath to break laws. A fourth factor is that there must be some sort of leadership; without this, dissatisfaction will rarely turn into rebellion. Fifth, many people will want to feel that there really is some *point* in demonstrating; why take risks if little or nothing will be achieved? Finally, the authorities might introduce concessions before a riot emerges, taking the wind out of a potential demonstration's sails. Points four and five are not universal—spontaneous actions do sometimes occur; but then we are back with the point that they emerge as a response to some specific event.

(v) *Factors leading to external intervention*

The reasons for external intervention are complex, but reflect principally leadership politics in the Soviet Union and elsewhere; the contemporary state of international relations; and Soviet strategic concerns. Let us apply these factors to various cases of intervention.

The decision to use Soviet troops in the GDR in 1953 reflected both Soviet leadership politics, the state of East–West relations (still at a low ebb, despite Stalin's death), and the fears the Soviets had that a mass uprising, if allowed to get out of hand, might lead to an eventual reunification of the GDR and the FRG into a unified anti-Soviet Germany.

In 1956, the decision to invade Hungary seems to have been finalized when Nagy declared Hungary a neutral country; this frightened the Soviets even more than Nagy's commitment to a proper multi-party system. In other words, this is a case of a strategic concern. To this must be added, however, Soviet leadership politics and the state of East–West relations. It has already been pointed out that Khrushchev's policies—towards Yugoslavia, Austria, Togliatti, and above all Stalin—were major factors in the buildup to the 1956 troubles. By late 1956, Khrushchev was being subjected to an increasing amount of criticism from many around him. The pressure from the conservatives—notably Molotov and Kaganovich—could no longer be resisted given the massive unrest and potential collapse of communist rule in Eastern Europe. Had Khrushchev not intervened in Hungary, it is highly probable that he would have lost his leadership position; there were certainly attempts along these lines by some top-ranking conservatives *anyway* from the end of

1956 through to the ouster of the 'anti-party group' in June 1957. If Khrushchev had not given orders for the use of force, his support would almost certainly have been much less than it was when the assault on his position was
mounted. In late 1956, the West was preoccupied with the Suez crisis; since
the West had done virtually nothing about the East Berlin crisis of 1953, and
given the other pressures on him, Khrushchev was prepared to take a calculated risk in sending troops to Budapest. In the event, the gamble paid off—
from the Soviet perspective at least.

  In the early 1960s, the Soviet Union suffered considerable international
humiliation, the most extreme case being the Cuban Missile Crisis of 1962
(see, for example, Shevchenko 1985, esp. p. 118). Humiliation was not
limited to relations with the West. In the communist world, too, the Sino–
Soviet rift was not only undesirable in itself, but was also leading some of the
East European states either to leave the Soviet fold or else attempt to assert
themselves far more within it (on all this see chapter 14). These international
humiliations were one of the reasons for Khrushchev's ouster in 1964. The
new leadership was not prepared to allow the USSR to become a laughing-
stock, which was one reason why it was so sensitive to the Prague Spring. If
the Soviets could successfully control that, it would not only be in the
Soviets' strategic interests, but would also show the world that the USSR was
once again able and willing to assert itself. There was, as ever, the possibility
of a Western counter-attack. But the Soviets correctly read the signs that this
was improbable; the West was already up to its eyes in fighting communists
in South-East Asia. Moreover, the new Soviet leadership was able to acquire
more favour amongst some of the East European hard-line leaders (notably
Ulbricht and Gomulka) by their actions—though the fact that both of these
fell, seemingly with Soviet connivance, within two or three years of the
Czechoslovak events means that one should not make too much of this particular factor. The new Soviet leadership was happy to have such support,
but it was not dependent upon it.

  But what of the cases where the USSR/Warsaw Pact has not intervened? On
balance, the Soviet Union would always prefer to not to have to invade
another socialist country. Although communist ideology can justify much in
the name of 'internationalism', the Soviets are not so thick-skinned that they
are completely oblivious to the charges of imperialism when their troops
march into another sovereign state. They will therefore always prefer an indigenous leadership to sort problems out itself. It is when the commitment of
such leaders to 'socialist internationalism' and even Leninist-oriented socialism itself is in question that the Soviets will consider an invasion. This helps
to explain the interventions in Hungary 1956 and Czechoslovakia 1968—and
the lack of invasion of Poland so far. I would argue that none of the Polish
leaders' basic commitment to socialism and/or the Soviet Union was ever in
question, and that this was as much an explanatory factor for the absence of
Soviet intervention as those such as 'common Slavic roots', the fear of civil

war, the size of the country, and the reaction of the West to the Soviet invasion of Afghanistan (in the case of the latest Polish troubles) that are often
put forward. One final factor—an important one—is that intervention costs
money. The costs are not just short-term (i.e., the military actions themselves), but can also be longer-term, in the sense that the Soviets will be seen
by many in the invaded country as having taken responsibility for the solution of the country's economic problems. In recent years, the USSR has had
enough of these of its own, without wanting to bail out other countries unless
its own strategic interests are really under serious threat.

(*vi*) *How successful is mass protest?*

A comparative analysis of mass unrest in the communist world reveals that
large-scale demonstrations almost always lead to some change, but that the
nature and scale of the change varies considerably. A new leader is one common—though not universal—outcome. But the way in which the new
leader—or a continuing one—will behave, and what concessions will be
made, is difficult to predict. Kadar gradually liberalized both the economic
and the political system of Hungary, whereas Husak rapidly moved towards
greater repression in Czechoslovakia. Lenin liberalized economically, but
clamped down politically. Ulbricht made some concessions, but these were
either short-lived and/or of marginal significance. Gomulka initially
appeared to be relatively liberal, but became increasingly repressive. His successor, Gierek, attempted to improve Poland's economic situation; but his
policies backfired and only led to further tensions. Jaruzelski soon revealed
that he was prepared to use draconian methods to bring the Polish population under control, but now seems to be taking tentative, cautious steps
designed to improve the relationship between his regime and society. In sum,
mass protest can sometimes lead to improvements for a given population,
but at least as frequently leads to a clampdown, especially in the medium
term. On balance, demonstrations may be a necessary release-valve for many
frustrated citizens in communist countries, but are not conspicuously successful at leading to major improvements in their lives.

(*vii*) *How political are the mass demonstrations?*

The final question to consider is whether the demonstrations are political. In
one sense, everything can be seen as political, and the term is used so broadly
by some people that it becomes almost meaningless. For our purposes, the
term 'political' is used here to mean that demonstrators etc. are calling fairly
explicitly for some redistribution of power (e.g. the establishment of workers'
councils to weaken the decision-making powers of managers; or for free elections, to give the electorate more say over who is going to rule them) as distinct from a call merely to revoke a price increase.
      Montias has argued that:

. . . the primary demands made by strikers are economic, (but) secondary demands regarding workers' participation and representation play an important subsidiary role in the interaction between the authorities and the strikers. Abstract 'system demands'—such as the institution of full-fledged parliamentarism or the restoration of capitalism—have so far been conspicuous by their absence. (1981, p. 185.)

This is not strictly accurate; although Montias does exclude Czechoslovakia from his analysis, he includes the GDR 1953, and Hungary 1956. In fact, workers in the GDR not only demanded the abolition of the work norms, but also free elections, free speech, and freedom of the press (Baring 1972, pp. 72–4). Political demands were also made by protestors in Hungary (see Lomax 1976, *passim* and esp. pp. 200–3). Moving beyond Montias' period of investigation, many of the 21 demands made by Gdansk workers in August 1980 were explicitly political, and some concerned the very nature of the political system. Moreover, it is not clear that specific 'secondary' demands made by protestors in the various countries regarding representation and participation are quite as distinct from 'abstract system demands' as Montias seems to be suggesting. Were these 'secondary' demands to be implemented, they could well lead in the long run to basic change in the system. It should also be borne in mind that, even in a bargaining situation, demands are usually made that are at least within the realm of political/economic possibility. Thus if one discovers a shortage of overtly systemic demands—the point about the absolute absence has already been disproven—this does not *necessarily* mean that protestors are fundamentally satisfied with the system and are only making narrow economic demands. They might simply be aware that it is easier to remove a mountain by chipping away at it than by trying to push the whole to one side. In Poland between August 1980 and December 1981, demands and criticisms became increasingly openly anti-system as some of the narrower demands were met. If protestors in other countries were free to do so, it would be fascinating to see how many 'abstract system demands' they would make.

Basic further reading

N. Ascherson, 1981.
A. Baring, 1972.
Z. Brzezinski, 1967, esp. chs. 9, 10, 11, 14.
C. Harman, 1983.
B. Lomax, 1976.

J. M. Montías, 1981.
K. Ruane, 1982.
H. G. Skilling, 1972; 1976.
P. Zinner, 1962.

13

NATIONALISM AND ETHNIC POLITICS

ONE of the most difficult political problems of all facing communists is that of unofficial nationalism. Communist leaderships find it difficult to cope with this, partially because of their over-dependence on Marx's analysis of nationalism, and partially because of contradictions in their own policies. Looking at the first of these, Marx greatly underestimated the power of nationalism (see e.g. Petrus 1971), arguing that nationalism was essentially only a bourgeois ideology; this is explored in more detail below. This meant that for a long time communist leaderships did not tackle the phenomenon in their own countries with nearly the vigour they should have done. This particular weakness—of seeing nationalism as essentially only a bourgeois phenomenon—has been compounded by the fact that most Western non-Marxist writers on nationalism also see the phenomenon emerging at about the same time as the industrial revolutions in Europe and thus some temporal, if not necessarily causal, link between nationalism and capitalism (see e.g., Kedourie 1960, p. 9; Plamenatz 1973, p. 23). Too many communist leaderships have therefore wrongly assumed that the problem of nationalism would simply disappear as socialism was consolidated. As for contradictions, one of the many reasons why ethnic conflict has not disappeared is that communists themselves have encouraged some forms of nationalism, which has helped to keep national awareness very much alive in the communist world. Once the concept of 'socialism in one country' had been officially adopted by the Soviets in 1925—which was criticized by some as a renunciation of Marxist and Leninist ideas of socialist internationalism—the scene was set for an assimilation of aspects of nationalist ideology into Marxism–Leninism, and problems were virtually bound to arise. There are inherent dangers in promoting 'official' nationalism in a communist state. Such nationalism can easily get out of hand. It can promote anti-state or unofficial nationalism amongst ethnic minorities. It can produce a set of values and attitudes which undermine and may even be stronger than many of the other communist values. These are the sorts of dilemmas that will be elaborated and analysed in this chapter. But let us begin by considering some definitions.

WHAT IS NATIONALISM?

Before discussing nationalism itself, we need to define a number of closely related terms—nation, race, national identity, and patriotism.

Etymologically, the word nation is from the Latin 'natio', meaning breed or race. Both of these terms have become ever less meaningful as people from different parts of the globe have interbred over the centuries. There is no English *race*—let alone an American race, for example—in the sense that the *biological* homogeneity implied in the term 'race' has long since been diluted. Although we can still distinguish between whites, blacks, yellows, etc., even these distinctions are—slowly—eroding. So the original meaning of nation is not terribly useful. Let us therefore consider some more modern definitions.

For a long time, one of the analyses of nationalism most widely adopted by communists was that produced by Stalin in 1913; it is still sometimes used by Soviet scholars (Rutland 1984, p. 152). This is too long a document to consider in detail here, but we can at least analyse Stalin's definition of a nation:

A nation is a historically constituted, stable community of people, formed on the basis of a common language, territory, economic life, and psychological make-up manifested in a common culture. ... It must be emphasised that none of the above characteristics taken separately is sufficient to define a nation. More than that, it is sufficient for a single one of these characteristics to be lacking and the nation ceases to be a nation. (Cited in Lane, 1978, p. 471.)

There are a number of problems with this definition. The concept of a 'stable community', for instance, is problematic. The Italians are constantly changing their governments—does this render Italy an 'unstable community'? If 'stability' is assured primarily through terror and/or high levels of coercion, then how useful is the 'stable community' concept in showing the existence of a nation? The notion of a common language is also not without problems. Many writers, such as Seton-Watson (1965, p. 9), refer to the Jewish nation; yet not only is there dispute over which of two languages (Hebrew and Yiddish) should be the accepted Jewish tongue, but many Jews speak neither, do not live in Israel—but still identify with the Jewish nation. Switzerland has four official languages—yet that does not mean that German- or French-speaking Swiss do not identify with or constitute part of the Swiss nation. As for territory, the Jewish nation once again provides an excellent example of a nation which existed for centuries without having a common territory, and indeed was scattered across the globe. Moreover, a potential problem is that individuals can identify with different periods of the past in making territorial claims, and there is no acceptable way of telling any group that it should identify with one period rather than another. The Argentinians stake their claim to the Falkland Islands (which they call the Malvinas) by reference to the pre-1833 situation; the British have ruled the Falklands since then, however, and can argue that the rights of the present Falklanders have been established over many generations. Turning to Eastern and Central Europe, it could be argued that there was once a Habsburg Empire or an Ottoman Empire, so that there should be a return to these political units. Without labouring the point, we can summarize by stating that claims by a given nation to some 'traditional' territory are often open to question; one group can refer to one period, another to a different one. A common economic life is ever less of a distinguishing feature of a nation, since the former is increasingly internationalized and standardized anyway, through the spread of the transnational corporations, the increase of economic integration via organizations such as the European Community or the Council for Mutual Economic Assistance, etc. 'Psychological make-up' is an extremely vague concept. We might have an image of volatile Italians, wily Chinese, arrogant Germans or the 'sang-froid' of the English, but these are stereotypes, not necessarily very reflective of reality. Moreover—and this is important—if we are looking at how the existence of a nation can be transformed into nationalism, then we are in most cases concerned very much with the activities of an intellectual *élite* in the nation. The stereotypes described above are probably even less accurate when applied to élites—who in most nations are better educated, more widely travelled, and therefore conform even less to standard national images than 'ordinary' citizens. As for culture—a Marxist should surely point to significant *class* differences within a given country, which make the notion of a common culture questionable.

The above criticisms of Stalin's definition do not render it completely useless; a common language or territory or religion, for instance, often *is* a distinguishing feature of a particular nation, and certainly these factors do frequently act as symbols around which nationalists rally. All we are saying is that an attempt at such a rigorous definition, incorporating specific variables, conceals the many real problems that exist in trying to define a nation.

But we do not have to be entirely negative. Like so many concepts in social science, the fact that a neat, watertight definition of the concept cannot be produced does not mean that the phenomenon itself does not exist. Knowledge of the world, and especially of its wars, are ample proof that nationalism—for which a prerequisite is the concept of nation—is a very real phenomenon indeed. Thus less specific, but more honest attempts at defining nation focus on people's *perceptions*. Seton-Watson, for instance, has defined a nation as follows:

... it seems to me, after a good deal of thought, that all we can say is, that a nation exists when an active and fairly numerous section of its members are convinced that it exists. Not external objective characteristics, but subjective conviction is the decisive factor. (Seton-Watson, 1965, p. 5; see too Seton-Watson, 1977, p. 5.)

A similar, if slightly more detailed definition is provided by R. Emerson—

The simplest statement that can be made about a nation is that it is a body of people who feel that they are a nation. ... To advance beyond it, it is necessary to attempt to take the nation apart and to isolate for separate examination the forces and elements which appear to have been the most influential in bringing about the sense of common identity which lies at its roots, the sense of the existence of a singularly important national 'we' which is distinguished from all others who make up an alien 'they'. This is necessarily an overly mechanical process, for nationalism, like other profound emotions such as love and hate, is more than the sum of the parts which are susceptible of cold and rational analysis. (Cited in Rakowska-Harmstone, 1974, pp. 3–4.)

The above definitions of a nation, though more general than Stalin's, are also more satisfactory for the reasons given. Emerson's emphasis on the 'them' and 'us' mentality is a particularly useful point; moreover, it highlights the fact that, contrary to what some Marxists argue, class is not the only really basic and significant division between people.

The mere existence of a nation does not in itself suggest that active nationalism exists. If people believe that a nation exists and that they are part of it, there is *national identity*. In one sense this national identity—or, if it is particularly strong, *patriotism* (usually defined as love of one's country)—is a form of nationalism. But this is for most purposes too broad a conception of nationalism, since the term usually connotes something more active than national identity, national pride, or even patriotism. It will comprise a specific ideology, and some form of political activism (e.g. organizing a campaign for recognition by other groups, for self-rule, etc.). The ideology will state that the interests of the nation come before all other interests (e.g. they should override class differences). If a nationalist movement is particularly aggressive towards other nations and claims superiority over them, we call it *chauvinist*.

Although we have now narrowed nationalism down, and shown it to be distinguishable from mere patriotism, it should also be emphasized that there are several different *types* of nationalism. The most superficial knowledge of, for instance, the Nazis and the Welsh nationalist group Plaid Cymru will reveal this. In attempting to distinguish the different kinds of nationalism, we need to start by drawing a basic division between the nationalism of a group in power, ruling a country (*official nationalism*) and that of a particular group of citizens within a country (*unofficial nationalism*). A further distinction can be drawn between those forms of nationalism that are basically *integrative*—i.e., where a group is encouraging citizens to identify with a bigger unit than they have traditionally done—and those which are *particularist* or *disintegrative*. In the latter case, nationalists have tried to resist integrative nationalism and encourage citizens to identify with smaller units. Although most official nationalism nowadays is integrative and most unofficial nationalism disintegrative, we shall see that this is not always the case. Having made these distinctions, and having considered official nationalism in chapter five, we can now classify the most common forms of unofficial nationalism. For our purposes, there are four reasonably distinct types of unofficial nationalism—unitarist, autonomist, separatist (or secessionist), and irredentist.

(a) Unitarism

Here, members of the biggest and/or dominant ethnic group want either to expand the political unit or further to integrate other ethnic groups into an existing political unit; it is thus intended to be integrative. Although such unofficial nationalism will sometimes harmonize with the official nationalism of the central authorities, there are times when it becomes dysfunctional to the leadership.

(b) Autonomism

The next three kinds of nationalism are essentially disintegrative, in that they are directed against the integrative official nationalism of a given state. Autonomists will accept that their nation will have to be part of some larger political unit (state), but will seek more autonomy within it, in such fields as language and economic decision-making.

(c) Separatism/Secessionism

Separatist or secessionist nationalism is more radical than autonomist, in that a given national group would not be content with merely a higher degree of independence within an existing state. Rather, it wants to be completely independent (i.e., break away from an existing state and establish its own sovereign state). In practice, the line distinguishing autonomist from separatist/secessionist nationalism is sometimes hazy, since the former may be just the first step on the path to the latter.

(d) Irredentism

Here, nationalists want the control of their territory transferred from one state to another with which they feel a closer affinity. Unlike the separatists/ secessionists, they do not want to rule themselves, but merely be part of another state.

WHAT IS ETHNIC POLITICS?

Many writers use the terms nationalism and ethnic politics virtually, if not completely, interchangeably. There are perfectly sound etymological grounds for this, in that *ethnos* is essentially the classical Greek equivalent of the Latin word *natio*. Moreover, unofficial nationalism of all kinds can be seen on one level as a form of conflict between groups, the members of which identify with a nation and/or race above all other political identifications.

However, there are at least two distinct political phenomena that can be covered by the term 'ethnic politics'; since one of these is well described by the term nationalism, it makes sense to use the term ethnic politics here only in the second, *narrow* sense. In this context, ethnic politics can be defined as conflict within one state either between groups of different ethnic origin and/or an ethnic group and the state, but where there is no demand for a basic restructuring of the existing political unit(s). Demands may well be made, but for what are believed to be rights to which the state is committed by its pronouncements (e.g. equal access to jobs, a 'fair' slice of the national investment cake, etc.) rather than for major structural change. This particular form of ethnic politics in the communist world has been much less documented than others. But the phenomenon certainly exists—there is racial tension between Chinese and Vietnamese in Vietnam, between black students and white students in the USSR, etc.

Although the term ethnic politics tends to be used in the narrow sense in this chapter, we will follow normal practice and, largely in order to avoid excessive repetition, use the terms ethnic group, nationality, nation and national group interchangeably unless otherwise specified.

MARX ON NATIONALISM

As is the case with so many other political phenomena, Marx's views on nationalism are not entirely clear (see Zwick 1983, pp. 15–31). However, Marx does seem to have believed that contemporary nationalism was essentially a bourgeois ideology designed to make proletarians identify with 'their' state (as the bourgeoisie would have it) rather than with any other political entity; in other words, he was mainly concerned with official nationalism. According to Marx, this served to mask class conflict, and to lessen the possibility that the proletariats of different countries would realize their common interest in struggling against their respective national bourgeoisies. For Marx, workers ultimately have no nations of their own. On the other hand, Marx also argued that the moves towards international socialism would have to proceed along the lines of national revolutions; the proletariat would take power in individual states, and only then begin to break down national boundaries. By the time the proletariat reached this stage, however, the internationalization of economics would have meant that the national differences between groups of workers would have become marginal; levels of development would be similar, for instance.

Up to this point, Marx's analysis seems fairly clear. However, his overemphasis on the *economic* aspects of political and social development meant that he did not deal adequately with other aspects of national identity and, in particular, with the factors leading to various kinds of unofficial nationalism. This vagueness in Marx helps to explain why twentieth-century communists have sometimes differed quite considerably both in their analyses of the reasons for and the treatment of unofficial nationalism within their states.

Another important point is that one particular aspect of Marx's conception of nationalism, has, to the extent that it has been adopted by communist leaderships, in fact stimulated unofficial nationalism and ethnic politics. Thus Marx, in line with the vast majority of political writers in the nineteenth century, distinguished between progressive and reactionary nationalism, and favoured the creation of large, centralized political units led by the most 'civilized' nations. For example, he favoured the expansion of the German nation, which he saw as progressive, and criticized the Croats, Czechs, Danes in Schleswig, and others for resisting the extension of this nation in the 1840s. From this, it follows that the Russians' notion that they are spreading civilization (i.e., their form of socialism) by intervening in the affairs of others is not as clearly out of line with classical Marxism as is sometimes maintained.

NATIONALISM AND ETHNIC POLITICS IN THE COMMUNIST WORLD: SOME CASE-STUDIES

In each of the following case-studies, a brief ethnographic survey of the particular country will be followed by a summary of official policy on nationalism and ethnic politics. After this, there will be a short history of nationalist and ethnic tensions in the country. Having looked at the situation in the USSR, Yugoslavia, and China, we shall take a comparative look at the nature of and reasons for nationalist and ethnic politics in the communist world.

(*i*) The USSR

Well over 100 nationalities are now officially recognized in the USSR, of which 20 account for approximately 95 per cent of the total population. The biggest group are the Russians (sometimes known as Great Russians), who account for about half the population; they are followed by the Ukrainians, the Uzbeks, the Belorussians, and the Kazakhs. Table 2 gives a detailed breakdown, based on the 1959, 1970, and 1979 Soviet censuses.

In the early days of the Russian Social Democratic Labour Party (one wing of which later became the Bolsheviks), there were serious disagreements over the question of how nations and nationalities within what was then the Russian empire should be treated following a revolution. Some believed that, although integration between nations should be encouraged, some autonomy should be left to every national group. Others believed in maximum integration. Lenin seemed to take a contradictory view, in that he argued simultaneously that the existence of nationally autonomous groups would weaken the proletarian struggle and that every national group should have the right to secede. Perhaps Lane (1978, p. 431) is correct when he argues that this apparent contradiction can be partially resolved by assuming that Lenin is talking about different stages of the revolution. Thus the right to secede would be associated with the bourgeois revolution, following which proletarian internationalism should take top priority. This said, Lenin was clearly

Table 2   Ethnic Composition of the USSR according to Official Censuses (in percentages)

	1959	1970	1979
Russians	54.6	53.4	52.4
Ukrainians	17.8	16.9	16.2
Uzbeks	2.9	3.8	4.8
Belorussians	3.8	3.7	3.6
Kazakhs	1.7	2.2	2.5
Tatars	2.4	2.5	2.4
Azerbaidzhani	1.4	1.8	2.1
Armenians	1.3	1.5	1.6
Georgians	1.3	1.3	1.4
Moldavians	1.1	1.1	1.1
Tadzhiks	0.7	0.9	1.1
Lithuanians	1.1	1.1	1.1
Turkmens	0.5	0.6	0.8
Germans	0.8	0.8	0.7
Kirghiz	0.5	0.6	0.7
Jews	1.1	0.9	0.7
Chuvash	0.7	0.7	0.7
Latvians	0.7	0.6	0.5
Bashkirs	0.5	0.5	0.5
Mordvinians	0.6	0.5	0.5
Others	4.5	4.6	4.6
(Total population in millions)	(208.8)	(241.7)	(262.1)

Sources: calculated by the author on the basis of *Narodnoe Khozyaistvo SSSR v 1972 g.* (Moscow: Statistika, 1973), p. 35 (for 1959 and 1970 figs.) and *Narodnoe Khozyaistvo SSSR 1922–1982* (Moscow: Financy i Statistika, 1982), p. 33 (for 1979 figs).

not anxious to encourage secession, since it would go against his view—shared with Marx—that economic development implied ever larger units, which in turn would help to break down differences between nations. Hence, in that he favoured any moves which would bring socialism and communism nearer, he was always loath to encourage any form of nationalism which, ultimately, draws distinctions between people rather than breaks down barriers. His long-term aim was for first a 'merging' then a 'fusion' of the national groups comprising the USSR. In practice, his ideas led him to adopt a form of federalism in the USSR, based on national groups. This was seen as a way of integrating nations, and in the long term breaking down national barriers. This federal system has remained to the present day.

Stalin, too, did not in theory favour any actual encouragement of what could be seen as disintegrative or particularist nationalism. This said, he did not see national identity or nations dying out under socialism. Rather, he saw them changing, so that new socialist nations would arise. He de-emphasized the internationalism of both Marx and Lenin—to some extent because the hoped-for revolutions in other countries after the First World War had either not materialized or else failed—and encouraged 'socialism in one country'. Despite this official nationalism at the level of the USSR, Stalin played down minority particularist nationalisms *within* the country, arguing that class would replace nation as the prime unit of identification. But he was also sufficiently pragmatic to realize that it would be unwise and probably impractical to attempt to centralize all decision-making at the top of a large politico-economic unit; he therefore advocated regional autonomy to replace national autonomy.

Like his predecessors, Khrushchev was ambiguous in his views on nations and nationalism. Thus in the 1961 Programme of the CPSU—in the writing of which Khrushchev played a major role—there are references to the Leninist concept of 'merging' of nations, the weakening of national borders and a future 'single world-wide communist culture'. But Khrushchev saw this process as a very long one, even admitting that 'the effacement of national distinctions is a considerably longer process than the effacement of class distinctions'-(in Rutland 1984, p. 159). What is unclear is how such effacement is to come about, and whether there will actually be increases, even under socialism, in national and ethnic tensions before the unified culture emerges.

The ambiguity continued into the Brezhnev era. On the one hand, there were claims that the nationality problem had in essence been solved, as revealed in the Central Committee statement made on the 60th anniversary of the October Revolution that, 'genuine brotherhood of the working people, irrespective of nationality, has been established' (adapted from Gitelman 1983, p. 38). On the other, Brezhnev also recognized the continuing problem of nationalism even in a society at the highest stage of socialism—and therefore, by implication, preparing for the transfer to communism: 'Nationality relations, even in a society of mature socialism, are a reality that is constantly developing and putting forth new problems and tasks' (statement made in 1972, quoted in Rakowska-Harmstone 1974, p. 9); or 'The unity of Soviet nations is now closer than ever. This does not mean, of course, that all questions of nationality relations have been solved already' (1981 statement, quoted in Gitelman 1983, p. 37).

The Andropov era witnessed a similar confusion as to whether nationalism has in essence been overcome or not (see, e.g. Andropov's speech on the 60th anniversary of the founding of the USSR, translated in the *Current Digest of the Soviet Press*, vol. xxxiv, no. 51, pp. 1–8). Indeed, the question of merging—a term revived by Andropov, Brezhnev having preferred the even weaker term 'coming together' of nations—let alone fusion, has now been deferred to some, distant, unspecified point in the future, which might reflect Soviet leadership perceptions that an over-hasty attempt to eradicate national differences would be politically dangerous. It is certainly the case that some Soviet writers now see nationality problems as being more difficult to cope with than even class differences (à la Khrushchev); indeed one scholar is quoted as saying off the record that the 'most crucial matter facing Soviet society' is the ethnic problem (cited in Allworth 1980, p. xv). Such scholars are also more explicit in casting doubts on the notion of a merging of nations than are the politicians, although even Andropov, in the speech just cited (p. 4), argued that 'the economic and cultural progress of all nations and nationalities is accompanied by an inevitable growth in their national self-awareness'; this hardly implies a merging. In short, Soviet policy on nationalities and nationalism has been and continues to be rather confused.

The threat of nationalism and ethnic politics will be discussed in the last part of this chapter; for the present, let us consider briefly some of the main examples in recent years of nationalist and ethnic politics in the USSR. We shall adopt Reddaway's method (1978), and much of his information, for considering specific groups by republic and territory—as simple and effective a method as any.

Perhaps surprisingly, one of the most vocal forms of nationalism in recent years has been Great Russian nationalism itself; this is an example of unitarism. In 1964, 'Fatherland' clubs emerged within what is by far the largest Soviet republic, the RSFSR; these preached the virtues of Russian culture, and for most of the 1960s were treated with extreme tolerance by the Soviet authorities. Presumably, it was felt that such nationalism coincided to some extent with official nationalism, at least in the RSFSR. However, these nationalists became increasingly embarrassing to the authorities after the 1968 Warsaw Pact intervention in Czechoslovakia, since they were justifying the invasion on the almost racist grounds of Russian 'great powerism'. Moreover, the authorities were beginning to realize the dysfunctions of allowing the largest national group to indulge in nationalism, since it can encourage similar sentiments in other parts of the country—either by example, or because minority national groups feel threatened by the majority group and therefore develop greater national awareness. Hence there was a clampdown on the Russian nationalists in 1970. But this was not completely effective, and a new *samizdat* journal, *Veche* began to be published in 1971. The head of this movement was Osipov, and it was closely linked to the Russian orthodox faith. The religious element—as well as the dysfunctions mentioned above—led the authorities to attempt to keep the movement within bounds. But they could not do this to their satisfaction, and eventually closed *Veche* down in 1974. With the expulsion of Solzhenitsyn in the same year, the movement has declined in significance. However, Andropov told the Soviet minorities that they should be grateful to the Russians for all their achievements, and that the Russian language should play an even greater role in the integration of all nationalities; this policy—which is being continued at the time of writing—could well inspire a rekindling of the Russian nationalist spirit.

The Baltic region (i.e., the republics of Estonia, Latvia, and Lithuania), has witnessed ethnic politics (meaning here tension between Balts and Russians living in the area), autonomist and secessionist nationalism in recent years. The Baltic states were not even part of the USSR until 1940 when, taking advantage of the Nazi–Soviet non-aggression treaty, the Soviets forcibly and violently annexed them. Memories of that period seem to have lived on in the minds of many Balts, and surfaced in various nationalist outbursts in the 1960s and 1970s. The most widespread outbursts were in Lithuania, which is the only Soviet republic in which nationalism has been an overtly mass movement. Lithuanian nationalism is closely linked to the strong Roman Catholic tradition of the area. The violence of the early 1970s can be traced back to the late 1960s, when a number of Catholic priests started demanding greater religious freedom. In 1971, the arrest of two priests served as a rallying call for all those Lithuanians who were dissatisfied with the Soviet regime. The movement peaked in May 1972, after a student burnt himself to death; there were riots in Lithuania's second largest city, Kaunas, and demands for greater religious and national freedom. The riots were forcibly suppressed, and tension simmered for about 18 months. In November 1973, the KGB launched an all-out attack on the Lithuanian religious movement, and many of the dissidents were arrested. Sentences of up to six years were imposed, and the back of the movement seems to have been broken. However, nationalist sentiment has not been entirely eradicated, and there are still occasional reports of nationalist activity, often associated with the Catholic church. In terms of overt activity, nationalism has been less widespread in Estonia and Latvia than in Lithuania, and is far less obviously related to religion. Yet here too, nationalism has been an irritant to the central authorities. For example, in 1971 a group of Latvian communists wrote to a number of West European communist parties criticizing the fact that, as they saw it, the Soviet authorities were attempting to eradicate Latvian culture; such actions caused a great deal of embarrassment and annoyance in Moscow, and were soon clamped down upon.

The second-largest republic in the USSR, in terms of population though not territory, is the Ukraine; autonomist, separatist, and even irredentist (wanting Western Ukraine to be under Polish control) nationalism has a long history there, but we shall deal exclusively with the post-Khrushchev period. In 1965 and 1966, 22 Ukrainian intellectuals were arrested for nationalist activity; following this, the nationalists were relatively quiet. But in 1971, the Ukrainian party chief Shelest seemed to be showing sympathy towards the nationalists. Given this, and news of what was happening elsewhere, Ukrainian nationalism experienced a resurgence. The KGB mounted a counter-offensive, and in January 1972 at least 50 nationalist dissidents were arrested. This was followed in May by the replacement of the over-sympathetic Shelest by the more hard-line Shcherbitskii. Although this led to a decline in overt action by Ukrainian nationalists, signs that it continues to simmer emerge every so often. For instance, the poet Irina Ratushinskaya was imprisoned in March 1983 for nationalist, 'anti-soviet agitation and propaganda'.

Georgia experienced a rather similar fate to the Ukraine in 1972, in that its party chief Mzhavanadze was replaced (by Shevardnadze) partly because of his over-tolerant attitudes towards nationalism. In 1978, the CPSU tried to make Russian a second official language of Georgia (i.e., in addition to Georgian itself) but backed down following mass demonstrations in the capital, Tbilisi, in April.

Some commentators (e.g. Carrère d'Encausse, 1981) see the biggest *potential* area of national dissent in the USSR as being the Central Asian republics (i.e., Kazakhstan, Kirghizia, Tadzhikistan, Turkmenistan, and Uzbekistan). It is certainly the case that the populations of these republics are growing faster than any others within the USSR, and that their standards óf living fall well below those of virtually all other parts of the Soviet Union—both of which have been cited as reasons why we should expect to see more nationalist activity in the future. Even more important, however, is the fact that Islam is widespread in the Central Asian republics, and provides an alternative ideology to Marxism–Leninism. It has been argued by some that the revival of Islamic fundamentalism in Iran and elsewhere in recent years, plus sympathy for the Muslims of Afghanistan, is tending to raise political consciousness in the area, and that this will probably erupt into mass nationalist unrest in the future. This may be true, although the fact that the vast majority of the 43 million Muslims living in Central Asia are Sunni—a sect which has suffered a great deal under the Shi-ite Muslims in Iran—means that one should be careful in making inferences. Certainly, there is remarkably little evidence of nationalist activity in this area at present. Moreover, according to Bennigsen (1980, pp. 47, 49), many Soviet Muslim intellectuals initially welcomed the Soviet occupation of Afghanistan, seeing it as an opportunity to liberate the Afghans from imperialism and feudalism, to introduce a progressive new order in which communism and Islam could coexist, and to gain concessions (e.g. more investment funds for their own areas) from Moscow in return for support of the Soviet effort. Although this situation soon began to change (for details see Bennigsen 1980, pp. 47–8), this example shows that one must be wary of drawing over-hasty conclusions about Islamic nationalist tendencies.

In sum, although unofficial nationalism is not the force in Soviet politics today that it was fifteen years ago, it continues to simmer and *could* under certain circumstances become a major problem for Moscow.

(ii) *Yugoslavia*

It has been argued that 'In Yugoslavia all political problems are intimately linked with the issue of nationalism' (Klein and Klein 1981, p. 261); although this assessment is somewhat exaggerated, it does give us some indication of just how important nationalism is in contemporary Yugoslav politics. It was observed in chapter 2 that one of the reasons the Western allies supported Tito at the end of the Second World War was that his was the only pan-Yugoslav movement. All the other movements were unacceptable, not *only* because they had collaborated with Germans, but also because they represented individual nations within Yugoslavia and were often hostile to other nations. This said, Tito's partisans were not unaware of the problems of national, religious, and linguistic antagonisms, and the Yugoslav authorities have consistently been among the most sensitive in the communist world to the problem of integrating various national groups. Before elaborating upon this, however, let us consider briefly the ethnic composition of the Yugoslav population (see Table 3).

Table 3   Ethnic Composition of Yugoslavia According to Official Censuses (in percentages)*

	1948	1971	1981
Serbs	41.5	39.7	36.3
Croats	24.0	22.1	19.8
Muslims	5.1	8.4	8.9
Slovenes	9.0	8.2	7.8
Albanians	4.8	6.4	7.7
Macedonians	5.1	5.8	6.0
Montenegrins	2.7	2.5	2.6
Hungarians	3.1	2.3	1.8
Others (including citizens who declare their nationality to be 'Yugoslav')	4.7	4.6	9.0
(Total population in millions)	(15.8)	(20.5)	(22.4)

* N.B. Censuses were also held in 1953 and 1961.

Sources: All figures have been calculated by the author on the basis of *Jugoslavija 1945–1964—Statistiki Pregled* (Savezni Zavod za Statistika; Belgrade, 1965), p. 45 (1948 figs); *Statistical Pocket Book of Yugoslavia* (Federal Statistical Office; Belgrade, 1979), p. 28 (1971 figs); *Facts about the Federal Republic of Yugoslavia* (Federal Secretariat for Information; Belgrade, 1982), p. 11 (1981 figs).

As in the USSR, the Yugoslav communists decided from the beginning that they would recognize national differences within the state by creating a federal system. But the Yugoslav authorities have made a clearer distinction than the Russians between 'nations' and 'nationalities'/'national minorities'. 'Nations' are ethnic groups whose traditional territory lies wholly inside Yugoslavia, whereas 'nationalities'/'national minorities' are groups of some larger nation, a sizeable proportion of which lives in countries bordering on Yugoslavia. This is reflected in the organizational structure of Yugoslavia. Thus the five major Slavic nations were granted a republic each, in addition to which a sixth republic was established (Bosnia-Hercegovina) for the various Slavic Muslim groups which dominated that part of the country. The two biggest non-Slavic nationalities—the Hungarians and Albanians—were given an autonomous province (the Vojvodina) and an autonomous region (Kosovo) respectively; Kosovo was granted the status of autonomous province in 1963, at a time when the status of such provinces was enhanced. To endorse this policy of national representation at the central level, a Council of Nationalities was established as the Upper House of the legislature in 1946.

Despite the formal federalism, the period 1946–65 has been characterized by Bertsch (1973, p. 3) as a unitarist one, in which the party and government sought to minimize awareness of national differences and encourage a Yugoslav national identity. However, such a policy seemed to be increasingly at odds with the more general policy of decentralizing the political process (i.e., workers' self-management and all that went with it), and in any case did not appear to be as successful as had been hoped. Thus from about 1966 to 1971, following the ouster of the authoritarian and pro-centralism leader Alexander Rankovic, there was a more decentralized federalist approach. This gave more autonomy to the republics and provinces, though not to such an extent that it might endanger Yugoslavia as a whole. For example, twenty-three amendments to the constitution were enacted in 1971, including the establishment of a collective presidency comprising three members from each republic and two from each autonomous province. This was all intended to make the centre appear as fairly representative of each ethnic group as possible. Moreover, various additional powers and rights were given to Kosovo and Vojvodina in 1968 and 1971 which brought them even closer to republican status, in practice if not formally in title. However, such measures actually encouraged greater national awareness in some areas—so much so that the central leadership felt by the end of 1971 that the situation was getting out of control. Signs of serious disquiet at the top came with the forced resignations of several leading Croatian politicians (e.g. Miko Tripalo, Secretary of the Croatian League of Communists) in December 1971, following their demands that Croatia be allowed to retain all the foreign currency it earned for investment; hitherto, the Croats, like everyone else, had had to exchange most of the foreign currency they acquired for dinars at the National Bank in Belgrade, at what many considered to be very unfavourable rates. Months later came the dismissal of many top politicians from other republics. These included the President of the Serbian League of Communists' Central Committee, Marko Nikezic—showing that the campaign was not just an anti-Croat phenomenon. This period (i.e., the early 1970s) was the first time since the Second World War that the senior leadership, including Tito himself, had referred to a 'national crisis' threatening the very existence of Yugoslavia. The Party Presidium devoted special attention to the problem of nationalism at a meeting in 1972, at which both unitarist (represented above all by the Serbs) and separatist (represented in particular by the Croats) trends were observed and criticized.

Yugoslav policy since the crisis of 1971–2 has been very ambiguous. In 1973 Bertsch (1973, p. 3) called the period from 1972 a 'confederational' one, in that the functions of the central government were further limited to the benefit of local units. But to look only at the state machinery would give a distorted picture. The role of the communist party was reasserted in the aftermath of the crisis (most visibly at the 10th Congress in 1974) with the result that some powers, especially of policy-making, have been recentralized in recent years. This has led to what many Yugoslav theoreticians themselves see as an ambiguous and problematic political situation. As the LCY journal *Politika* put it in September 1982, the most fundamental political problem in Yugoslavia today is that the state is confederal whereas the LCY is federal; in fact, the 10th Congress of the LCY explicitly forbade federalization of the party. This has fairly obvious implications for nationalism, in that one part of the political system is encouraging most ethnic groups to take a greater role in running their own affairs, whilst another is discouraging it—a situation which is almost bound to lead to conflict. At present, the LCY is undergoing its most dramatic self-examination for years, mainly on the question of how centralized or decentralized power should be; the debate is far from over, but one indicator of which tendency has been gaining the upper hand is the fact that Rade Končar, a leading member of the Belgrade city committee of the LCY, was forced to resign in September 1982 for having advocated an over-centralist conception of the party, in which the republican and provincial tiers would have virtually disappeared. At present, therefore, the leadership still seem to be attempting to tread a middle path between over-centralization (which can be criticized as undemocratic) and excessive devolution of powers to ethnic groups, which in the past has been shown to contain the danger that Yugoslavia could actually break up.

Having considered official policy, let us now examine some of the most important examples of unofficial nationalism in Yugoslavia.

In the period to the mid-1960s examples of overt nationalist activity were rare and quickly dealt with. But with the policies of political and economic devolution of the mid-1960s, examples of nationalistic behaviour—some unitarist, but more often autonomist or separatist—became increasingly visible among virtually all of the ethnic groups in Yugoslavia. A good example is that of the Croatian cultural society Matica Hrvatska, which in 1967 demanded that the Croat language be separate from Serbian, so that the principal language of Yugoslavia (Serbo-Croat) would be replaced by two main languages (i.e., Serbian and Croatian). However, it needs to be emphasized very strongly that such examples of nationalism were largely displayed in their early stages *not* by the grass roots population, but by the republic-level politicians and a few intellectuals. It was only *after* politicians and intellectuals had encouraged nationalist orientations that ordinary Croats, Serbs, Montenegrins, and others began to channel the frustrations they had been experiencing in recent years (particularly in the economic and cultural spheres) into nationalist demands. The movement seems to have gathered momentum earliest and most rapidly in Croatia, and culminated in big demonstrations in Zagreb in November 1971. The dissatisfaction was fanned not only by politicians such as Tripalo, but in particular by the writer Sime Djodan, who, like the party chief, argued that Croatia was being exploited by the rest of Yugoslavia. Whilst Croatian nationalism was primarily of the separatist sort, there was also growing Serbian unitarist nationalism; Serbs were claiming that the other ethnic groups were threatening to wreck the Yugoslav federation—in which the Serbs were politically dominant.

By 1974, the leadership had not only identified nationalism as a major problem but had also decided to deal with it firmly. The powers of the security police, which had declined in 1966 following Rankovic's ouster, were now increased again. There were a number of arrests and prison sentences. Some of the latter were very harsh; for example, fifteen Croats were found guilty in February 1975 of plotting the secession of Croatia, and received sentences of up to fifteen years. All this was a relatively new development, in that there had been almost no imprisonments for nationalism (or indeed other forms of dissidence) until 1971 (Klein and Klein 1981, p. 262). There were other examples of nationalism—e.g. Muslim nationalism in Bosnia-Hercegovina— in the mid-1970s, but the authorities' clampdown seems to have helped to quell them.

The relative calm of the late 1970s was shattered in the early 1980s by nationalist activities in the autonomous province of Kosovo. As pointed out earlier, this province is predominantly Albanian, and has become increasingly so in the last two decades. There were nationalist outbreaks there in 1968, 1975, and 1980, but nothing nearly as serious as the demonstrations which broke out less than a year after Tito's death, in the period March–May 1981. The 1981 problems started as student demonstrations, mainly over conditions at Pristina (the capital of Kosovo) university. However, one group was demanding the creation of a Kosovar republic. The troubles soon spread to some of Kosovo's factory workers, and became a clear case of nationalist conflict. One of the main features of this nationalism was that it was *not* a unified movement. Although the nationalists were agreed that they wanted change, the majority called for a Kosovar republic (i.e., autonomist nationalism) whilst a more extremist group advocated the separation of Kosovo and its incorporation into Albania (i.e., unofficial irredentist nationalism). Despite the varied nature of the nationalism, it caused severe problems for the central authorities, who responded by declaring a state of emergency in the province and sealing its borders. In June, the Minister of the Interior (Hrlevic) announced that eight demonstrators and one policeman had been killed, and 257 people wounded (including 133 policemen) during the riots; 506 people had been sentenced for their activities in the riots. In May 1981, the head of the Kosovar communist party, Mahmut Bakali, was dismissed; he had long been encouraging close ties with Albania, which some politicians from other republics felt was fanning Albanian nationalist feeling in Kosovo. This was followed by the dismissal of the Kosovar security police chief, Mustafa Sefedini, and a number of other senior officials (including twelve members of the collective presidency of Kosovo) in the period June to September.

Despite the purges and the hard-line policy of the federal authorities, the situation is still volatile. There were more demonstrations in 1982 and 1983 although these seem to have been *relatively* peaceful and were in most cases dispersed without too much trouble. More trials took place in the summer of 1982 and the autumn of 1983, and these again highlighted the diverse nature of Kosovar nationalism; various illegal groups were cited at the trials, including the 'Voice of Kosovo', the 'Communist–Marxist–Leninist Party of Albanians in Yugoslavia' and the 'Group of Marxist–Leninists in Kosovo'.

Although Kosovo has been the scene of the most serious outbreaks of nationalism in Yugoslavia in recent years, incidents have been occurring elsewhere. For instance, five Albanians were tried and imprisoned in Macedonia in May 1981 for wanting to transfer half of that republic to Albania. Macedonia has a long history of nationalism problems, in that there is another group of irredentist nationalists who would like to see Macedonia become part of Bulgaria. A third group—one that has been well tolerated by the authorities (see Meier 1983, p. 51)—wants parts of Greece and Bulgaria to be incorporated into Yugoslav Macedonia, whilst a fourth group wishes to see Macedonia separated from all existing states and made into a sovereign land in its own right. The Yugoslav authorities are going to have to keep tight control of nationalist outbreaks in the future, since history has shown that any success by one group will often trigger the aspirations of others. And this is not the only problem. The words and deeds of Albanian nationalists in Kosovo have led many Serbs—the second-largest group in the province—to become anti-Albanian (i.e., an example of ethnic politics) and more nationalist (unitarist) than before. The list could go on. But this is unnecessary; the reader will by now be aware of just how big a problem nationalism is in today's Yugoslavia.

(*iii*) *China*

Despite its enormous population, China is dominated by one nationality to a much higher degree than either of the two states considered so far. The vast majority of Chinese citizens—approximately 93 per cent—are Han Chinese. This said, fifty-five national minorities are officially recognized; according to the various Chinese censuses, the ethnic composition has been as shown in Table 4.

As in the USSR and Yugoslavia, official Chinese policy on the nationalities has varied over time, fluctuating between what Dreyer (1975) calls the 'gradualist pluralist' and the 'radical assimilationist' approaches. The following periodization of official policy is based principally on those produced by Dreyer (1975) and Derek Waller (1981, pp. 164–8).

In the pre-1949 period, Mao and the CCP leadership pursued a policy basically aimed at encouraging national groups to break away from China which, it will be recalled, was at that time principally under Chiang Kai-shek's Nationalist (Guomindang) regime. Thus, the 1931 constitution for the Chinese Soviet Republic specified that nationalities had the right to secede from China and to establish sovereign states. Following their takeover, the

Table 4 Ethnic Composition of the PRC according to Official Censuses (in percentages)

	1953	1964	1982
Han	93.9	94.2	93.3
Zhuang	1.1	1.2	1.3
Hui (Muslims)	0.6	0.6	0.7
Uighur	0.6	0.6	0.6
Yi	0.6	0.5	0.5
Miao	0.4	0.4	0.5
Manchu	0.4	0.4	0.4
Tibetans	0.5	0.4	0.4
Mongols	0.3	0.3	0.3
Tujia	n.a.	0.1	0.3
Bouyei	0.2	0.2	0.2
Koreans	0.2	0.2	0.2
Others	1.0	0.9	1.3
(Total population in millions)	(582.6)	(691.2)	(1,003.9)

Sources: 1953. Based on figures in Nai-Ruenn Chen, *Chinese Economic Statistics* (Chicago: Aldine, 1967), p. 126.
  1964. Based on figures in *Beijing Review*, 18 June 1984, p. 23.
  1982. Based on figures in *Beijing Review*, 23 May 1983, pp. 19–20.

communists initially pursued a gradualist policy of assimilation. Although the CCP proclaimed China a unitary state (i.e., the PRC has never had a federalized arrangement, unlike the USSR or Yugoslavia), they also recognized its multi-national aspect and allowed for the possibility of national groups having some degree of autonomy. Thus the concept of an 'Autonomous Region' (AR) was introduced—in fact, even before power had been consolidated throughout mainland China, in that the inner-Mongolian AR was established in 1947. In addition, a number of autonomous provinces, which have fewer rights than regions, were set up. The leaders do not appear to have been anxious to encourage the establishment of too many ARs, and the only other one to have been established in the period before 1958—when the Ningxia (Hui) and Guangxi (Zhuang) ARs came into being—was the Xinjiang (Uighur) AR in 1955. There were a number of reasons for this. One was that the communist leaders were unsure of how to deal with some groups, and preferred to interfere minimally when in doubt; this included not complicating matters, by not establishing new units. Moreover, the establishment of too many ARs could possibly have led to demands for a proper federalized state, an arrangement the leadership was anxious to avoid. Hence, rather than create new ARs, the communists preferred simply to come to an agreement with ethnic minority leaders not to interfere excessively in the affairs of the particular group and its territory. For example, the Beijing regime signed an agreement with the Tibetan religious and political leader, the Dalai Lama, in 1952, according to which the communists agreed not to change the existing political arrangements. Although the period is characterized as a gradualist one, it should be emphasized that in most cases there were some moves to integrate minorities more into the PRC system. Thus, although Inner Mongolia became an AR, the number of Han political cadres sent into the area during this period was so great that there were eventually more Hans than Mongols in the region, a development which led to ethnic tensions.

It became evident in the period preceding the Great Leap Forward of 1958 that the basically gradualist policy was beginning to change. In 1956, despite the fact that the newly adopted party statute had referred to the need for communists to respect the special features of the various minorities, the regime began to forge ahead in the minority areas with various reforms that had been under way in the main Han areas for some years. In the following year, when the Hundred Flowers Campaign got out of hand and led to various minority nationalist demands, an anti-rightist campaign was mounted; one of the campaign's targets was 'local nationalism'. These moves towards radical assimilation received a major boost in 1958, when the Great Leap Forward was introduced. Now, all languages other than Mandarin (Han) Chinese were discouraged. Moreover, people's communes were set up in most parts of the country (Tibet being a notable exception), which often brought both Hans and a minority group together in one residential- and work-unit. The radical policy did not last long, however, since signs of major ethnic tensions soon became evident. Already in 1959 some communes were disbanded in the areas of greatest minority hostility.

The early 1960s saw a return to a more gradualist policy, and many proposed reforms in minority areas were deferred. But the GPCR led to pressure from the radical assimilationists once again. A policy of destroying 'the four olds' (ways of thinking; culture; customs; and habits) was mounted, directed on one level against ethnic minorities who wished to maintain a distinctive identity. During this time, the Inner Mongolian AR was almost decimated, approximately 50 per cent of its territory being distributed to adjoining provinces. Many communes were re-established, and they were introduced for the first time in Tibet. However, as Dreyer (1975, p. 55) points out, the fact that the radical assimilationists were able to have much more influence on policy than before is not to say that Chinese policy at this time reflected only their views. In fact, the political infighting at the top was reflected in an ambiguous policy on the national minorities. Thus, while some local leaders, such as the Mongolian Ulanhu, were in essence punished for their nationalism— Ulanhu was accused in 1967 of trying to be a 'ruler in an independent kingdom' and lost all his posts—others of allegedly rather similar views survived the height of the GPCR virtually intact (e.g. Seypidin of the Xinjiang AR).

If the radical assimilationists seemed, on balance, to be winning during the height of the GPCR, the moderate gradualists became increasingly assertive after the death of Lin Biao in 1971; Lin was in fact criticized in the mid-1970s for having sabotaged the CCP's policy on ethnic groups. Minority languages and religious beliefs were tolerated again and, in order to ensure that there would be more native cadres in the autonomous regions and areas in the future, the Central Nationalities College in Beijing was reopened in 1972. In the same year, the CCP agreed to a programme of renovation of Tibetan religious buildings damaged or destroyed during the GPCR, although the CCP nowadays tries to give the impression that this more tolerant policy is a feature solely of the post-1978 changes (see *Beijing Review*, 22 November 1982, p. 15). Finally, some of the politicians who had suffered during the GPCR were now rehabilitated—most notably Ulanhu, who was once again elected onto the Central Committee by the 10th Congress in 1973. The new constitution of January 1975 affirmed the equality of all ethnic groups—even though its section on nationalities was very brief in comparison with the 1954 constitution, perhaps suggesting that the gradualists were still not sufficiently dominant over the radicals to emphasize this policy too forcefully.

Although the moderates had been in the ascendancy ever since late 1971, the real consolidation of a gradualist and tolerant policy has been obvious in the years since 1978. When the PRC's third constitution was adopted in March 1978, for instance, article four emphasized the equality of nationalities, and the right of all nationalities to use and develop their own language and customs. This was in marked contrast to the policy against the 'four olds' during the GPCR, even though there was still far less detail on minority rights than in the 1954 constitution. In the same year, the State Council's 'Nationality Affairs Commission' was re-established, and in 1979 this body resolved to direct a higher proportion of investment funds to minority areas and to the training of more ethnic cadres. As a result, a number of Han cadres have been leaving various minority areas in the 1980s and handing their work over to minority cadres. Indeed, according to the most recent (1982) constitution, the chairpersons and vice-chairpersons of the local state executive of an AR *must* in future be members of the local nationality; the top state posts in Xinjiang, for example, could not be held by Han Chinese (such explicit stipulations were not contained in the 1978 constitution). This basic principle was further elaborated and extended to autonomous prefectures and counties in May 1984 (for an analysis of the 'Law on Regional Autonomy for Minority Nationalities' see Ngapoi Ngawang Jigme, 1984).

In short, the gradualist rather than the radical assimilationist policy is dominant at present. The leadership continues to criticize both 'big nation chauvinism' (i.e., Han nationalism) and 'local-national chauvinism' (i.e., unofficial nationalism among the ethnic minorities).

We see yet again from the Chinese case that communists in power can have very divergent views on how to treat national groups within the state. Let us now consider some of the examples of nationalist conflict in the PRC since its establishment.

Some ethnic minorities were very opposed to being incorporated into the PRC after 1949, which is one of the reasons the new communist leadership took a particularly gradual and cautious approach in some areas. Typically, according to both Dreyer and Waller, the less developed a minority was economically and politically, the more potential hostility the leadership sensed, and thus the more cautious the handling of the minority (Dreyer 1975, p. 50; D. Waller 1981, p. 165). There were various examples of Hui (Muslim) hostility to the Chinese at this stage, but nothing that reached serious proportions. However, the Great Leap Forward of 1958 did lead to a number of disturbances in minority areas—again, for example, in the Hui areas. The most serious problems arose in Xinjiang (see Dreyer 1968, p. 100) and Tibet. In the latter, for instance, trouble had been building up since 1956; the collectivization drive in adjacent Sichuan had led many shepherds to flee to Tibet where they encouraged resistance to the Hans amongst the Tibetans. The situation was exacerbated by the Great Leap Forward, and culminated in the Tibet rebellion of March 1959. This rebellion—possibly encouraged by India and the USA (Brugger 1981, p. 199)—was soon squashed by the Chinese army, and the Dalai Lama fled to India. The regime clearly decided that this was a good opportunity to commence Tibet's further integration into China, which is why it became an AR (called Xizang) in 1965. There was more fighting between Tibetans and Chinese both before and during the GPCR, but the more tolerant policy of the 1970s saw a relaxation of tension between the two groups. The situation was helped by the release of many of the 1959 Tibetan rebels in the early 1970s. Since 1978, the Beijing government has made even greater attempts to improve relations with the Dalai Lama than they were already doing in the early 1970s, knowing that many Tibetans still owe their primary allegiance to him. This resulted in the Dalai Lama making a trip to China in 1982 to discuss the future of Tibet with the Chinese authorities. Unfortunately, the Dalai Lama made rather greater demands than his hosts had expected. He requested that Tibet be granted the same status the PRC has offered to grant Taiwan, and that areas inhabited by Tibetans in the provinces bordering Tibet be incorporated into a new, bigger Tibetan Autonomous Region. At present, both of these proposals have been rejected out-of-hand, and a *Beijing Review* editorial makes it quite clear that even the more liberal leadership now running China is not prepared to concede to what they see as excessive nationalist demands. In an article which refers disparagingly to 'separatists and others with ulterior motives' who 'continue to flaunt the misleading banner of an "independent Tibet"', the editors write that—

Neither is the request for merging all areas inhabited by Tibetans realistic. For centuries, the Tibetan people have lived in separate communities within four other provinces in addition to Tibet itself. Just like other minority nationalities in China, they exercise national regional autonomy and are organised into an autonomous region, several autonomous prefectures and autonomous counties. It is not reasonable to change the historically determined administrative divisions simply according to the distribution of nationalities. (*Beijing Review*, 15 November 1982, p. 3.)

Such statements, and the references to separatists etc., make it clear that nationalist sentiment in Tibet is still a force the Chinese have to reckon with; time will tell whether such nationalism will become a serious problem for the PRC leadership.

Although we have concentrated on Tibet, there have been many other cases of unofficial nationalism in modern Chinese history. These cannot be elaborated here; the important point to note is that even the unitarist Chinese state, dominated by one national group, has experienced a number of ethnic tensions and clashes.

WHAT CAUSES UNOFFICIAL NATIONALISM AND ETHNIC CONFLICT?

There are a large number of factors that lead to the rise—and, it should not be forgotten, sometimes the demise—of nationalism in its various forms. Sometimes, there are very particular factors playing an important role in a specific case of nationalism, and these cannot be examined here. Given their range, even the general factors will have to be analysed superficially. We can begin by making the obvious but not always sufficiently appreciated point that the different kinds of nationalism will be triggered by different factors. The second caveat is that, as with so many other phenomena analysed in this book, the factors have been separated here merely for the sake of better understanding; in the real world, many of them overlap and are difficult to disentangle. Once again, a mixture of hard evidence and informed guesswork is used in the analysis.

(a) Historical tradition

In many cases, nationalism and ethnic conflict in a given state predates communist rule; this is true of the three countries examined in depth here, but also of many others. The continuing tensions between the Aulaqis and Dathina in South Yemen, between the Kongo, Vili, Teke, M'bochi, and Sangha in the Congo—or numerous other examples one could cite—merely testify to the fact that communists have in most cases so far been unable to overcome traditional ethnic rivalries, which may be based on religion, territorial claims, feelings of exploitation, etc.

(b) Official and unitarist nationalism

Ironically, much unofficial nationalism can either be triggered or exacerbated by the regime itself, and is sometimes even a response to official nationalism. For instance, in their endeavour to create a national consciousness, the Bulgarian authorities no longer officially recognize ethnic differences in the population; this has led to hostility among some of the national minorities (e.g. the Turks), who wish to preserve aspects of their traditional culture. In 1960, in a somewhat similar attempt to break down ethnic differences between Czechs and Slovaks, the new Czechoslovak constitution specified that there were to be no more separate Slovak political institutions, which led to increased Slovak nationalist activity. Sometimes, one communist state's hostility to another can lead to increased ethnic tension within the former's own borders. For example, both Vietnam and Mongolia have had strained relations with China in recent years, and this has led to tensions between the Chinese living in Vietnam or Mongolia and other ethnic groups (as well as the state authorities).

Sometimes, as part of the attempt to create a new national consciousness for the whole country, communist authorities can be, or may be perceived as being, over-sympathetic to the unofficial unitarism of the dominant/largest ethnic group. For instance, the authorities might insist on the dominant group's language being learnt by all citizens, which can put the survival of minority languages at risk. This, too, can increase ethnic tensions. Minority groups may feel that their culture is threatened in such a situation and protest about this. Thus the nationalist wave in the USSR of the late 1960s/early 1970s was in part a response to the regime's toleration of Great Russian nationalism, whilst much of the Croatian nationalism of the same period was a response, amongst other things, to Serbian unitarism.

(c) Political structures

We have seen that communist attempts to integrate minorities on a gradual basis can be reflected in a federalized political system. Sometimes this will help the integration process, at other times it can help to perpetrate awareness of ethnic differences; whether the effect is beneficial or harmful really depends on other variables given in this listing.

Not only the nature, but also the size of a political system may be important. It is often argued that alienation caused by the growth of political and economic units is one of the factors leading to nationalism in the liberal democracies. Thus the integration moves taken during the establishment and development of the Common Market, for example, coincided with the rise in nationalist sentiment in some parts of Western Europe. If this is the case in the liberal democracies, there seems to be no obvious reason why this should not pertain also to the communist states, with the development of international organizations such as Comecon.

(d) Regime sycophancy towards a foreign power

Closely related to the last point is the fact that excessive sycophancy by a given communist leadership towards another communist party-state is likely to lead some citizens to feel that 'their' state has little real identity of its own, which can encourage allegiance to some smaller group. This has been happening to some extent in Afghanistan.

(e) Poor regime performance

Poor performance by a regime—especially in the economic sphere—can inspire unofficial nationalism. If the economy generally is performing poorly, many citizens will listen more sympathetically to local nationalist claims that the particular republic, autonomous region, etc. would do better were it to have more autonomy or even become a sovereign state.

(*f*) *Political climate*

The general political climate—whether the regime is being more oppressive or more liberal towards dissidence—can be seen to correlate with the state of unofficial nationalism. A liberal period can encourage nationalists to give vent to feelings of frustration which may have been suppressed at earlier stages. Conversely, when the situation gets out of hand, the regime can become more repressive again, deal harshly with a few nationalist leaders, and thus discourage others from pursuing nationalist activity. Thus the relative liberalization in Yugoslavia after Rankovic's fall in 1966 was accompanied by a rise of unofficial nationalisms, whilst the clampdown on these from about 1971/2 saw a decline in them. It is not only when the leadership consciously pursues a more liberal line on dissidence that nationalist aspirations are often more openly and widely articulated. If nationalists believe that the leadership is either explicitly disunited or at least unclear in its policies, they may take advantage of this. This is one part of the explanation for the recent troubles in Kosovo, which are worse than they ever were under Tito.

(*g*) *Rapid modernization*

If a communist leadership attempts to modernize (economically) a region associated with a particular ethnic group too rapidly, this too can lead to an increase in unofficial nationalism. Very rapid economic modernization—involving the breakdown of traditional life-styles and peer-group relationships as people transfer from the countryside to town, higher levels of education and political awareness, etc.—can lead to grave social tensions, which in turn can produce a nationalistic backlash. This was a major explanatory factor for the Tibetan rebellion of 1959, for instance. At a later stage of the modernization, and as part of it, *new national minority élites*—of industrial managers, party cadres, etc.—emerge, and these often aspire to run the affairs of their own area with less interference from the nation that was originally responsible for implementing the development process. The differences between the two sorts of nationalism just described—traditional backlash, and the growing aspirations of newly created élites—are analysed well in the Soviet context by Teresa Rakowska-Harmstone, who describes the latter phenomenon as 'new' nationalism (1974, esp. pp. 9–14).

(*h*) *Perceptions of unequal or unjust treatment*

Perceptions of unequal and/or unjust (the two terms are *not* synonymous) treatment can inspire nationalism. Given that communists often take power in countries with enormous regional differences, in terms of wealth and levels of development, it follows that they are going to have to treat different areas and therefore ethnic groups unequally (e.g. in terms of investment) if their long-term goal of an equal level of development in all regions (a more just society) is to be reached. The equalization policy can lead to the problems of rapid modernization just described in more backward areas. On the other hand, there may well be claims by some nationalists in these areas that the central authorities are not equalizing rapidly enough. This can create a dilemma for the authorities, since if they channel *too* much of the national cake into the less developed areas, this can encourage nationalism in the more advanced regions. Croatia and Slovenia constitute excellent examples, in that many Croatian and Slovene nationalists feel resentful of the fact that they are having to pay for the modernization of the less developed southern parts of Yugoslavia. This form of nationalism is not encountered only *within* states; citizens of wealthier states within Comecon, such as the GDR or Hungary, often express their resentment of the 'fact' (whether it is or not is a debatable point) that their own standards of living are being held back because of having to contribute towards the development of less developed countries such as Vietnam or Cuba. Finally, it should be noted that communist regimes are sometimes unequal *and* unfair, investing more in the better-off areas; this leads to feelings of deprivation in the less developed areas, which in turn can lead to nationalism.

There may also be a feeling amongst minority groups that the central leadership's interest in them and their territory is less because of a desire to create a harmonious society of equal but different nations than because of strategic and/or economic interests. For instance, many Ukrainians are very aware that their republic is of vital strategic interest to the Russians, since it is part of the corridor along which Germans have in the past marched into Russia. The Uighurs in the Xinjiang Autonomous Region and the Mongols both know that the Han Chinese are concerned with keeping both regions well under control on one level because both border onto the USSR. At another level, Georgian nationalists in the USSR, Croatian nationalists in Yugoslavia and Xinjiang nationalists in China feel that one of the reasons why the Soviet, Yugoslav, and Chinese leaderships respectively are so interested in keeping these areas within the fold is because of their above-average economic usefulness to the state. Georgia is seen as the garden of the USSR; Croatia is one of the most productive industrial areas of Yugoslavia; whilst Xinjiang is rich in important mineral deposits, including iron, oil, and uranium.

(i) Direct and indirect external stimulation

Sometimes, the government and/or the citizens of one country will encourage nationalist activity in another; we can call this direct external stimulation. For example, Albania has done and is doing this in Kosovo (although Meier 1983, pp. 59–60 gives an interesting and convincing argument as to why this is kept within bounds), whilst Bulgaria sometimes encourages Macedonian nationalism in Yugoslavia, and Hungary has urged Hungarians in Romania to stand up for their rights on various occasions in the past. By indirect stimulation, we mean that knowledge of the existence of and, in particular, any successes of other nationalist movements, either within the same state or elsewhere, can be an impetus to nationalists. The close temporal proximity of so much nationalist activity in both Eastern and Western Europe in the late 1960s/early 1970s was not merely coincidental.

(*j*) *Alternative organizations and leadership*

A final factor that can encourage or prolong nationalist feelings is the existence of an alternative organization to the state, around which nationalists can rally; this will often be a church (e.g. Lithuania, Tibet). This relates to the larger point—an appropriate one with which to finish this section—that any form of dissatisfaction, including nationalist ones, needs leadership if it is to become a political movement.

ARE PERCEPTIONS OF UNFAIR TREATMENT JUSTIFIED?

As we have seen, one of the many factors that can exacerbate ethnic tensions is the feeling among minorities that they are not being treated 'fairly' by the central authorities and/or the dominant ethnic group. But are such perceptions well founded? In order to begin to answer this, we need to look beyond the general policy statements outlined earlier to the actual treatment of minorities in communist states. There are numerous variables that could be looked at—numbers of books and journals published in minority languages, educational levels among minorities, etc.—but space is limited, and we have restricted our analysis to two significant areas, political representation and economic development. Unfortunately, the data available on these are patchy, and those who write on different countries do not always present data in directly comparable format. Hence, we can do no more than produce a sketch; in years to come, the picture should become clearer.

(*a*) *Political representation*

In this section, we shall consider briefly the representation of nationalities in both party and state organs.

Looking first at the USSR in recent years, the evidence suggests that, proportionately, Russians and Georgians have been overrepresented in the CPSU, the Ukrainians, Belorussians, and Armenians are just about right, whilst the other nationalities are underrepresented, especially the Central Asians and the Moldavians (for further details see Rigby 1968b, p. 378; Rakowska-Harmstone 1974, esp. p. 5; and *Partiinaya Zhizn'*, no. 14, 1981, p. 18). The pattern is such that Hill and Frank (1983, p. 39) have concluded that 'it will be a long time before the party is "representative" of nationalities in a sociological sense'. Miller (1982, pp. 16–17) has given a more detailed picture, which shows that minorities which are large enough to have a republic have been doing better in recent years in terms of gaining admission to the party (i.e. their admission rate is higher than the Soviet norm), whereas the smaller minorities (e.g. Tatars, Jews, etc.) have been doing worse. In sum, the pattern is complex. The picture at the top of the CPSU is also hazy. The Politburo itself has traditionally been dominated by Russians; this pattern changed slightly in the early 1970s, but has been reversed again recently (for a brief overview, see Lane 1982, p. 93); however, the numbers are relatively so small that one should not become too obsessed with percentages. But it does look as if the Russians are becoming more dominant in the Central Committee again, at the expense of minority groups (see Hough and Fainsod 1979, p. 648 and Lane 1982, pp. 92–3). At the local level, there has been a clear pattern of putting *local* nationals into *most* of the top party posts in recent years. For example, the First Secretary at almost all levels will be a member of the local ethnic group. This said, Russians are nearly always the Second Secretaries, so that the dominant ethnic group in the USSR certainly keeps its eye on the party officials of the minority nationalities.

Looking now at the state machinery, we see that the federal system itself is one way of giving 'proper' representation to the various nationalities of the USSR. Within the Supreme Soviet, not only is there one chamber specifically designed to give representation to national groups, but, overall, 61 different nationalities are represented in the Soviet, and only 43 per cent of deputies are Russians. The Presidium of the Supreme Soviet (i.e., the Soviet presidency) has to include 15 deputy chairpersons—one from each republic—among its 39 members. The Council of Ministers (i.e., the Soviet government) includes the chairmen of the 15 republic Councils of Ministers. However, the inner core of the Council of Ministers, the Presidium, does not appear to follow any policy of nationality representation. At the local level, the pattern adopted by the party seems to have been followed by the state—i.e., most of the top positions (e.g. members of republic Councils of Ministers) are held by local nationals, but Russians occupy certain key 'watchdog' positions. Thus local state security (KGB) and military chiefs will usually be Russian.

Yugoslavia has gone further than the USSR in attempting to ensure 'proper' representation for each national group, although success has been limited. Not until June 1982 did the LCY release figures on the ethnic composition of the party; when it did, it became obvious that there are huge differences between national groups in terms of membership of the LCY. For instance, only 4.6 per cent of Albanians have joined the LCY, whereas 20 per cent of Montenegrins have; over 12 per cent of Serbs are party members, but only 7 per cent of Croats. Although these figures might give the impression that the less satisfied groups are less likely to join the party, we must be cautious in drawing this conclusion, since the Slovenes—who enjoy the highest standard of living in Yugoslavia—are second only to the Albanians in *not* joining the party (all figures from Meier 1983, p. 54).

The situation at the centre is more satisfactory. Since 1969, many changes made in the equivalent of the politburo have been aimed at equal or near-equal representation of the major ethnic groups. Between 1972 and 1978, republics and autonomous provinces were given equal representation; before and since then, republics have slightly higher representation (now three members each) than autonomous provinces (two members each). This policy is repeated at the Central Committee level. The 11th Congress of the LCY (June 1978) elected a 165-member Central Committee, comprising 20 representatives from each republic and 15 representatives from the two autonomous provinces (plus 15 army representatives).The situation at the local level cannot be directly compared with that of either the USSR or China, since there is no ethnic group in Yugoslavia which dominates in quite the same way as the Russians or the Hans; in Kosovo, however, Serbs have done better than Albanians in terms of occupying the top political offices.

The central Yugoslav state organs have consistently been staffed in ways that show sensitivity to the multi-ethnic nature of the country. The federal principle applies not only to the assembly, but also to the state presidency, on which, since 1974, all the republics and autonomous provinces have one seat each. In contrast, the Yugoslav government (the Federal Executive Council) has kept to the principle of equality of the republics, but slightly lower status for the autonomous provinces.

Before moving on to China, we must briefly consider the special case of Kosovo; given the recent troubles there, the reader might wonder why the central Yugoslav authorities have not made what would seem to an outsider to be the relatively simple but symbolically important gesture of granting Kosovo republican status. As writers such as Remington (1979, pp. 232–3) have pointed out, the biggest problem here is that many Serbs would be very upset—and might demonstrate this overtly—if they felt that the Albanians were essentially being granted even greater autonomy, in the form of what the Albanians would doubtlessly see as their own republic. Early in this chapter, we referred to the fact that different groups can cite different points in history in their present claims of historical rights to a given territory; Kosovo is one such area, since both Serbs and Albanians can point to past centuries when they were dominant in the area. Hence the central authorities do not want to jump out of the frying pan into the fire (i.e. invite Serbian unrest in placating Albanian dissatisfaction), which largely explains why they have been improving the political lot of the Albanians in Kosovo without upgrading the autonomous province to a republic.

The problem of political representation in China is rather different from that in either the USSR or Yugoslavia, given the massive preponderance of one ethnic group. But an analysis of the ethnic composition of various party and state bodies suggests that even the Chinese have attempted to give some say at the centre to the ethnic minorities. Unfortunately, data on the ethnic composition of the CCP is not available. Some picture of the representation of ethnic minorities at the top of the CCP is available, however, if we concentrate on the five autonomous regions referred to earlier in the chapter. In general, the major minorities have done rather well at the top, both in the Politburo and the Central Committee (although Tibet and Ningxia have never been represented in the Politburo); further details can be found in Bartke 1981. This said, not all the representatives of autonomous regions have been natives of the area (i.e., they were not necessarily themselves members of the ethnic minority). At the local level of the party, the policy of increasing the proportion of local cadres and withdrawing Han cadres has been intensified in recent years. However, the evidence available suggests that many of the key posts at the local level (e.g. Party First Secretaries) were still—at least until very recently—frequently in the hands of Han Chinese (see e.g. Goodman 1980, pp. 50–2, D. Waller 1981, pp. 167–8).

Data on ethnic representation within the state organs used to be very scarce, but are now increasing. Within the unicameral National People's Congress, there is now explicitly a policy of allocating seats to every minority nationality. In the 5th National People's Congress elected in 1978, deputies representing minority nationalities accounted for 10.9 per cent of the total (i.e., they were proportionately overrepresented); this overrepresentation increased to 13.5 per cent in the 6th Congress (1983). Figures on representation in the State Council are not available, and there does not appear to be any policy of explicitly including representatives of the ethnic minorities (see e.g. the communique in *China Daily*, 21 June 1983, p. 1). The Deputy President of China since June 1983 is the Mongol Ulanhu, whilst several vice-chairpersons of the 6th (1983) NPC Standing Committee were explicitly chosen as representatives of minority nationalities. At the local level, the practice described for the party appears to apply to state offices too—that is, there is an increasing number of representatives of local nationalities, although many of the top posts have until recently been occupied by Han Chinese.

(b) *Economic development*

The data available on the relative economic development levels of republics, etc. in the three countries we are focusing on suggest that there may be *some* correlation between levels of development and nationalism/ethnic tensions, but also that the relationship is a highly complex one. The first difficulty is that a number of technical problems arise in trying to measure levels of development; these are way beyond the scope of this book. This problem notwithstanding, there is general agreement among analysts on certain overall patterns. Let us examine these, starting with the USSR.

It seems incontrovertible that people in the Baltic states are generally much better off than the 'average' Soviet citizen, whereas the Central Asians are worse off. Moreover, although the Central Asians were catching up the European Soviets for much of the period since the October Revolution, this process has virtually stopped since the mid-1960s, despite the greater proportion of investment in these less developed areas. There are several reasons for this, including the much higher birth rates in the poorer areas (for a survey see Clayton 1983, esp, pp. 76–7). This might lead one to expect more dissatisfaction in the Asian republics than in the Baltic; but we have seen that in fact the reverse seems to be true. To the extent that nationalism and ethnic tension in the Baltic area is related to economic issues—and we have seen there are other important factors involved, such as religion—it seems to be the case that many Balts *believe* they would have done even better had they not been part of the USSR; ultimately, of course, the validity of this belief cannot be conclusively proven one way or the other. On the other hand, Kazakhs, Uzbeks, etc. might compare themselves with Muslims in the Middle East, and decide that they have done better than they would have done in Iran, Tunisia, etc.

Turning to Yugoslavia, we see that the area that has experienced the most nationalist activity recently, Kosovo, certainly is the poorest area, and is in fact becoming poorer relative to other parts of the country. At present, the per capita income of Kosovars is approximately one-third of the Yugoslav average, and only one-sixth of that of inhabitants of Slovenia (Singleton 1983, p. 286). Moreover, growth rates in the period 1978 to 1980 were approximately half the national average. This is surprising given that Kosovo is naturally well endowed. It is perhaps even more surprising in view of the fact that Kosovo has received the lion's share of federal investments for regional development in recent years (well over one-third of the total in 1976–80, for instance—see *Yugoslav Survey*, no. 2, 1982, p. 15). There are a number of factors explaining this apparent paradox. Other Yugoslavs sometimes claim that it is because Kosovars are less diligent than, for instance, Croats; there *may* be some truth in this, but it is at most only part of the story. The second factor is that the Albanians—who constitute almost 80 per cent of Kosovo's population—have the highest birth-rate in Europe, so that there is some similarity to the situation in Soviet Central Asia (i.e., the ratio of non-working people, mainly children, to working people is becoming ever less favourable). Third, the deterioration of the economic situation in Yugoslavia as a whole in recent years has hit Kosovo harder than most of the more developed areas. This is related to the fact that investment in Kosovo in recent years has tended to be directed more towards infrastructure than productive capacity. In normal times, this makes sense; it seems pointless to build huge factories before one has a transport system capable of moving these factories' products to the shops. But in a recession, it means that recent large-scale investments yield little return. Also linked to all this is the fact that Kosovo has a shortage of trained personnel, and has therefore not always been able to make the best of what assistance it was given by the central authorities. Finally, the fact that the centre has attempted to decentralize much of the economy, especially since 1976, has meant that republics and autonomous provinces have been expected to take greater responsibility themselves for capital accumulation and investment. Expressing this another way, the decentralization policy means that the centre takes less from the republics and provinces (in the form of taxes, etc.), but consequently also has less to distribute. Thus, although more central funds are allocated to Kosovo than to anywhere else, these funds are small relative to what the province needs and is expected to produce itself. In such a situation, the already well-developed and wealthy areas tend to become richer, the poor poorer—a familiar enough situation in today's world.

Data on Chinese regional development are scarcer than on the other two countries being examined, but the general picture reveals similarities. Minorities that were already relatively well developed before the communists took power (e.g. the Zhuang, Koreans) have continued to maintain their position, whereas the early policy of not pushing assimilation too hard has meant that traditionally backward areas (e.g. Tibet) have remained well behind the rest of China. However, Mao did pursue a policy of reducing interregional inequalities from the late 1950s, and appears to have had *some* success in this; at times, central subsidies to some of the autonomous regions accounted for over 50 per cent of local expenditure, whereas the wealthy regions not only received no help but had to contribute towards the subsidies for the poorer regions (see Lardy 1978, passim and esp. 77–8, 130, and 181–4). More recent data suggest that the post-Mao leadership is continuing to subsidize the autonomous regions, at a higher per capita level than any ordinary province (see Donnithorne 1983, p. 100). However, it is not clear how much impact all this has had in terms of reducing differences, and Donnithorne has pointed out (1983, p. 103) that the central authorities have spent considerably less on developing more backward areas than they have on defence.

Do the data and the analyses we have on political representation and interregional inequalities in the USSR, Yugoslavia, and China tell us much? In fact, they reveal a great deal. To start with, they tell us something about how general policies are translated into practice, and give us *some* hints as to why groups feel underprivileged. Beyond this, they reveal many of the dilemmas faced by communists in dealing with ethnic tensions. For instance, we begin to appreciate how difficult it is to decide what is 'fair' and what is not. Let us consider the question of proportionate versus equal representation of ethnic groups, both of which have been tried in the communist world. If groups are represented proportionately, then one or two large nationalities could continually outvote smaller ones. On the other hand, equal representation for all nationalities can lead to the tyranny of a minority over the majority (i.e., several small groups forming a bloc to outvote a few large ones). In addition, it has to be remembered that ethnic cleavages are only one of many in any society, and communist leaderships have to strive for 'fair' representation— however this is defined—of groups distinguished by all sorts of other criteria (functions in the division of labour, sex, age, etc.). It is surely obvious that it is an extremely difficult task to achieve a mix that will be satisfactory to everybody. We have also seen how difficult it is to find an optimal pace and method of interregional equalization, one that will not trigger ethnic conflict. Above all, perhaps, we see that the more information and analyses we have on representation etc., the more scope there is for widely differing interpretations of these. For instance, some nationalists will actually resent the fact that more of their fellow nationals are participating in central political bodies, on the grounds that this represents a form of capitulation to whatever ethnic group dominates the centre. The low rate of Albanian membership in the LCY, for instance, may thus be more a reflection of Albanian hostility to Serbs than of the centre's opposition to—or 'unfair' treatment of—the Albanians. It has been suggested that regime tolerance of minority languages *might* be partially because a given regime feels it can socialize minorities into the official culture better by publishing more in their own languages (Dreyer 1975, pp. 60–1), which can give such a policy slightly sinister overtones. And Donnithorne (1983, p. 101) has argued that the centre's investments in roads and other facilities in Tibet has been less to improve the lot of Tibetans than to meet the needs of the Chinese military—which again casts the notion of 'fairer' treatment of ethnic minorities in a rather different light. In sum, communist leaderships can be accused of being unjust and/or having ulterior motives whether they appear to be attempting to improve the lot of minorities or not. We are back with the point that even 'hard facts' may mean different things to different people and that *perception* is all important. Thus it is not possible conclusively to answer the question 'are perceptions of unfair treatment justified?', because the notions of what is fair and what is unfair are so subjective.

IS UNOFFICIAL NATIONALISM A THREAT TO COMMUNIST RULE?

Many writers have argued that unofficial nationalism is growing in the communist world, and that such a development could undermine the communist regimes in years to come. Is this argument convincing? We would suggest that it largely depends on the particular communist country; this needs elaboration. First, it should be acknowledged that several communist states— including Cuba, Poland, Hungary, and Albania—have experienced and are likely to experience very little problem with nationalism or ethnic conflict, either because of ethnic homogeneity (e.g. Albania) or because of traditionally good relations between ethnic groups (e.g. Cuba—see Lambert 1977, pp. 241–2). But we must also be careful not to overemphasize the significance of ethnic politics in several of those countries which have experienced such problems (e.g. Vietnam, Romania, and the countries analysed in depth in this chapter). To start with, just as many Welsh nationals are not only not Welsh nationalists but are positively opposed to Plaid Cymru, so not every Tibetan or Kosovar or Ukrainian is fundamentally opposed to the central regime, and may well support it. Many members of ethnic minorities believe that the communist authorities genuinely intend to bring their standard and style of living up to that of the leading ethnic groups, but appreciate that this is a long and difficult process. Even if an individual's support for the centre is weak, he or she may feel that the situation would be even worse if local nationalist 'hotheads' were in charge. Second, it must be remembered that nationalism comes in waves, and surges tend to be followed by demise. Hence, if we witness a growth of nationalism/ethnic conflict in a given country, we should be wary of reaching over-hasty conclusions as to when this is going to 'finish'; in most cases, there is no obvious conclusion to the outburst, certainly not in terms of *major* change in existing political structures. Third, as McAuley (1984b, p. 180) and others have argued, if liberal democracies can cope with nationalism/ethnic conflicts, then it is far from obvious that most communist states will be unable to. Of course, liberal democracies have the escape valve of the ballot box—nationalist groups can stand for election, which often shows the weakness of their support and leads to a decline in activity—which the communist states do not. On the other hand, the communist states do have powerful security organs, which can keep most dissident political activity within manageable proportions.

This all said, some of the newer communist states are still not well established, and ethnic conflict in some of them (e.g. Afghanistan, Angola) *could* seriously undermine communist rule. In addition, in the event of a major crisis such as a war, nationalism could become a major political force in other, more established communist states; it is conceivable that this would result in a redrawing of the world map of sovereign states, such as occurred after the First and Second World Wars.

CONCLUSIONS

We have seen that nationalism takes many forms and is caused by many factors. We have also seen that communists have tried a variety of methods for overcoming unofficial nationalism, but with only limited success. It is probable that there are other paths to explore. The language problem, for instance, could perhaps be overcome if all citizens in a given communist state had to be bilingual—speaking their traditional tongue and some new one (e.g. Esperanto or, for practical reasons, English) which even the dominant group would have to learn. If the dominant nationality were in basically the same position, as regards language, as the minorities, the perception of what is sometimes called 'linguistic imperialism' would surely disappear. But this is only one possible solution to only one of the causes of friction. At the end of the day, communists seek change, and change invariably brings conflict to a greater or lesser extent. All that communist leaderships can hope for is to minimize ethnic conflict, not totally eradicate it, at least until the basic causes of tension—economic, political, social etc.—have been overcome. We are back yet again with the point that communists usually take power in economically relatively underdeveloped and often very unequally developed countries. It is easy enough to criticize the dominant ethnic group for sending specialists and politicians into the more backward areas in order to develop them—some see this as a form of imperialism—but skills need to be learned, and natives of the more backward areas will not always be able to use investments, etc. to the maximum advantage until they have been taught new techniques. This said, it is a highly subjective matter as to *when* the more backward ethnic groups are ready to take over from the dominant and more advanced nationalities.

For the foreseeable future, then, most communist states—certainly the more legitimate ones—should be able to cope with but not fully solve the problems of nationalism and ethnic conflict. Only when there is enough for all and no competition for resources (broadly understood) is it conceivable that nationalism—though not necessarily national identity and patriotism, which may well be psychological needs—will disappear. That day is a long way off. For now, at least it is a healthy sign that an increasing number of communist politicians and theoreticians (e.g. in Yugoslavia, and now also in the USSR) have come to realize that classical Marxism provides an inadequate analysis of nationalism, and are attempting a more sophisticated, less blinkered approach to the problems so many of them face.

Basic further reading

P. Artisien and R. Howells, 1981.
A. Bennigsen, 1980; 1984.
G. Bertsch, 1973.
W. Connor, 1984.
J. Dreyer, 1975; 1976.

G. Klein and M. Reban (eds.), 1981.
V. Meier, 1983.
T. Rakowska-Harmstone, 1974.
H. Seton-Watson, 1977.

14

RELATIONS BETWEEN COMMUNIST STATES

In the last chapter we considered ways in which ethnic tensions and territorial disputes between groups could erupt and affect relations *within* states; to some extent, many of the tensions *between* communist states can be analysed from a similar perspective. As has been emphasized at several points in this book, despite Marx's and Lenin's commitment to socialist internationalism, communist states almost invariably put their own interests—however these may be interpreted—above socialist internationalism if and when the two come into conflict.

Since this book is primarily concerned with domestic politics, the relations between communist states can be analysed only cursorily; readers whose appetites have been whetted can follow up their interests via the bibliography at the end of this chapter. The chapter is divided into two main sections—integrative and disintegrative forces. In the former, we shall look at two of the main organizations for integration in the contemporary communist world, Comecon and the Warsaw Pact; as shall be demonstrated, integrative moves do not invariably proceed smoothly. In the latter, one of the most troublesome relationships in the communist world—that between the USSR and China—will be analysed; there will also be brief references to a number of other conflicts between communist states. At the end of the chapter, an analysis of the reasons for the successes and failures of communist attempts at socialist internationalism will be made.

INTEGRATIVE FORCES

(i) Comecon

Comecon (the Council for Mutual Economic Assistance, or the CMEA) was founded in Warsaw in January 1949. It was established largely as a reaction to the Marshall Aid Programme—also known as the Marshall Plan—which was announced by the US in June 1947. Under this, the USA had offered to finance the recovery of national economies in Europe, including even the USSR, in the aftermath of the Second World War. Initially, the Soviets had responded very negatively to this plan, seeing it as a ploy by the Americans to increase their influence in Europe—including Eastern Europe, which had been coming increasingly under Moscow's influence. However, the Soviets did send a delegation to Paris in July 1947 to attend the conference that had been organized to discuss the details of the recovery plan; for a very brief period, the Soviets reversed their initially hostile position on the US proposal. But the Americans made it very clear in Paris that there were conditions attached to the offer. One very important one was that the countries participating should work towards greater economic integration and interdependence; trade barriers, for instance, were to be progressively reduced. On one level, the US was attempting to ensure that Germany would never again distance itself from its neighbours, as had happened in the 1930s with such disastrous consequences. But the Soviets (correctly) saw another side to the offer—that the US was hoping to develop Europe as a pro-US, liberal-democratic bloc. This, too, can be seen in terms of the US desire to avoid the horrors of 1939–45; but, of course, it can also be seen as a way of undermining Soviet influence in Eastern Europe. Thus, although the Soviets were as anxious as the Americans to keep Germany under control and ensure that it never again became the starting-point for a global war, Moscow had a fundamentally different approach to the problem. The USSR would maintain a buffer-zone of communist or pro-communist states around itself and, in particular, between itself and Germany. The Soviets therefore forbade the East European regimes from accepting the US offer. But Moscow had briefly favoured the US proposal, and countries such as Czechoslovakia and Poland had already declared their willingness to participate in the programme. The Soviet ban therefore led to tensions between Moscow and the capitals of several East European countries, and Stalin felt the need to do something, both to overcome the tensions and to appear to be providing an alternative to the Marshall Plan. The initial response was both coercive and vague. In September 1947, delegations from several European countries (all the East European communist states excluding Albania and East Germany, plus the two West European states in which the communists were strongest, Italy and France) met in Poland under Soviet auspices; this led to the establishment of a new organization, the *Cominform* (the Communist Information Bureau). This body was basically intended to bring the major European communist parties under stricter Soviet control, although its aims and raison d'être were never clearly defined. Although some Westerners saw it as essentially an updated version of *Comintern*—the Third (communist) International, 1919–43—this perception was not an accurate one. The Comintern had originally been designed to spread communist and Soviet influence throughout the world, whereas the Cominform was much narrower in scope, designed essentially to consolidate the Soviet gains in Eastern Europe—and possibly add one or two extra countries—following the World War II negotiations. In fact, the Cominform remained a very weak organization with vague aims of political and ideological integration; its role declined during the early 1950s, and it was finally dissolved in April 1956. As it became clear that Cominform was not capable of consolidating Soviet influence in Eastern Europe, so the more concrete notion of an organization designed to co-ordinate and eventually integrate the economies of Eastern Europe and the USSR came to the fore. The idea gained momentum as the West made rapid progress with its plans for economic collaboration. Thus, in line with the aims of the Marshall Aid Programme, the Organization for European Economic Co-operation (OEEC) was established in April 1948; this involved eighteen European nations plus the USA and Canada. Thus developments in the West and the USSR's perceived need to counter this effectively were the major factors leading to the establishment of Comecon—although classical Marxist notions of breaking down national barriers were also used as justification for the new organization.

The founding members of Comecon were Albania, Bulgaria, Czechoslovakia, Hungary, Poland, Romania, and the USSR; subsequently, the ranks were swelled, with the GDR joining in 1950, Mongolia in 1962, Cuba in 1972, and Vietnam in 1978. Only one country, Albania, has left Comecon (in practice by 1961, formally in 1968). In addition to the member-states, a number of other communist countries have special relationships of one kind or another with Comecon. Thus Yugoslavia has had 'limited participant' status since 1964, whilst many of the newer communist states (Afghanistan, Angola, Ethiopia, Laos, Mozambique, South Yemen) have observer status.

Formally, the highest body in Comecon is the Council, which has existed since 1949; it consists principally of heads of government from the member-states, and meets on average once per annum. In practice, however, the Executive Committee (established 1962, comprising mainly deputy-premiers, and scheduled to meet at least four times per annum) and the Secretariat (established 1954 and comprising largely full-time Comecon officials) are in many ways at least as powerful. The Secretariat is concerned very much with the day-to-day running of Comecon; its headquarters are located in Moscow. Several 'Council Committees' have also been created since 1971, and there are a number of other institutions and agencies attached to Comecon (for details see van Brabant 1980, pp. 179–218). But above all these is an informal Comecon body, the conference of First/General Secretaries of the communist parties. This has been meeting—very frequently—since 1958, and has potentially more influence on the general direction adopted by Comecon than any other body.

The official aims of Comecon are several, and are laid down in the Comecon Statute, which was adopted in December 1959 and came into effect in April 1960. They include raising the level of economic integration between the member-states; deepening the international division of labour between countries; accelerating economic and technical progress; constant raising of labour productivity in each member-state; bringing the economic development of the less developed states up to that of the most developed; and creating the conditions for a virtually simultaneous transition to communism by all the member countries.

Despite the formal aims of Comecon and the reasons for its establishment, it was a relatively ineffectual body in the early years, as might be inferred from the fact that there was no statute for more than a decade. Various steps were taken in the 1950s, but few were implemented in any meaningful sense. For instance, it was proposed in 1954 that member-states co-ordinate their national economic plans; this did not result in anything very concrete, however, and it was not until the 1970s that such plans really began to be co-ordinated (even then, this was mostly at a very general level). Specialization agreements were also signed in the mid-1950s; but, again, little came of these.

If the 1950s were characterized by inactivity in Comecon, the early 1960s were characterized by strife. In June 1962, at a conference of party secretaries held in Moscow, the USSR made concrete proposals for a much deeper international division of labour within Eastern Europe than had existed hitherto; the step was probably taken largely as a reaction to the increasing integration in Western Europe at the time, particularly within the EEC. The basic idea behind the new proposal was that some countries would concentrate on industrial manufacturing, whereas those naturally better endowed would concentrate on the primary industries (e.g. mining and agriculture). Such a plan received warm support from some countries (notably the GDR and Poland), but incensed some of the more agrarian countries, especially Romania. The Romanians argued that Marx's vision of socialism was one in which all countries would be highly industrially developed, and that the implications of the Soviet proposal were that some countries would remain backward rural communities. At the November 1962 Plenum of the Central Committee of the Romanian communist party, the Romanians decided not to accept any such plan. In February 1963, the Executive Committee of Comecon met and issued instructions to Romania which amounted to an order to abide by the Soviet-inspired policy. Romania responded by making it clear that it was indifferent to the order and to any threats of expulsion; as a country with more natural resources than many in Eastern Europe, Romania was in a better position for resisting the Soviets than many of its neighbours. The Romanians claimed that Comecon was supposed to encourage *co-ordination* rather than integration, and as a symbol of their view of the way this should be done began establishing formal bilateral ties with several communist states. This was all happening during one of the peaks of the Sino–Soviet conflict, and Romania received verbal support from both China and Yugoslavia. In this context, the Soviets were running the risk that if many other countries agreed with the Romanian position, then they would be able to leave the Soviet camp and possibly join the Chinese, as the Albanians had already done. It is therefore not surprising that the Soviets largely conceded to the Romanian demands. In July 1963, the party leaders again met in Moscow, and Gheorghiu-Dej's formula of co-ordination, bilateralism and full sovereignty was adopted. Khrushchev's notion of a supra-national Comecon organ (i.e., a body with powers to issue binding orders on individual communist states) was rejected. For the time being, Comecon remained a relatively weak, essentially consultative and symbolic organization.

The situation began to change in the mid-1960s. One major reason for this is that the new Soviet leadership (from October 1964) was both less impetuous and more firm in its convictions than Khrushchev had been. Having suffered the various international embarrassments of the early 1960s (e.g. the Cuban missile fiasco, the Romanian challenge), the new leadership was not prepared to allow the USSR to be humiliated again. One of the most important symbols of the new, firmer approach was the Warsaw Pact invasion of Czechoslovakia in 1968. Following this, the USSR reasserted itself in a number of ways, including the renewed attempt to turn Comecon into a significant organization. Romania had by this time a new leader too; although no less nationalistic than his predecessor, Ceausescu seems to have seen the writing on the wall following the August 1968 events, and reluctantly began to fall more into line within both Comecon and the Warsaw Pact. In 1969, Comecon held its 23rd (Special) Council session, which has been described by the Soviets as 'a *new landmark* in the development of socialist integration' (Senin 1973, p. 255—original emphasis). The session resolved to work out a 'complex and comprehensive programme' of economic development and integration, and this 'Complex Programme' was formally adopted at the 25th Council session in Bucharest in June 1971. This envisaged higher levels of both co-ordination and specialization between member-states. However, whereas the proposals of the early 1960s had been directed largely towards a *sectoral* division of labour (e.g. agriculture, heavy industry, light industry), the new programme was mainly concerned with a division of labour by *branch* (i.e., subdivisions of sectors). Thus the specialization proposals did not mean that any country would have to remain predominantly agricultural in the future.

The practical ramifications of the 1971 programme were several. First, there were a number of organizational developments, which were referred to briefly above. Both the Council and the Executive Committee remained essentially unchanged; neither became supra-national, and Comecon to this day has no supra-national body (member-states are, in theory, sovereign and not subject to instructions from any outside body). But three new bodies were created, and have subsequently proven to have considerable influence within Comecon. These were the Council Committees—one for planning and co-operation, another for scientific and technical co-operation, and a third for materials and technical supply. Second, joint financing of projects began in the early 1970s, with the establishment of the International Investment Bank, based in Moscow. Moreover, joint planning received a major boost with effect from the 1975–80 plan period. The policy of equalizing economic levels of development was pursued more actively in the 1970s, although the achievements were less than in some other areas of Comecon activity.

Finally, the international division of labour has deepened in recent years. For example, Hungary is the principal manufacturer of buses within Comecon; Poland, the USSR, and the GDR are the principal shipbuilders; Romania produces much of the oil-drilling equipment, etc.

But the fact that Comecon became considerably more active in the 1970s does not mean that all sources of tension between member-states had now been overcome. To some extent, tensions that either continued or arose were however tempered by forces outside the communist world altogether. Most notably, the tendency of countries such as Poland to turn towards the West in the early 1970s for finance and trade was cut short by the 1973 oil crisis and its aftermath. As the West sought to solve its own economic problems, so the East European states had to turn back towards Comecon and the USSR. But they were to find that there were problems here too. Although the Soviets initially claimed that the oil crisis was a capitalist phenomenon, it soon became clear that the economies of Eastern Europe were being affected too. One clear sign of this came in 1975, when the Soviets pushed through a pricing reform (the so-called 'Bucharest Formula') within Comecon which, in essence, advantaged those countries rich in natural resources—notably the USSR and, to a lesser extent, Romania—and disadvantaged those countries whose exports were principally of manufactured goods. The new arrangement linked prices for certain raw materials—notably oil—more closely to world prices, which meant in practice that prices for raw materials rose much more steeply than prices for manufactured items (for details see Kux 1980, pp. 27–34). Although the individual Comecon members did not complain as publicly as they might have done in the early 1960s, many hints of dissatisfaction were dropped, particularly in the heavily industrialized communist states of Northern Europe.

The opposing trends of integrative policies and disintegrative forces within Comecon have continued into the 1980s. As the Comecon economies have slowed down and many communist states have found that their debt situation *vis-à-vis* the West has either deteriorated or else not substantially improved, so the vested economic interests of individual countries have often been highly visible to the public. In short, there have been several signs in recent years of continuing disagreements within Comecon. Perhaps the most important one at present is one of mutual dissatisfaction between, on the one side, the USSR and, on the other side, the smaller member-states, particularly those of Eastern Europe. The basic problem is that the USSR often seems to feel that its commitment to its Comecon neighbours is holding back its own development. For instance, it has for many years supplied them with oil at prices linked to but still below those it could obtain on the world market, at a time when it could well have done with the higher prices—and the hard currency—the West would have paid. The Soviets have also made it clear that they feel that if the East Europeans want Soviet raw materials, then they are going to have to become more involved in the extraction of these. Although the USSR is enormously rich in minerals, for instance, many of these are located a considerable distance from the main areas of population and in inhospitable regions (e.g. Siberia). Hence the costs and difficulties of extracting them are huge, and the Soviets frequently complain that their Comecon neighbours are making insufficient contribution—in terms of investment, skills, labour, etc.—to the overall effort. Finally, the Soviets resent the fact that their East European neighbours often prefer to sell their best products to the West rather than to Moscow; the problem is that the East Europeans also want to maximize their incomes of hard currency. On the other side of the coin, many East Europeans in particular feel that they would do better if they were less tied to the USSR (via Comecon) and at liberty to trade on a much larger scale with the advanced Western economies. Moreover, they resent the fact that the USSR sometimes arbitrarily reduces supplies of raw materials—as it did with oil at the beginning of the 1980s—knowing that these countries are not in a position to make up the deficit from other sources. Signs of this disagreement were visible at the 1983 Council session held in Berlin (see, e.g. *The Financial Times*, 1 November 1983, p. 4) and more recently at the June 1984 conference of First/General Secretaries held in Moscow; the latter was in fact to have been held in May 1983, but was postponed because of differences between the USSR and Romania over the provision of energy and raw materials. It should be noted that the tensions do not arise *only* between the smaller states and the USSR. There have in recent years been several instances of bilateral projects between the smaller states themselves being deferred to some distant date, and of countries arbitrarily imposing restrictions on other Comecon members' imports and/or exports.

In sum, although Comecon has achieved much in terms of integration of the communist states' economies, there is still a very long way to go, and conflicts between the various member-states continue to hinder progress. One sign of just how far the communist states still have to go is revealed in the fact that, according to many analysts both in the West and in Eastern Europe, the international division of labour within Western Europe's EEC is far in advance of that within Comecon. This is almost certainly to some extent a function of the existence of the transnational corporations in the West, which have done a great deal to rationalize the division of labour between countries (i.e., the division of labour is not solely or necessarily primarily the result of goodwill between member-states of the EEC). However, this is not the whole story. Despite all the bickering within the Common Market, the general perception that one member is dominating all the others—which in turn feel they are over-dependent on one source—is not a feature of that organization as it is of the CMEA. Moreover, there is not the sense of restriction within the EEC that there is within the CMEA; any West European country is relatively free to leave the Common Market if it really wants to, whereas this would be considerably more difficult for a member of Comecon. These facts, and the feelings they engender, mean that moves towards greater economic integration in Comecon will continue to be faltering and problematic.

(*ii*) *The Warsaw Pact*

The Warsaw Pact (formally the Warsaw Treaty Organization or WTO) is the major international military organization in the communist world; it was established 14 May 1955. The reason given by the communists for its establishment is that it was a reaction to the Paris Agreements of October 1954, which became operative in May 1955, and which permitted the remilitarization of West Germany and its inclusion in NATO (the North Atlantic Treaty Organization). This undoubtedly *was* a—perhaps the—major reason for the establishment of the Warsaw Pact; certainly, the organization did not come into being as an immediate reaction to the setting up of NATO, which had occurred some six years earlier, in April 1949. Moreover, the Soviets had let it be known at the end of 1954 that they would retaliate in some way were West Germany to be admitted to NATO. But there was almost certainly more to the establishment of the WTO than this. Following the Second World War, not only Germany but also Austria was occupied by allied troops. According to the Austrian State Treaty—which the Soviets knew they would be signing on 15 May 1955—all occupying troops were to withdraw from Austria after the signing of the treaty. In addition, Austria was to become a neutral, with no military ties to any country. As pointed out in chapter 12, this notion of neutrality found considerable support throughout Eastern Europe, especially in Hungary. Thus the Soviets were probably attempting to pre-empt such demands by bringing the countries of Eastern Europe together in a military alliance just before the signing of the Austrian treaty. A related point is that, under the terms of the peace treaties the USSR had signed with both Hungary and Romania in 1947, the Soviets had the right to maintain a military presence in these two countries in order to protect the lines of communication between the Soviet Union and Austria; once the Soviets had withdrawn from Austria, this right would disappear. The establishment of the Warsaw Pact thus meant that the Soviets now had a justification for maintaining Soviet troops in both countries. Soviet military personnel did indeed stay on in both, although they were forced to leave Romania in 1958 when Bucharest refused to renew the 'status-of-forces' agreement with Moscow.

Unlike Comecon, all the members of the Warsaw Pact other than the USSR are European communist states. The original members were Albania, Bulgaria, Czechoslovakia, the GDR, Hungary, Poland, Romania, and the USSR; Albania in practice left the pact in 1961, although its formal resignation was not announced until 1968, when Tirana strongly criticized the Pact's invasion of Czechoslovakia. Again unlike Comecon, there are no countries with observer status at Warsaw Pact meetings, although China did enjoy such status in the 1950s.

The major official aims of the Warsaw Pact are to safeguard the security of member states and to increase military co-operation. The WTO is thus form-ally a defensive organization, and article eleven of the treaty provides for the dissolution of the organization should a 'General European Treaty of Collec-tive Security' ever be signed and become operative. Although self-defence against outside aggression is a major *raison d'être* of the Warsaw Pact, this is not necessarily its only aim. One *possible* long-term aim is aggression against the Western liberal democracies. A more significant aim up till now has been identified by Robin Remington, who argues that the principal function of the WTO is to act as a 'channel for communication or even conflict resolution among the European Communist states' (1971, p. 8). She provides case-studies of conflicts between the USSR and three of its WTO allies (Romania, Czechoslovakia, and the GDR), and shows how the pact has been used in dif-ferent ways to resolve these conflicts. In short, this interpretation of the Warsaw Pact sees it as an organization more concerned with relations between communist states than between communist and non-communist states.

The notion that the WTO is an organ for political co-ordination and inte-gration as well as a military bloc is to some extent reflected in its organiza-tion. This has become increasingly complex over the years, so that even specialists do not fully agree on the details (compare e.g. Caldwell 1975, esp. p. 8; Cason 1982, esp. pp. 138–41; Herspring 1980, esp. pp. 5–7; A. R. John-son *et al.*, 1982, esp. pp. 151–5). However it appears that the main bodies now are the Political Consultative Committee (the PCC) and its Permanent Commission and Secretariat; the Committee of Defence Ministers; the Mili-tary Council; the Joint Staff; the Committee for the Co-ordination of Weapons and Technology; the Committee of Foreign Ministers and its Sec-retariat; and the Joint Command. As may be inferred from their titles, several of these organs are staffed primarily by politicians rather than by military personnel. Most notably, the PCC—which is the most senior body within the WTO—comprises the heads of party, heads of government, foreign and defence ministers of the member-states. It was established in 1955, and meets on average less than once a year (although supposed to meet twice annually), primarily to determine general political and military developments of the member-countries. What of other bodies? Following the invasion of Czecho-slovakia, there were a number of organizational reforms—the so-called Budapest Reforms—within the WTO. As Erickson (1981, p. 151) points out, demands had been building up for these for some time *before* the invasion; but it seems reasonable to assume that the events of 1968 brought the whole question of WTO organization and the relationship between the USSR and its East European neighbours very much to the fore. It was as a result of discus-sions held by the PCC in Budapest in March 1969 that four new bodies (those listed immediately after the PCC above) came into being. It is sometimes ar-gued that the Soviets permitted the establishment of these new bodies pri-marily in order that they may have even more channels through which to be able to exert influence on the East Europeans. Whilst this may be true, it is just as plausible to suggest that the Soviets felt the need to consult more with the East Europeans, and to give them at least the appearance of having more say in the pact decision-making process— these two explanations are to a large extent mutually compatible—than had been the case hitherto. In all events, the four bodies were established. The Committee of Defence Ministers (CDM) was to meet 'when necessary'; in practice it has met on average once a year. One of its main tasks is to discuss and ratify decisions of the Military Council. The latter consists solely of military personnel, tends to meet twice a year, and has as one of its primary functions to decide on the major activities of the armies, navies, and air forces of the member-states for the following year. The Joint Staff consists of the chief of staff of the Joint Command (a Soviet) plus the first deputy chief of staff from each member and country of the WTO; it works particularly closely with the Committee of Deputy Ministers and the Military Council. The Committee for the Co-ordination of Weapons and Technology is staffed by military personnel and is concerned—as its name suggests—with the integration and modernization of weapons systems and other military equipment; very little is known about this body. A second major set of reforms was introduced in 1976. Most importantly, yet another consultative body—the Committee of Foreign Ministers—was established. This usually meets once or twice a year, and is designed to increase the level of co-ordination of member-states' foreign policies. The final body, the Joint Command, is responsible for the actual organization of military activity; it has been in existence since the establishment of the WTO.

As with Comecon, so the level of activity within the Warsaw Pact has fluctuated over the years. In the 1950s, the organization was relatively inactive. One of the few major developments at this stage was a move away from sheer numbers of soldiers towards greater dependency on technology and equipment, which resulted in an overall reduction in the size of the military establishments in most member-states. But from the early 1960s, the situation began to change dramatically. There were at least three reasons for this. First, the new Commander-in-Chief of the joint armed forces from February 1960, Marshal Grechko, appeared to be far keener to promote military integration and generally to upgrade the role of the WTO than his predecessor, Marshal Konev, had been. Second, the international situation was becoming very tense again, as evidenced by the Bay of Pigs episode in April 1961, the Berlin crisis of August 1961 and the Cuban missile crisis of 1962. Third—and despite these tensions—Khrushchev wanted to keep Soviet military spending in check so as to be able to invest more in agriculture and other areas of the economy; by emphasizing *joint* operations, some of the pressure on Soviet defence spending could be reduced. In short, the WTO became a far more active organization. For instance, whereas there had only been one joint military exercise during the 1950s, there were no less than nineteen in the period

1961–8 (Herspring 1980 p. 4). Another significant development in the 1960s was the major updating of military equipment; this in itself was important, but of particular significance was the fact that the modernization was selective. Basically, the 'Northern Tier' states (i.e., the GDR, Poland, and Czechoslovakia) were developed much more than the 'Southern Tier' states (Romania, Bulgaria, and Hungary).

As the Warsaw Pact became more active, so conflicts between the member-states became more visible. Two of the major issues of contention in the mid-1960s concerned the nationality of the commander-in-chief, and the right of control over nuclear weapons. In the case of the former, Romania and Czechoslovakia in particular criticized the fact that the military head of the Warsaw Pact had always been a Soviet; despite the complaint, Grechko was replaced in 1967 by yet another Soviet, Yakubovskii—who was in turn replaced by Soviet Marshal V. Kulikov, the present commander-in-chief, in 1977. As regards the latter issue, the Soviets made it very clear in 1968, at the time of the signing of the nuclear non-proliferation treaty, that they intended to keep a monopoly over all nuclear weapons within the Warsaw Pact.

But the single most important event in the history of the WTO during the 1960s was the invasion of Czechoslovakia in August 1968. This was and remains the first and only time that the WTO had engaged in real as distinct from simulated military activity. The Romanians refused to participate in the action, reflecting once again the great differences that exist between them and, in particular, the USSR.

Following the invasion of Czechoslovakia, the Warsaw Pact entered a third phase—one in which, as we have seen, its organization was made considerably stronger and more complex. Joint exercises were also significantly increased. It was in this period that the West started referring to the 'Brezhnev Doctrine', according to which the Soviets are said to allow their bloc partners freedom in their domestic politics as long as this is not perceived to have major negative implications for other members of the bloc (in particular the USSR itself). In short, it is a doctrine of limited sovereignty of states. In this atmosphere of a newly confident USSR, even the Romanians fell into line for a while; for instance, they participated in Warsaw Pact joint exercises on a much larger scale than hitherto.

By the beginning of the 1970s, the Soviets had firmer control over the WTO, and the organization had grown in importance. Partially because of this enhanced Soviet confidence, and partially because of the marked improvement in East–West relations in the early 1970s, the number of joint exercises in the WTO declined markedly after 1972. Relations between member-states also appeared to improve at this time. But by the mid-to-late 1970s, there was a resurgence of overt tensions within the WTO. In particular, there was a renewed upsurge of overt Romanian dissatisfaction. For example, when NATO announced in May 1978 that its members' defence budgets were to increase by 3 per cent, Moscow made a proposal for a similar increase in the defence budgets of WTO members. The Romanians made it very clear that they could not and would not increase defence spending on this scale. Nor were they prepared to integrate their forces more with the WTO as Moscow had requested. The Romanians did receive some support for their position from other states, although most of this was relatively well hidden from outside observers. Poland is one of the countries that is rumoured to have supported Romania; but its economy was already in such a sorry state that the Soviets agreed to exempt it from the 3 per cent increase anyway.

Conflicts within the Warsaw Pact have continued into the 1980s. For instance, both the GDR and Czechoslovakia have been less than totally enthusiastic about the deployment of the new Soviet-controlled nuclear missiles on their territory since the end of 1983. This debate is essentially an updated version of the 1960s dispute over 'trigger-control'. Moreover, Romania and Bulgaria have been advocating a nuclear-free zone in the Balkans. At present, this is not a major concern for the Soviets, since the area is not due to receive nuclear weapons anyway. But if the arms race and a deterioration in East–West relations were to lead the Soviets to want to install nuclear missiles in Bulgaria or Romania, it would almost certainly lead to another major conflict within the Warsaw Pact. One sign of Romania's concern about its position within the WTO generally is the fact that in early 1985 it showed some unwillingness to renew its membership of the pact, which was to expire in May 1985; in the event it did renew this, but with some reluctance. Finally, there is also rumoured to be considerable, continuing dissatisfaction amongst several East European states at the fact that the Soviets rarely provide them with the latest military technology and equipment. It is not merely that the Soviets themselves have the more advanced equipment, but—even worse— that they sometimes provide non-WTO members, notably in the Middle East, with this.

In sum, the history of the Warsaw Pact bears a marked similarity to that of Comecon. In both cases, the organization has become much more active since the 1960s, after a relatively inactive beginning. But in both cases, the smaller partners have often been critical of Soviet policies and dominance, with Romania being the most outspoken critic within both organizations. The Romanians have even criticized the use of the term 'socialist internationalism' when the Soviets have wanted to include this in Warsaw Pact communiqués. Bucharest argues that this term is often a synonym for Soviet domination, and has on various occasions successfully insisted that a term which it feels is less loaded—'international solidarity'—be employed. This is just one example of many one could cite to show that although the USSR dominates the Warsaw Pact, it is not able to have its own way all the time. The smaller countries do sometimes stand up to the USSR, and do manage to extract concessions. Moreover, the smaller countries have sometimes been able to use the WTO for their own ends, in support of foreign policy stances of major importance to them; Edwina Moreton (1978) has provided a very interesting case-study of the East Germans doing this. In short, we must be wary of an over-simplistic and inaccurate picture of the relationship between the USSR and the other members of the Warsaw Pact. Moreover, it should be borne in mind that many of the kinds of conflicts that have arisen within the WTO bear some resemblance to disputes within other military alliances, such as NATO and ANZUS.

Before moving on to a consideration of the more explicitly disintegrative forces within the communist world, a few words on the alliances and position of those communist states not in the Warsaw Pact are in order. Most of these states belong to an essentially Third World organization called the Non-Aligned Movement (NAM). This began to emerge after the Second World War, largely on the initiative of the Indians, Burmese, and Egyptians. The idea was to create an alliance of countries that did not wish to side with either the West or the communist bloc. Two meetings were held in Delhi in the late 1940s, and the Bandung Conference of 1955 was a milestone in the development of the NAM. The first summit conference was convened in Belgrade in 1961; 25 countries were represented, including Vietnam, Cuba, and Yugoslavia. By the time of the fifth summit, which was held in Sri Lanka in 1976, the movement's membership had risen to 86 countries, mostly from Asia, Africa, and Latin America, and including many communist states. However, tensions between communist states have emerged at NAM conferences. Perhaps the most significant example became very visible at the sixth summit, held in Havana in September 1979. At this, the Yugoslavs (and others) questioned the alleged non-alignment of Cuba. During the 1960s—and despite Cuba's moves towards communism—the Cubans and Soviets had frequently displayed profound disagreements in foreign policy, especially regarding the scale and nature of assistance to be given to revolutionary groups in the Third World (see Edmonds 1983, p. 54). In a nutshell, the Cubans felt that the Soviet policy of 'peaceful coexistence' with the West was overriding the communist superpower's commitment to the spread of revolutionary change. But these differences began to disappear after 1968, and the Soviets and Cubans worked closely together on various projects, especially in Angola and Ethiopia, in the mid-1970s. It was in this context that the Yugoslavs argued that Cuba's status as a non-aligned country was now in serious doubt. Certainly, the sheer numbers of Cuban military personnel in Africa revealed the huge growth of Cuban involvement in that continent; in 1966, it was estimated that there were less than a thousand such people in Africa, whereas the 1978 figure was 38–39,000 (figures cited in Eckstein 1982, p. 208). This in itself would not have been so important had it not been public knowledge that the Soviets were directing much of the activity of these soldiers. At the Havana conference, the Cubans retorted that they were not tied to the Soviets, and had always supported revolutionary movements. Although they managed to secure the backing of most members of the NAM at the summit, they did have to compromise on their original position, which was that there was a 'natural alliance' between the NAM and the communist world. They are now aware of a fairly widespread feeling that they are militarily and politically too close to one of the superpowers to be considered truly non-aligned, and will have to be wary of further involvement with the Soviets in the Third World in the future if they are to retain their position within the NAM. Indeed, they are currently winding down their activity in Africa. It is ironic that it was another communist state that brought the whole issue into the open and caused the Cubans so much embarrassment within the movement in the late 1970s (for further details see Leogrande 1980, esp. pp. 45–52).

Parenthetically, we can note that in the 1970s Moscow often perceived it as being in its own interests to be involved *vicariously* in Third World countries via an allegedly non-aligned Third World state (i.e. Cuba); this probably still pertains. There are various reasons for this. One is that many developing countries have become highly suspicious of Soviet motives, and see the USSR essentially as another industrialized expansionist power that does not always fully appreciate or care about their problems. Another is that Moscow knows that the West finds it more difficult to criticize indirect involvement by the Soviets than direct, especially in the military sphere. Thus, until such time as the Cuban-Soviet relationship is explicitly and more forcefully condemned by the NAM, the Soviets have a useful 'back-door' entrance to Third World countries undergoing revolutionary upheaval. Of course, it is another question as to whether they always *want* such involvement, since they often discover that they are then expected to provide substantial economic and technical aid to such countries. This, too, can and does lead to tensions within the communist world.

DISINTEGRATIVE FORCES

As will already be clear from the above analysis, even integrative moves within the communist world have often come into conflict with national interests. Many of these national interests are rooted in traditional territorial claims, most of which predate communist power in the various states. Brzezinski has summarized this well—

The list of potentially disruptive and far from dormant territorial disputes capable of bitterly complicating the stability of the Soviet-East European bloc ... was quite impressive. At some critical juncture Bulgaria could have claims on Yugoslavia (Macedonia); Albania on Yugoslavia (Kosmet [i.e., Kosovo]); Hungary on Rumania (Transylvania); Rumania on the Soviet Union (Bessarabia); Poland on Czechoslovakia (Teschen); Poland on the Soviet Union (Lvov, etc.); East Germany on Poland (Szczecin or Wroclaw). In the first four cases, the situation could be emotionally dramatised by the presence in the disputed territories of sizeable minorities of the same nationality as the potential claimant and, generally, subjected to traditional discrimination. ... If the conflicting Chinese–Soviet claims and the Chinese–Mongolian aspirations were also listed, territorial irredenta in the Communist camp become quite impressive indeed. (It would seem that of all the communist countries, Cuba alone did not have a territorial claim to make on another Communist country!)   (1967, p. 440.)

Since Brzezinski wrote this we have seen examples of territorial conflict between countries not listed by him—e.g. the Sino-Vietnamese dispute and its implications for Kampuchea and Laos. Although many of the squabbles between communist states are essentially reflective of official irredentist claims, some involve much more than this. Similarly, although many of the conflicts are essentially localized and have relatively little impact on third communist states, this is not invariably so.

The first major publicly visible conflict between communist states emerged in 1948, when the Soviets and the Yugoslavs fell out with each other to such an extent that the former had the latter expelled from Cominform. This was not a territorial dispute as such, although both the Yugoslavs and the Bulgarians were irritated at the fact that the moves they had recently taken towards a federalized Balkan union—moves which Stalin had earlier encouraged—were now being frowned upon by Moscow. But this incident only reflected a deeper irritant to the Yugoslavs, namely the fact that the Soviets wanted to force conformity on Cominform members from above. The Yugoslavs felt that this went against their understanding of socialist internationalism, which permitted both greater diversity and greater equality between countries all allegedly building socialism. Tito did not have the same feeling of deference and gratitude towards Stalin and the USSR that some of the other communist leaders of Eastern Europe had, to no small extent because the Yugoslav communists had come to power largely through their own efforts. In all events, this represented one of the earliest examples of Soviet views on 'socialist internationalism' being perceived by some communists in power as synonymous with the USSR's attempt to dominate the communist movement.

Since then, there have been numerous conflicts. Many of these have been between the smaller states and the USSR (some of which were considered above). Others have been between China and the smaller states, whilst a third group have been between the smaller communist states themselves. A good example of the latter is that between Albania and Yugoslavia. Tensions between these two have been visible on numerous occasions since at least 1944 (for general analyses of tensions between the Balkan communist states see King 1973 and Lendvai 1969) and reflect both the territorial dispute mentioned by Brzezinski, and fundamental ideological differences. Whereas Yugoslavia has a reputation for being the most liberal and tolerant of the communist states, Albania still has an essentially Stalinist system (which helps to explain why the Albanians fell out with the Chinese in the late 1970s, as the latter moved towards the less authoritarian political style of Deng Xiaoping).

Given the sheer number of conflicts, and the fact that some have already been touched upon, I have decided to look at only one conflict in detail. Since it is the most important conflict—in terms both of the size of the countries involved and the repercussions for other states—the obvious choice is the Sino-Soviet dispute. The bizarreness of this conflict is reflected in the fact that—through much of the 1970s at least—both the USSR and the PRC had warmer relations with the capitalist world than with each other.

The Sino-Soviet Conflict

The Sino-Soviet conflict began to emerge in the 1950s, became very overt in the 1960s, and festered throughout the 1970s. In recent years, there have been signs that the two giants of the communist world are now more willing than they have been for many years to work at overcoming their differences. But there is still a very long way to go, and a 1984 article in *Beijing Review* claims that, despite recent negotiations, 'the nature of the Sino-Soviet relationship remains unchanged' (9 July 1984, p. 31).

The nature of the conflict is highly complex, and cannot be fully understood without examining both Moscow's and Beijing's relationships to third countries. Nevertheless, we can at least identify both historical landmarks in the conflict and the major factors involved; as with almost any process occurring over many years, the relative balance of the component factors varies over time.

When Mao came to power in 1949, he did so almost in spite of Stalin. Stalin had maintained an ambivalent attitude towards the Chinese communists since the 1920s, often supporting the Guomindang and urging the communists to work with them. Although Stalin did change his attitudes somewhat by the late 1940s, he was urging caution on Mao well into 1949; the Chinese communists owe very little to the Soviets for their successful take-over. Mao never forgot this, as revealed in the fact that in 1962, he traced the Sino-Soviet dispute back to 1945, when Stalin had attempted to stop war between the CCP and the Guomindang and had urged Mao to collaborate with Chiang Kai-shek (Strong 1972, p. 23). Nevertheless, Mao did respect many of Stalin's ideas and policies, especially the notion of 'socialism in one country'. He also admired many of the Soviet achievements. Largely for these reasons, early communist China was highly emulative of the Soviet Union, and signed a Friendship Treaty with Moscow in 1950. But following Stalin's death in 1953, the situation slowly began to change. The Chinese were already disappointed at what they considered to be insufficient support from the Soviets in the fight against the West during the Korean War (1950–3); over the next few years, a number of other issues were to be added to this list. But the growing dissatisfaction was not one-sided. For instance, the Soviets were irritated by the Chinese in 1955, when Beijing made it clear that it did not feel the Soviets should attend the Bandung Conference, held in April, since this was supposed to be for African and Asian states only. In fact, the qualifications for attendance were less to do with geography than with economic levels of development, and China argued that it had far more in common with the Third World countries of Africa and Asia than did the highly industrialized USSR. But the Soviets felt that there was more to the Chinese position than Beijing was revealing. Moscow seems to have believed that the Chinese were trying to build up their influence in the Third World, so that the Soviets now retaliated by trying to improve relations with other Asian states (e.g. India, Burma, Afghanistan). Apparently, they believed that the Chinese would, if given the opportunity, attempt to build up a complex of satellites similar to the USSR's own in Eastern Europe. The Soviets had not demonstrated any major interest in Asia hitherto, but, as they thought they saw China trying to increase its influence in the region—sometimes by force, as with India in 1954—so they increased their activities.

The Chinese leaders, like most in the communist world, were taken aback by Khrushchev's de-Stalinization speech of February 1956. Nevertheless, they initially supported the new line on Stalin, especially since they were about to introduce their 'Hundred Flowers Campaign' of 1957. However, as the Chinese tightened up domestically by late 1957, so they reassessed the Soviet de-Stalinization policy. By the time of the celebrations of the fortieth anniversary of the October Revolution (November 1957), Mao was calling for an end to de-Stalinization and had started attacking what he saw as Soviet revisionism. Understandably, the Soviets objected to this, and retaliated by accusing the Chinese of dogmatism (for a useful survey of the ideological conflicts between China and the USSR at the end of the 1950s/early 1960s, and many of the key documents, see Dux 1963).

Yet another factor in the growing dispute was Beijing's charge that the Soviets had in June 1959 broken an agreement—made in October 1957—to provide nuclear weapons to the Chinese. Although the Chinese eventually overcame this problem by developing their own atomic bomb—first tested in 1964—the incident clearly left a bitter taste in the mouths of the Chinese leadership. The Chinese felt threatened by the West, and had been involved in major military confrontations with capitalist countries throughout the 1950s (e.g. the Korean War, the Formosan Straits crisis of 1955, the Quemoy crisis of 1958). They argued that these incidents testified to the real dangers facing China, which they felt the USSR should acknowledge and appreciate. After all, in each of these cases the Chinese were facing a superpower which, only a few years before, had used atomic bombs in the area (i.e., the USA in Hiroshima and Nagasaki).

The mounting tensions came to a head in 1960. In April of that year, the Chinese published a series of articles, 'Long Live Leninism', in which they accused the Soviets of having renounced their original Leninist aims; it was a very strong attack. The Soviets responded by withdrawing economic aid and advisers to China later in the year, leaving many major projects in which the Soviets had been involved, such as the bridge over the Yangzi at Nanjing, incomplete. The dispute was now out in the open, and each side continued to show its disapproval of the other. In 1961, Chinese premier Zhou Enlai insulted the Russians by walking out of the 22nd CPSU Congress. In the following year, the Soviets actually supported a non-communist power in its struggle with a communist power, when they took the Indian side in the Sino-Indian war. And in 1963, there was a very public exchange of letters between the CCP and the CPSU, in which each side blamed the other for the poor state of relations.

Although the change of Soviet leadership in 1964 led to hopes in some quarters of an improvement in Sino-Soviet relations, this did not materialize. Mao was in a radical mood, as reflected in the GPCR, and thus in no mood to start compromising with the Soviets. In fact, relations worsened still further in the late 1960s, culminating in actual border fighting between Chinese and Soviet troops on the Ussuri river in 1969. This appeared at the time to be so serious that some commentators felt it could develop into a full-scale Sino-Soviet war (see e.g. Salisbury 1969). Partially because both sides realized how easily the situation might escalate, the border fighting was in fact short-lived. Moreover, the Chinese now slowly began to change their attitudes towards the West, which had practical ramifications for the Sino-Soviet dispute. Hitherto, the Chinese had adopted a very hostile posture towards the capitalist world; largely under the influence of premier Zhou Enlai, they now began to warm to the West, especially to the USA. To some extent, this change reflected Chinese fears of the possible effects on China of the growing *rapprochement* between Moscow and Washington (see Ulam 1983, p. 42). The new Chinese policy was warmly welcomed by the West; the US was keen to use the Sino-US *rapprochement* as a lever in its negotiations with the USSR (see Kissinger 1979, p. 886). Signs of the fundamental change in attitude in both East and West included the admission of China to the UN in 1971 and President Nixon's visit to China in 1972. Thus the bilateral Sino-Soviet relationship had now changed into a trilateral one involving the West, with each communist state attempting to gain some support for its position in the dispute from a third party.

Following Mao's death in September 1976, there was soon speculation that the Sino-Soviet relationship could change significantly. For some time, in fact, the Chinese seemed to be so preoccupied with their domestic political arrangements that the big, thorny question of the relationship with Moscow (and as a corollary with Washington) was not a major focus of attention. However, as Deng consolidated power, so signs began to emerge of a possible improvement in relations; many Western observers felt that Deng's more pragmatic approach to politics in general would probably result in a less hostile approach towards Moscow. This is in fact what has happened.

The beginning of the new phase has been traced back to 1979 (Griffith 1983, p. 20). At that time, the Soviets urged the Chinese to renew the 1950 Sino-Soviet Treaty of Friendship; China refused, but did agree to discuss its relationship with the Soviets providing the latter were prepared to talk about a range of Chinese concerns in addition to the question of the Sino-Soviet border. The situation looked relatively good. But then the Soviets intervened in Afghanistan, which led to a rapid deterioration in relations between Beijing and Moscow once again. However, the Chinese appeared to have begun a major reassessment of foreign policy in 1981, one major ramification of which was that Beijing now started to view the two superpowers more equally. In other words, the USA was now seen in a less positive light than before (largely because of the Taiwan issue and the strongly anti-communist rhetoric of President Reagan), whereas the USSR was seen in a somewhat less negative light than hitherto. Expressed crudely, China seemed to be saying that the superpowers were virtually as bad as each other, but that China must maintain a realistic relationship with both. Moscow was quick to recognize this, and made a number of proposals for negotiations. The Chinese were slow to accept, but eventually agreed to the October 1982 discussions between deputy foreign ministers. Andropov warmly welcomed the then Chinese foreign minister, Huang Hua, at Brezhnev's funeral in November 1982, and both sides seemed optimistic about the future of the relationship. Since then there have—as of early 1985—been four more rounds of negotiations. As mentioned above, the relationship has in fact essentially stalemated of late—although the negotiations continue, which in itself shows how far the situation has improved in comparison with the 1960s and 1970s. Let us now examine the major points of contention in the current negotiations.

At present, the Chinese have spelt out four major problem-areas which must be resolved before a normal relationship can be established with the USSR; these points are considered below. For their part, the Soviets maintain that the Chinese are being insensitive to legitimate Soviet security concerns and the alleged intentions of the West to become more involved in the affairs of a number of Asian states. What, then, are the four major issues?

The first is the question of the Sino-Soviet border; at over 4,000 miles, this is the longest land-based frontier between two states in the world. The Soviets have withdrawn many of their troops from the Ussuri and Amur regions since 1969, but there has been a buildup of Soviet troops and weaponry in the Soviet Far East as a whole in recent years, which is hardly conducive to a lessening of tensions. The territorial issue is a complex one, with claims and counter-claims going back at least as far as 1689, when the first treaty on the Sino-Russian frontier was signed; the point made in chapter thirteen about different groups referring to different periods in history to endorse a current claim is highly apposite here. In fact, there are signs that both sides would be willing to make compromises on the border issue. However, not only is this to some extent contingent upon the Soviets making concessions on other issues, but there is a fundamentally different approach to the question anyway. Basically, the Soviets would prefer to settle the issue on a piecemeal (i.e., section by section) basis, whereas the Chinese would prefer to consider the whole frontier and reach a once-for-all solution as they have done *vis-à-vis* their border with several other countries. According to Bonavia (*The Times*, 5 February 1970, p. 9), Moscow's reticence is largely because the Soviets fear that the Chinese want more territory than the Chinese actually do want. The problem is further complicated by at least three sub-issues. Firstly, many of the weapons—including nuclear missiles—located in the Far East of the USSR could be directed at 'bourgeois' enemies (e.g. the USA, and perhaps in the long term Japan) as much as at China, so that the Soviets will not willingly remove them. Conversely, it is understandable why the presence of such weapons so near to their border causes concern to the Chinese (see Griffith 1983, p. 28 for evidence of Chinese concern at the stationing of SS-20 missiles in the Soviet Far East). The second aspect of the problem is that there are a number of ethnic groups that straddle the border (e.g. Uighurs and Kazakhs), and both the Soviets and the Chinese are fearful that the other side will attempt to exploit this fact to its own advantage (i.e., will encourage irredentist claims to the other country's disadvantage). Finally, there are important resources along some stretches of the disputed frontier. Probably most important are the uranium deposits in Xinjiang (Griffith 1964, p. 14); until 1954, the USSR had enjoyed the right to joint mineral exploration of the region, and no doubt wishes it still had that right—although this factor does not appear to have figured prominently in the most recent period of the dispute.

The second problem-area specified by the Chinese is the People's Republic of Mongolia (formerly known as Outer Mongolia). This is in fact closely linked to the territorial/border dispute. The Chinese have long felt that the Soviets have too much influence in what is supposed to be a sovereign state. Outer Mongolia was largely under Chinese control during the Qing dynasty; it gained autonomy following the 1911 Chinese revolution, and became a People's Republic in 1924 following the 1921 revolution. Since then, Ulan Bator has been very much under Moscow's influence, which irritates the Chinese; for example, they have been very critical of Mongolia's membership of Comecon since 1962 (on all this see Wallace 1983, p. 459). However, of late the main issue has been the existence of Soviet troops in Mongolia—the Chinese would like to see them removed.

Third, there is the question of Soviet support for the Vietnamese occupation of Kampuchea. For many years it was unclear whether the Vietnamese were closer to Moscow or to Beijing; although they have consistently shown that they still intend to maintain some independence of Moscow, they have nevertheless clearly moved towards the USSR and away from China since about the mid-1960s (Comecon membership is one sign of this). To no small extent, this is all in line with traditional (i.e., pre-communist) hostilities between Vietnam and China. China was highly supportive of Pol Pot's regime in the mid-1970s, largely because of its hostility to Vietnam. It is hardly surprising, then, that China was very critical of Vietnam's invasion of

Kampuchea at the end of 1978 and the installation of a pro-Hanoi government, which Beijing refused to recognize. It is since that time that there have been a number of skirmishes between Vietnamese and Chinese troops on their mutual border. The Chinese want the Soviets to condemn the Vietnamese presence in Kampuchea and to recognize the Kampuchean communist government of the mid-1970s. But the Soviets now have access to strategically very important military bases in Vietnam (at Da Nang and Cam Ranh Bay), and—for this and other reasons—are highly unlikely to accede to this demand.

Finally, there is the issue of Soviet occupation of Afghanistan. Although the Afghan-Chinese border is a short one, Beijing is nervous at the thought of being increasingly encircled by heavily pro-Soviet states. One of the problems with the Soviet desire to have buffer states along as much of its frontier as possible is that what Moscow sees primarily as protection may be perceived as further encirclement and partial aggression by Beijing (or indeed other capitals). The Soviets do not appear to appreciate this, and feel that the Afghan issue should not be China's business. This all said, the Afghan issue in itself is, as Segal (1984, p. 210) points out, probably the least important of the four, and there could almost certainly be a marked improvement in Sino-Soviet relations, even if the Soviets stayed in Afghanistan, if agreement could be reached on the other issues. After all, Soviet involvement in Afghanistan gives Moscow a bad image in the rest of the world—not only the West, but also the Third World. From the Chinese point of view, this factor is a major compensation for the encirclement problem.

Some of the key differences of the past are now no longer contentious issues between Beijing and Moscow. For instance, the fact that the USSR and the PRC were at very differing stages of development and, to a large extent as a consequence, had very different views on ideology, domestic and foreign policies, has now become much less of a source of tension. An excellent reflection of the fundamentally different approaches to and perceptions of the world that once existed between the USSR and China is contained in the following extract from a 1963 CPSU letter to the CCP

To follow their [the CCP's] line of thinking, it transpires that if a nation walks in rope sandals and eats watery soup out of a common bowl—that is communism, and if a working person lives well and wants to live even better tomorrow—that is almost tantamount to the restoration of capitalism. (*Pravda*, 14 July 1963, p. 3.)

The Chinese are now much more sophisticated and pragmatic in their policies, and in this sense are better able to appreciate the Soviet way of thinking. Closely linked to this is the fact that the Chinese have, fortunately, dramatically reassessed their attitudes towards war; they now accept that widespread death and suffering is just as undesirable for citizens in communist countries as for citizens in other types of political system. Moreover, the sudden major decline of Soviet economic and technical aid to the Chinese in the late 1950s and 1960s embittered the Chinese at the time, but made them look even more to their own resources, so that nowadays they do not feel the need for Soviet assistance in the way they once did. This, too, has helped the relationship.

But there are still significant long-term differences between the two sides, in addition to the specific points elaborated above, and it is far from obvious that a compromise position can be reached on some of them. The most basic problem is a long-standing fundamental difference between the Soviet and Chinese approaches to sovereignty. The Soviets—more explicitly the Russians—have always had a basically expansionist drive, which they now attempt to justify in terms of spreading 'socialist internationalism'. Admittedly, they tend only to attempt further expansion when this does not appear to endanger the Soviet Union itself in any way (i.e., expansionism is always secondary to the security of the USSR, and Moscow will not normally attempt to bring more countries into its sphere of influence if it suspects that third parties—notably the USA—will react violently). Nevertheless, this is a different approach from the Chinese. Although the Chinese communists have not been above 'spreading the message to' (i.e., annexing) neighbouring areas, such as Tibet, this is the exception, and the Chinese have long criticized Soviet expansionism. In the 1960s and early 1970s, the derogatory term used by the Chinese to describe this aspect of Soviet foreign policy was 'social imperialism', a term used particularly frequently after the intervention in Czechoslovakia. This term has in recent years been replaced by the somewhat tamer 'hegemonism', but the basic criticism is no less valid. China has been subject to too much foreign interference in its own affairs in the past not to be nervous at Soviet long-term intentions, and it will be many years—if ever—before the Chinese overcome their suspicions. This all said, the present Chinese interpretation of US global intentions means that Beijing will have little reason to permit a major deterioration of its relationship with the USSR until and unless either of the superpowers begins to adopt a fundamentally different position on world affairs.

There are a number of other underlying and ongoing factors which neither side mentions much nowadays but which could hinder an improvement of relations in the future. One factor that has played a role in the past and *could* be important again in the future is personality clashes between the leaders of the two countries. Reference was made earlier to Mao's ambivalent attitude towards Stalin; Mao was more explicit in his criticisms of Khrushchev, whom he genuinely seems to have believed was reneging on the aims and aspirations of the 1917 revolutionaries. The Chinese leaders were less sympathetic towards Chernenko than they were towards Andropov. Although this question of personality clashes should not be overemphasized—one would expect it to be secondary to other variables—it must nevertheless be incorporated into any analysis of the Sino-Soviet conflict. The same argument applies to the issue of racial tensions between the two states. There is abundant evidence to show that many European Soviets (especially Russians) have racist attitudes towards Asians, including the Chinese. For example, Yevtushenko's poem 'On the Red Snow of the Ussuri' (written after the 1969 border conflicts) carries on a 'yellow peril' tradition in Soviet literature that can be traced back to Blok's 'Scythians' and beyond. The Chinese themselves have criticized Soviet racism on various occasions in the past (see e.g. the quotations cited in Ionescu 1965, p. 103). Although there is less evidence of Chinese racism towards the Soviets, the latter have certainly accused the former of being racist towards them (see, e.g. *Pravda*, 14 July 1963, p. 1).

The rift between the communist giants has in the past led them—particularly the Chinese—to adopt some extraordinary positions in international relations. For instance, China supported West Pakistan against East Pakistan (now Bangladesh) during the Pakistani civil war (1971), to some extent because the Soviets were supporting the latter. Soviet condemnation of General Pinochet's regime in Chile was one of the factors that led the Chinese to recognize it. While the Soviet Union has traditionally been hostile towards the European Community—even though it now reluctantly accepts it as a reality—the Chinese welcomed it, seeing in such integrative moves the formation of a bloc in Western Europe to counter and check Soviet influence elsewhere in Europe. From this short list, it becomes clear how little meaning 'socialist internationalism' has when applied to some sets of relations between communist states.

CONCLUSIONS

We have seen that, unfortunately, there are at least as many disintegrative as integrative forces operating in communist international relations. As Western socialist writer Christopher Chase-Dunn has put it, 'Proletarian internationalism has long been endorsed by socialist movements, but the concrete achievements of this endorsement have been disappointing.' (1982b, p. 282.) Why is this?

Marx's expectation that socialism would come about in highly developed industrial states, in which national differences had already largely disappeared, is one of the reasons he devoted so little attention to the question of relations between socialist states. As with so many other problems in the communist world, the fact that communists have usually taken power in countries which, by classical Marxist standards, were not yet ripe for socialism is one of the factors explaining the tensions that exist and have existed between communist states. Such countries are often at different levels of development from each other, and often do not fully appreciate the problems and perceptions of other states. Closely connected to this is the fact that different countries—and even different leaders within these countries—interpret both Marxism and socialism/communism in different ways, and are frequently aggressive in defending their own interpretations. This is hardly conducive to a marked improvement in communist international relations. Then there are the traditional territorial disputes, which further complicate international relations. The existence of one or two very large states is a fourth source of tension, since smaller states often justifiably feel that they are being treated as inferior within a movement they feel should be one of equals. It is all very well for the Soviets to claim that they have a duty to defend 'socialism' in Czechoslovakia or Afghanistan or Hungary if there are political developments of which they disapprove taking place in those countries, but if the Czechoslovaks or Afghans or Hungarians felt that socialism was under threat in the USSR, there is precious little they would be able to do about it. Even *if* Marx's writings can be invoked to justify the notion of a more developed and civilized country incorporating and/or interfering in the affairs of less developed countries, Soviet and Warsaw Pact interference in Czechoslovakia in 1968 does not fit this description. In my opinion, there is no justification in any version of Marxism for the 1968 invasion; it was the action of a superpower looking after its own interests, and should be seen clearly as such. It had little if anything to do with socialism. That one action has been the source of many tensions between communist states ever since. This notion of inequality in communist international relations does not refer only to size. Another major factor is the proximity of smaller communist states to the communist giants—particularly the USSR—and even to non-communist states. Thus Albania and Yugoslavia are small, but they are able to criticize Moscow more than, say, Czechoslovakia, Poland, or the GDR simply because they have no common border with the USSR and are not as strategically located (i.e., they do not lie between the USSR and West Germany). However, the existence of a rift between the two biggest communist states has given some of the smaller ones opportunities to assert their independence of one or other of the giants in a way that might not otherwise have been possible. Thus, not only was Albania able to leave the Soviet camp in the 1960s, but Romania was able to assert itself more, by implicitly threatening to move into the Chinese camp. Conversely, Vietnam and North Korea have on various occasions sided more with one of the giants than the other, and in doing so have been able to maintain a relatively high level of independence of both (although this is currently more true of North Korea than of Vietnam). Although particular relationships will fluctuate, tensions will continue in the communist world for the foreseeable future, largely because many of the factors listed above still pertain. Moreover, the experiences of the most advanced industrial states do not bode particularly well for the communist world. Admittedly, the leading capitalist states have not fought each other now for more than four decades. But the internationalization of capital, the spread of the transnational corporations, etc. have not reduced national differences to anything like the extent Marx had predicted. Tensions exist between the US and its West European allies, and between the West Europeans themselves. The US and the West Europeans have their differences with the Japanese. At the time of writing, there were tensions between New

Zealand and the US. And so the list goes on. Some Marxists might retort that these states are all capitalist, and as such are constantly seeking to increase profits, production, consumption, etc., and that the natural limits of the world's resources are going to come into conflict with this drive. This, they would argue, in turn leads to conflict between these states. This may well be so. But if it is, it does not suggest any better future for the communist states. As argued at length in chapter five, they have generally accepted the same basic philosophy of growth in production and consumption that Western states have, so that the sources of tension in both are very similar. The future of 'socialist internationalism' is not going to be without problems.

Basic further reading

J. van Brabant, 1980.
Z. Brzezinski, 1967.
R. Clawson & L. Kaplan (eds.), 1982, esp. Pt. 1.
K. Dawisha and P. Hanson (eds.), 1981.
R. Edmonds, 1983.

G. Evans and K. Rowley, 1984.
W. Griffith, 1983.
G. Ionescu, 1965.
R. Remington, 1971.
J. Steele, 1985.
W. Wallace, 1983.

15

TOWARDS AN UNDERSTANDING OF THE NATURE OF COMMUNIST SYSTEMS

HAVING studied the politics—formal and informal, domestic and international—of the communist states, we are now in a position to examine various approaches to and interpretations of such politics. Are communist states typically totalitarian, as many writers in the mass media still maintain? Are they state capitalist, as many Western Marxists would argue? Or are they something else altogether? In analysing the major approaches to communist politics it is appropriate to make three broad divisions—into Marxist exceptionalist, non-Marxist exceptionalist, and convergence (both Marxist and non-Marxist) approaches. We shall find that in this topic, even more than the others we have studied, the field has been dominated by approaches to *Soviet* politics. In assessing the usefulness of such concepts, however, I shall when possible and appropriate consider them on a comparative basis. One final introductory remark is that some of the approaches have already been dealt with—either cursorily or at length—in earlier chapters; these approaches will be listed and only *briefly* analysed.

MARXIST EXCEPTIONALIST APPROACHES

Before examining the two major Marxist exceptionalist approaches (i.e., ones which see communist systems as being basically different from other kinds of system), the point should be made that one such approach is that of the regimes themselves. Thus, according to the particular country, the label for the political system may be 'developed socialism', 'socialism', 'building the basis of socialism', etc. Such terms are principally ideological, however, in the sense that they are designed to reflect a regime's achievements and goals rather than be a penetrating analysis of the strengths, weaknesses, and actual nature of the system. Let us therefore move on to a consideration of the degenerate workers' state and state capitalist arguments.

(i) Degenerate (deformed) workers' state

The degenerate or deformed workers' state approach is associated above all with Leon Trotsky. In exile from the late 1920s until his murder by Stalin's henchmen in Mexico in 1940, Trotsky tried to analyse what had gone wrong in his native Soviet Union. What he saw was a society in which the means of production had been largely taken into social ownership, but one in which there was still a ruling group. He called this group the ruling 'stratum' (some-times 'caste'), and identified it very much as the Soviet bureaucracy. For Trotsky, this bureaucracy had distanced itself from the masses, who were in fact *atomized* (i.e., the subgroupings in society, between the individual and the state, had broken down). One of the major reasons for this was that the October Revolution had not triggered the international revolution the Bolsheviks had been expecting. Therefore, the Soviet economy had had to develop largely through its own devices, starting from a *relatively* backward position. In order to catch up with the advanced industrial societies, the USSR had had to undergo a draconian phase in which power was highly centralized.

Since the means of production in the USSR were not privately owned, Trotsky argued that there could not be the property-based class system typi-cal of capitalism. One important ramification of this for him was that wealth could not be accumulated and inherited, so that class-based privilege was not transferred from generation to generation. Moreover, Trotsky argued that distribution in the Soviet Union was based on a plan—even if an imperfect one—rather than the market, and that production was principally for use rather than for the sake of production (and hence profit-making) itself. In these senses, the term 'capitalism', even if modified to 'state capitalism', seemed to him to be an inappropriate one for the USSR.

On the other hand, Trotsky did see the Soviet workers' state as having degenerated or been deformed by the power of the bureaucracy, so that it was far from being a genuinely socialist—let alone communist—society. In that it was neither capitalist nor socialist, Trotsky described the USSR as a *transitional* society, and argued that a second revolution would be necessary to convert it into a genuinely socialist system (on all this see Trotsky 1967).

Others who have taken an essentially similar approach to Trotsky's in-clude Isaac Deutscher and Ernest Mandel. The latter argues that the commu-nist states are at an early stage of the transition to real socialism and communism, and that, under certain circumstances (which he calls a 'social counter-revolution') they could become capitalist. But if they did, they would be capitalist in the sense that Western states are, rather than what the next group of Marxists to be considered call 'state' capitalist (see e.g. Mandel 1970 and 1974); Mandel and a number of other Western Marxists explicitly reject the notion of state capitalism as a contradiction in terms, for reasons that are dealt with in the next section.

(ii) State capitalism

The 'state capitalism' theorists—e.g. Tony Cliff, Bruno Rizzi—started from a Trotskyist base and accept several of the premises of the degenerate workers' state argument. For instance, they accept that the mass of the popu-lation has been atomized by the state (see e.g. Cliff 1974, pp. 18–22), and that society is a transitional one. They also accept that the root of the problem is the fact that the USSR (the country they concentrate on) underwent an allegedly socialist revolution before the conditions for a genuinely socialist revolution were ripe. They acknowledge that this was understandable in the circumstances, and that the non-realization of the socialist revolution in the advanced capitalist countries was largely to blame for the degeneration of the Soviet system. However, their analysis of this system now begins to diverge from that of the degenerate workers' state approach. Most notably, they draw what is in essence a distinction between form and substance. Thus they accept that there is a form of planning in the USSR, but argue that the driving force behind this is very similar to that in capitalism, namely commodity fetishism (in this context meaning production for the sake of exchange and profit rather than for use, and the social relations such production engenders). Indeed, in its competition with capitalism proper, state capitalism increasingly adopts the values of its competitor. This started as the USSR's need to protect itself against capitalist attack, which meant that huge sums had to be extracted from the workforce to spend on defence. But the USSR has gone further than mere self-defence now, and has become involved in an arms race with the West. This in turn means that more and more surplus created by the workers is used to finance a massive defence bill rather than an improvement in their own lifestyle (not just in terms of goods, but of education, health, etc.). Inasmuch as the Soviet Union is involved in competition with basically market-oriented economies, its own ability to plan and distribute in a rational, socialist manner is severely limited.

Another major plank of the state capitalism argument is that there is a new type of ruling class in the Soviet Union. The basis of this argument can be traced to the writings of Milovan Djilas. Djilas—who had at one time been number two politician in communist Yugoslavia—wrote a swingeing critique of the communist system from a Marxist perspective. Like Trotsky, he was appalled at the distortion of socialist ideals he saw all around him. But Djilas did not accept Trotsky's analysis of the nature and problems of Soviet (and other communist) society. Most fundamentally, the Yugoslav argued that the concept of a 'ruling stratum' was grossly inadequate and, in its implications, potentially misleading. Developing a line of thought writers such as James Burnham had used *vis-à-vis* industrial managers, Djilas argued that the notion that class is based solely on formal *ownership* of the means of production is an overly rigid application of Marx's ideas. According to Djilas, it is *control* of the means of production that is all important, and that forms the basis of class division; in Marx's time, ownership and control were virtually identical, so that no clear conceptual differentiation had been made. Although Djilas himself was not fully satisfied with the 'state capitalism' label for communist states, his argument is close on several features to that of Cliff, and his position on class at least is accepted by the state capitalist writers (for further details see Djilas 1966).

But a major component of Marxist class analysis is that the ruling class is able to maintain its position largely through the transfer of its privileged class position from one generation to the next. Surely this does not pertain in the 'state capitalist' societies? Cliff argues that privileged position *is* passed on, even if wealth itself is a less salient feature of class antagonism than in 'pure' capitalism. Thus

> The state bureaucracy . . . possesses the state as private property. In a state which is the repository of the means of production, the state bureaucracy—the ruling class— has forms of passing on its privileges . . . Every bureaucrat will try more to pass onto his son his 'connections' than he would, let us say, a million rubles (even though this has importance). Obviously, he will at the same time try to limit the number of com- petitors for positions in the bureaucracy by restricting the possibilities the masses have of getting a higher education etc. (Cited in Lane 1978, pp. 175–6.)

The state bureaucracy has, in this view, essentially the same position *vis-à-vis* the masses as the bourgeoisie has in a capitalist state. It is these non-elected bureaucrats who decide how to distribute the surplus created by the indus- trial and agricultural workforces rather than these workforces themselves. In this sense, there is class antagonism.

The class analysis in the state capitalism argument has been the subject of much criticism, from Marxists and non-Marxists alike. If the ruling class is the 'state bureaucracy', where does the communist party—which many would see as the single most important repository of power in communist systems—fit in? Djilas is more vague than Cliff on this. But even Cliff is imprecise on where to draw the line in defining 'the bureaucracy', and the identity of the new ruling class is difficult to ascertain.

Some (e.g. Burnham) have argued that the very notion of 'state capitalism' is a nonsense if by this we mean that the state owns all (or nearly all) of the means of production rather than just a part of them. The reason is that capi- talism is a system of private ownership and competition; if both of these are missing, there is no longer capitalism. Cliff *et al.* would argue that it is the social and political ramifications of private ownership rather than the legal concept *per se* that matters, and that the *international* competition means that communist economies are in competition anyway. Clearly, the argument starts to go around in circles, since much hinges on mutually exclusive definitions.

Without elaborating these two Marxist approaches any further, certain points should already be clear. The first and most important is that they adopt a radically different approach to the question of class. The degenerate workers' state adherents maintain that there is no ruling class, only a ruling stratum/caste in the USSR (and other communist states). Typical of their approach towards property is Deutscher's, in which it is argued that what

> . . . this so-called new class lacks is property. They own neither means of production nor land. Their material privileges are confined to the sphere of consumption. Unlike the managerial elements in our [i.e., Western] society, they are not able to turn any

part of their income into capital ... They cannot bequeath wealth to their descendants; they cannot, that is, perpetuate themselves as a class. (Cited in Brown, 1974, p. 25.)

Thus, despite the fact that both approaches are allegedly Marxist, they cannot agree on a Marxist definition of class—which is a reflection of the imprecision of the original concept. The degenerate workers' state adherents' argument that the existence of a planned economy in the USSR and elsewhere means there is a fundamental difference between such countries and the capitalist states is rejected as an essentially marginal point by the state capitalist writers. Without going any further, it is obvious that the two approaches place their major emphasis on different aspects of the social, political, and economic systems, and that they cannot agree on basic Marxist concepts such as class and exploitation. One reason for this is that, as Konrad and Szelenyi (1979, pp. 39-44) point out, the types of society with which we have been concerned in this book were simply not considered by Marx. It is thus an understandable—though not necessary—consequence that classical Marxist analysis is going to be either insufficient or inappropriate for an analysis of such societies. The Marxist method becomes problematic if basic concepts used in it are unclear. One other weakness of the Marxist approaches is that, precisely because of Marx's own emphasis on the importance of the economic relations to all the other aspects of the state and society, the more obviously *political* dimensions of such countries are often overlooked or insufficiently analysed. This difference of emphasis and focus is one of the major factors distinguishing most Marxist approaches from most non-Marxist approaches. Let us now turn to a consideration of the latter.

NON-MARXIST EXCEPTIONALIST APPROACHES

The range of non-Marxist approaches is very wide and, as is the case with the two major Marxist 'schools' outlined above, no two individuals adopting a given approach will agree entirely on even that one analytical framework. Nevertheless, there have been a number of major discernible schools; we shall deal in this section with totalitarianism, the bureaucratic approach, and the cultural approach—in short, with approaches that treat communist states as fundamentally different from Western ones. Some of these have been both elaborated at much greater length and much more influential than others, and this is to a limited extent reflected in the different lengths of the following subsections.

(i) *Totalitarianism*

In the early years of Western academic study of the USSR and other communist states, the most widely accepted approach to these systems was the totalitarian. To no small extent, this reflected the general atmosphere in the West during the late 1940s and the 1950s—a period nowadays often referred to as the First Cold War—when memories of the Second World War were still fresh and at a time when Stalin's Russia seemed to many to be in practice little different from Hitler's Germany. Thus much of the totalitarian writing was largely—and probably understandably—a product of a particular historical epoch.

The actual term 'totalitarianism' predates the Cold War period, having first been used in the 1920s; even Trotsky used it on occasions to describe the USSR. Writers who have used it have mostly (but not exclusively—see Barber 1969, p. 7) emphasized the differences between totalitarian dictatorships and other forms of dictatorship and autocracy (see e.g. Friedrich 1969, p. 124). In particular, they emphasize that totalitarianism is very much a product of the twentieth century, when technology has provided the possibilities for much deeper and wide-scale involvement by the state and its dictator in the lives of ordinary citizens than in any earlier period. Although the concept has been increasingly discarded by Western scholars since the 1960s, there are still some analysts (e.g. Odom 1976) who maintain that it remains the single most useful key to an understanding of politics in the communist world.

One perceived feature of communist societies that adherents of both the major Marxist and most totalitarian approaches agree upon is atomization. Thus Hannah Arendt has written that 'The chief characteristic of the mass man' (which she sees as the typical condition under totalitarianism), 'is ... his isolation and lack of normal social relationships' (Arendt 1958, p. 317); while William Kornhauser had essentially the same phenomenon in mind when he referred to a 'massified' society (1960).

Of all the analyses of totalitarianism, still the best known and most influential is that of Friedrich and Brzezinski, who in a 1956 book identified what they saw as the six principle features of a totalitarian dictatorship. These were:

(i) an official ideology, consisting of an official body of doctrine covering all vital aspects of man's existence to which everyone living in that society is supposed to adhere, at least passively; this ideology is characteristically focused and projected toward a perfect final state of mankind, that is to say, it contains a chiliastic claim, based upon a radical reflection of the existing society and conquest of the world for the new one;

(ii) a single mass party led typically by one man, the 'dictator', and consisting of a relatively small percentage of the total population (up to ten per cent) of men and women, a hard core of them passionately and unquestioningly dedicated to the ideology and prepared to assist in every way in promoting its general acceptance, such a party being hierarchically, oligarchically organised, and typically either superior to, or completely intertwined with the bureaucratic government organisation;

(iii) a system of terroristic police control, supporting but also supervising the party for its leaders, and characteristically directed against not only demonstrable 'enemies' of the regime, but against arbitrarily selected classes of the population; the terror of the secret police systematically exploiting modern science and more especially scientific psychology;

(iv) a technologically conditioned near-monopoly of control, in the hands of the party and its subservient cadres, of all means of effective mass communications, such as the press, radio, motion pictures;

(v) a similarly technologically conditioned near-complete monopoly of control (in the same hands) of all means of effective armed combat;

(vi) a central control and direction of the entire economy through the bureaucratic coordination of its formally independent corporate entities, typically including most other associations and group activities. (Friedrich and Brzezinski 1956, pp. 9–10.)

In a later (1965) edition of this book, two further characteristics were added—namely expansionism and the administrative control of justice. Friedrich and Brzezinski included as examples of such totalitarian dictatorships not only the USSR, but also other communist states, such as the PRC and Cuba as well as various fascist regimes.

How valid is the totalitarian approach? If we consider the eight variables individually, it becomes clear that several of them are now very much outdated. Moreover, not only some of the outdated variables, but also some of the others are not very useful as *distinguishing* features, since they pertain to other kinds of system. Since the approach has in the past been so influential, and since the term 'totalitarian' is even now frequently used in media reports on the communist states, let us examine each of the variables more closely.

It was argued in chapter 5 that ideology in the communist world increasingly plays a legitimating and justificatory role, and that politicians in communist states are ever less guided by the long-term, distant-goal aspects of the ideology. In this sense, communist ideology can be argued to be playing a role increasingly similar to that of ideology in the liberal democracies. There are still very important differences, of course—for instance in the 'languages' of the different ideologies and in some of the limitations imposed by such ideologies—but the distinction is less clear-cut than was once supposed.

The single mass party is still typical of communist states, even in those with allegedly multi-party systems. However, the notion of a single dictator has become increasingly questionable as the communist states have, in general, moved away from the supreme leader. Moreover, the concept of a 'hard core' of party members who are 'passionately and unquestioningly dedicated to the ideology' is also dated. Not only is the ideology itself in most countries ever more complex and contradictory, but the fact that past ideology has often been strongly criticized by present leaders and ideologues tends to undermine the passion and dedication of ordinary party members. The hierarchical and oligarchic organization of the party *is* still largely valid, and democratic centralism continues to be a key feature of communist systems.

This said, there are elements of hierarchy and oligarchy in most political parties.

The terroristic political control is seen by several writers (e.g. Arendt, Friedrich) as the essence of totalitarianism. But terror is much less a feature of most communist states than it once was. Moreover, examples of arbitrary violence by the state against innocent citizens can be found in so many countries in the contemporary world that this is not a particularly distinctive feature.

A near monopoly of the media is still a feature of most communist states. However, the communist media have become slightly more pluralistic in recent years. In addition, the West is more able to beam alternative views and information into many communist states, so that citizens in such states are often more familiar with non-communist views, etc. than is commonly realized in the West.

The fifth variable is still largely valid, but it pertains to most states, and is therefore not a salient distinguishing feature.

The communist states certainly have centrally planned economies. However, it must be acknowledged that the degree of central control has varied over time, and that the impact of economic reforms in some communist states (e.g. Hungary, Yugoslavia, Bulgaria) has had a perceptible effect on the number of plan indicators coming to enterprises, etc. from the centre. In addition, the encouragement of small-scale private enterprise in some communist states in recent years, particularly in agriculture, also undermines the image of the highly directed economy. One final point is that it should not be overlooked that there has been a widespread increase in government intervention in the economies of the Western world in recent years; whilst such interference is still on a very small scale in comparison with the communist world, it does at least mean that we have to be careful of drawing over-stark contrasts between the two kinds of system.

Expansionism is very much more a feature of the Soviet Union than it is of other communist states; one should therefore be cautious in seeing this as a feature of communist states in general. Furthermore, many Western states have been expansionist in the past, at a time when their political systems would not have been described as totalitarian. Hence, this variable is not a particularly useful distinguishing one.

Finally, it does seem that political/administrative interference in the judicial system is more a feature of communist systems than of liberal democracies (though not necessarily of many non-communist Third World countries). However, the clear distinction that is made in the USA between a constitutional court, for example, and the rest of the political system is not drawn in many other Western countries. For instance, the law lords in the UK are technically part of the non-elected chamber of the legislature. Thus the significance of an absence of such bodies in almost all communist states should not be over-emphasized. Furthermore, the communist states in general—certainly the older ones—have been placing far more emphasis in the last ten-to-fifteen years on the rule of law at the same time as politicians and administrators have interfered less in the administration of justice. Although this process still has a very long way to go before it reaches the levels of autonomy of the judicial system in liberal democracies, some allowance for changes that have occurred and are occurring should be made.

In sum, there are a number of problems with the classic eight-point syndrome. There have been many changes in the USSR since Stalin's time, for example, and an approach that cannot adequately incorporate these is of limited value. Certainly, totalitarianism has come in for considerable criticism for being an essentially static description, applicable to a large extent to Stalin's Russia (and the earliest days of Mao's China and the communist states of Eastern Europe), but incapable of adaptation. It can also be argued that the totalitarian approach not only lacks a dynamic component, but also an explanatory one; to describe a phenomenon—even if this is done accurately—is not to explain how and why it exists, how and why it might disappear, etc. Moreover, critics such as Inkeles (1966, p. 4) have argued that even when the approach is applied only to the most terroristic phases in communist history, it still omits several salient features of communist societies. Most notably, he argues, the approach does not acknowledge that there was considerable support for Stalin, his political style, and his policies amongst large sections of the Soviet population, especially in the early period of his leadership. The approach also makes insufficient distinction, in some commentators' opinion, between fascist regimes with little coherent ideology and communist ones, which typically have a far more sophisticated ideology and, arguably, do more for their citizenry over time than do fascist regimes. In other words, it can be argued that there were sufficient differences between Stalin's Russia or Mao's China on the one hand and Hitler's Germany or Mussolini's Italy on the other for the use of one blanket term to describe both to be put in serious question.

Although this list of criticisms of totalitarianism is far from exhausted, it will already be clear that there are a large number of problems with the approach. Does this mean that the term should be completely abandoned now? My own opinion is that it would not be a serious loss were we to jettison the concept, but that if we are to retain it as a heuristic device, then it is considerably more useful as an ideal-type than as a model. Since these two terms are widely used, sometimes incorrectly, and since several of the approaches to be considered can be used either as models or ideal-types, an understanding of the differences between the two concepts is necessary. Now that one non-Marxist approach has been examined in some detail, the distinction will be easier to draw than it would have been had we no concrete example to which to refer.

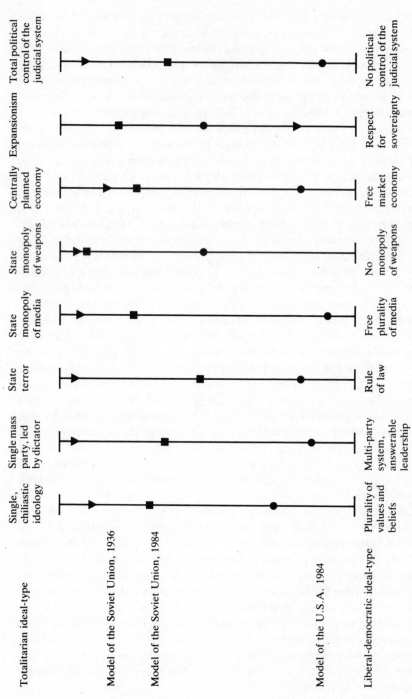

Fig. (iii) Ideal Types and Models: the triangles represent the USSR in 1936, the squares represent the USSR today, and the circles represent the USA today.

Ideal-types and Models

As Archie Brown (1974, p. 32) points out, writers often use the terms ideal-type and model interchangeably. This is unfortunate, since there are important distinctions to be drawn between at least two separate conceptual phenomena. Let us start with a model. Basically, a model is an abstract, systematized picture of perceived reality, either as it is (descriptive and analytical models—see chapter 10) or as it realistically could be (predictive models). In other words, social scientists will observe a given complex phenomenon, such as a political or economic system, identify as discrete variables what they believe to be the salient features of that system, and construct a model of it in terms of those variables. In the case of economic models, they might use existing known data and trends, and produce likely models of the future based on these; such models are, however, still based on what are perceived as realistic/attainable goals. Having created a model, social scientists may wish to test other realities—the political and/or economic system of another country, for instance—against it. In contrast, an ideal-type is not meant to be a reflection of reality, but rather a pure form of the salient features identified in reality. Expressed differently, the aspects of a society, economy, or polity that have been singled out for the creation of a model are pushed in the ideal-type to their extreme forms, the 'ideas'. The word 'ideal' is thus being used here in its philosophical rather than its everyday sense. An advantage of the ideal-type over the model is that it can be used to show change over time and/or between countries or systems, whereas major changes in an observed phenomenon would normally require a new model. For our purposes, the latter point is best elaborated in terms of *two* ideal-types, against which actual societies can be measured. Most readers will be familiar with multi-channel sliding volume or tone controls on sophisticated record-players (a graphic equalizer will do equally well), and these can be used to make the distinction between models and ideal-types very easily. Let us suppose that each channel on our record-player or equalizer represents not the volume/tone of a given instrument or human voice but, rather, an axis between each of the eight variables suggested by Friedrich and Brzezinski and their opposite. Let us further suppose that the totalitarian ideal-type is represented by the maximum volume/tone position (probably the figure ten on our record-player), whereas the minimum volume/tone position (indicated by the figure zero) represents the liberal-democratic ideal-type. We can now create models of different societies and/or the same society at different points in time. This has been done in Fig. (iii). It is *not* meant to be definitive in any sense, but rather is designed as a didactic device. The various slides have been located somewhat arbitrarily, and another person performing the exercise may well position them differently. At this point in the argument, this is of marginal relevance.

As already suggested, some readers will disagree with the location of the triangles, squares, and circles in Fig. (iii); this is not important. Some readers will also disagree with the variables chosen as the salient features of such societies; this does not matter either, although it must be noted that I have merely used the eight variables suggested by Friedrich and Brzezinski. The important point is that the distinction between a model and an ideal-type should now be clear. It should also be obvious why the ideal-type is more adaptable and dynamic than many models (certainly descriptive models). Although the ideal-type itself is static, we can measure actual societies against it, as has been done in Fig. (iii). In doing this we can show—if this is what we want to argue—that the USSR is further away from the totalitarian ideal-type than it was at the height of the Stalin terror, but that it is still closer to the totalitarian ideal-type than the USA is. At the same time, we can also see that the USA is not a 'pure' liberal-democracy either, but is much closer to the Western democratic ideal-type than it is to the totalitarian. Thus I would argue that the concept of totalitarianism is much more useful as an ideal-type than as a model—although some of the criticisms of it (e.g. of the absence of any indication of social support for the political system) still pertain. Some of the following approaches have been presented by their advocates as both ideal-types and models.

(ii) The Bureaucratic Approach

As it became clear following Stalin's death that profound changes were occurring in the USSR and Eastern Europe, so there was a move away from the term 'totalitarian' to describe such societies. One of the least radical new approaches was that of Allen Kassof, who in 1964 produced the 'administered society' ideal-type and argued that it would be useful to employ this for a better understanding of changes that were taking place in Soviet-type systems. Kassof describes his ideal-type as follows

The administered society can be defined as one in which an entrenched and extraordinarily powerful ruling group lays claim to ultimate and exclusive scientific knowledge of the social and historical laws and is impelled by a belief not only in the practical desirability, but the moral necessity, of planning, direction, and coordination from above in the name of human welfare and progress... The elite believes, and through a far-reaching program of education and propaganda tries to teach its subjects, that the only possible good society is one that is *administered*. (1964, pp. 558–9.)

The emphasis in this approach is on a group that takes upon itself the direction of society in the name of a long-term and all-embracing ideology, and in this sense it is very close to the totalitarian approach. Indeed, Kassof actually subtitled his 1964 article 'Totalitarianism without Terror', which shows how relatively little he had moved from the approach of Friedrich and Brzezinski, Arendt, and others.

But many scholars in the early 1960s felt that the changes that had occurred in recent years in the USSR and elsewhere represented a more significant move away from the Stalinist political system than writers such as Kassof had acknowledged. They also felt that there was more real politics (in the sense of conflict)—albeit within very limited parameters—than the essentially monolithic image of 'the administered society' allowed for. Finally, this group felt that the concept of totalitarianism was no longer applicable, and hence wanted to abandon it rather than merely modify it as Kassof had done. It was in this context that the 'bureaucratic' approach was born.

The leading exponent of this in the 1960s/early 1970s was Alfred Meyer, who was arguing from 1961 that the USSR could usefully be compared to a Western bureaucratic organization—such as an industrial corporation (he specifically cited General Motors), an army or a church—but on a much larger scale. The essence of his argument is contained in the following quotation:

... at least one Communist system can be understood adequately by comparing it with complex modern bureaucratic organisations anywhere. Like modern bureaucracy, Communist rule is essentially an attempt to impose rational management over social life by means of complex organisation ... An important difference which remains is that Communist systems are sovereign bureaucracies, whereas other bureaucracies exist and operate within larger societal frameworks, so that a Communist state becomes one single bureaucratic system extended over the entire society, or bureaucracy writ large. (Meyer 1967, p. 5.)

Meyer does not entirely reject the totalitarian 'model' (his word), but, rather, argues that it applies to communist states for only a limited period of their development. In contrast, he maintains that his bureaucratic model applies to the 'presumably much longer period of settled existence within a well-established system' (1967, p. 5). Meyer does argue that the relative strength of the various features he enumerates in his model (e.g. industrialization as the chief aim and effect of communism; the emergence of new patterns of social stratification in communist societies, etc.) will vary from country to country and from one period to another, but he also maintains that the model applies to 'most or all' communist societies.

One of the problems with Meyer's approach is that the kind of organization and politics typical of one bureaucracy, such as a modern corporation, will differ in a number of significant ways from that of another, such as an army. The analogy is thus at best impressionistic and imprecise (for an excellent critique see Lane 1978, pp. 172–4). Moreover, it too concentrates only on some aspects of society at the expense of others. Meyer shows some awareness of this when he says that whichever model is used to describe communist systems 'several features more readily associated with the democratic way of life than with the totalitarian or bureaucratic have to be added' (1967, p. 5). If this is the case, it becomes unclear why Meyer wishes to retain the 'bureaucratic' label.

The bureaucratic model has been amongst the most popular approaches to communist politics, largely because it simultaneously implies a very hierarchical polity and society, but also one in which there is real politics, especially within the higher echelons. Variations on the theme have been produced by, amongst others, John Armstrong (1965), Carl Beck (1968) and T. Harry Rigby (1964, 1976, 1980, 1982).

(iii) The Cultural Approach

So far in this overview of the many approaches to communist politics, the focus has been on those that stress the uniqueness of communist systems, the ways in which they differ from other kinds of political system. Before moving on to approaches that play down the uniqueness of the communist world, let us consider very briefly one approach that concentrates on each communist system separately in an endeavour to explain why the political climate can vary so much in countries with allegedly similar ideologies and political structures. That approach is the cultural one, and it appeared more recently than those already considered. The leading exponent of this approach has been Archie Brown, who since the 1970s has been arguing that a study of 'the specific historical experience of particular nations and people's perception of this experience' (1974, p. 103) should be incorporated into any attempt to understand the communist systems. It should be emphasized that neither Brown, nor other advocates of the cultural approach (e.g. White, especially 1979) see this as the sole or even the main way of understanding communist politics. Rather, they see it as an important additional factor to incorporate into any attempt at distilling the essence of politics in communist countries. Thus, unlike some of the advocates of the other approaches examined, the culturalists cannot be accused of focusing on some aspects of a society and ignoring others.

Let us now turn to a consideration of approaches which explicitly play down the differences between communist and other types of political, social, and economic system.

CONVERGENCE APPROACHES

Many commentators, both Marxist and non-Marxist, have argued that the communist states have much more in common with other kinds of system than the approaches so far considered would lead us to believe. They maintain that economic and technological development render systems of radically different ideologies increasingly similar, and that, on balance, the similarities outweigh the differences. However, we shall see that such observers can also differ fairly considerably amongst themselves, both in their assessments of the level of similarity between communist and other types of system, and in the aspects of such systems that they most want to analyse and emphasize.

(i) The developmental (modernization) approach

According to the developmental approach, communist systems are best understood as countries undergoing or having undergone rapid development (modernization) under an ideologically motivated intellectual élite. The term development is understood here primarily in economic and social terms, and involves such factors as a change from a predominantly agricultural to an industrial economic base, the concomitant urbanization, raised levels of education, etc. The best-known exponent of this approach is John Kautsky, who sometimes uses the term 'mobilizing' (e.g. 1973, esp. pp. 142–4) as well as 'developing' and 'modernizing' to describe what communist regimes are or have been. Kautsky stresses that communist regimes have a great deal in common with other modernizing systems, such as Mexico, the Dominican Republic, Egypt, or Turkey, and argues that in most respects they are not a distinctive type of system. For him, the most important distinguishing feature is the ideology of Marxism–Leninism, but he maintains that this is not as salient a feature of such systems as is often suggested. For instance, the distinction that is sometimes drawn between communist and non-communist developing countries in terms of their orientation towards nationalism is questioned by Kautsky. His own research interests led Kautsky to be primarily interested in what he sees as the developing world, rather than the developed world. However, Kautsky does argue that, just as the similarities between communist and non-communist developing states are greater than the differences, so the similarities between developed communist and non-communist states are such that it is ultimately artificial to draw neat distinctions between them.

Kautsky's approach does largely overcome the lack of dynamism problem that is seen by many as a major weakness of totalitarianism. On the other hand, the developmental approach has been criticized for the neglect of important differences between communist and non-communist states. Certainly, the 'mobilization' regimes of the communist world differ in some important ways—not only in terms of the ideology, but also political organization, the economic structure, the status of women—from the non-communist modernizing regimes. It is a highly subjective matter whether an individual analyst places greater emphasis on the similarities or the differences between states, which in turn means that this approach is just as subjective as all the others.

(ii) Industrial society approaches

A number of Western observers have argued that high levels of industrialization and technological development bring with them increasingly homogeneous patterns of social and political organization. There are several variants of this, but the most widespread and influential one is represented by writers such as Clark Kerr (1962) and Talcott Parsons (1960). On the basis of such arguments, David Lane (1978, pp. 184–6) has produced an eight-point model of this most common image of industrial society; he himself is wary about using the model, and is primarily concerned to encapsulate the essence of the thesis. His model is somewhat lengthy for our purposes, and I shall merely list the main points, making marginal alterations to Lane's wording when this seems to me to be appropriate. This industrial society model can be summarized thus:

(1) Rapid growth of the population and control of this growth. Labour becomes more valuable relative to capital, and there is no expendable class. The extended family is replaced by the nuclear family, and relations between men and women are on a more egalitarian basis.

(2) A diffusion of political power and greater equality of wealth.

(3) A highly developed division of labour and greater social mobility, with 'equality of opportunity' becoming a widely accepted goal. A highly differentiated social hierarchy, based on education and occupation, is typical.

(4) An ideology of diligence, technical change, 'progress', and status differentiation. The search for a utopian social order—whether 'true democracy' or 'communism'—is in practice abandoned. The state's ideology is oriented towards system-maintenance rather than radical change.

(5) The legal system is relatively independent of the government, and applies a more or less equal law to individuals from all status groups. Laws are extensive and complex.

(6) Although the forms of government control vary, the national government organizes the whole society in the interest of collective goals. Its direct and indirect role in the control of the economy, science, and education distinguishes it from non-industrial societies.

(7) Human relations tend to be specific and achievement-oriented.

(8) Large-scale urbanism generates a form of social life and social relationships independent of the political setting. The size of communities means that communications become indirect; political power is delegated to representatives, whilst the cultural sphere is dominated by the mass media.

Although Kerr and like-minded sociologists accept that individual societies approximate to this model to varying degrees, they do argue that the differences are less significant than the similarities, and that the trend is towards increasing uniformity.

A number of political scientists—among them Gabriel Almond (1970), Robert Dahl (1971), and Karl Deutsch (1963)—have adopted essentially similar approaches, but have been more concerned with the particularly *political* aspects of the industrial society model. For instance, they are interested in the pluralizing effects of the deepening division of labour. These writers have recognized that the communist states are still authoritarian in comparison with Western societies, but they see change in the direction of a greater pluralism as inevitable. In this sense, such writers have adopted a deterministic approach, something they share in common with the Marxists.

However, they do not accept the theory of class polarization, whether applied to liberal-democratic or communist industrial societies. Indeed, most find the concept of class outdated and/or of limited value.

Among the many criticisms that can be levelled against this version of the industrial society approach is that it is excessively deterministic—it has been labelled 'technological determinism'. Moreover, many feel that it is insufficiently sensitive to significant differences between advanced industrial societies. Whilst it is quite true that there are many factors in common between East and West Germany, for example, anyone who has visited both will know that there are important differences between them, and that these are perceived as such by many of the citizens living in those two states.

In an attempt to test empirically one major aspect of the industrial society thesis—namely the notion that societies become more pluralistic as they become more economically developed and the division of labour deepens—Stephen White analysed the meetings of the Supreme Soviet and the CPSU's Central Committee over the period 1954–75. He chose these two bodies on the grounds that they are the most important centres of 'authoritative societal decision-making' to which representatives of functional groups in the USSR have potential access. White argued that there should, according to what he called the industrial society approach's 'iron law of pluralism', be signs of increasing levels of debate, frequency of meetings, etc. In fact, his research revealed that 'the nearer one comes to the present day the greater the tendency for pluralism, on almost all the indicators we have chosen, to decline' (White 1978, p. 115). White's study is concerned with only one communist state—albeit a major one—and with what is, on the scale of world history, a relatively brief timespan. Some would also question his choice of decision-making bodies and other aspects of his methodology (for a critique see Brown 1984c, p. 91). Consequently, one must be careful not to place excessive emphasis on his findings. Nevertheless, the trend he has identified is quite an interesting one. Taken in conjunction with other Western analysts' perceptions of patterns of political change over time in other countries such as Czechoslovakia (see, for example, Rupnik 1981), White's analysis does raise doubts about the validity of claims concerning the emergence of something akin to Western-style pluralism in the communist world.

Although White, in his study of the USSR, is not searching for *all* the manifestations of pluralism associated with the West (e.g. he does not look for signs of anything like a multi-party system), he does expect group politics to be somewhat akin to group politics in the West if we are to use the term pluralism. Others have implicitly suggested that we should expect at this stage only a very particular and limited kind of pluralism, even in terms of group politics and a plurality of views. An attraction to *some* aspects of the industrial society approach, coupled with a desire to acknowledge what can be seen as significant changes in the Soviet political system since Stalin's time, led to the emergence of the *institutional pluralist* approach. The actual term 'institutional pluralism' was coined by the American Jerry Hough in the early 1970s (see Hough 1972, esp. pp. 27–9). It must be emphasized that institutional pluralism was for Hough a model of a feasible development pattern in the USSR, and that, contrary to what many writers have subsequently maintained, he did not argue that the USSR had actually become an example of institutional pluralism. Hough has in fact recently revealed that he bowed to editorial pressure when he coined the term, and himself now prefers to use less problematical concepts such as 'communist regime' or 'Soviet system' (1983, pp. 49 and 57). Nevertheless, the term is now in common usage, and should be briefly considered.

Whereas the totalitarian approach emphasizes the all-important position of the leader in decision-making, and the bureaucratic approach that of the administrators of the party-state complex standing above society, institutional pluralism is a step nearer the pluralism of the West. In this approach, power is still concentrated in relatively few hands, but there is conflict—politics—not only between the various institutions of the party-state complex (e.g. party apparatus, state bureaucracy, etc.), but also those close to but not explicitly of this complex (e.g. industrial managers). There are, moreover, relatively open conflicts *within* the various institutions (e.g. a ministry, etc.). Thus this approach is markedly different from those that see communist systems as highly monolithic and controlled. On the other hand, it is still an image of a polity in which the masses play a very minor political role. The approach has been criticized for placing insufficient emphasis on the role of the communist party. Furthermore, it can once again be argued that the use of a term so widely applied to Western societies, even if this term is prefixed with the adjective 'institutional', is potentially misleading. Despite the fact that there is evidence of conflict within and around the party-state complex, the near impossibility for ordinary citizens to form new political parties, protest openly, set up 'alternative' political magazines, etc, means that there is still a very wide gap between the liberal democratic and communist political systems. Thus it is understandable why, just as some Marxists (e.g. Mandel) object to the use of the term 'state *capitalism*' when applied to communist countries, so some non-Marxists object to the use of the term 'pluralism', however modified.

Towards the end of the 1970s Valerie Bunce and John Echols (1980) argued that it would be more appropriate to see the USSR as a *corporatist* state. Fot them, this had a number of advantages over the term 'pluralism'. First, it implies a political arrangement somewhat akin to institutional pluralism without making use of the actual term pluralism. Second, they advocated this approach at a time when some Western analysts were arguing that Western societies, too, were becoming more corporatist; it was thus felt to be a sounder basis for comparison than notions of pluralism which were already in question *vis-à-vis* Western societies anyway. What does the term corporatism mean? Like all such terms, there is some disagreement on this. However, in its most widely accepted contemporary usage, corporatism implies that the major decisions in society are taken by government in conjunction with key groups ('corporate bodies'), such as business organizations and trade unions. When applied to Western societies, it is argued that pluralism has led to the emergence of a hierarchy of pressure groups, the most significant of which have become so powerful that governments have actually sought to integrate (incorporate) them into the decision-making process. In return, such groups are expected to keep firm control over their members. In the West, such corporatism tends to be a feature more of labour governments (e.g. the Wilson–Callaghan government in the UK in the mid-to-late 1970s, the Hawke government in Australia in the mid-1980s, etc.) than of more conservative ones, and it has come in for much criticism when used as a general term to describe Western politics. This is not our concern, however, and we need to consider the applicability of the term only to communist societies.

Like all approaches, the corporatist one provides some insights and also suffers limitations. On the one hand, it does imply the less monolithic political system that institutional pluralism does, and which does seem to be a feature of many older communist states. On the other hand, it suffers from essentially the same problem as pluralism, namely that the same word is used to describe quite different political arrangements and phenomena. For example, although trade unions might be consulted by party and state leaders and involved in decision-making in the communist world, this happens because the leaders have chosen to do this, not because of the perceived power of the unions. The party-state leaders do enter into deals with the trade union leaders, and the latter would not normally threaten to bring their members out on strike if they felt that their interests were not being sufficiently heeded. Furthermore, the key organizations being consulted and incorporated by the party-state complex have been *established* by those complexes, and their leading officials are subject to party control via the *nomenklatura* system. This is all very different from the situation of most Western organizations that are 'incorporated'. Bunce and Echols themselves try to overcome this problem by describing two very different types of corporatism ('societal' and 'state') and arguing that the USSR falls somewhere in between these. Indeed, they refer to the USSR as a 'mixture of corporatist types' (1980, p. 19), and emphasize that the Soviet system differs in significant ways from the corporatism of the liberal democracies. Unfortunately, this only tends to make the image of corporatism more blurred, and we are back with the problem of using one catch-all term to describe admittedly very different phenomena. For these reasons, Fleron's less value-laden term of *a cooptative political system* (1968, esp. pp. 239–44) would seem to me to be more appropriate than corporatism. Such a term allows for the fact that key functional groups in society are being listened to more by the politicians, but does not imply a very high level of similarity between liberal-democratic and communist politics. But even Fleron's approach at best captures only a part of the complexity of politics in the communist world, in that it is concerned only with an (admittedly important) part of the input side of the policy process.

We have seen that a number of writers believe that industrialization brings with it certain changes in society and the political system, but that there is disagreement on the levels of similarity engendered. Writers such as Kerr wish to emphasize the commonalities, whereas others, such as Giddens (1973) argue that there are two major types of industrial society (capitalist, and what he calls 'state socialist'), and that there are both commonalities and important differences between them. But what of the future? In the final part of this section, we shall briefly consider some of the different conclusions analysts have reached in projecting the perceived convergent effects of industrial society in both liberal democratic and communist states into the distant future. Once again, there are in one sense as many versions of approaches to future convergence as there are people writing on it. But for analytical purposes, we can discern two main groups, the 'optimists' and the 'pessimists'.

As will readily be inferred, the optimists are analysts who see industrialization bringing a better society. But they are divided amongst themselves on the nature of this better society. Some, such as W. Rostow (1960), see the communist states becoming essentially the same as liberal democracies, and believe that this is not only a necessary development but a *desirable* one too. Such writers look forward to the day when the USSR and other communist states become much more like the USA. It should be noted, however, that some American scholars who would no doubt *like* to think that this was going to happen have dismissed such projections—and indeed notions of convergence generally—as wishful thinking (Brzezinski and Huntington 1964, esp. pp. 9–14 and 419–36). A second group of 'optimists' believes that there will be increasing state intervention in the economy in liberal democracies and a reduction of central control of the economy in the communist states; a reduction of class antagonisms and both increasing and more egalitarian political pluralism in both kinds of system; and that people will increasingly control technology, rather than vice versa, in all industrial societies. This approach envisages a future of 'democratic socialism' in both the liberal democracies and the communist states, which they see as desirable. Isaac Deutscher and Maurice Duverger have been typical of this school.

A much more pessimistic vision has been described by Alfred Meyer as the 'apocalyptic' view, which he summarizes as follows

A composite version of the apocalyptic theories of convergence I have in mind can be roughly described. Both the Communist world and the highly developed nations of the West are said to be moving toward a social and political system marked by centralization and authoritarianism, with gross political inequalities perpetuated by irresponsible elites wielding unprecedented power. In this world of the future, state and society will have merged into one bureaucratized order. True politics openly and freely pursued by all citizens will have disappeared, and all social life will have become politicized, meaning that it will have become a matter of public concern and political control, regulation, and coordination. Bureaucratic techniques and regulations will have supplanted and replaced law ... Order, stability and compliance with rules and regulations will have assumed primacy in the hierarchy of social values ... In sum, there are some theories direly predicting the convergence of developed systems, Communist and capitalist, within a framework of bureaucratic or fascist-like authoritarianism ... (Meyer 1970b, pp. 329–31.)

Meyer goes on to describe such Orwellian or Kafkaesque societies as a new form of totalitarianism. But they are very different from earlier forms, not only in style, but also in that they are to be found in the West as well as in the East. The role of the state bureaucracy, the police and the military is enhanced in such societies. A leading proponent of this view is Jacques Ellul (1965). These futuristic convergence theories are interesting (if sometimes frightening), but are by definition untestable since they refer to societies that do not yet exist and they do not incorporate timetables against which we could check actual developments. Even if they did, there is no reason at all to suppose that scholars will in the future agree on what constitute the salient features of any given society any more than they do now; it should by now be abundantly clear that a number of scholars—even scholars of very similar background—can observe the same phenomenon yet see very different things.

CONCLUSIONS

Although a wide range of approaches has been considered in this chapter, there are many more—both Marxist and non-Marxist—that could have been included. Such an exercise would have had some benefits in terms of comprehensiveness, but would not have altered the basic points of my argument concerning approaches to the study of communist societies, which can now be summarized.

The first point is that there is much common ground between several of the approaches. Both Marxists and non-Marxists have referred to the totalitarian and bureaucratic aspects of communist societies. Both Marxists and non-Marxists have adopted deterministic and dynamic approaches to communist systems, even if they reach different conclusions as to the direction in which such systems are heading. All approaches accept that there is a gap between rulers and ruled, and that there are still many problems to be solved in the communist world.

Second, it should by now be obvious that none of the approaches is entirely satisfactory—yet all have *something* to offer. One of the problems is that the models, in particular, are often based on an observation of very different countries and/or periods, and one would hardly expect an analysis that fitted one's own perception of contemporary Hungary or Czechoslovakia to be particularly appropriate for Mozambique—although something that fitted the *early* Chinese or Cuban system might be more apt. Some of the convergence approaches partially overcome this in emphasizing that countries are at different stages along an essentially similar path; but they suffer from other weaknesses already elaborated.

A third point is that the various approaches focus on different dimensions of communist societies. As mentioned earlier, Marxist approaches tend to concentrate on the economic aspects of communist systems, and play down the complexities of the political systems. The totalitarian approach tries to cover the politics, the economy, and society of communist countries—even though it does omit important aspects of each of these—whereas the bureaucratic or corporatist approaches are primarily concerned with the political system (especially the input side), and only tangentially with other aspects of these countries. Finally, some approaches are designed principally to *describe* communist systems, whereas others are more interested in *explaining* them. Thus the fact that different observers reach different answers is to some extent because they are asking different questions and performing different exercises.

Does the fact that no approach is fully satisfactory mean that we should abandon them altogether? The inadequacies of the existing approaches, and the seemingly endless plethora of new approaches mean that one can sympathize to a large extent with people such as Hirschman (1970) or Hough (1983) when they argue that labels and approaches often obfuscate more than they clarify, and that it might be time to abandon them. But were we to do this, we would in my view run the risk of throwing the baby out with the bathwater. For all their drawbacks, the various models, ideal-types, etc. do collectively give us many insights into the communist world—perceptions that we might not have had had the advocates of these approaches not alerted us to them in their endeavours to capture the essence of communist systems. In one sense, every communist system is unique, *sui generis*. But at another level, there *are* common factors, and the existence of differences should not blind us to these. At the end of the day, Archie Brown's suggestion (1974, esp. p. 104 and 1978) that we adopt an eclectic approach—whereby we pick and choose from among the various approaches as seems most appropriate to a better understanding of a specific dimension of the particular communist system and period we are examining—is a very sensible one.

We shall never fully understand any one communist system or the group of countries that collectively constitute the communist world, anymore than we shall ever fully understand our own societies. Human organization is far too complex for that. But just because we can never finish our task does not mean that we should not start it. In addition to any instrumental advantages, greater knowledge and a deeper understanding of any phenomenon—including communism—is a desirable end in its own right.

Basic further reading

A. Brown, 1974.

V. Bunce and J. Echols, 1980.

T. Cliff, 1974.

F. Fleron (ed.), 1969.

C. Friedrich, M. Curtis, B. Barber, 1969.

G. Ionescu, 1972.

D. Lane, 1976, pt. 1; 1978, ch. 6.

E. Mandel, 1970; 1974.

A. Meyer, 1970b.

L. Schapiro, 1972.

L. Trotsky, 1967.

APPENDIX

Basic Data on the Political System of Each Communist State

The following appendix is for the most part self-explanatory. However, certain points need to be noted.

(i) *Population*. Figures are for mid-1983, and are taken from R. F. Staar, 'Checklist of Communist Parties in 1983', *Problems of Communism*, March–April 1984, pp. 43–51.

(ii) *Ethnic Composition*. These are mostly rounded to the nearest whole figure. I have included the latest available figures known to me—taken from a very wide range of sources—but these are in some cases several years old. The data should therefore not be treated as definitive, but are designed merely to give the reader an impression of the ethnic balance in a given country.

(iii) *Membership of Communist Party*. Source as for 'population' except that the Mozambique figures are from A. & B. Isaacman, 1983, p. 124.

(iv) *Percentage of Population in Communist Party*. These are rounded to one decimal place except in those cases where the percentage is so small that it is necessary to give a more specific figure. A more meaningful percentage would be that of *adults* in the party, which would give a higher figure; unfortunately, full data are available on too few countries to make this exercise feasible at present.

(v) *Social Composition of Party*. Official sources have been used in most cases. Unfortunately there is no standardized system of social classification in the communist world, so that data are not directly comparable across countries.

(vi) *Year of Most Recent Constitution*. Details are from A. Blaustein and G. Flanz (eds.), *Constitutions of the Countries of the World* (New York: Oceana Publications, ongoing), currently in eighteen volumes.

(vii) *Electoral System*. Details are for the national/central legislature, and refer to the *formal* rules (e.g. the rule on frequency of elections may not be observed in practice). It has not been possible to obtain full details for all countries; gaps have been left where details do not appear to be available, both to indicate my inability to obtain these, and so that they may be inserted at a later date by readers who have obtained them.

(viii) *Leaders Since Communists Assumed Power*. Two important points need to be made about this section. The first is that there is sometimes disagreement over the year in which the communists actually took power in a given country. Some cases—e.g. the USSR and China—are clear-cut, in the sense that there is common agreement. But in many countries, the communists *gradually* assumed power over a number of years (this was the case in several East European countries, for example). Moreover, the leaders who took power in some revolutionary coups became communists only later (e.g. Cuba, arguably Congo, Ethiopia, etc.). Thus it is often not possible to provide a date that would be accepted by everyone. The practice adopted in this appendix *vis-à-vis* disputed cases has been to give the year in which the communists either consolidated power (e.g. by banning all other parties, declaring a people's democracy, etc.) or in which leaders who later became communists took power; this seems to me to be the optimal solution. Second, it is not always clear who is the head of the party, head of state, etc. For instance, Lenin was never General Secretary of the Central Committee of the CPSU, despite the fact that this post is accepted as the number one post in the Soviet communist party. Where this sort of problem arises, I have given the name of the person most widely accepted as 'the' party (or government, or state) leader. Even this method is not without problems, however. For instance, the person widely perceived as 'the' Chinese leader at present—Deng Xiaoping—does not figure in the appendix, since there are generally recognized heads of the Chinese party, government, and state respectively. The Chinese case is a rare exception, however, and the reader will in the vast majority of cases discover who was perceived as 'the' leader of a given country in a given year by looking up the 'Head of Party'.

(x) *Introductory bibliography.* Between one and six basic sources are included. These are mostly *general* analyses of the political system and/or the communist party, and are not *necessarily* what I perceive to be the most scholarly or interesting works on a given country. The reader is advised to start his/her search with B. Szajkowski (ed.), *Marxist Governments—A World Survey*, which is a three-volume collection of country-studies by specialists on these countries. Another useful starting point is G. E. Delury (ed.), *World Encyclopedia of Political Systems and Parties*, in two volumes. For the developments in a particular country in a given year, the most useful initial source is the annual *Yearbook on International Communist Affairs*, currently edited by Richard Staar. The most valuable journals specifically on comparative communism are *Communist Affairs*, *Problems of Communism*, and *Studies in Comparative Communism*; another very useful periodical for keeping up to date with recent developments in the communist world (and elsewhere) is *The World Today*. Other reference sources in English include *Keesing's Contemporary Archives*; The Economist's *Quarterly Economic Review* of individual countries; *The Statesman's Yearbook*; the BBC's *Summary of World Broadcasts* (SWB); the *U.S. Foreign Broadcast Information Service* (FBIS); and A. Day and H. Degenhardt, *Political Parties of the World*.

Afghanistan

Official name of state: Democratic Republic of Afghanistan

Capital: Kabul

Nature of state: unitary

Population: 14.2m.

Ethnic composition: Pushtuns 50%; Tadzhiks 25%; Hazaras 11%; Uzbeks 9%; Others 5%

Principal religion: Islam (Sunni)

Formal title and usual abbreviation of communist party: People's Democratic Party of Afghanistan (PDPA)

Membership of communist party: 90,000

Percentage of population in communist party: 0.6

Social composition of party: no data available

Other legal political parties: none

Year of most recent constitution: 1980 (Provisional—actually called 'The Basic Principles')

Electoral system: direct—other details not yet available

Local representative organs: local jirgahs (to be formed)

Central legislature: Loya Jirgah (Supreme Council)

State executive organ: Council of Ministers

Leaders since communists assumed power (1978):

Head of Party	Premier	Head of State
N. Taraki (1978–9)	N. Taraki (1978–9)	N. Taraki (1978–9)
H. Amin (1979)	H. Amin (1979)	H. Amin (1979)
B. Karmal (1979–)	B. Karmal (1979–81)	B. Karmal (1979–)
	S. A. Keshtmand (1981–)	

Introductory bibliography:

A. Arnold, 1983.
L. Dupree, 1979, 1980.
F. Halliday, 1978, 1980.
A. Hyman, 1984.
Z. Khalilzad, 1980.

Albania

Official name of state: People's Socialist Republic of Albania

Capital: Tirana

Nature of state: unitary

Population: 2.8m.

Ethnic composition: Ghegs 67%; Tosks 29%; Others 4%

Principal religion: Banned since 1967—previously Islam (Sunni)

Formal title and usual abbreviation of communist party: Albanian Party of Labour (ALP)

Membership of communist party: 122,000

Percentage of population in communist party: 4.4

Social composition of party (1981): 'Nearly 38%'—Workers (blue-collar); 29.4%—Co-operativists (peasants); 32.6%—Workers (white-collar)

Other legal political parties: none

Year of most recent constitution: 1976

Electoral system: direct; no choice; elections every four years; vote at 18; single-member constituencies

Local representative organs: People's Councils

Central legislature: People's Assembly: unicameral; 250 seats

State executive organ: Council of Ministers

Leaders since communists assumed power (1946):

Head of Party	Premier	Head of State
E. Hoxha (1946–85)	E. Hoxha (1946–54)	O. Nishani (1946–53)
R. Alia (1985–)	M. Shehu (1954–81)	H. Lleshi (1953–82)
	A. Carcani (1982–)	R. Alia (1982–)

Introductory bibliography:

N. Pano, 1968, 1979.
P. Prifti, 1978.

Angola

Official name of state: People's Republic of Angola

Capital: Luanda

Nature of state: unitary

Population: 7.6m.

Ethnic composition: Ovimbundu 35%; Mbundu 25%; Bakongo 10%; Others 30%

Principal religion: Catholicism

Formal title and usual abbreviation of communist party: Popular Movement for the Liberation of Angola—Party of Labour (MPLA—Party of Labour)

Membership of communist party: 31,000

Percentage of population in communist party: 0.4

Social composition of party: no data available

Other legal political parties: none

Year of most recent constitution: 1975 (with major amendments in 1980)

Electoral system: indirect;   choice; elections every three years; vote at 18; -member constituencies

Local representative organs: People's assemblies

Central legislature: National People's Assembly; unicameral; 203 seats

State executive organ: Council of Ministers

Leaders since communists assumed power (1975):

Head of Party	Premier	Head of State
A. Neto (1975–9)	L. de Nascimiento (1975–8)	A. Neto (1975–9)
J. dos Santos (1979–)	(Post abolished—December 1978; the head of state heads the government)	J. dos Santos (1979–)

Introductory bibliography:
K. Brown, 1979.
D. and M. Ottaway, 1981, ch. 5.
M. Wolfers & J. Bergerol, 1983.

Benin

Official name of state: People's Republic of Benin

Capital: Porto-Novo

Nature of state: unitary

Population: 3.7m.

Ethnic composition: Fon 60%; Somba 10%; Yoruba 10%; Bariba 9%; Fulani 6%; Others 5%

Principal religion: Animism

Formal title and usual abbreviation of communist party: People's Revolutionary Party of Benin (PRPB)

Membership of communist party: 200

Percentage of population in communist party: 0.005

Social composition of party: no data available

Other legal political parties: none

Year of most recent constitution: 1979

Electoral system: direct; no choice; elections every five years; vote at 18; -member constituencies

Local representative organs: Revolutionary councils

Central legislature: National Revolutionary Assembly; unicameral; 196 seats

State executive organ: National Executive Council

Leaders since communists assumed power (1972):

Head of Party	Premier	Head of State
(Party founded November 1975)	A. Kerekou (1972–)	A. Kerekou (1972–)
A. Kerekou (1975–)		

Introductory bibliography:
S. Decalo, 1979.

Bulgaria

Official name of state: People's Republic of Bulgaria

Capital: Sofia

Nature of state: unitary

Population: 8.9m.

Ethnic composition: (1956)—Bulgarians 85.5%; Turks 8.6%; Macedonians 2.5%; Others 3.4%

Principal religion: Eastern orthodoxy

Formal title and usual abbreviation of communist party: Bulgarian Communist Party (BCP)

Membership of communist party: 826,000

Percentage of population in communist party: 9.7

Social composition of party (1978): Industrial Workers 41.8%; White-collar workers 30.3%; Peasants 22.4%; Others 5.5%

Other legal political parties (membership in brackets): Bulgarian Agrarian People's Union (BAPU) (120,000)

Year of most recent constitution: 1971

Electoral system: direct; no choice, elections every five years; vote at 18; single-member constituencies

Local representative organs: People's Councils

Central legislature: National Assembly; unicameral; 400 seats

State executive organ: Council of Ministers

Leaders since communists assumed power (1947):

Head of Party	Premier	Head of State
G. Dimitrov (1947–9)	G. Dimitrov (1947–9)	M. Neichev (1947–50)
V. Chervenkov (1950–4)	V. Kolarov (1949–50)	G. Damyanov (1950–8)
T. Zhivkov (1954–)	V. Chervenkov (1950–6)	D. Ganev (1958–64)
	A. Yugov (1956–62)	G. Traikov (1964–71)
	T. Zhivkov (1962–71)	T. Zhivkov (1971
	S. Todorov (1971–81)	
	G. Filipov (1981–)	

Introductory bibliography:

J. Brown, 1970.
R. King, 1979a.
N. Oren, 1973.

China

Official name of state: People's Republic of China

Capital: Beijing (formerly Peking)

Nature of state: unitary

Population: 1,008m.

Ethnic composition: Han 93%; Others 7%

Principal religions/philosophies: Confucianism, Daoism, Buddhism

Formal title and usual abbreviation of communist party: Chinese Communist Party (CCP or CPC)

Membership of communist party: 40m.

Percentage of population in communist party: 4.0

Social composition of party: no data available

Other legal political parties (total membership—120,000): Association for Promoting Democracy

Democratic League
Democratic National Construction Association
Jiusan Society
Peasants and Workers Democratic Party
Revolutionary Committee of the Guomindang
Taiwan Democratic Self-Government League
Zhi Gong Dang

Year of most recent constitution; 1982

Electoral system: indirect; limited choice; elections every five years; vote at 18; single-member constituencies

Local representative organs: Local People's Congress

Central legislature: National People's Congress; unicameral; 2,997 seats

State executive organ: State Council

Leaders since communists assumed power (1949):

Head of Party	Premier	Head of State
Mao Zedong (1949–76)	Zhou Enlai (1949–76)	Mao Zedong (1949–59)
Hua Guofeng (1976–81)	Hua Guofeng (1976–80)	Liu Shaoqi (1959–68)
Hu Yaobang (1981–)	Zhao Ziyang (1980–)	(Position vacant until 1975, then dropped until 1982, and not filled until 1983)
		Li Xiannian (1983–)

Introductory bibliography:

H. Hinton, 1978.
F. Kaplan and J. Sobin, 1982.
A. Saich, 1981.
F. Schurmann, 1968.
D. Waller, 1981.
J. Wang, 1980.

Congo

Official name of state: People's Republic of the Congo

Capital: Brazzaville

Nature of state: unitary

Population: 1.7m.

Ethnic composition: Kongo 45%; Teke 20%; M'bochi 15%; Sangha 7%; Others 13%

Principal religion: Catholicism

Formal title and usual abbreviation of communist party: Congolese Party of Labour (CPL)

Membership of communist party: 7,000

Percentage of population in communist party: 0.4

Social composition of party (1975): Workers 34%; Farmers 32%; 'Revolutionary' Intellectuals 22%; Soldiers 12%

Other legal political parties: none

Year of most recent constitution: 1979

Electoral system: direct; choice; elections every five years; vote at 18; -member constituencies

Local representative organs: People's Councils

Central legislature: People's National Assembly; unicameral; 153 seats

State executive organ: Council of Ministers

Leaders since communists assumed power (1968):

Head of Party	Premier	Head of State
(Party established Dec 1969)	(No premier until 1973)	M. Ngouabi (1968–77)
M. Ngouabi (1969–77)	H. Lopes (1973–5)	J. Yhombi-Opango (1977–9)
J. Yhombi-Opango (1977–9)	L.-S. Goma (1975–9)	D. Sassou-Nguesso (1979–)
D. Sassou-Nguesso (1979–)	D. Sassou-Nguesso (1979)	
	L.-S. Goma (1979–84)	
	A. Poungui (1984–)	

Introductory bibliography:

S. Decalo, 1979.

Cuba

Official name of state: Republic of Cuba

Capital: Havana

Nature of state: unitary

Population: 9.9m.

Ethnic composition: 'European' (Caucasian) *c.* 49%; Blacks and Mesticos (mixed ethnicity) *c.* 45%; Others *c.* 1%.

Principal religion: Catholicism

Formal title and usual abbreviation of communist party: Communist Party of Cuba (CPC or CCP)

Membership of communist party: 434,000

Percentage of population in communist party: 4.4

Social composition of party (1979): White-collar workers and intelligentsia 49.3%; Blue-collar workers 44.9%; Peasants 1.3%; Others 4.5%

Other legal political parties: none

Year of most recent constitution: 1976

Electoral system: indirect; limited choice; elections every five years; vote at 16; single-member constituencies

Local representative organs: Organs of Popular Power

Central legislature: National Assembly of People's Power; unicameral; 499 seats

State executive organ: Council of Ministers

Leaders since communists assumed power (1959):

Head of Party	Premier	Head of State
(Party not properly established until 1965)	F. Castro (1959–)	M. Urratio (1959)
		O. Dorticos (1959–76)
F. Castro (1965–)		F. Castro (1976–)

Introductory bibliography:

J. Dominguez, 1978 and 1982a.
E. Gonzalez, 1974.
I. Horowitz, 1984.
C. Mesa-Lago, 1978.
H. Thomas, 1977.

Czechoslovakia

Official name of state: Czechoslovak Socialist Republic

Capital: Prague

Nature of state: federal

Population: 15.4 m.

Ethnic composition: Czechs 64%; Slovaks 30%; Hungarians 4%; Others 2%

Principal religion: Catholicism

Formal title and usual abbreviations of communist party: Communist Party of Czechoslovakia (CPCS)

Membership of communist party: 1.6m.

Percentage of population in communist party: 10.4

Social composition of party (1982): Industrial workers 45.3%; Co-operative workers 5.7%; Others 49.0%

Other legal political parties:
Czechoslovak People's Party
Czechoslovak Socialist Party
Slovak Freedom Party
Slovak Reconstruction Party

Year of most recent constitution: 1960 (with major amendments in 1969)

Electoral system: direct; no choice; elections every five years; vote at 18; single-member constituencies

Local representative organs: National Committees

Central legislature: Federal Assembly; bicameral; 350 seats

State executive organ: Government

Leaders since communists assumed power (1948):

Head of Party	Premier	Head of State
K. Gottwald (1948–53)	K. Gottwald (1948)	E. Benes (1948)
A. Novotny (1953–68)	A. Zapotocky (1948–53)	K. Gottwald (1948–53)
A. Dubcek (1968–9)	V. Siroky (1953–63)	A. Zapotocky (1953–7)
G. Husak (1969–)	J. Lenart (1963–8)	A. Novotny (1957–68)
	O. Cernik (1968–70)	L. Svoboda (1968–75)
	L. Strougal (1970–)	G. Husak (1975–)

Introductory bibliography:

A. Oxley, A. Pravda, and A. Ritchie, 1973.
D. Paul, 1981.
H. G. Skilling, 1976.
O. Ulc, 1974.

Ethiopia

Official name of state: Socialist Ethiopia

Capital: Addis Ababa

Nature of state: unitary

Population: 31.3m.

Ethnic composition: Amhara 37.7%; Galla 35.3%; Tigrean 8.4%; Gurage 3.2%; Others 15.4%

Principal religions: Orthodoxy and Islam

Formal title and usual abbreviation of communist party: Until September 1984 there was a 'Commission for Organizing the Party of the Working People of Ethiopia' (COPWE); now there is a 'Workers' Party of Ethiopia' (WPE)

Membership of communist party: 'Guesstimate'—2,000

Percentage of population in communist party: 0.006(?)

Social composition of party: no data available

Other legal political parties: none

Year of most recent constitution: Ethiopia currently works to a set of proclamations made over the years since 1974, pending a new constitution

Electoral system: not yet specified

Local representative organs: Kebeles (in towns only)

Central legislature: Dergue (Provisional Military Administrative Council)

State executive organ: Council of Ministers

Leaders since communists assumed power (1974):

Head of Party	Premier	Head of State
(Party established Sept 1984)	Aman Andom (1974)	King Merid Azmatch Asfa Wossen (1974–5)
Mengistu Haile Mariam (1984–)	Teferi Banti (1974–7)	
	Mengistu Haile Mariam (1977–)	Mengistu Haile Mariam (1977–)

Introductory bibliography:

F. Halliday and M. Molyneux, 1981.
J. Harbeson, 1979.
P. Henze, 1981.
R. Lefort, 1983.
D. and M. Ottaway, 1981, ch. 6.
M. and D. Ottaway, 1978.
P. Schwab, 1985.

Germany (East)

Official name of state: German Democratic Republic

Capital: Berlin (East)

Nature of state: unitary

Population: 16.8m.

Ethnic composition: German 99%; Others 1%

Principal religion: Protestantism

Formal title and usual abbreviation of communist party: Socialist Unity Party (SED or SUPG)

Membership of communist party: 2.2m.

Percentage of population in communist party: 13.1

Social composition of party (1981): Workers 57.6%; Members of the Intelligentsia 22.1%; Others 20.3%

Other legal political parties (membership in brackets):
Christian Democratic Union (125,000)
Democratic Farmers' Party (103,000)
Liberal Democratic Party (82,000)
National Democratic Party (91,000)

Year of most recent constitution: 1968 (with major amendments in 1974)

Electoral system: direct; limited choice; elections every five years; vote at 18; multi-member constituencies

Local representative organs: Local People's Representative Bodies

Central legislature: People's Chamber; unicameral; 500 seats

State executive organ: Council of Ministers

Leaders since communists assumed power (1949):

Head of Party	Premier	Head of State
O. Grotewohl and W. Pieck (1949–50)	O. Grotewohl (1949–64)	W. Pieck (1949–60)
W. Ulbricht (1950–71)	W. Stoph (1964–73)	W. Ulbricht (1960–73)
E. Honecker (1971–)	H. Sindermann (1973–6)	W. Stoph (1973–6)
	W. Stoph (1976–)	E. Honecker (1976–)

Introductory bibliography:
D. Childs, 1983.
M. Grote, 1979.
L. Legters, 1978.
M. McCauley, 1979, 1983.
J. Starrels and A. Mallinckrodt, 1975.

Hungary

Official name of state: People's Republic of Hungary

Capital: Budapest

Nature of state: unitary

Population: 10.7m.

Ethnic composition: Hungarians 96%; Others 4%

Principal religion: Catholicism

Formal title and usual abbreviation of communist party: Hungarian Socialist Workers' Party (HSWP)

Membership of communist party: 852,000

Percentage of population in communist party: 8.0

Social composition of party: Workers 42.9%; Co-operative Peasantry 7.6%; Others 49.5%

Other legal political parties: none

Year of most recent constitution: 1949 (with major amendments in 1972)

Electoral system: direct; limited choice; elections every five years; vote at 18; single-member constituencies

Local representative organs: Councils

Central legislature: National Assembly; unicameral; 352 seats

State executive organ: Council of Ministers

Leaders since communists assumed power (*1949*):

Head of Party	*Premier*	*Head of State*
M. Rakosi (1949–56)	I. Dobi (1949–52)	A. Szakasits (1949–50)
E. Gero (1956)	M. Rakosi (1952–3)	S. Ronai (1950–2)
J. Kadar (1956–)	I. Nagy (1953–5)	I. Dobi (1952–67)
	A. Hegedus (1955–6)	P. Losonczi (1967–)
	I. Nagy (1956)	
	J. Kadar (1956–8)	
	F. Munnich (1958–61)	
	J. Kadar (1961–5)	
	G. Kallai (1965–7)	
	J. Fock (1967–75)	
	G. Lazar (1975–)	

Introductory bibliography:
B. Kovrig, 1979a, 1979b.
M. Molnar, 1978.
P. Toma and I. Volgyes, 1977.

Kampuchea (Cambodia)

Official name of state: People's Republic of Kampuchea

Capital: Phnom Penh

Nature of state: unitary

Population: 6.0m.

Ethnic composition: Khmers 80%; Others 20%

Principal religion: Buddhism

Formal title and usual abbreviation of communist party: Kampuchean People's Revolutionary Party (KPRP)

Membership of communist party: 700 est.

Percentage of population in communist party: 0.01

Social composition of party: no data available

Other legal political parties: none

Year of most recent constitution: 1981

Electoral system: direct; limited choice; elections every five years; vote at 18; multi-member constituencies

Local representative organs: Local People's Revolutionary Committees

Central legislature: National Assembly; unicameral; 117 seats

State executive organ: Council of Ministers

Leaders since communists assumed power (*1975*):

Head of Party	*Premier*	*Head of State*
Pol Pot (1975–9)	Penn Nouth (1975–6)	Prince Sihanouk (1975–6)
Pen Sovan (1979–81)	Pol Pot (1976–9)	Khieu Samphan (1976–9)
Heng Samrin (1981–)	Heng Samrin (1979–81)	(No formal head 1979–81)
	Pen Sovan (1981–2)	Heng Samrin (1981–)
	Chan Si (1982–4)	
	Hun Sen (1985–)	

Introductory bibliography:
D. Chandler and B. Kiernan, 1983.
B. Kiernan and C. Boua, 1982.
M. Vickery, 1984.

Korea (North)

Official name of state: Democratic People's Republic of Korea

Capital: Pyongyang

Nature of state: unitary

Population: 18.8m.

Ethnic composition: Koreans 99.7%; Others 0.3%

Principal religions/philosophies: Confucianism Buddhism

Formal title and usual abbreviation of communist party: Korean Workers' Party (KWP)

Membership of communist party: 3m.

Percentage of population in communist party: 16.0

Social composition of party: no data available

Other legal political parties: Korean Social Democratic Party; Chongu (Friends') Party

Year of most recent constitution: 1972

Electoral system: direct; no choice; elections every four years; vote at 17; single-member constituencies

Local representative organs: People's assemblies

Central legislature: Supreme People's Assembly; unicameral; 615 seats

State executive organ: Administration Council (under supervision of the Central People's Committee)

Leaders since communists assumed power (1948):

Head of Party	Premier	Head of State
Kim Il-sung (1948–)	Kim Il-sung (1948–72)	Kim Tu-bong (1948–59)
	Kim Il (1972–6)	Choe Yong-gon (1959–72)
	Pak Song-chol (1976–7)	Kim Il-sung (1972–)
	Yi Chong-ok (1977–84)	
	Kang Song-san (1984–)	

Introductory bibliography:
B. Cumings, 1974.
I. Kim, 1975.
C-S. Lee, 1978.
R. Scalapino and C-S. Lee, 1972.
D-S. Suh, 1981.

Laos

Official name of state: Lao People's Democratic Republic

Capital: Vientiane

Nature of state: unitary

Population: 3.6m.

Ethnic composition: Lao Lum 56%; Lao Theung 34%; Lao Soung 9%; Others 1%.

Principal religion: Buddhism

Formal title and usual abbreviation of communist party: Lao People's Revolutionary Party (LPRP)

Membership of communist party: 35,000

Percentage of population in communist party: 1.0

Social composition of party: no data available

Other legal political parties: none

Year of most recent constitution: (none valid—the equivalent of the Constitution are the 'Organic Documents' of December 1975)

Electoral system: not yet specified

Local representative organs: People's revolutionary committees

Central legislature: Supreme People's Council (unicameral, 45 seats) until election of a National Assembly.

Leaders since communists assumed power (1975):

Head of Party	Premier	Head of State
Kaysone Phomvihane (1975–)	Kaysone Phomvihane (1975–)	Souphanouvong (1975–)

Introductory bibliography:

J. van der Kroef, 1981.
M. Stuart-Fox, 1982.

Mongolia

Official name of state: Mongolian People's Republic

Capital: Ulan Bator

Nature of state: unitary

Population: 1.8m.

Ethnic composition: Khalkha 75%; Turkic Kazakhs 5.2%; Others 19.8%.

Principal religion: Buddhism (Lamaism)

Formal title and usual abbreviation of communist party: Mongolian People's Revolutionary Party (MPRP)

Membership of communist party: 76,000

Percentage of population in communist party: 4.2

Social composition of party: Workers 33%; Peasants 18%; Others 49%

Other legal political parties: none

Year of most recent constitution: 1960 (with several amendments since)

Electoral system: direct; no choice; elections every four years; vote at 18; single-member constituencies

Local representative organs: Khurals of people's deputies

Central legislature: People's Great Khural; unicameral; 370 seats

State executive organ: Council of Ministers

Leaders since communists assumed power (1924):

Head of Party	Premier	Head of State
Ts. Dambadorj (1924–8)	B. Tserendorj (1924–9)	
D. Losol (1928–)	A. Amar (1930–2)	Z. Sambuu (1954–72)
Y. Tsedenbal (1940–54)	P. Genden (1932–6)	S. Lusan (1972–4)
D. Damba (1954–8)	A. Amar (1936–8)	Y. Tsedenbal (1974–84)
Y. Tsedenbal (1958–84)	K. Choibalsan (1939–52)	J. Batmunkh (1984–)
J. Batmunkh (1984–)	Y. Tsedenbal (1952–74)	
	J. Batmunkh (1974–84)	
	D. Sodnom (1984–)	

Introductory bibliography:

W. Brown and U. Onon, 1976.
R. Rupen, 1979.

Mozambique

Official name of state: People's Republic of Mozambique

Capital: Maputo

Nature of state: unitary

Population: 13.0m.

Ethnic composition: Makua-Lomwe 37%; Thonga 23%; Shona 10%; Others 30%

Principal religion: Animism

Formal title and usual abbreviation of communist party: Mozambique Liberation Front (Frelimo)

Membership of communist party: 110,323

Percentage of population in communist party: 0.8

Social composition of party: Workers 53.5%; Peasants 18.9%; Others 27.6%

Other legal political parties: none

Year of most recent constitution: 1975

Electoral system: indirect; no choice; elections every five years; vote at 18; -member constituencies.

Local representative organs: People's Assemblies

Central legislature: National People's Assembly; unicameral; 226 seats

State executive organ: Council of Ministers

Leaders since communists assumed power (1975):

Head of Party	Premier	Head of State
S. Machel (1975–)	(None—the President heads the Council of Ministers)	S. Machel (1975–)

Introductory bibliography:

A. and B. Isaacman, 1983.
B. Munslow, 1983.
D. and M. Ottaway, 1981, ch. 4.

Poland

Official name of state: Polish People's Republic

Capital: Warsaw

Nature of state: unitary

Population: 36.6m.

Ethnic composition: Poles 99%; Others 1%

Principal religion: Catholicism

Formal title and usual abbreviation of communist party: Polish United Workers' Party (PUWP)

Membership of communist party: 2.3m.

Percentage of population in communist party: 6.3

Social composition of party (1980): Workers 45.9%; Peasants 9.4%; White-collar employees 33.2%; Others 11.5%

Other legal political parties (1978 membership in brackets):
United Peasant Party (428,000)
Democratic Party (96,500)

Year of most recent constitution: 1952 (with several major amendments, especially in 1976)

Electoral system: direct; limited choice; elections every four years; vote at 18; multi-member constituencies

Local representative organs: People's Councils

Central legislature: Sejm (Diet); unicameral; 460 seats

State executive organ: Council of Ministers

Leaders since communists assumed power (1947):

Head of Party	Premier	Head of State
W. Gomulka (1947–8)	J. Cyrankiewicz (1947–52)	B. Bierut (1947–52)
B. Bierut (1948–56)	B. Bierut (1952–4)	A. Zawadski (1952–64)
E. Ochab (1956)	J. Cyrankiewicz (1954–70)	E. Ochab (1964–8)
W. Gomulka (1956–70)	P. Jaroszewicz (1970–80)	M. Spychalski (1968–70)
E. Gierek (1970–80)	E. Babiuch (1980)	J. Cyrankiewicz (1970–2)
S. Kania (1980–1)	J. Pinkowski (1980–1)	H. Jablonski (1972–85)
W. Jaruzelski (1981–)	W. Jaruzelski (1981–5)	W. Jaruzelski (1985–)
	Z. Messner (1985–)	

Introductory bibliography:

A. Bromke, 1967.
M. Dziewanowski, 1976.
A. Korbonski, 1979.
M. Simon and R. Kanet, 1981.
J. Woodall, 1982.

Romania

Official name of state: Socialist Republic of Romania

Capital: Bucharest

Nature of state: unitary

Population: 22.6m.

Ethnic composition: Romanians 88%; Hungarians 8%; German 2%; Others 2%

Principal religion: Romanian Orthodoxy

Formal title and usual abbreviation of communist party: Romanian Communist Party (RCP)

Membership of communist party: 3.3m.

Percentage of population in communist party: 14.6

Social composition of party: Workers 55.4%; Peasants and Agricultural Workers 22.7%; Intelligentsia 22%

Other legal political parties: none

Year of most recent constitution: 1965 (with major amendments in 1974)

Electoral system: direct; limited choice; elections every five years; vote at 18; single-member constituencies

Local representative organs: People's Councils

Central legislature: Grand National Assembly; unicameral; 369 seats

State executive organ: Council of Ministers

Leaders since communists assumed power (1947):

Head of Party	Premier	Head of State
G. Gheorghiu-Dej (1947–54)	P. Groza (1947–52)	C. Parhon (1948–52)
G. Apostol (1954–5)	G. Gheorghiu-Dej (1952–5)	P. Groza (1952–8)
G. Gheorghiu-Dej (1955–65)	C. Stoica (1955–61)	I. Maurer (1958–61)
N. Ceausescu (1965–　)	I. Maurer (1961–74)	G. Gheorghiu-Dej (1961–5)
	M. Manescu (1974–9)	C. Stoica (1965–7)
	I. Verdet (1979–82)	N. Ceausescu (1967–　)
	C. Dascalescu (1982–　)	

Introductory bibliography:

S. Fischer-Galati, 1969.
G. Ionescu, 1964.
R. King, 1979b and 1980.
M. Shafir, 1985.

Soviet Union

Official name of state: Union of Soviet Socialist Republics (USSR)

Capital: Moscow

Nature of state: Federal

Population: 272.3m.

Ethnic composition: Russians 52%; Ukrainians 16%; Uzbeks 5%; Belorussians 4%; Others 23%

Principal religions: Russian Orthodoxy and Islam (Sunni)

Formal title and usual abbreviation of communist party: Communist Party of the Soviet Union (CPSU)

Membership of communist party: 18.3m.

Percentage of population in communist party: 6.7

Social composition of party (1981): Workers 43.4%; Collective Farmers 12.8%; Intelligentsia and others 43.8%

Other legal political parties: none

Year of most recent constitution: 1977

Electoral system: direct; no choice; elections every five years; vote at 18; single-member constituencies

Local representative organs: Soviets of People's Deputies

Central legislature: Supreme Soviet; bicameral; 1500 seats

State executive organ: Council of Ministers

Leaders since communists assumed power (1917):

Head of Party	Premier	Head of State
V. Lenin (1917–24)	V. Lenin (1917–24)	Y. Sverdlov (1918–19)
J. Stalin (1924–53)	A. Rykov (1924–31)	M. Kalinin (1919–46)
N. Khrushchev (1953–64)	V. Molotov (1931–41)	N. Shvernik (1946–53)
L. Brezhnev (1964–82)	J. Stalin (1941–53)	K. Voroshilov (1953–60)
Y. Andropov (1982–4)	G. Malenkov (1953–5)	L. Brezhnev (1960–4)
K. Chernenko (1984–5)	N. Bulganin (1955–8)	A. Mikoyan (1964–5)
M. Gorbachev (1985–)	N. Khrushchev (1958–64)	N. Podgorny (1965–77)
	A. Kosygin (1964–80)	L. Brezhnev (1977–82)
	N. Tikhonov (1980–5)	Y. Andropov (1983–4)
	N. Ryzhkov (1985–)	K. Chernenko (1984–5)
		A. Gromyko (1985–)

Introductory bibliography:

A. Brown, J. Fennell, M. Kaser and H. Willetts, 1982.
L. Churchward, 1975.
D. Hammer, 1974.
R. Hill and P. Frank, 1983.
D. Lane, 1978, 1985.
M. McAuley, 1977.

Vietnam

Official name of state: Socialist Republic of Vietnam

Capital: Hanoi

Nature of state: unitary

Population: 57.0m.

Ethnic composition: Vietnamese (Kinh) 87%; Others 13%

Principal religion: Buddhism

Formal title and usual abbreviation of communist party: Vietnamese Communist Party (VCP)

Membership of communist party: 1.7m.

Percentage of population in communist party: 3.0

Social composition of party: no data available

Other legal political parties:
Democratic Party
Socialist Party

Year of most recent constitution: 1980

Electoral system: direct; limited choice; elections every five years; vote at 18; single-member constituencies

Local representative organs: People's Councils

Central legislature: National Assembly; unicameral; 496 seats

State executive organ: Council of Ministers

Leaders since communists assumed power (1945/75):

Head of Party	Premier	Head of State
Ho Chi Minh (1945–69)	Ho Chi Minh (1945–55)	Ho Chi Minh (1945–69)
Le Duan (1969–)	Pham Van Dong (1955–)	Ton Duc Thang (1969–80)
		Truong Chinh (1981–)

Introductory bibliography:

J. M. van der Kroef, 1981.
D. Pike, 1978.
W. Turley, 1980.
R. Turner, 1975.

Yemen (South)

Official name of state: People's Democratic Republic of Yemen

Capital: Aden

Nature of state: unitary

Population: 2.08m.

Ethnic composition: Arabs 75%; Indians 11%; Somalis 8%; Others 6%

Principal religion: Islam (Sunni)

Formal title and usual abbreviation of communist party: Yemeni Socialist Party (YSP)

Membership of communist party: 19,000

Percentage of population in communist party: 0.9

Social composition of party: no data available

Other legal political parties (membership in brackets): People's Democratic Union (500)

Year of most recent constitution: 1970 (with major amendments in 1978)

Electoral system: direct; some choice; elections every three years; vote at 18; single-member constituencies

Local representative organs: Local People's Councils

Central legislature: Supreme People's Council; unicameral; 111 seats

State executive organ: Council of Ministers

Leaders since communists assumed power (1969):

Head of Party	Premier	Head of State
(Party founded 1978) Abdul Fattah Ismail (1978–80) Ali Nasser Mohammed (1980–)	Mohammed Ali Haithem (1969–71) Ali Nasser Mohammed (1971–85) Haider Abu Bakr al Attas (1985–)	Salem Rubayi Ali (1969–78) Ali Nasser Mohammed (1978) Abdul Fattah Ismail (1978–80) Ali Nasser Mohammed (1980–)

Introductory bibliography:

R. Bidwell, 1983.
N. Cigar, 1985.
F. Halliday, 1979.
R. Stookey, 1982.

Yugoslavia

Official name of state: Socialist Federal Republic of Yugoslavia (SFRY)

Capital: Belgrade

Nature of state: federal

Population: 22.8m.

Ethnic composition: Serbs 36%; Croats 20%; Moslems 9%; Slovenes 8%; Albanians 8%; Others 19%

Principal religions: Orthodoxy and Catholicism

Formal title and usual abbreviation of communist party: League of Communists of Yugoslavia (LCY)

Membership of communist party: 2.2m.

Percentage of population in communist party: 9.6

Social composition of party (1976): White-collar employees 41.8%; Blue-collar workers 28.1%; Peasants 5.1%; Others 25.0%

Other legal political parties: none

Year of most recent constitution: 1974

Electoral system: indirect; limited choice; elections every four years; vote at 18, or 16 if employed; single-member constituencies

Local representative organs: Assemblies

Central legislature: Assembly of the SFRY; bicameral; 308 seats

State executive organ: Federal Executive Council

Leaders since communists assumed power (1945):

Head of Party	*Premier*	*Head of State*
J. Tito (1945–80)	J. Tito (1945–63)	I. Ribar (1945–53)
S. Doronjski (1980)	P. Stambolic (1963–7)	J. Tito (1953–80)
L. Mojsov (1980–1)	M. Spiljak (1967–9)	L. Kolisevski (1980)
D. Dragosavac (1981–2)	M. Ribicic (1969–71)	C. Mijatovic (1980–1)
M. Ribicic (1982–3)	D. Bijedic (1971–7)	S. Kraigher (1981–2)
D. Markovic (1983–4)	V. Djuranovic (1977–82)	P. Stambolic (1982–3)
A. Sukrija (1984–5)	M. Planinc (1982–)	M. Spiljak (1983–4)
		V. Djuranovic (1984–5)
		R. Vlajkovic (1985–)

Introductory bibliography:

R. Remington, 1979, 1984.
D. Rusinow, 1977.
P. Shoup, 1979.
F. Singleton, 1976.
S. Zukin, 1975.

LIST OF SOURCES CITED

ALLWORTH, E. (ed.) (1980). *Ethnic Russia in the USSR* (New York: Pergamon).

ALMOND, G. (1970), *Political Development* (Boston: Little Brown).

—— and S. VERBA (1963), *The Civic Culture* (Princeton, N.J.: Princeton University Press).

ALTHUSSER, L. (1979), *For Marx* (Harmondsworth: Penguin).

AMALRIK, A. (1969), 'Will the Soviet Union Survive until 1984?', *Survey*, no. 73, pp. 47–79.

AMNESTY INTERNATIONAL (1984a), *Torture in the Eighties* (London: Amnesty International Publications).

—— (1984b), *China—Violations of Human Rights* (London: Amnesty International Publications).

ARENDT, H. (1958), *The Origins of Totalitarianism* (London: George Allen & Unwin).

ARMSTRONG, J. (1965), 'Sources of Administrative Behavior: Some Soviet and Western European Comparisons', *American Political Science Review*, vol. lix, no. 3, pp. 643–55.

ARNOLD, A. (1983), *Afghanistan's Two-Party Communism* (Stanford: Hoover Institution Press).

ARTISIEN, P. and R. HOWELLS (1981), 'Yugoslavia, Albania and the Kosovo Riots', *The World Today*, November, pp. 419–27.

ASCHERSON, N. (1981), *The Polish August* (Harmondsworth: Penguin).

AVTORKHANOV, A. (1967), *The Communist Party Apparatus* (Cleveland: World Publishing).

BAHRO, R. (1978), *The Alternative in Eastern Europe* (London: NLB).

BAHRY, D. (1983), 'Politics, Succession and Public Policy in Communist Systems: A Review Article', *Soviet Studies*, vol. xxxv, no. 2, pp. 240–9.

BARBER, B. (1969), 'Conceptual Foundations of Totalitarianism' in Friedrich, Curtis, and Barber (1969), pp. 3–52.

BARGHOORN, F. (1971), 'The Security Police' in Skilling and Griffiths (1971), pp. 93–129.

BARING, A. (1972), *Uprising in East Germany* (Ithaca: Cornell University Press).

BARTKE, W. (1981), *Who's Who in the People's Republic of China* (Brighton: Harvester).

BAYLIS, T. (1971), 'Economic Reform as Ideology: East Germany's New Economic System', *Comparative Politics*, vol. iii, no. 2, pp. 211–29.

—— (1972), 'In Quest of Legitimacy', *Problems of Communism*, vol. xxi, no. 2, pp. 46–55.

—— (1974), *The Technical Intelligentsia and the East German Elite* (Berkeley and Los Angeles: University of California Press).

BECK, C. (1968), 'Bureaucratic Conservatism and Innovation in Eastern Europe', *Comparative Political Studies*, vol. i, no. 2, pp. 275–94.

BECK, C. *et al.* (1973), *Comparative Communist Political Leadership* (New York: David McKay).

—— W. JARZABEK and P. ERNANDEZ (1976), 'Political Succession in Eastern Europe', *Studies in Comparative Communism*, vol. ix, nos. 1 and 2, pp. 35–61.

BECK, F. and W. GODIN (1951), *Russian Purge* (London: Hurst & Blackett).

BENNIGSEN, A. (1980), 'Soviet Muslims and the World of Islam', *Problems of Communism*, vol. xxix, no. 2, pp. 38–51.

—— (1984), 'Mullahs, Mujahidin and Soviet Muslims', *Problems of Communism*, vol. xxxiii, no. 6, pp. 28–44.

BENTLEY, A. (1908), *The Process of Government* (Chicago: University of Chicago Press).

BENTON, G. (1980), 'China's Oppositions', *New Left Review*, no. 122, pp. 59–78.

—— (1982a), *Wild Lilies, Poisonous Weeds* (London: Pluto Press).

—— (1982b), 'China Spring', in Benton (1982a), pp. 1–15.

BERKI, R. (1982), 'The State, Marxism and Political Legitimation' in Rigby and Feher (1982), pp. 146–69.

BERTSCH, G. (1973), 'The Revival of Nationalisms', *Problems of Communism*, vol. xxii, no. 6, pp. 1–15.

—— (1982), *Power and Policy in Communist Systems* (New York: Wiley).

—— and T. GANSCHOW (eds.) (1976), *Comparative Communism* (San Francisco: Freeman).

BEZUGLOV, A. (1973), *Soviet Deputy* (Moscow: Progress).

BIDWELL, R. (1983), *The Two Yemens* (Harlow: Longman).

BLACK, C. (1964), 'The Anticipation of Communist Revolutions' in C. Black and T. Thornton (eds.) (1964), *Communism and Revolution* (Princeton: Princeton University Press), pp. 417–48.

BLECHER, M. and G. WHITE (1979), *Micropolitics in Contemporary China* (New York: M. E. Sharpe).

BLOCH, S. and P. REDDAWAY (1978), *Russia's Political Hospitals* (London: Futura).

BONAVIA, D. (1982), *The Chinese* (Harmondsworth: Penguin).

BOTTOMORE, T. (1966), *Elites and Society* (Harmondsworth: Penguin).

BRABANT, J. VAN (1980), *Socialist Economic Integration* (Cambridge: Cambridge University Press).

BROMKE, A. (ed.) (1965), *The Communist States at the Crossroads* (New York and Washington: Praeger).

—— (1967), *Poland's Politics* (Cambridge, Mass: Harvard University Press).

—— and D. NOVAK (eds.) (1978), *The Communist States in the Era of Detente* (Oakville: Mosaic).

—— and T. RAKOWSKA-HARMSTONE (eds.) (1972), *The Communist States in Disarray* (Minneapolis: University of Minnesota Press).

BRONFENBRENNER, U. (1970), *Two Worlds of Childhood* (New York: Russell Sage Foundation).

BROWN, A. (1971), 'Policy-Making in the Soviet Union', *Soviet Studies*, vol. xxiii, no. 1, pp. 120–48.

—— (1974), *Soviet Politics and Political Science* (London: Macmillan).

—— (1977), 'Introduction' in Brown and Gray (1977), pp. 1–24.

—— (1978), 'Policymaking in Communist States', *Studies in Comparative Communism*, vol. xi, no. 4, pp. 424–36.

—— (1980), 'The Power of the General Secretary of the CPSU' in Rigby, Brown, and Reddaway (1980), pp. 135–57.

—— (ed.) (1984a), *Political Culture and Communist Studies* (London: Macmillan).

—— (1984b), 'Conclusions' in Brown (1984a), pp. 149–203.

—— (1984c), 'Political Power and the Soviet State: Western and Soviet Perspectives' in Harding (1984), pp. 51–103.

—— J. FENNELL, M. KASER and H. WILLETTS (eds.) (1982). *The Cambridge Encyclopedia of Russia and the Soviet Union* (Cambridge: Cambridge University Press).

—— and J. GRAY (eds.) (1977, 1979), *Political Culture and Political Change in Communist States* (1st and 2nd eds.) (London: Macmillan).

—— and M. KASER (1978), *The Soviet Union Since the Fall of Khrushchev* (London: Macmillan).

BROWN, J. (1970), *Bulgaria under Communist Rule* (London: Pall Mall).

BROWN, K. (1979), 'Angolan Socialism' in Rosberg and Callaghy (1979), pp. 296–321.

BROWN, W. and U. ONON (eds.) (1976), *History of the Mongolian People's Republic* (Cambridge, Mass: Harvard University Press).

BRUGGER, B. (1981), *China: Liberation and Transformation 1942–1962* (London: Croom Helm).

BRZEZINSKI, Z. (1967), *The Soviet Bloc* (Cambridge, Mass: Harvard University Press).

—— and S. HUNTINGTON (1964), *Political Power: USA/USSR* (New York: Viking).

BUNCE, V. (1981), *Do New Leaders Make A Difference?* (Princeton: Princeton University Press).

—— and J. ECHOLS (1980), 'Soviet Politics in the Brezhnev Era: "Pluralism" or "Corporatism"?' in D. Kelley (ed.) (1980), *Soviet Politics in the Brezhnev Era* (New York: Praeger), pp. 1–26.

BURDA, A. (1978), *Parliament of the Polish People's Republic* (Wroclaw: Ossolineum).

BURKS, R. V. (1964), 'Eastern Europe' in Cohen and Shapiro (1974), pp. 38–79.

BURNHAM, J. (1950), *The Coming Defeat of Communism* (London: Jonathan Cape).

CALDWELL, L. (1975). 'The Warsaw Pact: Directions of Change', *Problems of Communism*, vol. xxiv, no. 5, pp. 1–19.

CAREW HUNT, R. (1963), *The Theory and Practice of Communism* (Harmondsworth: Penguin).

CARRERE D'ENCAUSSE, H. (1981), *Decline of an Empire* (New York: Harper and Row).

CARRILLO, S. (1977), *'Eurocommunism' and the State* (London: Lawrence and Wishart).

CASAL, L. and M. PEREZ-STABLE (1981), 'Party and State in Post-1970 Cuba' in Holmes (1981b), pp. 81–103.

CASON, T. (1982), 'The Warsaw Pact' in Clawson and Kaplan (1982), pp. 137–62.

CHAMBERLIN, W. H. (1965), *The Russian Revolution—Vol. 1* (New York: Grosset and Dunlap).

CHAMBRE, H. (1967), 'Soviet Ideology', *Soviet Studies*, vol. xviii, no. 3, pp. 314–27.

CHANDLER, D. and B. KIERNAN (eds.) (1983), *Revolution and Its Aftermath in Kampuchea* (New Haven: Yale University Southeast Asia Studies).

CHANG, P. (1981), 'Chinese Politics: Deng's Turbulent Quest', *Problems of Communism*, vol. xxx, no. 1, pp. 1–21.

CHASE-DUNN, C. (ed.) (1982a), *Socialist States in the World System* (Beverly Hills: Sage).

—— (1982b), 'The Transition to World Socialism' in Chase-Dunn (1982a), pp. 271–96.

CHERNENKO, K. (1980), *Voprosy Raboty Partiinogoi Gosudarstvennogo Apparata* (Moscow: Izdatel'stvo Politicheskoi Literatury).

CHIANG HSIN-LI (1981), 'De-Maoification in Communist China: Its Development and Prospects' *Issues and Studies*, vol. xvii, no. 1, pp. 27–42.

CHILDS, D. (1969), *East Germany* (New York: Praeger).

—— (1983), *The GDR* (London: George Allen & Unwin).

CHURCHWARD, L. (1975), *Contemporary Soviet Government* (London: Routledge & Kegan Paul).

CIGAR, N. (1985), 'State and Society in South Yemen', *Problems of Communism*, vol. xxxiv, no. 3, pp. 41–58.

CLAWSON, R. and L. KAPLAN (eds.) (1982), *The Warsaw Pact* (Wilmington, Del: Scholarly Resources).

CLAYTON, E. (1983), 'USSR Regional Issues: Growth vs. Equality', *Problems of Communism*, vol. xxxii, no. 5, pp. 75–7.

CLIFF, T. (1974), *State Capitalism in Russia* (London: Pluto Press).

COHEN, L. (1977), 'Political Participation, Competition, and Dissent in Yugoslavia: A Report of Research on Electoral Behavior', in Triska and Cocks (1977), pp. 178–216.

—— and J. SHAPIRO (eds.) (1974), *Communist Systems in Comparative Perspective* (New York: Anchor).

CONNOR, W. (1980), 'Dissent in Eastern Europe: A New Coalition?' *Problems in Communism*, vol. xxix, no. 1, pp. 1–17.

—— (1984), *The National Question in Marxist–Leninist Theory and Strategy* (Princeton: Princeton University Press).

CONQUEST, R. (1971), *The Great Terror* (Harmondsworth: Penguin).

COX, M. (1975), 'The Politics of the Dissenting Intellectual', *Critique*, no. 5, pp. 5–34.

CPSU (1961), *Programme of the Communist Party of the Soviet Union* (Moscow: Foreign Languages Publishing House).

CUMINGS, B. (1974), 'Kim's Korean Communism', *Problems of Communism*, vol. xxiii, no. 2, pp. 27–41.

DAHL, R. (1971), *Polyarchy* (New Haven: Yale University Press).

—— (1976), *Modern Political Analysis* (Englewood Cliffs: Prentice-Hall).

DALLIN, A. and G. BRESLAUER (1970), *Political Terror in Communist Systems* (Stanford: Stanford University Press).

DAWISHA, K. (1972), 'The Roles of Ideology in the Decision-Making of the Soviet Union', *International Relations*, vol. iv, no. 2, pp. 156–75.

—— and P. HANSON (eds.) (1981), *Soviet—East European Dilemmas* (London: Heinemann).

DAY, A. and H. DEGENHARDT (eds.) (1980), *Political Parties of the World* (Harlow: Longman).

DECALO, S. (1979), 'Ideological Rhetoric and Scientific Socialism in Benin and Congo/Brazzaville' in Rosberg and Callaghy (1979), pp. 231–64.

DELURY, G. (ed.) (1983), *World Encyclopedia of Political Systems and Parties*, 2 vols. (New York: Facts on File).

DEUTSCH, K. (1963), 'Cracks in the Monolith: Possibilities and Patterns of Disintegration in Totalitarian Systems', in H. Eckstein and D. Apter (eds.) (1963), *Comparative Politics* (New York: Free Press), pp. 497–508.

DEUTSCHER, I. (1966), *Stalin* (Harmondsworth: Penguin).

DITTMER, L. (1983), 'Comparative Communist Political Culture', *Studies in Comparative Communism*, vol. xvi, nos. 1 and 2, pp. 9–24.

DJILAS, M. (1966), *The New Class* (London: George Allen & Unwin).

DOBBS, M. (1979), 'Three Mile Island fuels Rebellion in Yugoslavia', *The Guardian* (Manchester), 24 April, p. 9.

DOMINGUEZ, J. (1978), *Cuba* (Cambridge, Mass: Harvard University Press).

—— (ed.) (1982a), *Cuba—Internal and International Affairs* (Beverly Hills: Sage).

—— (1982b), 'Revolutionary Politics: The New Demands for Orderliness' in Dominguez (1982a), pp. 19–70.

DONNITHORNE, A. (1983), 'New Light on Central-Provincial Relations', *Australian Journal of Chinese Affairs*, no. 10, pp. 97–104.

DRAGNICH, A. (1983), 'Yugoslavia' in R. Wesson (ed.) (1983), *Yearbook on International Communist Affairs 1983* (Stanford: Hoover Institution Press), pp. 367–78.

DREYER, J. (1968), 'China's Minority Nationalities in the Cultural Revolution', *China Quarterly*, no. 35, pp. 96–109.

—— (1975), 'China's Quest for a Socialist Solution', *Problems of Communism*, vol. xxiv, no. 5, pp. 49–62.

—— (1976), *China's Forty Millions* (Cambridge, Mass: Harvard University Press).

DUPREE, L. (1979), 'Afghanistan under the Khalq', *Problems of Communism*, vol. xxviii, no. 4, pp. 34–50.

—— (1980), *Afghanistan* (Princeton: Princeton University Press).

DUX, D. (1963), *Ideology in Conflict* (Princeton: Van Nostrand).

DYKER, D. (1977), 'Yugoslavia: Unity out of Diversity?', in Brown and Gray (1977), pp. 66–100.

DZIEWANOWSKI, M. (1976), *The Communist Party of Poland* (Cambridge, Mass: Harvard University Press).

ECKSTEIN, S. (1982), 'Cuba and the Capitalist World Economy' in Chase-Dunn (1982a), pp. 203–18.

EDMONDS, R. (1983), *Soviet Foreign Policy* (Oxford: Oxford University Press).

EHLERT, W. *et al.* (eds.) (1973), *Worterbuch der Okonomie Sozialismus* (East Berlin: Dietz).

ELLIOTT, D. (1975), 'North Vietnam Since Ho', *Problems of Communism*, vol. xxiv, no. 4, pp. 35–52.

ELLUL, J. (1965), *The Technological Society* (London: Jonathan Cape).

ERICKSON, J. (1981), 'The Warsaw Pact—the Shape of Things to Come?' in Dawisha and Hanson (1981), pp. 148–71.

ESHERICK, J. and E. PERRY (1983), 'Leadership Succession in the People's Republic of China: "Crisis" or Opportunity?' *Studies in Comparative Communism*, vol. xvi, no. 3, pp. 171–7.

EVANS, A. (1977), 'Developed Socialism in Soviet Ideology', *Soviet Studies*, vol. xxix, no. 3, pp. 409–28.

EVANS, G. and K. ROWLEY (1984), *Red Brotherhood at War* (London: Verso).

FAGEN, R. (1969), *The Transformation of Political Culture in Cuba* (Stanford: Stanford University Press).

FAINSOD, M. (1954), *How Russia is Ruled* (Cambridge, Mass: Harvard University Press).

FALKENHEIM, V. (1978), 'Political Participation in China', *Problems of Communism*, vol. xxvii, no. 3, pp. 18–32.

FARRELL, R. B. (ed.) (1970), *Political Leadership in Eastern Europe and the Soviet Union* (London: Butterworths).

FEI XIAOTONG (1981), 'Reflections of a Judge' in *A Great Trial in Chinese History* (1981), pp. 1–11.

FEJTÖ, F. (1974), *A History of the People's Democracies* (Harmondsworth: Penguin).

FEUER, L.(1969), *Marx and Engels: Basic Writings on Politics and Philosophy* (London: Collins).

FISCHER-GALATI, S. (1969), *The Socialist Republic of Rumania* (Baltimore: Johns Hopkins).

—— (ed.) (1979), *The Communist Parties of Eastern Europe* (New York: Columbia University Press).

FISCHER, A. and H. WEBER (1979), 'Periodisierungsprobleme der Geschichte der DDR', *Deutschlandarchiv*, Sonderheft, pp. 17–26.

FLERON, F. (1968), 'Toward a Reconceptualisation of Political Change in the Soviet Union—The Political Leadership System', *Comparative Politics*, vol. i, no. 2, pp. 228–44.

—— (ed.) (1969), *Communist Studies and the Social Sciences* (Chicago: Rand McNally).

FRANK, P. (1978), 'The Changing Composition of the Communist Party' in Brown and Kaser (1978), pp. 96–120.

FRIEDGUT, T. (1979), *Political Participation in the USSR* (Princeton: Princeton University Press).

FRIEDRICH, C. (1969), 'The Evolving Theory and Practice of Totalitarian Regimes' in Friedrich, Curtis, and Barber (1969), pp. 123–64.

—— and Z. BRZEZINSKI (1956), *Totalitarian Dictatorship and Autocracy* (Cambridge, Mass: Harvard University Press).

—— M. CURTIS and B. BARBER (1969), *Totalitarianism in Perspective* (London: Pall Mall).

GEHLEN, M. (1969), *The Communist Party of the Soviet Union* (Bloomington: Indiana University Press).

GERTH, H. and C. WRIGHT MILLS (eds.) (1970). *From Max Weber* (London: Routledge & Kegan Paul).

GIDDENS, A. (1973), *The Class Structure of the Advanced Societies* (London: Hutchinson).

GILBERG, T. (1981), 'Modernization, Human Rights and Nationalism: The Case of Romania' in Klein and Reban (1981), pp. 185–211.

GILL, G. (1982), 'Personal Dominance and the Collective Principle: Individual Legitimacy in Marxist–Leninist Systems' in Rigby and Feher (1982), pp. 94–110.

—— (1984), 'The Decline of the General Secretary? The Structure of Soviet Leadership in the 1980s', Unpublished Paper, 34 pp.

GITELMAN, Z. (1983), 'Are Nations Merging in the USSR?', *Problems of Communism*, vol. xxxii, no. 5, pp. 35–47.

GONZALEZ, E. (1974), *Cuba Under Castro* (Boston: Houghton Mifflin).

GOODMAN, D. (1980), 'The Provincial First Party Secretary in the People's Republic of China, 1949–78: A Profile', *British Journal of Political Science*, vol. x, no. 1, pp. 39–74.

—— (ed.) (1984), *Groups and Politics in the People's Republic of China* (Cardiff: University College Cardiff Press).

GRAY, J. (1977), 'China: Communism and Confucianism' in Brown and Gray (1977), pp. 197–230.

A Great Trial in Chinese History (Beijing: New World).

GRIFFITH, W. (1964), *The Sino-Soviet Rift* (Cambridge, Mass: MIT Press).

—— (1983), 'Sino-Soviet Rapprochement?', *Problems of Communism*, vol. xxxii, no. 2, pp. 20–9.

GRIPP, R. (1973), *The Political System of Communism* (London: Nelson).

GROTE, M. (1979), 'The Socialist Unity Party of Germany' in Fischer-Galati (1979), pp. 167–200.

GUILLERMAZ, J. (1972), *A History of the Chinese Communist Party 1921–1949* (London: Methuen).

GUINS, G. (1956), *Communism On The Decline* (The Hague: Martinus Nijhoff).

HALLIDAY, F. (1978), 'Revolution in Afghanistan', *New Left Review*, no. 112, pp. 3–44.

—— (1979), 'Yemen's Unfinished Revolutions: Socialism in the South', *Middle East Research and Information Project Reports*, vol. ix, no. 8, pp. 3–20.

—— (1980), 'The War and Revolution in Afghanistan', *New Left Review*, no. 119, pp. 20–41.

—— and M. MOLYNEUX (1981), *The Ethiopian Revolution* (London: Verso and NLB).

HAMMER, D. (1974), *USSR: The Politics of Oligarchy* (Hinsdale: Dryden).

HAMMOND, T. (ed.) (1975a), *The Anatomy of Communist Takeovers* (New Haven: Yale University Press).

—— (1975b), 'A Summing Up' in Hammond (1975a), pp. 638–43.

—— (1975c), 'The History of Communist Takeovers' in Hammond (1975a), pp. 1–45.

HANHARDT, A. (1975), 'East Germany: From Goals to Realities' in Volgyes (1975), pp. 66–91.

HARALAMBOS, M. (1980), *Sociology—Themes and Perspectives* (Slough: University Tutorial Press).

HARBESON, J. (1979), 'Socialist Politics in Revolutionary Ethiopia' in Rosberg and Callaghy (1979), pp. 345–72.

HARDING, N. (1981), 'What Does It Mean to Call a Regime Marxist?' in Szajkowski (1981a), vol. 1, pp. 20–33.

—— (1983), *Lenin's Political Thought* (London: Macmillan).

—— (ed.) (1984), *The State in Socialist Society* (London: Macmillan).

HARDT, J. and T. FRANKEL (1971), 'The Industrial Managers' in Skilling and Griffiths (1971), pp. 171–208.

HARMAN, C. (1974), *Bureaucracy and Revolution in Eastern Europe* (London: Pluto).

—— (1983), *Class Struggles in Eastern Europe* (London: Pluto).

HAVEMANN, R. (1974), 'Die Regierung soll dem eigenen Volk Vertrauen schenken', *Deutschland Archiv*, vol. vii, no. 1, pp. 46–9.

HAYNES, V. and O. SEMYONOVA (eds.) (1979), *Workers Against the Gulag* (London: Pluto Press).

HENZE, P. (1981), 'Communism and Ethiopia', *Problems of Communism*, vol. xxx, no. 3, pp. 55–74.

HERSPRING, D. (1980), 'The Warsaw Pact at 25', *Problems of Communism*, vol. xxix, no. 5, pp. 1–15.

HILL, R. (1980), *Soviet Politics, Political Science and Reform* (Oxford: Martin Robertson).

—— (1983), Book Review in *Communist Affairs*, vol. ii, no. 2, pp. 275–6.

—— and P. FRANK (1983), *The Soviet Communist Party* (London: George Allen & Unwin).

HINTON, H. (1978), *An Introduction to Chinese Politics* (New York: Praeger).

HIRSCHMAN, A. (1970), 'The Search for Paradigms as a Hindrance to Understanding', *World Politics*, vol. xxii, no. 3, pp. 329–43.

HOLMES, L. (1981a), *The Policy Process in Communist States* (Beverly Hills: Sage).

—— (ed.) (1981b), *The Withering Away of the State?* (London: Sage).

—— (1981c), 'Conclusions: Whither the Party and State?' in Holmes (1981b), pp. 245–80.

—— (1981d), 'The GDR: "Real Socialism" or "Computer Stalinism"?' in Holmes (1981b), pp. 125–50.

HOROWITZ, I. (1984), *Cuban Communism* (New Brunswick: Transaction).

HOUGH, J. (1969), *The Soviet Prefects* (Cambridge, Mass: Harvard University Press).

—— (1972), 'The Soviet System: Petrification or Pluralism?', *Problems of Communism*, vol. xxi, no. 2, pp. 25–45.

—— (1976), 'Political Participation in the Soviet Union', *Soviet Studies*, vol. xxviii, no. 1, pp. 3–20.

—— (1979), 'The Generation Gap and the Brezhnev Succession', *Problems of Communism*, vol. xxviii, no. 4, pp. 1–16.

—— (1980), *Soviet Leadership in Transition* (Washington DC: Brookings Institution).

—— (1983), 'Pluralism, Corporatism and the Soviet Union' in S. G. Solomon (1983), pp. 37–60.

—— and M. FAINSOD (1979), *How the Soviet Union is Governed* (Cambridge, Mass: Harvard University Press).

HU QIAOMU (1982), 'On the Practice of Communist Thought', *Beijing Review*, 18 October 1982, pp. 12–15.

HUBER, M. and H-G. HEINRICH (1981), 'Hungary—Quiet Progress?' in Holmes (1981b), pp. 151–74.

HYMAN, A. (1982), 'Afghan Intelligentsia 1978–81' *Index on Censorship*, no. 2, pp. 8–10.

—— (1984), *Afghanistan Under Soviet Domination* (London: Macmillan).

INKELES, A. (1966), 'Models and Issues in the Analysis of Soviet Society', *Survey*, no. 60, pp. 3–17.

IONESCU, G. (1964), *Communism in Rumania 1944–1962* (London: Oxford University Press).

—— (1965), *The Break-Up of the Soviet Empire in Eastern Europe* (Harmondsworth: Penguin).

—— (1967), *The Politics of the European Communist States* (London: Weidenfeld & Nicolson).

—— (1972), *Comparative Communist Politics* (London: Macmillan).

ISAACMAN, A. and B. (1983), *Mozambique* (Boulder: Westview Press).

ISMAEL, T. (1981), 'People's Democratic Republic of Yemen' in Szajkowski (1981a), vol. iii, pp. 755–83.

JANCAR, B. (1978), *Women under Communism* (Baltimore: Johns Hopkins).

JOHNSON, A. R., R. DEAN, and A. ALEXIEV (1982), *East European Military Establishments* (New York: Crane Russak).

JOHNSON, C. (ed.) (1970), *Change in Communist Systems* (Stanford: Stanford University Press).

JORAVSKY, D. (1966), 'Soviet Ideology', *Soviet Studies*, vol. xviii, no. 1, pp. 2–19.

JUVILER, P, and H. MORTON (eds.) (1967), *Soviet Policy-Making* (London: Pall Mall).

KANET, R. (1968), 'The Rise and Fall of the "All-People's State": Recent Changes in the Soviet Theory of the State', *Soviet Studies*, vol. xx, no. 1, pp. 81–93.

KAPLAN, F. and J. SOBIN (1982), *Encyclopedia of China Today* (London: Macmillan).

KARDELJ, E. (1978), *Democracy and Socialism* (London: Summerfield).

KARPINSKI, J. (1982), *Countdown* (New York: Karz-Cohl).

KASSOF, A. (1964), 'The Administered Society: Totalitarianism Without Terror', *World Politics*, vol. xvi, no. 4, pp. 558–75.

KAUTSKY, J. (1973), 'Comparative Communism Versus Comparative Politics', *Studies in Comparative Communism*, vol. vi, nos. 1 and 2, pp. 135–70.

KAVANAGH, D. (1972), *Political Culture* (London: Macmillan).

KEDOURIE, E. (1960), *Nationalism* (London: Hutchinson).

KERR, C. *et al.* (1962), *Industrialism and Industrial Man* (London: Heinemann).

KERSHAW, R. (1982), 'Lesser Current: The Election Ritual and Party Consolidation in the People's Republic of Kampuchea', *Contemporary Southeast Asia*, vol. iii, no. 4, pp. 315–39.

KHALILZAD, Z. (1980), 'Soviet-Occupied Afghanistan', *Problems of Communism*, vol. xxix, no. 6, pp. 23–40.

KHRUSHCHEV, N. (1970), *Khrushchev Remembers* (Boston: Little Brown).

KIERNAN, B. and C. BOUA (eds.) (1982), *Peasants and Politics in Kampuchea 1942–1981* (London: Zed Press).

KIM, I. (1975), *Communist Politics in North Korea* (New York: Praeger).

KING, R. (1973), *Minorities under Communism* (Cambridge, Mass: Harvard University Press).

—— (1979a), 'Bulgaria' in Rakowska-Harmstone and Gyorgy (1979), pp. 168–88.

—— (1979b), 'Romania' in Rakowska-Harmstone and Gyorgy (1979), pp. 145–67.

—— (1980), *History of the Romanian Communist Party* (Stanford: Hoover Institution Press).

KISSINGER, H. (1979), *White House Years* (Boston: Little Brown).

KLEIN, G. and P. (1981), 'Nationalism vs. Ideology: The Pivot of Yugoslav Politics' in Klein and Reban (1981), pp. 247–79.

—— and M. REBAN (eds.) (1981), *The Politics of Ethnicity in Eastern Europe* (New York: Columbia University Press).

KLUG, H-J. (1974), *Lernwortschatz Englisch* (East Berlin: Volk und Wissen).

KOLAKOWSKI, L. (1978), *Main Currents of Marxism*, 3 vols. (Oxford: Oxford University Press).

—— (1981), 'An Unique Revolution' *Times Higher Education Supplement*, 26 June 1981, p. 11.

KOLANKIEWICZ, G. and R. TARAS (1977), 'Poland: Socialism for Everyman?' in Brown and Gray (1977), pp. 101–30.

KONRAD, G. and I. SZELENYI (1979), *The Intellectuals on the Road to Class Power* (Brighton: Harvester).

KORBONSKI, A. (1976), 'Leadership Succession and Political Change in Eastern Europe', *Studies in Comparative Communism*, vol. ix, nos. 1 and 2, pp. 3–26.

—— (1979), 'Poland' in Rakowska-Harmstone and Gyorgy (1979), pp. 37–70.

KORNHAUSER, W. (1960), *The Politics of Mass Society* (London: Routledge and Kegan Paul).

KOROM, M. (1983), 'Further Development of the Hungarian Election System', *Information Bulletin of the Central Committee of the Hungarian Socialist Workers' Party*, no. 3, pp. 27–32.

KOSZEGI, F. and E. P. THOMPSON (n.d.), *The New Hungarian Peace Movement* (London: END and Merlin).

KOUSOULAS, G. (1975), 'The Greek Communists Tried Three Times—and Failed' in Hammond (1975a), pp. 293–309.

KOVRIG, B. (1979a), 'Hungary' in Rakowska-Harmstone and Gyorgy (1979), pp. 71–99.

—— (1979b), *Communism in Hungary from Kun to Kadar* (Stanford: Hoover Institution).

KROEF, J. VAN DER (1981), *Communism in South-east Asia* (London: Macmillan).

KUSIN, V. (1979), 'Challenge to Normalcy: Political Opposition in Czechoslovakia, 1968–77' in Tökes (1979), pp. 26–59.

KUX, E. (1980), 'Growing Tensions in Eastern Europe', *Problems of Communism*, vol. xxix, no. 2, pp. 21–37.

LAMBERT, F. (1977), 'Cuba: Communist State or Personal Dictatorship?' in Brown and Gray (1977), pp. 231–52.

LANE, D. (1976), *The Socialist Industrial State* (London: George Allen & Unwin).

—— (1978), *Politics and Society in the USSR* (London: Martin Robertson).

—— (1982), *The End of Social Inequality?* (London: George Allen & Unwin).

—— (1985), *State and Politics in the USSR* (Oxford: Blackwell).

—— and G. KOLANKIEWICZ (eds.) (1973), *Social Groups in Polish Society* (London: Macmillan).

LANGE, P. and M. VANNICELLI (eds.) (1981), *The Communist Parties of Italy, France and Spain* (London: George Allen & Unwin).

LARDY, N. (1978), *Economic Growth and Distribution in China* (Cambridge: Cambridge University Press).

LEE, C-S. (1978), *The Korean Workers Party* (Stanford: Hoover Institution).

LEFORT, C. (1977), 'La première révolution anti-totalitaire', *Esprit*, no. 1, pp. 13–19.

LEFORT, R. (1983), *Ethiopia* (London: Zed Press).

LEGGETT, G. (1981), *Cheka* (Oxford: Oxford University Press).

LEGTERS, L. (ed.) (1978), *The German Democratic Republic* (Boulder: Westview).

Lektsii po Partiinomu Stroitel'stvu (1971) (Moscow: Mysl').

LENDVAI, P. (1969), *Eagles in Cobwebs* (London: Macdonald).

LEOGRANDE, W. (1980), 'Evolution of the Nonaligned Movement', *Problems of Communism*, vol. xxix, no. 1, pp. 35–52.

LEONHARD, W. (1968), 'Politics and Ideology in the Post-Khrushchev Era' in A. Dallin and T. Larson (eds.) (1968), *Soviet Politics since Khrushchev* (Englewood Cliffs: Prentice-Hall), pp. 41–71.

LESLIE, R. F. (ed.) (1980), *The History of Poland Since 1863* (Cambridge: Cambridge University Press).

LEVI, A. (1979), 'Eurocommunism: Myth or Reality?' in della Torre (1979), pp. 9–34.

LEWIS, P. (ed.) (1984), *Eastern Europe: Political Crisis and Legitimation* (Beckenham: Croom Helm).

LIEBMAN, M. (1975), *Leninism under Lenin* (London: Merlin).

LIEBERTHAL, K. (1978), *Central Documents and Politburo Politics in China* (Ann Arbor: Center for Chinese Studies, University of Michigan).

LIPPMANN, H. (1970), 'The Limits of Reform Communism, *Problems of Communism*, vol. xix, no. 3, pp. 15–23.

LIU, A. (1983), 'The Politics of Corruption in the People's Republic of China', *American Political Science Review*, vol. lxxvii, no. 3, pp. 602–23.

LOMAX, B. (1976), *Hungary 1956* (London: Allison and Busby).

LOTARSKI, S. (1975), 'The Communist Takeover in Poland' in Hammond (1975a), pp. 339–67.

LÖWENHARDT, J. (1981), *Decision Making in Soviet Politics* (London: Macmillan).

—— (1982), *The Soviet Politburo* (Edinburgh: Canongate).

LÖWENTHAL, R. (1970), 'Development vs. Utopia in Communist Policy' in C. Johnson (1970), pp. 33–116.

LUKES, S. (1974), *Power: A Radical View* (London: Macmillan).

MACRIDIS, R. (1983), *Contemporary Political Ideologies, Movements and Regimes* (Boston: Little, Brown).

MANDEL, E. (1970), *The Mystifications of State Capitalism* (London: I.M.G. Publications).

—— (1974), 'Ten Theses on the Social and Economic Laws Governing the Society Transitional Between Capitalism and Socialism', *Critique*, no. 3, pp. 5–21.

MANNHEIM, K. (1936), *Ideology and Utopia* (London: Routledge & Kegan Paul).

MAO ZEDONG (1965), *Selected Works of Mao Tse-tung*, vols. ii and iii (Peking: Foreign Languages Press).

MARX, K. and F. ENGELS (1967), *Manifesto of the Communist Party* (Moscow: Progress).

—— (1970), *The German Ideology—Part One* (London: Lawrence and Wishart).

MCAULEY, M. (1977). *Politics and the Soviet Union* (Harmondsworth: Penguin).

—— (1984a), 'Political Culture and Communist Politics: One Step Forward, Two Steps Back' in Brown (1984a), pp. 13–39.

—— (1984b), 'Nationalism and the Soviet Multi-ethnic State' in Harding (1984), pp. 179–210.

MCCAULEY, M. (ed.) (1977), *Communist Power in Europe 1944–1949* (London: Macmillan).

—— (1979), *Marxism–Leninism in the German Democratic Republic* (London: Macmillan).

—— (1981), 'Official and Unofficial Nationalism in the GDR', *GDR Monitor*, no. 5, pp. 13–20.

—— (1983), *The German Democratic Republic Since 1945* (London: Macmillan).

McCLOSKY, H. and J. TURNER (1960), *The Soviet Dictatorship* (New York: McGraw-Hill).

McLELLAN, D. (1975), *Marx* (Glasgow: Collins).

—— (1977), *Engels* (Glasgow: Collins).

—— (1979), *Marxism after Marx* (London: Macmillan).

—— (1980), *The Thought of Karl Marx* (London: Macmillan).

—— (1981), 'Marx, Engels and Lenin on Party and State' in Holmes (1981b), pp. 7–31.

MEDVEDEV, R. (1979), 'The Future of Soviet Dissent', *Index on Censorship*, no. 2, pp. 25–31.

—— (1980), *On Soviet Dissent* (London: Constable).

MEIER, V. (1983), 'Yugoslavia's National Question', *Problems of Communism*, vol. xxxii, no. 2, pp. 47–60.

MESA-LAGO, C. (1978), *Cuba in the 1970s* (Albuquerque: University of New Mexico Press).

MEYER, A. (1966), 'The Functions of Ideology in the Soviet Political System', *Soviet Studies*, vol. xvii, no. 3, pp. 273–85.

—— (1967), 'The Comparative Study of Communist Political Systems', *Slavic Review*, vol. xxvi, no. 1, pp. 3–12.

—— (1970a), 'Historical Developments of the Communist Theory of Leadership' in R. B. Farrell (1970), pp. 5–16.

—— (1970b), 'Theories of Convergence' in C. Johnson (1970), pp. 313–41.

—— (1983a), 'Cultural Revolutions: The Uses of The Concept of Culture in the Comparative Study of Communist Systems', *Studies in Comparative Communism*, vol. xvi, nos. 1 and 2, pp. 5–8.

—— (1983b), 'Communism and Leadership', *Studies in Comparative Communism*, vol. xvi, no. 3, pp. 161–9.

—— (1984), *Communism* (New York: Random House).

MILIBAND, R. (1973), *The State in Capitalist Society* (London: Quartet).

MILLER, J. (1982), 'The Communist Party: Trends and Problems' in A. Brown and M. Kaser (eds.) (1982), *Soviet Policy for the 1980s* (London: Macmillan), pp. 1–34.

MINAGAWA, S. (1975), 'The Functions of the Supreme Soviet Organs and Problems of Their Institutional Development', *Soviet Studies*, vol. xxvii, no. 1, pp. 46–70.

MOLNAR, M. (1978), *A Short History of the Hungarian Communist Party* (Boulder: Westview).

MONTAPERTO, R. (1973). 'The Maoist Approach', *Problems of Communism*, vol. xxii, no. 5, pp. 51–63.

MONTIAS, J. M. (1981), 'Observations on Strikes, Riots and Other Disturbances' in Triska and Gati (1981), pp. 173–86.

MOORE, B. (1950), *Soviet Politics—The Dilemma of Power* (Cambridge, Mass: Harvard University Press).

—— (1966), *Terror and Progress—USSR* (New York: Harper & Row).

MORETON, E. (1978), *East Germany and the Warsaw Alliance* (Boulder: Westview).

MUKHERJEE, T. (1983), *The Social, Economic and Political Ideas of the Great President Kim Il Sung* (Pyongyang: Foreign Languages Publishing House).

MUNSLOW, B. (1983), *Mozambique* (Harlow: Longman).

MUSHABEN, J. (1984), 'Swords to Plowshares: The Church, The State and the East

German Peace Movement', *Studies in Comparative Communism*, vol. xvii, no. 2, pp. 123–35.

NELSON, D. (ed.) (1980a), *Local Politics in Communist Countries* (Lexington: University Press of Kentucky).

—— (1980b), 'Workers in a Workers' State: Participation in Romania', *Soviet Studies*, vol. xxxii, no. 4, pp. 542–60.

—— and S. WHITE (eds.) (1982), *Communist Legislatures in Comparative Perspective* (London: Macmillan).

NETHERCUT, R. (1983), 'Leadership in China: Rivalry, Reform and Renewal', *Problems of Communism*, vol. xxxii, no. 2, pp. 30–46.

NGAPOI NGAWANG JIGME (1984), 'Explaining Regional Autonomy Law', *Beijing Review*, 25 June 1984, pp. 17–19.

O'CONNOR, J. (1970), *The Origins of Socialism in Cuba* (Ithaca: Cornell University Press).

ODOM, W. (1976), 'A Dissenting View on the Group Approach to Soviet Politics', *World Politics*, vol. xxviii, no. 4, pp. 542–67.

OKSENBERG, M. (1974), 'Occupational Groups in Chinese Society and the Cultural Revolution' in Cohen and Shapiro (1974), pp. 335–57.

—— (1982), 'Economic Policy-Making in China: Summer 1981', *The China Quarterly*, no. 90, pp. 165–94.

OLESZCZUK, T. (1980), 'Group Challenges and Ideological De-Radicalization in Yugoslavia', *Soviet Studies*, vol. xxxii, no. 4, pp. 561–79.

—— (1982), 'Dissident Marxism in Eastern Europe', *World Politics*, vol. xxxiv, no. 4, 527–47.

OREN, N. (1973), *Revolution Administered* (Baltimore: Johns Hopkins University Press).

OTTAWAY, D. and M. (1981), *Afrocommunism* (New York: Holmes & Meier).

OTTAWAY, M. and D. (1978), *Ethiopia* (New York: Holmes & Meier).

OXLEY, A., A. PRAVDA and A. RITCHIE (eds.) (1973), *Czechoslovakia* (London: Allen Lane).

PANO, N. (1968), *The People's Republic of Albania* (Baltimore: Johns Hopkins Press).

—— (1979), 'Albania' in Rakowska-Harmstone and Gyorgy (1979), pp. 189–212.

PARSONS, T. (1960), 'Some Principal Characteristics of Industrial Societies' in C. Black (ed.) (1960), *The Transformation of Russian Society* (Cambridge, Mass: Harvard University Press).

PAUL, D. (1981), *Czechoslovakia* (Boulder: Westview).

PELIKAN, J. (ed.) (1971), *The Czechoslovak Political Trials 1950–1954* (Stanford: Stanford University Press).

PETRENKO, F. (1981), *Socialism: One-Party and Multi-Party System* (Moscow: Progress).

PETRUS, J. (1971), 'Marx and Engels on the National Question', *Journal of Politics*, vol. xxxiii, no. 3, pp. 797–824.

PIKE, D. (1978), *History of Vietnamese Communism 1925–1976* (Stanford: Hoover Institution Press).

PLAMENATZ, J. (1973), 'Two Types of Nationalism' in E. Kamenka (ed.) (1973), *Nationalism* (Canberra: Australian National University Press), pp. 22–36.

PRAVDA, A. (1978), 'Elections in Communist Party States', in G. Hermet *et al.* (eds.) (1978), *Elections Without Choice* (New York: Wiley), pp. 169–95.

PRAVDA, A. (1979), 'Industrial Workers: Patterns of Dissent, Opposition and Accommodation' in Tökes (1979), pp. 209–62.

PRIFTI, P. (1978), *Socialist Albania Since 1944* (Cambridge, Mass: MIT Press).

RAKOWSKA-HARMSTONE, T. (1974), 'The Dialectics of Nationalism in the USSR', *Problems of Communism*, vol. xxiii, no. 3, pp. 1–22.

—— and A. GYORGY (eds. (1979), *Communism in Eastern Europe* (Bloomington: Indiana University Press).

RAMET, P. (1984), 'Church and Peace in the GDR', *Problems of Communism*, vol. xxxiii, no. 4, pp. 44–57.

REDDAWAY, P. (1978), 'The Development of Dissent and Opposition' in Brown and Kaser (1978), pp. 121–56.

—— (1980), 'Policy Towards Dissent Since Khrushchev' in Rigby, Brown, and Reddaway (1980), pp. 158–92.

REMINGTON, R. (1971), *The Warsaw Pact* (Cambridge, Mass: MIT Press).

—— (1979), 'Yugoslavia' in Rakowska-Harmstone and Gyorgy (1979), pp. 213–43.

—— (1984), 'Yugoslavia', in T. Rakowska-Harmstone (ed.) (1984), *Communisn in Eastern Europe* (Bloomington: Indiana University Press).

RIGBY, T. H. (1964), 'Traditional, Market and Organizational Societies and the USSR', *World Politics*, vol. xvi, no. 4, pp. 539–57.

—— (ed.) (1968a), *The Stalin Dictatorship* (Sydney: Sydney University Press).

—— (1968b), *Communist Party Membership in the USSR 1917–1967* (Princeton: Princeton University Press).

—— (1970), 'The Soviet Leadership: Towards a Self-Stabilizing Oligarchy?', *Soviet Studies*, vol. xxii, no. 2, pp. 167–91.

—— (1976), 'Politics in the Mono-Organisational Society' in A. Janos (ed.) (1976), *Authoritarian Politics in Communist Europe* (Berkeley: University of California Institute of International Studies).

—— (1980), 'Some Concluding Observations' in Rigby, Brown, and Reddaway (1980), pp. 193–7.

—— (1982), 'Introduction: Political Legitimacy, Weber and Communist Mono-organisational Systems' in Rigby and Feher (1982), pp. 1–26.

—— A. BROWN and P. REDDAWAY (eds.) (1980), *Authority, Power and Policy in the USSR* (London: Macmillan).

—— and F. FEHER (eds.) (1982), *Political Legitimation in Communist States* (London: Macmillan).

RILLING, R. (ed.) (1979), *Sozialismus in der DDR*, 2 vols. (Cologne: Paul Rugenstein).

RITVO, H. (1960), 'Totalitarianism without Coercion?', *Problems of Communism*, vol. ix, no. 6, pp. 19–29.

ROGERS, R. (1976), 'Policy Differences Within the Hanoi Leadership', *Studies in Comparative Communism*, vol. ix, nos. 1 and 2, pp. 108–28.

ROSBERG, C. and T. CALLAGHY (eds.) (1979), *Socialism in Sub-Saharan Africa* (Berkeley: University of California Institute of International Studies).

ROSTOW, W. (1960), *The Stages of Economic Growth* (Cambridge: Cambridge University Press).

RUANE, K. (1982), *The Polish Challenge* (London: British Broadcasting Corporation).

RUBLE, B. (1981), *Soviet Trade Unions* (Cambridge: Cambridge University Press).

RUPEN, R. (1979), *How Mongolia is Really Ruled* (Stanford: Hoover Institution).

RUPNIK, J. (1981), 'The Restoration of the Party-State in Czechoslovakia since 1968', in Holmes (1981b), pp. 105–24.

RUSH, M. (1968), *Political Succession in the USSR* (New York: Columbia University Press).

—— (1974), *How Communist States Change Their Rulers* (Ithaca: Cornell University Press).

—— (1976), 'Comment by Myron Rush', *Studies in Comparative Communism*, vol. ix, nos. 1 and 2, pp. 23–6.

RUSINOW, D. (1977), *The Yugoslav Experiment 1948–1974* (London: Hurst).

RUSSO, G. (1979), 'Il compromesso storico: the Italian Communist Party from 1968 to 1978', in della Torre (1979), pp. 69–111.

RUTLAND, P. (1984), 'The "Nationality Problem" and the Soviet State', in Harding (1984), pp. 150–78.

SAICH, T. (1981), *China: Politics and Government* (London: Macmillan).

SAKHAROV, A. (1968), *Progress, Coexistence and Intellectual Freedom* (London: Andre Deutsch).

SALISBURY, H. (1969), *The Coming War Between Russia and China* (London: Secker and Warburg).

SANFORD, G. (1981), 'Polish People's Republic', in Szajkowski (1981a), vol. iii, pp. 553–88.

SAWER, M. (ed.) (1978), *Socialism and Participation* (Adelaide: Australian Political Studies Association).

SCALAPINO, R. and C-S. LEE (1972), *Communism in Korea*, 2 vols. (Berkeley and Los Angeles: University of California Press).

SCHAPIRO, L. (1972), *Totalitarianism* (London: Macmillan).

SCHÖPFLIN, G. (1977), 'Hungary: An Uneasy Stability', in Brown and Gray (1977), pp. 131–58.

—— (1984), 'Corruption, Informalism, Irregularity in Eastern Europe: A Political Analysis', *Sudosteuropa*, vol. xxxiii, nos. 7 and 8, pp. 389–401.

SCHRAM, S. (1969), *The Political Thought of Mao Tse-tung* (Harmondsworth: Penguin).

SCHULZ, D. and J. ADAMS (eds.) (1981), *Political Participation in Communist Systems* (New York: Pergamon).

SCHURMANN, F. (1968), *Ideology and Organization in Communist China* (Berkeley and Los Angeles: University of California Press).

SCHWAB, P. (1985), *Ethiopia* (London: Frances Pinter).

SCHWARTZ, J. (1973), 'The Elusive "New Soviet Man"', *Problems of Communism*, vol. xxii, no. 5, pp. 39–50.

—— and W. KEECH (1968), 'Group Influence and the Policy Process in the Soviet Union', *American Political Science Review*, vol. lxii, no. 3, pp. 840–51.

SEGAL, G. (1984), 'Sino-Soviet relations: the road to detente', *The World Today*, vol. xl, no. 5, pp. 205–12.

SELIGER, M. (1976), *Ideology and Politics* (London: George Allen & Unwin).

SENIN, M. (1973), *Socialist Integration* (Moscow: Progress).

SETON-WATSON, H. (1956), *The East European Revolution* (London: Methuen).

—— (1960), *The Pattern of Communist Revolution* (London: Methuen).

—— (1965), *Nationalism Old and New* (Sydney: Sydney University Press).

—— (1977), *Nations and States* (London: Methuen).

SETON-WATSON, H. (1980). *The Imperialist Revolutionaries* (London: Hutchinson).

SHAFIR, M. (1981), 'Socialist Republic of Romania' in Szajkowski (1981a), vol. iii, pp. 589–639.

—— (1985), *Romania* (London: Frances Pinter).

SHARLET, R. (1967), 'Concept Formation in Political Science and Communist Studies: Conceptualising Political Participation' reprinted in Fleron (1969), pp. 244–53.

—— (1978), 'Dissent and Repression in the Soviet Union and Eastern Europe: Changing Patterns since Khrushchev', *International Journal*, vol. xxxiii, no. 3, pp. 763–95.

SHER, G. (1977), *Praxis* (Bloomington: Indiana University Press).

SHEVCHENKO, A. (1985), *Breaking with Moscow* (London: Jonathan Cape).

SHOUP, P. (1979), 'The League of Communists of Yugoslavia' in Fischer-Galati (1979), pp. 327–80.

SHUB, D. (1966), *Lenin* (Harmondsworth: Penguin).

SHUHACHI, I. (1984), *Modern Korea and Kim Jong Il* (Tokyo: Yuzankaku).

SIMON, M. and R. KANET (eds.) (1981), *Background to Crisis* (Boulder: Westview).

SIMONS, W. (ed.) (1980), *The Constitutions of the Communist World* (Alphen: Sijthoff and Noordhoff).

—— and S. WHITE (eds.) (1984), *The Party Statutes of the Communist World* (The Hague: Martinus Nijhoff).

SINGLETON, F. (1976), *Twentieth-Century Yugoslavia* (London: Macmillan).

—— (1983), 'Yugoslavia: Economic Grievances and Cultural Nationalism'. *The World Today*, July–August, pp. 284–90.

SKILLING, H. G. (1966), 'Interest Groups and Communist Politics', *World Politics*, vol. xviii, no. 3, pp. 435–51.

—— (1972), 'Czechoslovakia' in Bromke and Rakowska-Harmstone (1972), pp. 43–72.

—— (1976), *Czechoslovakia's Interrupted Revolution* (Princeton: Princeton University Press).

—— (1981), *Charter 77 and Human Rights in Czechoslovakia* (London: George Allen & Unwin).

—— (1983), 'Interest Groups and Communist Politics Revisited', *World Politics*, vol. xxxvi, no. 1, pp. 1–27.

—— (1984), 'Czechoslovak Political Culture: Pluralism in an International Context' in Brown (1984a), pp. 115–33.

—— and F. GRIFFITHS (eds.) (1971), *Interest Groups in Soviet Politics* (Princeton: Princeton University Press).

SLUSSER, R. (1972), 'Aspects of Political Terror', *Studies in Comparative Communism*, vol. v, no. 4, pp. 428–33.

SOLOMON, R. (1971), *Mao's Revolution and the Chinese Political Culture* (Berkeley and Los Angeles: University of California Press).

SOLOMON, S. G. (ed.) (1983), *Pluralism in the Soviet Union* (London: Macmillan).

SOLZHENITSYN, A. (1973), 'Letter to the Soviet Leaders' in *The Sunday Times* (London), 3 March 1974, pp. 33–6.

STAATS, S. (1972), 'Corruption in the Soviet System', *Problems of Communism*, vol. xxi, no. 1, pp. 40–7.

STANKOVIC, S. (1982), 'Yugoslavia' in Staar, R. (ed.) (1982), *Yearbook on International Communist Affairs 1982* (Stanford: Hoover Institution).

STARRELS, J. and A. MALLINCKRODT (1975), *Politics in the German Democratic Republic* (New York: Praeger).

STEELE, J.(1985), *The Limits of Soviet Power* (Harmondsworth: Penguin).

STERN, G. (1980), 'Afghanistan and East–West Relations', *Journal of International Studies*, vol. ix, no. 2, pp. 135–46.

STOOKEY, R. (1982), *South Yemen* (Boulder: Westview).

STRONG, J. (1972), 'The Sino-Soviet Dispute' in Bromke and Rakowska-Harmstone (1972), pp. 21–42.

STUART-FOX, M. (ed.) (1982), *Contemporary Laos* (St. Lucia: University of Queensland Press).

SUH, D-S. (1981), *Korean Communism 1945–1980* (Honolulu: University Press of Hawaii).

SUMMERS, L. (1981), 'Democratic Kampuchea' in Szajkowski (1981a), vol. ii, pp. 409–36.

SZAJKOWSKI, B. (ed.) (1981a), *Marxist Governments*, 3 vols. (London: Macmillan).

—— (1981b), 'Albania, Bulgaria, Romania: Political Innovations and the Party', in Holmes (1981b), pp. 33–50.

—— (1982), *The Establishment of Marxist Regimes* (London: Butterworths).

TATU, M. (1970), *Power in the Kremlin* (New York: Viking).

TEIWES, F. (1979), *Politics and Purges in China* (New York: M. E. Sharpe).

THAYER, C. (1981), 'New Evidence on Kampuchea', *Problems of Communism*, vol. xxx, no. 3, pp. 91–6.

THOMAS, H. (1977), *The Cuban Revolution* (New York: Harper & Row).

TING WANG (1977), 'Leadership Realignments', *Problems of Communism*, vol. xxvi, no. 4, pp. 1–17.

TÖKES, R. (ed.) (1979), *Opposition in Eastern Europe* (London: Macmillan).

TOMA, P. and I. VOLGYES (1977), *Politics in Hungary* (San Francisco: Freeman).

TORRE, P. F. della *et al.* (eds.) (1979), *Eurocommunism* (Harmondsworth: Penguin).

TOWNSEND, J. (1969), *Political Participation in Communist China* (Berkeley and Los Angeles: University of California Press).

TRISKA, J. (1977), 'Citizen Participation in Community Decisions in Yugoslavia, Romania, Hungary and Poland', in Triska and Cocks (1977), pp. 147–77.

—— and BARBIC, A. (1980), 'Evaluating Citizen Performance at the Community Level: The Role of Party Affiliation in Yugoslavia' in Nelson (1980a), pp. 54–89.

—— and P. COCKS (eds.) (1977), *Political Development in Eastern Europe* (New York: Praeger).

—— and C. GATI (eds.) (1981), *Blue-Collar Workers in Eastern Europe* (London: George Allen & Unwin).

TROTSKY, L. (1967), *The Revolution Betrayed* (London: New Park).

TUCKER, R.(1968), 'Paths of Communist Revolution, 1917–67' in K. London (ed.), *The Soviet Union: A Half Century of Communism* (Baltimore: The Johns Hopkins Press), pp. 3–39.

—— (1973), 'Culture, Political Culture and Communist Society', *Political Science Quarterly*, vol. lxxxviii, no. 2, pp. 173–90.

—— (ed.) (1975), *The Lenin Anthology* (New York: Norton).

TUCKER, R. (ed.) (1977), *Stalinism* (New York: Norton).

—— (ed.) (1978), *The Marx—Engels Reader* (New York: Norton).

TURLEY, W. (ed.) (1980), *Vietnamese Communism in Comparative Perspective* (Boulder: Westview).

TURNER, R. (1975), *Vietnamese Communism* (Stanford: Hoover Institution Press).

ULAM, A. (1983), *Dangerous Relations* (New York: Oxford University Press).

ULC, O. (1974), *Politics in Czechoslovakia* (San Francisco: Freeman).

UNGER, A. (1981), 'Political Participation in the USSR: YCL and CPSU', *Soviet Studies*, vol. xxxiii, no. 1, pp. 107–24.

VALENTA, J. (1979), *Soviet Intervention in Czechoslovakia 1968* (Baltimore: Johns Hopkins University Press).

VICKERY, M. (1984), *Cambodia: 1975–1982* (Sydney: George Allen & Unwin).

VINOGRADOV, N. (1980), *Partiinoe Rukovodstvo Sovetami* (Moscow: Mysl').

VOLGYES, I. (1974), 'Political Socialization in Eastern Europe', *Problems of Communism*, vol. xxiii, no. 1, pp. 46–55.

—— (ed.) (1975), *Political Socialization in Eastern Europe* (New York: Praeger).

WALLACE, W. (1983), 'Sino-Soviet Relations: An Interpretation', *Soviet Studies*, vol. xxxv, no. 4, pp. 457–70.

WALLER, D. (1981), *The Government and Politics of the People's Republic of China* (London: Hutchinson).

WALLER, M. (1979), 'Problems of Comparative Communism', *Studies in Comparative Communism*, vol. xii, nos. 2 and 3, pp. 107–32.

—— (1981), *Democratic Centralism* (Manchester: Manchester University Press).

—— (1982), 'A Movement is a Movement is a Movement', *Communist Affairs*, vol. i, no. 1, pp. 40–4.

WANG, J. (1980), *Contemporary Chinese Politics* (Englewood Cliffs: Prentice-Hall).

WANG RENZHONG (1982), 'How to View our Party's Style of Work', *Beijing Review*, 5 April, pp. 16–17.

WANG XIZHE (1980), 'For a Return to Genuine Marxism in China', *New Left Review*, no. 121, pp. 33–48.

—— (1982), 'China's Democracy Movement', *New Left Review*, no. 131, pp. 62–70.

WEINTRAUB, W. (1950), 'Marx and the Russian Revolutionaries', *The Cambridge Journal*, vol. iii, no. 8, pp. 497–503.

WESTOBY, A. (1981), *Communism since World War II*, (Brighton: Harvester).

WHITE, S. (1977), 'The USSR: Patterns of Autocracy and Industrialism', in Brown and Gray (1977), pp. 25–65.

—— (1978), 'Communist Systems and the "Iron Law of Pluralism" ', *British Journal of Political Science*, vol. viii, no. 1, pp. 101–17.

—— (1979), *Political Culture and Soviet Politics* (London: Macmillan).

—— (1982), 'Some Conclusions', in Nelson and White (1982) pp. 191–5.

—— (1983), 'What is a Communist System?', *Studies in Comparative Communism*, vol. xvi, no. 4, pp. 247–63.

—— J. GARDNER and G. SCHÖPFLIN (1982), *Communist Political Systems* (London: Macmillan).

WOLFERS, M. and J. BERGEROL (1983), *Angola in the Front Line* (London: Zed Press).

WOODALL, J. (ed.) (1982), *Policy and Politics in Contemporary Poland* (London: Frances Pinter).

ZANINOVICH, M. G. (1983), 'Yugoslav Succession and Leadership Stability', *Studies in Comparative Communism*, vol. xvi, no. 3, pp. 179–90.

ZASLAVSKY, V. (1982), *The Neo-Stalinist State* (New York: M. E. Sharpe).

—— and R. BRYM (1978), 'The Functions of Elections in the USSR', *Soviet Studies*, vol. xxx, no. 3, pp. 362–71.

ZASLOFF, J. and M. BROWN (1979), 'The Passion of Kampuchea', *Problems of Communism*, vol. xxviii, no. 1, pp. 28–44.

ZAWODNY, J. (1962), *Death in the Forest* (Notre Dame: University of Notre Dame Press).

ZIEGLER, C. (1983), 'Worker Participation and Worker Discontent in the Soviet Union' *Political Science Quarterly*, vol. xcviii, no. 2, pp. 235–53.

ZINNER, P. (1962), *Revolution in Hungary* (New York: Columbia University Press).

ZINOVIEV, A. (1984), *The Reality of Communism* (London: Victor Gollancz).

ZLOTNIK, M. (1984), 'Chernenko Succeeds', *Problems of Communism*, vol. xxxiii, no. 2, pp. 17–31.

ZUKIN, S. (1975), *Beyond Marx and Tito* (London: Cambridge University Press).

ZWICK, P. (1983), *National Communism* (Boulder: Westview).

INDEX